Mastering™

Revit® Architecture 2008

Mastering™
Revit® Architecture 2008

Tatjana Dzambazova

Greg Demchak

Eddy Krygiel

Wiley Publishing, Inc.

Acquisitions Editor: Willem Knibbe
Development Editor: Jim Compton
Production Editor: Eric Charbonneau
Copy Editors: Tiffany Taylor, Judy Flynn
Production Manager: Tim Tate
Vice President and Executive Group Publisher: Richard Swadley
Vice President and Executive Publisher: Joseph B. Wikert
Vice President and Publisher: Neil Edde
Book Designer: Maureen Forys, Judy Fung
Compositor: Craig W. Johnson, Happenstance Type-O-Rama
Proofreader: Ian Golder
Indexer: Ted Laux
Anniversary Logo Design: Richard Pacifico
Cover Designer: Ryan Sneed
Cover Image: © Pete Gardner / Digital Vision / Getty Images

ISBN: 978-0-4701-4483-1

For general information on our other products and services or to obtain technical support, please contact our Customer Care Department within the U.S. at (800) 762-2974, outside the U.S. at (317) 572-3993 or fax (317) 572-4002.

Wiley also publishes its books in a variety of electronic formats. Some content that appears in print may not be available in electronic books.

Library of Congress Cataloging-in-Publication Data

Krygiel, Eddy, 1972-
  Mastering Revit architecture 2008 / Eddy Krygiel, Tatjana Dzambazova, Greg Demchak.
    p. cm.
  ISBN 978-0-470-14483-1 (pbk.)
 1. Architectural drawing--Computer-aided design. 2. Architectural design--Data processing. I. Dzambazova, Tatjana. II. Demchak, Greg. III. Title.
  NA2728.K793 2008
  720.28'40285536--dc22

10 9 8 7 6 5 4 3 2 1

Dear Reader,

Thank you for choosing *Mastering Revit Architecture 2008*. This book is part of a family of premium quality Sybex books, all written by outstanding authors who combine practical experience with a gift for teaching.

Sybex was founded in 1976. More than thirty years later, we're still committed to producing consistently exceptional books. With each of our titles we're working hard to set a new standard for the industry. From the paper we print on, to the authors we work with, our goal is to bring you the best books available.

I hope you see all that reflected in these pages. I'd be very interested to hear your comments and get your feedback on how we're doing. Feel free to let me know what you think about this or any other Sybex book by sending me an email at `nedde@wiley.com`, or if you think you've found a technical error in this book, please visit `http://sybex.custhelp.com`. Customer feedback is critical to our efforts at Sybex.

Best regards,

Neil Edde
Vice President and Publisher
Sybex, an Imprint of Wiley

To my dad Aleksander and my brother Igor who I miss so much. To all the authors who are brave enough to write books that live much longer than themselves. And to a part of my life that went into writing this book.
—Tatjana

To all my students over the years; you make this worth the effort.
—Greg

To all my critters.
—Eddy

Acknowledgments

Hats off to the innovators who conceptualized, designed, and made Revit happen. You have changed the world! Huge thanks to all the faithful followers! Without you, Revit wouldn't be what it is today.

Personal thanks to the Grand Master Philippe Drouant, without whose expertise, generous help, and amazing illustrations we wouldn't have been able to make this book. Many thanks to Guillermo Melantoni and Erik Egbertson, whose participation was crucial to getting this book out the door. To all our friends who have contributed to this book, the inspirational leaders Mario Guttman and Ken Sanders for their contributions and to the development of Revit, we wish to extend our sincerest gratitude.

And finally, huge thanks are due to our excellent support team at Sybex: Jim Compton, for his great editorial insight and patience; Craig W. Johnson at Happenstance Type-O-Rama, copy editors Tiffany Taylor and Judy Flynn, and proofreader Ian Golder for making us look good in print; Eric Charbonneau for managing the schedule; and our friend Willem Knibbe for his constant support and positive attitude in the face of our deadlines. Janet Chang and Pete Gaughan also helped out behind the scenes.

About the Authors

Tatjana Dzambazova was the product manager for Revit Architecture in Autodesk for the last two years and has recently moved into a new position where she explores emerging technologies, immersive experiences, and the impact of the Web 2.0 on our lifestyles. Before joining Autodesk in 2000, she practiced architecture for 12 years in Vienna and London. At Autodesk, she has focused on evangelizing technology and established herself as an internationally renowned speaker who has fostered relationships with architects and industry leaders around the globe. Powered with seemingly unlimited resources of energy, Tanja manages to make three days out of one, and when she is not working (is that ever?) or coauthoring technology books, she is advocating wildlife conservation and sustainability, reading books like a maniac, and getting inspired at the theater. If you're lucky enough to be in the Bay Area, you might catch a glimpse of Tanja cruising the streets on her Ducati Monster.

Greg Demchak is a designer, technology advocate, urban explorer, and post-apocalyptic webisode producer. He holds architectural degrees from the University of Oregon and Massachusetts Institute of Technology. He is a product designer for Revit Architecture and has been working with Revit since the year 2000 (Release 2.0, if anyone's counting). He has been teaching Revit and BIM technology at the Boston Architectural College since 2003. He currently lives in Massachusetts.

Eddy Krygiel is a registered architect, a LEED Accredited Professional, and an Autodesk Authorized Author at BNIM Architects. He has been using Revit since version 5.1 to complete projects ranging from single-family residences to office buildings as large as 1.12 million square feet. Eddy is responsible for implementing BIM at his firm and consults for other architecture and contracting firms looking to implement BIM. For the last three years, he has been teaching Revit to practicing architects and architectural students in the Kansas City area and has lectured around the nation on the use of BIM in the construction industry. Eddy also coauthored a paper on sustainability and BIM that was presented at the 2006 AIA Technology in Architectural Practice conference.

Contents at a Glance

Introduction . . . . *xxi*

Chapter 1 • Understanding BIM: From the Basics to Advanced Realities 1

Chapter 2 • Revit Fundamentals. 13

Chapter 3 • Know Your Editing Tools 61

Chapter 4 • Setting up your templates and Office Standards. 81

Chapter 5 • Customizing System Families and Project Settings in Your Template . . 127

Chapter 6 • Modeling Principles in Revit 153

Chapter 7 • Concept Massing Studies 201

Chapter 8 • From Conceptual Mass to a Real Building. 229

Chapter 9 • Working with Design Options 259

Chapter 10 • Creating Custom 3D Content. 279

Chapter 11 • Extended Modeling Techniques 309

Chapter 12 • Presenting Your Design. 395

Chapter 13 • Fine-Tuning Your Preliminary Design 427

Chapter 14 • Evaluating Your Preliminary Design: Sustainability 451

Chapter 15 • Annotating Your Model 471

Chapter 16 • Developing the Design with Smart Workflows. 515

Chapter 17 • Moving from Design to Detailed Documentation. 541

Chapter 18 • Advanced Detailing Techniques 581

Chapter 19 • Tracking Changes in Your Model 601

Chapter 20 • Worksharing 617

Chapter 21 • Troubleshooting and Optimizing Tips 635

Appendix A • The Bottom Line. 647

Index *667*

Contents

Introduction . . . . *xxi*

Chapter 1 • Understanding BIM: From the
Basics to Advanced Realities **1**
The Advantages of Building Information Modeling 1
   A Brief History of Design and Documentation 1
   Building Information Modeling 2
What to Expect from BIM 4
   Be Creative 4
   Every Element in Revit Has Properties 6
   Elements Interact with Other Elements—All the Time 6
   Duplicating a View Takes Two Clicks 6
   Problem-Solve Your Designs 7
   You Create a Full Range of Documents with BIM, Not Just a 3D Model 7
   Embrace the Family Editor 8
   Forget About Layers and X-References 9
   BIM Is More Than a Technology: It's a Change in Process 9
   Revit Is Relatively New Technology 10
Where Can You Go From Here? 10
The Bottom Line 12

Chapter 2 • Revit Fundamentals **13**
Working with Revit Parametric Elements 13
   Model Categories 15
   Annotation Categories 17
   Subcategories 17
   Imported Categories/Subcategories 18
   Views 18
   Type and Instance Parameters 19
   Bidirectional Relationships 19
   Constraints 22
   Revit Families 23
   Overriding the Representation of Elements 29
The Revit User Interface 30
   The View Window 30
   The Design Bar 32
   The Options Bar 33
   The Project Browser 33
Using the Project Browser 34
   Views 34
   Working with Views and View Properties 39
The Bottom Line 58

Chapter 3 • Know Your Editing Tools **61**

Selecting, Changing, and Replacing Elements 61
  Selection 61
  Copy/Paste 63
  Place Similar 64
Editing Elements Interactively 64
  Moving Elements 64
  Copy 67
  Rotating and Mirroring Elements 67
  Arraying Elements 70
  Resizing Elements 71
  Aligning Elements 72
  Trimming and Extending Lines and Walls 73
  Splitting Lines and Walls 74
  Offsetting Lines and Walls 74
  Keeping Elements from Moving 75
Other Useful Tools 76
  Join Geometry 76
  Split Face and Paint 76
  Keyboard Shortcuts (Accelerators) 78
The Bottom Line 79

Chapter 4 • Setting up your templates and Office Standards **81**

Starting a Project with a Custom Template 81
  Strategies for Making Templates 83
Settings for Graphic Consistency 84
  Object Styles 84
  Line Styles 85
  Line Patterns 87
  Materials 88
  Fill Patterns (Hatch) 90
  Dimension Styles 96
  Text 100
Creating Custom Annotation Tags 101
  View Tags 102
  Customizing Element Tags 116
  Keynotes and Text Notes 119
Creating Custom Title Blocks 121
Creating a Custom Title Block with the Family Editor 122
The Bottom Line 125

Chapter 5 • Customizing System Families and
                Project Settings in Your Template. **127**

Wall Types 127
  Creating Custom Wall Types 128
Floor and Roof Types 133
Ceiling Types 134

Door and Window Types 135
Stair Types 135
    Properties of Stairs 135
Types and Type Catalogs 139
    Creating Types in the Project Environment 140
    Creating Types in the Family Editor 140
    Creating Types with Type Catalogs 140
    Loading from a Type Catalog 142
Graphic Overrides of Host Objects with Complex Structure 143
Additional Global Project Settings 145
    Room and Area Settings 145
    Units 146
    Keynote Settings 147
    Setting Up Default Elements 147
The Bottom Line 151

Chapter 6 • Modeling Principles in Revit **153**
Modeling with Revit 153
    Sketch-Based Design 154
    Working with Work Planes 162
Principles of Modeling in Revit 170
    Principles of Modeling Techniques 172
    Solids and Voids 196
Where Can You Go From Here? 197
The Bottom Line 198

Chapter 7 • Concept Massing Studies **201**
Massing Studies 201
    Massing Study Workflows 203
    Massing Tools 206
    Starting a Conceptual Massing Study 208
    Putting Theory into Practice: Making a Parametric Mass Family 215
    Tagging and Scheduling Mass 223
    Importing 3D Conceptual Models Created in Other Applications 224
    Rapid Prototyping and 3D Printing 225
The Bottom Line 227

Chapter 8 • From Conceptual Mass to a Real Building **229**
Conceptual Design and Early Studies 229
    Getting Site Data and Building the Context 230
    Building the 3D Context 233
    Program Check and Feasibility 235
    Building Maker 238
    Massing Best Practices 244
    Using Imported Geometry from Other Applications for Massing 251
    Using Smart Relationship between Building Mass and the Underlying Mass . . . 255
The Bottom Line 257

Chapter 9 • Working with Design Options **259**

Revit Design Options 259
    Enabling Design Options 260
    Design-Option Sets 260
    Adding Elements to a Design Option 261
    Editing a Design Option 264
    Displaying Design Options 266
    Deciding on a Final Design Solution 266
    Putting Design Options into Practice 268
    Showing Quantities and Cost Schedules for Multiple Options 272
    Working with Rooms and Design Options 273
    The Bottom Line 276

Chapter 10 • Creating Custom 3D Content **279**

Modeling Parametric 3D Families 279
Choosing the Right Family Template 280
Types of Families 280
    Host-Based Families 282
    Profile Families 283
    2D Line-Based Families 285
    3D Line-Based Families 285
    Work Plane– and Face-Based Families 287
    Rich Photorealistic Content (RPC) Families 288
    Detail Component Families 289
    Generic 3D Families 289
    Curtain Panel Families 290
    Family Categories and Parameters 291
Smart Workflow: Nesting One Family into Another 293
    Scheduling Nested Families 294
    Linking Parameters 295
    Linking Parameters (Conditional Visibility) 296
Parametric Arrays in the Family Editor 297
    Making the Array Parametric 297
Encoding Design Rules 298
    Example: Using a Formula to Control Dimensions 299
    Using a Formula to Control an Array 300
Building a Parametric 3D Family 303
    Nesting the Chair 303
    Creating a Parametric Array 304
    Controlling Chair Visibility 306
The Bottom Line 307

Chapter 11 • Extended Modeling Techniques **309**

Basic Walls: Advanced Modeling Techniques 309
    Wall Core 309
    Layer Join Cleanup 311
    Editing Wall Joins 312
    Disjoining Walls 313

Stacked Walls 313
Adding Wall Articulation 315
Wall Wrapping 319
Sweeps and Reveals 319
Creating Custom In-Place Walls 324
Curtain Walls: Advanced Design Techniques 325
Designing a Curtain Wall 326
Curtain Panels 330
Curtain Wall Doors and Windows 330
Complex Curtain Wall Panels 330
Roofs 332
Footprint Roofs 332
Roof by Extrusion 336
In-Place Roofs 337
Sloped Glazing 338
Sloped Arrows 343
Roof Typologies 345
Roofs and Slabs: Advanced Shape Editing 370
Sloped Roofs 371
Warped Surfaces 374
Railings and Fences 374
Railings 375
Sub-elements and Principles of the Railing Element 378
Railing Construction 380
Setting Up Rail Structure 380
The Bottom Line 393

Chapter 12 • Presenting Your Design **395**
Drawings with Shadows 395
Analytical Drawings: Sun and Shadow Studies 397
Expressive Drawings with Shadows 399
Performance 401
Color-Coded Plans and Sections 401
Color Fill Schemes 402
Creating Presentation Plans and Sections 405
Elevations That Convey Depth 408
Linework 408
Drafting Lines 409
True-Color Elevations 410
Elevations with Transparent Materials 411
Using Images in Elevation Views 411
Working with Perspective Views 412
Silhouetted Edge Display 414
Rendering 415
The Rendering Design Bar 416
Materials 419
Raytracing the View 422
Rendering Best Practices 423

Creating Animated Walkthroughs 423
Exporting to Other Formats 424
The Bottom Line 425

Chapter 13 • Fine-Tuning Your Preliminary Design 427
Preliminary Design Tools 427
The Foundation Model 427
Calculating Areas 429
Room Tags 429
Area Plans 430
Making a Rentable Area Plan 433
Adding Areas and Tags 436
Schedules 437
Making a Simple Schedule (Rentable Area) 439
Placing the Schedule on a Sheet 443
Additional Schedule Capabilities 445
Using Schedules for Preliminary Cost Estimates 446
Editing the Graphic Appearance of a Schedule 448
The Bottom Line 449

Chapter 14 • Evaluating Your Preliminary Design: Sustainability 451
Sustainability in Architecture 451
Preliminary Design Tools 452
The LEED Rating System 452
Sun Studies 452
Tracking Recycled Materials 463
Window Surface Percentage vs. Room Area 465
Energy Analysis 466
IES <VE> 467
gbXML 467
Green Building Studio 468
The Bottom Line 469

Chapter 15 • Annotating Your Model 471
Annotating Your Views 471
Displaying Information about Rooms 472
Placing and Tagging Rooms 472
Room Separation Lines 475
Selecting Rooms 476
Rooms in Section Views 478
Room Properties 478
Room Area and Volume 479
Schedule Keys 481
Creating a Schedule Key 481
Tags 484
Loading Tags 485
Placing Tags 485
Changing a Tag Value 486
Tagging Untagged Elements 486

Shared Parameters 489
    Creating a Custom Project Parameter 489
    Creating Shared Parameters 491
    Shared Parameter Notes and Cautions 501
Text and Keynotes 502
    Text 502
    Keynotes and Textnotes 503
    Keynote Behavior and Editing 504
    Keynote Filenaming Conventions 505
    Keynote Settings 505
    Adding Keynotes to a View 506
    Keynote Legends 507
    The Keynote Family 508
    Predefining Keynotes 512
The Bottom Line 513

Chapter 16 • Developing the Design with Smart Workflows **515**
Working with Repetitive Elements 515
Groups 516
    Using Groups for Repetitive Rooms 516
    Creating and Managing Groups 517
    Creating and Placing Repetitive Units Using Groups 517
    Adding Rooms to a Group 521
    Nesting a Group into Another Group 523
    Adding Detail Elements to Groups 524
    Nesting a Group from a Previous Project 525
    Making Variations to a Group Instance 525
    Repeating Groups to Other Levels 528
    Making the Group a Part of the Project 529
    Editing a Group in a Separate File 531
    Detail Groups 531
    Best Practices for Grouping 532
Links 533
    Common Link Use Cases 534
    Linking Files 535
    Special Link Features 536
    Controlling the Visibility of Links 537
Groups, Links, or Both? 538
    Final Considerations 539
The Bottom Line 539

Chapter 17 • Moving from Design to Detailed Documentation **541**
Advancing the Design 541
Creating Drafting Views 541
Importing and Linking 542
    Linking vs. Importing 543
    Importing CAD Details 545
Detail Groups 547

Detail Components 548
Masking Regions 548
Creating a Repeating Detail Element 548
   Detail Component Properties 550
   Creating Custom Line Types Using Repeating Details 551
Miscellaneous Line Tools 552
   Insulation 552
   Filled Region 553
   Show Hidden Lines 554
Linework 555
Using Callouts 556
Adding Information to Your Details 557
   Embellishing the Wall Section: The SIM (Similar) Condition 560
   Embellishing the Wall Section: The Model Details 566
General Tips for Detailing 578
The Bottom Line 579

Chapter 18 • Advanced Detailing Techniques **581**
Creating 3D Details 581
   Enabling a Section Box in 3D View 583
   The Second Technique: Orienting to View 584
   Adding Annotations to the 3D Detail 585
Embedding Details within Families 586
Visibility Settings 591
Adding Additional Information Using Symbolic Lines 592
Reusing Details from Other Revit Projects 594
   Exporting Details from Revit Projects 594
   Importing Views into Revit Projects 595
The Bottom Line 599

Chapter 19 • Tracking Changes in Your Model **601**
Adding Revisions to Your Project 601
   Placing Revision Clouds 603
   Tagging a Revision Cloud 606
Parametric Modeling and Supplemental Drawings 607
Using Autodesk Design Review 607
   The Design Review User Interface 609
   Pubishing to Design Review 610
   Marking Up the Model Using Design Review 613
   Importing a Design Review Markup 614
The Bottom Line 615

Chapter 20 • Worksharing **617**
Worksharing Using the Workset Methodology 617
   Worksharing Basics 619
   Workset Organization 621
   Moving Elements between Worksets 623

Workflow 625
    Making a Central File 626
    Making the Local File 626
Saving Shared Work 627
    Loading Work from Other Team Members 628
Element Ownership 628
    Borrowing Elements 629
    Requesting Permission 629
    Granting Permission 630
The Bottom Line 632

Chapter 21 • Troubleshooting and Optimizing Tips **635**
Performance 635
Best Practices 637
File Corruption 642
Tips for Getting Started in Revit 643
Additional Resources 645
The Bottom Line 646

Appendix A • The Bottom Line **647**

Index *667*

Introduction

Welcome to the first edition of *Mastering Revit Architecture*, based on the Revit Architecture 2008 release.

This is the second book we've written for you. The feedback we received for our first book, *Introducing Revit Architecture 2008 (Wiley, 2007)*, was so stimulating that we decided to invest some more time in writing a second, more comprehensive and in-depth book to share more of what we know about Revit with you.

Writing this book has been another great experience. We've enjoyed the synergy of three friends, three designers, three educators, three authors collaborating to bring this project into reality. But mostly, we were all driven by the feeling that we're doing something important: sharing knowledge and best practices about Revit and Building Information Modeling (BIM) to those who have already been acquainted with its incredible power and feel the need to go deeper and further to fully leverage its abilities and values. We want to help you make better designs and be more efficient in creating correct documentation and put some fun back into using software.

We wanted to make a book that is as much about architectural design and practice as it is about software. We think we've succeeded, because the book follows real-life workflows and scenarios; it's full of real-world examples that show how to use Revit practically and creatively.

Who Should Read This Book

This book is written for architects who have already gotten their feet wet with Revit and are eager to learn more so they can optimize workflow and leverage the full power of this tool. It's for architects of any generation—you don't need to be a high-tech wizard to dive into this book. However, a basic understanding of Revit will make it easier to work through the book. Revit is very rich, and the topics we've selected include both the areas most widely used and those least understood. Many more books need to be written to cover the entire world of Revit.

This book is also for the seasoned user who has already received training or has started working on projects with Revit and is looking to discover useful best practices and tips that will make the work on a project smoother and the implementation easier. We've added many timesaving and inspiring concepts to the book, supported with examples from architect friends and colleagues from all around the world, to motivate you and help you on your journey into the new era of Building Information Modeling. The book also offers insights for BIM managers into the best practices for creating good project or office templates; these managers should also take a sneak peek into the powerful world of building content and Revit families.

What You Will Learn

This book will help you take the basics of Revit and BIM that you already know and grow those skills by using real-world examples. It is intended to go beyond an introduction to Revit. Thus, we won't be starting a project from scratch and teaching you how to build a simplified BIM model from the ground up (if you are interested in that approach, please see *Introducing Revit Architecture 2008 (Wiley, 2007)*, which is meant to be complementary to this book). Instead, we show you how to take a very preliminary model and add layers of intelligence to help analyze and augment your designs.

Our book begins with a brief overview of the BIM approach. As you are already aware, BIM is more than just a change in software; it's a change in architectural workflow and culture. To leverage the full advantages of both BIM and Revit in your office structure you will need to make some changes to your practice, and the book is designed around an ideal, integrated workflow to help you make this transition.

Starting with the workflows for conceptual design and feasibility studies, it continues through best practices for design iteration and refinement. You'll learn about powerful modeling techniques, design documentation, presentation graphics, and some strategies for sustainable design. The book concludes with a chapter on troubleshooting and best practices so you can avoid common pitfalls. But throughout the book we've tried to share our practical experience with you, particularly in the form of Real-World Scenario sidebars.

Whether you're studying Revit on your own or in a class or training program, you can use the Master It questions in the Bottom Line section at the end of each chapter to test your mastery of the skills you've learned.

Also featured is a color project gallery containing inspirational Revit projects.

All the tutorial files necessary to complete the book's exercises plus sample families are hosted online at www.sybex.com/go/masteringrevit2008. To download the trial version of Revit Architecture, go to www.autodesk.com/revitarchitecture, where you'll also find complete system requirements for running Revit.

Enjoy! Revit has changed our lives. Maybe it will change yours as well.

We welcome your feedback! Please feel free to email us at GoRevit@gmail.com.

Go Revit!

Tanja, Greg, and Eddy

Chapter 1

Understanding BIM: From the Basics to Advanced Realities

In this chapter, we'll cover the principles of a Building Information Modeling (BIM) approach and summarize how BIM differs from a traditional 2D CAD tool. We'll explain fundamental characteristics of Revit, how Revit delivers the benefits of a true BIM tool, and why Revit is the tool best suited for a process motivated by an integrated and collaborative practice.

In this chapter, you'll learn the following:

◆ The advantages of Building Information Modeling

◆ What to expect from Building Information Modeling

The Advantages of Building Information Modeling

The production of design documents has traditionally been an exercise in drawing lines to represent a building. These documents become instruction sets: an annotated booklet that describes how the building is to be built. The plan, section, and elevation are all skillfully drafted—line by line, drawing by drawing, sheet by sheet. Whether physical or digital, these traditional drawing sets are composed of graphics—each line is part of a larger abstraction meant to convey design intent so that a building can eventually be constructed. By and large, this is still the reality we face today, but the process of creating these drawings is being fundamentally changed as a result of BIM. Let's put this into a historical context for a moment and briefly walk through the evolution of architectural design and documentation.

A Brief History of Design and Documentation

Andrea Palladio's *Four Books of Architecture* (trans. Robert Tavernor and Richard Schofield, MIT Press, 1997) presents an amazing array of drawing techniques that show buildings cut in plan and section and even hybrid drawings that show elevations and sections in one drawing. There are drawings complete with dimensional rules for laying out the relative proportions of rooms. You can even see hints about construction techniques and structural gestures in the form of trusses, arches, and columns.

These representations were simplified expressions of a project, and often they were idealized versions of the building—not necessarily how the building was built. The drawings were communication and documentation tools, themselves works of detailed craftsmanship. In those days (14th–17th centuries), the architect was brought up in the tradition of building and had integral knowledge of how buildings were constructed. Palladio, like many other architects of his day, grew up as a stone mason. Building techniques were deeply embedded in the construction trades, which in turn spawned the great architects of the time. Other master masons and sculptors include the likes of Filippo Brunelleschi, Giovanni Bernini, and Francesco Borromini. These architects are often referred to as the master builders—they were integrated into all facets of the design and construction of architecture.

Over time, however, architecture became more and more academic as building typologies solidified, and classical reconstructions on paper and in model form became part of the formative education of the architect. The design profession began its gradual separation from the building trades. The notion of design process and iterative problem solving became critical attributes of a design professional—in many cases superseding knowledge of construction means and methods.

With modern architecture, solving abstract spatial problems, accommodating programmatic elements, and experimenting with new materials became driving forces. The machine age and the promise of mass production were idealized and fully embraced. Le Corbusier's (1887–1965) romantic vision of steamships and automobiles inspiring a new generation of architecture took hold, and buildings became increasingly machine-like. Consider all the office towers and commercial office parks that have emerged, with their internal mechanical systems used to keep the building operational.

As buildings continued to grow in complexity, both technically and programmatically, the architect grew more removed from the act of physical construction. Modern materials such as steel and reinforced concrete became prevalent, and complex building systems were introduced. In turn, the production of more detailed drawings became a legal and practical requirement. Structural engineers and mechanical engineers were added to the process, as specialized knowledge of building systems grew. No longer could the architect expect to produce a few simple drawings and have a building erected. Complexity in building systems demanded greater amounts of information, and this information was delivered in the form of larger and larger construction document sets. Architects today find themselves drafting, producing details, working with a wide range of consultants, and still having to create sketches for contractors in the field.

The traditional production of plans, sections, and elevations continues to this day, but with far more drawings than in the days of Palladio. At the same time, we ask: Will all these drawings be necessary in the near future? Will the adoption of BIM lead to new delivery methods, new forms of construction, and new roles for the architect? Can a shift in technology lead to a shift in thinking about building?

Building Information Modeling

Fast-forward to the present context and the advent of Building Information Modeling: In this landscape, complexity is still very high, but the production of drawings is now the by-product of building a virtual 3D model composed of constructive elements. These elements are loaded with data that describe not only geometry, but also cost, manufacturer, count, and just about any other metadata you can imagine. With an integrated parametric 3D model, it's possible to detect spatial clashes between the multitudes of systems in the building. You can know with confidence whether duct work will interfere with the structural steel long before construction starts.

The goal of reducing errors and smoothing out the construction process is driving firms to be more efficient, effective, and productive. In this reality plans, sections, and elevations are all derivative representations—producing them isn't a set of isolated, discontinuous tasks. A data-rich model means that more analysis and iterative searching for optimal solutions can occur early in the design process. As detail is added, the model becomes an increasingly accurate representation of what will actually be built. The model itself can be used to generate part lists, shop drawings, and instructions for industrially produced elements. If you can send a digital file that can instruct machines to produce components, the need for traditional annotated drawings disappears. Of course, that day has yet to arrive; but the idea can get you thinking about future directions and possibilities. The ultimate benefits of BIM are still emerging in a market primed to radically change the way buildings are designed and built. A shift in process and expectation is happening in the Architecture, Engineering, Construction (AEC) world, with private and public sector owners beginning to demand BIM models as part of the delivery package.

The shift from traditional 2D abstractions to on-demand simulations of building performance, usage, and cost is no longer a futuristic fantasy but a reality. In the age of information-rich digital models, all disciplines involved with a project can share a single database. Architecture, structure, mechanical, infrastructure, and construction can be coordinated in ways never before possible.

Models can now be sent directly to fabrication machines, bypassing the need for traditional shop drawings. Energy analysis can be done at the outset of design, and construction costs are becoming increasingly predictable. These are just a few of the exciting opportunities that a BIM approach offers. Designers and contractors can begin to look at the entire building process, from preliminary design through construction documentation into construction, and rethink how buildings come together. The whole notion of paper-based delivery may become obsolete as more players adopt up-to-date, accurate, digital models.

As we've mentioned, with a Revit Building Information Model, a parametric 3D model is used to generate traditional building abstractions such as plans, sections, elevations, details, and schedules. The drawings produced aren't discrete collections of manually coordinated lines, but interactive representations of a model. Working in a model-based framework such as Revit guarantees that a change in one view will propagate to all other views of the model. As you shift elements in plan, they change in elevation and section. If you move a level height, all the walls and floors associated with that level update automatically. If you remove a door from your model, it's simultaneously removed from all other views, and your door schedule is updated. This unprecedented level of coordination allows designers and builders to better control and display information, ensuring higher quality and a leaner process.

The immediate 3D design visualization of the building and its spaces improves understanding of the building and gives you the ability to show a variety of design options to all members of a project, at any moment. Integrated design and documentation keeps the data centralized and coordinated. This in turn leads to live and up-to-date schedules and quantity take-offs. That information can then be used to make decisions earlier in the design process, reducing risk and cost overruns. Not only that, but with the coordinated BIM model, you can start running energy analysis, solar studies, daylighting simulations, and egress analysis much earlier in the process, allowing you to iterate through design decisions earlier, not later.

Coordination with BIM is now required for many buildings to come into existence. Consider Daniel Libeskind's recently completed Denver Art Museum and its extreme geometric configuration (Figure 1.1). Integrating the mechanical and structural systems into a 3D model was essential to the building's successful completion. Exact spatial organization of structural members could be modeled, which in turn led to fewer field errors and fewer requests for information. In addition, parts could be sent directly to fabrication from the model, eliminating the need for 2D drawings entirely.

FIGURE 1.1
BIM makes it possible to build more complex buildings with fewer errors. Denver Art Museum, Daniel Libeskind

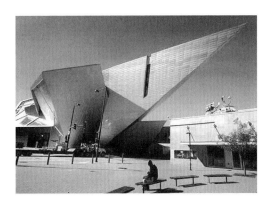

Let's not leave out some of the more pleasurable aspects of BIM that go beyond all the technical, economic, and ecological benefits. With a 3D model, you can expect to see changes in how you interact with your team and your clients and in the way you produce presentations. No longer are you stuck with using 2D drawings or outsourcing to create perspective images. You'll find yourself working with your team in close quarters, sharing a model, and exploring it together. With your clients, you can now take them through the building, in full 3D, from the beginning. The experience of working with and visualizing 3D space can't be overemphasized, and people enjoy it immensely. In the BIM era, 3D experience is the norm, not the exception.

What to Expect from BIM

When moving to a BIM work environment, you'll experience a change in process and workflow. Perhaps the most immediate and obvious difference is that a traditional CAD system uses many separate files to document a building, whereas a BIM project typically has only one file. With CAD, all the separate files are created individually and have no intelligent connection between them. Each drawing represents a separate piece of work to be managed and updated throughout the design process. With such an unwieldy process, the possibility of uncoordinated data is very high. The change management required by CAD is a tedious and error-prone process that requires diligent project management and lots of red lines. BIM provides a different approach to the problem: Rather than many files, you work with one file. With BIM, all information is consolidated and networked together for you, and the resulting drawings all relate back to a single underlying database, guaranteeing an internally consistent model.

If you understand the basic premise of an integrated building model, then you'll by now have realized that BIM removes the concept of drawing lines to represent objects. Instead, you build walls, roofs, stairs, and furniture. You model the building and its systems. Figure 1.2 shows a 3D sectional view of a Revit model. You can see that the model incorporates façade elements, floors, roofs, parapets, curtain walls, and materials. All this information is modeled and must be designed as it is to be built. You then add layers of information to the drawings to explain the model, in the form of parametric tags and keynotes. Although the end result is still a set of printed lines, you rarely draw these lines. This concept of modeling is so simple, so natural, that you'll get used to the idea in no time and find yourself dreading the idea of ever having to go back into the 2D realm.

Revit is excellent at managing changes and keeping your model interconnected. Unlike CAD, the intent of BIM is to let the computer take responsibility for redundant interactions and calculations, providing you, the designer, with more time to design and evaluate your decisions. As the architect, you hold the design decision process in your hands. With a BIM tool such as Revit, be prepared to change your expectations of how to use design software. Remember—you are modeling a building now, not drafting lines. You're doing what you do best: solving complex 3D problems.

As you move into a more advanced Revit workflow, we want you to keep some concepts in the back of your mind.

Be Creative

Revit's tools are clustered in easy-to-access groups such as modeling, drafting, rendering, structural, and so on. Most of these tools will get you where you need to go with minimal effort. For more complicated conditions, be prepared to put your creativity to use. Remember, Revit is a 3D modeling application that will let you build almost anything you want. For example, if you can't create the wall or roof you want with the explicit Wall or Roof tool, you can create your own walls and roof using 3D solid geometry. Figure 1.3 shows an example of custom-designed railings, curtain walls, and structural elements—all possible for a creative and engaged designer.

FIGURE 1.2
The BIM model keeps you honest and focused on 3D problem solving.

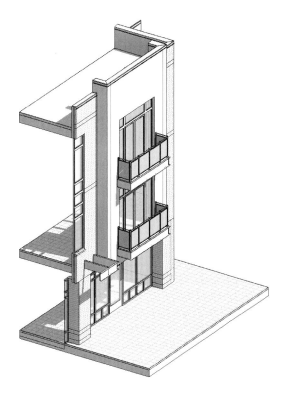

FIGURE 1.3
Be creative, and work out your design solutions in 3D.

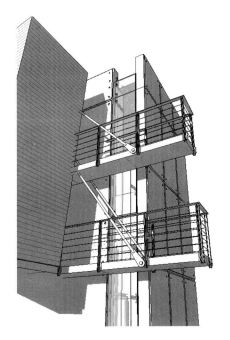

Every Element in Revit Has Properties

You'll interactively adjust elements, and you'll also frequently change the model through properties. Get used to the idea of clicking the Element Properties button to make changes to the model. A member of the Basic Wall family, for example, has properties like width, height, bearing or non-bearing, demolished or new, interior or exterior, fire rating, and material. You can even define how layers wrap when inserts are placed in the wall, add integrated wall sweeps, and build stacked walls. Figure 1.4 shows the assembly options embedded in the type properties of a Revit wall.

Elements Interact with Other Elements—All the Time

The wall interacts with other walls to join geometries and clean up connections. It connects to floors, levels, and roofs, and it affects rooms and areas. Windows and doors placed in a wall move with the wall. Deleting the wall will delete all the windows and doors in the wall and all dimensions associated with the wall. If you move a level, expect floors, roofs, walls, and all the plumbing and electrical features to also move as their parameters change. Keep the interaction of elements in mind, especially in multi-user scenarios where your changes to the model will affect many views at once.

Duplicating a View Takes Two Clicks

With Revit, you can duplicate floor plans quickly, allowing you to generate plans as in-progress working drawings, others for presentation purposes, and still others for final Construction Documents (CDs). Note that this is very different from making a copy of a drawing: you are simply duplicating a view then changing how to look at the model. Remember, no matter which view you change the model in, the change will immediately be updated in all views. And in each view, you have total control over what information you want to display. Think of a view as a pair of glasses that can filter what you see; but the underlying model is still there, all the time.

FIGURE 1.4
The Element Properties dialog contains many powerful features.

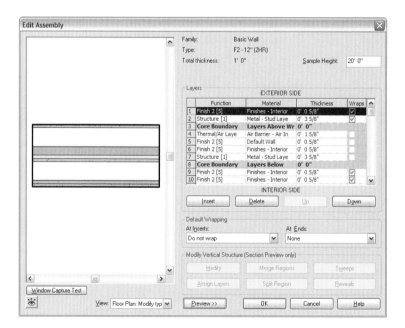

Problem-Solve Your Designs

An advantage of a BIM methodology is that you can't cheat your design. Because the elements have properties based on real-life constraints, you'll find it difficult to fake elements within the design. When you get stuck trying to resolve a roof condition, it's most likely that you have a complex roof to solve. You can't just fake the elevations and call it a day. Of course, in CAD-based systems, fakery has always been possible and has no doubt led to some messy Construction Administration work. As you move into the BIM world, be prepared to take on some early design challenges.

Figure 1.5 shows what appears to be a simple house model, but it's more complex than it looks. With Revit, you model the dormers, the trusses, and the fascia and soffits. You need to determine how the walls and roofs connect to one another—and Revit is well suited to figuring these things out.

You Create a Full Range of Documents with BIM, Not Just a 3D Model

Other software packages, like SketchUp, Rhino, and 3ds Max, are excellent modeling applications. However, these modeling applications don't have the ability to document your design for construction, nor can they be leveraged downstream. While these tools are not BIM, they can still play a role in a BIM workflow; many architects use them to generate concept models, which can then be brought into a BIM application and progress through design, analysis, and documentation. If you prefer to work with other tools for concept modeling, doing so isn't a problem. When the design starts to gel, import the geometry into Revit and start taking advantage of BIM.

Not everything is modeled in 3D in Revit. You can create 2D details in Revit, import CAD details, and reuse details from other Revit projects. The tools may be a bit different than AutoCAD, but there is nothing you can draw in CAD that can't be drawn in Revit. By using the intelligence of Revit families, you can build your details into individual components, thereby embedding drafting into the object. Figure 1.6 shows an example of a detail drawn entirely in Revit.

FIGURE 1.5
To build a BIM model, you need to problem-solve 3D problems, from dormers to trusses.

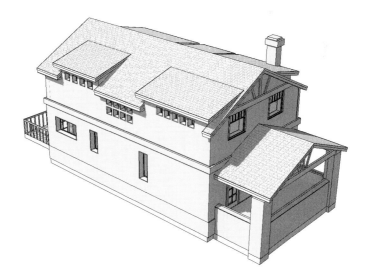

FIGURE 1.6
2D details can be drawn directly over the 3D model, allowing you to add as much more information to the model.

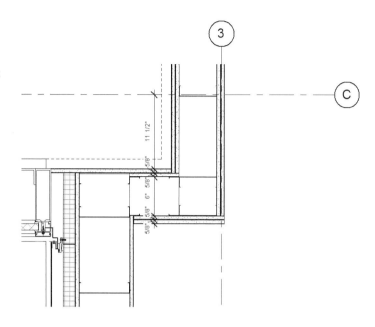

Embrace the Family Editor

Most elements (families) in Revit are made with the Family Editor and can be built with incredible features. Don't be afraid to dig in to the editor and explore your creative side. We've seen many beautiful families and clever tricks put to use that make Revit fun to use. Figure 1.7 shows a curtain-wall system with nested panels and attachment clamps. As we'll discuss in Chapter 5 and reinforce in chapter 10, making such families isn't too difficult, and requires no programming or scripting knowledge. Using 3D modeling tools and parametric dimensions, you can create reusable and dimensionally flexible components for any architectural element. By taking your time, being patient, and problem solving, you'll be producing custom content in no time.

FIGURE 1.7
Using the Family Editor, you can model intelligent part assemblies.

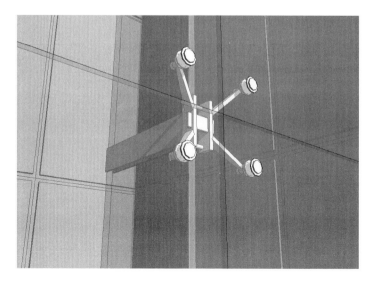

Forget About Layers and X-References

If you've already made the jump into Revit, then this will already be obvious: Rather than user-defined layers, you use an intelligent architectural classification system to manage visibility, graphics, and selection. This may seem stringent at first, but once you get the hang of it, you'll see the benefits. Because a building model is an assembly of meaningful, to-be-built objects, you control the visibility and graphics of those objects using a rational list of well-understood categories. This also makes it easy to select similar elements and edit them. Figure 1.8 shows the list of classifications that manage visibility. You can't add to or alter this list, which means every project enjoys the same level of visual predictability. And of course, with an integrated model, you don't need to worry about referencing other drawings to keep the drawings up to date and in sync.

FIGURE 1.8
The Visibility/
Graphics Overrides
dialog expresses the
entire range of elements used in Revit.

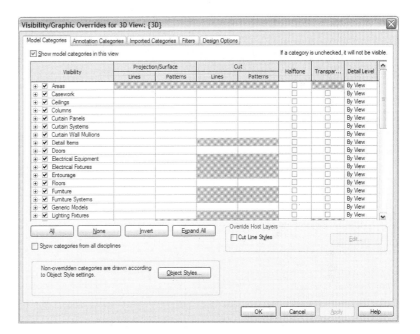

BIM Is More Than a Technology: It's a Change in Process

One of the powers of Revit is the ability to work in a single-file environment where the design and documentation of the building happens on a holistic model. This can be a disadvantage if it isn't taken seriously. Users who are quick to make changes without thinking about how such changes will ripple through the model can cause unintended problems. Revit is a parametric modeler—it creates relationships between building elements to streamline the design process. For example, deleting a roof underlay in a view doesn't just delete the roof in that view—it deletes it *everywhere* in the model. You need to think before you delete that wall or ignore that warning message!

Be prepared to work in much tighter, collaborative teams. As soon as you enter the BIM multi-user world, you absolutely need to be communicating with your team all the time. The changes that you make in the model will impact the whole model and other people's work. We think this is a great—perhaps unintended—consequence of moving into a model-based design paradigm.

Anticipate that tasks will take different amounts of time when compared to a CAD production environment. You'll perform tasks in Revit that you never had in CAD; and, conversely, some CAD tasks that took weeks (such as chamfering and trimming thousands of lines to draw walls properly or making a door schedule) take almost no time using Revit. On the other hand, some tasks may seem to take longer in Revit. This may initially seem true; but remember that as you're modifying or adding something in plan, you're also adding it in section, elevation, and detail. Be prepared to discover and embrace new tasks with BIM that were never part of a 2D workflow.

Speaking of 2D workflows, in Revit, you'll often feel as if you are working in traditional types of 2D views—just keep in mind that it's still a 3D model. Moving walls, windows, and doors in plan feels like a 2D operation, but of course it's not. If you've never worked in a model-based environment, it can be jarring at first to see the drawing you've been working on change as a result of an edit in a different view. As we mentioned, this becomes even more dramatic when you start working in a team and sharing a model. You'll learn that preventing movement of elements becomes just as critical as being able to edit elements to the model. Pinning down grids, levels, and exterior walls will become part of your workflow, especially in larger projects with many users working in a single file.

Revit Is Relatively New Technology

Revit is the newest and most technologically advanced BIM application, and it's under constant development. What began as a single tool for architects has expanded to include structural and mechanical engineers. The evolution of the Revit software platform will continue. As with any new technology, you'll run into problems, get flustered, and no doubt pull out some hair. That said, no other application on the market delivers the advantages of BIM as well as Revit does. Consider this for a moment: Most other architectural products in today's market are based on technology that is 20+ years old, whereas Revit is a new technology that was designed from the ground up as a BIM tool to specifically address the AEC industry. From its inception, Revit has had the goal of improving design communication, coordination, and change management. It has a patented parametric change engine that is unmatched in sophistication. It's also the leading software package in the international market. Revit is not the only BIM package out there, but we feel it offers the most holistic approach.

As you complete more projects with Revit, you'll begin to understand some of its advanced functionality. In this book, we'll delve into advanced concepts and guide you through some really cool features. We'll touch on the fact that Revit is now a technological platform that supports architectural, structural, and mechanical disciplines. The fact that you can share a model with your structural and mechanical, engineering, and plumbing (MEP) engineers is an exciting new prospect, and one that will continue to drive changes in process.

Where Can You Go From Here?

Building Information Modeling is a revolutionary approach to the design, analysis, and documentation of buildings that takes full advantage of modern-day computational technology. At its core, BIM manages the flow of information throughout the lifecycle of a building-design process, allowing you to experience the building before it is built. Using BIM from early conceptual design through construction documentation and into construction administration and beyond, it's possible to better predict, plan, and execute the complex task of creating architecture to meet today's demanding requirements.

The flow of information in this new world consists of virtually all imagined inputs that go into a building design: the gross area of the building; its impact on the environment; the number of windows, doors, and plumbing fixtures; the cost of materials; the size of heating and cooling equipment; you name it. All this information is stored in a digital model—a virtual 3D database chock full of information primed for extraction, analysis, and representation. The input turns into output in the form of coordinated document sets, which can be shared across multiple disciplines and which serve as a centralized design-management tool for an entire project.

The AEC industry is at the cusp of a major shift in technology and the resulting impact on building and, by extension, the greater environment will be revolutionary. We can no longer build without considering the impact of the building, without considering the building as part of a larger network of interconnected flows. The promise of BIM lies in the ability to visualize and understand how a building participates in these complex networks: how it performs, how it will age, and how it will accommodate and adapt to dynamic economic and spatial requirements. This software, along with a change in process, can change the way you do business, structure your office, present ideas to clients, win new jobs, and ultimately build a new architecture.

Armed with the skills you'll develop in this book, you'll be able to take Revit to the edges of creative expression and maybe create something as ambitious as the skyscraper in Figure 1.9.

FIGURE 1.9
Taking Revit to the edges of creative expression

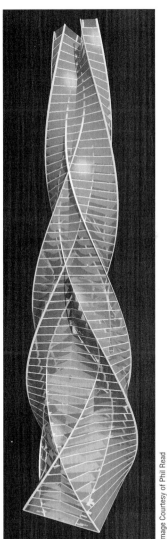

Image Courtesy of Phil Read

The Bottom Line

The advantages of Building Information Modeling   The traditional architectural design tools you've mastered are probably serving you well. New software and a new conceptual model of the building process will inevitably involve some adjustments, so they need to provide significant benefits.

Master It   What are some of the advantages of using BIM over traditional CAD tools?

What to expect from Building Information Modeling   A BIM project is based on a single, centralized database of information. You need to anticipate how that change can affect workflows based on more independent functions.

Master It   How can the work process be affected by the adoption of BIM?

Chapter 2

Revit Fundamentals

The power of a database is that information can be easily accessed, managed, and updated. By using a fixed categorization structure in Revit, you're able to quickly identify elements, control their visibility and graphics, and generate reports based on this information. The data is highly structured, but you have tremendous liberty when it comes to the representation of that data. This flexibility lets you have as many views as you want and/or need to convey your design intent. Every view is a filtered, graphical representation of an underlying database, and you're free to make as many views as you deem necessary.

The sooner you embrace this concept and start exploring the opportunities it presents, the better. If you can't get your drawing to look just right, chances are you just haven't dug deep enough. Throughout this book, we'll give you more suggestions and techniques that we hope will inspire you to go that extra mile and start thinking outside the box.

In this chapter, you'll learn the fundamental principles of Revit parametric elements and how data is organized in Revit. You'll also get an overview of the graphical user interface and walk through the basics of selection and object manipulation.

In this chapter, you'll learn how to do the following:

◆ Work with and understand Revit parametric elements

◆ Use the Revit user interface

◆ Use the Project Browser

◆ Navigate views and view properties

Working with Revit Parametric Elements

Every element in Revit is considered a *family*, and each family belongs to a *category*. Figure 2.1 shows the basic Revit object model. In this section, we'll discuss how Revit organizes all these families into categories and why this makes sense from a workflow and consistency point of view. Then, we'll look at the different types of families, the principles of their behavior, and how to create them.

FIGURE 2.1
The essential
categorization of
Revit elements

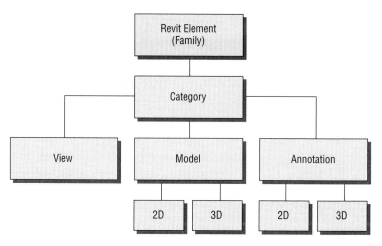

FIGURE 2.1
The essential
categorization of
Revit elements

Revit uses a classification system to organize all the families (content) in the model. This system of organization is based specifically on the AEC industry and is set up to help manage relationships between classes of elements as well as the graphical representation for each class. To see all the categories available in a Revit Project, go to Settings ➤ Object Styles (see Figure 2.2).

FIGURE 2.2
The Object Styles
dialog box

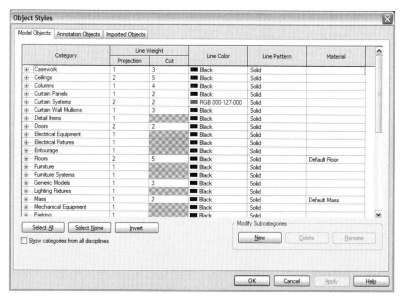

At the core of this organization is a fixed list of *categories* to which all elements ultimately belong. Although this may seem stringent, it works well and will help you maintain a consistent graphical representation across your projects. As you can see, every element belongs to a category, and that category is either a model or an annotation object. In addition, each element is either 2D or 3D in nature. Whenever the mouse hovers over an element, a tooltip appears and tells you what kind of element it is and what category it belongs to (see Figure 2.3). If you aren't working in a worksharing (multiuser) project, then the first bit of text in the tooltip tells you what category the element belongs to. If you're in a worksharing project, the category is preceded by the name of the workset containing the element. (See Chapter 20 for more detail on worksharing.) The next part of a tooltip tells you the family name, and then comes the family type. So, the tooltip follows this logic:

Workset : Category : Family Name : Family Type

FIGURE 2.3
Using tooltips to define elements. The element on the left is part of an unshared project and omits the workset name; the element on the right is part of a workset named Shell and Core.

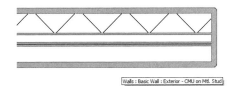

Model Categories

Model Object categories, the first tab in the Object Styles dialog, includes all the real-world types of objects typically found in buildings. These object categories include the usual elements such as walls, floors, roofs, and furniture, along with other categories that makes sense in an architectural project. For 2D elements that represent real-world objects, the category *Detail Element* is provided. Examples of 2D detail elements are insulation and detail components that represent real objects but are represented only in detail views. In Revit, these objects are not modeled as 3D elements, but added as 2D representations, as shown in Figure 2.4.

FIGURE 2.4
Details such as this steel connection at the roof are composed of 2D elements.

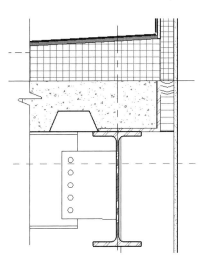

For elements that don't fit into any obvious category, there is the *Generic Models* category. This can be used for objects such as fireplaces, theatre stages, and other specific design elements. If you're not sure exactly what you're making, you can always create it as a generic element. If you later decide that any element needs to be recategorized, that's not a problem—you can reassign the element to a new category at any point.

With the exception of the detail elements, model elements appear by default in all views. In other words, if you draw a wall in plan, it will show up in any other applicable plans, elevations, sections, and 3D views. Remember, you're working on a single building model—all views in Revit are just different ways to look at the model. Detail components, on the other hand, appear only in the view in which they were placed.

As we'll discuss in more detail shortly, you can turn on and off the visibility of any category or element, in any view. For example, say you've placed furniture in your model. The furniture is 3D geometry and will be visible by default in many views. Revit lets you turn off the visibility of the furniture in one floor plan while leaving it visible in another floor plan. The furniture isn't deleted; it's made visible or not depending on the information you need to convey in particular drawings.

Because model elements appear in all other views, two types of graphic representation are defined for each category: projection and cut, as shown in the Object Styles dialog in Figure 2.2. The *projection* graphics define the graphics for the element in elevation, 3D views, or any other view where the element isn't being cut by the view. The *cut* graphics define how the element will look when cut by sections and plan views. Typically, the section cut graphic is bolder than the projection lines, to emphasize that the element is being cut by the view plane. (Surface and cut patterns are always drawn with line weight 1 and can't be made thicker.) Figure 2.5 shows how wall line weight differs between the cut and projection. Also notice that patterns are applied to the walls and floors. Patterns can be added to give additional graphic representation to a material and are always drawn with a thin line weight.

FIGURE 2.5
Cut and projection graphics are defined for each element.

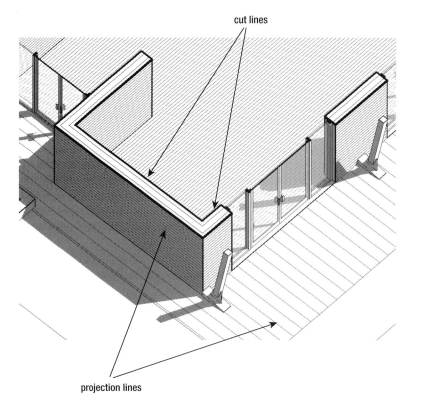

cut lines

projection lines

Categories also make it easy to interchange elements. You can swap out elements of the same category with a few clicks of the mouse. This streamlines the process of editing the model by limiting choices to those that make sense. For example, you can swap a lighting fixture with another lighting fixture by selecting the element and then seeing what other lighting fixtures are available in the Type Selector. Choosing another type swaps out the type instantly.

Revit is smart about this interchange—it offers only different types of the same category of elements. For example, when you select a door, you don't get a list of plumbing fixtures to swap it with; you get a list of other door families.

Annotation Categories

Annotation object categories include all the annotations, symbols, and descriptive data added to a view to describe the building. These are listed in the second tab of the Object Styles dialog. Most annotations are view-specific 2D elements and appear only in the view in which they were created. Examples include dimensions, tags, callouts, and text notes. Annotations such as sections, levels, and grids are 2D graphics, but they have 3D characteristics and appear in other views. These elements (levels, grids, sections) appear in many views thanks to BIM application functionality. Levels, grids, and section marks extend throughout the model and can be edited from multiple views. You don't need to draw these elements in each view as separate, disconnected graphics. With Revit, they're truly 3D annotations. The only caveat to this statement is that they don't appear in 3D views.

DEPENDENT VIEWS

There is an exception to the rule that annotations appear in only one view. With *dependent views*, annotations are shared between views, so that if you change the annotation in one view, it affects other views as well. This feature was added in the 2008 release.

Subcategories

Within each category can be many subcategories that let you control graphics with finer precision. This is what makes the concept of categories so much more powerful and natural to work with than layers. For example, looking at a door, you can see that the category Doors (Figure 2.6) has a set of subcategories that relate to sub-elements in the door assembly. For example, you see Elevation Swing, Frame/Mullion, Glass, Opening, Panel Swing, and any other user-defined elements that can be made when creating a door family. Each subcategory can be assigned an independent line weight, color, and pattern.

FIGURE 2.6
Subcategories allow finer graphic control over categories.

Doors	2	2	■ Black	Solid
Elevation Swing	1	1	■ Black	Dash 1/16"
Frame/Mullion	1	3	■ Black	Solid
Glass	1	4	■ Black	Solid
Hidden Lines	2	2	■ Blue	Dash
Opening	1	3	■ Black	Solid
Panel	1	3	■ Black	Solid
Plan Swing	1	1	■ Black	Solid

Imported Categories/Subcategories

When a CAD file is imported into Revit, all of its layers are represented as subcategories in the Imported Objects tab of the Object Styles dialog. Layers have a projection line weight, a color, and a pattern.

IMPORTED FILE LIMITATIONS

There is no Cut line style for DWG, DXF, and DGN files. These files are just sets of lines, and lines can have only one line weight thickness.

These can be overridden at any time to suit your requirements. Each import appears as a category in this dialog, as shown in Figure 2.7. There is no need to remap CAD layers into Revit taxonomy. If you're used to the layer conventions set up in CAD, these will be mapped directly into the Object Styles dialog with same names, line weights, and colors.

FIGURE 2.7
Imported CAD layers represented as subcategories

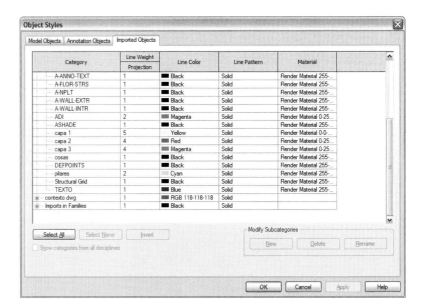

Views

Views are also considered parametric elements in Revit, and they have many properties to help you define how they should display information. A view doesn't change the model in any way—it only acts as a filter through which you view the model. This also applies to schedules and material take-offs. Although these are more abstract to think of as views, they're still parametric windows into the model. Throughout the book, you'll be asked to make views, and we'll guide you through various methods for making views convey specific information about your design.

Type and Instance Parameters

A *parametric* element is something that can change size, material, and graphic look but is still the same fundamental element. Most elements in Revit are designed with parameters that allow for the creation of variations of a base type. Take a typical Revit door family as an example. Each family can have many types built into it. Each type typically represents a variation in size, material, color, or other defining characteristic. Although each type can vary in shape and size, the base geometry for each type is derived from the same family.

THE DIFFERENCE BETWEEN BLOCKS AND FAMILIES

In a typical CAD environment, you might create each door as a block; each of those blocks would be a separate element unrelated to any of the others. So, 20 door sizes would mean 20 floor-plan blocks, 20 section blocks, 20 elevation blocks, and 20 3D blocks if you were going to use them as liberally as we use them in Revit. All of those in Revit are represented with *one* family that can display itself in 2D and 3D and whose size, material, and visibility can be changed at any time.

Depending on how the family is built, parameters can affect either the *type* or the *instance*. *Type parameters* affect all families used in the model, whereas *instance parameters* affect only the family you've selected. This is an important distinction: You can change instance properties only when you have an element selected, but you can change type properties without selecting anything.

Consider a round table. You might define its shape using a type parameter for the radius. If you placed 20 types of tables with a 2′ radius and then changed that radius to 3′, all 20 tables would update automatically. Now, if the radius parameter was an instance parameter, changing the radius would affect only the type of table you currently had selected. The same logic can be applied to other dimensional constraints and materiality. Revit forces you to consider what an element is and what it means to change the element's defining characteristics. For example, most content in Revit doesn't let you arbitrarily change dimensions of every instance, on the fly, whenever you want—this would make tracking the notion of object type difficult and would make mass-updating more tedious. Think of a type as something you'll eventually have to schedule, spec, and install as a real-world commodity.

Bidirectional Relationships

Objects with parameters that can be edited are nothing new in the world of software. But what makes Revit unique is its ability to go beyond mere parameters and create relationships *between* objects. This ability has been referred to as the *parametric change engine*, and it's a core technological advantage built into Revit.

For example, walls can be attached to roofs, and if the roof changes to a new shape or size, all walls attached to the roof automatically adapt to the roof shape. Figure 2.8 shows that changing a roof pitch automatically adjusts other roofs and walls to keep them joined.

FIGURE 2.8
Changing the roof pitch updates walls automatically.

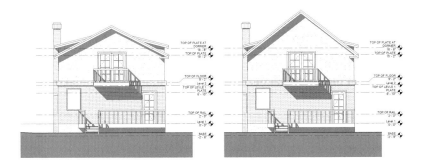

Another powerful manifestation of interrelated relationships occurs between walls, floors, roofs, components, and levels. They all have explicit relationships to levels, so that if a level changes elevation, all elements associated with that level update automatically. Not only does the base of the walls attached to a level change, but the tops of the walls attached to this level also change. This is fundamentally different from many other BIM software applications, where elements understand where they're placed in plan but not in section. Similarly, when you change the size of a room by moving walls, you're changing not only the wall, but also everything that wall affects in the model: the size of the room (area and volume), color-fill diagrams, ceilings, and floors. The doors and windows within the wall move with the wall, and any dimensions to that wall automatically update.

🌐 Real World Scenario

ADJUSTING A LEVEL AND ROOF SLOPE TO MEET DESIGN REQUIREMENTS

In a real-world project, the height of a level is bound to change in the design process, which in turn will change floor-to-ceiling heights and roof locations and will influence the building's overall height. Consider a scenario in which keeping the top of the roof below a maximum height was a design requirement. Not to worry—with Revit, changing the height of levels at any point in the process updates all dimensions and elements associated with that level.

Changing the Top of Roof level pushed the roof peak too high. By editing the roof and changing its slope parameter, we lowered the roof height, and all the walls attached to the roof updated to reflect the change. There was no need to edit the walls independently in order to get the correct results.

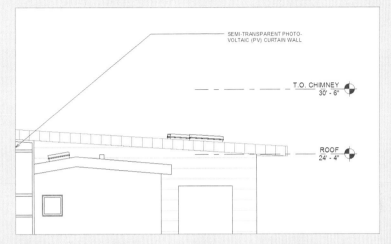

With one edit, we changed the level height. The walls and roof updated immediately.

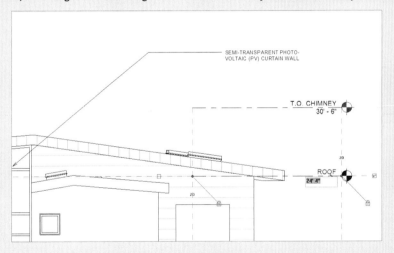

With an edit to the roof property for slope, the roof updated, as did the walls attached to it.

Revit tries to keep things joined and connected in order to eliminate huge amounts of tedious editing. You'll begin take it for granted after a few days with Revit, but remember: When you drag a wall that has other walls attached to it, those other walls will automatically stretch with your move. Not only that; but rooms, dimensions, floors, components, and tags will also move. Of course, if you don't want all this intelligent behavior, Revit provides escape hatches. For example, if you right-click a wall's end control, you can disallow it from joining other walls (see Figure 2.9). Or, you can select Disjoin from the Options bar once you've selected a wall and then select the move command—doing so will detach the smart relationships between the wall and the rest of the model and treat the wall as an independent entity.

FIGURE 2.9
By right-clicking the end of a wall join, you can stop the wall from auto-joining to other walls.

This parametric behavior extends to annotations and sheet management, as well. Tags aren't simple graphics and text: They're interactive graphical parameters of the element being tagged. To edit a tag is to edit the element or tag family, and vice versa. This is also known as a *bidirectional association*: You can edit the elements and the tag and maintain consistent data. A great example is easily demonstrated with a view and a sheet. When you place a section view onto a sheet, the section key automatically references the sheet number and detail number on the sheet. Change the sheet number, and the section tag updates instantly. *This* is what a real parametric engine is and what ensures total coordination of documentation. You've probably heard this phrase before, but it's worth repeating: The parametric engine guarantees that a "change anywhere is a change everywhere."

Constraints

During the design phase, you may want to apply some dimensional rules to the design and make sure they aren't altered. These rules might be a minimum hallway width for code compliance, or a maximum office square footage for a particular user. Whatever the restriction, Revit dimensions make it possible to lock it down and create a constraint. This constraint is independent, but it's related to the dimension. If you delete the dimension, you can keep the constrained condition and know that the model will maintain those relationships. The point is that a dimension can be much more that a 2D annotation.

These design rules are used all the time, but not many software applications let you capture this design intent in the model. If you run a dimension string from level to level and lock the dimensions (as in Figure 2.10), you're locking the relationship between these elements in the whole model. By locking down elements, you make it harder for other elements in the model to break this important design intent, and thus you keep the model more intact and predictable.

Here's another example: You may want your door jamb always positioned 4″ (25cm) from the wall corner; or you may want three windows in a room to be always positioned at equal distances. By locking this relationship, you embed design intent into the model. If one element moves, the other element also moves. Revit also provides a less explicit, automatic way to associate elements to other elements. When an element is selected, there is an option to make the element move with nearby elements; Revit will make its best guess as to which elements drive other elements to move.

FIGURE 2.10
Design intent can be locked down by adding constraints.

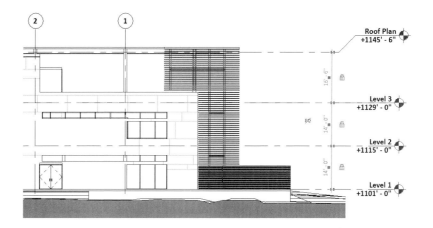

Revit Families

Revit families are used to create your model. There are three over-arching methods for creating families in Revit:

◆ System families

◆ Standard families

◆ In-place families

The difference between them lies in their creation method, in what context they're created, and the types of parameters available. Let's review each of these types of families.

SYSTEM FAMILIES

Model system families are made up of a limited set of types: walls, roofs, ceilings, stairs, railings, ramps, mullions, curtain panels, and toposurfaces (topography). See Figure 2.11 for examples of system families. These families are created in the context of each project using some predefined types. These families also have various creation methods that are specific to the type of the family. For example, to make walls, you can just start drawing (placing a wall), whereas to make a floor or roof, you enter a *sketch mode* in which you define the outer shape with lines that then generate a 3D model of the floor. For stairs and railings, you enter a more detailed sketch mode that has additional features not available in floors or roofs. When making toposurfaces, you use a sketch mode that lets you edit 3D points specific to toposurfaces.

You can create new types of system families by duplicating existing types and editing their parameters. If you've been using Revit for any length of time, then this method of duplicating a type to create new types should be familiar territory for you.

(You can't create new categories in Revit. These categories are predefined within Revit and limited to the list available. This is primarily to maintain control over the graphics from project to project.)

System Families

FIGURE 2.11
System families

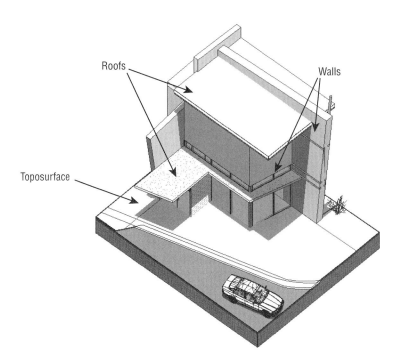

If you aren't sure whether an element is a system family, open the Element Properties dialog and check the family name. Embedded in the family name, you can see whether the element is a system family. Figure 2.12 shows that a Basic Wall and a Section are both system families.

FIGURE 2.12
System families
include model and
annotation elements.

System families are also used for many annotation categories such as sections, elevations, levels, grids, text, and dimensions—they aren't limited to model elements.

Although you can't save a system family outside of your project to a shared library as a stand-alone component, it's possible to reuse system families in other projects. To transfer system families between projects, choose File ➢ Transfer Project Standards to display the Select Items To Copy window (Figure 2.13). This dialog gives you a feel for the number of different types of system families used in a Revit project.

FIGURE 2.13
The Select Items
To Copy dialog

FIGURE 2.13
The Select Items
To Copy dialog

STANDARD FAMILIES

Standard families (see Figure 2.14) are created outside of the project environment using the Family Editor. They're stored in an external library and can be loaded into a project for use at any point. Every standard family belongs to a specific Revit category so that when it's loaded into a project, it adopts the graphic rules defined for its category in the Object Styles dialog. This guarantees graphic consistency throughout your project without your having to constantly manage changes to new families. This also guarantees that when you schedule a category, you get all elements that belong to that category.

For example, if you find a lighting fixture family on the Web and load it into your project, it will use the Lighting Fixtures object style in your project to represent the family. It will be scheduled with other lighting fixtures. You aren't forced to open the family and adjust line weights or colors, or add metadata to the element, because this is all controlled at the project level. This illustrates the value of having a fixed number of categories to manage—you can rest assured that the project won't inflate with endless, oddly named layers that are difficult, if not impossible, to decode.

FIGURE 2.14
Standard families

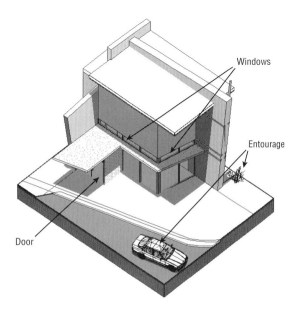

Standard families have their own file format extension (.rfa) and can be stored outside the project environment for later use in other projects. Revit ships with a predefined folder structure to help manage the vast numbers of families available. Choose File ➢ Load Library ➢ Load Family to see how Revit organizes information (see Figure 2.15).

FIGURE 2.15
The Load from Library dialog box

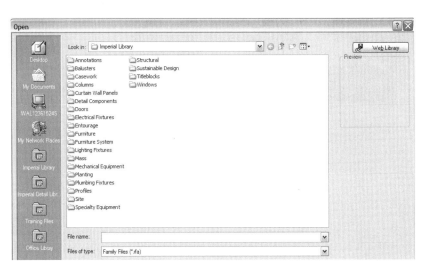

ORGANIZING YOUR OFFICE LIBRARY

In your office, you're free to organize your families in whatever way makes the most sense. You can use a read-only, shared office library, or per-project mini-libraries. Whatever route you go, be sure to add your library locations to your Revit file load dialog.

To do this, choose Options ➢ File Locations, and add a new path to the Libraries table.

Once you do this, a new link appears in the Open dialog with the name of your library. Clicking the icon takes you directly to your office library.

To create a new standard family, either duplicate an existing one in the project and modify its properties, or open it in the Family Editor if you need to make more radical geometric changes. (The first method only allows for slight dimensional and material modifications and *not* geometry modifications.) The process of editing a family supports an iterative design workflow: By selecting any family, you have the option either to edit its properties, or to open it in the Family Editor and make changes to it and then load it right back into your project. Families can be complex, but at least you won't need to learn any specialized scripting languages in order to create smart, parametric content. This goes for all forms of standard families, from totally parametric windows and doors to one-off pieces of furniture or lighting fixtures.

Revit provides a set of starting family templates you can use to make content from scratch. When you want to start creating a new library element (family), you first need to select the correct template. To open a template, choose File ➤ New ➤ Family. Choose the type of element you want to make, and the template will open. Embedded in each template are smart behavior characteristics of the family you're creating. Figure 2.16 illustrates a door family template, where geometry, parameters, and dimensions are already in place to help you get started.

FIGURE 2.16

The template for this door family includes geometry, parameters, and dimensions to help get you started.

Doors, windows, balusters, casework, columns, curtain wall panels, entourage, furniture, massing elements, generic objects, and plantings are all examples of standard Revit families.

To move families between projects, you can use copy-paste or save your families to disk and then load them into another project.

IN-PLACE FAMILIES

In-place families are custom elements that are specific to a project and the specific conditions of the project. An in-place family opens functionality available in the Family Editor in the context of a project environment. The model grays out and becomes unselectable when you make such families. A complex sweep as a railing fence on a site is an example of an in-place family.

You can copy-paste in-place families from project to project, but you can't save them as RFA files as you can with standard families. Figure 2.17 shows an in-place family added to a facade in order to create some non-orthogonal mullions.

FIGURE 2.17
Example of an in-place family used to add skewed mullions to the facade

Overriding the Representation of Elements

As we mentioned earlier in this book, there are no layers in Revit. Instead of using layers, Revit uses object categories and subcategories to define the graphics for each element class as well as to control visibility (which is the purpose of layers in other software). The Object Styles dialog establishes the default graphics for every category; however, in any view, you can override these graphics using the View ➤ Visibility/Graphic Overrides dialog shown in Figure 2.18. The two dialogs look very similar—the difference is that Object Styles shows the defaults preset for a project, whereas Visibility/Graphic Overrides is the place to review and make changes to those default settings on a per-view basis. The same familiar categories and subcategories displayed in the Object Styles dialog are displayed in this dialog as well.

FIGURE 2.18
The Visibility/Graphic Overrides dialog box

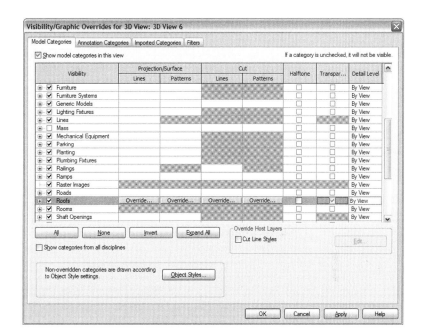

The same level of visual control for line weight, color, and pattern is provided here, but in a slightly different interface. In addition to line overrides, you can also override cut and surface patterns and choose to show a category as halftone, transparent, or at a different level of detail. Figure 2.19 shows the Roof category overridden to be transparent in the 3D view, allowing you to see through the roof and look into the rooms beneath while keeping the shape of the roof visible. The changes made in the dialog are applied only to the current view.

FIGURE 2.19
The Roof category has
been overridden to
be transparent in the
3D view.

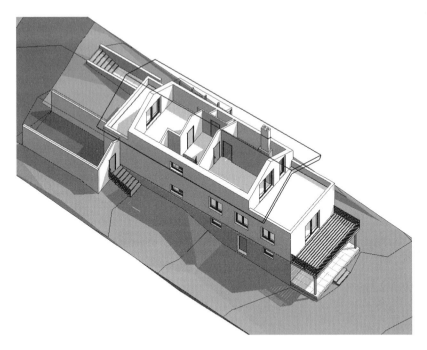

The same categories are used to control the visibility of elements in a view. You can turn off entire categories, subcategories, or individual elements in any view.

The Revit User Interface

As you'll notice, the Revit interface isn't overburdened by a lot of toolbars. It may seem as if there are too few buttons to build an entire building. Don't worry, all the tools are there—they're just not visible all the time. The UI is divided into five major components, shown in Figure 2.20: the *View window*, where all the views and drawing take place; the *Design bar*, where you access all the creation tools; the *Project Browser*, where all the views and families are stored and which is used to navigate the projects; the *Options bar*, where you choose types, access properties, and edit context-sensitive options; and the *toolbars*, where you invoke various editing tools. Next, we'll take a quick look at each of these components.

In addition to these major UI components, the Status bar is located along the bottom of the application frame. It contains information about active commands, what is selected, progress meters, and the Communications Center.

The View Window

The View window is where all the action takes place. Here, you add elements, modify them, and construct and document your model. The view area can tile multiple views, allowing you to visualize the model from multiple vantage points concurrently. We don't recommend tiling the views if you have more than six open views, because the views get too small, and it becomes difficult to work.

FIGURE 2.20
The Revit user
interface

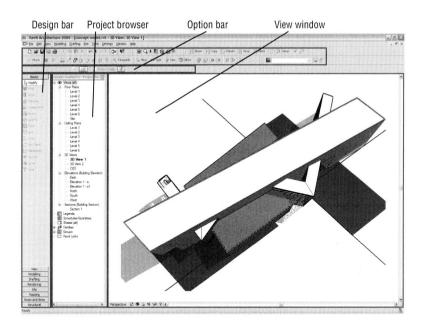

To arrange views, go to the Window menu and try the Cascade or Tile option. You'll also see the option to Close Hidden Windows.

This feature is a great way to clear your workspace when you have a unmanageable number of views open. Clicking the button closes all but one view for each project or family you have open. This is especially advisable for better performance on a complex project.

To see an example, open two views of the model, and then tile the views. Select an element in one view; you'll see that it becomes selected in both views. This simple interaction shows that when you make a change to an element in one view, the change is instantly reflected in other views. This is a great way to conceptually understand the reality of a true BIM modeler.

Each view has properties, and some of these properties are exposed at the bottom of the View window in what is called the View Control bar.

These controls allow you to quickly change the display of the view without having to dig into a properties dialog. The available controls include View Scale, Detail Level, Display Type, Shadows, Crop View, Show Crop, Temporary Hide/Isolate, and Reveal Hidden Elements.

The Design Bar

The Design bar is a group of tabs located on the left side of the application that contains creation tools organized based on common tasks, as shown in Figure 2.21.

FIGURE 2.21

The Design bar

The tools are grouped into tabs that suggest a certain task: Drafting, Modeling, Site, Massing, and so on. Some tools are repeated on multiple tabs because they're used for various tasks. The Dimension tool is an example: Dimensions are used when modeling, drafting, and laying out structures. Which tabs are visible is entirely up to you.

TURNING TABS ON AND OFF

The Massing tab can be turned off if you don't use massing. The same is true for the Structural and Site tabs. To see the full selection of tabs, right-click anywhere on the Design bar, and select only those you wish to view.

Clicking a tab opens it and makes the tools available. You can hide/reveal design tabs using the context menu when the mouse is hovering over the Design bar. On some smaller monitor resolutions (less than 1280×1024), you may not see all the tools available in a design tab. To access these tools, click the More Tools flyout at the bottom of the tab, as shown here.

All the tools located in the Design bar are also available from the menu at the top of the application. You may also notice that some tools aren't enabled, depending on the type of view you're currently working in. If you open a perspective view, almost all the tools in the Design bars appear grayed out. This is because Revit doesn't let you create new elements in perspective views (don't be discouraged; you can place objects in any orthographic 3D view).

The Options Bar

The Options bar contains several parts: the Type Selector, properties button, and dynamic option controls. The Type Selector becomes active when you're making new elements or when an element is selected. The tool is used to swap types of family elements—and works on all types of Revit objects—whether model or annotation. The Options bar looks like this when a wall is selected:

The Properties button takes you to the element properties of whatever you've selected. Everything to the right of the Properties button is dynamic and changes depending on what you're creating, what tool you're using, or what element is selected. For example, when the Move tool is activated, you'll notice some new options appear:

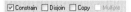

Look to the Options bar whenever you're using a tool, placing elements, or selecting elements, because it will show you options specific to the current task. It's easy to forget the Options bar exists, so train yourself to scan it, and get familiar with what it offers.

The Project Browser

The Project Browser allows you to navigate to all your views, create new views, access element properties, and place elements. All the views of your project are stored here, making it possible to organize and navigate a project from one location. This feature is the backbone of your project, so we'll spend more time exploring its functionality in the next section.

Figure 2.22 shows a collapsed view of a typical Project Browser. As you can see, the browser contains all your views, families, schedules, sheets, and linked files.

The Project Browser is such an important tool that we'll devote the rest of this chapter to exploring its use.

Using the Project Browser

There are a number of ways to navigate through a Revit project. As you start working in real projects, the number of views and drawings that accumulate will become quite large. Being able to find your views and effectively move between them is critical to support an effective workflow. We'll look at the various methods of moving between views, best practices, and how to customize the display of these views using the Project Browser.

Views

A *view* is a graphical way to look at the database of information you're creating. Plan, section, schedule table, 3D view—all of these are just different ways to look at and query the same underlying database of information that describes your building. Revit organizes all the views of your project in the Project Browser. Your plans, sections, elevations, 3D views, and schedules are all stored there. Double-clicking a view name opens the view in the View window. When you close a window, you don't need to save first—it's always accessible from the Project Browser.

The default organization is based on the view type, which is why the views are divided into separate nodes in the tree. The default organization when all the nodes are collapsed looks like this:

With a node expanded, right-click a view name to access additional options for any view (see Figure 2.23). From this menu, you can open views, rename them, duplicate them, and apply view templates.

Note that you can multiselect views in the Project Browser. When more than one view is selected, you can right-click to bring up the context menu:

For example, from the context menu, you can create and apply view templates. This is a way to give views a consistent scale and graphical appearance, among other things. Let's look at how to use the Project Browser as a way to drive properties from one view to another:

1. Open `Foundation.rvt` from the `Chapter 2` folder on this book's companion website (`www.sybex.com/go/masteringrevit2008`).

2. Open Plan: Level 1.

3. Right-click the view, and duplicate it.

4. Rename the view **Level 1 - Presentation**.

5. Press VG to open the Visibility/Graphic Overrides dialog.

6. Go to the Annotations tab, and turn off visibility of all annotations by selecting the "Show annotation categories in this view" check box at the top of the table.

7. Go back to the view in the Project Browser, and right-click the view. Select Create View Template From View (see Figure 2.24).

FIGURE 2.24
Creating a new view template

8. Name the template **Presentation Graphics**.

9. Duplicate Level 2, and rename it **Level 2 - Presentation**.

10. Right-click the view name, and choose Apply View Template.

11. Choose Presentation Graphics.

12. The plan how has the same properties as Level 1 - Presentation.

Working in a data-driven model, you can use view properties as a way to customize how the browser sorts and organizes all your views. This is a great way to manage the large number of views that will fill your project. Clicking the top of the Project Browser window (not a view) makes it the active selection. You'll notice the Type Selector in the Options bar activates, and some pre-defined options will be available to choose (see Figure 2.25). Selecting any of these will re-sort the views in your project based on criteria.

FIGURE 2.25

Browser organization options

MAKING A CUSTOM BROWSER ORGANIZATION

The following steps show how to customize the browser organization:

1. With the Foundation file still open, select the Views icon in the Project Browser.

2. The Type Selector lists Browser - Views : all.

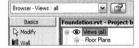

   Click the Properties button.

3. Change the type to "not on sheets". You'll see the browser reorganize the list and remove views that are on sheets.

Now, let's make a custom sort based on your name (or initials) by applying a new "Drawn by" parameter to all views and then using that parameter to sort the views in the browser:

1. Choose Settings ➤ Project Parameters.

2. In the resulting dialog, click the "Add a new parameter" button.

3. Choose the Views category on the right side of the dialog, and give the parameter the name **Drawn by**. In the Group Parameter Under drop-down list, select Identity Data (see Figure 2.26). Click OK.

4. Go back to the Project Browser.

FIGURE 2.26
Create a new project
parameter for views.

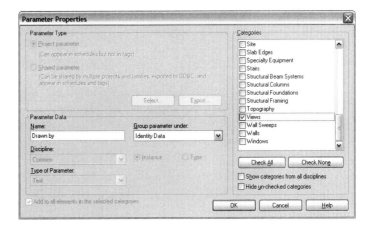

FIGURE 2.26
Create a new project
parameter for views.

5. Go to Properties, and choose Duplicate ➤ "not on sheets". Name the duplicate **My Drawings**.

6. Click the Folders button.

7. Change the "Group by" setting to "Drawn by" (Figure 2.27), and click OK.

FIGURE 2.27
Group views by the
new parameter,
"Drawn by".

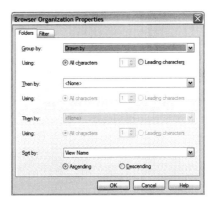

8. Go to any view, and open its view properties.

9. The project parameter you added appears in the Identity Data group as "Drawn by". Type your initials or name in the value field, and click OK (Figure 2.28).

FIGURE 2.28
Change the "Drawn
by" parameter for
any view.

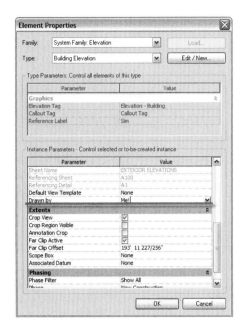

SHEETS

Sheets are special views that are your future documents—the actual sheets you'll be sharing with your contractor, client, or team members. These sheets can contain many other views. This is where the collections of drawings that eventually get printed are stored. Under each sheet node, you see all the views placed on that sheet. Like any other view in Revit, if you double-click the node, the sheet view opens in the View window.

To make a new sheet, use the View tab or the View menu, and choose Sheet. This lets you select a title block family to use.

FAMILIES

In the Project Browser, you can see all the loaded families in your project. From here, you can drag and drop elements into the drawing area, query element properties, create new types of elements, and even select all instances of a given element in the model in order to perform wholesale changes. The context menu for families (Figure 2.29) is different from that for views. Note that if you choose the option to edit a family, you'll open the family in the Family Editor, where you can make changes to the component and then reload it. If you expand the family node to expose all the family types, you can right-click a type and choose Select All Instances from the context menu. All instances in the model become selected, even if you can't see them in your current view. This lets you make edits to the family type in one interaction. For example, you can select all instances of a door family and swap it with a different door type.

LINKS

Starting with the 2008 release, Revit *links* (other Revit files that are linked into your project) are also listed in the Project Browser. Using the context menu, you can reload, unload, open, copy, and visually identify the links in your project.

ACTIVATING A VIEW ON A SHEET

Double-clicking a view placed on a sheet is the same as opening the view from the view's node. Double-clicking the sheet name opens the sheet. From the sheet, you can directly edit views on the sheet by right-clicking a view and choosing Activate View option. This opens the view and grays out the sheet context. You can then edit the view from the context of your sheet. To get back to the sheet, use the context menu again, and choose Deactivate View.

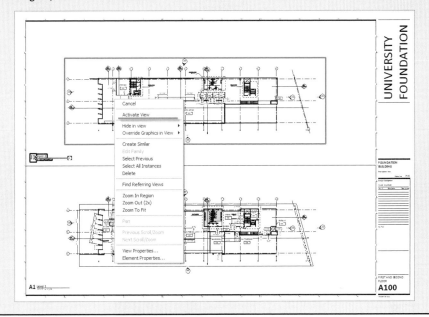

FIGURE 2.29
Options for families in
the Project Browser

GROUPS

Groups are associated collections of elements that can be repeatedly placed throughout the model. Groups are used for repeating entities (from furniture composed of a table and six chairs, to a typical bathroom type with fixtures and partitions, to a typical hotel room). When one group changes, all other instances of that group also change. Whenever a group is created, it appears in the Project Browser. You can place a group from the Project Browser by dragging it into the View window.

Working with Views and View Properties

As we've mentioned, all views have properties that determine characteristics such as scale, graphics display, and view depth. Each view type has special characteristics and options that are important to understand when you're using Revit. We'll look at the different view types and explain their defining features and how to use them. To access view properties, use any of these access methods:

◆ Right-click anywhere in the drawing surface of a view, and select View Properties.

◆ Right-click a view in the Project Browser, and select Properties.

◆ Select View ➤ View Properties.

◆ Use the keyboard shortcut VP to access the View Properties dialog directly.

FLOOR PLANS

Plan views are used to show horizontal slices through your 3D building. Each plan view in Revit is associated with a level. A *level* is a horizontal datum that establishes major floor-to-floor heights and other critical horizontal working planes. Figure 2.30 shows that each level generates a plan view. By default, the plan is cut 4′ above the actual level height, but this value can be customized to suit your requirements. Note that if you delete a level in your project, you also delete all plan views associated with that level—so be careful when deleting levels!

Each plan view can show a range of the model based on levels. This aspect of Revit is often misunderstood, so let's take a moment to demystify it.

FIGURE 2.30
Levels generate
plan views.

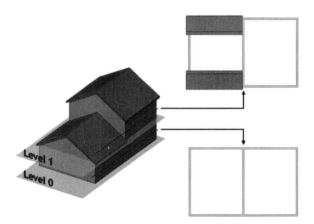

View Range

When creating your documents, you care about correct representation of your elements. Using the Object Styles dialog and graphic overrides, you can get your drawings to look exactly how you want them. However, you'll often wish to add some abstraction to the drawing that involves elements that aren't typically visible in the view. You may want to see roof lines overhead, or see down into an atrium a few levels below. This is where the View Range options come in handy.

The options available in the View Range dialog allow you to define how elements in a view are represented, depending on their location in space. View-range values are stored as a property of the view and are included when you save a view as a view template.

Figure 2.31 shows three ways to represent the same space and elements by using different view-range settings. Think of the mess you might end up with if you had to do this using a layering system!

FIGURE 2.31
Three different representations of the same model in plan view

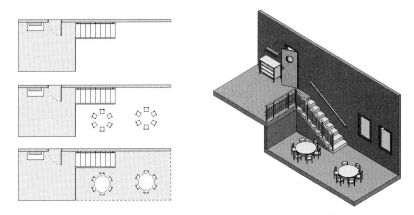

To access the View Range dialog, go to view properties of a plan or ceiling plan view, and choose to edit the View Range parameter. Doing so opens the dialog shown in Figure 2.32.

FIGURE 2.32
The View Range dialog

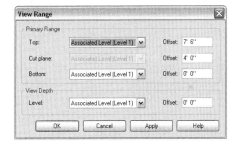

The View Range dialog is divided into two parameter groups: Primary Range and View Depth. The view range is defined by horizontal planes—three of them define the primary range (Top, Cut plane, and Bottom), and a fourth plane defines the depth of a view (View Depth):

- *Top*—Defines the top limit of the view range

- *Cut plane*—Defines the height of the Cut plane

- *Bottom*—Defines the bottom limit of the view range

Note that the positioning of these is *always* relative to a level. The Cut plane *always* references the level of the view in which you're working, and the other two can reference *any* level of the project.

There is no graphical presentation of the view-range settings, but it shouldn't be difficult to imagine their position in space. Look at Figure 2.33, a representation of different positions of the horizontal planes of a view range:

FIGURE 2.33
Various positions of
the view range (top)
and the associated
plan view (bottom)

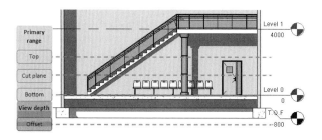

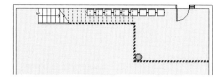

Floor plan In a floor plan view, the direction of the view is from top to bottom—so, you're looking from above.

Ceiling plan In a ceiling plan, the view direction is exactly the opposite—you're looking from below, upward (see Figure 2.34).

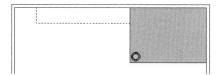

FIGURE 2.34
Position of the view
range for ceiling plans
(top) and the associated
plan view (bottom)

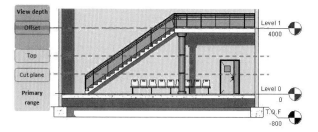

Depending on the positioning of the elements with respect to the view range and its parameters, the graphical display of those elements can vary. The "Cut plane" parameter can radically change the appearance of your view, because every element in Revit has a physical location in space. Elements look different depending on whether they're cut *by the Cut plane*, *above the Cut plane*, or *below the Cut plane*.

Cut Plane

Not all Revit elements behave the same with respect to the Cut plane. Some Revit categories don't support the notion of being cut (furniture families, for example); regardless at the height at which a Cut plane intersects them, they're always represented as if they're viewed from above (not cut). Figure 2.35 shows that a stool looks the same, no matter where the Cut plane happens to intersect it.

FIGURE 2.35
Elements are affected differently by the Cut plane.

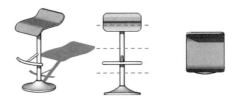

DOES A CATEGORY ALLOW CUTTING?

How do you determine whether a category allows its elements to be cut? A fast way is to look it up in the Revit Help file under "Creating your own Components (Families)" ➤ Visibility and Detail Level ➤ "Cuttable and non Cuttable Family categories."

There is another method, as well, which may be more practical: In the Visibility Graphics dialog or the Object Styles dialog is a Cut column. For certain categories, this column is grayed out; this is the indicator that the category doesn't allow cutting.

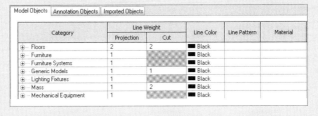

Category	Line Weight		Line Color	Line Pattern	Material
	Projection	Cut			
⊕ Floors	2	2	■ Black		
⊕ Furniture	1		■ Black		
⊕ Furniture Systems	1		■ Black		
⊕ Generic Models	1	1	■ Black		
⊕ Lighting Fixtures	1		■ Black		
⊕ Mass	1	2	■ Black		
⊕ Mechanical Equipment	1		■ Black		

The Primary Range

Now that you have a general understanding of how the Cut plane affects elements in a view, let's dig deeper into the primary range concept. As we mentioned, this range consists of two other planes, Top and Bottom, which are placed respectively above and below the Cut plane. The exact positioning of these two planes is defined by an offset value relative to a level:

The Top plane can reference any levels above the current one. The Bottom plane can reference any levels below the current one. Let's look at some examples:

◆ If an element is cut by a Cut plane, it's visible in the view as shown in Figure 2.36.

FIGURE 2.36
The cabinet is cut by the Cut plane and is visible.

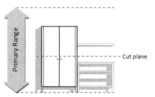

◆ If an element is *below* the Cut plane but within the primary range (partially or completely), it's visible in the plan view as if it were looked at from above, as shown in Figure 2.37.

FIGURE 2.37
The lower bookcase isn't cut but is visible.

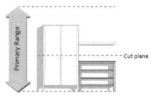

◆ If an element is *above* the Cut plane and completely within the view range, it doesn't appear unless it's the category Windows, Casework, or Generic Model. It appears as if seen from above, as shown in Figure 2.38. Because the wall shelf is the category Casework, and it's within the primary range, it appears in plan view.

FIGURE 2.38
The wall shelf appears.

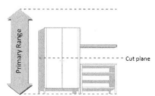

View Depth

The View Depth is defined by a horizontal plane that is below the view range. The positioning of this plane uses the same principle as the planes in the view range—it's defined by an offset referencing a level:

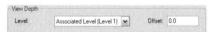

This plane is often confused with the Bottom plane of the view range: The View Depth *cannot* be above the Bottom plane. View Depth allows you to see elements below. The default is set to show nothing, because it's associated with the active level and has no offset.

The View Depth is easy to misunderstand; it sounds confusing to have a Bottom plane in the view range and also have this additional View Depth parameter. The idea here is that you need the ability to control the display of elements that are below the primary range but within the View Depth. Consider a wall with a footing. The wall is placed on Level 0 and goes up to Level 1. In the plan view of Level 0, using the default settings, you don't see the footing (see Figure 2.39).

FIGURE 2.39

With the default View Depth, the footings aren't visible in plan view.

Figure 2.40 shows the effect of the default view range when it's set to be coincident with the view's associated level, in this case Level 0. To make the footing visible in the Level 0 plan view, you need to do the following:

♦ Lower the height of the Bottom plane in the primary range, and define the View Depth to be coincident with it.

♦ Define the View Depth so that it's below the base of the footing.

In the second case, you don't need to change anything about the Bottom plane. In addition, you can obtain a different graphic presentation for the footings (without modifying the Visibility/Graphic Overrides settings). The View Depth allows elements that are below the current level to appear in a unique line style named *Beyond*. To control that line style, choose Settings ➤ Line Styles.

FIGURE 2.40

Modifying the view range for different visibility. Lowering the depth of the view makes the footings visible in plan view. They're represented with the Beyond line style, which in this example uses a dashed line.

To display the elements in view in a specific way, you'll need to play with various parameter settings in the view range (see Figure 2.41).

FIGURE 2.41
Changing the view-range settings (top) and the corresponding plan view (bottom)

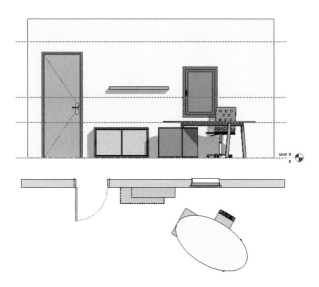

To fully understand this example, it's essential to understand the categories of the elements participating in this view (from left to right in Figure 2.41):

The door   The door belongs to the Door category. It's cut by the Cut plane. Its graphic presentation is controlled by the Cut style in the Object Styles or Visibility/Graphic Overrides dialog. The arc representing the door swing is a 2D symbolic element and thus can't be cut by the Cut plane.

The low cabinet   The low cabinet belongs to the Furniture category Because it's placed below the Cut plane but still within the View Depth, it's visible in plan view. It uses the Beyond line style.

The wall mounted shelf   The wall shelf belongs to the Furniture System category. The shelf is above the Cut plane but within the view range. Its category allows it to be represented in plan view. Its graphics are controlled by the Projection column in the Visibility/Graphic Overrides or Object Styles dialog.

The desk-chair-drawer family   The desk with a chair and a drawer (all one family) belongs to the Furniture category. This family is cut by the Cut plane. Its category doesn't allow for it to be cut, and its graphics are thus controlled by the Projection style in the Visibility/Graphic Overrides or Object Styles dialog.

The window   The window belongs to the Window category. It's cut by the Cut plane. Its graphics are controlled by the Cut style in the Visibility/Graphic Overrides or Object Styles dialog.

CREATING A PLAN VIEW USING VIEW RANGE AND A PLAN REGION

Figure 2.42 is a model of a simple space that we'll use to understand view range. We have chosen a split-level example to show you the power of various settings and resulting displays of the view-range parameters. The goal is to create a plan view of Level 0 that displays information from a lower level. We want to display elements placed on Level 00B with a dashed line style. Follow these steps:

FIGURE 2.42
Working with the view range

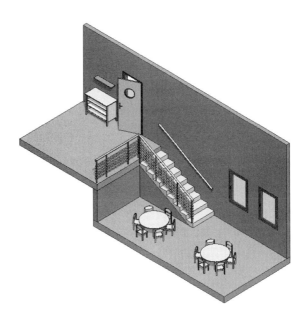

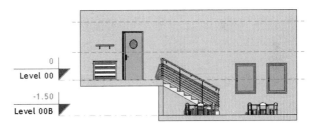

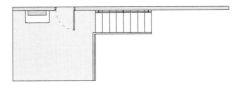

1. Open the File View_Range.rvt from the Chapter 2 folder on the book's website.

   In the elevation view, you can see the various planes (Figure 2.43). The View Depth is defined to be the same as the Bottom plane.

FIGURE 2.43
View-range settings

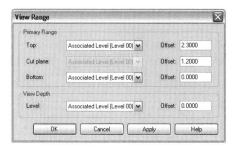

2. From the Level 00 plan view, go to View Properties, and open the View Range dialog.

   The default Revit settings are currently being used. Notice in Figure 2.44 that elements placed on Level 00B are *not* visible in this view. The low cabinet is visible in the view, because it's within the primary range. The wall shelf above the low cabinet belongs to the category Furniture Systems and is also visible, even though it's above the Cut plane.

FIGURE 2.44
You can see the effect of moving the Bottom and View Depth to Level 00B.

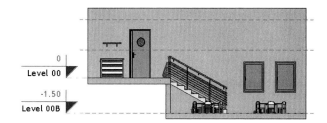

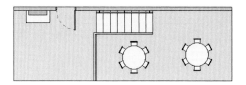

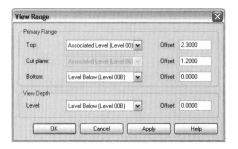

3. Change the Bottom and View Depth to Level Below (Level 00B), and click Apply.

Having defined the Bottom plane as well as the View Depth to be coincident to Level 00B, you've managed to show the elements of Level 00B in the Level 00 plan view. The problem is that it will be difficult to assign a dashed-line style to the elements placed on Level 00B, as you initially desired. You could manually override all the elements, but you'd have to do so in each view manually—let's look at a smarter way to do this.

4. The furniture in this level is below the Cut plane. To change the graphic display of it, you could use the Projection column in the Visibility/Graphic Overrides or Object Styles dialog; but in that case, the presentation of the furniture on Level 00 would be affected—and that isn't what you want to happen.

5. Set the Bottom plane to Level 00, and give the View Depth a –4′ (–1m) offset below Level 00. Click Apply. In the elevation in Figure 2.45, you can see the various planes in dashed-line style. As you'll notice, the chairs are now visible but not the table—this is because the chairs are partially within the view but the tables aren't (they're below the View Depth). The chairs belong to the Furniture category, which doesn't support a cut representation; they're shown as if they were seen from above, even though they're intersected by the View Depth.

FIGURE 2.45
Modifying the View
Depth settings

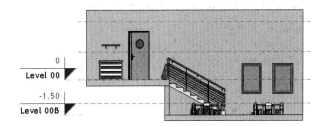

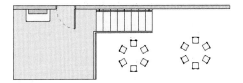

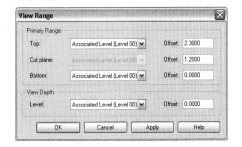

6. Set the View Depth to Level Below (Level 00B) and give it a –4′ (–1m) offset. In the elevation in Figure 2.46, you can see the various planes in dashed-line style.

By changing the View Depth, you have achieved your goal of seeing the furniture from below in a dashed-line style; however, the windows don't look quite right. To fix that, Revit provides a tool that allows you to selectively alter the view range for certain parts of the view using a *plan region*. This tool lets you draw a rectangle and then define the view range for that rectangle as a way to override the view-range settings of the view.

FIGURE 2.46
Lowering the
View Depth

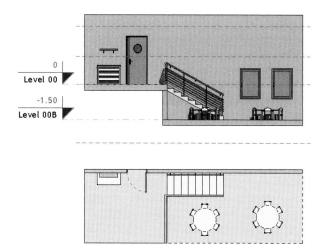

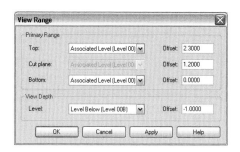

7. In the View Design tab of the Design bar, select the Plan Region tool, and sketch a rectangle around the windows as shown in Figure 2.47. This region will make it possible to show the windows as if they were cut.

FIGURE 2.47
Making a plan region,
annotated here by
the rectangle in the
upper right

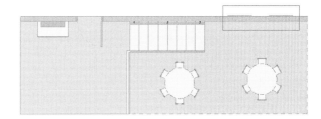

8. Click the View Range Properties button on the Design bar, and change the view range of the plan region. In this example, to show the window, set the level the Cut plane is referencing to Level 00B (see Figure 2.48).

FIGURE 2.48
View-range properties
of the plan region

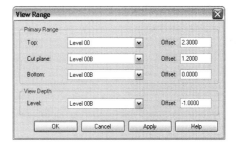

If you need to adjust the properties of the plan region later, select it and use the View Range button on the Options bar as a quick way to get back to the settings.

SECTIONS

Section views are placed using the Views or Basics tab in the Design bar. Like a plan view, a section is a live cut through the building model. You can place sections in plans, elevations, and other section views, and they will appear in other views. A section has two graphic symbols associated with it that appear at either end of the section line. Check the Options bar when placing a new section—you'll notice that you can choose a section type (Building, Wall, Detail) and also preset the scale. These are the options available when placing a section:

You define the section line by making two clicks in the view. Once a section has been created, you can move it by dragging it. The amazing thing is that when you move the section line, the view it references is automatically regenerated. A section line always shows what it's cutting when the view is displayed. It's impossible to have a section that is out of sync with the model.

Some special properties are available to sections, which help you create the drawings you want. We'll focus on those next.

Broken Section Lines

The default section graphic is shown as solid line with a section head and section tail at the ends. You can break a section cut line by clicking the little squiggle icon in the center of the line. Doing this lets you create a graphic as shown in Figure 2.49.

FIGURE 2.49
Clicking the squiggle icon breaks the section line.

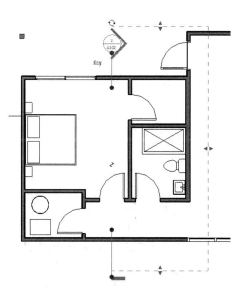

Jogged Sections

As you draw a section line, you'll notice that you can only draw a straight segment. Often, however, you'll want the section line to pass through important parts of the building that don't lie on the same line—you'll need to break the section line and make it jog. You can jog the section line around elements in plan to change what is shown in the view. To do this, click the Split Segment button on the Options bar when a section is selected. The cursor changes to a knife. Click to split the section, and begin dragging the segment. Figure 2.50 shows an example of a section split that jogs around an elevator core but cuts through classrooms.

FIGURE 2.50
Jogging a section line

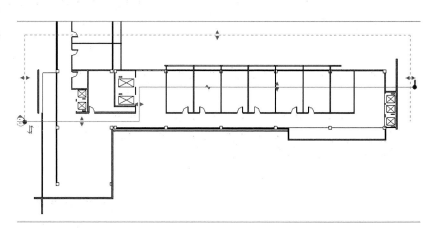

View Depth

When a section is selected, you can control the extents of the view interactively using the crop boundaries. The right and left sides directly affect the section-view size on a sheet. The far clip limits how much geometry is visible in depth. To improve performance and get the right representation, be aware of how deep your sections are. Show only what is needed. By default, a new section extends the entire depth of the model. To change that, pull the far clip closer to the cut plane (see Figure 2.51).

FIGURE 2.51
Controlling the section depth

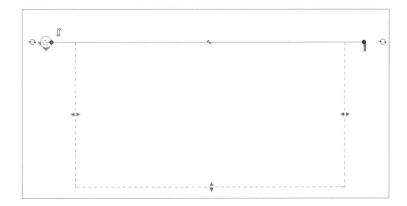

Auto-Hiding Sections/Elevations

It's possible for sections to disappear from time to time as you change the scale of a view. If you check the visibility settings or try Reveal Hidden Elements mode, it won't be clear why the sections aren't visible. This behavior is a result of a little-known feature: "Hide at scales coarser than." This parameter lets you set a scale beyond which the section will no longer be visible. In most circumstances, the benefit of this feature will be nearly invisible—Revit will do the right thing, and you'll go about your business as usual.

ELEVATIONS

Elevations are made by placing elevation tags in floor-plan views. Depending on where you place the elevation in the model, you'll get different resulting views. Revit assumes that if you place an elevation in the model (in a room, for example), you're creating interior elevations. The view shows only the walls visible in that room. If you place an elevation outside your model, a building elevation is created that shows the entire façade.

Elevations are a lot like sections in terms of how they behave in Revit: They have a clip plane, a crop boundary, and a symbol, and they can be opened directly by double-clicking the symbol. Elevation tags can have as many as four views related to one tag for the purpose of creating interior elevations of rooms. This is great for interior elevations but limits your ability to customize the graphics of these tags.

Real World Scenario

HIDING SECTIONS AT COARSER VIEW SCALES

In a ¼˝ floor-plan view, you may have many wall sections, building sections, and interior elevation tags visible. However, with a ⅛˝ plan, you only want to see the building sections and exterior elevation tags. Using the "Hide at scales coarser than" option, you can do this. Select your interior elevation tags, and set their type property to hide at scales coarser than ¼˝. (Make sure you select the view direction arrow, not the view reference part.) Next time you open the ⅛˝ plan, they won't be visible. Do the same for your wall sections. Because this is an instance property, you must first select the elements to which you want to apply this rule.

In many scenarios, the symbol used for an exterior building elevation is identical to the symbol used for section heads. Currently, in Revit, this can't be done with a standard elevation symbol. For this use case, we suggest a common workaround:

1. Create a building section, and open its properties. Click the Edit/New button, and then duplicate the section. Name the new type **Exterior Elevation**, as shown in Figure 2.52.

2. When you go to place an exterior elevation, choose the Section tool instead. Draw the section so that it creates an exterior view of the model.

3. Drag the section head to the middle of the model. Notice that the section extents stay where they are, so the view isn't affected by this graphical change.

4. Turn off the visibility of the section tail by clicking the cycle icon.

FIGURE 2.52
Making a new section
type for a building
section

5. Drag the section line so it disappears into the section head.

    ⊟···· Sections (Exterior Elevation)
            └···· Section 3

6. Check your Project Browser. A new node appears for your Exterior Elevations.

7. In Figure 2.53, the elevation still appears in the sections node, but it's appended with the Exterior Elevation type. You can rename the section if needed.

FIGURE 2.53
The elevation tag
looks like the
section tag.

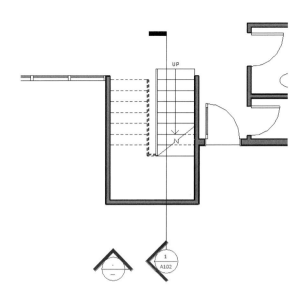

If you go this route, be aware that to adjust the cropping, you must select the section line you just worked so hard to hide. You'll need to zoom in close and use the Tab key to select that line again. Once it's selected, you'll have full access to the other controls associated with the section.

3D VIEWS

One of the most obvious benefits of working with BIM is the 3D nature of the model. When using Revit, you'll find yourself constantly making 3D views, examining the space from various vantage points, and making presentations you would not be able to do using a 2D application. You can create two types of 3D views in Revit—axonometric and perspective—and each has special characteristics that you need to be aware of.

Axonometric 3D Views

An *axon view* is a scaled drawing showing the model in three dimensions. These views allow you to dimension lengths in all three dimensions with no perspective distortion. The easiest way to make an axon view is to duplicate the default {3D} view using the Project Browser. Right-click the {3D} view name, and duplicate it. Once you do this, the next time you press the 3D icon, a new default {3D} view will be created automatically. Once you have a 3D view, use the mouse to spin around. Hold down Shift and the middle mouse button to orbit around the model. If you first select something and then orbit, you'll orbit around your selection. To pan the view, hold down the middle mouse button and pan. To zoom, scroll the mouse wheel back and forth.

Orienting to Other Views

Perhaps the most compelling feature of the axon view is its ability to orient to other views. When you do this, a 3D section box is enabled in the view that cuts the model in all six directions of the box. You can go from a very dense, hard-to-read model to a focused representation. Figure 2.54 shows a 3D view that was oriented to a section view. You're free to create new elements and edit the model from these types of views.

To create these types of views, open a 3D view and choose View ➤ Orient To Other View. Then, choose which view to orient to. The section box is turned on and matches the extents of the view being oriented to. You can then spin the model to get a 3D representation. With Revit, these types of views are easily generated; they suggest a new type of drawing to be included in standard construction and presentation document sets.

Perspective Views (Cameras)

Perspectives in Revit (bird-eye and frog-eye views) follow the metaphor of placing a camera in space. To make a new camera, start from a floor plan, and use the Camera tool from the View Design tab. The first click establishes where the camera is placed in the model. Look at the Options bar: You can set the camera height prior to placement if you want. The default puts the camera 5´6˝ (1.8m) above the active level you're on. You then give the camera a direction and set the center of rotation by clicking a second time. The view automatically opens for you to reveal what your camera sees. The camera placement is shown in Figure 2.55.

FIGURE 2.54
3D view oriented to a
section view and then
orbited

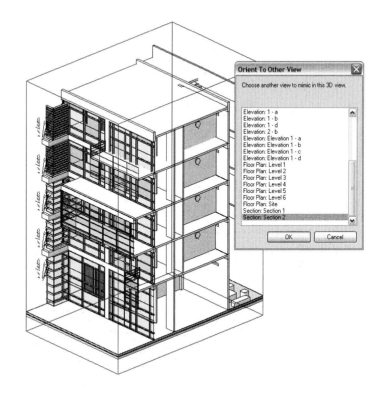

FIGURE 2.55
Camera placement

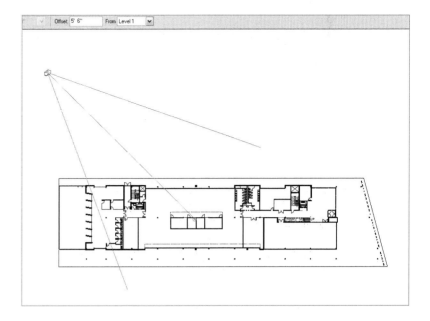

Once in the camera view, you can navigate around by using the mouse buttons to orbit and pan. For even more options, enable the Dynamic View dialog. Check the Walkthrough and Field of View tabs for some less-obvious options that are available (shown in Figure 2.56).

FIGURE 2.56
Dynamic View options

In the Field of View tab, you see a button labeled In/Out. This lets you change the focal length of the camera, which you can think of as zooming a lens in and out. The camera stays in same location when you use this feature.

Once a camera has been placed, you won't see it in other views. Its default state is to be invisible. To make a camera visible, select the view in the Project Browser, and choose Show Camera from the context menu. You'll see a graphic of the camera and its available controls such as the camera, target, and far clip plane (if it's enabled). Select any controls, and drag them around to alter the location of the camera. Clicking empty space or another element deselects the camera; it will disappear.

Unlike axon views, perspective cameras don't have a view scale that determines how big the view is. A perspective has no scale, so you use the crop region to define the size of the image. Select the crop region of a perspective view, and click the Size button on the Options bar.

The width and height are controlled here—this is the size of the image if it was printed out on paper. If you start editing the values, you'll see the crop boundary resize. The default option ("Field of View") adjusts the width and height independently, and the model becomes more or less cropped. Figure 2.57 shows the effect of changing Width from 16″ to 12″.

If you choose the "Scale (locked proportions)" option and change either Width or Height, the image looks exactly the same but is scaled up or down. If you like the proportions of your shot, but you want a bigger version of it, choose this option.

The Bottom Line

The Revit user interface is fairly straightforward. Once you know how to access settings, add elements to a view, and navigate views, you'll be off and running. Get use to the idea of editing properties of elements to change their appearance and behavior. This applies to model elements, annotations, and views.

Work with and understand Revit parametric elements   Although you can find references to objects, families, instances, and components, in the end everything is an element.

Master It   What are Revit elements, and how are they managed graphically?

Use the Revit user interface   As in any software application, you need to know where all the major components are and what tasks they support.

Master It   How do you change the graphics of a category for all views? What if you need to change the graphics for only one view?

FIGURE 2.57
Changing the size of
perspective views

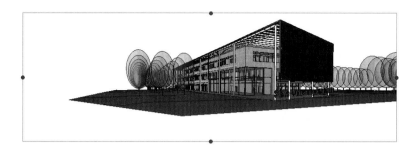

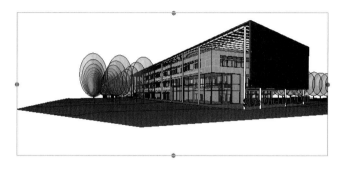

Use the Project Browser   This UI component provides access to all elements in your model. Get used to using it to locate views, families, groups, and links.

   Master it   Knowing how to navigate views in Revit is essential to completing work. What are some of the ways to open views in Revit?

Navigate views and view properties   Views are also elements. Just like the walls, floors, and roofs you add to the model, you'll also add views. They have properties you should become familiar with.

   Master it   You need to change the scale of a plan view from ⅛″ to ¼″. How do you do this with Revit?

Chapter 3

Know Your Editing Tools

Get to know Revit's basic commands, tools, and techniques. The faster you learn to work with the interface, the more productive you'll become. The more you use Revit, the more you'll find that certain commands are better suited for certain tasks. For example, you'll develop a sense of when to copy and paste an element and when to move it; and when to use the spacebar instead of the Rotate tool.

There are also some tools that are less obvious, but that you should still get acquainted with, such as the Join Geometry tools and the Split Face and Paint tools. These tools will help you produce the drawings you need with the added value of being intelligent and parametric.

In this chapter, you'll learn how to take advantage of Revit selection and editing features and learn a few new tips and tricks along the way.

In this chapter, you learn how to do the following:

◆ Select, change, and replace elements

◆ Edit elements interactively

◆ Use other useful tools

Selecting, Changing, and Replacing Elements

Knowing how to select, change, and replace elements of a Revit building model is fundamental to working with the software. These basic interface operations are the building blocks that you'll use throughout the process of making edits to your model.

Selection

Selection is straightforward in Revit. Hover your mouse over an element, and it highlights (turns gray)—click the highlighted element, and it turns red, meaning you have it selected. Once the item is selected, the Options bar adjusts to show you relevant options (Figure 3.1).

FIGURE 3.1
The tool set offered by the Options bar depends on the type of element you've selected.

You can select multiple elements several ways:

Additive selection   Hold down the Ctrl key while clicking new elements to add them to your selection. To remove elements from the selection, hold down the Shift key and click selected elements.

Window selection   You can select many elements by dragging a selection window across the view. Do this by holding down the left mouse button and dragging. A right-to-left drag selects only elements completely within the selection window; a left-to-right drag selects anything within or intersecting the selection window.

Chain selection   You can select connected lines and walls by holding down the Tab key and selecting a wall or line. All walls/lines that are end-joined to that wall become selected.

Select all Instances   This option allows you to select all instances of a particular family in the entire model. This is great when you need to perform a wholesale swap of a certain family. For example, if you placed some generic wood doors in your project, and you now want to swap all those with metal doors, this command is perfect. To use it, you select one door, right-click, and choose Select All Instances from the resulting menu to select all the wood doors. Then, use the Type Selector in the Options bar to change the door type. With this command, elements become selected that may not be visible in your view, because this type of selection isn't limited to what you manually clicked. Remember: You're selecting all instances of that family type in the *entire* model.

FILTERING YOUR SELECTION

You can filter what you've selected based on categories using the Filter button located on the Options bar. This allows you to make large, nonspecific box selections and then focus your selection by removing categories from it. For example, if you box-select an entire floor plan, you'll end up selecting many categories of elements. Using the Filter dialog, you can limit the selection to just the windows category (or the doors, or whatever element you need).

You can try this on a model you have open. Using a box selection, draw a big box around a portion of your model, and then click the Filter button. You'll get a dialog like the one shown in Figure 3.2. Here, you can deselect categories to limit what you've selected. Think of this as a short-cut. Let's say you need to change the properties of 20 doors in a plan view. It's much faster to box-select an area of your model and then filter out all elements but doors than it is to Ctrl-pick all 20 doors one at a time.

FIGURE 3.2
Use the Filter dialog to limit what you've selected.

USING THE TYPE SELECTOR

One of the most effective ways to change your model is to swap out types of elements progressively. For example, you may start with some generic walls, floors, doors, and windows initially, and then over time refine the details of those elements. Using Revit, you don't have to redraw the elements when you decide to get more specific with your design. You make new types or load new content, and then swap out the elements using the Type Selector on the Options bar. The elements on the Options bar are all of the same category, making it easy to locate relevant content.

You can take advantage of this feature the moment you start placing any Revit families. During creation, you can use the Type Selector to choose the type of element being placed. Once you select an element, the same list is available, making it simple to change the types.

SELECTING BY MATCHING PROPERTIES

The Match Properties button allows you to select one type of element and then apply its properties (type and instance) to another element of the same category. Once you select an element, the eyedropper appears filled. Each subsequent click on elements of the same category will replace the selected element with the type currently in the eyedropper.

Be careful when you use this tool with walls, because it changes top and bottom constraints of the elements being matched. For walls, if you need to change the type but don't want any of the level constraints to change, use the Type Selector, not the Match Properties tool.

Copy/Paste

Copying and pasting is a familiar technique used in almost all software applications, and Revit provides the basic features you'd expect with a copy-paste interaction (Ctrl-C and Ctrl-V). It also has some additional time-saving options that are specific to working on a 3D building model.

To copy any element to the Clipboard, select it and press Ctrl-C. Elements are now ready to be pasted. To paste, press Ctrl-V. In the majority of cases, Revit pastes the elements with a dashed bounding box drawn around them. You then determine where to place the elements by clicking. In the Options bar, you can also choose Quit to abandon the operation, Finish to complete the paste, or Edit Pasted Elements to move the element prior to finishing the paste.

PASTE ALIGNED

Once you've copied elements to the Clipboard, you can paste them into other views with a variety of options. This allows you to quickly duplicate elements from one view to another (from one floor to another floor, for example) while maintaining a consistent location in the XY coordinate plane. After selecting elements and copying them to the Clipboard using Ctrl-C, choose Edit ➢ Paste Aligned from the main menu, as shown in Figure 3.3.

FIGURE 3.3

Paste Aligned options

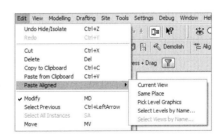

Five options are available. Depending on the view from which you copy and what elements you copy, the availability of these options will change. For example, if you select a model element in a plan view, you'll have all the options shown in the figure. The options are as follows:

Current View   This pastes the elements from the Clipboard into the currently active view, in the same relative spatial location. For example, if you copy a series of walls in one view, switch to another view, and choose Current View, Revit pastes the walls into exactly the same XY locations in that view.

Same Place   This option places an element from the Clipboard in the exact same place from which it was copied or cut. One use for this tool is copying elements into a design option; see Chapter 9 for an explanation of design options.

Pick Level Graphics   This is a mode you can use to copy-paste elements between different floors. Once you select the elements and choose this option, you're placed into a pick mode where you can select a level in section or elevation. You must be in an elevation or section view to have this option available. The level you select determines the Z location of the paste and preserves the XY location. You might use this type of paste to copy balconies on a façade from one floor to another.

Select Levels by Name   This method is similar to the previous one, but the selection of levels doesn't happen graphically. Instead, you choose levels from a list in a dialog box, and you can paste to multiple levels at once. This is useful when you have a multistory tower; in such a case, manually selecting levels in a view can be tedious. Similar to other options, the XY position is maintained, and the pasted elements are translated in the vertical dimension.

Select Views by Name   This option allows you to copy elements to other views by selecting views in a dialog box. In the list available for selection, you don't see levels listed but rather a list of parallel views. For example, if elements are copied from a plan view, all other plan views are listed. Likewise, if you copy from an elevation view, only elevation views appear as possible views to paste into.

Place Similar

Rather than hunting through a list of families or making copies using copy and paste, try using the Place Similar tool to add new instances of an element to your model.

The tool is on the main toolbar, all the way to the right. To use this tool, think about the type of element you need to make, and select an instance of it. Then, click the Place Similar tool, and you'll immediately be put into a placement/creation mode. If you use this tool to create a similar floor or roof (or any other sketch-based element), you're taken directly into sketch mode, where you can start sketching your new element.

Editing Elements Interactively

Revit provides a range of options to interactively edit elements in the model. The most obvious is to select elements to drag around the screen or use the blue control grips to extend walls and lines. At the same time, you often need more precise methods for moving and positioning things. Let's look at some ways to do this.

Moving Elements

Revit provides several ways to move elements, ranging from traditional tools to using intelligent dimensions that appear on the fly when you select elements. Become familiar with each method, and find what works best for your workflow.

USING TEMPORARY DIMENSIONS

You should have noticed by now that when elements are selected, dimensions appear. These dimensions are called *temporary dimensions* and are there to help you position elements relative to other elements. Clicking the blue dimension value makes it an active, editable value. Type in a new value, and *the element you selected* moves to that point. Keep this in mind: Dimensions always move elements that are selected. By the same token, you can't edit a dimension if nothing is selected.

If a temporary dimension isn't referencing a meaningful element, you can choose a different reference by dragging the small blue square attached to the dimension witness line to a new parallel reference (Figure 3.4). Parallel references highlight when the mouse moves over them.

FIGURE 3.4
Drag or click the small blue grip to change the temporary dimension

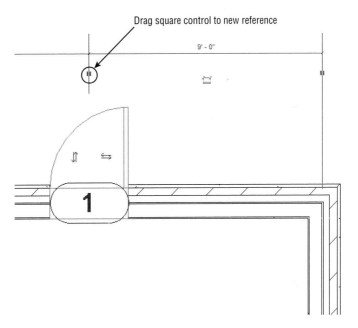

If you click a blue grip, it cycles to other possible reference in the element. For example, clicking the blue grip of a dimension to a door or window cycles between the left and right openings and the center of the element. The same is true for walls: Try clicking the blue grip control, and see how the temporary dimension cycles through the various references in the wall (interior face, centerline, exterior face).

To change which references temporary dimensions go to first, use the Settings ➤ Temporary Dimensions dialog (Figure 3.5). Here, you can set how dimensions default to walls, doors, and windows independently.

FIGURE 3.5
The Temporary Dimension Properties dialog lets you define default behaviors.

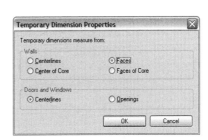

If you have many elements selected, temporary dimension sometimes don't appear. Check the Options bar for the Activate Dimensions button; clicking it adds dimension to the view for you to use.

USING THE MOVE TOOL

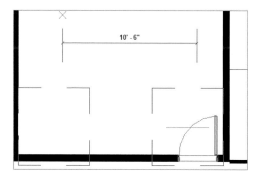

Use the Move tool to move elements precise distances by typing in values or using the temporary dimensions as helpers. When you have an element selected, the Move tool becomes enabled.

Moving elements is a two-click process: First you define a start point, and then you click to define an end point. If you know you need to move something to the left 10′6″, it doesn't matter where your two picks take place; all that matters is that the distance between the two clicks is 10′6″. (Figure 3.6 shows the graphics provided during a move operation.)

FIGURE 3.6
Use the Move tool to move elements precisely.

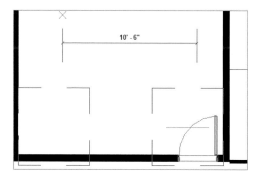

When the Move command is active, there are a few options to be aware of on the Options bar:

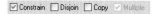

Constrain   When this option is selected, it constrains movements to horizontal and vertical directions. Deselecting it gives you free movement if the element is freestanding. Hosted elements such as windows and doors always move in a constrained manner parallel to their host axis.

Disjoin   Hosted elements such as windows and doors can't change host and move to another host without explicitly being disjoined from their host. This option lets you disconnect inserts from their host and move them to new hosts. For example, if you need to move a door from one wall to another, you select the door, select the Move tool, select Disjoin on the Options bar, and move the door to another host.

Copy   This option lets you make a copy of the element without moving the original element. In the strictest sense, this isn't really a *move* operation but a shortcut to making a *copy*.

NUDGING ELEMENTS (REPOSITION IN SMALL INCREMENTS)

Nudging is a great way to push things around quickly and with a bit less precision. When an element is selected, you can use the arrow keys on the keyboard to move the element horizontally and vertically in small increments. Each press of an arrow key nudges the element a specific distance based on your current zoom factor. The closer you zoom, the finer the nudge is. Likewise, as you zoom out, the nudge moves elements by larger increments. This is a good tool when you're working with views placed on sheets.

MOVES WITH NEARBY ELEMENTS

Another way to move free-standing elements, but in a more automatic ways, is to use the Moves With Nearby Elements feature. This tool is designed to capture logical relationships between elements. When furnishing a space, you probably want to align the bed or dresser with a wall. If you change your design, you want the furniture to follow the wall to the new location. For this purpose, select the furniture and then select the option to Moves With Nearby Elements on the Options bar. By doing so, you create an invisible relationship between the bed and the wall so that each time you move the wall, the bed moves with it (Figure 3.7).

FIGURE 3.7
When the bed is selected, the option to have it move with nearby elements is available on the Options bar.

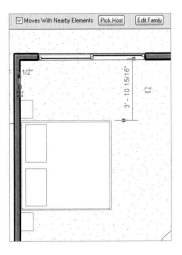

Copy

This is an interactive tool that is nearly identical to the Move tool but makes a copy of the selected element at the location of the second pick. This tool doesn't copy anything to the Clipboard; it copies an instance of an element or selection of elements in the same view. If you change views while using this tool, your selection is dropped.

To activate this tool, first choose the element(s) you want to copy, and then select the tool. Using the Options bar, you can choose to make multiple copies of the element in one interaction by selecting the Multiple option:

Rotating and Mirroring Elements

It's common to need to rotate an element. Just as with Move, Revit provides a few methods for rotating elements. The time-saving spacebar is a quick way to rotate elements in 90-degree increments. For more precision, the Rotate tool is provided, which you can use to rotate elements to any angle you require.

USING THE SPACEBAR

Revit uses the spacebar to rotate elements both at the time of placement and once an element has been placed. This is a great time-saving command to become familiar with, because you can forgo using more traditional tools such as Rotate and Mirror by taking advantage of the spacebar. Here are a few examples:

Doors and windows   If you have a door with its swing in wrong direction, select it and press the spacebar. You can cycle through all four possible orientations of the door with a few clicks. The same holds true for windows; however, many window families are built to only let you flip the window from inside to outside, because many windows are symmetrical in elevation. If you have asymmetrical windows, be sure to add flip controls to the family—these allow the spacebar to work on hosted elements. Figure 3.8 shows the window opened in the Family Editor and where to access the flip controls for placement from the Design bar and Options bar.

FIGURE 3.8

Flip arrows are used to flip elements. These can be added to families from the Family Editor.

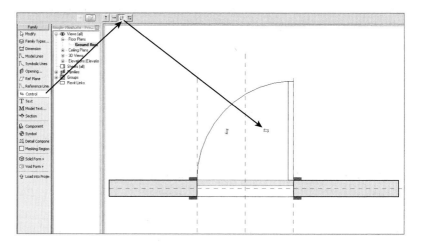

Walls   If you select a wall, pressing the spacebar flips the element as if it were being mirrored about its length. Walls flip based on the Wall Location Line, which often isn't the wall centerline. If you aren't sure which direction your wall is facing, select it and look for the flip-control arrows. These are always drawn on the exterior side of walls (Figure 3.9).

Freestanding elements   If you select a freestanding element like the loveseat shown in Figure 3.10, the spacebar rotates the element about the center reference planes defined in the family. Depending on how the family was built, the rotation origin may not make the most sense, but you can quickly orient your furniture and casework. If you decide to edit a family to change the location of the geometry relative to the center reference planes, be careful: When loaded back into a project, all your elements will jump to a new XY location based on the changes you made!

FIGURE 3.9
The flip arrow is another way to reorient an element. For walls, the flip arrow is always on the exterior side.

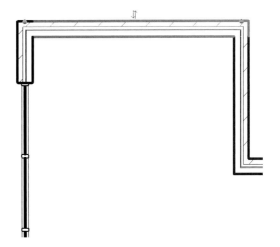

FIGURE 3.10
Center reference planes defined in the family determine the rotation origin.

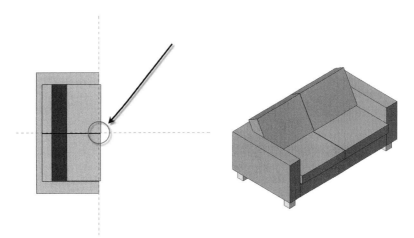

USING THE ROTATE TOOL

To rotate an element, select it and click the Rotate tool. This is a two-pick operation similar to the Move and Copy tools; or you can enter numeric values. Revit locates the geometric center of the element(s) and uses that as the default center of rotation. This is fine if you don't need to be precise and just want to rotate something by a known angle. However, in most cases, you first need to designate a meaningful center of rotation.

To do so, select and drag the rotation cursor to a new location before clicking to set start and end picks. Once the origin is established, begin rotating the element using the temporary dimensions as a reference or by typing in the angle of rotation explicitly.

You'll notice that while moving the origin, you lose the ability to pan and zoom the view. To overcome this, drag the origin into the Project Browser and release the mouse button; then, move the mouse back into the view. The cursor changes to a rotation icon, and you can freely pan and zoom all you want. The next click you make places the origin, and you can then designate the rotation.

USING THE MIRROR TOOL

The Mirror tool allows you to mirror elements across an axis in order to create a mirror image of an element, like the sinks in Figure 3.11. You can either pick an existing reference in the model (the arrow icon) or draw the axis interactively (the pencil icon). In the example shown, a mirror axis was drawn through the center of the top wall.

FIGURE 3.11
The sinks, toilet fixtures, and door are mirrored about the middle of the wall at the top of the view.

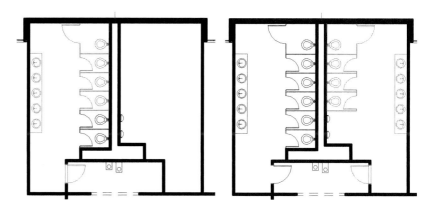

Use the pick method when you have an existing element with a meaningful center axis. If nothing in the model exists as a mirror axis, use the draw mode and draw your own axis.

Arraying Elements

An *array* allows you to copy instances of an element with equal spacing between each instance. Revit provides intelligent arrays that can be parametrically grouped and associated, as well as one-off, unassociated arrays. Like all the other tools we've reviewed, the creation options are presented on the Options bar.

You have two ways to array: *linear* and *radial*. Linear arrays are set as the default because they're the most common. As you would expect, a linear array creates a series of elements in a line. Each element in the line can be given a set distance from the previous element or be spaced equally based on a maximum line length. Figure 3.12 shows a linear array where the Move To 2nd option was selected in order to set the initial spacing correctly. Think of this type of array as additive/subtractive: If you change the number, the length expands or contracts.

FIGURE 3.12
This array uses the Move To 2nd option to set a fixed distance between each group.

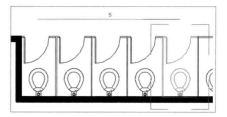

If you need to space elements in a fixed space, and the exact spacing between elements is a less important factor, use the Last option. Figure 3.13 shows an array where the location of the last element in the array was picked, and the elements (in this example, windows) were placed equally between the first and last elements in the array. With this option, the length is fixed, and the array squeezes elements within that constraint as the number changes. These two examples show that depending on your design criteria, you can use different arrays.

FIGURE 3.13
This array uses the Last option and back-fills instances between the first and last group.

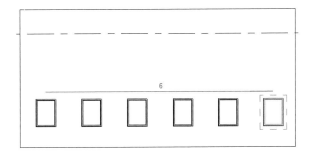

A radial array works in a similar fashion, but it revolves around a center point. With a radial array, elements auto-rotate so that each element faces the center of the array, as shown in Figure 3.14.

FIGURE 3.14
When you're making a radial array, you can specify the number of instances interactively.

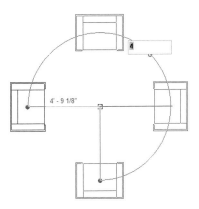

The Group And Associate option allows you to treat the array as a group that can be modified later to adjust the number and/or spacing of the array. If this option is unchecked, then the array is a one-off operation, and you have no means of adjusting the array after you create it.

When an element in a *grouped array* is selected, a control appears, indicating the number of elements in the array. Editing that number changes the number of elements in the array. This tool comes in handy when you're making certain families, because the array number can be parameterized. See the Chapter 10 section "Parametric Arrays in the Family Editor" for a detailed exercise.

Resizing Elements

The Resize tool lets you scale certain objects that make sense to scale, such as imported raster images and 2D lines. In Figure 3.15, the Resize tool was used to make the lines surrounding a door tag a bit larger. The first pick was the center of the family, the second pick was the center of one of the lines, and the final pick finished the resize.

FIGURE 3.15
The Resize command
sequence is a three-
click process.

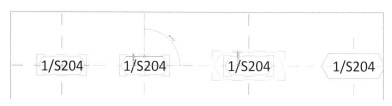

This tool is also well suited for working with imported images that need to be scaled to match real-world dimensions. For example, it's common to import an aerial photograph of a site to use as a contextual underlay; the Resize tool works great to get the image to the right scale.

This tool is active once you select an image. After you select the Resize tool, click a point to enter an origin (say, the lower-left corner of the image); the second point you click is the width of the image that you want to fit within a certain size; finally, the third click is the new length you want.

Keep in mind that you're working with a Building Information Modeling application full of real-world objects, not abstract primitive forms. Don't expect to resize most elements in Revit—it's not practical or meaningful. For example, you can't scale the size of a door or sink.

Aligning Elements

If you've been using Revit for any amount of time, you should have discovered the incredible power of the Align tool. If not, take time to get acquainted with this tool, because it's a real time-saver and supplants the need to use many of the tools we've already discussed. Basically, the Align tool lets you line things up in an easy, quick, and intuitive manner.

With this tool, you explicitly align references from one element to another. For example, you can align windows in a façade so their centers are all in alignment. To use the Align tool, first select a target reference, and then select what you want to align to that reference. The second element picked always moves into alignment. This selection sequence is the opposite of the other editing tools we've looked at so far, so remember: First you select the aligning reference, and then you select the element to move/align to the reference.

As soon as you make your second pick, a lock icon appears so you can constrain the alignment. Once you click the lock icon, if either element moves, it brings the constrained element along with it.

Figure 3.16 shows the use of the Align tool to align windows on a façade. The left opening of the topmost window was used to align multiple windows using the Multiple Alignment option on the Options bar.

FIGURE 3.16
The Align tool is great
for lining up edges of
windows in a façade.

The Align tool also works for aligning geometry with surface patterns like brick or stone. Select a line in the surface pattern, and then select the geometry you want aligned. Figure 3.17 shows how you can align the edge of a window to a brick pattern.

FIGURE 3.17
You can also align model elements to surface patterns.

Trimming and Extending Lines and Walls

You can trim and extend lines and walls to one another using the Trim tool. With the Trim tool, you first select the tool and then operate on elements in the model. Again, like all the other tools we've covered, the Options bar gives you a number of ways to use this tool.

The first option is the default, Trim/Extend To Corner. It trims elements to one another, creating a cleaned-up end join between walls and lines. For example, Figure 3.18 shows two walls before and after using the Trim/Extend To Corner tool.

FIGURE 3.18
The result of trimming two walls to one another is a clean corner join.

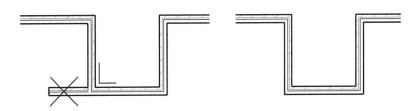

The second and third options are for extending lines and walls. First, you select a target wall; then select walls you want option, not options, to extend to that target (Figure 3.19). The second option, Trim/Extend Single Element, is for extending a single wall, and the third option lets you extend many walls in one interaction.

FIGURE 3.19

Trim can be used to extend walls as well

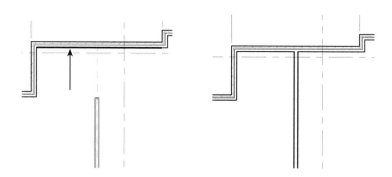

The Trim tool is used a lot for editing sketches of floors and roofs, because it's easy to end up with overlapping lines that need to be neatly trimmed. Keep in mind that with the Trim tool, you're selecting pairs of elements to *remain*, not be removed. Use the temporary preview graphics to help you. If you do trim the wrong thing, you'll see it immediately—just undo, and pick again.

Splitting Lines and Walls

The Split tool operates on walls and lines. This tool lets you slice a line or wall into pieces. To cut a wall, move the mouse over the edge of the wall—you'll see a preview of the split line prior to clicking.

The Options bar has a nice feature that removes the need to use the Trim tool: Delete Inner Segment. In Figure 3.20, you need to remove the middle section of the wall and end up with a clean set of wall joins. Using the Split tool with the Delete Inner Segment option selected, you can accomplish this with two clicks.

FIGURE 3.20

Use Split with the Delete Inner Segment to get a clean condition without having to come back and use the Trim command

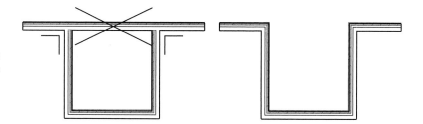

Offsetting Lines and Walls

Offset is similar to the Move and Copy tools in that it makes a copy of an element by offsetting it parallel to an edge you select. You can find the Offset tool either on the Edit toolbar or on the Options bar when you're sketching lines or walls.

This tool is especially useful in the Family Editor when you're making shapes that have a consistent thickness in profile, such as extruded steel shapes. Offset is also handy when you're making roof forms or soffits with known offsets from a wall. You can either offset a line and maintain the original (copy) or offset the line, removing the original. Figure 3.21 shows the offset of sketch lines in the Roof Editor where the offset has been defined as 1′0″. Each pick of the wall offsets the line by 1′.

FIGURE 3.21
Offset lets you pick existing elements and create new elements with a specific offset distance.

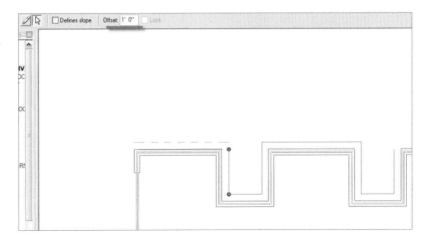

Keeping Elements from Moving

In many cases, you'll want to make sure some elements don't move, because the consequences could be bad. Imported drawings, grids, levels, and exterior walls are some of the most obvious cases. Revit provides a couple ways to deal with this.

PINNING ELEMENTS

You can restrict an elements' ability to move by pinning it down with the Pin tool. This tool is located in the upper-right corner of the toolbar. Select the element you want to pin down, and click the Pin tool. If you try to move the element, nothing happens—you don't even get a ghost preview of a potential move.

Use this tool to lock down critical elements that need to remain fixed for long periods of time. This is a great feature for imported CAD files, because it's *very* easy to accidentally select an import and drag it or move it. This kind of accident can lead to coordination problems, even in a BIM environment. Use pins to lock down gridlines as well, because you certainly don't want those to move accidentally.

To unpin an element, select it and look for the pin icon. Clicking the pin removes it and frees the element.

CONSTRAINTS

Constraints aren't as rigid as the Pin tool, but they do allow you to create dimensional rules in the model so that elements remain fixed relative to one another. You can create a constraint using dimensions and alignments and then click the Lock icon.

A simple example is keeping a door a fixed distance from a side wall, so that if the wall moves, the door also moves. At the same time, if you try to move the door, you can't. Look at Figure 3.22: The door has been locked to be 5⅜″ from the wall face. If the wall moves, the door moves as well; but if you try to drag the door to a new location, you can't.

Another example is to lock the head height of a series of windows relative to a level. This prevents users from accidentally dragging windows into undesired locations while guaranteeing that if the level moves, the windows also move.

FIGURE 3.22
A constrained door
can't be moved
independently.

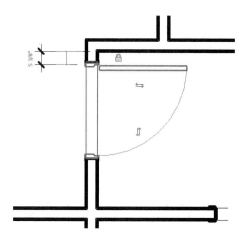

Other Useful Tools

A range of other tools are available in Revit, and these will be covered in subsequent chapters where they're used in specific operations. There are a few tools you should know about now, however, because they're generic tools that you can put to use on any project immediately.

Join Geometry

Revit does a good job of cleaning up joins between elements; however, in many cases elements don't look right unless they're explicitly joined. This is where the Join Geometry tool is useful. This tool creates joins between floor, walls, ceilings, roofs, and slabs. A common place to use this tool is in your building sections, where floors and walls appear overlapped and not joined. Figure 3.23 shows a floor intersecting some walls that aren't joined. Using the Join Geometry tool, these conditions can be cleaned up nicely.

To fix this condition, select the Join Geometry tool, and then select the floor and wall in sequence.

Split Face and Paint

To support painting of surfaces without having to make new types of elements, Revit provides the Split Face and Paint tools. You can paint the exterior faces of walls, floors, roofs, and ceilings with a material. This material has no thickness, but you can schedule (with a materials takeoff schedule) and tag it. A typical use case for this feature is the application of a carpet material or tile to a floor.

Figure 3.24 shows the floor being split with the Split Face tool. Once the face has been split, activate the Paint tool. The Type Selector lists all the materials in your project (Figure 3.25). Choosing a tile material and then clicking the split face applies the material. The result is that the floor is unchanged structurally, and the bathroom appears with a tile finish (Figure 3.26).

FIGURE 3.23
Joining floors to walls and walls to floors creates cleaner looking drawings.

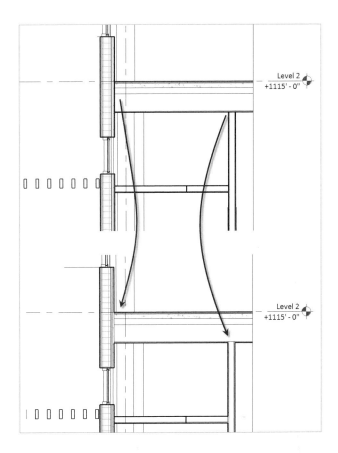

FIGURE 3.24
Use Split Face to sketch an area of the floor to be painted with a new material.

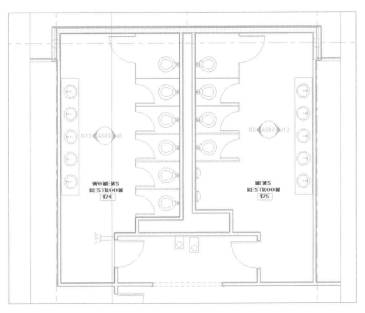

FIGURE 3.25
The Paint tool lists all materials in your project in the Type Selector.

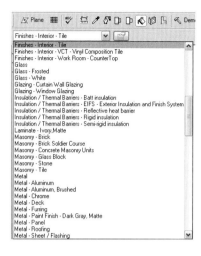

FIGURE 3.26
You can paint the split face with a tile material to get the desired effect.

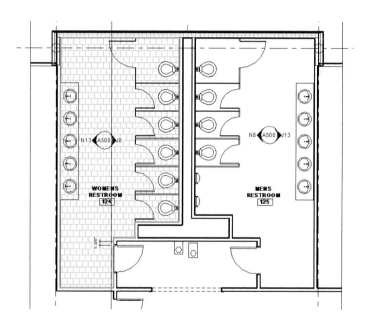

Keyboard Shortcuts (Accelerators)

Many users like using keyboard shortcuts to speed up common commands and minimize the need to interrupt workflow. When you open any of the menus in the menu bar, the keyboard shortcut is indicated to the right of the tool name:

Revit contains preset keyboard shortcuts when installed, but you can modify the default short-cuts by editing the `Keyboard.txt` file located in the `C:\Program Files\Revit Architecture 2008\Program` folder. Revit's shortcuts are two-key shortcuts and are available only for commands that already exist. When you change the shortcuts in the `Keyboard.txt` file, Revit shows these abbreviations in the menu.

The Bottom Line

Get to know the basic commands with Revit. The faster you become, the more productive you'll be. The more you use Revit, the more you'll find that certain commands are better suited for certain tasks.

Selecting, changing, and replacing elements   Learning the basic mechanics of the interface is crucial to just about everything you'll do in Revit.

Master It   Selecting elements in the model happens all the time. What are some of the affor-dances that the Revit UI provides when you select elements?

Editing elements interactively   The architectural process inevitably involves revision, so be sure you know how to make changes on the fly.

Master It   You need to make some major changes to a floor plan, moving the bathroom 20′ down a corridor. How might you do this with Revit?

Using other tools   Revit provides a wide range of tools for making changes in a project.

Master It   In a section view, you notice that the walls and floors aren't cleaning up neatly— you're seeing lines overlap. What tool could you use to try to clean that up?

Chapter 4

Setting up your templates and Office Standards

In this chapter, you'll learn how to set up your office standards and how to prepare a project template that will be rich with information that goes beyond the out-of-the-box content. You'll learn how templates assure graphic consistency in your projects and how the reuse of work will increase productivity downstream, making the process of creating documents more seamless. We'll tackle the Family Editor and the creation of custom annotation symbols, title blocks, object styles, and view templates.

In this chapter you'll learn how to do the following:

◆ Create your own template with custom annotations and settings

◆ Create custom annotation families in the Family Editor

◆ Create custom title blocks in the Family Editor

Starting a Project with a Custom Template

Depending on the type of building you're planning, the geographical area in which your building will be built, and even the style of the building you're designing, it's likely that the default elements and general settings provided by the out-of-the-box Revit template won't be what you need. Software vendors make a great effort to provide locale-specific content libraries that respect local traditions as well as incorporate local regulations in their documentation, but as we all know, that is only a good starting point and can't cover all the types of elements you'll need in the course of a project. Like many other software packages, Revit allows you to start with a basic template and then spawn your own custom templates to suit your specific requirements.

As your knowledge of the software progresses, you'll soon see that the default selection of wall types, roof types, ceilings, stairs, and other families aren't sufficient to satisfy all your design and documentation needs. This is also the case with the graphical language that you or your firm has established over the years *and* probably want to continue using with Revit. How you graphically present elements like text, dimensions, annotations, keynotes, and hatch patterns defines your style of design documentation. The reality of the architectural profession is that we tend to develop customized graphics, and Revit respects this need by letting you stylize your content and use that in your starting templates. One possible example of graphic style in a CD phase of a project done by BNIM Architects is shown in Figure 4.1.

FIGURE 4.1
Example of stylized annotations used in a custom template

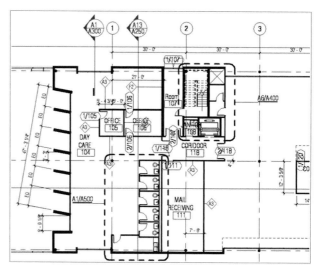

With Revit, you can expect to set up your templates by doing one or more of the following:

◆ Defining all the project settings to meet your graphic requirements

◆ Preloading model and annotation elements

◆ Defining system families before you start a project

Once everything is in place, you can then save the file as a template (.rte) and use that template whenever you start a new project. Once you've saved a new template, you can have Revit open that template by default by setting options in the File Locations dialog. Follow these steps:

Choose Settings ➢ Options, and click the File Locations tab.

The first option in the dialog shows the default template location. Click the Browse button to choose a new path to your default template (Figure 4.2).

FIGURE 4.2
Change the path to your default template once you've made one.

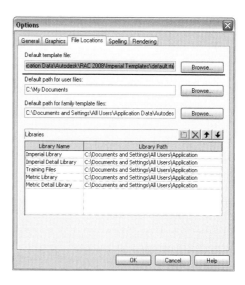

Creating and reusing templates can increase your productivity and keep your documentation looking consistent. Specifically, using templates allows you to do the following:

- Reuse work that you've already created whenever you can

- Maintain consistency in a project, especially when many team members participate in its creation

- Assure graphic consistency across projects

In this chapter, we focus on personalizing (customizing) the Revit template file (`.rte`). The following list lays out items we suggest you go through one by one when setting up templates. This doesn't represent *all* possible settings you can predefine in a template, but it includes those that we think are most pertinent:

Settings for graphics:

- Object styles

- Materials

- Line styles

- Line patterns

- Fill patterns (hatches)

- View templates

Setting up annotations:

- Dimension styles

- Text styles

- View tags

- Annotation tags

Setting up title blocks

Setting up global project settings:

- Keynoting external file locations

- Project units

Strategies for Making Templates

Different architectural firms address template files in one of two ways: generic, one-size-fits-all office templates; or project-type–specific templates. Some companies focus on one type of building (healthcare, office, retail, and so on) where a single template is sufficient, and others do a wide range of projects and may even work across cultures with very different requirements between project types. If you work all over the globe or have many types of projects, then a generic office template probably isn't the best strategy. Instead, create new templates for each type of project. On the other hand, if you're focused on predictable, similar projects, you can start each project from one template.

Don't overburden your template with too many elements—especially if you don't intend to use them all. You'll experience better performance when launching Revit and reduce the file size footprint of your model by starting out with a lean template.

When creating your own personalized template, avoid starting from an empty file (No Template); use an existing RTE file. You'll save yourself a lot of time by doing this.

Settings for Graphic Consistency

One of the goals of using a template is to assure graphic consistency across a project or even across Office. To achieve that, you need to set up the object styles that control the graphic appearance of your Revit elements as well as drafting elements such as lines, line and hatch Patterns, materials, and so on.

Object Styles

As we mentioned in Chapter 2, the Object Styles dialog controls the graphics for all the categories in your project. To access the dialog, choose Settings ➢ Object Styles. This dialog has three tabs: Model Objects, Annotation Objects, and Imported Objects. In this section, we'll discuss the first two types of objects. (Under the Tab for Imported objects is where all DWG, DXF, or DGN files that you have imported in your Revit file appear. These file types are based on a layering system. Revit doesn't work with layers, however it can read layers from imported files and classifies them in the Revit project as subcategories which can be controlled graphically similar to the way we control model and annotation categories.

When you define a template, you should focus on the first two tabs: Model and Annotation Objects. They're organized in a similar way: They list all main categories and their subcategories in a tree structure. You can define different graphics for the main category as opposed to its subcategory. If we take a door family as an example, you can define different graphic settings for the panel, the frame, and the door swing. The settings on these tabs are as follows:

Model Objects As shown in Figure 4.3, six columns are used to control graphic properties of model elements. The first holds the list of all available categories and their subcategories of model elements in Revit.

The next two columns define the line weight that will be used when these elements are drawn in projection (elevation and 3D) or section (plan or section) view. In some of the categories, you'll notice that the Cut column is grayed out; this is typical for elements that are never cut by Revit. The line weight used in these columns can vary between 1 and 16.

The next two columns define the color and pattern of the lines used to draw the geometry of these elements. The last column on the right lets you define a default material that will be associated with the category or subcategory in the event that elements in that category don't have materials explicitly defined. In an element, if you set the material to By Category, it looks to the material set in the Object Styles dialog.

Annotation Objects This tab is similar to the Model Objects tab. The difference lies in the material definition (lines don't have materials!) and the line weight (there is no distinguishing between projection and cut line weight), because annotation objects are 2D only.

FIGURE 4.3
The Object Styles dialog gives you independent graphic control of all Revit categories and subcategories.

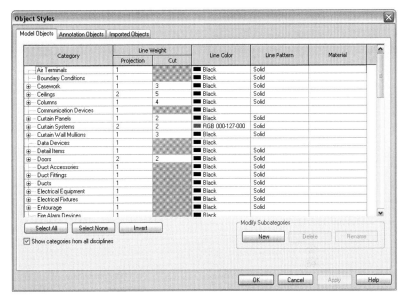

All these settings may look like overkill at first, but you usually only need to set up these values at the beginning of a process when building your office templates. Once you've assigned all the desired line weights, colors, and materials, you shouldn't mess around with them, because the effect will be global. While Object Styles are global, you do have the ability to change the graphic style of any element for a specific view, using overrides (View ➢ Visibility Graphic Overrides).

Object styles allow you to establish the graphical standard for the drawings that leave your office, contributing to an appearance of professionalism; take your time, and invest in getting them right. These powerful settings shouldn't scare you; they will make sure that your drawings have a consistent look and feel.

Line Styles

A line style is composed of a *line weight*, *line color*, and *line pattern*. To access the line styles, choose Settings ➢ Line Styles.

The dialog that opens (Figure 4.4) has four columns to control the appearance of each line type.

The Category column is organized in a tree structure with all line styles listed as subcategories of lines. As you can see, each style is defined by Line Weight, Line Color, and Line Pattern. Line Weight can have a value between 1 and 16, corresponding to a physical pen thickness that varies slightly based on view scale. This is the actual thickness of the line when printed on paper at 100 percent. Notice that lines have different thickness as you zoom in and out of a view, indicating that the lines have a real thickness.

line weights are managed from the Settings ➢ Line Weights dialog (Figure 4.5). As the scale gets coarser, line weights adjust so the drawing is still readable. For example, notice how the line thickness varies for heavy pens between scales.

FIGURE 4.4
The line styles define weight, color, and pattern for all lines used in a project.

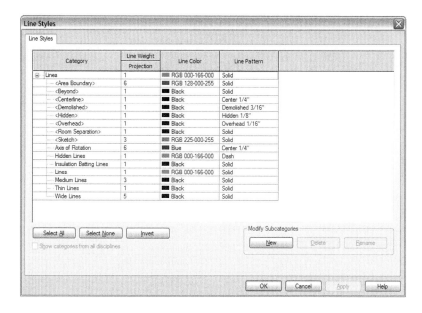

FIGURE 4.5
Model line weights vary depending on the view scale.

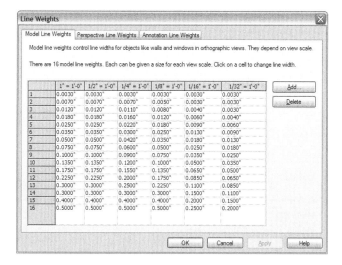

Back in the Line Styles dialog, notice that some of the line style names are bracketed, but others aren't. The bracketed line styles are internal, permanent types of lines, which can't be renamed or deleted. Any unbracketed line style can be renamed or deleted at any time. When deleting a line style that was already used by Revit elements in the project, those elements cannot reference that line style anymore and will automatically reference the first line style that was above the deleted one in the Line Style dialog. This may create undesirable results, so you should be aware how lines update.

To create a new line style, click the New button in the Modify Subcategories group. Enter a new name in the dialog that opens, and confirm it by clicking OK. The new style appears in the tree structure on the left; you can now set the rest of the parameters (Line Weight, Line Color, and Line Pattern) to suit your needs.

Line Patterns

A *line pattern* is a repetitive series of line segments, spaces, and/or points. To create a new line pattern, choose Settings ➤ Line Patterns. The dialog displays a list of existing line patterns in the project. On the right side of the dialog are four buttons: New, Edit, Delete, and Rename (see Figure 4.6).

FIGURE 4.6

Line patterns are made of dashes, spaces, and/or dots.

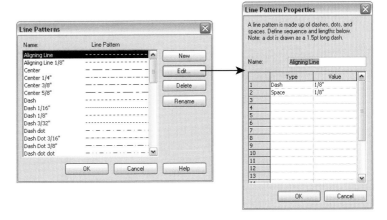

The dialog is fairly simple: To edit an existing line, click the Edit button. To create a new line pattern, click New. You can then create a line pattern by specifying line and space lengths that form a repeating sequence. To rename a pattern, click Rename. Be careful when naming line patterns: If you give a line pattern a name that already exists in the list, Revit overrides the existing pattern with the new one and overrides all elements that use that line pattern.

A pattern sequence can contain line segments, points, and spaces. For line segments and the spaces, you need to define their length; for points, a value isn't necessary. The construction of a sequence is simple: In the Type column, you select Dash or Dot from the drop-down list; and in the Value column, you provide a length (if it's a dash or space). For each row you add, only the available choices are shown in the drop-down list. Notice that in the first row, the drop-down only offers Dash and Dot as options, because Revit doesn't accept a sequence that begins with a space. Following the same logic, you can't have a dot after a dash or the opposite, because they will merge and the result won't graphically read.

Before deleting any line pattern, you must verify that it hasn't been used anywhere in your project. If you fail to do so, you'll lose information used and needed elsewhere in the project. This can only be done manually by checking line patterns used in the Visibility/Graphic Overrides dialog.

CREATING A NEW LINE PATTERN

Follow these steps to create a new line pattern:

1. Choose Settings ➤ Line Patterns.

2. In the Line Pattern dialog, click New.

3. Give the new line pattern a name.

4. Define the sequence, as shown in Figure 4.7.

5. Confirm by clicking OK.

6. The resulting line pattern looks like this:

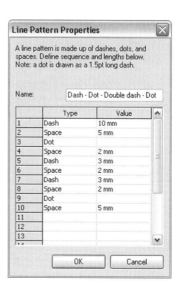

FIGURE 4.7
Make a new pattern
using this sample as
a guide.

Materials

Defining materials in your project template is definitely something you shouldn't neglect. Materials are essential for the graphical behavior of elements, and they merge with other materials when elements are joined. For example, concrete walls join and appear contiguous with concrete floors when the elements' geometry is joined together. A material also defines how an element's surface looks in shaded views, when cut in plan/section, and when seen in 3D and elevation views. In Figure 4.8, the surface patterns and colors are all derived from the material they're assigned to.

To access the Materials Editor, choose Menu Settings ➤ Materials. You'll see the dialog shown in Figure 4.9.

The Materials Editor has two components: a list and a tabbed properties interface. On the left is a list of all available Revit materials in the project. Below the list are options to duplicate, rename, and delete materials:

Duplicate   Use this button each time you need to create a new material. As with most elements you want to customize in Revit, always duplicate a material before you change any of its properties—if you fail to do so, you may change a material definition already used in the project and risk losing a lot of work. To create a new material, find an existing material that closely matches what you want to make. Once you click the Duplicate button, you'll be prompted to provide a name for the newly created material.

Rename   This works like all other Rename buttons in Revit. Clicking the button lets you rename the material. If you use a name that's not unique, Revit will warn you and prompt for a unique name.

Delete   You'll rarely delete an existing material. If for some reason you decide to do so, select the material that you wish to delete, and click the Delete button. You'll need to click OK to finalize the deletion. Be sure you don't delete a material that is already being used by elements.

FIGURE 4.8
Materials define the surface and cut patterns, color and render material of the elements.

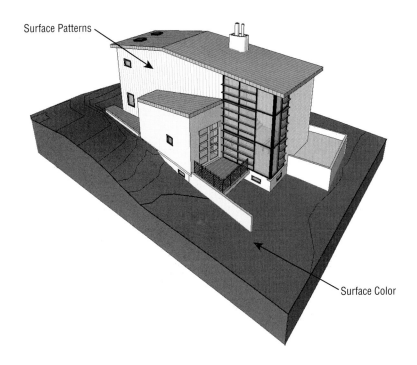

Surface Patterns

Surface Color

FIGURE 4.9
Use the Materials Editor to create the hatch patterns on elements.

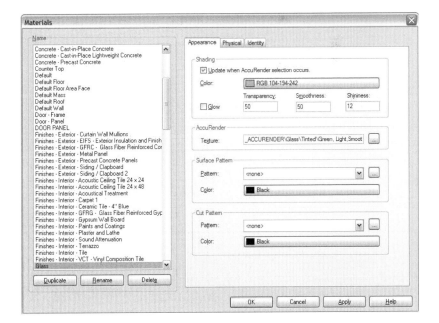

On the right side of the editor are three tabs that contain material properties:

◆ *Appearance*—Defines graphical and rendering attributes

◆ *Physical*—Defines structural properties of a material (used for structural analysis)

◆ *Identity*—Defines schedule values and keynotes

We'll concentrate on the Appearance tab, because it includes the graphical properties of materials. The other tabs are used for scheduling and structural analysis and aren't critical to this chapter. Here are the Appearance tab's options:

Shading   In this group, you define the color used for the selected material when a view is set to Shaded or Shaded with Edges display mode. Note that the color can be dependent on the associated texture. (See the next description.) In that case, the option "Update when AccuRender selection occurs" is checked, and the dominant color of the texture is displayed as color in shaded views.

AccuRender   In this group, you select an AccuRender (rendering) texture to be used when that element is rendered. There are various methods to create your own materials (from a bitmap or procedural materials). We'll get into rendering in more detail in Chapter 12.

Surface Pattern   In this group, you select a model pattern that will be displayed on the faces of the elements in elevation, plan, and 3D views.

Cut Pattern   The fill pattern that you select here is a drafting pattern, and it will be the pattern displayed when an element is cut through. Some Revit elements can't be cut, as we discussed in Chapter 2; in these cases, this parameter has no effect on the graphic display.

It may seem impossible to imagine all the materials you'll need in a project, making building a template seem daunting. Think of the basic materials you're likely to use: woods, brick, concrete, glass, and so on, and build from those. Remember, a template is just a starting point, and you can always expand it. If you end up making a lot of nice materials over the course of a project, use Transfer Project Standards functionality to move materials back into your template(s).

Fill Patterns (Hatch)

Materials are often represented with simple hatch patterns. For any material used in Revit, you can define a *surface pattern* and a *cut pattern*. For simple parallel hatches and crosshatches, you can use the patterns already supplied in Revit or you can also make your own custom hatches. For more complex patterns, you need to import an external pattern file (.pat). To access the Fill Pattern settings, choose Settings ➤ Fill Patterns (see Figure 4.10). On the left side of the Fill Patterns dialog, you can view the names and small graphic previews of the patterns that help you visualize as you select and edit the patterns. Below those are the Pattern Type options, where you choose what type of patterns you wish to create or inform you what type is the pattern you wish to edit (drafting or model). Similar to the Line Styles dialog, the New, Edit, and Delete buttons appear on the right.

There are two types of fill patterns: *model patterns* and *drafting patterns*. Use the model patterns when you want to convey real-world dimensional patterns to represent a material. Use drafting patterns for symbolic representations. For example, a model pattern is used to show a brick pattern in 3D and elevation views, whereas a drafting brick pattern is used to represent the cut pattern in plan and section. Figure 4.11 shows how concrete masonry units (CMUs) are represented with a running bond pattern (model) as well as a crosshatch (drafting).

FIGURE 4.10
Fill patterns are defined separately for drafting and model representations.

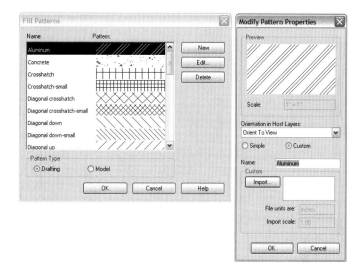

FIGURE 4.11
The CMU wall has both a drafting pattern (cut) and a model pattern (surface) defined.

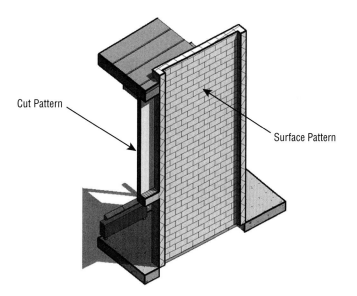

Model and drafting patterns have specific behaviors. In our example, we have a CMU wall with blocks that measure 16″ × 8″ (40mm x 20mm), regardless of the view scale. With a drafting pattern, the opposite is true: The pattern adjusts with the view scale so the pattern looks identical in all scales.

To create a new pattern, first choose either Model or Drafting, and then click the New button. A generic pattern appears in the New Pattern dialog. You can then design your pattern and assign some behaviors.

FIGURE 4.12
From left to right:
pattern orientation
Orient To View, Keep
Readable, and Align
With Element

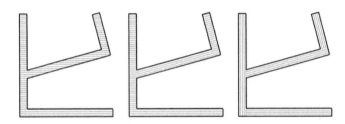

The option to Orient In Host Layers is particularly useful when you're making drafting patterns. This allows you to specify how a pattern orients itself relative to host elements such as walls, floors, roofs, and ceilings when they're represented as cut. (Note that the option isn't available for model pattern types.)

The three options shown in Figure 4.12 are described here:

Orient To View When this orientation is applied, the patters used in the project all have the same orientation and the same origin. They're always perfectly aligned with the origin of the view.

Keep Readable This orientation is best understood when compared with the Keep Readable attribute of text that is always readable regardless of its orientation.

Align With Element This orientation ensures that the pattern orientation depends on the orientation of the host element. Patterns essentially run parallel with the element.

You can choose to make either simple or custom patterns with this dialog, using the radio button options. Figure 4.13 shows the result of each option:

Simple These patterns are generated with parallel or crosshatch lines that can have different angles and spacing. With both the crosshatch and parallel options, you can specify only one angle for the entire pattern. Using crosshatch, you can set two spacing values. The exercise in the sidebar "Creating a Simple Fill Pattern" demonstrates creating a fill pattern.

Custom This pattern requires you to import a pattern from an external source. This is often necessary due to Revit's limited customization of pattern functionality. Your office may have a set of established patterns they've been using for years, and this allows you to import those without having to make new patterns from scratch. Custom patterns let you import a PAT file from anywhere on your hard drive or on a network and use it as a base pattern for a new fill pattern in Revit. The next section shows some best practices for importing a PAT file.

FIGURE 4.13
From left to right:
simple fill
pattern, simple fill
pattern with the cross-
hatch option selected,
and a custom fill
pattern

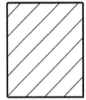  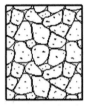

Real World Scenario

CREATING A SIMPLE FILL PATTERN

Often, the default templates don't have all the patterns you need. Following these steps, you can make a new simple fill pattern:

1. Choose Settings ➤ Fill Patterns.

2. In the Fill Patterns dialog, choose to make either a Model or a Drafting pattern, and click New.

3. In the New Pattern dialog, enter a new name for the fill pattern.

4. If Drafting is selected, also choose an option from the Orientation in Host Layers drop-down.

5. In the Simple group, enter a line angle. Choosing to create a crosshatched pattern lets you define the line spacing in both directions of the crosshatch. Note that a crosshatch always makes the second set of parallel lines perpendicular to the first.

6. The preview window shows the pattern. Click OK to commit the pattern to the model.

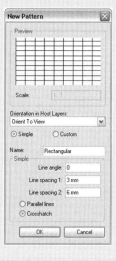

CREATING A CUSTOM PATTERN USING A PATTERN FILE (.PAT)

Custom patterns require an external file that contains the definition of the pattern. The file extension of that pattern should be `.pat`, which is what you'll make in this section by editing an existing AutoCAD PAT file. An advantage of specifying patterns in the template file is that the PAT file won't need to be installed on each computer where Revit is installed; Revit stores each pattern internally, in each project.

Before modifying PAT files, always make a copy of the file you intend to use in Revit; you don't want to risk messing up other files that might use that PAT file. PAT files can be edited with Notepad, but any text-editing application will do. For this exercise, you'll choose the AutoCAD pattern called Grass, which you can find in `acadiso.PAT` (in metric units) or `acad.pat` (imperial units) located in the Chapter 4 folder on the book's website (`www.sybex.com/go/masteringrevit2008`).

IMPORTING A CUSTOM PATTERN

Follow these steps to make a custom fill pattern by importing an existing pattern definition:

1. Using Notepad, open the file `acadiso.PAT` or `acad.PAT`.

2. Highlight the lines that define the patterns, and select them:

```
45, 6.35, 0, 4.49013, 4.49013, 1.5875, -5.80526, 1.5875, -8.98026
*GRASS, turfed surface
90, 0, 0, 17.9605, 17.9605, 4.7625, -31.1585
45, 0, 0, 0, 25.4, 4.7625, -20.6375
135, 0, 0, 0, 25.4, 4.7625, -20.6375
*GRATE, grid
0, 0, 0, 0, 0.79375
```

3. Choose Edit ➢ Copy.

4. Open a new text file, and paste the selection. (Note that you can also open the PAT file in which all Revit patterns are already saved. In that case, paste the selected text in that file.)

5. This is the important part: In the new text file where you pasted the selected text, add the following lines:

```
;%UNITS=MM

*GRASS, turfed surface
;%TYPE=DRAFTING
90, 0, 0, 17.9605, 17.9605, 4.7625, -31.1585
45, 0, 0, 0, 25.4, 4.7625, -20.6375
135, 0, 0, 0, 25.4, 4.7625, -20.6375
```

The first line that you write before the pattern text ;%UNITS=MM, can appear only once in the text file. It defines the value for the units used in the pattern. In the example, the units are millimeters (MM); if you wanted to work in imperial units, it would be ;%UNITS=INCH. (If you followed our second option to not create a new note for each file but collect them in one file, then this line already exists and you don't need to add it.)

The second statement, ;%TYPE=DRAFTING, helps define whether you're creating a drafting or model pattern. In this example, the pattern is the Drafting type. It's important to know that when you import a new pattern, the type of pattern needs to be the same as the new type of pattern you're making. In other words, if you're making a new model pattern, you can't import a drafting pattern. If you try to do so, you'll see a warning message like the one shown in Figure 4.14.

6. Save your text file with a `.pat` file extension.

7. In Revit, choose Settings ➢ Fill Patterns.

8. In the Fill Patterns dialog, verify that the Drafting option is selected, and click New.

9. In the New Pattern dialog, select the Custom option. The lower part of the dialog offers new options.

FIGURE 4.14
If you try to assign a drafting .pat pattern to a Revit model pattern, you'll see a warning.

10. Click Import.

11. Navigate to the place on your hard drive or network where you saved the PAT file, and click Open.

12. In the list that appears to the right of this button, you can see the name of the pattern you created: Grass. (If you have a PAT file with many patterns defined, you see all the other drafting patterns available in that list.) The name of the pattern automatically becomes the name of your fill pattern, but you can change that if you like. See Figure 4.15.

FIGURE 4.15
The New Pattern dialog displays the imported PAT file in the Custom group.

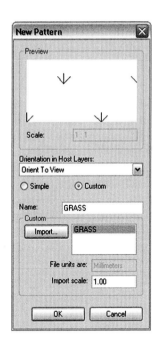

13. If necessary, you can adjust the scales of the imported pattern. The Preview window displays the graphic of the pattern, always in 1:1 scale. This informs you if you need to scale the pattern up or down. You'll know that you need to scale the pattern if the preview appears as a solid black box—that means the pattern is too dense.

14. If you're happy with the result, confirm by clicking OK.

Dimension Styles

Dimension styles are system families used to dimension the model. Dimensions can be linear, angular, or radial, each of which has a set of type parameters that control their graphic characteristics. By default, predefined type parameters are set for each of these dimension styles. When placing dimensions in the project, you can choose between aligned, linear, angular, radial, and arc length dimensions. Depending on the choice you make, a corresponding dimension style will be chosen for you:

◆ Aligned, linear, and arc length dimensions are associated with the system family Linear Dimension Style.

◆ The angular dimensions are associated with the system family Angular Dimension Style.

◆ The Radial dimensions are associated with the system family Radial Dimension Style.

PROPERTIES OF DIMENSION STYLES

Dimension styles can vary from a rigid technical appearance to more creative and sketchy types. Figure 4.16 shows three variations of a liner dimension style, each using a different type of tick mark. The range of graphic controls at your disposal is wide. Most conventions can be achieved using the options located in the type properties of your dimension types. The options include tick marks, length of dimension lines, extension, text type, spacing of text, spacing between the text and the dim line, and so on. Figure 4.17 shows the type properties of a linear dimension.

Let's look at the various ways you can customize the appearance of dimensions:

Tick Mark This option allows you to select the type of graphic called a *tick mark* that marks the crossing between the dimension line and the extension lines. You can select the type of the tick mark but not its size. Adjusting the size isn't possible directly from the dimension dialog. To edit a tick mark or make a new one, choose Settings ➤ Annotations ➤ Arrow Heads. You'll see the Type Properties dialog shown in Figure 4.18.

FIGURE 4.16
You can create a variety of graphical dimension styles with Revit.

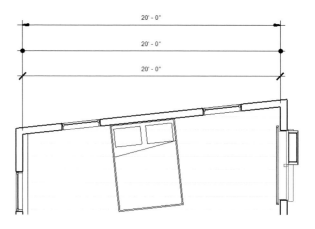

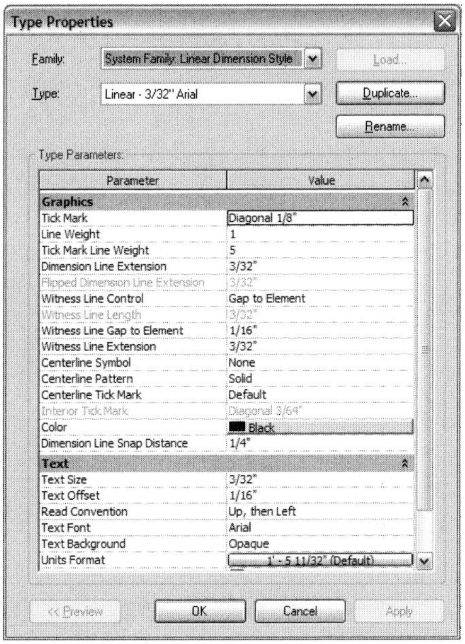

FIGURE 4.17
Type properties are
used to define different
graphic styles for
dimensions.

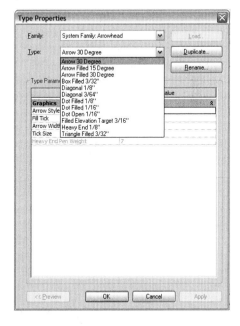

FIGURE 4.18
Type Properties of a
tick mark

Line Weight   This sets the thickness of the line that represents the dimension line and can be any value from 1 to 16. These numbers correspond to the weights defined in the Settings ➢ line weights ➢ Annotation line weights dialog.

Tick Mark Line Weight   You can set the thickness of the tick mark to any value from 1 to 16.

Dimension Line Extension   This setting allows you to define the length of the extension of the dimension line beyond the tick mark. In this example, the line extension has been highlighted in bold:

Flipped Dimension Line Extension   This setting is grayed out unless Tick Mark is set to Arrow Head. It inverts the direction of the arrows when the space between them is too small to accommodate both arrows in the dimension space. This parameter controls the length of the extension of the dimension line after the arrow symbol.

Witness Line Control   This setting controls the position of the witness lines with respect to the element that is dimensioned. You can choose one of the following options: Gap to Element or Fixed to Dimension Line.

Witness Line Length   This parameter defines the length of the witness line. It's active only when Witness Line Control is set to Fixed to Dimension Line.

Witness Line Gap to Element   This parameter sets the distance between the element that is dimensioned and the witness line. It's active only when Witness Line Control is set to Gap to Element.

Witness Line Extension   This parameter controls the length of the witness line above the dimension line.

Centerline Symbol   Some local standards require a specific graphic representation of the dimensions that reference to center axis of an element. By loading custom annotation symbol families into your project, you'll be able to choose which one is best suited for your needs.

Centerline Pattern   Using this parameter, you can define a line style when you're dimensioning to the center axis of an element. Again, this is to accommodate various local standards that require the center of elements to be graphically different from other dimensions.

Centerline Tick Mark   This is the third graphical way to make the axes or centers of elements easily recognizable. This parameter allows for a different graphic to be used as a tick mark when dimensioning centerlines of elements.

Interior Tick Mark   If more than one set of arrows doesn't fit in the space in a dimension chain, you can define smaller or simpler tick marks for the interior portions of the dimension segment.

Color   This parameter allows you to define any color for a dimension style (text and lines are both affected).

Dimension Line Snap Distance   Before you click the second line in a dimension chain, a dimension help line in a dashed green style appears, to help with positioning. The snap distance defines the automatic offset between two dimension lines. When you place a second dimension chain, the second one snaps to this designated offset.

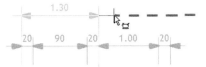

Text   Text height, offset from the dimension line, reading convention, text font, background (opaque or transparent), and unit format can all be set, allowing for a high level of customization when you create your own style.

Show Opening Height   When selected, this parameter displays the opening height of the element that is dimensioned, as shown here:

You can customize and rename the existing types and also create your own. To create your own type, you need to select an existing type (Duplicate), give it a name, and then edit the parameters:

Create a new type   In the Type Properties dialog, click Duplicate, give the new type a name, and click OK.

Rename a type   In the Type Properties dialog, select a type from the Type list, click Rename, give the type a new name, and click OK.

Delete a type   To delete a type, choose File ➢ Purge Unused. In the Purge Unused Elements dialog, select the dimension types you wish to delete, and click OK.

Text

Text is used to add notes to your drawings and can be customized to suit your needs. By default, Revit provides a couple of styles for you—feel free to edit these and add more as you see fit. Standard graphical control over size, font, color, and style are provided as well as the ability to add leaders to text.

Text is another form of system family and offers a range of graphic options for customization. To be realistic, we should say that Revit isn't a full-blown text-editing application, so you won't see the same level of font and paragraph stylization that you might find in regular text editors. However, a number of common parameters let you change the appearance of text.

PROPERTIES OF TEXT

Some parameters are also exposed directly in the Options bar when text is selected for editing, such as justification and the bold, italic, and underline options:

Most properties are managed through the Element Properties dialog. The following text properties can be accessed by selecting text and going to the Element Properties dialog:

Color   Text can be assigned any color using a standard color-pick dialog.

Line Weight   Any text note can be accompanied by leader lines—this parameter controls the weight of the leader lines. Line Weight can have any number from 1 to 16.

Background   The background on which text is written can be opaque or transparent. An opaque background is solid white and obscures other elements beneath it; a transparent background lets elements show through the text area. The usage of this parameter depends on the style of graphics you want to show. In busy drawings, setting the background opaque can help keep text readable. Figure 4.19 shows the effects of this parameter.

FIGURE 4.19
Text with (a) opaque and (b) transparent backgrounds

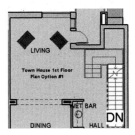

Leader Arrowhead   This parameter defines the leader arrowhead used in the leader line. You can't define the size of the leader arrowhead here. If you wish to create another size of leader arrowhead, choose Settings ➢ Annotations ➢ Arrowheads.

Read Convention   This parameter accommodates different reading conventions for the text with respect to the screen and sheet.

Text Height   This parameter controls the height of the text in dimensional values. Revit doesn't support the use of standard point sizes; you type in values in inches (mm).

Tab Size   This parameter controls the length of text when a tabulator is included in the text string.

Bold   This parameter forces the text to be bold.

Italic   This parameter forces the text to be in italic style.

Underline   This parameter forces underlining of text.

Width factor   This parameter lets you control the length of text without affecting its height. The default value is 1. If you want the text to be narrower, change this value to less than 1. If you need the text to be wider, the value must be greater than 1. In the example shown here, on the left the width factor is 0.5, in the center it's 1.0, and on the right side it's 2.0:

You can customize and rename the existing types and also create your own. To create your own type, you need to select an existing type (Duplicate), give it a name, and then edit the parameters to suit your requirements:

Create a new type   In the Type Properties dialog, click Duplicate, give the new type a name, and click OK.

Rename a type   In the Type Properties dialog, select a type from the Type list, click Rename, give the type a new name, and click OK.

Delete a type   To delete a type, choose File ➢ Purge Unused. In the Purge Unused Elements dialog, select the dimension types that you wish to delete, and click OK.

Creating Custom Annotation Tags

Many kinds of annotations are used in design and construction documents. These range from door and window tags, to wall and room tags, to view tags for sections and elevations. You can see the full list of annotation categories in the Object Styles dialog, under the Annotations Objects tab (Figure 4.20). Using the Family Editor, Revit allows you to customize all of these tags (elevation tags only minimally) to meet your graphic conventions. In this section, we'll walk through the creation of some common tags and show you how to make your own.

ARCHIVING AND MANAGING YOUR CUSTOM FAMILIES

Many new users of Revit are unsure where to store custom created families. It isn't advisable to save them in the folders provided by Revit, because you may lose track of them or inadvertently delete them when you reinstall the software. Keeping them on a shared network drive is the recommended strategy.

You should keep your templates up to date as you add more content; that way, you need to maintain only a few template files rather than dozens of separate family files. It's even better if you can establish this as a role within the office so everyone isn't making graphical changes to your templates.

FIGURE 4.20
The Annotation
Objects tab of
the Object Styles
dialog

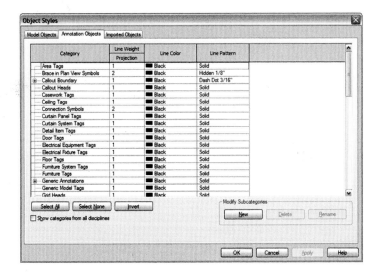

View Tags

Section, callout, and elevation tags are graphic indicators that reference other views in your project. The graphics for these elements can be customized to meet most scenarios. To create a custom section tag, for example, you have to first create a custom section tag family. To access the view tags, choose Settings ➤ View Tags. From here, you can customize a view tag through its Type Properties. By default, there is a predefined view tag for each view type. This can vary depending on the language version of Revit you have installed on your machine. The tags shown here are displayed and available by default in the USA English version:

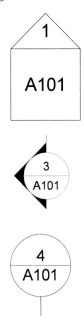

You can use the existing one, rename it or duplicate it, and amend its properties to create your own custom tag.

The creation of custom view tags differs depending on which view tag you're working with. Some require you to load a family file (.rfa) that can be fully customized with the Family Editor; others don't have corresponding family files and allow only limited customization, directly within the project.

SECTION VIEW TAGS

Before selecting a section tag, you can load multiple section tags from the family library. For example, you may decide to use different section tags for building sections and wall sections, and maybe even different tags for presentation plans than for construction documents. To implement these options in your project, you need to create each set of tags and load them into the project environment so they're available to select from the tag's Type Properties. All the section tags are defined in Settings ➤ View Tags ➤ Section Tags. In the Type Properties dialog that appears, you can find the following parameters:

Section Head   With this parameter, you can select different symbols for the section head. The drop-down list contains all loaded section view tag families (RFA files). Note that you can create your own fully customized section head using the Family Editor. Once selected from the list, the section head family appears at the beginning of the section line.

Section Tail   In some countries, a section line is described with the same symbol at the beginning and the end; in others, a section head appears on only one end of a section line, and at the other end is a section tail (a simplified graphic). This parameter lets you select the tail graphic; like the section head, this symbol can be fully custom-created in the Family Editor and loaded as a family (RFA file). Once selected from the list, the section head family appears at the beginning of the section line.

Broken Section Display Style   It's usual practice when documenting a building to make *non-linear sections*—sections that change direction and cut through the more important aspects of the design. With the section line selected, and using the Split Segment tool from the Options Bar, you can split a section in many segments. This property allows for graphical definition of the segmented section line. There are two options: Continuous and Gapped (dotted lines).

`Split Segment`

When you select the section line, a small break symbol appears in the middle of it (see Figure 4.21).

FIGURE 4.21
Click the break icon in the middle of the section line to split the line.

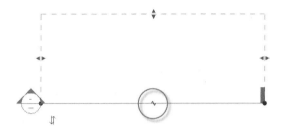

Creating a Custom Section Tag

To create your own section tag, you first need to select the tag family to which your new tag will belong. You have two options:

◆ The family already exists in your library, in which case all you need to do is load it into the template.

◆ The RFAs from the library don't correspond to your needs, and you wish to create a custom section tag. In this case, you first need to create a section tag in the Family Editor and then load it in the template.

This section's examples show how to create a custom tag family that you'll then use for your custom section tag.

Static Text and Parametric Labels

Creating annotation families in the Family Editor is by no means difficult, but you need to understand the principle of using parametric labels and text:

Text In the Family Editor, placing text in an annotation or title block means you're defining text that will always be the same and is unchangeable when that annotation is placed in the project environment. Figure 4.22 shows the words *AREA* and *VOLUME* as text. Regardless of where this room tag is placed, the text will always say *AREA* and *VOLUME*. Section tags work the same way: If you add static text, that text appears exactly the same for all section marks. This isn't typically used for sections, because each section is a reference to a unique view, and you want that information to be dynamic and parametric. That is where label functionality comes into play.

FIGURE 4.22
A custom room tag showing room name, number, area, and volume

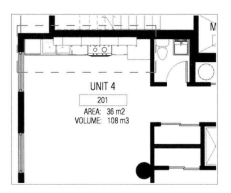

Labels A label offers textual information, but unlike static text, it's a live reference to a parameter value of an element in the project. It pulls information about a parameter directly from the BIM model. So, if you add an Area label, it will pull the value of the Area of the room, if you add a Sheet Number label in a Section Head family in the Family Editor environment and then use that section head in a project, the label will automatically display the actual sheet number on which this section is placed in the project. If you move the section from one sheet to another; the label will automatically report the new sheet number.

In Figure 4.22, Unit 4 is a label of the room name; the number 201 is a label of the room number. The label behaves as a dynamic text and is always fully coordinated with the value of the parameter it represents.

Like text, labels have graphical properties such as height, color, and font.

Creating a Custom Section Tag Family

An exercise will clarify what we just discussed. Imagine you would like to create a section tag that looks like the one shown in Figure 4.23. You need to create it first as a section tag family in the Family Editor and then load it into your template before you can create the tag in the project. Follow these steps:

FIGURE 4.23

Custom section tag

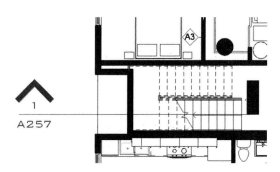

1. Choose File ➢ New ➢ Annotation Symbol.

2. In the Open dialog, select the family called `Section Head.rft` or `M_Section Head.rft`, and click Open.

3. The Family Editor environment automatically opens, and the drawing area shows a view in which three green reference planes (two vertical and one horizontal) have already been drawn. Do *not* change the position of the horizontal reference plane nor of the vertical reference on the right. In some templates, this is indicated with help text in red (which can you later remove):

    Intersection of horizontal & right ref planes define connection location with system section line. This means that your annotation will be located on the intersection.

    A proposed geometric shape is drawn for the annotation: a circle (two arcs) and a horizontal line. You're free to delete this default geometry and create your own tag shape. The default shape is there to help you visually understand where to begin drawing your new tag geometry.

4. Select the arcs that create the circle (use the Ctrl key for faster selection), and delete them.

5. Click the Label button in the Design bar. Position your mouse between the two vertical reference planes and below the horizontal plane, and click to position the start of the label. The cursor changes as shown here:

6. In the dialog box, select Sheet Number. In the Value group, you can enter a value; the default is A101.

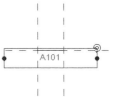

This isn't an actual value that will be displayed—it's a sample value that is visible only in the Family Editor. The text is a placeholder for an eventual real parameter value and is only here to help as a reference with layout. Once you load the family into a project template or project, this value will be replaced with the actual parameter value pulled from the database of your model. Usually, the proposed value is logical, so you can confirm by clicking OK. The label is placed and displays blue grips when selected. These let you redimension the length of the label. The length is important, because any value that is added (in a project) that is longer than the length of this box will begin to wrap and could mess up your graphics.

7. Following the same principle, place the label **Detail Number** above the horizontal reference but still between the vertical references.

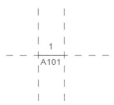

8. You can at any time reposition a label by selecting it and using the Move button to move it around. For more precise positioning, use the arrow keys on your keyboard to nudge elements in small increments. You can also help yourself by zooming in for a better view. (Note that zooming in makes the increment for the nudge tools finer.)

9. On the Design bar, click the Filled Region button. You'll be put into sketch mode. Using the Line tool, draw the shape shown here. Make sure the lines form a closed loop (no gaps or overlapping lines).

⬜ Filled Region

10. On the Design bar, click Finish Sketch. If you did everything correctly, you should have a custom designed family, as shown here:

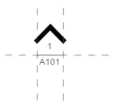

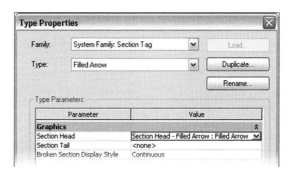

Save the tag you just created somewhere on your hard drive or network, and you're ready to use it in the template or a project. To load it into your project, click the Load Into Projects button on the Design bar. Choose the project you want to use the symbol in, and click OK.

In the next exercise, you'll assign this tag to a section mark in the context of a project.

Creating a Section Tag with a Custom Head/Tail Graphic

To create a section type that utilizes the section head family you created previously, you need to load the created section head in the template file:

1. Choose File ➢ Load from Library ➢ Load Family.

2. In the Open dialog, find the section head you created previously, select it, and click Open.

3. In the Settings dialog, click View Tags ➢ Section Tags.

4. In the Properties dialog, select Duplicate.

5. In the Name dialog (Figure 4.24), name the new tag **Filled Arrow** tag and click OK.

FIGURE 4.24
Give new section view tag a name.

6. In the section head's Type Properties dialog, click the drop-down menu and select your custom head family. For Section Tail, click <none>. This means the other end of the section line will be free of any symbol (Figure 4.25). Click OK.

FIGURE 4.25
You just created a new section tag that you now wish to associate with a section type.

Type Properties		
Family:	System Family: Section Tag	Load...
Type:	Filled Arrow	Duplicate...
		Rename...

Type Parameters:

Parameter	Value
Graphics	
Section Head	Section Head - Filled Arrow : Filled Arrow
Section Tail	<none>
Broken Section Display Style	Continuous

7. In the View menu of the Design bar, select Section.

8. From the Options bar, select Properties.

9. In the Element properties dialog, click Edit/New and then Duplicate.

10. Name the new type **Filled Arrow - No Section Tail**, and click OK (Figure 4.26).

FIGURE 4.26
Create a new
section type with a
unique name.

11. Under Section Tag, click the drop-down menu, select the tag you created, and click OK.

You can now place a section in your drawing area and see the results shown in Figure 4.27.

FIGURE 4.27
Draw one of your new
sections—it should
look like this.

Note that each time you create a new section type, Revit creates a new folder for it in the Project Browser. Our example uses two types of sections: building sections and detail sections. When you place one of each in a project environment, they're each placed in a new folder named by section type.

As you'll see next, the same principles apply when you make callout views.

CALLOUTS

In order to have a variety of different callout tags in the project environment, you need to load some customized tags into the project. The properties of callout tags offer a few options:

Callout Heads   This parameter defines the family and the callout type that will be used. The drop-down list contains all loaded callout head families (RFA files); you can also use no family (None). Using the Family Editor, you can create callout head families just as you can for section heads and tails.

Corner Radius   A callout in Revit usually has a rectangular shape with chamfered edges. This parameter lets you define the radius of those arcs on the corners of the callout tag.

Creating a Custom Callout Head

Figure 4.28 shows on the left the callout tag family you'll create in this exercise. Follow these steps:

FIGURE 4.28
(left) Custom callout
annotation; (right)
custom callout anno-
tation associated with
callout boundary

1. Choose File ➤ New ➤ Annotation Symbol.

2. In the Open dialog, select the family template called `Callout head.rft` or `M_Callout Head.rft`, and click Open.

3. The Family Editor opens, and a view with two crossing reference planes appears. Again, if you want to avoid problems later, don't move either of these two planes. In red, you'll see important guideline text: Always read it before deleting it. This text informs you that the tag will be positioned in the center of the crossing of the two reference planes and that the call-out leader will trim (be adjusted) to match the width of the drawn elements. Select the help text and delete it.

4. On the Design bar, click the Label button. Click the vertical reference plane and above the horizontal one to position the label.

5. In the dialog that opens, select Detail Number; in the Value zone, you can place a value as explained in step 6 of the exercise in the section, "Creating a Custom Section Tag Family."

6. Following the same principle, add another label—this time using "Sheet Number," position it below the horizontal reference plane.

7. On the Design bar, select Filled Region. Revit goes into sketch mode. Using the Line tool, draw the shape that represents the graphic of the callout tag you wish to create. Make sure the filled region uses a solid fill black pattern by editing its Type Properties.

8. Click Finish Sketch on the Design bar.

9. You can also adjust the text to be a different font or font size, if desired. The final appearance of the annotation in the Family Editor should look like this:

10. Save your callout tag, and load it into your project.

11. In the project, choose Settings ➢ View Tags ➢ Callouts. Make a new type, or edit an existing type by choosing the family you just loaded in. You need to do this in order to take advantage of your custom tag. Simply loading it into your project won't automatically assign it to a callout.

CHANGING THE GRAPHIC APPEARANCE OF THE FILLED REGION

You may want to use colors other than black for the filled region, and you may want to make it transparent or opaque. This will result in a different graphic presentation when you place the tag in the project and a different graphical presentation when it's printed, because most reprographics companies don't print full-size sheets in color.

Callout Views—Type Properties

The following are the Type Properties of a callout view:

◆ *Callout Tag*—Lists all available callout tags

◆ *Reference Label*—The default label for referenced callouts

Creating Callout Tags

You've already created your Callout Head family. Now you'll load it in the template file and associate it with a callout tag:

1. Choose File ➢ Load from Library ➢ Load Family.

2. In the Open dialog, find the callout head you created previously, select it, and click Open.

3. In the Settings dialog, click View Tags ➢ Callout Tags.

4. In the Properties dialog, select Duplicate.

5. In the Name dialog, name the new tag **Filled Rectangle**, and click OK (Figure 4.29).

FIGURE 4.29
Give the callout tag
type a unique name.

6. Under Callout Head, click the drop-down list and select your callout family. Under Corner Radius, set the angle that will be applied to the corners of the callout boundary line (Figure 4.30).

FIGURE 4.30
Choose the callout
head, and set the
radius for the callout
corners.

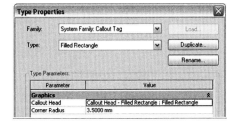

7. Click OK.

You just created a new callout tag that you can now associate with a callout type.

8. In the View menu of the Design bar, select **Callout**.

9. From the Options bar, select Properties.

10. In the Element Properties dialog, click Edit/New and then Duplicate.

11. Give the new type a name (**Filled Rectangle - Corner radius 3.5mm**), and click OK (Figure 4.31).

FIGURE 4.31
Create a new callout
view type.

12. Under Section Tag, click the drop-down list and select the callout tag you created.

13. Click OK.

You can now place a callout in your drawing area and see the results shown in Figure 4.32.

FIGURE 4.32
The final appearance
of the new callout type

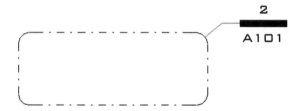

ELEVATION TAGS

Unlike all other tags in Revit, elevation tags don't reference a family file and are customizable only
to a limited extent. You can't create custom elevation tags—the only thing Revit lets you do is choose
between a round or square shaped elevation tags and make a few small modifications to those shapes.
However, you can create different elevation tags for exterior and interior elevations. Figure 4.33
shows the properties for elevation tags.

FIGURE 4.33
Elevation tag
Type Properties

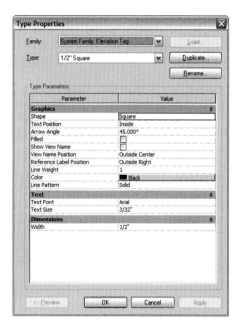

Elevation Tag Properties

The following parameters are available in the Type Properties of elevation tags:

Shape This provides the two possible shapes for elevation tags. The only possible selections
are Circle and Square.

Text Position Each elevation tag allows text to show the number of the view when placed on
a sheet. This value is empty until that elevation view is placed on a sheet. You can also decide
to add the name of the view to the elevation tag. This can make the tag busy and illegible, so
consider your options carefully. Figure 4.34 shows the options from left to right: Outside Left,

Outside Center, Outside Right, and at the end Inside. In the last case, it's preferable for better legibility to select an empty arrowhead.

FIGURE 4.34
Elevation variations, left to right: Outside Left, Outside Center, Outside Right, Inside

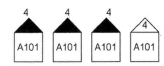

Arrow Angle The arrow indicates the direction of the view, and this parameter controls the angle of the arrow.

Filled This fills or doesn't fill the arrow associated with the tag. Depending on your graphical requirements, you may want to have the arrow filled or empty.

Show View Name This parameter allows you to add the information about the name of the view in the elevation tag.

View Name Position If you've decided to add the view name in the elevation tag, this parameter allows you to control the position of the name.

Reference Label Position This parameter controls the position of the reference label with respect to the tag. Figure 4.35 shows the different positions, from left to right: Outside Left, Outside Center, Outside Right.

FIGURE 4.35
The name of the elevation can appear on each arrow.

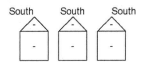

Line Weight This parameter defines the weight of the lines used for the entire tag. The Line Weight value can be any number from 1 to 16.

Color This parameter defines the color of the lines.

Line Pattern This parameter defines the line pattern for lines used in the tag.

Text Font This parameter defines the font used in the tag.

Text Size This parameter defines the height of the text used in the tag.

Width This parameter defines the size of the shape: If you choose Circle, this value is the diameter; if the tag is square, this is the size of the square.

As we mentioned previously, elevation tags are the only tags in Revit for which you can't create your own graphics using the Family Editor. For example, many firms use the same symbol for sections as they do for exterior building elevations. A common workaround to this problem is to use sections in lieu of elevations to get the right graphic appearance.

This workaround works well and is simple. The only downside is that your building elevations will be grouped with sections in the Project Browser.

Elevation View Type Properties

The following parameters are available as elevation Type Properties:

Elevation Tag   This parameter lists all available elevation tags in the project. You create elevation tags in the Settings ➢ View Tags ➢ Elevation Tags dialog.

Callout Tag   This parameter lists all available callout tags in the project. You create callout tags in the Settings ➢ View Tags ➢ Callout Tags dialog.

Reference Label   This parameter defines the default label for referenced elevations.

Creating an Elevation Tag

Unlike section and callout tags, to create a new elevation tag you don't need to load an elevation family, because there are none. As we mentioned previously, elevation tags are the only ones you can't fully customize, and no elevation tag family template exists in the Family Editor. You can change the appearance of the elevation tag to a degree, and then you associate it with a new elevation view type. Follow these steps:

1. In the Design bar's View menu, select Elevation.

2. From the Options bar, select Properties.

3. In the Element Properties dialog, click Edit/New and then Duplicate.

4. Give the new type a name (Interior), and click OK.

5. Under Elevation Tag, click the drop-down list and select the elevation tag you created.

6. Click OK.

You can now place an elevation in your drawing area and see the results as shown here:

Assigning a Family to a View Tag

We discussed how to create custom annotation families that are used to create custom tags. To put these annotations to use, you need to assign them to a view tag type. For sections and callouts, you use a section head family and a callout family. To assign an annotation to a section or callout view tag, choose Settings ➢ View Tags ➢ Section Tags. From there, you can choose what symbols to use for the section head and tail. The same concept is used for callouts.

LEVELS

Levels in Revit are represented with a line and a symbol that can be placed at one or both ends of the level line. Creating level types allows you to define the graphical characteristics of the level line, family symbol, and Z-coordinate system used by the level tags. All these parameters are stored in the level Type Properties; you can create as many as you please.

Level Properties

The following properties are available for levels:

Elevation Base   You'll find two options for Elevation Base: Project and Shared. When you select Project, the project's coordinate system is used. When you select Shared, the coordinates correspond to the shared coordinates.

Line Weight   This parameter allows you to set the line weight of the level line. Line Weight can be any number from 1 to 16. These numbers correspond to virtual pens with various thicknesses, which can depend on different scales applied to a view. To review the current settings, choose Settings ➢ line weights ➢ Annotation line weights.

Color   This parameter defines the color of the level line.

Line Pattern   This parameter defines the pattern of the line used for the level line.

Symbol   This parameter provides a list of all available level symbols that can be placed at the ends of the level lines. This list shows all level head family files currently loaded into your project. Just as with other tag families, you can create custom level tags and load them in your template. To create a custom level tag family, you need to use the correct family template: Level Head or M_Level Head.rft.

For the level tags shown in Figure 4.36, we created a custom level tag family and selected it in the custom level tag.

FIGURE 4.36
Level tags can be fully customized.

Symbol at End 1/2 Default   These options allow you to define whether to place the level head symbol at both sides of the level line (in which case this and the next option should be selected) or just one of them. End 1 is the start point when you draw the level line; End 2 is the end point.

GRIDS

The principle of customizing and creating grid types is similar to that of levels. The one parameter that grids don't have is Elevation Base. You can fully customize the appearance of a grid line, design your own symbol family, and define these in the Type Properties of grids. For custom symbols, there is a Grid Head.rft or M_Grid head.rft family template to use when you need to create your own.

Customizing Element Tags

During the construction documentation phase of a project, architects need to annotate various building components with symbolized descriptions (tags) in order to give additional information about the elements to be built. In the majority of cases, Revit allows automatic placement of the tags when the building component is created. If you don't want to fill your drawings with annotations early in the process, you can choose to not tag elements on creation. You can add the tags later, in a manual or automated way (see chapter 15, Tag all not Tagged). The tags use annotation families in their definition. This means you create your custom tag family, however you wish to imagine it, in the Family Editor, load the family in the project, and then use the tags wherever you need them.

It's advisable to load all tag families that you intend to use in your project or office template. That way, you can guarantee coherence and consistency in the way you document your project across the project team or office.

You can load the various tags in the template using several tactics:

◆ Choose File ➢ Load Library ➢ Load Family.

◆ Using Microsoft Explorer, select .rfa tag families and drag and drop them to place them in the Revit project environment. (You'll need to have the template file open.) When you try to load more than one family at the same time, Revit prompts you either to open each of those files in an independent window (so you can modify them) or to load them all in the current project. Choose the second option.

◆ Use the tool available in Settings ➢ Annotations ➢ Loaded Tags (Figure 4.37). The advantage of this method is that you have a preview of all loaded and preset tags that will be used throughout the project.

FIGURE 4.37
Tags dialog

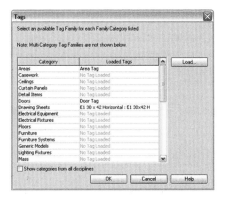

Certain tags are indispensable in a project template. These include door tags, window tags, room tags, revision tags, material tags, keynotes, and area tags. Out of the box, Revit offers at least one of each of these tags; but you'll probably want to create your own in the Family Editor and load them into your template.

CREATING A CUSTOM DOOR TAG

As an example of creating custom tags for a basic element, the following steps show you how to create the custom door tag shown in Figure 4.38:

FIGURE 4.38
The custom door tag you'll create in this exercise

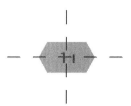

1. Choose File ➢ New ➢ Annotation Symbol.

2. In the Open dialog, select the family template called `Door Tag.rft` or `M_Door Tag.rft`, and click Open.

    The Family Editor opens in a view with two crossing reference planes. To avoid problems later, don't move the two reference planes. The intersection point is the center point of the tag.

3. On the Design bar, select Label. Click the intersection of the two planes to position the label.

4. In the dialog that opens, select Mark. In the Value group, you can enter a value that will be a symbolic value visible only in the Family Editor and that will be replaced by the number of the door to which this tag is associated. In this case, accept the proposed value and click OK.

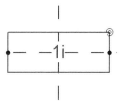

    Everything you learned about repositioning and changing the length of the section tag label in the exercise in the section "Creating a Custom Section Tag Family" applies here as well.

5. Click to select the label you just placed. On the Options bar, select Properties.

6. In the Element Properties dialog, click Edit/New.

7. In the Type Properties tab, select the text color, set the background to Transparent, and select a font style and size consistent with your office standards.

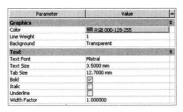

8. Click OK. Your graphic should look like this if you've followed the steps so far:

9. In the Design bar, click the Filled Region button, and sketch the shape of the tag.

10. Click Element Properties on the Design bar, and click Edit/New. In the Type Properties dialog, change the color of the fill pattern (select a color that allows you to see the color of the text—gray or yellow). Set Cut Fill Pattern to Solid Fill.

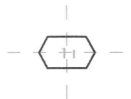

11. Click OK in all open dialogs.

12. While holding down the Ctrl key, click one of the lines in the sketch; from the Type Selector, select <Invisible Lines>. Doing so defines the shape of the tag, which has colored fill but no drawn boundary, as shown in Figure 4.38.

Invisible lines are for reference only in the Family Editor and in sketch mode. They're selectable but not visible in the project environment, and they never appear on printed documents.

13. On the Design bar, click Finish Sketch. The result should look like this:

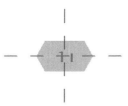

14. Save your tag. It's ready to be reused in a project or a template.

Creating Tags for Other Categories that Don't Have Family Templates

While creating custom tags, you'll notice that family templates aren't available for some available Revit categories you may need to create. For example, if you need to create a furniture tag, you won't find a corresponding template for it. What do you do? For such tags, you use the template called Generic.rft or M_Generic Tag.rft. As a first step when starting the template, you assign it to the category you wish it to be associated with. Here are the steps to do that:

1. Choose Settings ➢ Family Category and Parameters. (This exists *only* in the Family Editor.)

2. In the dialog, select the desired category (Furniture, in this case), and click OK.

3. Select the red information text, and delete it.

You can now proceed, using the techniques shown in our previous examples.

Keynotes and Text Notes

Notes are a critical part of communicating design and construction intent to contractors, subs, and owners. No drawing set would be complete without textual definitions and instructions on how to assemble the building. *Keynotes* are element-specific and can be scheduled and standardized in the Revit database.

Keynotes are textual annotations that relate text strings to specific elements in the model, which are in turn linked to an external text file. You can format font style, size, and justification in the same manner as for standard text, but keynotes behave like a Revit family. This means you can insert different text family types in Revit, just as you would door or window families.

KEYNOTE TYPES

The Keynote command is located on the Drafting tab in the Design bar. Adding keynotes in Revit gives you three options similar to those mentioned in our discussion of adding tags:

Element This option allows you to note an element in the model, such as a wall or a floor. This type of note is typically used if you want to note an entire assembly, such as a wall assembly. You can find this value in the family properties of that element.

Material This note type lets you note a specific material in Revit. You can add a note to concrete, gypsum board, or acoustical tile, for example.

This value can also be found in the Settings ➢ Materials dialog. The Identity tab lets you add keynote values directly to each material.

User This option allows you to select any model-based component in Revit and define a custom keynote for it. Notes defined this way differ from those defined under Element or Material because they're unique to the particular object selected. They can be used in conjunction with element and material notes.

CREATING A CUSTOM KEYNOTE

To create a custom keynote, follow these steps:

1. Choose File ➤ Open, select the Imperial library (or Metric, depending on your installation), and then choose Annotations ➤ Keynote Tag.rfa. You'll use an existing note block to edit in lieu of making one from scratch; this note is great to use as a template because it has each type of note already created.

 The Family Types include Keynote Number, Keynote Number Boxed, and Keynote Text note types; check boxes under each allow you to customize the notes further. As an example, here is Keynote Number Boxed:

$$\boxed{1}$$

2. For your keynote, select the Keynote Text option from the drop-down list, and click OK. As we discussed with the other tag families, you can add labels, text, lines, filled regions, and other graphic tools to customize your keynote.

3. Because you're using the text and not the numbers for this note, delete the box surrounding the note.

4. Select the label for the note (the 1), and go to the label properties. Here, you can adjust the font size and style. Also change the justification from Center to Left. Click OK to exit the dialog boxes when you're finished editing.

5. A critical part of a keynote is the note length. The overall length of the note before the texts begins to wrap to a new line is controlled by the size of the box for the note label. In this case, you want your notes to be 25 characters long (roughly 2¼″ at ³⁄₃₂″ scale). The best way to do this is to number the characters. Remember: The value you enter in this box now is only an aide to create the family.

$$12345678901214567890123 45$$

When you insert notes into the model and annotate a wall, you can see how the text responds on one line or on two (Figure 4.39).

FIGURE 4.39
Examples of
material keynotes

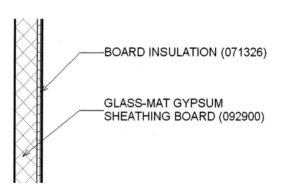

BOARD INSULATION (071326)

GLASS-MAT GYPSUM
SHEATHING BOARD (092900)

Creating Custom Title Blocks

While you're building a rich BIM model and adding more detail and intelligence in each phase of the project, you also have to document each phase and deliver drawings (sheets) for others. No matter whether you share this information digitally (DWF, PDF) or via printed documents, you need to place information that is company specific (logo and contact information), project specific, and sheet specific on those sheets. Consistency between the sheets is essential.

Sheets in Revit can be created in the project environment. Their creation starts with the selection of a title block that can have any shape, graphic layout, and size. Figure 4.40 shows a couple of examples; you'll create the second in this section's exercise. Title blocks are external families—you can create any kind of a title block in the Family Editor and add project-, sheet-, or company-specific information on it, both textual and images. (You can include your logo, an image of your project, and any other graphic.) Companies have different title block styles for document-sharing with different parties.

FIGURE 4.40
Different title blocks:
left for presentations,
right for construction
documents

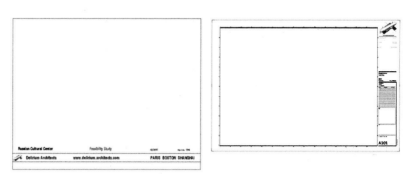

To use the title block families you've created in the Family Editor on a sheet, they need to be loaded in the project. If you've created office standards, the project templates are the best place to store title block families you created on your own. There is no need to create final sheets in the template file—loading the title block families is sufficient. However, different offices have different strategies.

Creating a Custom Title Block with the Family Editor

Sheets usually have standard dimensions depending on commonly agreed, standard paper sizes. These vary from country to country but are more or less standardized. Revit lets you easily create sheets to any standard you require.

The first thing to think about when creating a title block is the paper size on which it will be printed to which it will be cut. You then think about the layout graphics as well the information you want included on the sheet. Various world standards (DIN 680, BS 4264, SFS 2488, ISO 11180, ANSI/ASME Y14. 1, and U.S. National CAD Standards) define precise layout requirements for sheets and the content displayed in them.

Revit accommodates all these requirements, many of them in an automated manner. You can add any shapes, graphics, and textual information as well as use parametric labels capable of extracting information from the project. As you'll see, labels are part of the coordinated BIM concept and will help streamline your process. The following steps demonstrate how to create the custom title block illustrated in Figure 4.41:

1. Open the Family Editor by choosing File ➤ New ➤ Titleblock.

2. From the list, either select one of the prepared sheet sizes or select New Size. This opens a title block template where you can start laying out your title block. Let's assume that the size you need to duplicate doesn't exist in the list; select New Size.

3. A blank template file opens with nothing but a rectangle. Click the lines of the rectangle to activate temporary dimensions. You can then edit the dimension text value to drive the size of the rectangle. Make the sheet 42″ × 32″.

4. Draw lines with the Line tool, creating a layout as shown in Figure 4.41. For each variation in line thickness or color, you'll need to make a new line style using the Line Styles dialog. Add new subcategories to the Titleblock category.

FIGURE 4.41
The vertical title block you'll make

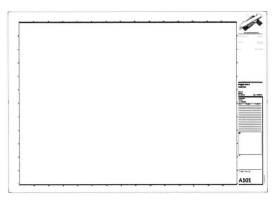

Once you're finished with the lines, you'll continue by adding images, fill patterns, text, labels, and symbols.

1. Add an image by choosing File ➤ Import ➤ Image and selecting the example on the book's website or any image on your computer. Place it anywhere, resize it using its grips when selected, and position it on the title block. This is how you can place your company logo into your title blocks.

2. Add fill patterns with the Filled Region tool to add a color banner or hatched area to your sheets. You can't add a fill pattern on a sheet in the project environment, so you need to add them in the Family Editor.

   Fill patterns added in the title block are always displayed *in front* of any views placed on the sheet. In other words, you can't use a filled region to create a colored backdrop view. There are other ways to achieve that, as covered in chapter 12.

3. Add text with the Text tool. Text is always the same and is unchangeable from the project environment. *Drawn by*, *Scale*, and *Date* are all examples of text. For each variation in font and/or size, you need to create a new type of text.

4. Add labels with the Label tool. These are textual fields that report information stored in individual projects. Like text notes, you need to create new types for every variation in font or size. By adding the label *Project Name* to the title block, you can reuse the title block in many projects; the label will update in each project with the appropriate name. The same principle works for the other labels, shown in the Select Parameter dialog (Figure 4.42).

   Figure 4.43 illustrates the difference between text and label elements, which behave as described in "Static Text and Parametric Labels" earlier in the chapter.

FIGURE 4.42
In this example, Project No. is text and remains unchanged in the project environment. The number 2000.01 is a label and will reflect the number of the project set in the project information.

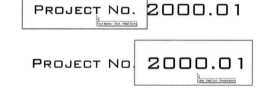

FIGURE 4.43
Place labels with standard parameters.

5. Place text and labels on the sheet to reflect the example shown in Figure 4.44.

FIGURE 4.44
Continue to build out
the title block.

6. Add a revision schedule to the title block so you can track changes in your document set. Changes are stored as revisions and can be displayed parametrically in your title blocks. We'll review the revisions in more detail in Chapter 19, but you'll add the revision schedule now.

Choose View ➤ New ➤ Revision Schedule (Figure 4.45). The Revision Schedule dialog opens, and you can choose which parameters to schedule. Choose Revision Number, Description, and Date. To adjust the font and size, use the Appearance tab. When you're finished, click OK. An empty schedule appears—close that view.

FIGURE 4.45
Place a revision
schedule.

7. In the Project Browser, click the Views node, and then open the Schedules node. Drag and drop the revision schedule into the title block to place it. The revision schedule appears empty, but not to worry—it will be filled automatically when used in a project.

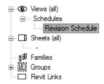

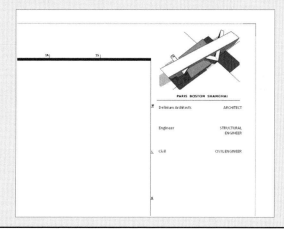

8. Once you've placed all these elements, the title block is good to go. Save it to your hard drive with a unique name, and click the Load Into Projects button. Choose a project file, and the title block will be loaded.

BEST PRACTICES AND WORKAROUNDS: POSITIONING VIEWS ON A SHEET

Currently, Revit has no automated way to place similar scaled floor plans in the same location across many sheets; you have to eyeball the placement. A useful aid is available to help, which takes advantage of the invisible line type. Choose an origin in your title block by drawing two intersecting invisible lines. These lines aren't visible in the project but provide a snappable intersection you can move views relative to. Another aid is to add tick marks to the title block to create a basic cell division.

The Bottom Line

If you set up your templates from the beginning, you'll save yourself headaches downstream. Experiment with object styles, annotations, and tags to get the right look and feel for your practice.

Create your own template with custom annotations and settings   Creating a template that incorporates your firm's styles and preferences is an essential first step in putting Revit to work.

> **Master It**   Your firm has some deeply established graphic conventions that were defined in AutoCAD. How would you go about matching these graphics and setting up a Revit template?

Create custom annotation families in the Family Editor   Styles for annotations, dimensions, and text are all governed by office standards, and the Family Editor is your tool for setting up those standards in Revit.

> **Master It**   You need to create dimensions, text, and annotations that match your office standards. How do you do this with Revit?

Create custom title blocks in the Family Editor   Title blocks are another important element of office standards that you can configure in the Family Editor.

> **Master It**   Most offices have several title blocks with lots of information embedded in them. How would you add multiple title blocks to your project template file?

Chapter 5

Customizing System Families and Project Settings in Your Template

In this chapter, we'll dig into customizing the Revit system families. Knowing how to leverage the adaptability of the system families by using type catalogs, view templates, and other global project settings can save you headaches early in the design process. In addition, the documentation process will be a lot easier because the assemblies are created correctly from inception.

You'll learn to do the following:

◆ Create new types in the Family Editor for common building components such as walls, floors, ceilings, roofs, and stairs

◆ Create type catalogs to quickly generate many types of the same family

◆ Create view templates for specific requirements

Wall Types

Walls are made from layers of materials that represent the construction materials used to build real walls. In Revit, these layers can be assigned functional values, allowing them to join and react to other layers in the model when walls, floors, and roofs meet. Each wall has at minimum a core, and then you have the option to add additional layers of material to the core to create the wall. These layers can be added inside the core or placed outside the core. As you'll see, this special wall *core layer* is a powerful element, and understanding it is essential to mastering Revit.

A wall core is much more than a layer of material. The core influences the behavior of the wall and how the wall interacts with other elements in the model such as floors or roofs, etc. Every wall type in Revit has a core material with a boundary on either side of it. These core boundaries are references in the model that can be snapped and dimensioned to.

What this means is: when you draw a floor above your exterior walls, you will use the pick creation method, select the exterior walls that should define the shape of the floor, and select in the Options bar if you wish the floor to extend only to the Core of the wall, have offset to it, or extend until the end of the wall. This floor creation method will result in a relationship between the floor and the underlying walls such that if those walls change their position, so too will the floor shape and position.

For example, you can constrain a floor sketch to the structural stud layer of walls by using the wall-core boundary to create the sketch (see Figure 5.1). If walls change size or are swapped, the floor sketch maintains its relationship to the core boundary and will auto-adjust.

Note: if you created your floor using the pick method, the locked relationship between the floor and the wall will happen automatically. If you decided to use the draw method instead of the pick method, you will need to manually lock the relationship so that the dependency is established. To get locks to appear, drag sketch lines so that they are co-incident with other lines, or use the align tool.

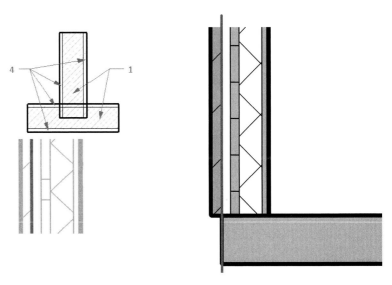

FIGURE 5.1
The sketch of a floor can be constrained to layers in a wall.

To access and edit wall-core boundaries and material layers, select a wall, go to the Element Properties dialog, click Edit/New to open the Type Properties dialog, and then select the Structure parameter to edit. Doing so opens a new Edit Assembly dialog. Here, you can define materials, move layers in and out of the core boundary, and assign functions to each layer (see Figure 5.2).

FIGURE 5.2
Each wall type is composed of layers of material, defined in the Structure/ Edit Assembly dialog

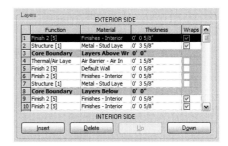

Creating Custom Wall Types

The creation of new wall types consists of modifying wall structure and function properties. If you have a series of wall types that are standard in your office, create them and add them to your project template. A wall can be a simple structure (single-component wall) or a complex structure (multi-component wall). The definition of the structure of the wall requires editing the wall's Type

Properties. You can create new wall types at any stage in a project by duplicating existing types and adjusting layers and other parameters.

The Structure (Edit Assembly) dialog, shown in Figure 5.3, is where you define the layers of the wall type. This dialog is divided into four zones: the Preview window, the Layers table, the Wrapping zone, and the Modify Vertical Structure zone (covered in detail in Chapter 11).

FIGURE 5.3
The Wall Edit
Assembly dialog

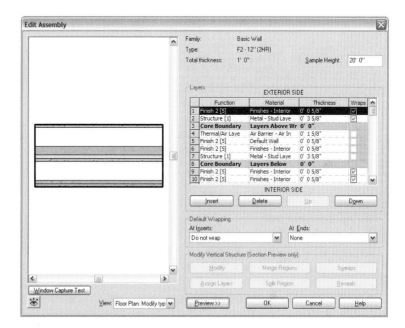

THE PREVIEW WINDOW

Located on the left side of the dialog box, you see a graphical preview of the wall structure in plan (the default) or section view. (If you don't see the preview, click the Preview button at the bottom left of the dialog.) To switch from the default plan view preview to section view preview and vice versa, click the drop-down list under View to choose another viewing option. In plan preview, the core boundaries of the wall are drawn with green lines. In section view, these lines aren't shown. In section preview, however, when you select a row or a layer in the layer properties, the layer will be highlighted in red.

THE LAYERS TABLE

This is where you add, delete, or move a layer of the wall structure. Each wall layer is represented as a separate row of information. Note that two of the rows are gray: They represent the boundaries of the core of the wall (the structural part of the wall). They don't represent any physical component but are just a visual representation of the separation between the structural and non-structural components of the wall. In between those two gray zones is the wall's structural core layer.

The table is divided into four columns: Function, Material, Thickness, and Wraps:

Function This column provides six options that relate to the purpose of the material in the wall assembly. Each layer has a priority assigned to it that determines how it joins with other walls, floors, and roofs:

Structure [1]: Defines the structural components of the wall that support that should be the rest of the wall components (layers). This layer is the highest priority and joins with other structural layers by cutting through weaker layers.

Substrate [2]: Forms a foundation for other layers (materials such as plywood or gypsum board).

Thermal/Air [3]: Defines the wall's insulation layer.

Membrane Layer: A zero thickness material that usually represents vapor prevention.

Finish 1 [4]: A finish layer to use if you have only one layer of finish (gypsum wall board).

Finish 2 [5]: A secondary, weaker finish layer (plaster, tiles, or brick).

With the exception of the membrane layer, all the other layers have a priority from 1 to 5. Revit uses the priorities of the layers in a wall to understand how to clean up/work out the intersections between various layers when two or more walls meet at an intersection. The principle is simple: Priority 1 is the highest in order; a layer that has a value of 1 cuts through any other layer with a lower priority value (2, 3, 4, 5). A layer with priority 2 cuts layers with priority 3, 4, or 5, and so on. Logically, the layer with priority 1 should be placed between the core limits and represents the core of the wall (the bearing component); the other layers should be outside the core. Revit starts sorting out wall joins by beginning with the highest-priority components and then working down the priorities (Figure 5.4).

FIGURE 5.4

Layers with same priority clean up when joined as shown on the right.

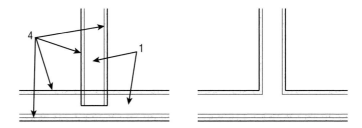

Material Associating a material to a wall layer provides graphical as well as physical characteristics for the wall. With a material, you can calculate the quantity of that material used in your project and schedule this information. The material also knows to clean up when it joins with other walls, floors, and roofs that are made of the same material.

How does a material definition affect the cleanup? The material usage informs Revit how to treat wall layers at intersections. If the priority of the layers is the same and the material is the same, Revit cleans up the join between these two layers, and they graphically show a consistent material. If the materials are different, even though their priority is the same, Revit separates the two layers graphically with a thin line (Figure 5.5).

Thickness This value represents the actual thickness of the material. Note that the membrane layer is the only layer that can have zero-thickness value.

FIGURE 5.5

Two layers with same priority but different materials: The clean-up between the layers isn't taking place because of the different materials used. The separation between the two layers is indicated with a thin line.

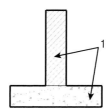

Wraps   Wall layers rarely end with a straight-cut finish at wall ends or wall penetrations (windows and doors). This option, when selected, allows a layer to wrap around other layers (Figure 5.6). You can define different settings for wrapping the end of walls or openings.

To create a wrapping solution that reflects a real-life condition, this setting probably won't be sufficient. All you can define in the Wall Editor is *if* a material layer will wrap and whether it's an exterior or interior wrap. The Wall Editor alone can only solve wrapping conditions in a generic way. To achieve more complex wraps like the one shown in Figure 5.6, you must define another set of rules in the Family Editor, while creating the window or door family itself. These additional settings, combined with the wrap function of the wall layer, will produce more complex wrap conditions such as the one shown.

FIGURE 5.6

Layer wrapping. Left: Wrapping is applied only to the first exterior component of the wall, and only that layer wraps around the window opening. Right: The first and second exterior components have wrapping active, so they both wrap around the opening of the window.

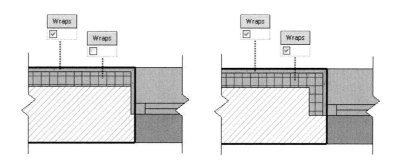

To summarize, editing the wall structure means adding or deleting wall layers. Each of those layers needs to be associated with a priority, a material, thickness, and wrap information. To move layers up and down in the table, or to add and remove layers, use the buttons at the bottom of the dialog.

Once layers have been defined and positioned, you need to consider a few more properties.

DEFAULT WRAPPING

Each wall layer can either wrap or not wrap at the ends of the wall or at inserts (windows, doors, openings). To make this happen in the project, you need to decide whether the wrapping should occur at openings or wall ends or at both conditions. For inserts, you can choose Do Not Wrap, Exterior, Interior, or Both. Similarly, for wall ends, the options are None, Exterior, and Interior. The default wrapping parameters appear in both the Edit Assembly window (Figure 5.3) and the wall's Type Properties dialog, as shown here:

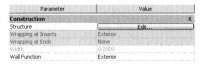

Level of Detail

Walls have only two different styles of graphic display for the three levels of detail: one for Coarse and another for Medium and Fine views. You will notice that changing from Medium to Fine view and vice versa will have no effect on the graphic display of the wall.

Coarse display   This is defined as a type property for each wall family. You can set both Coarse Scale Fill Pattern and Fill Color. If no Coarse Scale fill is set, then what you will get in coarse display will be the material that is set for the wall category in the Object Style and no interior layers will be displayed.

Medium/Fine display   Defined in the Type Properties dialog, in the Wall Assembly area where materials are defined that establish the cut and surface pattern for the each layer of the wall.

In Figure 5.7, Coarse Scale Fill Pattern is set to a solid fill and Color to black. You can see the difference in how these walls present in the same plan.

MANAGING LAYER POSITION

When you insert new layers, the newly created layer is always positioned below the active layer (the selected layer) in the layer table. To position your new layer properly, you can either click the Insert button and use the Up or Down buttons to position the new layer wherever you need it, or you can select the layer you want to reposition with the mouse (place the mouse at the beginning of the line and select the entire line as shown in Figure 5.3) and again, using the Up and Down buttons reposition it where you need it. By default, each time you insert a new layer, it has a Priority value of Structure [1], a Material setting of By Category, and a Thickness value of 0, and Wrap is selected:

Note that you can not delete the layer between the two gray lines (the structural portion of the wall) if it is the only or the last one. A structural layer must exist and have at least one layer that has a value greater than zero. If you make a wall that has only one material (like a concrete foundation wall), you must place that one concrete layer between the gray core-boundary lines.

FIGURE 5.7
The difference be-
tween (left) coarse and
(right) fine views is
that layers aren't
shown, and you can
define a drafting pat-
tern if you wish.

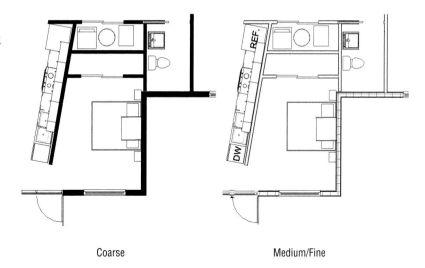

Coarse   Medium/Fine

Wall Function

Each wall has a function whose value is Interior, Exterior, Foundation, Retaining, or Soffit. Changing this parameter doesn't affect the geometry of the wall but is useful for controlling the visibility
of walls and for scheduling purposes. Another important aspect of this categorization is during
export to DWG: You can assign each functional wall type to a different CAD layer for export.

Floor and Roof Types

The process of creating floor and roof types is similar to that of walls. Editing the floor structure follows the same principles as for the wall structure. The only parameter that is different is Wraps—
in the Floor Editor, this parameter is always grayed out. On the other hand, multilayered floors
have an additional parameter that wall layers don't have that allows the layer to vary in thickness
if the floor is sloped. This appears in the Layers table as a new column named Variable (Figure 5.8).

With the 2008 release, Revit allows you to slope floors and roofs by adding points and ridges
that can then be manipulated to create creases and sloping forms. You do so using Shape Editor
tools, which are available in the Options bar when a floor or roof is selected. The Shape Editor tools
are explained in more detail in Chapter 11.

Floors or roofs that have been dynamically edited with these tools enable the Variable parameter.
If you select the Variable property, that floor layer can have a nonuniform thickness, as shown in
Figure 5.9.

FIGURE 5.8
The "Variable"
parameter available
only for Floor and
Roof Layers

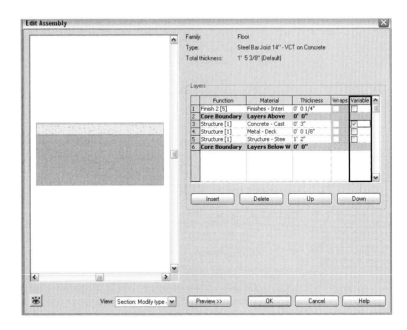

FIGURE 5.9
The property Variable
is selected, so the
floor layer has a non-
uniform thickness.

If the Variable property variable isn't selected, as in Figure 5.10, the layer in question has a uniform thickness, and it will be so that the entire floor structure is going to be sloped.

FIGURE 5.10
The Variable property
isn't selected, so
the floor layer has
uniform thickness
and the entire
structure slopes.

Ceiling Types

Ceilings are also system families. Revit includes two different ceilings families: a simple ceiling that has no thickness or internal layers, and a multilayered ceiling that is identical to floors and roof in terms of functionality. Specific to ceilings is that they don't support the variable-layer thickness functionality and don't have a wrap function.

Use the simple ceiling to model drop ceilings that are hung from the structure. These are typically only as thick as the acoustical tiles and don't need to be modeled as fully 3D forms. The multi-layered ceiling is good for gypsum ceilings placed on studs.

Door and Window Types

Doors and windows are external families (RFA files) and are loaded into a project as needed. You should include file door and window families that you use most frequently in your templates. You create initial types using the Family Editor, but there is no limit to the number of additional types you can create in the context of a project. The same principle applies to other standard families such as furniture, plumbing fixtures, lighting fixtures, and so on.

Stair Types

Stairs are complex building elements and require a deep understanding of local standards, rules, and requirements. Check the local Building Code requirements (minimum width, maximum height) to confirm that you're using the correct stairwell dimensions and ensure proper headroom. Formulas for calculating stairs are based on common codes and ergonomics. These may have slight variations in different regions, based on local conditions.

As illustrated in Figure 5.11, a number of parameters define the representation of stairs, including rules for risers, treads, and stringers. All of these can be adjusted and made into types for use in your templates.

FIGURE 5.11
Various stair types representing different construction approaches and material selections

Properties of Stairs

In the Element Properties dialog for a stair, you can control the following properties:

Calculation Rules   In the stair's Type Parameters dialog, in the Construction/Calculation rules, click the Edit button to open the calculation rules. To use the calculation functionality, select the option at the top of the Stair Calculator dialog (see Figure 5.12). The calculation rule is based on the universal calculation formula that sets the value that should result depending on the size of the runs and risers. If this value can't be achieved, it should at least be within the minimum and maximum range you've defined.

FIGURE 5.12
Stair Calculation
Options

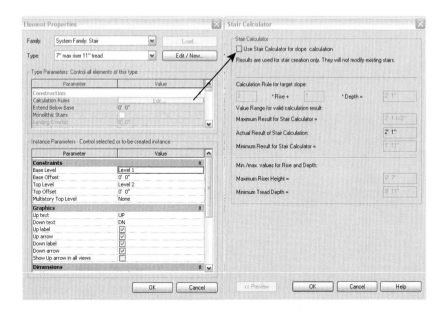

Extend Below Base   This field defines an offset between the base of the stair and the level where it starts. A positive value means the stair starts higher than its base level, and a negative value starts the stair below the base level. The top of the stair isn't affected by this parameter. This option is needed for conditions where the floor material demands that the stair start a bit higher or lower than the level.

Monolithic Stair   When this option is selected, it changes the stair into a monolithic form where the stringers, risers, and treads are treated as the same material. This is great for making concrete stairs.

Landing Overlap   This option is active only when the Underside Of Winder option is selected (see following explanation).

Underside Of Winder   This option is available only with Monolithic Stairs and has two values: Smooth and Stepped. They represent the treatment of the underside of the stairs, as show in Figure 5.13.

Break Symbol in Plan   This parameter shows a break line in plan. If it's selected, the break symbol appears at the cut height of the stair. The part of the stair that is beyond the break symbol (above the cut plane of the view) is shown with special subcategories of stairs: "Stairs beyond cut line" and "Stringers beyond cut line." Each can be assigned a different color and line type. This setting is unique to the rest of the graphics used for the stair.

Figure 5.14 shows on the left a stair with visible break symbol and on the right the same stair with no break symbol.

Text Size and Font   These properties of the text can be automatically added (up and down from the instance properties of the stair).

FIGURE 5.13
Monolithic stairs with
Underside Of Winder
set to (a) Stepped and
(b) Smooth

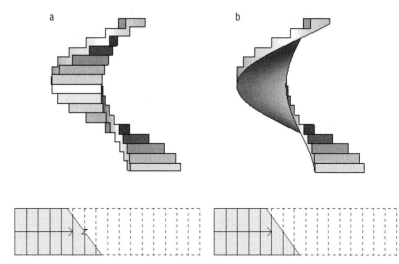

FIGURE 5.14
The same stair with
and without the break-
line graphic enabled

Material   You can set different materials for various components of the stairs. When the Mono-lithic Stair option is selected, some of the options under Material will become grayed out.

Minimum Tread Depth   This parameter controls the depth of a tread. Once you place a stair in a project, you can set the Actual Tread Depth in the stair's instance parameters. If this value is less than the type property Minimum Tread Depth, Revit gives you an error message alerting you to the problem.

Tread Thickness   This parameter controls the thickness of a tread.

Nosing Length   When this parameter has a value of 0, no nosing is applied to the stair. A pos-itive value for this parameters results in a nosing being exposed on all treads.

Nosing Profile   This is where you can set the nosing profile that is used when Nosing Length has a positive value. You can create any custom profile for the nosing—the Family Editor includes a Profile – Stair Nosing family template you need to use. Once you have the custom nosing family, you load it in the template (project) and associate it with a certain stair type.

Apply Nosing Profile   This determines where the nosing profile is placed relative to the tread. The available values are Front Only; Front and Left; Front and Right; and Front, Left and Right. No Back option is available.

Maximum Riser Height   This field defines the maximum allowed value for a riser. Usually, this setting depends on regulations set in the local Building Code as well as the type of building.

Begin with a Riser, End with a Riser   These settings control the start and end of the stair and the connection with the landing.

Riser Type   There are three possible types: None, Straight, and Slanted. As shown in Figure 5.15, this is fairly self-explanatory for the riser. For the slanted type, you can't define the angle of the slope; that value is a result of the length of the tread and the profile of the nosing.

Riser Thickness   This value defines the thickness of the riser material.

FIGURE 5.15

Riser types: left to right, (a) no riser, (b) straight riser, (c) slanted rise with value 1″ (2 cm) for nosing, (d) slanted riser with value 1.5″ (3cm) for nosing

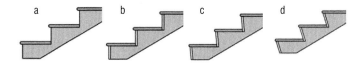

Riser to Tread Connection   There are two options: Extend Riser Behind Tread, as shown on the left; and Extend Tread under Riser, as shown on the right:

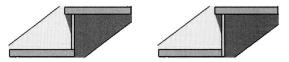

Trim Stringers at Top   This option controls how the stringer finishes its geometry at the top of the flight (see Figure 5.16).

FIGURE 5.16

Trim stringer options

- Do Not Trim: The stringer continues above the level.

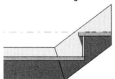

- Match Level: The height of the stringer is coincident with the level.

- Match Landing Stringer: The top of the stringer is cut at a height that matches the landing stringer.

Stringer Left/Right   This setting provides three options for stringer geometry:

None: There are no stringers.

Closed: The stringers are placed on the sides of the stair.

Open: The stringers are placed below the stair and are cut away by risers and treads.

Middle Stringers   This option allows you to add one or more stringers below the stair. When more than one is added, they're evenly spaced.

Thickness/Height of Stringers   This option gives you dimensional control over the stringers.

Open Stringer Offset   This option is active only if the stringers are defined as open. This parameter controls the position of the stringer relative to the stair.

Stringer Carriage Height   This is the value between the stringer height and the treads. The larger the value, the deeper the stringer goes below the treads (the tread position stays the same).

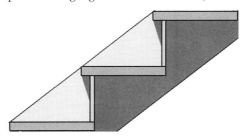

Landing Carriage Height   This value controls the distance between the bottom of the landing and the bottom edge of the stringer.

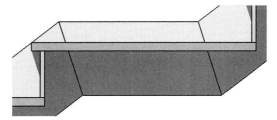

Types and Type Catalogs

To see why type catalogs are useful, you need to understand the various ways types of families can be created.

Library elements (families) are often the same shape and material but come in different sizes. Revit allows you to embed many variations of a single family by creating types. Each type corresponds to user-definable values that control the size and material of an element. In Figure 5.17, you can see three types of the same table that come in three different sizes and three different chair configurations. They're all the same family, but each variation in table size is captured as a separate type. The geometry and number of chairs are all controlled parametrically, allowing for many types to be generated.

FIGURE 5.17
One family with three types: 4 chairs type, 6 chairs type, and 8 chairs type

A Revit element can have many different combinations of sizes and materials. Those can be stored in different types so that efficiency and consistency across a team are guaranteed. You can create types of Revit elements in different ways and places, depending on the elements as well as of the intended purpose of the types or their number. You can create types of families in the project environment using the duplication method, you can set them in the family environment, and you can also use a type-catalog approach. The last is used in cases where you need more than five or six types, such as 50+ different sizes of a manufactured steel columns, etc.

Creating Types in the Project Environment

New types created in a project exist only in that project. You create a new type of an element by duplicating an existing type and giving it new values. As an example, you select a wall, in its properties select Duplicate, give it a new name, and change it to reflect the new type you wish to create. If you need to reuse that new type in another project, you can copy and paste the element from one project to another or use the Transfer project Standards.

Creating Types in the Family Editor

Unlike the creation of types in the Project Environment that can be applied to both System and Standard Families, this method applies only to standard families. You create new types using the Family Types dialog on the Design bar in the Family Editor. By creating the types in the Family Editor, you save time downstream by providing a collection of common sizes that will be available when loaded into a project. Creating types in the Family Editor also ensures consistency of library components across projects. If you make unintended changes in a project, you can always reload the original file and override the values you changed. When doing so, you get a warning dialog that asks if you want to override family type values.

The strategy of defining types in the Family Editor isn't always applicable, depending on the number of types you need per element. If you think you'll have more than five different types, consider using the type-catalog strategy instead of making the types in the family. This is a way to define many types by entering textual information that a family then uses to construct a list of possible types.

Creating Types with Type Catalogs

Each family type uses a certain amount of disk memory for its definition. When you load a family into a project, every type in that family is loaded. There is no way to selectively load types of a given family created in the Family Editor. If you have lots of families with lots of types, this can consume unnecessary memory and bloat your file size. Additionally, when you have many types defined in a family and you load them in a project, the list of available types can become long and difficult to search through.

This is where type catalogs can help. They allow you to define many different types (size combinations) of an element, which can then be selectively loaded into your project. A *type catalog* is a text-format list that contains all the dimensions of the family for each type variation and this can be an infinite number of types. The catalog is a separate TXT file related to the family. When you load a family associated with a type catalog, you get the option to choose which types to load in.

When you're creating a type catalog, it's imperative that it has the same name as the RFA family and is located in the same folder as the family. To create a type catalog file, all you need is a simple text editor (Notepad, for example). Figure 5.18 shows a steel column that comes in many different sizes (more than 20 types) and what the corresponding type catalog looks like in a text editor.

FIGURE 5.18
The type catalog lets you make many types using a text editor.

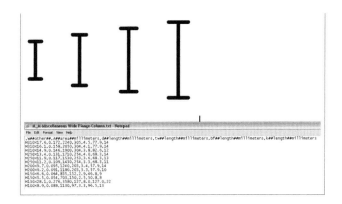

TYPE-CATALOG SYNTAX

To make and edit a type catalog, you need to know and follow some syntax rules.

The type catalog must have the exact same name as the family it's associated with. The only difference should be file extension (.txt). In the example in Figure 5.18, the family is called M-Miscellaneous Wide Flange-Column.rfa and the matching type catalog is M-Miscellaneous Wide Flange-Column.txt.

The type catalog has to be stored in the same directory as the family. The example mentioned can be found in the following standard installation locations:

Imperial sizes: C:\Documents and Settings\All Users\Application Data\Autodesk\ RAC 2008\Imperial Library\Structural\Columns\Steel

Metric sizes: C:\Documents and Settings\All Users\Application Data\Autodesk\ RAC 2008\metric Library\Structural\Columns\Steel

Each value must be separated with a comma or period, depending on the regional settings of your PC.

The first line in the type-catalog file declares the parameters that will be taken into account in the type catalog:

```
,W##other##,A##area##inches,d##length##inches,tw##length##inches,bf##length##
inches,tf##length##inches,k##length##inches
```

or

```
;Width##Length##millimeters ;Height##Length##millimeters;Frame##other##
```

Let's look at the second example in more detail. The essential rule can be stated as follows:

```
Name of Parameter##Type of Parameter##Units
```

Name of Parameter corresponds to the name of a parameter in the family. You have to be careful when typing, because this value is case sensitive. For example, if you have a Width parameter in the family, it should be shown as Width in the catalog as well. This parameter must be followed by two # symbols. *Type of Parameter* also must correspond to a type parameter in the family. The supported types are Length, Area, Volume, Angle, Force, and Linear Force. If the parameter in the family doesn't correspond to any of these, type **Other##s**.

Next, you enter the units. These are the valid units that will work in a type catalog:

For length: Inches, Feet, Meters, Centimeters, and Millimeters

For surfaces: square_feet, square_inches, square_meters, square_centimeters, square_millimeters, acres, and hectares

For angles: decimal_degrees, minutes, and seconds

For forces: newtons, decanewtons, kilonewtons, meganewtons, kips, kilograms_force, tonnes_force, and pounds

For linear forces: newtons_per_meter, decanewtons_per_meter, kilonewtons_per_meter, meganewtons_per_meter, kips_per_foot, kilograms_force_per_meter, tonnes_force_per_meter, and pounds_per_foot

For Others, you don't specify a value; it can be anything. In our case, it's Yes/No.

In the example, Width is a Length parameter defined in millimeters, Height is also a Length parameter defined in millimeters, and Frame is a parameter that has Other as its value and no defined units.

After editing the first line in the catalog, you then begin to type in values to define types. Here is an example showing four types. Notice that each definition consists of name, length, height, and frame:

```
900mm x 400mm - D;900 ;400 ;1
900mm x 400mm;900 ;400 ;0
1200mm x 600mm - D;1200 ;600 ;1
1200mm x 600mm;1200 ;600 ;0
```

By having set this in the type catalog, you create four types for one family. The first type is named 900mm x 400mm – D. The width of the element is 900mm, the height is 400mm, and there is a frame (Frame is defined in a family as a Yes/No parameter; in the type catalog, this value uses 1 for Yes and 0 for No). To better understand the principle of the type catalog, it's best to see it in table form:

Type Name	Width	Height	Frame
900mm x 400mm – D	900	400	1
900mm x 400mm	900	400	0
1200mm x 600mm – D	1200	600	1
1200mm x 600mm	1200	600	0

Loading from a Type Catalog

When you have a type catalog associated with a family and you load the family into a project, you'll see in the lower part of the dialog a table where the various types are listed. Select one or many of these types (use Shift or Ctrl for multiple selections), and then click the Open button to load the family and selected types. Figure 5.19 shows a Shift-selection, and Figure 5.20 shows a selection using the Ctrl key.

FIGURE 5.19

When you load a family with a type catalog, you see a list of types at the bottom of the dialog box.

Type	Width	Height	Frame
(all)	(all)	(all)	(all)
600mm x 200mm - D	0.6000	0.2000	1
600mm x 200mm	0.6000	0.2000	0
900mm x 400mm -- D	0.9000	0.4000	1
900mm x 400mm	0.9000	0.4000	0
1200mm x 600mm – D	1.2000	0.6000	1
1200mm x 600mm	1.2000	0.6000	0
1500mm x 800mm – D	1.5000	0.8000	1

FIGURE 5.20

Using the Ctrl key, you can select several types that aren't sequential.

Type	Width	Height	Frame
(all)	(all)	(all)	(all)
600mm x 200mm - D	0.6000	0.2000	1
600mm x 200mm	0.6000	0.2000	0
900mm x 400mm -- D	0.9000	0.4000	1
900mm x 400mm	0.9000	0.4000	0
1200mm x 600mm – D	1.2000	0.6000	1
1200mm x 600mm	1.2000	0.6000	0
1500mm x 800mm – D	1.5000	0.8000	1

Graphic Overrides of Host Objects with Complex Structure

When dealing with multi-component walls, Revit uses object styles to define a single cut-line style for all walls. As shown on the left in Figure 5.21, this cut line applies to the wall's outermost layer. This isn't flexible enough for some representations, where you may want to show only the core as a thick line and reduce the line weight of finish layers, as shown on the right in Figure 5.21. To address richer and more descriptive graphics to complex host structures, you need the ability to assign line thickness, type, and color to individual layers in a host structure. You can do so on a per-view basis using graphical overrides; however, the settings can be stored in a view template and applied to other views.

FIGURE 5.21

(Left) The default representation of a cut line. (Right) The core layer can be made bolder and the finish layers thinner.

To do this, open the Visibility/Graphic Overrides dialog from a plan view. Then, choose the Overrides Host Layers option for Cut Line Styles (Figure 5.22).

When the Host Layer Line Styles dialog opens, you see that the wall functions are listed with options to adjust the line weight, color, and pattern. Changing these values lets you generate wall graphics as shown in Figure 5.23.

You can also control the line styles for *common edges*. A common edge is a line that is common between two layers of different functions. The common edge is drawn with the line weight of the higher of the two layers that touch. If both layers are drawn in line styles with the same pen weight, the properties assigned to Common Edges are used. Common Edges is a property of every host, and you can set its style in the Object Styles dialog (Figure 5.24).

FIGURE 5.22
You can change the line weight, color, and pattern of host layers.

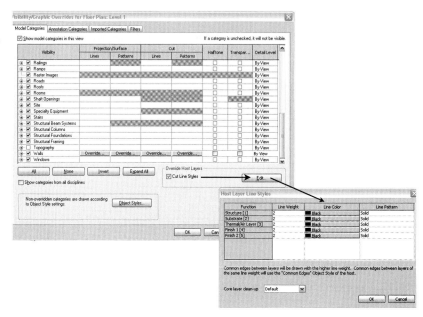

FIGURE 5.23
The effect of changing line weight, color, and pattern for walls

FIGURE 5.24
In the Object Styles dialog, you can set graphic rules for common edges in walls, floors, and roofs.

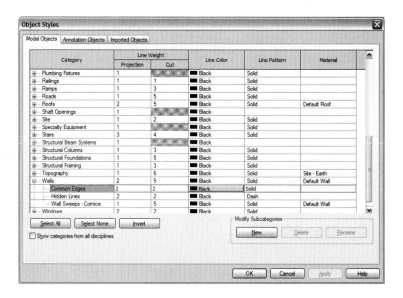

The Host Layer Line Style dialog also lets you define how the core layers should clean up:

Default   All line weights, colors, and patterns use standard behavior.

Use Function   This setting ignores the material settings (the line is never invisible) and sets the style of the separating line based on the layers' functional priorities. The style of a separating line is determined by the layer with the higher functional priority.

Use Common Edge Style   This setting ignores the functional priorities and material settings and always uses the common edge style.

No Edge   This option sets the separating line to invisible whenever the layers have the same fill pattern.

Additional Global Project Settings

In addition to setting up the graphic-object styles for your templates, you should also set up some other common settings in advance. In the Settings menu (Figure 5.25), you'll find the following global project settings that can be stored on a per-template basis.

FIGURE 5.25

The Settings menu

Room and Area Settings

Room and Area Settings include several predefinitions for you to consider. In this dialog (Figure 5.26), you can set the rules for room surface calculation (the cut height at which room areas are calculated) and enable automatic calculation of room volumes. We don't suggest enabling the volume calculation option at all times because it can slow down overall performance when you're working on your model. Do it only when you need the information or need to print out the documents that contain that information.

USE VIEW TEMPLATES

If you want these settings to be available in every project, it's strongly advisable to define them in your project templates as separate view templates.

FIGURE 5.26

Room and area calculations are based on the height of the cut plane and the layer in a wall to which the calculation is measured.

Finally, you can apply different rules for room calculations that relate to boundary options in walls. These include wall finish, center, core layer, and core center.

These setting affect Area plans which are used to convey building usage that extends beyond the shape and size of individual rooms, such as rentable area or office space. You access area plans from the View list of the Project Browser.

Units

Depending on where the project is located or what country you work in, you'll use either metric or imperial units. In the Project Units dialog (Figure 5.27), you can set the units for length, angles, surface, and volume. Under each of these options, you can define a rounding value, rounding increment, and units suffix and decide whether you wish to show the symbol + for positive values.

Note that Revit allows for combination of imperial and metric units within the context of the same project. For each unit type in the Project Units dialog, you can specify any formatting that is most suitable. Also note that while the project settings establish a consistent baseline, you can override project unit settings for elements such as dimensions and schedules.

IMPERIAL UNITS: FEET OR INCHES?

When you're using Revit for the first time and working in imperial units, you'll notice that numeric values resolve in feet instead of inches, which is different from the way AutoCAD works. A majority of Revit users have extensive experience (and thus established habits) with AutoCAD, so this can be frustrating at first. If you want to make sure your workflow isn't inhibited by this issue, you can modify the setting here to work in inches in lieu of feet.

FIGURE 5.27

Set up your units and rounding in advance in your templates.

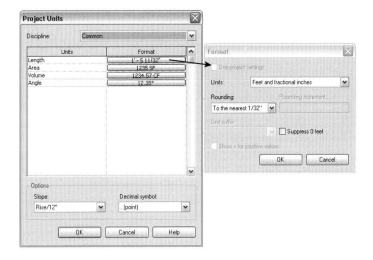

Keynote Settings

If you use keynotes, define the following Keynoting Settings at the onset. First, set the keynote table path, as shown in Figure 5.28. The path defaults to the Revit library locations, but you may want to change this if you're using customized keynote files located on the office network. From this dialog, you establish whether the numbering method for keynotes is By Keynote or By Sheet. We'll go into more detail about how to use keynoting in Revit in Chapter 15.

FIGURE 5.28

The Keynoting Settings dialog

Setting Up Default Elements

Whatever type of element you set in the project template will be the default setting for any Revit element until you specifically modify an element to another type. Revit remembers the most recently used settings across sessions. It's therefore important that you set the types of your selected Revit elements as defaults so that when you start a project, those types are set as defaults.

DEFAULT WALL

To set a default wall type, activate the Wall tool. Then, under the Type Selector, select the wall type that you wish to be the default choice. In the properties or from the Options bar, select the wall height or set a top level, and select the wall location line. You never know which wall type you'll need in the next project, so we suggest setting this to a Generic type. The selection of exact wall types can come later.

DEFAULT DOORS AND WINDOWS

Your project template is loaded with common windows and doors that are typically used in projects. Activate the window or door tools, then using the type selector, choose default door and window families, and then save your template. The last selected door and window are the default elements in the Type Selector when you place new elements. This applies to all other family elements in your template.

DEFAULT DIMENSION TYPES

To streamline your workflow, set the dimension style used most commonly in your template. You can consider presetting many settings in the Options bar:

◆ The type of dimension (we suggest selecting Linear).

◆ The reference selection that will be used when dimensioning a wall (to or from). Here the choices are the usual wall references: wall center, face, core face, and core center.

◆ The selection method or what we call *manual* versus *automated* dimensioning. In Revit, the Pick method can be Individual, where you're asked to click each instance you wish to dimension, or Entire Walls, where you click an element and it's dimensioned automatically. With the Entire Walls option, another dialog prompts you to further define what elements are used as autodimension references when you pick walls (Figure 5.29).

FIGURE 5.29
Dimensions can be preset in your template to be automatic if need be.

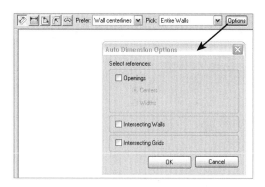

ALIGN TOOL

Chapter 3 describes the Align tool, which many users find to be one of the most helpful tools in Revit; it aligns selected elements to a reference target that can be another element or a datum. Setting its options correctly will aid in smoothing your workflow. Preset which wall layer you want the Align tool to default to. The options available for a wall are shown in Figure 5.30.

FIGURE 5.30
Set up a default
alignment preference
with respect to wall
references.

LEVELS/PLAN VIEWS

Set up levels and corresponding plan views in advance in your template to save time downstream. You can predefine the number of levels, their typical height, and naming convention (Figure 5.31).

FIGURE 5.31
Levels in the Project
Browser and in
section view

ELEVATIONS

If you've started building your template from an existing Revit template, you already have four default exterior elevations defined. If you started from scratch with no template, you'll need to create all four base elevations (south, east, north, and west) by placing elevation markers. (Note that we don't recommend that you ever start Revit using the None option under Template file as you'll have to define a great many things to make Revit work that are already defined in the default template.) It's very important that you also set the width and depth of the elevations. To do so, select the arrow of the elevation mark that will activate the current width and depth; then you can adjust them accordingly (Figure 5.32).

FIGURE 5.32
Two different settings
for elevation tag
depth and width

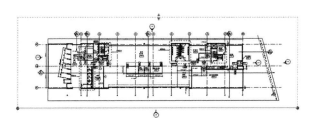

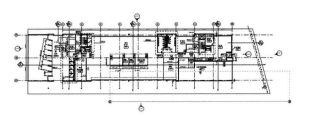

VIEWS

For each view that you preset in the Revit template, you can predefine a scale, a level of detail, the state of the crop region (visible or not), and display settings (hidden lines, shaded view, and so on). But mostly, think of view templates when you preset your views, because they're the biggest time savers—setting them in the templates will bring you increased productivity and graphical consistency.

View Templates

View templates let you define a desired set of view properties for any of your view types. This is a great way to enforce graphic consistency across views. For example, if you want your architectural plan views to always show furniture as half-toned, you can define this in your plan view template. If someone changes the appearance of furniture to no longer be half-toned, you can reapply the view template to get the drawing back to its original configuration. To do this, right-click the view name in the Project Browser, and choose the Apply View Template option. Choose the desired template, and click OK.

Look at the view templates that ship with the default template, and adjust these to suit your requirements. For example, the architectural plan scale (1:100) is set to 1/8″=1′-0″. If this is too coarse for your needs, change the value to 1/4″=1′0″ (1:50).

Every view can have a default view template assigned to it (Figure 5.33). This doesn't automatically keep the view in sync with the view template, but it lets you multiselect many views in the project browser and push their default view template back into the view. To do this, multiselect multiple views in the Project Browser, and choose to apply the view template. Choose the option Default View Template (Figure 5.34).

FIGURE 5.33

Views can have a default view template assigned to them to help streamline updating the view later in the process.

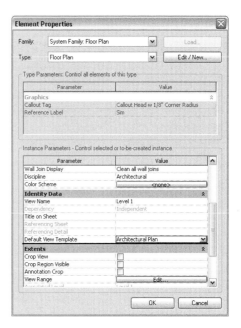

FIGURE 5.34
To apply the view's default template, use the Default View Template option.

COLOR SCHEMES

Color Fill Schemes let you apply color to room and area parameter values to help graphically illustrate spatial organization. Applying a color fill scheme to a plan view color-codes room properties such as department, name, usage, etc. It's good practice to predefine different color schemes that you're likely to use. Once a color scheme is defined, it can be applied to any number of plan views. Keep in mind that color is applied only to spaces that have been populated with room or area elements. If you want to make department-usage plans, think about pre-populating your color schemes with commonly used department/usage names. This will make the value available for rooms later so you don't have to manually type them in each time. For example, if you add "Accounting" as a value to a color scheme in your template that colors by department, then when you later go to a rooms element properties to assign it a department, you'll see "Accounting" as a predefined choice in the drop-down list.

The Bottom Line

Project templates save you time by capturing repetitive settings in a pre-set file and keeping look and feel consistent across different projects. Templates allow you to load a set of commonly used families in advance, so that you won't have to search and load those elements with each new project you start. These affordances will help create a more efficient and productive working environment.

Creating new types in the Family Editor for common building components such as walls, floors, ceilings, roofs, and stairs Incorporating common building components in your project template is fundamental to using Revit effectively.

> **Master It** How do you add/remove wall, floor, and roof types to your template?

Creating a type catalog to organize types for accessibility Revit's type catalogs are an important tool for keeping the types you create accessible in a project.

> **Master It** What are type catalogs used for?

Creating view templates for specific requirements View templates allow you to tailor views according to the requirements of a project.

> **Master It** How would you set up a new view template for plan views where the surface pattern of floors is turned off?

Chapter 6

Modeling Principles in Revit

Creating a BIM model requires modeling in 3D. This is very different from working with abstract 2D lines in order to represent your design. To work with Revit and be able to build a BIM model, you need to have an understanding of how objects are constructed at various scales ranging from the building mass down to furniture assemblies. You'll need to know how various building elements interact with each other and depend on each other, what materials they are made of, and how are they constructed and assembled. To this end, Revit provides a set of tools that enable you to build your model and all the elements that go into the model. Understanding the principles of modeling in the context of Revit will be essential to your success as you move deeper into building information modeling.

In this chapter you will learn the basic modeling principles that support the design process in Revit:

◆ The underlying concept of Sketch Based design

◆ How Work Planes, Datums, and Reference Planes are used in modeling

◆ Using Revit's essential form making tools (Extrusion, Sweep, Revolve and Blend)

◆ Combining Solids and Voids to create complex and intriguing forms

Modeling with Revit

Designers have a long tradition of modeling before building. This activity involves the use of pliable and tactile materials such as clay and wood to model designs fluidly. With these materials, form can be explored with ease, and designs allowed to iterate directly in our own hands. The use of software to model form has become a popular extension of this activity, and you only need to look so far as the latest animated film to see how far the technology has come.

There are many software modeling tools that allow direct editing and intuitive shaping of form. Tools such as Rhinoceros, 3ds Max, Maya, and SketchUp allow you to create free-form shapes with relative ease. These tools are great for modeling, but they are not geared for a BIM approach to design and documents. The elements created with these modelers are meshes, nurbs, acis solids, and other generic geometrical shapes that are used to represent walls, slabs, roofs, and windows but they do not have any embedded intelligence or relationships among themselves or with other elements in the model. Further, they barely contain any metadata that can be quantified and analyzed. So, as it stands today—you will find great modelers that are not BIM and BIM applications that are not powerful modelers. One way that Revit approaches this problem is to allow the import and smart re-use of free-form geometries into the project and family environment.

The entire modeling concept in Revit is based on four base class modeling forms—extrusion, revolution, sweep, and blend—and the combinations that these can produce.

Each of the four base modeling techniques can produce either a positive or negative shape that can be combined to create more complex forms. Each form is derived from 2D sketches that are drawn on Work Planes. We'll explore in more detail what sketch based forms are in the next section.

While there is clearly room for improvements when it comes to the generic modeling capabilities of Revit, you will be pleasantly surprised with the variety of 3D geometry you can generate in a short amount of time. Figure 6.1 shows an example of what's possible.

FIGURE 6.1
Example of expressive architecture using Revit

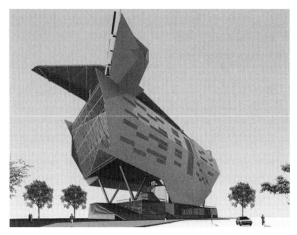

IMAGE COURTESY OF ARCHITECT KAMAL MALIK

Sketch-Based Design

All internal modeling techniques in Revit rely on an approach called *sketch-based design,* where you draw a shape in a special sketch mode by creating 2D lines that then generate 3D forms. When you start modeling Revit elements, you are basically starting a sketch: Revit enters a mode in which everything but the sketch itself is grayed out so that the focus is given to the sketch, represented in strong magenta colored lines. Once you've defined the shape by creating closed loops of lines, you click Finish Sketch, and the geometry is generated. This sketch mode is used throughout Revit.

The Floor and Roof tools both require you to first sketch 2D shapes and then generate the form by "finishing the sketch." Revit then applies a thickness based on the element type to the sketch. Even walls have an underlying sketch but in the case of the walls this is a sketch that can be edited in Elevation, not plan view, as shown in Figure 6.2.

To edit the elevation of a wall, select the wall in an Elevation or 3D view and click and click the Edit Elevation Profile button in the Options bar. Note that this only applies to linear walls.

FLOORS

One of the first places you'll encounter sketch-based modeling is with the Floor and Roof tools. When you initiate either of these tools, you are instantly placed in sketch mode. The design bar will change (Figure 6.3), and you'll get a set of tools specific to the task of creating 2D sketch lines and creating lines with relationships to other model elements.

FIGURE 6.2

Moorish architectural example: (A) Standard straight rectangle shaped wall, (B) elevation profile of that wall changed to the desired shape using simple lines, (C) wall shape result achieved by simple editing of the sketch in elevation; (D) the wall used in a building.

A
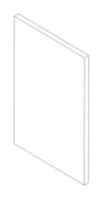

B
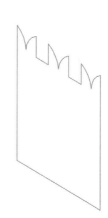

C
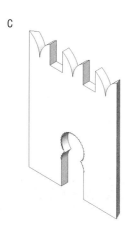

D
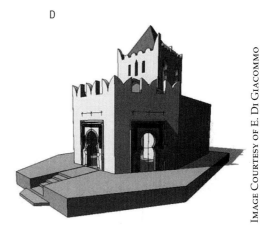

IMAGE COURTESY OF E. DI GIACOMMO

FIGURE 6.3
The Design bar in sketch mode

Sketch
⬎ Modify
⊟ Dimension
⌐ Lines
⌿ Ref Plane
⊤ Pick Supports
⊩ Pick Walls
◇ Slope Arrow
⚏ Set Work Plane
⬚ Floor Properties
⦿⦿ Finish Sketch
⬤ Quit Sketch

For example, you can either draw lines freely, or use the Pick Walls tool to generate the floor or roof sketch lines for you by picking on walls. When using the pick walls method, you create an explicit relationship between the sketch and the walls. The result is that when walls move, the sketch (and thus the floor or the roof made of it) will adapt and update with the walls.

The rules for creating a valid sketch are straightforward:

◆ The line sketch has to form a closed loop of lines, and the lines have to be perfectly trimmed at edges. You cannot have gaps or overlapping lines in the sketch. Whenever a sketch is not complete or has overlaps, you will not be able to finish the shape and Revit will indicate that something is wrong with an error message.

◆ When creating certain types of elements, you are allowed to sketch more than one shape within the same sketch—this is OK as long as the two sketches do not intersect. If the one loop of lines is within the boundaries of the other, that second loop of lines will create a hole in the shape defined by the bigger one (Figure 6.4).

FIGURE 6.4
Creating a closed loop within another closed loop of lines results in an opening

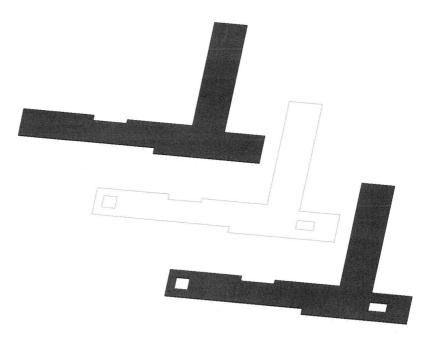

If you were to draw another shape within those openings, it would be positive and create another solid piece of floor of the same type. The logic of the loops is: one is positive, the next one within it is negative, the next one within it is positive. Remember that. (Figure 6.5)

FIGURE 6.5
An additional loop of lines results in a positive shape.

◆ To edit a sketch you need to be in a view that is parallel to the sketch, or a 3D view. For example, it is not logical to edit the sketch of a wall profile in a plan view as you would not be able to see the sketch in a way that is relevant to edit it. If you attempt to do this in plan view, Revit will alert you and propose other views in which you CAN execute the task. The same goes for a floor—only in plan views or 3D will you be able to edit the sketch.

◆ Sketch mode cannot be activated in Perspective (camera) view. If you select a wall or any other element and want to edit its shape but cannot find the Edit Shape button in the Options bar, you must be in Camera view. Switch to any other view in which the sketch makes sense to edit.

WORK PLANES

Reference Planes, Reference Lines, Datum Planes, Work Planes…what are they? In order to master modeling techniques in Revit, you will need to understand the concept of Work Planes.

The Work Plane is nothing more than a 2D plane that is used to sketch on. For example, when you are in a plan view and start sketching a floor, the Work Plane is set to the level associated with the plan view you are working in. The majority of views in Revit (plans, 3D views, or views set in the Family templates) have predefined Work Planes set automatically when they are created. Views such as Sections and Elevations require you to manually pick a Work Plane in order to add 3D elements to those views.

A Work Plane can be understood as a surface on which you draw something. To understand this better, imagine you are holding a marker in your hand and have a space in front of you—can you draw with the marker in the space? No. you need a piece of paper, glass, wall, some kind of a surface to draw on. So, a Work Plane defines a surface on which you can draw something as a base to build geometry. You can define a Work Plane by drawing a Reference Plane, picking a face from an existing element, or use an existing Level (datum) as a reference. Let's look a bit more closely at the types of Work Planes available in Revit:

Reference Planes

These are 2D planes that exist in 3D space. They are not visible in 3D views, but can be seen "edge on" in other views (plan, section, elevation) and are represented as green dashed lines. These lines are not view-specific and will appear in other perpendicular views such as plans, sections and elevations. Even though Reference Planes look and feel like ordinary lines, they do not have a "real" beginning nor an end. They are symbolic representations of infinite planes. This means you cannot reference to the beginning or end of a Reference Plane in order to make something like an angular constraint or dimension.

Reference Planes are the essence of content creation in the Family Editor as they are used to create the parametric skeleton to which geometry is then attached. They can also affect how other elements relate to the family by giving the Reference Planes various states. A Reference Plane can be set as Not A Reference, Weak, or Strong; and it can be defined as a reference for the Left, Right, Front, Bottom, Back, or Center position. The selection of these options is important in the Family Editor environment as they define references for snapping. Just to give you an idea, when you have two crossing references that are set as Strong, they will define the insertion point of an element when placing it in the Project environment (as shown in Figure 6.6). In Figure 6.6, the two centrally positioned Strong references define the insertion point of the element. The Weak references serve only as secondary snaps.

In a project, Reference Planes can be used to drive geometry (see Figure 6.7).

FIGURE 6.6
A working desk

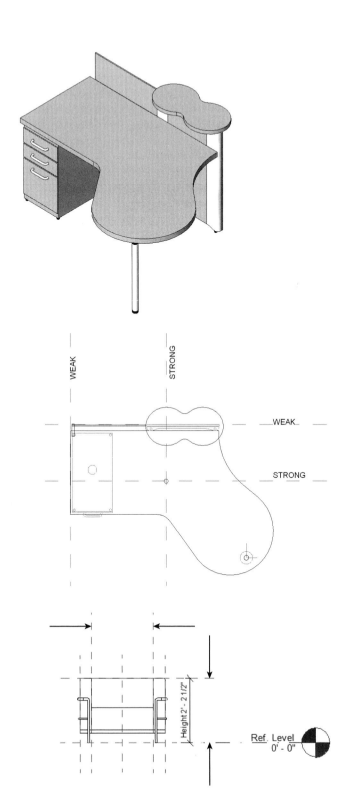

FIGURE 6.7
Reference Planes are used extensively in the family editor to create parametric constraints that can drive forms and define snapping references

Reference Lines

These were designed to overcome the limitation of the Reference Planes and their inability to define constraints that reference a point, direction, and angle. Unlike with reference Planes, the start and end points of a Reference Line can be referenced and used for dimensioning. A popular use of a Reference Line is to define door swing openings by creating an angular relationship between the door leaf position and the closed state of the door leaf. Other differences between Reference Lines and Reference Planes are that you cannot name the Reference Lines and you can only select them graphically.

Reference Lines define two workplanes—one is the plane on which the Reference Line was drawn, and the other is perpendicular to it (see Figure 6.8).

FIGURE 6.8
Reference Lines are used to control door swings and opening angle in families.

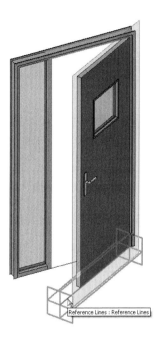

Reference Lines : Reference Lines

Levels

These are horizontal Datum planes that define the levels in a building and can also be used to denote important horizontal references in a building (attic height, etc.). Levels are only created and visible in Section or Elevation views. Each level commonly has a corresponding floor plan view associated with it, although it is possible to make levels with no associated floor plan. For example, a level may define the Top Of Steel in a building section, but there is no need to have a floor plan view of that level. For that case, you can create levels without plans by unchecking the option Make Plan View in the Options bar when the level tool is activated. This will create a level that appears black and white, rather than blue—indicating that there is no hyperlinked view. Note that when you create new levels using the Copy tool, the newly created level an elevation view, the newly created levels will appear as this black-and white version, as copying levels will not auto-generate new floor plans. If you need to convert a level that has no view associated with it to a level with a view associated, use the Floor Plan… tool in the View design tab in the Design bar. You will then be able to choose to add a view to any existing Level in the project.

When placing elements, they are automatically associated with the Level they are drawn on so that when the level changes position, so will the elements on that level. All sketch based families such as floors, roofs, ceilings, and stairs will be associated with at least one level. Levels can define both the bottom and top constraints for several elements in Revit, including walls, stairs, and ramps.

Grids

These are vertical planes used as standard references in the construction industry for creating location grids on the site as well as a communication reference between the building participants. These construction data are used to accurately define locations for elements such as columns and beams or position of main structural walls or exterior shell. You can associate elements with the Grids so that when the grid system changes, it controls the position of the associated elements. A good example for that would be columns associated with grid intersections. As with a level, when a grid is moved, associated elements move with the grid. The creation, graphic representation, and control editing of grids is similar to that of levels (see Figure 6.9).

FIGURE 6.9
Grids are datum planes that can be used to control other elements such as beams and columns.

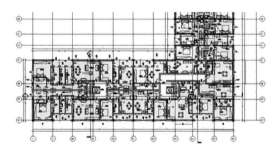

Once all the Datum planes in Revit have been defined, they will appear in all views that they intersect.

EXTENDING DATUM PLANES

If you wish to expand grids or levels to encompass a larger portion of your model, you can use the Context Menu of the grids and select Maximize Extents. This will extend the datum planes you have selected to the maximum extents of the model geometry.

So, if you work on a project in a system of grids, you need only draw the grid system once in a floor plan view, and the grids will be visible in every other plan or ceiling view. This may not always be a desired behavior, for example, if your project has a base of 5 floors of shopping with a 30-story hotel above, (like the model shown in Figure 6.8) it's likely you'll have separate structural bays for each part of the building. You don't need to see all grid lines of the shopping base in the tower, and vice versa. To deal with these scenarios, you can use a *Scope Box*. This will allow you to control in which views a grid will appear.

Important note: Grid lines will show in Section or Elevation view ONLY if the view is cut perpendicular to the Grid line. In no other case will the grid line appear. This is done to avoid confusion on construction site due to misleading graphic description.

SCOPE BOXES

These are used when you have multiple floor plans where the gridlines aren't the same for all levels. This tool limits the range in which data elements (grid lines, levels, and reference lines) appear. In our example of a building with a base and tower, two separate scope boxes are created for each major volume of the building. The grids in each part of the building are then assigned to appropriate scope boxes. Figure 6.10 shows how scope boxes work in a 3D view.

Scope boxes are visible in 3D views (although not in camera views), and you can easily manipulate their extent directly using the grip controls. Assigning gridlines or other datums to a scope box is easy: Select the gridlines, Select the gridlines and in the Element Properties choose Scope Box and select the scope box where the datums should belong. Figure 6.10b shows the Element Properties dialog box for the gridlines and the associated scope box.

FIGURE 6.10
(A) This building consists of two main volumes, low volume with shopping function and a tower with hotel use. These two volumes use separate grid systems and thus two different Scope Boxes are created to control the visibility of the separate Grids. (B) Grid element properties indicate the Scope box to which the grid belongs.

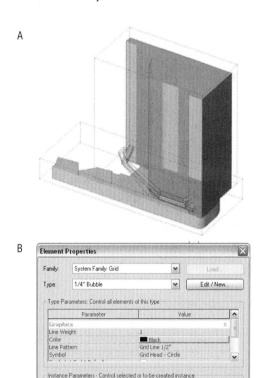

WORK PLANES IN A NUTSHELL

Before moving on to look at using work planes in practice, let's take a moment to summarize the basic theory.

A Work Plane is the *active plane* you are working on in any given graphic view. It is used when you are creating objects by sketching or placing. Think of it like the "UCS" (user coordinate system) in AutoCAD that allows you to work in specific orientations and directions. Every view has an active Work Plane. Figure 6.11 graphically explains the Work Plane. There are a few simple rules when using or understanding a Work Plane:

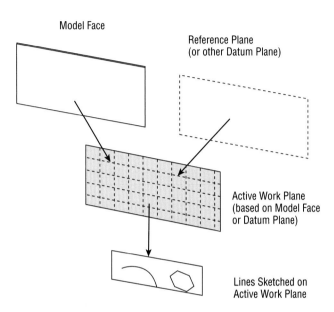

Model Face

Reference Plane
(or other Datum Plane)

Active Work Plane
(based on Model Face
or Datum Plane)

Lines Sketched on
Active Work Plane

◆ The Work Plane is set by selecting a Reference Plane/Reference Line; a Datum Plane (like a Level, Grid) or a planar face of a Model element. Often it is pre-set and you do not need to explicitly set it.

◆ Many elements in Revit use the active Work Plane to know where to sketch or place objects (some objects are limited to only horizontal or vertical Work Planes).

◆ The Work Plane is also used when you are modifying objects. When you drag or move an object it is typically constrained to be along that plane.

◆ When you set the Work Plane to be based on other selectable elements it creates a "dependency" or relationship to the underlying reference you selected. If the underlying object is moved, the Work Plane is moved to stay aligned to it. Any objects created on the Work Plane will also update.

Working with Work Planes

When creating elements that are not standard (orientation or geometry) or not automatically connected to a Work Plane, to create them you will need to will need to select the Work Plane tool from the Toolbar. This displays the Work Plane dialog shown in Figure 6.12; it's a good idea to understand its options.

Name   This option displays either the available Levels and Grids in the project or the Reference Planes that you have created—if you have named them. This is why naming a Reference Plane is a very important thing.

5. You will be prompted to select a Work Plane:

From the Name list, select the named Reference Plane you just drew. You'll be asked to open a view to begin sketching. Choose the South Elevation.

6. Sketch a roof in arc shape as shown here and finish the sketch.

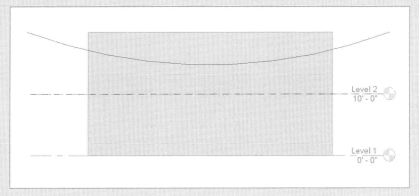

7. Go to the default 3D view and using the blue arrows, adjust the length of the roof to make sure it extends beyond the exterior walls as shown here.

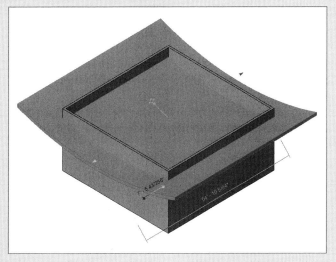

8. While still in the 3D view, select all the walls. Click the **Attach** button in the Options bar and then select the roof to attach the walls to the roof. The resulting roof should look something like this:

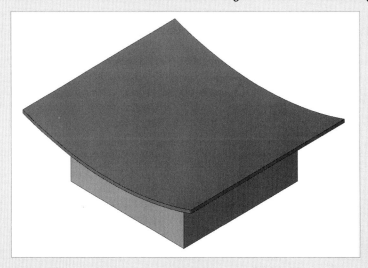

9. To make the roof end at the edge of the exterior walls, select the roof in plan view and select the option **Cut Plan Profile** in the Option bar. This allows you to cut off the extruded roof exactly at the edge of the building, regardless of its shape. In this example, draw two rectangles that cut the roof up to the face of the walls.

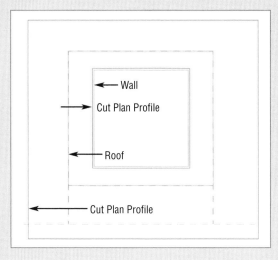

After using Cut Plan Profile, the final result for the first roof looks like this:

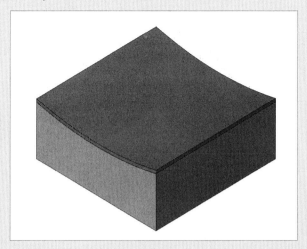

CREATING A ROOF USING A 45 DEGREE ORIENTED WORK PLANE AS A REFERENCE

To obtain the second roof (B), repeat all previous steps, but draw the Reference Plane at a 45 degree angle to the building as show below. Remember to give the Reference Plane a different name in the Element Properties dialog.

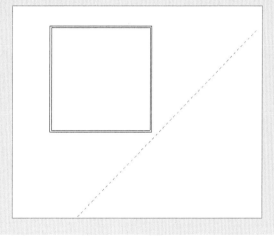

The finished roof looks like this:

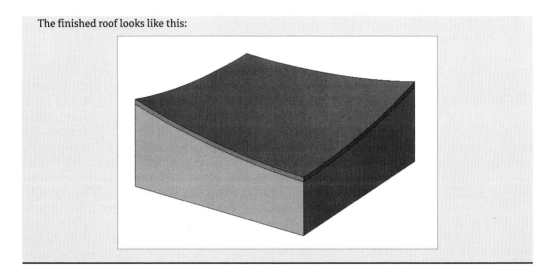

Principles of Modeling in Revit

Revit is much more than a 3D modeler. It is built specifically for architects and has behavioral rules built into many of the architectural elements that make up the building. For example, walls usually are vertically extruded rectangular shapes; floors and ceilings are horizontal extruded shapes with constant thickness. These major building elements (System Families) use a restricted sketch-based approach because those restrictions make sense for these types of elements. This is one of Revit's major differences compared with a generic modeler where you can model anything, any way you like. In Revit, the type of element you are modeling will present a more tailored set of creation tools.

You draw a wall by defining its start and end point, which will determine its position and length. The width of the wall and its height are determined by the wall properties. The wall becomes 3D immediately with each click of the mouse. Roofs and Floors, on the other hand, require a definition of a sketch that determines their outer shape while their thickness is what is defined in the Element properties of the Roof or the Floor.

Once the envelope of the building has been established with walls, floors, and roofs (the system families) you progressively add windows, doors, furniture, plumbing fixtures, and so on (standard families) to the model. These elements rarely depend on the context of the building and are usually built off site and manufactured in some factory in real life. In Revit, a good selection of these elements is pre-prepared and saved in a library for use across multiple projects. These loadable elements are all created in the Family Editor using a combination of simple geometric forms that can be associated with parametrically driven dimensions. For example, a chair can be created with a combination of sweeps, blends, extrusions, and revolves. The same applies to a lighting fixture, a sitting bench, a plumbing fixture—you name it. Figure 6.19 shows samples of standard "loadable" family types.

FIGURE 6.19
These windows and
doors belong to the
standard "loadable"
family types

In some cases, you need the full flexibility of the Family Editor in the context of your project. When you need to create a custom design feature tightly related to the context of the building or the landscape around it (entrance canopy, reception desk in welcome area, etc.) you'll need a robust set of tools that are not available using the basic walls, floors and roofs. These types of elements are created using the Create tool from the Modeling tab in the Design bar (Figure 6.20) and they use the same features available in the family editor, and are referred to as "in-place families." Figure 6.21 shows a fireplace built as an "In-Place" Family.

FIGURE 6.20
The Modeling
design bar

FIGURE 6.21
Example of an In Place
family

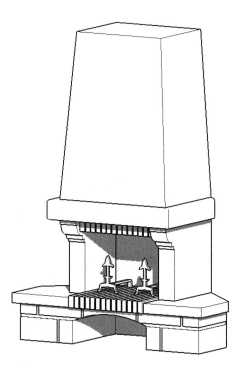

Another workflow where free-form modeling comes into play is at the early stages of conceptual design, where massing studies are explored. These mass forms are done with the Massing tools, as combinations of various geometric shapes made using extrusions, blends, sweeps, and revolves. Again, with massing, the tools need to be flexible and not constrained to a specific use case. In Revit, the same set of primitive form making tools is available when making massing geometry. Figure 6.22 shows a massing study using Revit form making tools.

Principles of Modeling Techniques

As we've mentioned, there are four basic form making options in Revit. With these forms you can create almost any shape you need for various scales of design, from large scale massing studies, down to sink faucets. By combining forms, and using forms as subtractive elements, nearly anything can be modeled in Revit. The four primary forms are:

- ◆ Extrusion
- ◆ Revolve
- ◆ Sweep
- ◆ Blend

All of these are accessible in a few places:

- ◆ The Family Editor when selecting Solid or Void shape (Figure 6.23 A)
- ◆ Under the Modeling Tab, when you select the Create Tool, Solid or Void (Figure 6.23 B)
- ◆ Under the Massing Tab , when you select Create Mass, Solid or Void (Figure 6.23 C)

FIGURE 6.22
Early Massing
Concept Studies

IMAGES COURTESY OF GENSLER

IMAGE COURTESY OF RMJM HILLIER

FIGURE 6.23
The (A) Family Editor,
(B) Modeling tab, and
(C) Massing tab all
enable you to create
solid or void forms,
which you can then
model by any of the
four basic techniques.

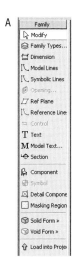  

Selecting Solid Form or Void Form from any of these toolbars displays the options shown in Figure 6.24.

FIGURE 6.24
Solid and Void Extrusion, Blend, Revolve, and Sweep options.

EXTRUSION

Extrusion is the simplest of all modeling transformations and it's based on a closed 2D sketch (shape) that is given a thickness value. The thickness is always perpendicular to Work Plane of the sketch. (Figure 6.25)

FIGURE 6.25
An extrusion is a 2D sketch shape with depth added.

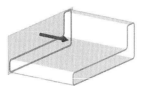

The Properties of an Extrusion allow you to set the thickness of the extrusion as well as an offset value from its Work Plane.

Extrusion start   This defines where the extrusion starts and has a default of 0, but it can have any positive or negative value. The effects of this parameter are shown in Figure 6.26.

FIGURE 6.26
(A) "Extrusion start" is set to 0; (B) has a positive value and the extrusion starts above the Work Plane; (C) has a negative value and starts below the Work Plane.

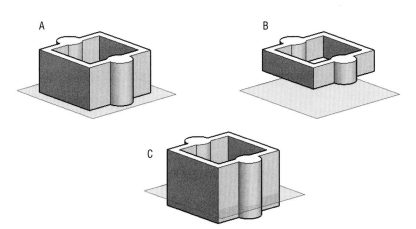

Extrusion end   This feature defines the end of the extrusion relative to the Work Plane. This value can be positive or negative. The default is set to 1'-0" (25mm). The total thickness of an extrusion is the difference between the "Extrusion end" and "Extrusion start".

When an extruded element is selected, check the Options bar for relevant options:

Edit   This feature takes you back to sketch mode so that you can make changes to the underlying shape. Once you have changed the shape, don't forget to click on "Finish Sketch".

Depth   Depth defines the value of the extrusion depth—this value can be positive or negative.

Visibility   Visibility defines which view types or levels of detail you want the extrusion to be visible. Figure 6.27 shows that the selected extrusion will be visible only in Plan and Reflected Ceiling Plan Views, and only in Medium and Fine Level of Detail.

FIGURE 6.27
Forms can be made visible/non-visible in different views and at different levels of detail.

Edit Work Plane   This feature allows you to change the Work Plane of the extrusion. Note that a new Work Plane is only valid if it is parallel to the one that you wish to change.

Figure 6.28 demonstrates how a Furniture Element can be constructed basically from two extrusions that create the entire shape. Tip: to make the lower element hollow the sketch needs to be double (a sketch in a sketch).

FIGURE 6.28
A cozy lounge chair made of two simple extrusions

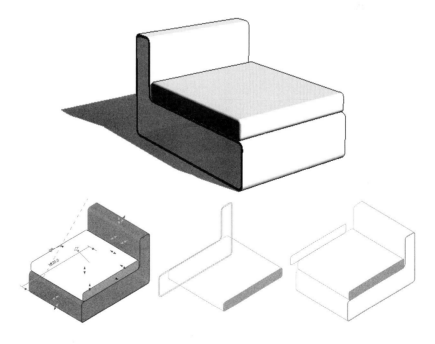

DIRECTIONS IN A REFERENCE PLANE

The direction in which one draws a Reference Plane determines which way is positive and which way is negative.

These images demonstrate in plan view how the different direction in which the Reference Plane was drawn affects the direction of the extrusion:

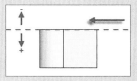

It is not easy to remember which way you drew each reference, thus we suggest this tip: Name each Reference Plane you create. If you do that, when the Reference Plane is selected you will see the name of the Reference Plane, and it is always placed at the END of the direction in which it was drawn.

When you use the *face* of an element as a Work Plan (rather than Reference Planes) as shown in Figure 6.29, the direction of the extrusion will depend on whether you are making it a solid or a void shape.

When you sketch a shape that is going to be a *Void*, the void will be extruded positively *toward the interior* of the object that we used to define the Work Plane.

When you add a *Solid* shape, the shape will extrude positively *away from the exterior* of the object face (Figure 6.30).

FIGURE 6.29
A void extrudes into
the solid face.

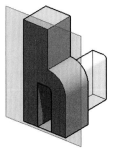

FIGURE 6.30
A solid extrudes away
from the solid face.

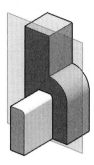

FIGURE 6.30
A solid extrudes away
from the solid face.

REVOLVE

Revolve takes a 2D profile and rotates it around an axis. A revolve is composed of two elements: a 2D profile (think of this as a cross section) that will define the surface once it is revolved, and an axis that the profile will revolve around. As with extrusions, the profile sketch must be a closed loop of lines for the revolve to be valid. The bollard shown in Figure 6.31 is an example of a revolved form.

FIGURE 6.31
A revolve consists of a
closed loop sketch and
an axis of rotation.

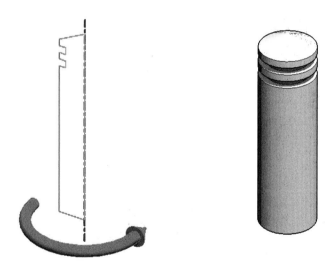

A revolve will follow a full 360 degree path by default. In the properties of a revolve you can adjust this angle, so that the profile can appear open, as shown in Figure 6.32.

End angle   This positions the sketch relevant to the Work Plane of the end of the revolution. Figure 6.32 shows a revolve with an end angle set to 270°.

FIGURE 6.32
End angle is set
to 270˚.

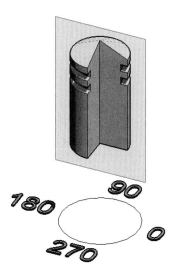

Start angle   This positions the sketch relevant to the Work Plane at the beginning of the Revolution. By setting the Start Angle to a value other than 0, you can get shapes like that shown in Figure 6.33.

FIGURE 6.33
"Start angle" is set to
90˚ and 'End angle' is
set to 270˚.

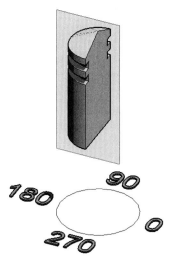

When an element that is revolved is selected, you will find the following Tools in the Options Bar:

These are similar to the options available when selecting other modeling forms. You can change the sketch that you used to execute the revolution with, set the Visibility, Edit the Work Plane or Rehost the form to another plane.

To understand the how sketches create revolution shapes, we will look at three different results based on three different types of sketches. Figure 6.34 shows a standard revolution made out of one closed loop of lines. Figure 6.35 shows a revolve made out of two closed loops, where one loop is a subtractive element; and Figure 6.36 shows another sketch with two closed loops, where each loops is an additive element.

FIGURE 6.34

One closed loop of lines revolved around an axis

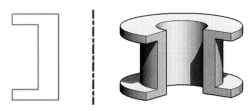

A revolve can be composed of multiple closed loops to define the profile sketch. Keep in mind that each sketch must not intersect another sketch, or the sketch will fail, and Revit will warn you when you try to "Finish Sketch". Depending on the positioning of the different loops, you can achieve different results, as shown in the Figures 6.35 and 6.36:

FIGURE 6.35

In this example, the two closed loops of lines are placed one inside the other. Following the principle of sketch based design, the inner loop creates a hole in the first loop.

FIGURE 6.36

The two loops are independent of one another and thus the resulting revolution creates two solid shapes.

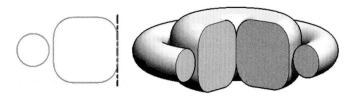

A common example of a revolve form is shown in Figure 6.37. The profile defines the cross section of a dome (cupola) roof. By rotating this profile around the center axis, a dome form can be generated.

FIGURE 6.37
The profile is revolved
around the center
axis, resulting in a
dome form.

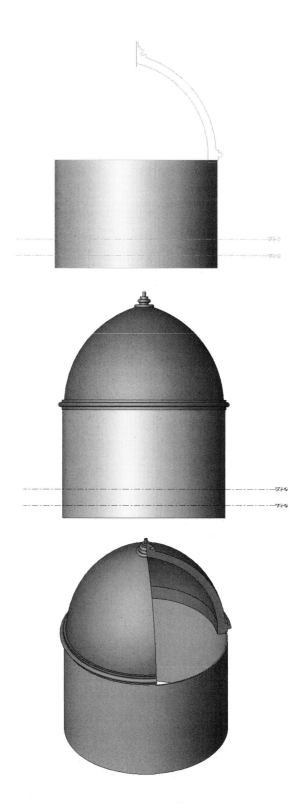

THE RULE OF THE AXIS

None of the shapes that are to be revolved can intersect the axis of the revolution. They can however have an angle different than 90 degrees to it and can be offset from the axis.

Another example of a revolve is this door knob (Figure 6.38), where the the cross section is drawn then revolved around an axis:

FIGURE 6.38
A revolve can be used to create elements such as door knobs as well.

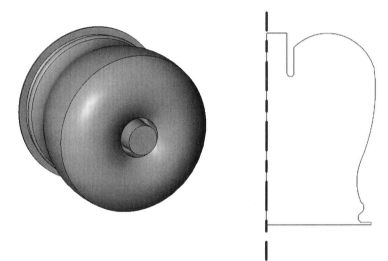

SWEEP

A Sweep is conceptually similar to an extrusion, but you define a path for the extrusion profile to follow. The resulting form is generated by sweeping the profile along path segments. The profile is always swept perpendicular to the path segment it follows.

A sweep is defined by two sketches: the Path and the Profile that you sweep along the Path. The path can be drawn on any Work Plane, and the profile will always be drawn perpendicular to the path. The first segment of the path you draw determines the default Work Plane for the profile sketch. To change the default location of the profile sketch plane, delete the line segment of the path that hosts it—the profile plane will jump to next available line segment in the path. Figure 6.39 shows a swept form, along with the path and profile used to create it.

FIGURE 6.39

Example of a sweep. In the sketch, the dashed rectangle is the profile plane—always perpendicular to the path.

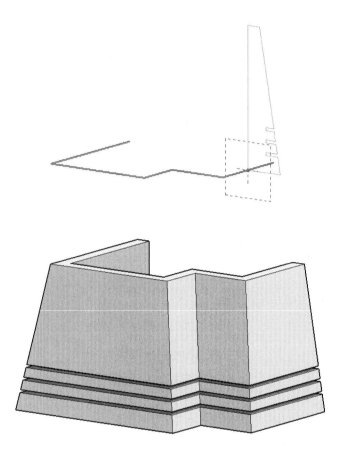

Defining the Sweep Path

You can make a path by either picking existing geometric edges to create new lines, or by or drawing lines. These options are available either from the design bar:

or the Options bar:

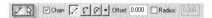

Sketch 2D Path allows you to draw the path using the various draw tools to make lines. You can use the pick command to pick edges and lines from the other elements to speed up creation:

Pick Path allows you to select existing lines or edges of geometry as the path for your sweep. With this method you create a dependency between the swept element and the object that you picked for edges to define the path. Thus, when the geometry of the referenced object changes, so too will the swept element. We strongly recommend working in a 3D view when using this method to make it easier to understand the relationships and effects of changing geometry (Figure 6.40).

FIGURE 6.40

Example of a sweeping path that is created by picking existing edges of a solid geometry (in this case a wall opening). Should the opening change its size, the sweep will also change because of the dependency established with the pick method.

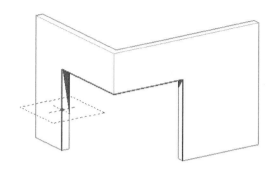

Defining the Profile

A profile can be created using one of two methods: by drawing the profile, or by using a loaded, pre-defined profile. These options are shown in the options bar when the sweep command is activated. The default is <By Sketch> and lets you draw the profile using standard draw tools. You can also select a profile from the pulldown list of profiles that can be loaded into the project/family. This method is applicable in cases where you will need to sweep the same profile on many paths. For example, you would first create a 2D profile family using the Profile (imperial) M_Profile (metric) template. The profile has to be a closed loop of lines. You then save the profile on your hard disk and then load it in your project.

Once you've made a sweep profile, the profile will be available in the dropdown list in the Options bar.

Figure 6.41 shows the Options bar with both options.

FIGURE 6.41

The default method for creating profiles is by sketching (top). You can also load pre-made profiles and use those (bottom).

If you use a loaded profile, you are given controls to position the profile relative to the X and Y axes (Figure 6.42). These values are distances from the point of insertion of the profile (the intersection of the two Reference Planes in the family editor) and the point of reference of the profile and the path (the green cross). You can also rotate the loaded profile by adding a value under the "Angle" option (Figure 6.43). The Flip button will mirror the profile, if you need it.

FIGURE 6.42
Offsetting the profile from the point of reference of the path. In this profile, the crossing of the references in the family editor was set to the lower left corner of the profile. Thus, the offset values start from that point.

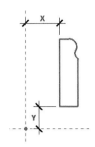

FIGURE 6.43
Angle of rotation is applied to the profile that is to be swept.

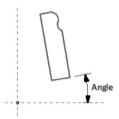

Once a sweep is created, you can always change the values that are available in the Properties of the sweep:

Parameter	Value	=
Constraints		
Work Plane	Level : Niveau 0	
Horizontal Profile Offset	0.1000	
Vertical Profile Offset	0.0500	
Angle	0.000°	
Construction		
Profile	Plinth : #01	

The advantage to using pre-made profiles is enormous. Figure 6.44 illustrates a concrete example of a sun shading family that needs to be edited.

If you drew your profile manually and then used the Copy Multiple command to repeat the shade, you will need to change each shade separately to apply a new profile. If you had drawn the shape as a loadable profile family and loaded it into the family, you'll only need to change the profile family once and re-load it. All instances of the profile will update automatically when re-loaded.

FIGURE 6.44
Sweeps can be used to create a sun shade.

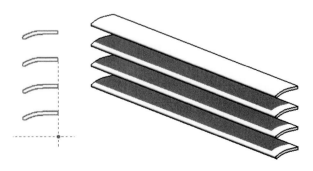

Real World Scenario

PUTTING THE SWEEP TOOL TO WORK

Here are some real life scenarios in which the Sweep tool is very handy. We'll let the pictures do most of the talking.

First consider the modern shower fixture in the bathroom shown here:

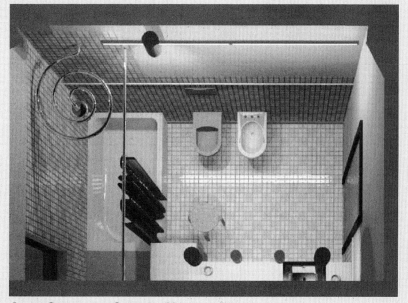

IMAGE COURTESY OF GIANLUCA NICHOLAS LANGE

This design was created as a simple sweep on a circular path.

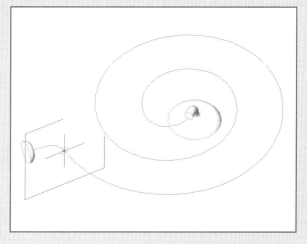

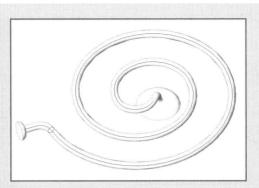

The architectural example shown here demonstrates another use of sweeps, to create a highly specific wall shape. The retaining wall was created as an in-place wall using the Create function and the Sweep method.

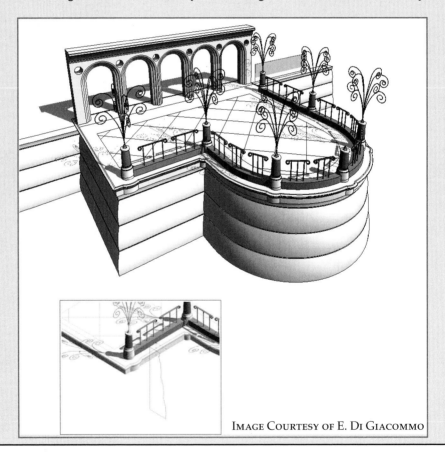

IMAGE COURTESY OF E. DI GIACOMMO

Trajectory Segmentation

This option (Figure 6.45) provides a way to segment smooth arcs into linear segments. This can be useful when rationalizing a form into planar, constructible elements. When the option is checked, it makes the parameter Maximum Segment Angle active. The value you set will define the maximum value of the angle between two segments of the arc. The smaller that value, the higher the number of linear segments that will replace the arc. Figure 6.47 shows the effects of this parameter.

FIGURE 6.45
Sweeps can be seg-
mented using the
"Trajectory Segmen-
tation" parameter.

FIGURE 6.46
An arc path can be
segmented using the
Maximum Segment
Angle parameter.

Trajectory before segmentation

Maximum Segment Angle = 30°

Maximum Segment Angle = 60°

Maximum Segment Angle = 90°

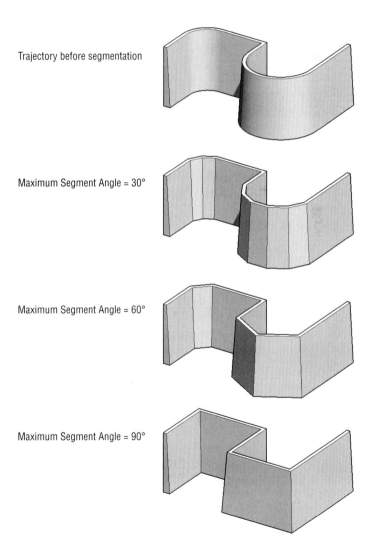

BLEND

A blend creates a form by connecting two different 2D shapes on two different planes along a linear path (Figure 6.48). The distance between the two shapes—the base and top, is what defines the depth of the blend. The two shapes for the top and base of the blend do not need to be the same shape or have the same number of segments. Revit can even blend arcs into linear segments.

When the top and base shapes are the same, the resulting form will look exactly like an extrusion or sweep along a single, linear segment. You can think of a blend as extrusion with two sketches—one for the base, and one for the top.

FIGURE 6.47
A blend is created from two sketches that blend together along a linear path

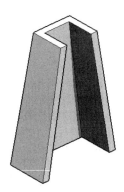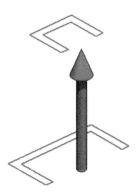

The properties of a blend are very similar to those of an extrusion. You can set the Blend Depth as well as the offset from the work planes on which the shapes will be drawn.

First end   This defines the offset of the base shape relevant to its work plane. This value can be negative or positive. The default value is set to 0.

Second end   This defines the offset of the top shape relevant to the work plane on which the blend is drawn. This value can be positive or negative. The default is set to 1′ 0″ (250mm).

The total depth of the blend is the resulting value between the First End and the Second End. When a blended element is selected, you will find new tools in the Options Bar:

These are the same as the options for extrustions, with addition of two other features that take to the sketch of the base or top of the blend. **Edit Base**: you can always go back to the base sketch by selecting this option and redefine its shape if needed. You will need to "Finish sketch" to exit that option.

Edit Top   Enters sketch mode where you can modify the top sketch.

Edit Base   Enters sketch mode where you can modify the base of the sketch.

Whenever you select one of those two options, the Options Bar will change as well as the design bar, as shown in Figure 6.48.

FIGURE 6.48

Options in the Design bar depend on whether you are editing the base (A) or the top (B) of the blend.

As you can see, when creating blends there is not one single work plane—this means that the two sketched shapes are always on work planes that are parallel.

Vertex connect is a tool specific to blends, and it shows up in the design bar when editing the blend sketch. This tool allows you to set the connection between the vertices that the two shapes have. Manipulating the vertexes will produce different results in the final blend.

When you click on the Vertex Connect tool, you will see graphic controls indicating existing connections between the vertexes of the blend shapes.

There are two different things you can do here:

Twisting   After selecting Vertex Connect, you will find two tools called Twist in the Options bar.

These control the number of twists between the two shapes. Figure 6.49A shows a basic blend between two 45 degree oriented square shapes. Figure 6.49B shows one additional twist and Figure 6.49C yet another additional twist.

Editing Vertices

This is another way to affect the blend in order to arrive at alternative shapes. By clicking one of the open blue circle controls that appear when you first select the Vertex Connect tool, you'll have the ability to change the direction of the vertexes by clicking on the control. Once you change the connection point, the circle will be filled in solid blue (Figure 6.51B) and a line will be drawn showing a preview of the connection from one vertex to another. Revit will connect the vertexes from the base shape to the top shape in automated way with each click. But each of the vertexes has an option to be connected to the top vertex that lies to the right of it, or left or both. The example shown in Figure 6.50 demonstrates how the same blend with the same base, top, and depth all look different depending on the vertex connections.

FIGURE 6.49

The forms shown can be a tower shape or a table leg: various looks for the same element depending on the number of vertex connections or twists.

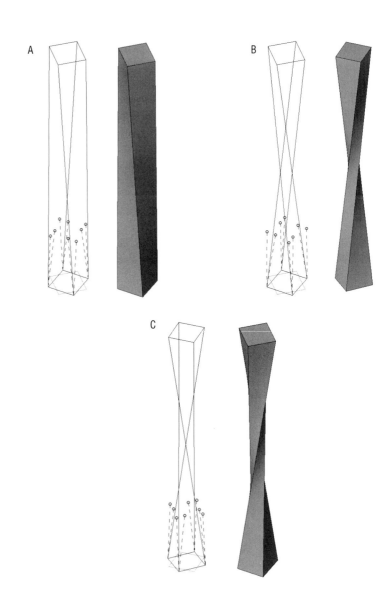

Troubleshooting Blends

When the base shape of a blend has the same number of vertices as the top shape, the results are pretty much predictable. But often the number is not the same and you may not get the results you expect or desire. A few tips to consider when working with more complex blends:

If one of the shapes is a circle, you might want to break it up into segments to get additional vertex points so that you arrive at a shape you need, as shown in Figures 6.51 and 6.52.

FIGURE 6.50
Changing vertex con-
nections will result in
different blend forms.

A

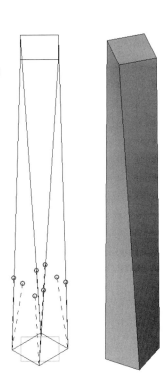

B

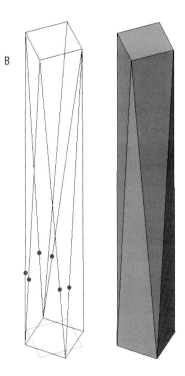

FIGURE 6.51
A standard blend you
will often see, with
base shape square and
top shape circle.

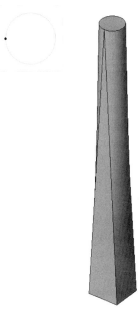

FIGURE 6.52
The same shapes with the circle split into 4 segments to add 3 more vertices. In example A, the vertex points are orthogonal; in B they are rotated 45 degrees. Note the difference in the results.

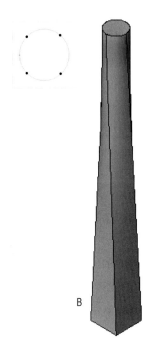

A

B

CREATING A LAMP WITH BLENDS AND SWEEPS

A real-world application of blends and sweeps can be seen in the Revit lamp family illustrated here.

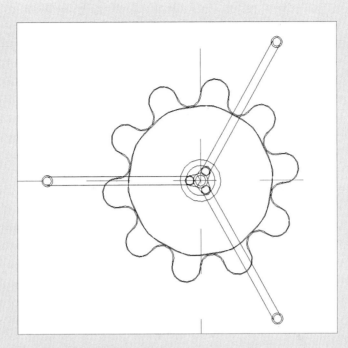

The shade is constructed using a blend between a segmented circle for the top (A), and a more complex series of arcs for the base (B).

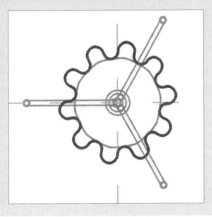

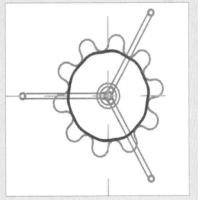

The top sketch has been divided into many segments to match the number of vertexes of the base. This file can be found in the Chapter 6 folder on the web site if you want to explore it some more on your own (PS Lamp.rfa).

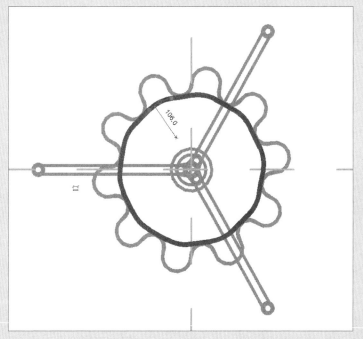

The legs of this lamp can be made using sweeps. A void extrusion was used to cut the bottom of the legs horizontally so that it sits flat on the floor.

EXAMPLES OF BLENDS IN PRACTICE

The following shapes (Figure 6.53) are inspired by the sculptor and designer Isamu Noguchi's lamps, but as you can imagine, they could just as easily represent a lamp, a column, or an entire shape of a building. They are constructed as simple combinations of connected blends.

FIGURE 6.53
A series of blends used to form a more complex form

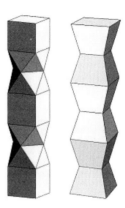

The blend sketches cannot contain more than one loop of closed lines. If your intention is to create something like the lamp shade shown in Figure 6.54, you will need to add a void. If you try to make such a shape, Revit will give you a warning message stating that "more than one loop is not allowed."

FIGURE 6.54
This blend sketch with multiple loops is not allowed and would generate a warning message.

To obtain the result needed, you will need to first create a solid blend and then a second one, done with void that has a smaller radius, as shown in Figure 6.55.

FIGURE 6.55
A lampshade can be made by creating a void blend that is smaller than the solid blend.

CONSIDER YOUR OPTIONS

Before making a digital model of your design, whether it is the shape of an entire building, a portion of specially modeled wall, a front desk or a door handle, you need to analyze and think about the basic geometric shapes that are used to create such a form. Is your object best modeled as an extrusion? A blend? A sweep? A blend with a void cut in it? Think carefully how the element is made, how it is assembled, and the tools that Revit provides to plan your modeling strategy.

Solids and Voids

Many complex shapes you wish to design go beyond the four basic form making techniques we just explored. Designs often require a combination of forms that are both additive and subtractive. To accommodate richer modeling, Revit approaches this problem by allowing any form to be solid or void. Solids are positive, physical elements, and voids are invisible, cutting elements that remove form from solids.

All the forms we covered (extrusion, revolve, sweep, blend) can be made as either a solid or a void. This is represented in the design bar, where you have the two options: Solid Form and Void Form.

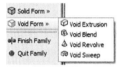

EXAMPLES SHOWING USE OF VOIDS

Voids can be used in many ways to arrive at some surprising geometric forms. Think of a void as a way to carving away from a solid chunk of clay—you can truly sculpt with this tool!

Vaults

In Figure 6.56, complex vaults have been created out of solid pentagonal extrusion and half circle void extrusions cutting through it. Note: you will need to use the Join Geometry tool to have the void cut the solid.

FIGURE 6.56
Vaulted space created out of combination of solid and void extrusions

COURTESY OF REVIT QA E.EGBERTSON

Tower shapes

The basic shape of the tower shown in Figure 6.57 is a simple blend. A plow shape is used at the base, and a triangular shape defined for the top. Then a simple curved shaped void extrusion is used to carve out the blend. The result is an interesting shape that is far more complex than what you'd expect to be able to do with the four basic modeling forms.

FIGURE 6.57
A blend with a void ex-
trusion results in
some very interesting
forms!

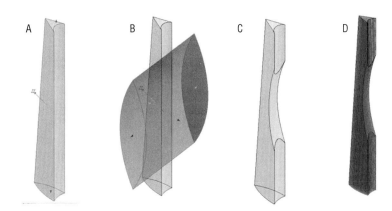

Complex roofs

A shape like the one shown in Figure 6.58 could be created using two revolved shapes and then cut
off using a void square around the edges.

FIGURE 6.58
Use of a simple void to
cut our geometry from
a revolved shape

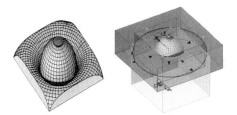

Where Can You Go From Here?

Mastering the modeling techniques in Revit and understanding the power of parametric relationships will open the doors to some powerful modeling skills. Even if it seems like science fiction that
you can make highly complex forms using Revit, with time, creativity, and practice, you will get
there. Figure 6.59 shows examples of some highly creative uses of solid and void forms.

FIGURE 6.59
These models are all made using Revit's native form making tools.

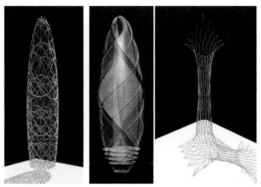

IMAGES COURTESY OF PHIL READ

The Bottom Line

Using Revit's essential form making tools (Extrusion, Sweep, Revolve and Blend)   These four tools are at the root of practically all form modeling.

Master it   Having learned the basics of Revit's form making tools, imagine how would you build this faucet designed by Philippe Starck.

Master it: In some cases, a form is made of multiple sketch lines to generate its form. What form making tools in Revit use more than one set of 2D sketches to generate the form?

The Underlying Concept of Sketch Based Design   Nearly every element you make in Revit has an underlying 2D sketch. Know how to edit and construct these sketches will be critical to your success.

Master it: Revit uses a 2D sketch based approach to modeling. What modeling elements in Revit use this 2D sketch principle to generate their form?

How Work Planes, Datums, and Reference Planes are used in modeling   When you create elements in Revit, they are tied parametrically to working planes.

Master it: In order to sketch a form, the form must reside on a Work Plane. How do you define and visualize the Work Plane in Revit?

Combining solids and voids to create complex and intriguing forms   Being creative with how you generate form means you have to think both in terms of both positive and negative forms making tools.

Master it: To make more complex forms, the use of both solids and voids can be used. Think of a case where the using voids as a subtractive element makes sense.

Chapter 7

Concept Massing Studies

In this chapter, we'll talk about the early stages of design and the first massing studies created that explore conceptual ideas. We'll introduce you to the principles of massing and the tools in Revit that are specifically designed to support workflows related to massing studies, and early conceptual design processes where form is explored and analyzed. You'll see how Revit allows you to maintain continuity as you move from massing study into real building elements that can be documented and eventually built. We'll discuss various approaches for creating massing studies and the underlying principles of creating parametric mass elements using the Family Editor.

You'll acquire the following skills in this chapter:

◆   Understand massing workflows supported by Revit

◆   Create massing elements in the Project Environment and Family Editor

◆   Understand how massing can be used downstream as the design progresses

Massing Studies

There are many ways to start a new design. It often starts as a napkin sketch while you listen to your client's needs and desires in a coffee shop. These first ideas encapsulate the essence of the design and, unless some unforeseen changes are demanded in the design, usually manifest themselves in recognizable form in the final building. Many architects are known for the remarkable similarity between the first napkin sketches and the final outcomes, as can be seen in drawings by architects such as Frank Gehry, Jorn Utzon, Daniel Libeskind, Frank Lloyd Wright, and countless others. Figure 7.1 shows a hand sketch using very gestural lines, tones, and hatches. The ability to sketch freely and with gestural expression is a fundamental aspect of design iteration and has been part of the architectural profession for centuries.-

FIGURE 7.1
An inspiring
early sketch

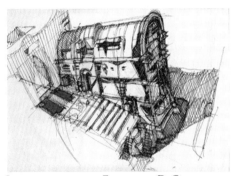

IMAGES COURTESY OF EMMANUEL DI GIACOMO

Architects have long realized that the only way to make an investor buy in into their early ideas and designs is to make that investor understand the designs. Many investors have difficulty reading technical drawings, so architects use creative methods to communicate the design, the space, and the experience of that space. Perspective drawings, photo collages, and 3D physical models made of wood, Styrofoam, cardboard, balsa, Plexiglas, and metals are all used to help the client, and sometimes the public, understand the implications of a given design.

In more sophisticated building studios, these models are constructed so that the design can be evaluated by deconstructing the model to examine individual stages of construction and integrated systems. Models can range in fidelity from very rough massing studies to highly photorealistic renderings, as Figure 7.2 demonstrates.

FIGURE 7.2
Models can range from very rough (a and b) to highly refined representations (c and d).

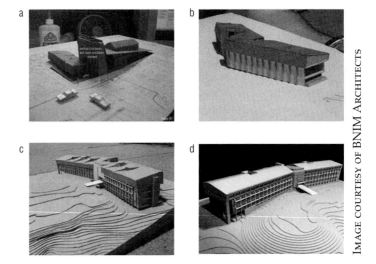

IMAGE COURTESY OF BNIM ARCHITECTS

3D physical models offer some obvious advantages for conveying design intent:

◆   You get an immediate feel for proportion, scale, and composition.

◆   You can get a feel for spatial volume.

◆   Light and shadow can be easily simulated.

◆   It's possible to model the surrounding site and understand how your design relates to its context.

3D physical models also have some potential disadvantages:

◆   They take a lot of time and patience to create.

◆   They require space for creation as well as storage.

◆   They are created in only one scale.

◆   They can't handle design options easily.

◆ They require manual work—both in the physical modeling and in performing calculations of area and space.

◆ They can be costly in terms of skilled personnel, materials, and equipment.

As clients become more demanding, they aren't satisfied with understanding how the future building will look, but also want to know how the building will perform in terms of lifecycle costs. They need the ability to compare and contrast multiple solutions in order to arrive with you at an optimized design solution that meets their taste, all the program requirements, and is sustainable economically.

To accommodate all that, architects and owners need to analyze the building and experience it in the early stages of design before it's built. Traditional hand-built models don't provide this kind of analytical flexibility. This is where using digital models backed up by real data comes into play. See Figure 7.3.

FIGURE 7.3
Early massing studies

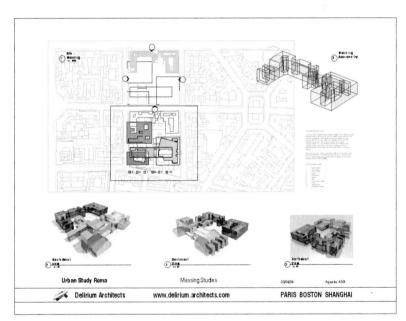

IMAGE COURTESY OF GIANLUCA N. LANGE

Massing Study Workflows

Regardless of how a massing study is done (digitally or in a physical medium), there has always been a break in the workflow from conceptual design to finished building. Physical massing models were made first and then, to create a digital project, the architect had to re-create the same concept from zero, usually in AutoCAD without having a way to reuse the information previously created.

When you make a digital study using tools such as Rhino, SketchUp, Form Z, or 3ds Max, you still need to start from scratch to begin the process of documenting your design because they are just modelers, not documentation tools, and the data created in them is not reusable in any intelligent way.

This has traditionally occurred in the form of 2D drawings using a tool such as AutoCAD. With the advent of Building Information Modeling, this is all changing.

An important part of using BIM is being able to use data throughout the design process, from start to finish—without needing to start over from ground zero once you've got the massing done. Revit provides specific tools for keeping the design process integrated. For early conceptual studies, Revit has massing tools that allow you to create a mass model that can later easily be transformed into walls, floors, and roofs. This capability is popularly called Building Maker, a set of tools for converting an abstract mass form into a full-fledged building model.

With the massing tools, you can create flexible preliminary designs and create massing models out of building blocks long before you make decisions about walls, roofs, and floors. You can create the pieces quickly, run though and visualize alternate configurations, and then, only when they're ready, generate a building shell.

 Real World Scenario

COMMON USES FOR THE MASSING TOOLS

Here are some commons scenarios where using Revit massing tools make sense.

SITE STUDIES: USING MASSING TO QUICKLY BUILD THE CONTEXT ENVIRONMENT AROUND THE BUILDING

You can use massing capabilities to quickly model the surrounding context of your building to get a feel for how it fits. This is a standard practice used to demonstrate to clients or for competitions how your design relates to its environment. Once you have modeled the environment around your building, you can make quick walkthroughs around your building and experience it from different points of view from various vantage points. You can also make initial solar studies to better understand how your building affects the environment and how the environment affects your design.

IMAGE COURTESY OF KUBIK-NEMETH-VLKOVIC

Massing Studies for Testing Different Design Options

You can do a quick conceptual massing study to work out a functional design arrangement, make more options, and look for an optimal solution. For each design, separate masses can be made and given color to indicate their form. This allows you to see spatial relationships in simplified geometric forms but also get precise area and volume values for each mass option you explore.

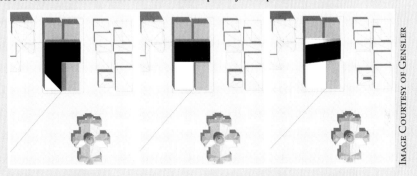

Feasibility Studies and Program Verification

You can take the massing study a step further and make a feasibility study, explore how you can fit the client's program on the site, calculate the Floor Area Ratio (FAR), and convert it into a building with walls, floor, roofs, and site elements. With mode information added to the model, you can get better estimates about building cost, energy analysis, and aesthetics.

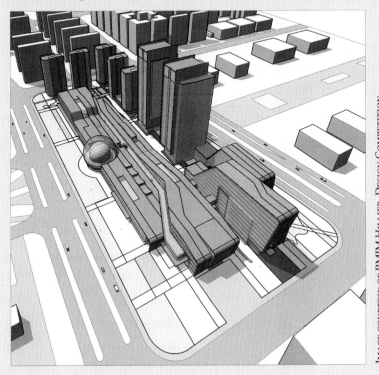

IMAGE COURTESY OF GENSLER

Massing Tools

The massing tools are located on the Design bar's Massing tab (Figure 7.4). If you don't see it, activate it by right-clicking anywhere on the Design bar and clicking Massing. To create a massing study, analyze it, and convert it to a building, you need to understand the available tools first; then, we'll walk through a real exercise.

FIGURE 7.4
The Massing tab
provides all the tools
needed to create a
massing study.

The tools for creating masses in Revit are directly connected to the modeling tools and techniques we discussed in Chapter 6. You'll use the same modeling tools (Extrusion, Blend, Sweep, Revolve) as well as the logic of work planes and placing by face whenever you create a mass, whether in the project environment or the Family Editor.

The Massing design bar is divided into three groups of tools that we refer to as mass-creation tools, Building Maker tools, and view tools.

The first group allows you to make masses from scratch or place massing families. The second group contains tools to support the concept of *Building Maker*—a term that doesn't exist in the Revit UI but is commonly adopted among Revit users to describe the process of converting a concept massing into a real building. Using the faces of a conceptual mass, you can attach walls, curtain systems, floors, and roofs to the mass form with a click of the mouse. Later in this chapter we'll refer to this grouping as *Building Maker*.

The third group contains the standard Section and Level tools; these are the most important additional tools to have at hand during creation of mass studies. They are the same Section and Level tools that you find on the Basic menu or in the views.

CREATING A MASSING ELEMENT

There are two ways to create a mass element in the project environment:

Select the Create Mass tool   This method allows you to create a new mass element.

Select the Place Mass tool   This method allows you to place a massing family or load a mass family from your library.

Before we look in detail at these two methods, you need to understand how massing visibility is handled in Revit, because you'll encounter this issue the moment you start creating masses.

Visibility of Masses

When you try to place mass or create mass for the first time, you may get the following message, which conveys information about the visibility of the mass elements:

This message can be disconcerting at first, so let's understand what is going on. Visibility of mass elements can be controlled via the toolbar or as a category in the Visibility/Graphic Overrides dialog. The toolbar control is a global on/off switch for massing that affects all views temporarily. It's located at the top of the screen, near the 3D button:

When you select this button, all masses in all views become visible. This is great for early massing studies, allowing you to move from view to view and see your mass without having to turn the category on/off for each view. When this mode is enabled, it *does not* affect the Visibility/Graphics Overrides state of your views.

To see the mass elements in specific views only, you should use the Visibility/Graphics Overrides settings for view control. Even when the Show Mass button is turned off, if you check the Mass setting in the Visibility/Graphic Overrides dialog, it will be visible in that view.

To print and export massing, you need to turn the mass category on using the Visibility/Graphic Overrides dialog. The Massing toggle is a temporary view control and doesn't affect printed output.

As you develop your design further and start creating the real building components (walls, floors, and roofs) by adding elements to the model, the mass will become obscured. A great way to maintain a view where only massing is visible is to create a 3D view where *all categories are turned off except massing*. Name the view Massing or something appropriate. Figure 7.5 shows two views: one with only the massing category visible and the other with all categories visible. This is handy, for example, when you want to make adjustments to the basic shapes that define the geometry (masses) without being distracted by the presence of the building elements. When you change the underlying mass, the architectural elements created from it follow the change automatically. You'll learn more about this workflow in Chapter 8.

FIGURE 7.5
The same view with different visibility states for massing and model elements

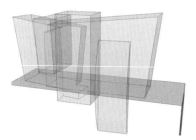 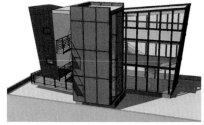

View with only the massing category visible   View with all categories visible

Masses in Revit appear with transparent materials in 3D views by default. When you switch to floor plan, however, they appear solid. Users of Revit have shared this experience and some suggest orienting a 3D view to a floor-level plan. You'll notice the difference with the behavior of the shadows as well: Although a floor-plan view of a mass displays a shadow, an oriented 3D view doesn't.

Starting a Conceptual Massing Study

You can create massing forms using Revit's 3D modeling tools. Use these tools to quickly generate site plans and initial building shapes in the early phase of design development.

CREATING A MASS

In the Massing Design Tab, when you select Create Mass, you're first prompted to name the mass you're about to create. Once you provide a name, the interface transforms into mass-creation mode, with a new set of tools on the Design bar (Figure 7.6). Using these tools, you proceed to create the massing form using combinations of solid and void forms.

FIGURE 7.6

The Design bar for massing creation

This creation mode is similar to that of the Family Editor, where a select set of tools are presented that are relevant to parametric creation of forms. You'll also notice some overlap with the Create tool in the Modeling Design bar. The underlying principles in all these environments (Family Editor, in-place Family Editor, and Massing Editor) are the same.

Most tools on this Design bar should be familiar. The only unique feature is the Place Mass tool. When selected, this tool does the same thing as the Place Mass tool on the Massing Design tab: It lets you place a mass family. This is a component-placement tool that only places components of the mass category.

When you're in mass-edit mode, you can create mass elements that are represented by a single shape or are a combination of shapes, solids, and voids. Everything you add is considered part of the mass you're creating. You can place as many different masses in this mode as you require. Your decision whether to make each shape a separate mass will depend on what you need it to represent and how you intend to interact with it. For example, one mass element could have five extrusions representing five buildings. Or, you could make five separate mass elements for each building. Do you want to move each building independently? Or will you likely want to move all the buildings together, as one element?

When you've finished modeling the mass, you click Finish Mass, and everything you modeled becomes one mass element. To edit a mass, select it and click the Edit button on the Options bar.

Be aware that a mass element must have solid geometry in it—it can't be made of voids alone. If you try to make a void massing, you'll get a warning message like the one shown in Figure 7.7.

FIGURE 7.7

Error message for a mass without solids

It's possible to get the same message even if you do have a solid but the void isn't cutting through the solid.

For example, if you draw the solid first and then the void, the message won't appear. If you do the opposite and add the void before the solid, you'll get the message. To solve this problem, you need to use the Cut Geometry tool to make the solids and voids intersect. Only by using this tool will this message be cleared so you can finish the mass. Figures 7.8 and 7.9 show this.

FIGURE 7.8
If you draw a void before you add a solid, they won't intersect or have any relationship—the mass can't be completed in this case.

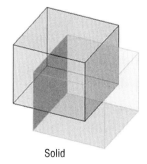

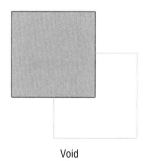

Solid

Void

FIGURE 7.9
Adding a void after placing a solid cuts it from the solid. The mass can then be completed.

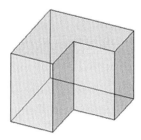

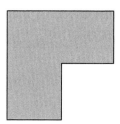

The Cut and Join Geometry tools are both available on the Options bar when forms are selected. These tools are important when you're dealing with massing, so let's look more closely at them:

Cut Geometry   This tool cuts voids out of solids. You select the tool, select a void, and then select what you want the void to cut. Voids can cut multiple solids.

Join Geometry   This tool joins solids (voids can't be joined together) to form one connected element. It merges the shapes (masses) into one, both graphically and as data (Figure 7.10). To use this tool, select the tool, and then select solids you want to join. Multiple solids can be joined together.

If you change the position of one of the joined masses, the intersection (called the *joining*) instantly updates. However, if you move one of the joined masses outside the boundaries of the other joined masses so they don't intersect any more, you'll get a warning message. To resolve the problem, you can use the Unjoin Geometry command. Note that even if the mass elements are joined, selecting the mass results in the selection of just one of them (Figure 7.11).

FIGURE 7.10
Joining two masses together creates a single, seamless element.

FIGURE 7.11
Joined masses can still
be selected and edited
independently.

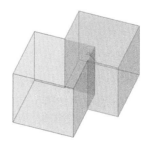

PLACING A MASS FAMILY

The other way to create a mass is to load it from the Family Editor. You do so with the Place Mass tool, which gives you access to the predefined massing families that represent basic geometric 3D shapes. You can load these into your project and start stacking them together to build the shape that you need (Figure 7.12). In practice, these predefined parametric mass families are great for building the context around your building in order to quickly create a sense of the environment in which your project will be situated.

FIGURE 7.12
Mass families ship
with Revit.

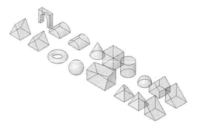

The difference between preloaded mass elements and those created in place is that you get different levels of interactivity with each method. For example, a mass created in place lets you edit its base sketch directly, whereas a family-based mass requires you to edit the family and then reload it if you want to change its sketch. You also get different grip controls when you select each type of massing form. If you select an in-place mass in a 3D view, you get drag controls that allow for dynamic manipulation. However, with a loaded mass family, you don't get the same grip controls.

Figure 7.13 shows two boxes of the same size: one created in the project using the Create Mass tool and the other placed in the projects using the Place Mass option.

By default, when you're loading a mass element for the first time, you may get the following message:

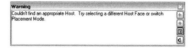

The message tells you that there is no host on which to place the massing based on the current placement mode. Host-based placement doesn't let you place an element floating freely in space.

To better understand this, look at the Options bar. You'll see two placement modes for massing: Place On Face and Place On Work Plane.

FIGURE 7.13

Loaded massing family on the left, and mass built in the project on the right

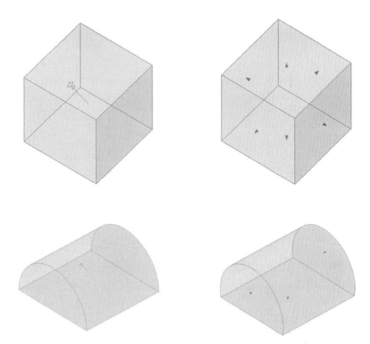

By default, this is set to Place On Face; if you try to drag and drop an element from the type list onto the workspace, your cursor looks like a crossed circle if it doesn't find any geometric face to be a placed on and you will not be able to place the mass. To switch out of this mode, change from Place By Face to Place On Work Plane to place masses freely. From then on, your mass elements will be placed on the current level or whatever the current work plane of the view is set to. The Place By Face option is usually used when you need to continue placement or creation of a mass on the face of another element. We covered this when discussing modeling techniques in Chapter 6.

One more option you should be aware of on the Options bar is Rotate After Placement. When this option is deselected, you place the mass element using one click. The click is the center of the mass element, which is placed at 0 degrees. When the option is selected, you use two clicks to place the mass element: the first one to position it, the second one to define the rotation angle.

In a new Revit session, try clicking Place Mass. In the Revit templates, no mass element is pre-loaded, so you're prompted to load one. If you confirm by clicking Yes, the Family Library opens so you can load masses from the Mass folder. The choices include arch, gable, box, sphere, pyramid, and other predefined shapes. You can load more than one at the same time with the familiar Shift or Ctrl selection. When you load a mass, don't expect it to immediately be dropped/drawn in the drawing area: Loading it just adds it to the project. To place it, you must select it from the Type Selector or the Mass folder in the Family Tree of the Project Browser and place it in the view.

CREATING A NEW MASS FAMILY

The mass element has its own family templates: Mass Element.rft and Mass.rft. If the shapes shown in Figure 7.12 don't represent what you need, and you wish to create your own custom shapes that you'll use in more than one project, you can start a new family using MassElement.rft and create your own parametric mass. Later in this chapter, we'll guide you through the creation of a parametric mass family in the Family Editor.

If you haven't been modeling much yet in Revit, you can learn a lot about how to model by editing one of these families. Load it in a project, select it, and click Edit Family in the Options bar, and the family will open in the Family Editor. Look at how the mass element was created.

MAKING A PYRAMID MASS FORM

The Pyramid Mass family (in the mass family folder) is an example that shows the use of solid and void extrusions. When you edit this family, you'll notice that it was created with the following elements: A solid box was created as a simple extrusion, and two void extrusions were added to remove geometry from the box and create the pyramid shape:

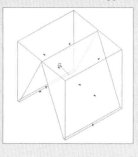 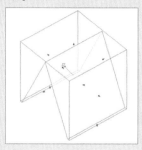 

When you're modeling it, a shape is nothing more than a static 3D object. To make a mass parametrically changeable, you can add labeled dimensions to it. That way, the mass can not just represent one shape and size, but also have several types of predefined sizes. Of course, once an element has parametric dimensions, you're free to make as many variations of that shape as necessary.

For example, if you open the Cylinder mass element from the library, you'll find that it has two parameters related to its size: Radius and Height. Defining parameters lets you predefine types (size combinations) that can be changed in the project environment. In the Family Editor, we made the Radius and Height dimensions into labeled dimensions, and thus they became parametric constraints (see Figure 7.14).

FIGURE 7.14
A cylinder mass element with two main parameters: Radius and Height

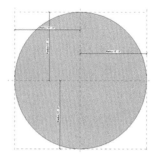 

The mass elements shown in Figure 7.12 are all simple, created from simple solids or combinations of solids and voids. You can create more complex mass elements by nesting one mass within another mass family. *Nesting* means you're importing one mass element into another to create a more complex assembly.

Putting Theory into Practice: Making a Parametric Mass Family

In the following exercise, we'll guide you through the creation of a simple parametric mass family so that you understand some of the principles of creating a mass in the Family Editor. (In the next chapter, we'll guide you through creation of a mass model within the project.)

The result will be the mass shape shown in Figure 7.15, which is parametrically adjustable in several dimensions.

FIGURE 7.15

The parametric mass family you'll create in this exercise

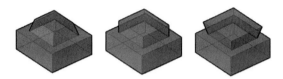

When you're creating a new family, it's essential to select the correct family template. In this case, you wish to create a new mass element, so you need to select `Mass.rft` or `Metric Mass.rft`. Follow these steps:

1. Choose File ➤ New ➤ Family. In the New dialog, select the template `Metric Mass.rft` and click the Open button.

   The Family Editor opens, and the drawing area shows the plan view. There are two pre-defined reference planes: The vertical one is called Center (left/right), and the horizontal one is called Center (Front/Back). The intersection of these two planes will define the insertion point of the family when you later place it in the project. You want to create a parametric family, not just a fixed mass, and thus you need to create reference planes to which you can constrain dimensional parameters that will allow you to change the size of the family by changing properties.

2. Using the Ref Plane tool from the Design Bar, add four more reference planes in the plan view:

   These will be used to control the size of the mass in plan.

3. In the front elevation, add two additional horizontal reference planes. These will be used to control the height of the mass:

4. Place dimensions between the reference planes in plan and elevation. You'll eventually convert these dimensions to labels that represent the future parameters to be tweaked; you'll do that by selecting the dimensions and clicking the Label button on the Options bar. For now, let's keep adding dimensions.

5. Select the reference plane you created in elevation and that is coincidental to the level: It isn't easy to see it (it can be completely covered by the level geometry), so use the Tab key and verify in the tooltip or in the command line that you have selected the reference plane and not the level. Click Properties on the Options bar, and change the value of the Is Reference parameter from Not Reference to Weak Reference. This makes the bottom of the massing form display blue grip controls when selected.

6. Look at the reference planes that define the center axis, because they need to remain centered relative to the other reference planes. You'll set an equality (EQ) dimension constraint between these three reference planes to keep the design symmetrically balanced.

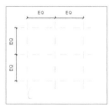

Select the two reference planes that define the axis, and set their Is Reference parameter to Not Reference.

7. Open the plan view Ref. Level. On the Design bar, click Dimension.

Click each reference plane to create the dimensions between them, and then click the EQ symbol:

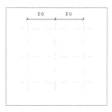

Repeat the same action in the other direction:

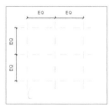

With these steps, you've ensured that the axes in both the X and Y directions will always be in the middle of the element. You now need to create the parameters that will control the size of the mass element: D for Depth and W for Width.

8. Still in plan view, select the Dimension tool, and place a dimension between the two outer reference planes. Don't worry about the value of the dimension:

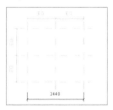

9. On the Design bar, click Modify, and select the dimension you just created. On the Options bar, click the drop-down list next to the label, and select Add Parameter.

10. In the Parameter Properties dialog (Figure 7.16), enter **W** for Name. In the list for Group Parameter Under, select Dimensions, and select the Instance radio button. Click OK to confirm your selections.

FIGURE 7.16
Defining the Width
parameter

Following the same principle, create a dimension in the other direction and name it **D** for depth:

Note that from now on the value in the dimension text has a prefix D or W.

11. Open the front elevation view, and add a dimension between the reference plane that is coincidental with the level (again, make sure that you select the bottom reference plane and *not* the level line) and the first horizontal reference plane above:

Add another dimension between the other two horizontal reference planes:

Following the principle previously described for labeling these, name them **H1** and *H2*:

12. You've created the framework that will drive the geometry, so all that is left to do is to make the geometry. But before that, you need to test the parameters you just created—what is called *flexing* the model:

On the Design bar, select Family Types. In the Family Types dialog (Figure 7.17), select the parameters you just created, and modify the values. Click the Apply button to see the effects in the view (the reference planes move as you change values).

Make sure you change the parameters one by one; if you get an error message, and you've changed many values at the same time, you won't know which one is the problem. If you try changing all the values and don't get any error messages, you have done well and are ready to create the geometry.

FIGURE 7.17

The Family
Types dialog

13. Open the plan Ref. Plane and, on the Design bar, select Solid and then Solid Extrusion:

    You're placed into sketch mode, and the Design bar changes to show only tools relevant to the extrusion sketch mode. On the Options bar, select the Rectangle shape:

    Click the intersection of the left and bottom reference planes to define the start point of the rectangle:

    Click the intersection of the top and right reference planes to define the diagonal finish point of the rectangle:

    Click the four padlocks that appear automatically—by doing so, you create constraints between the lines of the sketch and the reference planes on which they're drawn. This means that later—when you move the position of the reference planes by changing the values in the Family Types, the sketch lines of the geometry will follow the change and parametrically change.

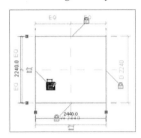

In the Design bar, click Finish Sketch.

14. Open the front elevation, and select the solid you just created. Click the blue arrow on the top of the solid, and move it up to the upper reference plane. It should snap to it.

When the geometry coincides with the reference plane, a padlock icon appears, allowing you to constrain the relationship. Click the padlock. You've now defined the relationship between the top of the solid and the reference plane, so that if you change the reference-plane position (the value of the parameter) again, the top of the solid will move with it.

15. Using the Family Type option from the Design bar, start changing the H1 and H2 parameters, and see what happens. While working with the family parameters, you can also change (flex) the values for W and D to verify how they affect the geometry. Note that to review the correct functioning of the parameters while flexing them, it's best to be in 3D view.

16. You'll now add a void to the solid. For that purpose, you'll use the Sweep tool. You'll start by adding a new reference plane that will control the position of the new shape in plan view.

Open the plan view Ref. Level, and add a reference plane:

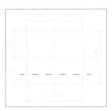

17. Add a dimension between this new reference plane and the one that defines the axis front/back, and transform this new dimension into a label as previously described. Name the new label **O** (for Offset).

18. Open a 3D view. On the Design bar, click Void Form ➤ Void Sweep.

19. Click the Pick Path tool. This time, instead of sketching the path, you'll use existing geometry for the path you want to define.

Click the solid's four top edges. For this exercise, make sure you first select the edge that is in the front:

On that first edge you picked, a cross appears, with a red spot in its center. This represents the work plane of the profile sketch. You can sketch the shape of your profile directly in 3D, but it's easier to draw the shape in the same plane as the profile work plane—especially when dimensions are important. Switch to a view that is parallel to the sketch's work plane—in this case, the left or right elevation.

On the Design bar, click Finish Path.

20. On the Options bar, select Sketch Profile. Open the right elevation. On the Design bar, click the Line tool, and then trace three sketch lines:

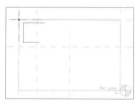

21. Click the Align tool, select the vertical reference plane, and then select the vertical line of the newly created sketch. By doing so, you align the sketch line to the reference plane. To establish the relationship, click the padlock icon.

Note: if you ever forget to click the lock, and the next time you want to do so the lock doesn't appear, click the sketch line, move it to the left or right, and reposition over the reference plane—the lock will appear again, and you can lock it.

22. Still using the Align tool, click the top horizontal reference plane and then the top horizontal line of the sketch, and again lock the padlock.

23. Click the horizontal reference plane just below the lower horizontal sketch line and then click that horizontal sketch line to align. Again, lock the padlock:

24. You have one more task, and it's more delicate. Zoom in closer in the lower-right corner of the sketch and the vertical reference plane.

Still using the Align tool, click the vertical reference plane (the second from the left, if you're in the right elevation), and then place your cursor next to the free end of the horizontal sketch line. A little square appears at the end of the sketch line, which fades slightly. (If this doesn't happen, try moving the cursor. Help yourself with the Tab key.) Once you see the small square at the end of the sketch line, click it to define the alignment to the vertical reference plane:

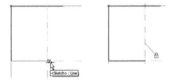

25. On the Design bar, click the Line tool, and draw the last line segment to close the sketch:

26. Click Dimension on the Design bar, and select Angular from the Options bar:

27. Add an angular dimension between the diagonal sketch line and the vertical reference. Create a label out of that dimension, and name it **A** (for an Angle):

28. On the Design bar, click Finish Sketch and then Finish Extrusion. Don't forget to finish both of these; otherwise, your drawing will look grayed out, indicating that you are still in the sketch mode.. Go to 3D view to see the result:

Congratulations! You just created your first fully parametric mass family! Save it as **My First Mass** somewhere where you can find it again. You can open a new project and load this newly created mass. In the project environment, start to flex the parameters and see how they affect the shape of the mass.

Also note that when you import the mass element in the project and select it, small blue controls appear on the edges of the solid. Using them, you can change the size of the mass element on the fly:

To change the angle of the shape you carved out with the void, change the angle in the parameters and see how it affects the look of your mass. The value of the angle can be positive or negative, allowing you to create variations in shape like those shown in Figure 7.15 at the beginning of this exercise.

Tagging and Scheduling Mass

The value of doing early massing studies in Revit is that they all contain information about the spaces you're designing. You can quickly tag the masses, visually categorize them, or schedule them to get feedback about the area and volume the building will occupy.

THE MASSING TAG

The Mass tag is Revit's tag for mass elements. By Default this type of tag is not loaded in Revit. When you decide to tag the mass families and select Tag/by Category from the Drafting Design Bar, you will get a message that a Mass tag has not yet been loaded and that you can load such a tag from the Library. If you confirm with Yes, the library folders open and you will find the Mass tag family under the Annotations folder. The default Mass tag extracts the gross floor area of each mass, but you can add any other instance property to be extracted by the tag or any shared parameters you may need in the process of a feasibility study for stacking and blocking diagrams (see Chapter 15 for more on tagging). There is no special `Mass tag.rft` template file. To create a new mass tag to match your graphic needs, you can either duplicate the existing one or start with a generic tag template.

PROJECT PARAMETERS AND SCHEDULING MASSING

To create schedules that can give you information about various functional groups to which mass elements belong, the departments they represent, or the space IDs, you can use project parameters. You can create project parameters for program group, department, or space ID; assign these to your masses; and then schedule them to analyze and track how your model fits the program.

To add a project parameter, choose Settings ➤ Project Parameters. Choose to add a new parameter, and then select Mass as the parameter's category. Once you do this, the parameter shows up in all mass instances, and you can assign values for this parameter in each of the mass instances. Should you also want to tag the properties in question (Program Group, Department, and so on), you'll need to create shared parameters instead. You'll learn more about shared parameters in Chapter 15.

Importing 3D Conceptual Models Created in Other Applications

You can import geometry from conceptual modeling applications (3D models, created in AutoCAD, SketchUp, Rhinoceros, and 3ds Max, among others) done in various formats into a mass instance or mass family in the same way you import geometry into other families. You may need or want to do this in several scenarios:

◆ You have users who are comfortable with 3D modeling tools like those listed. They prefer to do the massing there and then use Revit's analysis capabilities as well as the Building Maker to turn the mass into a building.

◆ There are shapes and NURBS forms that Revit doesn't do easily (or at all), so you need to create the shape in another application. You need not import a whole shape, as shown in Figure 7.18—it may be just a face of a shape that you'll need later to design a specific portion of a complex-shaped building, such as its roof.

FIGURE 7.18
NURBS shape created in Rhinoceros is converted to a real wall using the Wall By Face functionality of the Building Maker

 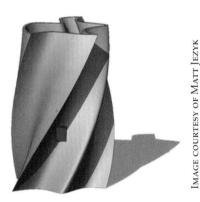

IMAGE COURTESY OF MATT JEZYK

You can import individual masses (a complex shape, for example) or a fully developed massing study model. Regardless what the import represents, the strategy is to never import it directly into the project file but to go through a family import:

◆ If the geometry is an individual element that you're likely to reuse, open the Family Editor by opening a mass template, and create a new mass by importing the geometry.

◆ If you have a full study model, it's advisable to import it as an in-place Mass family in the project (use the Create Mass tool and then File/Import CAD Formats to import the 3D geometry created elsewhere).

We'll talk more in Chapter 8 about how the behavior of the imported items depends on how they're imported, whether directly into the project, in a massing family in the family editor, or in an in-place Mass family.

It is important to note that Revit won't let you copy masses between a family and a model. You may encounter this limitation (and error message) when you mistakenly added more than one mass in one mass element but you needed to assign different parameters to each of them . To do so, you would need to move some of the masses to other mass elements. Be aware that there is no way to do it and you'll have to re-create the wrongly placed masses from zero.

Rapid Prototyping and 3D Printing

3D digital-massing studies allow architects to use advanced technologies and make physical prototypes for demonstration or testing purposes using the 3D printing services that are becoming more affordable. For many architects as well as investors, a physical model is still something they like to have in order to study the design.

Rapid prototyping is the automatic construction of physical objects using solid freeform fabrication. The first techniques for rapid prototyping became available in the 1980s and were used to produce models and prototype parts. Thanks to advanced and affordable technology, professionals in many different fields now rely on rapid prototyping—architects to create models, industrial designers to make first-draft prototypes, and even artists to sculpt complex shapes for fine arts. The process of rapid prototyping takes virtual designs from a CAD model, transforms them into virtual cross sections, and creates each cross section in physical space one after the next until the model is finished. This is often done by layering liquid and powdered material for each section and using glue or a laser; the material is fused together as shown in Figure 7.19.

FIGURE 7.19
3D physical models can be printed directly from a digital model.

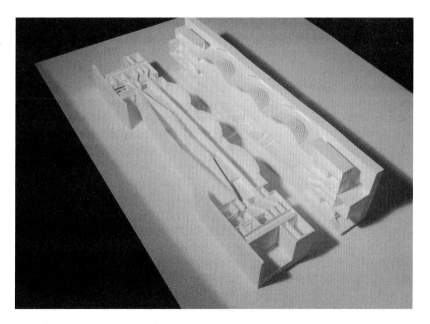

The most common file format for sending this data is .stl. You can 3D-print a Revit model by exporting it first to .dwg and then printing to .stl from 3ds Max, AutoCAD, Inventor, or other software that supports .stl exporting.

Figure 7.20 shows a rapid prototype model of an unbuilt Louis Kahn building.

FIGURE 7.20
Hidden-line view, shaded view, sectional 3D view, and a rapid prototype physical model from the same Revit model

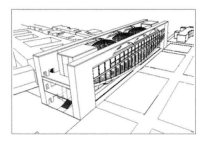

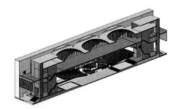

IMAGES COURTESY OF SIMONE CAPPOCHIN

The Bottom Line

Projects begin with broad, gestural strokes that are eventually refined with more detail. The ability to quickly generate conceptual 3D massing forms aids in the development of a project. With Revit, you can make parametric abstract mass forms and use those forms downstream in your process as the design progresses.

Understanding massing workflows supported by Revit   Using generic forms, you can create early conceptual models and then use the mass to create the walls, floors, and roofs.

> **Master It**   You need to explore a design idea early on, in 3D, using abstract forms. How would you do this with Revit?

Creating massing elements in the project environment and Family Editor   In the project environment, you can make massing forms at any time. For generic forms that might appear in multiple projects, consider using the Family Editor and create Mass Families.

> **Master It**   You've imported a 2D site plan, and now you need to start building up a massing study model in the project. How would you approach this with Revit?

Understanding how massing can be used downstream as the design progresses   Making a mass is one thing, but leveraging that mass for quantity take-offs can further aid and inform the design process.

> **Master It**   Once you've settled on a basic massing study, what information can you derive from it? How can this be represented?

Chapter 8

From Conceptual Mass to a Real Building

In this chapter, we'll describe the use of an early conceptual mass model to help you understand program fitness and early feasibility studies. You'll see how easy it is to convert a massing study, whether done within Revit or imported from another application, into building elements such as walls, floors, and roofs. The premise of a BIM approach to design is that a fluid workflow can be maintained as you move from early concept models into design development, and eventual construction documentation, all the while maintaining the same underlying geometry and design intent. Revit provides specifically designed tools that accommodate early massing model studies for program validation and feasibility studies, which can then be quickly converted to real building elements.

You'll acquire the following skills in this chapter:

◆ Leveraging a massing study for program validation and early feasibility studies

◆ Converting a mass into a building using the Building Maker tools

◆ Importing files from other sources when working on massing

Conceptual Design and Early Studies

A project usually starts with a very rough conceptualization of first ideas in which the architect's mind wanders between the creativity of fantasy and the reality of customer needs, merged with the influence of the genius loci.

Conceptual designs are the first graphical words an architect exchanges with a client to get approval for the architect's first thoughts and sense the temperature of the client's taste. When the initial idea is approved, the architect continues in the next stage of development of their design and makes more developed studies supported by concrete measurements and numbers that show the applicability of the design and its feasibility.

We'll review how this process can be done using Revit. Figure 8.1 shows an example of a very early massing study using Revit that has the semblance of a building. Let's walk through how this workflow is supported.

FIGURE 8.1
Massing study model

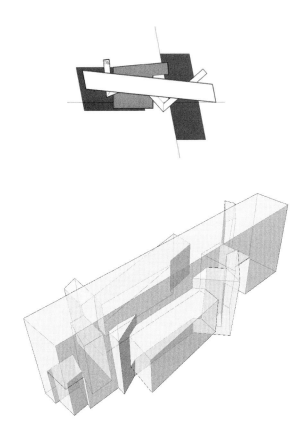

Getting Site Data and Building the Context

A project usually starts with a client's wish, vision, and hopes described during a conversation with the architect. A list of program requirements is compiled, listing the types of spaces the building will have and its rough area. The architect then starts gathering information and data about the site—aerial photos, photos of the site and context, site-survey files with land information, and building footprints and blocks. Using site analysis, program requirements, and creativity, the architect proceeds to study what shape and size building fits best. Variations of the design are studied, analyzed, critiqued, and presented to the client.

Getting site data into the digital model is the first step in moving from loose napkin sketches to a real project. By importing DWG/DGN site information into Revit, you'll have an underlay from which to work. (For small projects, this can also be a scanned image of a hand-drawn site situation.) CAD drawings with site information usually come with a rich amount of information that needs to be culled. Using the Visibility/Graphic Overrides dialog, you can hide unnecessary layers to make the drawings more legible. Setting the correct scale and orientation of the site relative to the building will be the most critical beginning steps and should be done during the import of the site file.

SCALE

In the Import dialog, setting the units to Automatic usually works well if the CAD file was drawn at 1:1 inch scale. If the drawing was scaled, you may find that the scale of the imported file is incorrect, and you need to re-import the file and set the scale units manually to get useful results.

ORIENTATION

The next step is to deal with the orientation of the imported site plan. Maps are usually created so that north is always at the top, and that is how site information should be displayed in final documents. When you're working on developing a site plan, you'll prefer to work in a way that is most comfortable for you, so the site is oriented parallel to your computer screen—not to true north.

ORIENTING A SITE PLAN TO FIT YOUR SCREEN

Suppose you're starting your design study, and you open a site plan view to import the CAD file with the site. An imported CAD drawing usually comes in its original coordinates' orientation, with north/south in the vertical axis:

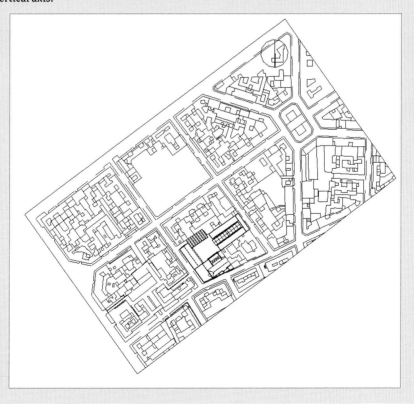

If you open the view's properties, you'll notice that the Orientation parameter indicates Project North:

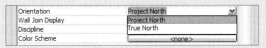

By default, the orientation of a view is set to Project North. By changing the Orientation parameter to True North and rotating the True North setting, you can work in a comfortably oriented plan relative to your screen.

In the View Properties change Orientation to True North, and rotate true north using Tools ➤ Project Position/Orientation ➤ Rotate True North. A rotation control appears in the view. Rotate to an angle best suited to work on. Note that this does not mean you've rotated the project but rather the world.

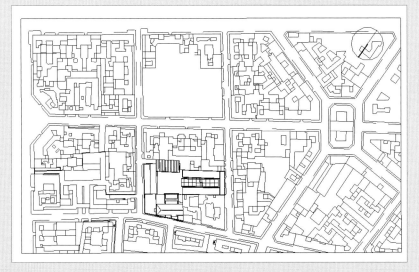

This procedure is more than enough if you don't intend to send information back to the person you received the file from. However, if you're collaborating with a civil engineer and need to send back the building footprint or an early mass study, you need to establish a connection between the two files so they have the same coordinates. This can be achieved using the Linking method as well as the Acquire Coordinates functionality.

POSITIONING IMPORTED FILES RELATIVE TO THE REVIT PROJECT

You can choose to automatically place or manually place an import. With Automatically Place (under the "Positioning" group in the Import dialog) you have the following options:

Center-to-center aligns the 3D center points of both models.

Origin-to-origin places the world origin of the linked file at the Revit model's origin point. If the linked model was created far from the origin point, linking with this option may put the linked file far away from the main model.

By shared coordinates places a linked file geometry according to the shared coordinate system created between the two files (this is available only if you're linking files). If no shared coordinate file has been created, Revit alerts you. The Shared Coordinates settings can be found in the Tools drop-down menu; you have the following options:

Acquire Coordinates allows you to take the coordinates of the linked file into the host model. There is no change to the host model's internal coordinates; however, the host model acquires the true north of the linked model and its Origin setting.

Publish Coordinates allows you to publish the Origin and True North settings to your linked model. Revit understands that there may be other things in your linked file and you may not want this to be a global change to the linked file. An additional dialog appears that gives you the option to name separate locations for each set of coordinates.

Specify Coordinates at a Point allows you to manually key in x, y, and z coordinates relative to the origin point or define where you want your 0,0,0 point to be.

Report Shared Coordinates shows the E/W (east/west) (x), N/S (north/south) (y), and elevation (z) coordinates of any point in the model.

You can import a CAD file so that it appears in all views, or you can import it in the Current view only. You will find these options under the Import or Link group box. Remember that for topography files, you should NOT select the "Current View only" option because you will not be able to convert the imported file into topography.

If you forgot this rule, we advise that you delete the import and re-import, making sure that the Current View option is NOT checked. You will most probably not want the Site file to be visible in all other views, so you can turn its visibility on in the other views later.

Building the 3D Context

After positioning the imported CAD file in your site plan and reorienting it to True north, you can start building the environment in 3D using the massing tools. The base shapes of buildings in the CAD file can be used to quickly generate a massing model of the surrounding site. Use photos or actual data to establish building heights.

To make a 3D study of the surrounding site, use the Create Mass feature and begin developing solids out of the existing geometry:

1. From the Massing tab in the Design bar, select Create Mass. Give the mass a name, such as **context buildings**.

2. Select the Extrusion solid form, and switch from Draw to Pick method using the Options bar. Select lines in the imported file to create the base sketches.

3. Change the Height of each mass to match the real-world conditions.

4. Give each massing a material that suits your graphic needs. A neutral gray or white is common. Figures 8.2–8.5 show the use of massing to create abstract forms that represent the context.

FIGURE 8.2
Massing used to add
surrounding context
buildings

IMAGE COURTESY OF KUBIK-NEMETH-VLKOVIC

FIGURE 8.3
Massing used for
abstract contextual
representation

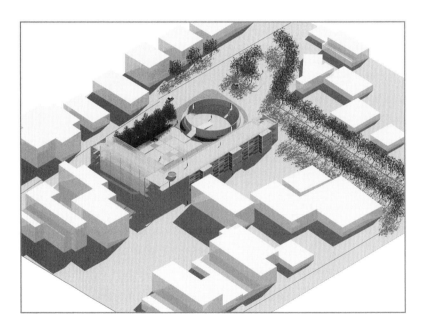

FIGURE 8.4
Massing used to
model existing
buildings on site

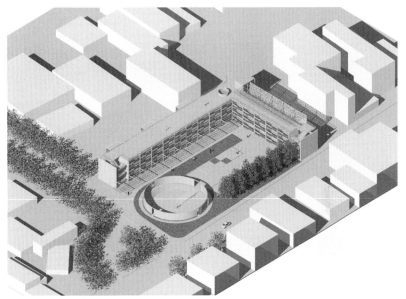

IMAGE COURTESY OF FELIPE MANRIQUE DIAZ, URUGUAY

FIGURE 8.5
Massing used to create
an initial form

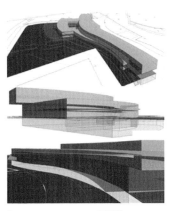

IMAGE COURTESY OF HOK

Program Check and Feasibility

Many of the activities in early design revolve around exploring the commercial viability of the site
and figuring out the right mix of uses (for example, residential versus office versus retail). All these
uses have different economic returns. Zoning regulations can be complicated in how they allow different amounts of total development based on the mix ratio. In essence, two numbers govern almost
all urban property: Floor Area Ratio (FAR) and Lot Coverage Ratio (LCR). FAR is a number that
says how many multiples of the site area the building area can be. LCR specifies the percentage area
of the site that can be covered by the building footprint. Usually the architect is required to maximize the FAR by determining the right mix of uses placed at the right location on the site.

At this stage, the problem is not only about forms or shapes but about the program, construction costs, and rents and the functional distribution on the site horizontally and vertically. The architect usually attempts to determine what physical forms, in what location, with what use, will provide the best economic return to the owner. This study then needs to be consolidated and documented. While studying this problem, the architect may generate tens if not hundreds of slightly different alternatives for numerical comparative purposes. A few of the most promising are then developed further for presentation purposes.

At early stages in design, you need to check the program and how well you fit into it. Programs can be less or more precise, depending on the client and the task in question. It can be as bold as 15,000 sq. ft. (4570 sq. meters) offices, 40,000 sq. ft. (12,200 sq. meters) hotel space, and 20,000 sq. ft. (6100 sq. meters) retail space for a bigger complex; or it can be an exact number of rooms and spaces when working on one building. Figure 8.6 shows an early massing study annotated to show usage and areas.

FIGURE 8.6

Early study documenting maximum allowed heights and total square footage of a proposed solution

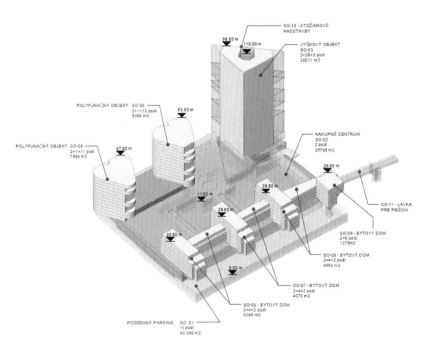

IMAGE COURTESY OF KUBIK-NEMETH-VLKOVIC

The architect is constantly thinking about architectural expression, fitting in the site, and accommodating the program. They're also evaluating whether the client's requirements can fit the allowed buildable area and height of the site, zoning regulations, land uses, traffic requirements (they usually always want more), and information about the number of parking spaces and other support functionalities. This phase of the project can also involve shadow studies and energy modeling, as discussed in Chapter 14.

The next step is to propose multiple solutions to the client, so proposals with different mixes of functions and spatial solutions can be reviewed and analyzed. This is where the Design Options tools you'll learn about in Chapter 9 come in handy.

CREATING MULTIPLE MASSING DESIGN OPTIONS

Here is a suggested workflow based on a real-world use case.

The architectural firm Gensler created an option set with three options, each with a distinct name. They duplicated 3D views and schedules to document project information early on. In each view, the Visibility/ Graphic Overrides were set to display each option (one set to Option 1, another to Option 2, and the third to Option 3). Doing so not only visually described the new option but also presented the data behind each design.

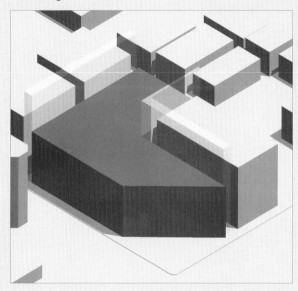
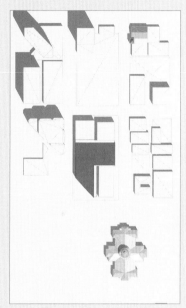
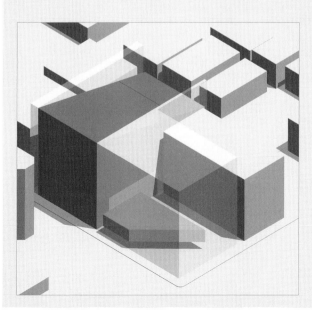
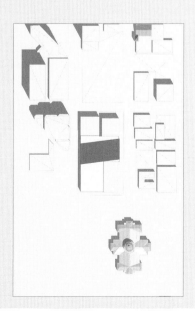

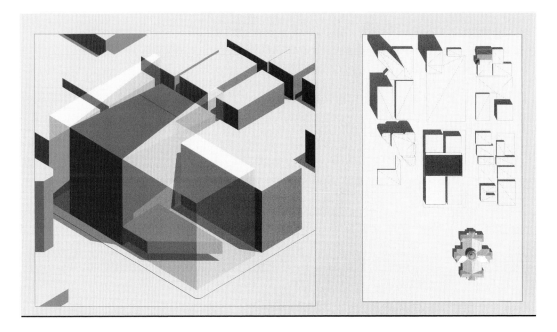

Building Maker

After several iterations and tweaking, the client makes up their mind. One of the solutions is selected to go forward, and you're ready to convert that early mass into a real building. Here is where the Building Maker tools come into play. With these tools, you can get more detailed information about the model by attaching walls, floors, and roofs to the massing shapes.

This approach has two major advantages over traditional 3D systems:

◆ The need to re-create the digital data from scratch is eliminated.

◆ An established connection exists between the building elements made by referencing the mass and the mass itself, so the massing design can iterate and update the building elements.

The nice thing about the Building Maker workflow is that it also supports the import of geometry from tools such as Rhino, 3ds Max, and SketchUp into mass shapes, to which you can then attach wall, floors, and roofs.

Chapter 6 discussed the principles of modeling, and Chapter 7 analyzed the bases of the massing tools for creation of massing studies. You should have a good understanding of how to create a mass element or an entire mass study. We'll now focus on the second group of tools located in the Massing tab of the Design bar: the so-called Building Maker tools.

Let's get an overview the available tools and then examine their real-life application.

FLOOR AREA FACES

Floor Area Faces

The first tool you should know about isn't visible in the Massing tab. It's the Floor Area tool, which is designed for getting early square-footage take-offs from the massing. This tool appears in the Options bar whenever a mass that you created is selected.

Assuming you've created a mass study in which you define the basic volumes and shapes that will form your building or complex of buildings, you're ready to start setting up levels. Depending of the type of building you're making, code regulations, and functional usage, you can begin to lay out levels for the building. Let's say the maximum height is 90˝ (22m), and your building is a hotel, which will usually have a 12´ (3m) floor-to-floor height. In that case, you can get approximately seven levels.

From any elevation view, add levels using the Level tool. It's obviously much easier to copy a level graphically using the Multiple Copy or Array command; however, with that method you won't create actual floor plans for each of the levels. If that's OK with you, go ahead. If not, you can either use the Level tool and draw each Level or use the copy method to create levels but then create floor plans from those levels by using the View/Floor Plan tool and selecting which levels should have a floor plan view associated with them.

Click the Floor Area Faces button when the mass is selected. You'll get a list of all levels in the project. If you check all levels, a floor area will be calculated for each level. If you want to skip a level because of double room height, for example, don't check that level. You can do this for all masses at the same time or separately for each volume.

When you OK the level selection, your mass is sliced by floor (see Figure 8.7).

Imagine that the other masses are for the conference center and parking structures, and apply the same concept. Add levels appropriate for each structure, then select each mass, click Floor Area Faces, and choose which levels you want to slice up the mass.

You now understand why the Level tool is handy on the Massing Design bar. Revit is fantastic because you can add, delete, and reshuffle levels at any moment in your project development without needing to redo work or losing any invested work. This *slicing* of volumes doesn't just visually help you understand the number of floors and divisions—it also calculates the floor area of the mass element in question and allows you to schedule the values (Figure 8.8).

VERIFYING YOUR DESIGN AND ITS FIT WITHIN THE DEFINED PROGRAM

You can schedule the parameters and values of the masses similar to how you schedule other Revit elements. In the earliest phase of the project, you'll probably want to schedule the functional zones. To create an understandable schedule, it's a good idea to give the mass elements you created names according to their function—Hotel Rooms, Conferences, Parking, Restaurants, and so on—and assign them different colors (materials) so it's easy to visually represent the data. If you need to rename the mass element once it is created you can do that from the project Browser—find the Mass Element in question and rename. As mentioned in Chapter 7, you can also add project parameters to the mass elements, such as Public or Private Space, Department, and so on. If you wish to tag those new parameters so that they are shown in the Mass Tag, you must make them shared parameters and add them in the Massing Tag family. See Chapter 15 for more on shared parameters.

Out of the box, the mass elements in Revit can report the following properties:

◆ Gross Floor Area

◆ Gross Surface

◆ Gross Volume

FIGURE 8.7
Floor areas slice up
the mass at each
designated level.

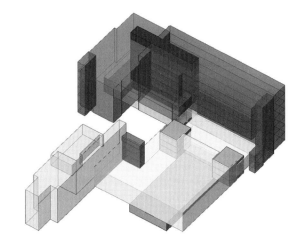

FIGURE 8.8
The other masses
can be sliced using
different levels.

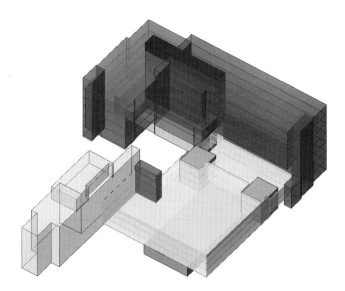

■	OBJECT A	224 m2	
■	OBJECT B	476 m2	
			$\sum 1 = 700$ m2
■	CORE	104 m2	
□	STAIRCASES	98 m2	
□	PARKING	1484 m2	$\sum 2 = 202$ m2
□	RAMPS	123 m2	
		2509 m2	$\sum 3 = 902$ m2

If you created an initial mass study and schedule the mass elements, you'll notice that the schedule reports Gross Surface and Gross Volume of the entire shape (Figure 8.9). You can't schedule the Gross Floor area without first adding levels and creating floor area faces.

Mass Schedule			
Family	Gross Floor	Gross Surfac	Gross Volum
Building 1		58080 SF	517251.44

By defining levels and creating floor area faces, you can add a total Gross Floor area to the schedule (Figure 8.10).

FIGURE 8.9
Example of a mass element without floor area faces

FIGURE 8.10
The mass is sliced into floor area faces.

The total gross floor area of the mass is the sum of all the floor slabs belonging to that one mass element. That probably isn't granular enough for your needs. You need to get separate data about the floor area per floor, probably sorted and grouped by usage/function. To get the floor area per level or at least per function, you need to use the floor element and build a floor schedule. This is due to a limitation of the current massing tools in Revit: The mass alone doesn't offer the ability to calculate floor area per level or per any other property of the mass without floor elements being added.

Mass Schedule			
Family	Gross Floor	Gross Surfac	Gross Volum
Building 1	52113 SF	58080 SF	517251.44

Floor by Face

Create Floors

To apply floors to the massing, click the Floor By Face tool, select each floor area face of the mass, and then click the Create Floors button in the Options bar.

Firms worldwide have found different ways to solve the problem of calculating a floor area per level. For example, you can create special massing templates in which floor elements are preset and assigned different functional properties and materials based on function. When you come to the stage in the design process where you need to get data about the individual floor area per floor or grouped by function per floor, you apply floors to the floor area slices and make a schedule of the floors.

For compelling graphics, you can give the mass and floor materials a transparency, as shown in Figure 8.11.

FIGURE 8.11

Transparency and color used to explain programming

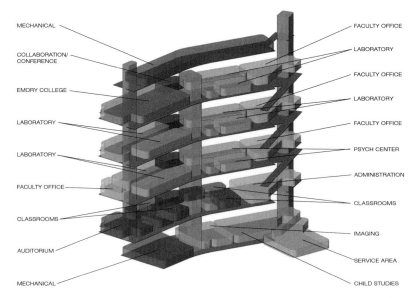

IMAGE COURTESY OF HOK ATLANTA, USA

Follow these steps to use floors both graphically and to drive a schedule:

1. Select the Floor tool, and go to the Type Properties of Generic Floor.

2. Duplicate the floor, and name it **Offices**.

3. Edit Structure in the Type Properties, giving it a new material that is 50% transparent blue. Set its thickness to 10´ (2.5m).

4. Give a mark number and comment/description to each floor slab so that later you can sort/group them in the schedule to achieve the desired result.

5. In the Element Properties (Figure 8.12), set The Height Offset From Level parameter to be identical with the floor height. You do this because the floor is always drawn from the level you choose (in this case, the thirty-third level) downward; to fill the space above the level, you should define an offset of the floor height. Figure 8.13 shows the resulting levels.

6. Repeat the same for Reception Level, Garages, Conference Center, and Hotel, applying different colors each time.

FIGURE 8.12
Element Properties—
set Height Offset
From Level to a
positive value.

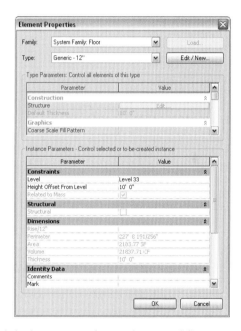

This process allows you to schedule the gross surface, volume, and floor area on a per-level and/or functional basis. Additionally, you can produce visual colored diagrams that are great for explaining to the client the spatial organization of the project.

This may sound like an odd workaround, but it's a great one, and it won't affect your future workflow. The moment you decide to switch to a real building and start applying walls, curtain systems, and roofs, you can exchange those floor types with normal floors, using the Type Selector and a few clicks of the mouse.

Because you can now quickly generate metrics and graphics showing the functional distribution of program elements, you should be able to get feedback on the fitness of the design early on. This will in turn allow you to fine-tune the design and make sure you're keeping pace with the client's requirements. Having built a parametric massing model, the elements are all adjustable in size and shape, and any change you make will instantly be reflected in the visual and schedule data.

FIGURE 8.13
Floor with positive
offset value

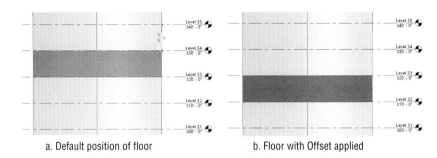

a. Default position of floor   b. Floor with Offset applied

Massing Best Practices

In the model shown in Figure 8.14, the differentiation of functions is simple, and the building has mixed uses. Currently, you can't assign different functions to sub-elements in a massing family, nor create a schedule of the three functional zones in the one mass. All the forms used in the family use one set of family parameters. To overcome this limitation, and for cases where you have more than one function in the same volume, you will need to make separate masses for each functional form. In Figure 8.15, a separate massing element were created for the retail, hotel, and restaurants sections of the building and stuck on top of each other.

FIGURE 8.14
Massing form with
mulitple uses—a chal-
lenge with Revit

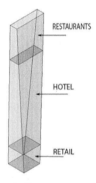

RESTAURANTS

HOTEL

RETAIL

When you make separate masses, be sure to create them one on top of the other, using the previous as a reference that you pick for the sketch of the next one. Be sure to also lock the sketches to another so that if the one form changes, the other one will also follow the change.

The usual scenario would be: you have the basic shape of the building established, but you need to divide it into separate functional zones: shops, then 20 floors of hotel, and then 10 floors of restaurants. Revit does not have tools to split a mass into separate masses so you will need to redo the mass and create three separate mass elements for each of the functional zones. By building each form on top of another, you can create parametric constraints between the elements.

Using the Pick option when sketching each shape, click existing geometry. That way, when one element's sketch changes, the change will propagate to other elements.

In this example, floor area faces were added to the original mass on the first, fifth and twenty-fifth floor in order to have geometry to pick when sketching the separate masses that describe different functions. The lower mass spans from Level 1 to Level 5, the middle mass spans from Level 5 to 25, and the top mass starts at 25 and spans upward. At each level, you can reference other geometry when sketching. Once you have made separate masses, they can be color coded per function—so you get a graphically clear mass and you can schedule them per function.

FIGURE 8.15

Make new masses based on the original, and then delete or hide the original. By having created each mass sketch based on and locked to the the sketch of the under-laying mass, any changes to the one mass will affect change of the shape of the other.

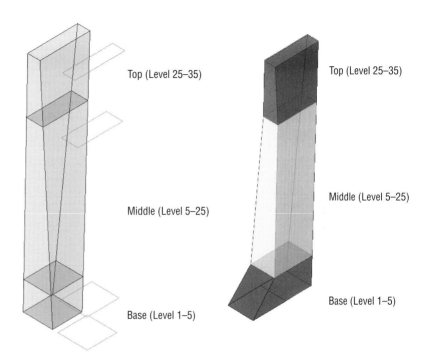

Top (Level 25–35)

Top (Level 25–35)

Middle (Level 5–25)

Middle (Level 5–25)

Base (Level 1–5)

Base (Level 1–5)

After you've reviewed a couple of design options with the client, a decision is made and you need to move forward. To the real project! Moving to the next stage is simple: You can convert the mass into building components using specially designed tools. Let's look at these tools now.

WALL BY FACE

Creating walls by face is simple: Click the Wall By Face tool on the Massing Design bar, and start applying it to faces of the masses. Note that you can create walls by face on vertical and inclined faces or arc faces of a mass exclusively. Wall by face cannot be applied to horizontal faces. You can begin applying generic walls that you later swap with exact wall types that you'll be using; or, if you want to make early renderings that convey color and texture, apply the types of walls that you believe represent your idea best and contain the texture/material/color information. Cost estimates are generated early in the process, so you'll soon need to move from abstract forms to the real wall types.

Many of the rules and principles behind standard wall creation should be followed here as well. It's important to correctly set your wall location (we advise using wall exterior face to keep the wall coincident with the outer boundary of the mass shape).

For example, imagine that you've created a conceptual mass study in SketchUp and imported it into Revit as a mass element. Using the Wall By Face tool, you can start applying generic walls to the mass immediately.

Keep these limitations in mind:

◆ Any wall in Revit can be converted into a curtain wall. Unfortunately, this isn't the case with walls created with the Wall By Face option. To make curtain walls, you need to use the Curtain System By Face tool.

◆ You can't edit the shape of the wall that is created with the Wall By Face tool. To do that, you must change the shape of the underlying mass.

FLOOR BY FACE

Only after you've applied floor area faces to the masses (as explained earlier in this chapter) can you apply real floor elements to them. Select the Floor by Face tool, and start selecting the floor area faces to which you want to assign a floor. You have to click the Create Floors button on the Options bar, or nothing will happen.

To accommodate floor creation in a tower with many floors, you can check the Select Multiple option on the Options bar; you can then begin picking all the floor area faces to which you wish to apply floors and finish with the Create Floors tool.

The Floor Area Faces tool slices the mass horizontally, creating horizontal floor plates. As shown in Figure 8.16, you can always slope those floors later by using the Floor Edit tools available from the Options menu when a floor is selected or edit the sketch of the floor and add a slope arrow while being in the sketch mode of the floor.

FIGURE 8.16
Click on a grip control to change the floor slope.

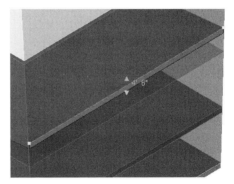

It's worth mentioning that when you create a floor by face, the Options bar includes an Offset parameter:

This isn't the vertical offset of the floor from the level you can find in the Floor properties; it's an offset of the floor sketch from the current floor area boundary. If you add a positive value to the offset, the floor plate becomes smaller than the actual floor area (Figure 8.17).

FIGURE 8.17
Use offset to make slab smaller or larger than the floor area face.

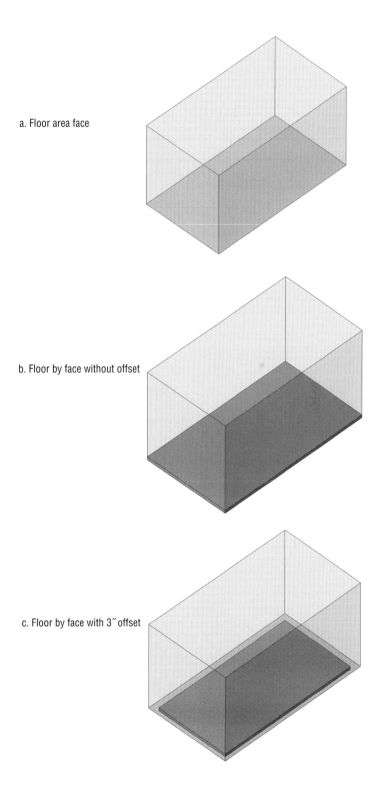

a. Floor area face

b. Floor by face without offset

c. Floor by face with 3″ offset

Roof by Face

You've learned how easy it is to apply walls and floors by face. Roofs follow the same basic principles but are more flexible. You can create roofs by face on planar faces, arcs, or other shapes defined by extrusions, revolves, sweeps, and blends. The only face on which you can't create a roof by face is a vertical surface.

Note these limitations:

♦ You can't pick a vertical face for a roof.

♦ Once a roof is created using the By Face method, you can't edit its sketch. If you created a roof by face and need to change its sketch, you must change the shape of the underlying mass from which the roof has been derived; only that way can you affect the shape of the created roof.

Curtain System by Face

Curtain systems is a handy tool. With one click, you can convert a face of a building into a curtain system that you can predefine with parameters to match your needs. Curtain systems can pick any nonplanar face and are composed of grids, panels, and mullions. Make sure the curtain system type you choose has a predefined Curtain Grid layout.

Keep these limitations in mind:

♦ You can't edit curtain system sketches. A curtain system made by face requires mass editing to change.

♦ You can't always predict the x or y coordinate system applied to the face. You may have to make new types in order to meet your requirements.

Technical Details You Should Be Aware of When Scheduling

It's important that your mass model be modeled properly from a geometrical point of view to support downstream applications of walls, floor, and roofs. Look at the towers shown in Figure 8.18. If you simply draw the two towers and schedule them, the schedule reports the values for the individual towers.

If you move the position of the towers so that they intersect, the schedule reports the same calculated values: Revit doesn't join the geometries and eliminate the overlapping areas automatically (Figure 8.19). If you place different masses that aren't joined but overlap, when using the Floor By Face tool, the intersecting portions of floor slabs overlap and cause duplicate area calculations. To resolve this issue, you need to join geometry.

To get the correct schedule that represents the actual volume, surface, and floor area values, use the Join The Geometry tool to join the two masses. Whichever mass you used first is the one that penetrates into the other mass. The schedule now reflects the values of the joined, merged geometries (Figure 8.20).

FIGURE 8.18
Unconnected mass
forms and their
schedule

Tower B

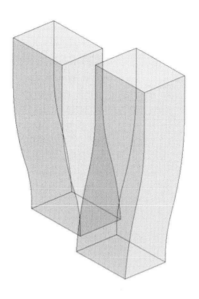

Tower A

Tower A   Tower B

Mass Schedule			
Family	Gross Floor	Gross Surfac	Gross Volume
Tower A		172052 m²	3915914.77 m³
Tower B		172052 m²	3915913.75 m³

FIGURE 8.19
Mass forms intersect
but are still not joined,
the schedule still re-
ports the sum of the
area and volume
(incorrect)

Tower A   Tower B

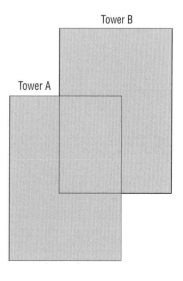

Tower B

Tower A

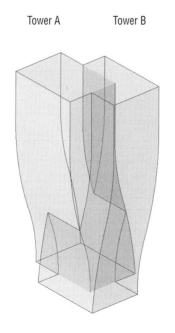

Mass Schedule			
Family	Gross Floor	Gross Surfac	Gross Volume
Tower A		172052 m²	3915914.77 m³
Tower B		172052 m²	3915913.75 m³

FIGURE 8.20
Mass forms joined.
The Schedule reports
correct surface and
volume.

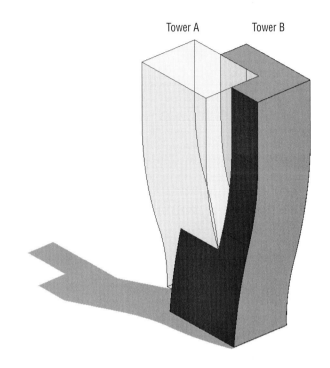

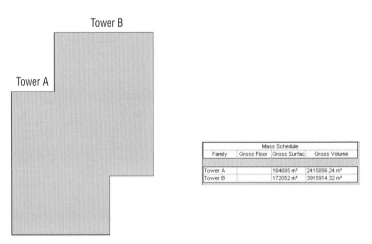

Joining the masses creates a relationship between the two masses. This means that if you move the location or edit the shape of one, the joined geometry automatically updates in a Boolean manner. Only in cases where you move one mass completely away from the other mass will you get an error message that the two masses don't intersect anymore and you need to use the Unjoin Geometry option to fix the error.

Once the masses have been joined, you can begin to apply elements by face (Figure 8.21).

Figure 8.21

Mass with applied
walls by face

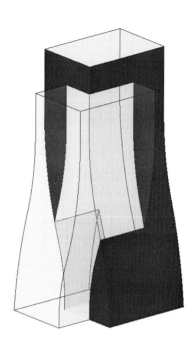

Using Imported Geometry from Other Applications for Massing

You can use various outside applications to create geometry to be imported into Revit for massing.
This section looks at using SketchUp, Rhino, and Inventor.

SketchUp

SketchUp is a fantastic piece of software. It's considered by many to be a beautiful concept modeling and visualization tool that is easy to use, produces great results, and really feels architectural.
Many architects adore SketchUp for conceptual studies or early images of design ideas. Revit users
use SketchUp to make initial massing and conceptual studies to produce nice graphic outputs for
their clients. They can then move the model into Revit for the documentation phase.

SketchUp files can be imported in either of two file formats, which are tied to different workflows and expectations:

- *SKP*—Use this format if you've created a complex geometric element in SketchUp that is
  pretty much final and you just need to import it into Revit using the direct import of the SKP
  file. An example is a building with a complex shape or roof that you couldn't easily do
  in Revit.

- *DWG*—If you expect a dynamic workflow where the models need to move back and forth
  and maintain some intelligence, use file linking and link in the DWG files. This way, if the
  DWG changes, the model will update to show the latest version of the DWG. Note: You can
  only leverage the linking functionality if you import the SketchUp model within the project
  environment. If you import it as a Mass, the reload link functionality will not work.

Here is how we suggest working with a SketchUp file:

1. In SketchUp, Make a quick and easy initial concept design like the one shown in Figure 8.22, and save it.

2. Before getting into too much detail, import the file into Revit (Figure 8.23). The best practice is to import it in a mass family by using the Create Mass tool in the Massing tab of the Design bar. Then, import the SKP file:

FIGURE 8.22
Massing created in
SketchUp

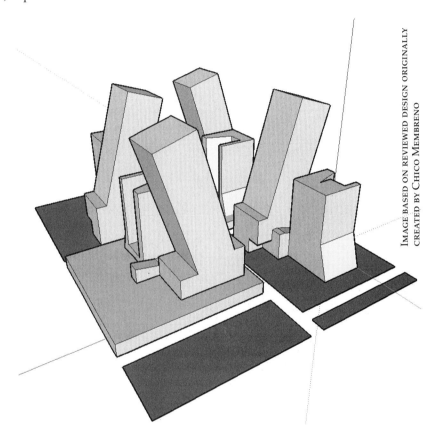

IMAGE BASED ON REVIEWED DESIGN ORIGINALLY
CREATED BY CHICO MEMBRENO

FIGURE 8.23
Import dialog

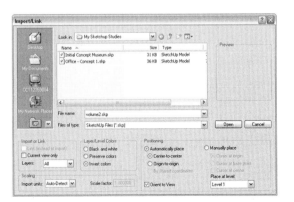

3. Finish the family.

4. Switch to 3D view, and switch the model graphics of the view to Shaded With Edges. The SketchUp model appears in Revit. You can also activate shadows to see the model better (Figure 8.24).

FIGURE 8.24
Imported SketchUp
file with shadows
turned on

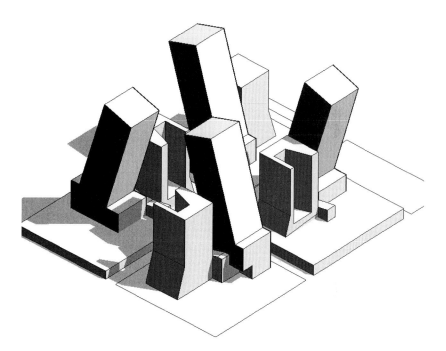

Often, when you finish the mass family after importing the SKP file, you'll get a Warning message:

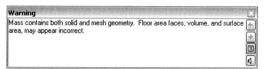

It's important to read this message in order to understand the future expectations for the import. If a mass family imports only non-volumetric geometry, you can't create floor area faces in Revit. However, if an imported mass family contains both volumetric and non-volumetric geometry, you'll be able to create floor area faces from the volumetric portions of the geometry.

When you're placing walls by pick face, the wall might be placed inside out. To flip the wall, select it, right-click, and choose Flip Orientation from the context menu.

RHINOCEROS

Rhinoceros is a neat application that many architects love for the powerful shapes it can create and its relative ease of use. The surfaces created by this modeler are NURBS surfaces. Revit doesn't natively create NURBS but can easily import them and transform them into a mesh.

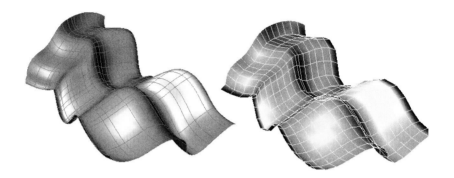

You can then use that mesh in a mass family as the basis for creating roofs. In this example, a draped form was created using Rhino and then imported into a Revit massing element (see Figure 8.25), just as you'd do with a SketchUp import. The form was then covered with a curtain system:

FIGURE 8.25
NURBS turned into curtain systems using the Curtain System by Face tool

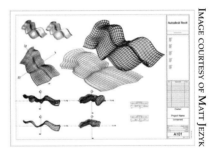

IMAGE COURTESY OF MATT JEZYK

To import an SAT file from Rhino into Revit, the best approach is to make a mass family in the project environment. When you're importing a mesh into the family, you get a message about calculation limitations:

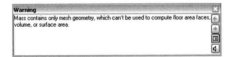

This can safely be ignored. Finish the family; then, from the Massing tab, select the Curtain System tool. You can select a different type from the Type Selector. Click the imported file geometry, and click the Create Roof tool on the Options bar.

The new object—a curtain system—is generated out of the underlying geometry (Figure 8.26). It's important to understand that glass panels don't conform to the surface—the panels remain planar and attempt to fit the surface as best they can. So, as the panel cell size gets smaller, deviance decreases. You can always change the type later, just as you can for any element in Revit. Once you're happy with the type and the size of the panels, you can apply mullions. Depending on the complexity of the imported file, this can take up to a few minutes; but don't worry, it's a one-time action! Note that tighter grids give better results but also increase the demand in performing processing.

FIGURE 8.26
You can apply a curtain system to a NURBS import.

You can import complex shapes created in Inventor and use them again to create faces out of which you can generate Revit building elements. The format in which you should export the Inventor file is SAT. Note that Inventor models have to be simplified prior to the export so to be optimal for use in Revit. If you use Inventor to easily create powerful shapes, then you should be OK. Save the file as an SAT file, and import it into a mass family either in the family editor or in the Project Environment just as you would a SketchUp or Rhino file.

Using Smart Relationship between Building Mass and the Underlying Mass

The idea behind attaching building elements to massing faces is that you can come back to the massing and make large gestural edits to the underlying form and have the walls, floors, and roofs update. In Revit, the update isn't automatic, but it's easy to keep in sync. When elements that are tied to a massing are selected, a Remake button appears on the Options bar. Clicking that button updates the element to match the current shape of the underlying mass form.

Figure 8.27 shows a series of elements updated.

FIGURE 8.27
A: Starting form;
B: Mass is made larger;
C: Wall is remade to
match the mass;
D: Roof and other
walls are remade to
match the mass

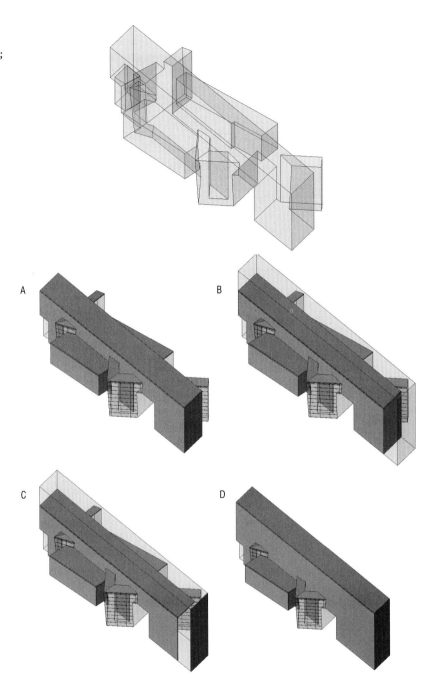

The Bottom Line

Leverage a massing study for program validation and early feasibility studies   You can use massing studies to validate a design against the program requirements.

Master It   Conceptual modeling is used early in the design process to explore building shape and program. How do you approach schematic design using Revit and perform feasibility studies?

Convert a mass into a building using the Building Maker tools   Moving from massing to actual building components is easily done with Revit.

Master It   You've got the basic massing nailed down, and now you need to study more details such as wall and window fenestrations. How do you approach this with Revit?

Import files from other sources when working on massing   You can make your own conceptual massing forms using standard Revit form-making tools or by importing geometry from other applications.

Master It   How can you reuse conceptual models created in other modeling applications and turn them into a measurable and documentable building in Revit?

Chapter 9

Working with Design Options

In this chapter, we'll explore how Revit supports workflows where multiple design options need to be explored, evaluated, and presented. This type of workflow is an integral part of developing a design solution. With Revit, design options can range in scale from entire façade studies down to kitchen layouts, all in the same integrated model.

You'll acquire the following skills in this chapter:

- ◆ Designing options work in Revit
- ◆ Creating new design options
- ◆ Presenting multiple design options
- ◆ Showing quantities and cost schedules for multiple options
- ◆ Consolidating your options and settling on a final solution

Revit Design Options

Revit provides a set of tools geared for developing multiple designs in the context of one project. These tools allow you to explore alternative designs without having to constantly save multiple independent versions of your model as you move in different directions. With Revit design options, you create, evaluate, and mock up a wide range of options in the context of your project file. You're free to mock up multiple roof configurations, entry canopies, furniture and office layouts, and stairs—anything that can be modeled. Figure 9.1 shows an example of the same model with two different entry canopies. Each canopy belongs to a separate design option that can be displayed or hidden in any view. This lets you create views that show each option so the two designs can be evaluated against one another.

FIGURE 9.1
Design options being used to explore alternative design solutions

Design options work in the following manner: You have a Main Model that includes all the elements you've modeled that are fixed and not affected by the options you want to explore. The Main Model can be thought of as a backdrop or stage on which different options play. Elements in the Main Model are always visible, whereas design options come and go—appearing and disappearing depending on what you're editing. The options could include different furnishing for the interior or different canopies over an entrance, and the Main Model includes everything else that's *not* in the option.

You can make as many options as you need—there is no limit. You can create views for each one and assign the view to show only specific options. You can then present them to a client, to the project architect, or to other stakeholders in the design process. Once a design option has been settled on, you take the option and accept it as the primary design solution going forward by adding it back to the Main Model. Doing so deletes all elements in the design options that aren't going forward.

Enabling Design Options

To enable design options, first make sure the Design Option group of tools is visible in the toolbar by right-clicking the toolbar and checking Design Options in the list. A new set of tools appears at upper right on the toolbar:

By default, only one button (Design Options) is enabled in a new file that has no design options. That button launches the Design Options dialog box, where you create and manage all the design options in a project. We'll cover the other buttons in the next few sections.

Enabling design options doesn't create anything at first—it simply sets up the work environment so you can begin making various designs using the feature.

Design-Option Sets

In Revit, every design option belongs to a *design-option set*, where a *set* is a way of structuring the design options into clusters to aid your workflow. For example, in a project you may have three design options for an exterior façade, two options for a bathroom configuration, and three options for room and furniture layout. Revit allows you to have several sets for each major type of option being explored. You may have a design-option set called Exterior Facades, one called Bathrooms, and another called Room Layout. In each set, you have two to three options for the design in question. This hierarchy is structured as a tree interface in the Design Options dialog box, as shown in Figure 9.2. Each option set is shown in a top-level node of the tree, and each design option is shown as a child of a set.

As you can see in the dialog in Figure 9.2, there is always a *primary* option in each set, designated by the "(primary)" suffix. This option is always visible by default in any view. You can change the primary option by selecting an option in the dialog and clicking the Make Primary button. In your views, the new primary option will then be visible by default, hiding the previously defined primary option.

When you reach a point in your design where you'd like to explore multiple design solutions, you're ready to start making option sets. Think about how you'd describe the option—Façade Studies, for example—and name your option set accordingly. Add at least two options to the set—more, if you think you'll be exploring more than two options. You don't have to define all the options in the beginning; you can always come back to the dialog and add/remove options if need be.

FIGURE 9.2
Design Options dialog showing some option sets and options

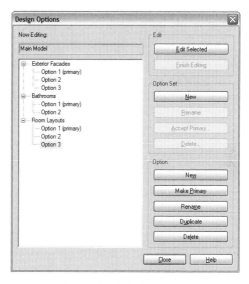

Creating new design option sets is straightforward. Click the New button, and a new set is created. To give the set a unique name, select it in the tree and click the Rename button. Adding new options follows the same pattern: Make a new one, and then give it a unique name.

You can delete sets and options at any time; doing so effectively deletes any elements added to a design variation you've made using that design option, so be wary of deleting before you're ready. The same effect is achieved when you click the Accept Primary button—all other options in that set are deleted.

Adding Elements to a Design Option

Once you've formally established design sets and design options, you can do a number of things depending on the scope of your options. You can add elements from the Main Model into each option to experiment with variations of the element—this is good if you want to explore different expressions of the same object without adding new elements. For example, if you want to show two roofs with the same footprint but different slopes, this method of adding the roof into each design option will work. Once the roof is added to each option, you edit the option and then edit the roof slope. The roof is essentially a copy and can be edited independently in each option (Figure 9.3).

Another way to work with options is to start editing the option directly, without first adding elements to the option. This approach works well if you have a design idea but don't want to add it to the Main Model just yet. When you begin editing an option, the Main Model grays out, and any new element you add is added to the active design option. For example, let's say you haven't yet designed the entry canopy for your model, and you want to experiment with some different ideas. Start editing the option, and you can then model whatever you want. The Main Model is still visible for reference, but it isn't editable.

FIGURE 9.3
Design options in the
same model

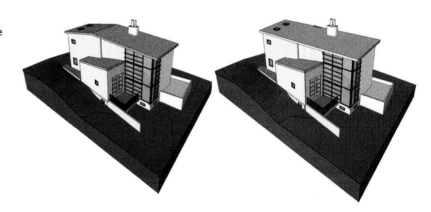

You can use both methods in combination as well. For example, you might add a wall from the Main Model to two options, and in each option add new, but different, window types to the wall. You'd use the Add To Design option-set button to put the wall into both options, and then you'd edit each option to add the new windows.

To add elements to an option, first select them, and then add them to the appropriate design options by clicking the Add To Design option-set button on the toolbar. Select only the elements you wish to make variations of—you don't need to add elements that you won't be editing. Once you click the Add To Design button, you're taken to a dialog that allows you to copy the elements into the desired design option(s). Again, this method is best if you know the elements will be essentially the same in each option and may vary only in type, material, or arrangement. Figure 9.4 shows the same walls in two options with different windows inserted, and using a different wall type to change material.

FIGURE 9.4
Add walls to multiple
options in order to
experiment with
different window
placements.

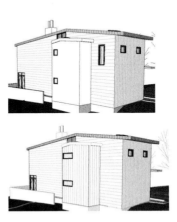

To edit a design option, click the Edit Option button, and choose an option to edit. You're taken to a special edit mode, and anything you create is added to the active design option automatically. Use this method if you're starting from a blank slate and laying out several options for furniture layout or exterior shading devices, like those shown in Figure 9.5.

FIGURE 9.5
Use this dialog to
choose the design
options into which
you want to add
elements.

When you're adding elements to design options, keep the following basic rules in mind:

◆ Host-based elements that cut the host (such as windows or doors) need to be included with the host when you make design options. Inserts are automatically copied with the host when you add hosts to design options. Using our example of a wall with a window in it, if you add the wall into a design option, the window is automatically added as well.

◆ By the same token, if you're editing an option and try to place a window or door into a wall that's not included in the option, you'll get a warning:

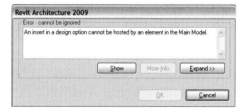

You need to add that wall to your design option if you want to place inserts in the wall. Host-based elements that *do not* cut their hosts *can* reside in different design options without the host. For example, a wall-hosted sink can reside in a different design option than the wall on which it's mounted (which resides in the Main Model), but a window that cuts a wall can't.

◆ When you're adding curtain walls from the Main Model to a design option, the grids, mullions, and panels are automatically added for you.

◆ When you're adding a roof to a design option, you should include all walls that attach to that roof. Otherwise, you won't be able to attach walls to the roofs in your design options.

◆ When you create groups or arrays within a design option, selected elements must be in the active option.

Once an element has been added to a design option, by default it's no longer selectable when you work on the Main Model. You can override this behavior by deselecting the Exclude Options check box on the Options bar.

Because the elements in a design option can't be selected from the Main Model, to edit elements, you'll need to use this feature or activate a design option. For example, if you add all your exterior walls to design options in the Exterior Facades option set, the walls won't highlight or be selectable unless you're editing the design option. If you add elements to a secondary option, they won't be visible by default in the Main Model.

Editing a Design Option

To start experimenting with design variations, you edit your design options. To do so, use the drop-down menu associated with the Edit Option button on the toolbar, and choose the option you want to edit (Figure 9.6).

FIGURE 9.6
Use the Edit Option button to access a drop-down list of available design options.

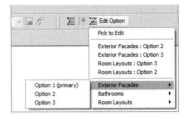

The Main Model grays out and becomes unselectable. This allows you to modify the elements in the design option without worrying that you'll mess up other parts of the model. Any element created while in the design option's edit mode is automatically added to the option. For example, if you're editing Option 2 of an Exterior Façade set, and you insert new windows in a wall in that option, the windows are added to the design option—they aren't added to the Main Model. Remember that the wall must be in the design option in order for you to place the window.

EDITING AN OPTION BY SELECTING AN ELEMENT

If you want to start editing an element in a design option directly, click the Edit Option button and choose the Pick To Edit option. Hover the mouse over the model, and elements in design options will highlight; you can then begin editing an element as soon as you click it. This shortcut lets you edit elements in a more direct manner and opens the desired option automatically.

Take the example of two views showing different roof options. In each view, to start editing the option, you choose Pick To Edit, select the roof, and start editing the roof—you don't have to think about the name of the option.

🌐 Real World Scenario

EXTERIOR SKINS

Using design options, we added the exterior skin of a building to two options in an option set. By creating a new wall type with different materials, we easily exchanged one wall type for another in each option. Once the wall types were swapped in each option, we duplicated the perspective view showing the exterior skin and changed it to show both options (spandrel glass o'n the left, wood on the right) using the Visibility/Graphic Overrides dialog. So that these northeast perspectives can be readily found in any list, we assigned the views meaningful names: Glass NE and Wood NE.

Displaying Design Options

To visualize different design options and have them represented in separate views that you can drop on a sheet, you create a new view that displays the desired option. To do this, right-click any view in the Project Browser, choose Duplicate, and give the view a name that indicates which design option it represents.

As you can see in Figure 9.7, once you've created option sets and design options, a new Design Options tab appears in the Visibility/Graphic Overrides dialog. The default visibility setting is Automatic, which shows the primary option and the Main Model. Using the drop-down menu under Design Option, you can override this setting and show any of your other options.

FIGURE 9.7
By default, views are set to show the primary design options and the Main Model.

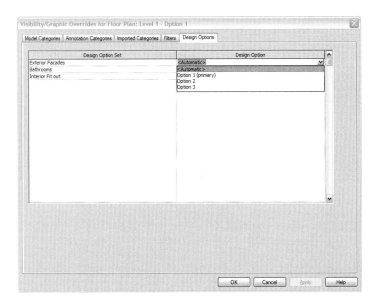

In Figure 9.8, three options are shown for a building façade: Option 1 has no canopy over the third-floor deck, Option 2 has a solid canopy, and Option 3 has a louvered canopy. All three options exist in the same model and can be visualized next to one another by duplicating the view and changing the Visibility value of the design option.

Deciding on a Final Design Solution

When you've decided which option to build, with one click you can make the chosen option become a part of the Main Model and get rid of the rest. First, decide which option you intend to keep, and designate it as the primary option by clicking the Make Primary button in the Design Options dialog. Then, select the option set, and click the Accept Primary button. Doing so brings up a confirmation dialog asking if you're sure you want to do this (Figure 9.9). As the message suggests, if you proceed, *all* secondary options will be deleted, and whatever is in the primary option will be pushed into the Main Model. (Make sure you're ready to implement the decision!) The elements will again become selectable without your having to edit a design option. This approach is recommended if you've made a definite design decision and intend to move forward with that decision. Keeping unused and out-of-date options in the project needlessly inflates the file size and adds unwanted complexity.

FIGURE 9.8

By duplicating views and changing the default design option visibility, it's easy to compare options and even place the views on sheets for printing.

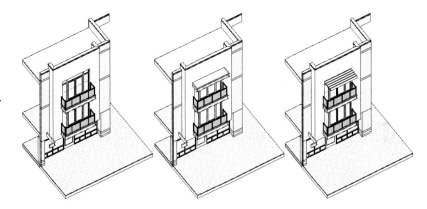

FIGURE 9.9

To add an option back to the Main Model, click the Accept Primary button in the Design Options dialog.

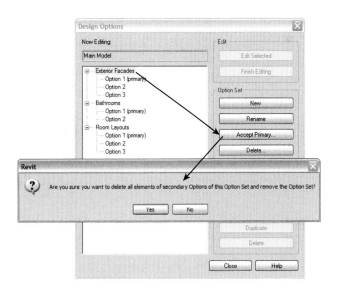

You're also asked to delete any views that were set up to display options that you're deleting (Figure 9.10).

FIGURE 9.10
You're prompted to delete views associated with options you're deleting.

Click Delete to continue, and the views will be removed from your project. You can't keep any views that were set to show secondary options that no longer exist.

Putting Design Options into Practice

In the following exercise, you'll make three different office layouts, shown in Figure 9.11, using design options. Option 1 is a hybrid design of open space and closed offices, Option 2 is an open office with cubicles, and Option 3 has only enclosed offices. Once created, all the options will exist in one file and can be separately displayed in different views and dropped on one sheet for comparison. Follow these steps:

FIGURE 9.11
The three office layouts you'll create as design options

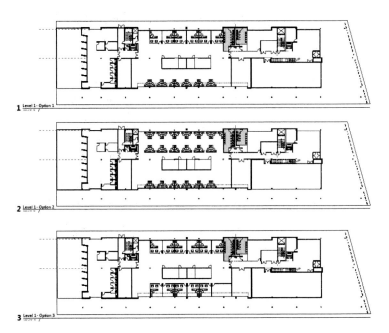

1. Open the Foundation model in the chapter 9 folder of the book's website (www.sybex.com/go/masteringrevit2008).

2. Open the Level 1 Presentation plan view.

3. Enable design options.

4. Create a new option set called **Interior Fitout**.

5. Create three options, and set Option 1 to be primary by clicking the Make Primary button, as shown in Figure 9.12 (this should be set by default).

6. Close the dialog.

7. Choose to edit Option 1, using the Edit Option drop-down menu.

8. While editing Option 1, place a series of workstation families (workstation.rfa), interior partitions, and offices, as shown in Figure 9.13.

FIGURE 9.12
Add a design option set and three design options.

FIGURE 9.13
Add a series of workstations to design Option 1.

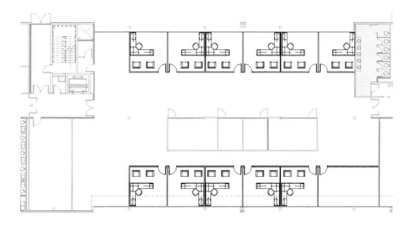

9. Finish editing the options by clicking the Edit Option button.

10. Choose Option 2 from the Edit Option drop-down menu.

11. Create the open floor plan shown in Figure 9.14. To speed up the process, you can choose Edit Option 1, copy the row of cubicle desks to the Clipboard, choose Edit Option 2, and paste them in using Edit ➤ Paste Aligned ➤ Same Place. Don't be thrown off by Same Place; this pastes the workstations only into the active design option.

FIGURE 9.14
Add cubicles to Option 2.

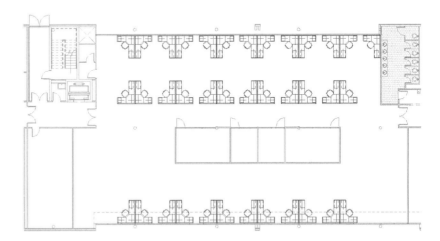

12. When you're finished, click Edit Option to return to the Main Model.

The elements in Option 2 disappear from the view. The primary option (Option 1) is set to be visible by default, and as mentioned earlier, you can't view more than one option per view.

13. To make a third option that has enclosed offices and no cubicles, choose to Edit Option 1, select all the offices in the top half of the space, and copy them to the Clipboard using Ctrl+C.

14. Choose Option 3 from the Edit Option drop-down menu.

15. Choose Edit ➤ Paste Aligned ➤ Same Place (Figure 9.15).

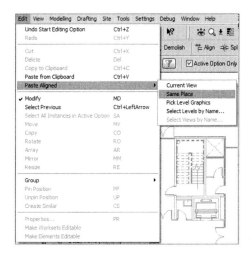

The workstations are copied into Option 3.

16. Continue to fill the space with offices, as shown in Figure 9.16. You can use the Mirror command to speed up the process.

FIGURE 9.16
Design Option 3
contains offices.

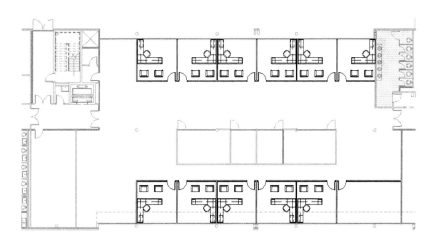

Next, you need to place each option on a sheet so you can show the options to your client and get feedback about the different layout options. Follow these steps:

1. Duplicate the plan view, and rename it **Level 1 - Option 1**.

2. Duplicate the view two more times, and give each view a unique name: **Level 1 - Option 2**, and **Level 1 - Option 3**.

3. In Level 1 - Option 3, open the Visibility/Graphic Overrides dialog, and go to the Design Options tab. Change the Design Option value from Automatic to Option 3.

4. Open Level 1- Option 2, and repeat step 3; but make sure Design Option is set to Option 2.

5. Create a new sheet view, and drag each of the plans onto the sheet, as shown in Figure 9.17.

6. You're now ready to present your alternatives.

FIGURE 9.17
All three options can be placed on a sheet by duplicating the plan views and adjusting the settings in the Visibility/Graphic Overrides dialog.

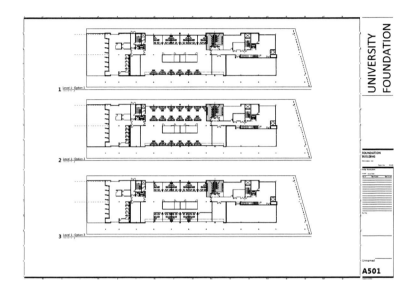

Showing Quantities and Cost Schedules for Multiple Options

Schedule/Quantities... You can compare design options and discuss with your client cost versus features desired, contrasting the cost of options using schedules. A schedule, like a view, can be tailored to show specific design options. To create a schedule of elements in a design option, first click the Schedule/Quantities tool from the View tab in the Design bar to make a new schedule. Choose the category you'd like to schedule, and the appropriate parameters. The properties of the schedule include a parameter for Visibility/Graphics Overrides (Figure 9.18). Clicking the Edit button brings you to the Design Options tab (in this case, the only tab in the dialog), where you can choose a design option to schedule. Only elements belonging to the selected category in the selected design option are included in the schedule.

FIGURE 9.18
From the schedule's
properties, you can
access the Visibility/
Graphic Overrides
dialog and change the
design option.

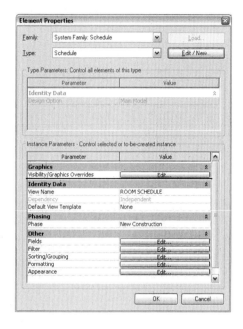

FIGURE 9.18
From the schedule's properties, you can access the Visibility/Graphic Overrides dialog and change the design option.

Working with Rooms and Design Options

You can create rooms in design options to compare areas and create color schemes for various options. For example, you can create two office layouts with different sizes and number of offices in each option and then add rooms to the offices. You can then create views of each option that are color-coded to provide a nice visual comparison. To get a feel for how this works, consider this simple example.

Start with a corridor and rooms on either side. You need to create two design options that show different room configurations. Follow these steps:

1. Draw a simple layout of walls, as shown here in plan view.

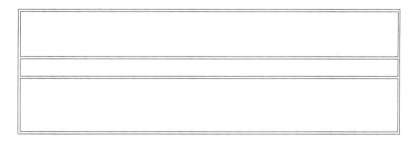

2. Open the Design Options dialog, and create an option set named **Office Configurations**. Add two design options to the set, as shown in Figure 9.19.

FIGURE 9.19
Adding the design options

3. Back in the plan view, duplicate the view from the Project Browser. Name the view **Level 1 Plan View - Option 2**. In the Visibility/Graphic Overrides dialog, go to the Options tab and set Option to Option 2.

4. Go back to your original view, and change the Options Visibility/Graphic setting to Option 1.

5. In the Option 1 plan view, choose to edit the option. Draw walls to create 12 offices:

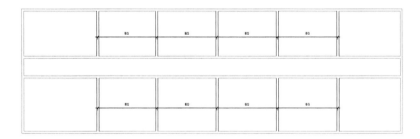

6. Add rooms to each office using the Room tool on the Basics tab of the Design Bar.

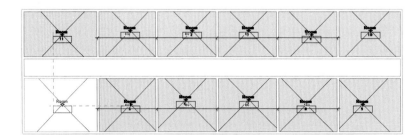

These rooms are added to the primary option.

7. Open Plan View - Option 2, and click to edit Option 2 from the toolbar. Place walls so that you make 10 offices rather than 12, and place rooms in each office space:

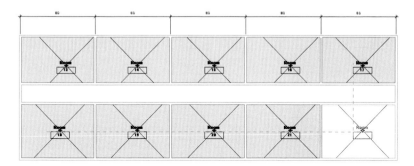

As you can see, Revit allow you to create two independent room layouts in the same model!

8. To create a schedule of the rooms in each option, select the Visibility/Graphics Overrides parameter in the Element Properties of the room schedule, and set the design option to the desired option (Figure 9.20).

FIGURE 9.20
Displaying the rooms in the schedule's design options

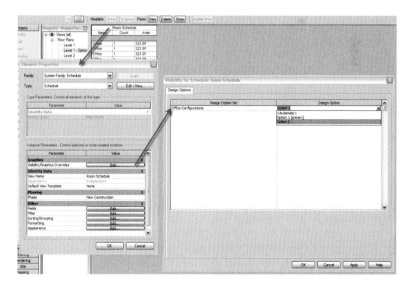

9. Make a schedule for each design option showing rooms, areas, and count. You can then place each schedule and plan view on a sheet for comparison (Figure 9.21).

FIGURE 9.21
The design options in schedule form

Room Schedule - Option 1		
Name	Count	Area
Office	1	254 SF
Office	1	254 SF
Office	1	254 SF
Office	1	254 SF
Office	1	299 SF
Office	1	299 SF
Office	1	299 SF
Office	1	299 SF
Office	1	316 SF
Office	1	267 SF
Office	1	323 SF
Office	1	381 SF
Grand total: 12		

Room Schedule - Option 2		
Name	Count	Area
Office	1	323 SF
Office	1	323 SF
Office	1	323 SF
Office	1	323 SF
Office	1	323 SF
Office	1	381 SF
Office	1	381 SF
Office	1	381 SF
Office	1	381 SF
Office	1	381 SF
Grand total: 10		

The Bottom Line

If you need to explore alternate design ideas in your model, try using design options. Doing so will save you from having to try to merge information downstream if you tend to make separate files for each design. Rather than going through a laborious copy-paste workflow and maintaining two or three models in separate files, you can use design options applied to the one and only model of your building and thus streamline your workflow. Just keep in mind that you're working with a 3D parametric model that creates lots of relationships between elements. Often, editing a floor or roof also involves editing walls that are attached to that roof, even if you aren't burdened with having to make the edits manually.

Understanding how design options work in Revit   Design options provide a means to maintain two or more alternative designs for the same project or component.

Master It   What are design options in Revit?

Creating new design options   Learning to add new options to a set is crucial to getting the most out of this tool.

Master It   Your client has asked you to explore an $8´ \times 8´$ seating arrangement option in their office space. It's currently designed for $8´ \times 10´$ and $6´ \times 8´$ options. Add a new design option to explore the new scheme.

Presenting multiple design options   Presenting multiple options makes it possible for your client and other project stakeholders to explore the alternatives.

Master It   You need to show a client five different design solutions for the new main entrance to the project you're working on.

Showing quantities and cost schedules for multiple options   Making quantitative differences visible is an essential part of presenting multiple alternatives.

> **Master It**   You need to look at some seating layout options for an auditorium space based on different-sized seating and show the seating counts.

Consolidating your options and settling on a final solution   The end result of exploring multiple options is to choose one alternative and implement that choice.

> **Master It**   You've explored a number of design options for an entry scheme. Your client has selected one, and you need to incorporate it into the rest of the model and remove the unwanted alternates.

Chapter 10

Creating Custom 3D Content

In this chapter, we'll explore how to build custom model elements for use in a project. We'll look at how parametric constraints and parameters can be used to build flexible and time-saving content. Building intelligent content is a key feature of Revit and deserves an entire book in its own right, but we will introduce you to some useful concepts and get you going. This chapter will take you through fundamental principles and some compelling use cases using the family editor.

You'll acquire the following skills in this chapter:

- ◆ Understanding the different types of families and their application
- ◆ Leveraging nested families for efficiency and flexibility
- ◆ Building relationships between parameters with formulas

Modeling Parametric 3D Families

As a design progresses from the generic to the more refined, you'll need to add more detail and realism to your components. This process involves more faithfully representing what will be built and will require you to start building your own families. Although many types of families are provided out of the box or can be downloaded from websites such as the Revit web library or revitcity.com, you'll inevitably reach a point where your design intent isn't matched by existing content (Figure 10.1). This is when you'll need to dig into the Family Editor and create new building components.

FIGURE 10.1
This sun-shading element was implemented as a custom Revit family.

Up to now, we've covered many of the basic principles of families, including family categories, form making, and constraints; but we haven't put this into practice beyond some simple shapes. In the following sections, we'll look at more advanced techniques used to make parametric families with embedded intelligent behaviors.

Choosing the Right Family Template

Every family belongs to a category, making it important to assign new families correctly so they can be controlled logically when loaded into a project. Revit provides a series of pre-made templates (Figure 10.2) for most families.

FIGURE 10.2
Premade model family templates

When you decide to create an element on your own you need to select the correct template. These premade templates are time savers, because they already have the right category assigned, provide the most important reference planes that drive the behavior and geometry, and in some cases include text notes to help explain how the family will work in the context of a project. Figure 10.3 shows a window template file, which includes text indicating the exterior/interior of the wall; parametric dimensions for width, sill height, and opening height; and a sample host wall.

The reference planes that appear in the family environment are the essential bones of any family. They establish the critical dimensional rules for the family, define the origin, and provide references that can be dimensioned to. All starting templates provide at least two reference planes to start with, because without reference planes, you can't make parametric content or dimension it in the project.

Types of Families

For model-based families, there are two high-level types: 2D and 3D. 2D families are used for making 2D details of the model, and 3D families are for making 3D geometric representations. Note that 3D families can contain nested 2D elements as a way to embed details directly into content.

For 2D families, you can make standard detail components and line-based (2-pick) detail components. 3D family types include various host-based types (floor, wall, roof, and ceiling), profiles, line based, work-plane based, and generic model. Depending on which template you use, you'll get different behavior in the model. To better understand what that means, let's drill deeper.

FIGURE 10.3

Plan, elevation, and 3D view of a template for windows. Text notes, reference planes, and dimensions have been preset.

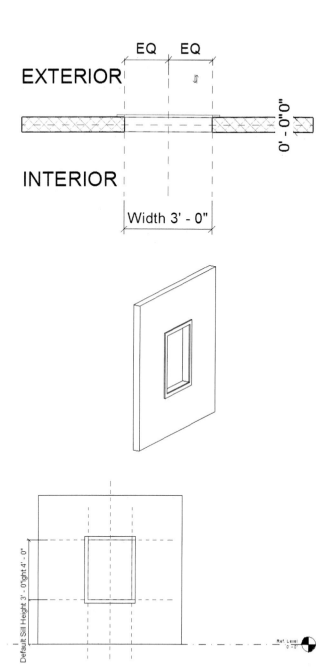

Host-Based Families

Windows, doors, skylights, and lighting fixtures are all discretely manufactured objects, but they have something in common: They're installed into something else. Without the wall, ceiling, or mounting surface, the object has no place to ground itself in a typical building project. For these types of elements, Revit provides host-based families and templates. When you need content to have an explicit relationship with a wall, floor, or roof, then a host-based family is absolutely the way to go. These are the most common types of families used in Revit, and include components such as doors, windows, skylights, solar panels, light fixtures, and balusters. Assuming you've placed some windows and doors in a Revit project, the benefits and behaviors of host-based families need not be covered here. Figure 10.4 shows several examples.

FIGURE 10.4
Examples of host-based families

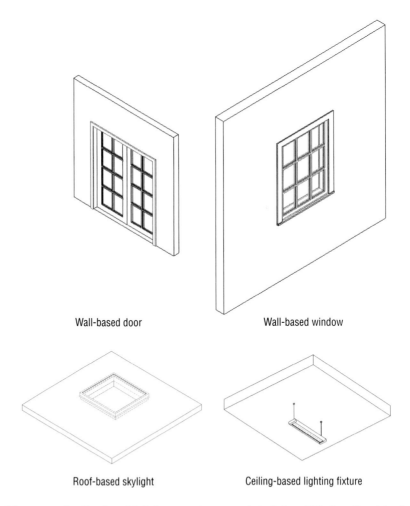

Wall-based door   Wall-based window

Roof-based skylight   Ceiling-based lighting fixture

When you're making a new family, first think from a category point of view: What am I making? Then, use an appropriate template as a starting point. For example, if you need to make a new window, start with the Window.rft template.

Windows and doors don't exist in the model in isolated, abstract form, but are always hosted by a wall. This is why you see a sample host element (a small wall, roof, or floor) when you open a host-based template. The sample host is used to help you construct the family so it behaves properly in the model—to give you a context in order to build the family so it correctly relates to wall thickness.

Note that the host that exists in the family template (such as the wall in the window template) isn't loaded in the project when you load the window—it's present in the Family Editor only as a reference to help you understand how the window will work when loaded into a project. Only the geometry and reference planes that you create end up in your project.

Profile Families

Many architectural details have distinct cross sections that run in a linear fashion. Geometrically, these details are constructed by extruding that profile along a path, which maps to how many of the elements are physically manufactured. Baseboards, cornices, handrails, and mullions are all examples:

Revit provides special templates designed for elements like these. To create one of these elements, you choose to make a profile family. Then, sketching with 2D lines, you define the shape of the profile cross section. Like many sketches in Revit, the profile must be made of *a single closed loop* of lines—multiple loops will lead to errors downstream. For example, if you loaded a mullion profile like that shown in Figure 10.5 and then tried to use it in a mullion family, you'd get a warning message. Delete the inner loop of lines to get the mullion to work properly.

FIGURE 10.5
Invalid profile:
Profiles with more
than one loop won't
work in a project.

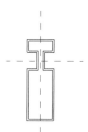

How do you make something like the shape shown in Figure 10.5? Although you can't have multiple loops in the profile family, you can import a detail component into the profile family, as there is no penalty for having multiple loops of lines in the detail component. To control when this level of detail is visible in the model, you can set the visibility of the detail component so it appears only at fine levels of detail. Continuing with the mullion example (Figure 10.6), take these steps:

1. Load a complex detail component derived from a manufacturer into the mullion profile family.

2. Trace the loaded component with a single loop of lines.

3. Set the options in the "Family element visibility settings" dialog to show the detail only in fine views.

FIGURE 10.6
On the left is the profile sketch, on the right a detail component.

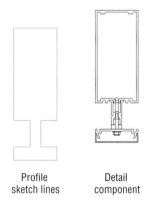

Profile
sketch lines

Detail
component

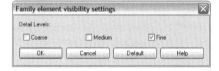

4. Load the family into the project.

5. From the Project Browser, locate the rectangular mullion profile and duplicate it. Open the Type Properties dialog, and assign the new profile to the mullion family (Figure 10.7).

FIGURE 10.7
Choose the profile from the mullion's Type Properties.

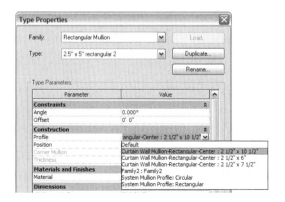

Once a profile is loaded into Revit, it doesn't take 3D form until it's assigned to system families such as rails, mullions, wall sweeps, and gutters. To do this, open the Type Properties dialog of any of these families and assign the profile to the family. You can use a 2D profile in the definition of a wall as a precast parapet cap, as shown in Figure 10.8.

FIGURE 10.8

Assigning a profile to a system family

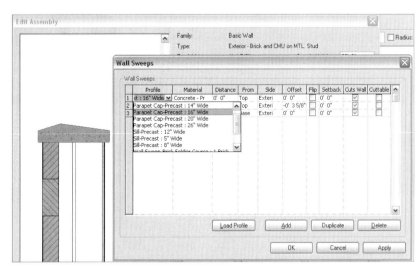

Many companies that sell finish moulding provide 2D CAD drawings that you can import directly into a Revit profile family. This is a great time saver and will keep you from having to draw complex profiles from scratch.

Profiles can be used for many different purposes. To accommodate more specific behavior as well as categorization, five different profile family templates are available: `Profile.rft`, `Profile-Rail.rft`, `Profile-Reveal.rft`, `Profile-Stair Nosing.rft`, and `Wall Sweep Profile.rft`. Be careful to select the correct one, because Revit looks only for specific profiles depending on what you're making. For example, a mullion family won't let you choose a wall-sweep profile; only mullion profiles will show up in the list.

2D Line-Based Families

Not all elements need to be modeled in 3D; some are represented using 2D detail drawings. Most details can be drawn using lines and filled regions, but these are inherently difficult to maintain and reuse. For details that are likely to be used in other drawings or projects, you should create detail families. With Revit, you can make stand-alone detail components or line-based families. The line-based family is great for making elements where length is the primary variable.

The 2D line-based template (`Detail Component line based.rft`) can be useful. These families let you draw a detail element as if you're drawing lines, but the component can contain as many lines and filled regions as you want. For example, you can draw a detail component that represents plywood (lines + wood hatch) with two clicks of the mouse.

3D Line-Based Families

Just like the 2D drafting line-based families, you can make 3D line-based families. For these families, use the template `Generic Model line based.rft`. Examples where you need such 3D line-based

MAKING A PLYWOOD LINE-BASED FAMILY

To make a plywood line-based detail, you can use the line-based detail template. In the line-based family template, you create a filled region between the left and right reference planes and assign a plywood fill pattern to the region. As long as the left and right lines of the filled region are coincident with the reference planes, they will follow the planes when the family is placed in a project, and drawn. The cross-sectional dimension of the filled region can be driven by a Thickness parameter, which is set to ¾″ and can later be modified if you need new types:

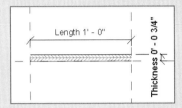

When the plywood family is loaded into the project, you can make a symbolic 2D plywood representation with two clicks that define the length. Once you've placed the plywood, you can reselect it and drag either end using the blue grips to stretch the detail. Compared to using a filled region in the project, this method provides parametric constraints, reusability, and incredible ease of use.

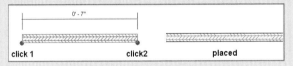

families are molding details, sun shades, grating, and any other elements that have length as their primary variable. Figure 10.9 shows a 3D chair family that adds chairs as the family is made longer.

FIGURE 10.9
3D line-based chair family

With two clicks of the mouse, you can quickly add rich 3D content to your model. Figure 10.10 shows a sun-shade example. The brackets at the left and right side were modeled in the family using solid extrusions and constrained to the left and right reference planes. The blades were modeled as sweeps between the two horizontal reference planes, using a profile. When placed in the model, the sun shade can be stretched dynamically.

FIGURE 10.10
3D line-based
sun shade family

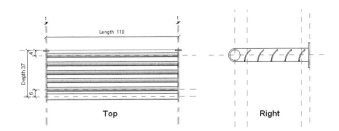

Work Plane– and Face-Based Families

For elements that need the flexibility to be placed on any model face, such as electrical outlets, signage, or coffee pots, there are work plane– and face-based families. These families attach to any surface of the model during placement; you can later rehost them to any other surface if need be. Any time you have a component that needs to be installed on multiple types of hosts, think of making the family face based.

FACE-BASED FAMILIES

You create face-based families with the template `Generic Model face based.rft`. When you open the template, you see an abstract host surface on which you can model your family. When you load your family into your project, the host surface in the family maps to whatever face you choose in the project, and your family reorients to sit on that face automatically. The face you choose can be anything from another family to geometry of a linked file. An example of a face-based family is an HVAC supply register, which you need to be able to place on walls, ceilings, or even floors. Figure 10.11 shows another application of a face-based component, where the curved surface doesn't have a work plane.

FIGURE 10.11
A sign is an example of
a face-based family.

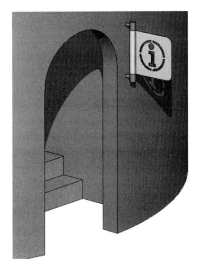

WORK PLANE–BASED FAMILIES

Work plane–based families are placed on the active work plane of the current view. Every view has an active work plane that you can manipulate using the Work Plane tool; see Chapter 6.

Be sure to give the family an appropriate category before loading it so you can control its visibility and graphics.

Rich Photorealistic Content (RPC) Families

When you're rendering a view, it's possible to substitute real model geometry (the family) for highly photorealistic images (such as Archvision content, available at http://www.archvision.com/). For example, a simplified stick figure can turn into a real-looking person when the view is rendered (Figure 10.12).

FIGURE 10.12
Left: Entourage family, non-rendered. Right: Same family when rendered

This can be a cool feature when you're rendering, and it makes rendering faster because there is no complex geometry to render. You can create plants, cars, and people using these families.

ASSIGNING A RENDERING APPEARANCE

RPC families are specialized and have specific behavior when rendered. In addition to the 3D and 2D representation that you normally add to a family, you can also assign a rendering appearance to the family. This appearance shows up only when you raytrace a 3D view.

You create RPC families using the template RPC Family.rft. RPC appearances can only be added to the Entourage and Planting families. When the family is set to either of these categories, a Rendering Type parameter is enabled in the Settings ➤ Family Category and Parameters dialog. RPC families in these categories have additional type parameters (located in the Family Types dialog; see Figure 10.13) to control the associated RPC file used when the family is rendered in a project, along with specific properties. In Figure 10.14, RPC properties of a car allow you to specify the license plate and window tinting!

FIGURE 10.13
RPC parameters in the Family Types dialog

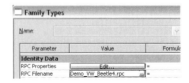

FIGURE 10.14
RPC Properties dialog
for a car family

Detail Component Families

As you'll see in Chapters 17 and 18, a typical workflow to complete a Construction Document set involves enriching the model with 2D details in detail views. These detail elements typically depict cross sections or elevation views of elements that don't need to be modeled in full 3D (to do so would only bog down the model and not add much value). For this use case, you can use detail-component families to add detail to model or drafting views; these details are visible only in the view in which they're placed. Examples include blocking, studs, steel sections, bolts, flashing, and so on:

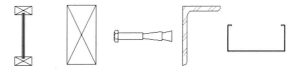

Detail components can contain lines, filled regions, masking regions, symbols, and other detail components. Detail components are meant to represent real building components and assemblies, so they scale with the model when the view scale is changed. To create a new detail component family, use `Detail Component line based.rft` or `Detail Component.rft`.

Generic 3D Families

If you can't find templates for element types, use generic families. These don't relate to any specific host but are rather used for free-standing components. Generic families allow you to create content such as fireplaces or other hard-to-categorize objects. These families have a relationship to the level in which they're placed but are otherwise free to move around the model and aren't connected to any host objects.

Many generic templates have been pre-made for you with the appropriate category selected. Examples include `Furniture.rft`, `Furniture Systems.rft`, `Mechanical Equipment.rft`, and `Plumbing fixture.rft`, to name a few.

Curtain Panel Families

Curtain walls and aluminum storefront systems are composed of mullions, glazing panels, operable windows, and doorways. In Revit, the Curtain Wall tool organizes all these components into an integrated system of parts. For panels, the default solid and glazed options are usually sufficient. Adding doors and windows to a curtain wall requires you to make custom panels in the Family Editor. Figure 10.15 shows a curtain-wall door family in the Family Editor—you'll notice that these templates don't contain host walls as other door-family templates do.

FIGURE 10.15
Double-panel curtain-wall door

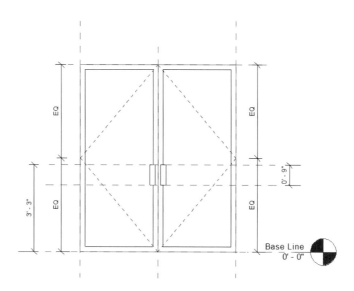

Keep this in mind: To add doors to a curtain wall, you must use one of the special curtain-wall doors—you can't place a standard door into a curtain wall. Use the Door - Curtain Wall.rft template to create these families. Essentially, they're like regular door families, but the width and height are dynamically tied to the size of the curtain-wall cell in which the door is placed. As the curtain-grid spacing changes, so does the size of doors placed in the wall. As you can see in Figure 10.16, the door family adapts to the size of the curtain-grid spacing.

FIGURE 10.16
Curtain-wall door

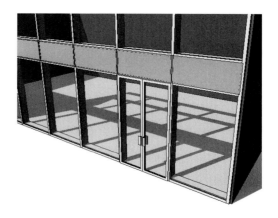

Family Categories and Parameters

In every Revit family, settings control specific behavior of the family and set the category. Depending on what category you assign the family, you can get a different set of type parameters and category-based parameters. For example, in a window family template, preset parameters for Sill height, Width, and Height are hard-coded into the family (Figure 10.17). In a furniture family template, you don't see these parameters.

FIGURE 10.17
Premade family parameters for windows

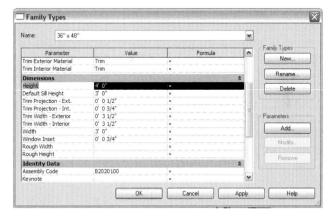

Another set of parameters affects the entire family based on the category it belongs to. You can access these settings by choosing Settings ➤ Family Category and Parameters. In the resulting dialog (Figure 10.18), you can set the category and also adjust some other parameters that affect how the family will behave when placed in a model.

FIGURE 10.18
Family Category and Parameters dialog

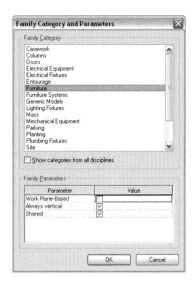

In the figure, the Furniture category has three family parameters listed: Work Plane–Based, Always Vertical, and Shared. Remember that changing the active category at the top of the dialog may enable or remove family parameters displayed in the bottom of the dialog. Let's briefly review what these parameters do:

Work Plane–Based Enabling this option allows the family to be hosted by the active work plane when placed in the project or nested into another family. Any nonhosted family can be set to be work plane–based. Any family using the generic template (furniture, site, casework, and so on) can be set to work plane–based, as such families aren't required to be hosted by another component (like doors or windows).

Always Vertical This parameter keeps a family oriented in the positive z direction when placed in a project. In most cases this is desired, because levels are always horizontal. But when you have sloped floors or sloped site conditions, you may want the component to be oriented perpendicular to the surface it's placed on. Parking stripes and cars placed on a sloped slab of a parking structure are examples where making the family *not* always vertical makes sense (Figure 10.19).

FIGURE 10.19
Family set to not be
always vertical

As another example, the Always Vertical parameter comes into play with trees placed on a topo-surface. As the site changes slope, you want to keep the trees vertical and not have them look like they're falling over.

Shared This parameter controls the visibility in a project of a family that is nested in another family component. You may choose to nest families to create assemblies or save time modeling components that repeat. Nesting has implications when you need to tag or schedule the family. For example, consider a window assembly with a main light and two side lights, one on each side. If the design intent is that the window is to be tagged and scheduled as a unit, then the families will be nested into a host family and the Shared parameter will remain unchecked. In this situation, only the host family (the family containing all nested windows) will schedule. If the intent is that the assembly is constructed from separately purchased units and assembled on site, then the nested families should have the Shared parameter checked. This will allow each nested window to appear on the schedule as if placed separately.

Rendering Type This parameter is enabled only for families set to the Entourage or Planting category. For Entourage, you can set the Rendering Type parameter to Geometrical or Archvision RPC. If you set the value to Archvision RPC, Revit adds the RPC Filename parameter to the Family Types dialog. You can then select the desired RPC filename for each type. For Planting, you can set the Rendering Type parameter to Geometrical, Accurender Procedural Plants, or Archvision RPC. If you set the value to Accurender Procedural Plants, then Revit enables type parameters to control the Accurender plant-material definitions used to render the family. If you set the value to Archvision RPC, Revit adds the RPC filename parameter to the Family Types dialog. You can then select the desired RPC filename for each type. When you render the family, Revit Architecture uses that RPC content and ignores the family geometry. If you set the Rendering Type parameter to Geometrical, Revit renders the actual family geometry regardless of the category.

Smart Workflow: Nesting One Family into Another

When you open a family in the Family Editor, you can load another family and place instances of it into your host family much as you would do in a project. This powerful feature allows you to manage your content and reuse existing work. For example, consider the workstation family illustrated in Figure 10.20.

FIGURE 10.20
Nested families used to create a workstation

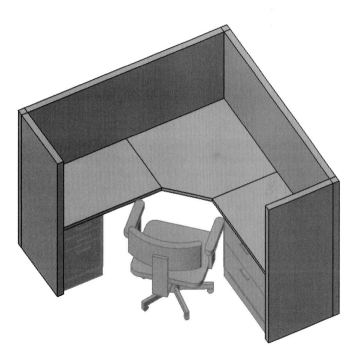

This family is composed of loaded filing cabinets, a desk top, partitions, and a chair. This makes building the family much more manageable and also makes it much easier to place and manipulate the family as a unit when placed in a project.

One common example of family nesting is the combination window. Rather than model the entire unit from scratch, you can load and insert existing window components into a base window family. You place the windows just as you would in a project. For example, you can place a fixed-window family in the center and two double-hung windows on either side (Figure 10.21). You can then save the family and load it into a project. The entire assembly acts as one element when placed in the model.

FIGURE 10.21
One family, created
from two nested
families

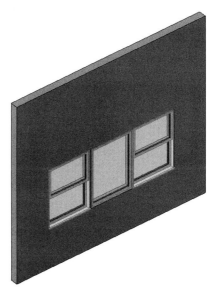

Choosing to use nested families not only saves modeling time but can also simplify your work in the Family Editor. It's often easier to manipulate and constrain an assembly of extrusions as a nested family than to model the same geometry in the host family. In another example, a bracket for a sunshade is modeled separately and nested into the host sunshade family (Figure 10.22). Two instances of the bracket can now be placed and constrained in the family much more easily than modeling the same elements as separate extrusions. Later in the chapter, we'll review some powerful features that you can use via family nesting.

FIGURE 10.22
Nesting a bracket into
a Sun Shade family
(host)

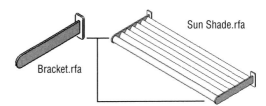

Sun Shade.rfa

Bracket.rfa

Scheduling Nested Families

When a family is nested in another family, by default it doesn't appear in project schedules and isn't taggable. For the most part, this is the desired behavior, because it avoids overburdening your schedules with unneeded subassembly elements. A nested family's geometry displays but is treated as part of the host family.

In some cases, you may want to schedule nested families: for example, if you've nested chairs within a table family. To expose nested families to tagging and scheduling, you need to enable a parameter called Shared. To do so, follow these steps:

1. Open the nested family.

2. Choose Settings ➤ Family Categories.

3. Select the Shared option in the Family Parameters group.

4. Reload the family into all its host families, and then reload those host families into your project.

Once all your nested families have Sharing enabled, they will be schedulable and can also be tagged in your project.

Linking Parameters

When families are nested, the parameters of the nested family *aren't visible in your project* by default. Only the parameters of the host family are visible. If the element you're nesting is unlikely to change parametrically, this may be desirable. However, if you want to control the element's parameters, you must explicitly link them to parameters in the host family.

In our example, the support bracket is a nested family, and you need to be able to drive its dimension from the context of the project. Let's look at how you do that:

1. In the host family, select an instance of a nested family, and go to its Type Properties dialog.

2. To the far right of the Value field, click the button to open the Associate Family Parameter dialog.

3. The parameters *in the host family* are listed. Select one that you want the nested family to be constrained to.

   Doing so ties the nested family to a parameter of the host family. Only parameters of the same type can be associated with one another. (Types include Text, Integer, Number, Length, Area, Volume, Angle, URL, Material, Yes/No, and <Family Type>.) For example, two lengths can be associated with each other, or two material parameters can be associated, but a length and a material parameter can't.

4. Click OK. Once the link is made, the small button in the Type Properties dialog displays an equal sign.

In Figure 10.23, the depth of the nested bracket family is associated with the depth of the host Sun Shade family. Changing the Depth parameter of the sun shade causes the depth of all support brackets to also change to the same value:

FIGURE 10.23
Linking a parameter in a nested family to the host

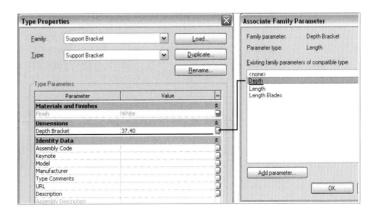

You can link any kind of parameter, from dimensions to materials to textual data. For example, the Sun Shade family has two material parameters: Material Supports and Material Blades. By selecting one of the nested brackets and going to its Type Properties dialog, you can assign its Finish Material parameter to the sun-shade (host) material parameter Material Supports. When this is done, you can control the bracket material from the project by assigning a material to the sun shade's Material Supports property.

Parameters in many nested families can be linked to a single parameter in a host family to provide powerful control over size, quantity, and even display of family subassemblies from within a project. This is a great way to limit exposing a family's internal complexity when the family is loaded into a project.

Linking Parameters (Conditional Visibility)

Every nested family or piece of solid geometry has a "Visible" parameter. You can control the visibility of nested families by creating a Yes/No parameter in the host family and then linking the nested family to that parameter. Enabling or disabling this check box controls the element's visibility in the host family when viewed in a project.

For example, take a window family that has a shutter family nested in it and two instances placed on either side of the window. You can create a Yes/No parameter called DisplayShutters in the window family and link the Visible parameter of the shutter family to this parameter (Figure 10.24).

FIGURE 10.24
Linking a Yes/No parameter to the Visible parameter

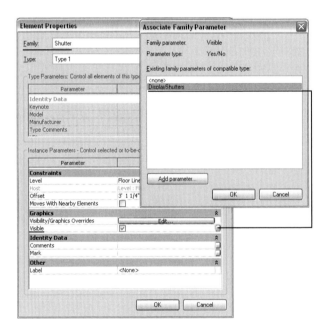

Two types are then created: Window w Shutters and Window w/o Shutters. The former has the DisplayShutters selected and the latter has it deselected. When loaded into the project, you can use the two types to control the display of the shutters (Figure 10.25).

Figure 10.25
Two types of a single family—conditional geometry display.

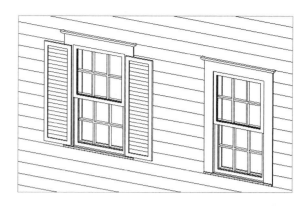

Parametric Arrays in the Family Editor

There are many examples of building components that have repetitive subcomponents built into them. Evenly spaced shelves, brackets, structural members, nested chairs, or other components—the list goes on. Figure 10.26 shows a perfect example where using an array to place vertical and horizontal shelves makes sense.

Figure 10.26
Arrays can help maintain element spacing in a family and allow you to control the number of grouped element instances.

In the family environment, you can use arrays on any geometry you've created or on any nested families you're using. The Array tool in the Family Editor works the same as it does in the project; but in the Family Editor, it can also be driven parametrically.

Making the Array Parametric

To make a parametric array in the Family Editor, you need to use the Group and Associate option on the Options bar. This allows you to parameterize the number of instances of the element in the array. When you select the array, a number appears that corresponds to the total number of groups in the array. If you change this number, the number of groups in the array updates. If the array was created with the option Move to: Last, elements are added or removed between the start and end of the array as defined when it was created. If the array was created with the option Move to: 2nd, elements are added or removed after the end of the array.

You can turn the array number into a parameter by selecting the array and labeling it as a parameter (Figure 10.27). Once the number is selected, the Options bar displays a Label drop-down menu. Select "Add parameter" to create a new number parameter.

FIGURE 10.27

Assigning an array number to a parameter

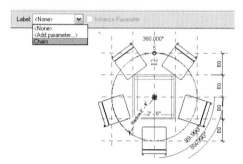

Once you make the assignment of the array number to a type parameter, the number of elements in the array can be controlled from the Family Types dialog. In Figure 10.28, the number parameter Chairs controls the number of chairs in the radial array. Changing the number automatically changes the number of elements in the array!

FIGURE 10.28

Array of chairs in `Table-Dining Round w Chairs.rfa.`

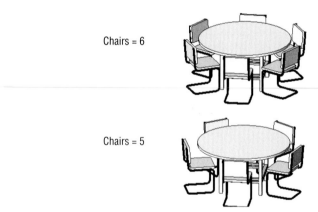

Chairs = 6

Chairs = 5

Encoding Design Rules

Proportion has been an important consideration in the design of objects for centuries. Relating width, height, and depth to a design rule informed the design of architecture dating back to early Greek and Egyptian times. The dimensional size of one element often drives the size of other related elements. Think, for example, of a window with muntins; the number of muntins often grows in proportion to the size of the window (Figure 10.29). To this end, Revit provides ways to relate parameters to one another using formulas. By changing one dimension of a component, you can effectively change many other dimensions and thereby maintain design intent. Often, your family will have parameters that determine its dimensions, and it's the relationship between these dimensions that you want to maintain.

FIGURE 10.29
Window with muntins added as function of width and height

Example: Using a Formula to Control Dimensions

In a simple case, you can imagine using a formula to set the width of a shutter in a window family. The window family may already have types that control its width and height. Knowing that the shutters should always be equal to the window height and half the width, you can use a formula and let Revit do the calculation for you. Follow these steps:

1. Load the shutter into your window family, and place two instances on either side of the window.

2. In the window Family Types dialog, create a new parameter by clicking the Add button:

3. In the Parameter Properties dialog (Figure 10.30), give the parameter the name **Half Width**, and set Type Of Parameter to Length. You can group the parameter under Dimensions to make it easier to find.

FIGURE 10.30
Use the Parameter
Properties window to
give the new parame-
ter a name and type.

4. Back in the Family Types dialog, in the parameter's formula field, enter **=Width / 2**
(Figure 10.31). This will ensure that the parameter is always half the window's width.
The Value field displays the calculated value; when the family is loaded into your project,
the parameter will display but won't be editable.

FIGURE 10.31
A simple formula for
Half Width

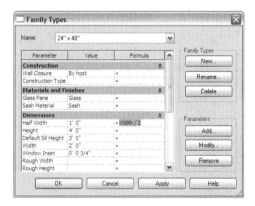

5. Select the nested shutter in your family, and link its dimensions to the window so they
change together. To do so, in the Associate Parameter dialog, click the button in the correct
row of the Shutter element properties. Associating the shutter's Width parameter with the
window's Half Width parameter and its Height to the window's Height connects the two
objects.

The shutter will now adapt its dimensions to the window whenever its shape is adjusted.

Using a Formula to Control an Array

In the next example, you'll see how you can use a formula to control the number of elements in
an array used to construct a sun-shading family (Figure 10.32). (You'll find this file on the book's
website, www.sybex.com/go/masteringrevit2008, as Sunshade.rfa.)

FIGURE 10.32
A sun-shade family
can be parametrically
defined with a formula.

This family is constructed of a support bracket and blades that make up the shade. The design calls for supports to be added dynamically as a function of length. In this example, both the brackets and the shades are arrayed so that their quantity is determined by the size of the family when placed in the project. The number of brackets is controlled by the *Support Quantity* parameter, and the number of blades in the shade is controlled by *Blade Quantity*. Both of these can be driven by formulas. The calculated value of a formula is always displayed in the Value column. Let's look deeper at this design problem and see how it can be solved.

Support Quantity uses a conditional statement to guarantee that there are always at least two support brackets in the family. A conditional statement takes this general form:

If (*condition*, do this, else do this)

In the support case, if Support Minimum is true, then the number of supports is set to "Length / 60". If it's false, then the value is 2.

Support Minimum is a Yes/No parameter that's also set to a formula. In this case, if Length (the length of the family) is greater than 135″, Support Minimum is Yes (true); otherwise, it's No (false).

In Figure 10.33, you see the default Length value is 110″. So, Support Minimum is false, and Support Quantity is set to 2. When the length exceeds 180″, Support Quantity equals 3, and an additional support bracket is introduced via the array.

Blade Quantity is simpler. The conditional statement determines whether the depth is greater than 15.75″. When it's larger (shown as 37″). the number of blades is one more than "Depth – 10″ / 6‴". When the depth is less than 15.75″, there are only two blades.

Figure 10.34 shows how changing the length to 180″ causes a new bracket to be added based on the formula.

FIGURE 10.33
Formulas used to
control arrays

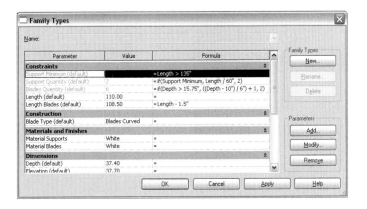

FIGURE 10.34
Different shade sizes evaluated via formula. On the left, two supports are added. On the Right, three supports are added.

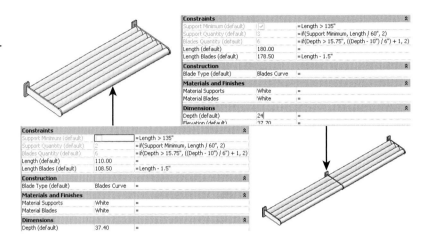

Constraints		
Support Minimum (default)	☑	= Length > 135"
Support Quantity (default)	3	= if(Support Minimum, Length / 60", 2)
Blades Quantity (default)	6	= if(Depth > 15.75", ((Depth - 10") / 6") + 1, 2)
Length (default)	180.00	=
Length Blades (default)	178.50	= Length - 1.5"
Construction		
Blade Type (default)	Blades Curve	=
Materials and Finishes		
Material Supports	White	=
Material Blades	White	=
Dimensions		
Depth (default)	24	=
Elevation (default)	37.70	=

Constraints		
Support Minimum (default)		= Length > 135"
Support Quantity (default)	2	= if(Support Minimum, Length / 60", 2)
Blades Quantity (default)	6	= if(Depth > 15.75", ((Depth - 10") / 6") + 1, 2)
Length (default)	110.00	=
Length Blades (default)	108.50	= Length - 1.5"
Construction		
Blade Type (default)	Blades Curve	=
Materials and Finishes		
Material Supports	White	=
Material Blades	White	=
Dimensions		
Depth (default)	37.40	=

 Real World Scenario

REAL-WORLD SCENARIO: MAKING A PARAMETRIC SUN SHADE

We constructed an advanced line-based family to model an exterior shading element. The family uses arrays with a formula to capture the design intent regarding the number of blades, proper support spacing, and blade angle. The resulting family can be quickly placed with two clicks, and the correct number of supports are placed. Once you place the family, you can experiment with different blade angles and numbers of blades in the system by changing a few properties:

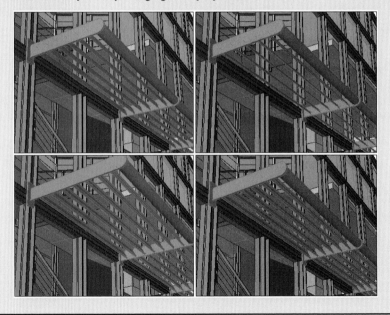

Building a Parametric 3D Family

In this exercise, you'll assemble a furniture ensemble consisting of a round table surrounded by chairs (Figure 10.35). To accomplish this, you'll do the following:

◆ Nest families

◆ Create an array

◆ Use a formula to lock in design intent

◆ Use parameter linking to control element visibility

FIGURE 10.35
Table family with
nested chairs

Nesting the Chair

To nest a chair into the table family so the whole family works as a unit, follow these steps:

1. Open `Table Round.rfa` from the `Chapter 10` folder of the book's website (www.sybex.com/go/masteringrevit2008).

2. Open the Ref. Level plan view using the Project browser, and fit the view to the screen.

3. Choose File ➤ Load from Library ➤ Load Family to load `Chair-Breuer.rfa` from the `Chapter 10` folder on the website.

4. Activate the Component tool on the Family Design bar.

5. The active component in the Type Selector should be Chair-Breuer.

6. Place a single instance of the chair, as shown in Figure 10.36. Use the spacebar to rotate the chair to face the table, and type **SI** to use the Intersection snap override to snap the chair origin to the reference-plane intersection.

FIGURE 10.36
Place an instance
of chair in the table
family

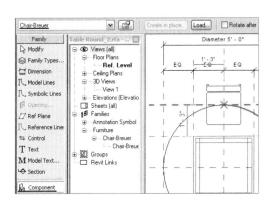

Creating a Parametric Array

Next, you'll make the chair array become parametrically driven. Follow these steps:

1. Click the Family Types command on the Design Bar to launch the Family Types dialog.

2. In the Parameters group, click Add.

3. In the Parameter Properties dialog, enter the information shown in Figure 10.37 for the parameter, and click OK.

FIGURE 10.37
Adding a new
Chairs parameter

4. Add a Radius parameter (Figure 10.38), and click OK.

FIGURE 10.38
New Radius
parameter added

5. For the Radius parameter, enter the following in the Formula column: **(Diameter / 2)**. This ensures that the radius is half the diameter.

6. For the Chairs parameter, enter the following in the Formula column:

   (Diameter *3.14)/2´6˝

   This formula sets the desired number of chairs relative to the circumference of the table.

7. Select the chair instance you placed earlier, and select the Array tool. Change the array type in the Options bar to from linear to radial. A red box appears around the chair, with a blue rotate control in the center. Drag the blue control to the intersection of the two reference planes at the center of the table to set the center of the array.

8. Define the start of the array by clicking at the origin of the chair, and then move your mouse into the Options bar area. Set the "Move to" radio button to Last, and enter **360** in the Angle field.

9. Press the Enter key twice. Revit creates three chairs.

10. To constrain the array to the radius of the table, activate the Dimension tool, and choose the Radial placement method from the Options bar:

11. Hold the tool over the table edge, and press Tab until the status bar reads *Array : Array : Reference*. Click in any whitespace to finish the dimension.

12. Select the dimension. In the Options bar, set the Label drop-down menu to the Radius parameter. This sets the radius of the array to match the radius of the table.

13. Select a chair group, and then the array reference (the line that connects the chair groups and displays the array number). You may need to press Tab until you see the status bar read *Array : Array : Reference*.

14. Once you make this selection, the number of chairs should change to match the value of the formula-driven Chairs parameter (Figure 10.39).

FIGURE 10.39
Assign the array reference to the Chairs parameter

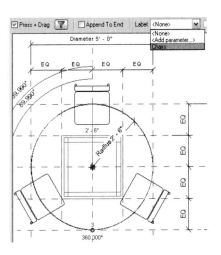

Controlling Chair Visibility

To modify the family so that chairs can be made visible (or not visible) as part of the family definition, follow these steps:

1. Click Family Types on the Design bar to open the Family Types dialog.

2. In the Parameters group, click Add.

3. In the Parameter Properties dialog, enter the data shown in Figure 10.40.

FIGURE 10.40
Fill out the Parameter Properties dialog as shown here.

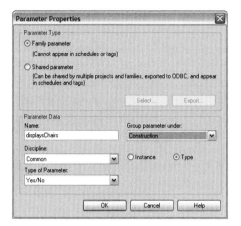

4. Click OK.

5. Select one of the chair groups, and choose Edit Group from the Options bar.

6. Select the chair, and edit its element properties, either by right-clicking and using the context menu or by clicking the Element Properties icon in the Options bar.

7. Under the Graphics group, find the Visible parameter. At the far right end of the row, click the button to launch the Associate Family Parameter dialog box.

8. In the dialog, choose the displaysChairs parameter you created earlier.

9. Click OK twice to dismiss the Associate Family Parameter and Element Properties dialogs; then, click Finish Group.

10. Click the Family Types Design bar command to launch the familiar Family Types dialog.

11. Choose the type 36″ Diameter in the Type drop-down list at the top of the dialog.

12. At right, in the Family Types group, choose New.

13. Type in the name **36″ Diameter no Chairs**, and then click OK.

14. In the Graphics group, select the displaysChairs parameter, and then Click OK to close the Family Types dialog.

15. Save the family. Choose Load Into Project from the Design bar to view the completed family.

16. You should have four types of families available. Place an instance of each to see the results (Figure 10.41).

FIGURE 10.41
Finished family types placed in a project. All four types are displayed, illustrating the use of the array with the formula and the conditional display of the chairs.

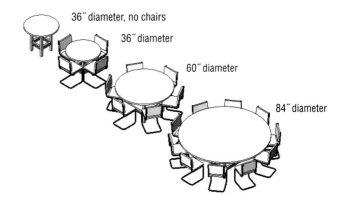

36″ diameter, no chairs

36″ diameter

60″ diameter

84″ diameter

The Bottom Line

Models are full of content, and at some point you'll need to make your own. Don't be afraid to dive into the Family Editor and start creating your own custom content. Begin with simple families, and elaborate as you go. When approaching an element you wish to model, think first of how it's constructed and what aspects of it you need to control parametrically—not all components need to be full-blown parametric objects. Also think about how you might break a component into subcomponents. Consider the eventual application of the family—will it be hosted in walls, ceiling, roofs? Or is it a stand-alone object? As you get more familiar with how parameters work, start considering formulas and parameter linking to save time and embed intelligent behavior.

Understanding the different types of model families you can make   When you're making a new family, consider how it will be used in the model, and choose an appropriate template.

> **Master It**   You found a ceiling-mounted lighting fixture that you want to use in your existing project, but you can't find a Revit family for it in any libraries or online communities. How would you start?

Leveraging nested families for flexibility and efficiency   The ability to nest families in other families lets you create content that's easier to manage and improves your workflow.

> **Master It**   Building components are often composed of a series of subcomponents that form an overall assembly. Think of some common examples and what strategies you could use to build such content in Revit.

Building relationships between parameters with formulas   Create smart connections between geometry and dimensions to create efficient and parametric content.

> **Master It**   You can use dimensional relationships to tie the size of one object to the size of another. How do you do this in the context of a family?

Chapter 11

Extended Modeling Techniques

In the previous chapters we covered basic modeling techniques for constructing a simple building. We skipped over many additional features to give you a handle on essential workflow, the user interface, and making modifications to the model. In this chapter we'll cover more-advanced features that are available anytime you're modeling in Revit. As you'll see, with a little refinement and creativity, you can make a wide range of building components with the standard tools.

In this chapter, you will learn how to do the following:

- ◆ Take advantage of advanced wall features
- ◆ Work with advanced roofs and slab editing
- ◆ Work with railings

Basic Walls: Advanced Modeling Techniques

Walls are made from layers of materials that represent the construction assemblies used to build real walls. In Revit, these layers can be assigned functions, allowing them to join and react to other, similar layers in the model when walls, floors, and roofs meet. The wall *core* is one of these special layers, and understanding it will help you when designing your walls.

Wall Core

Revit has a unique ability to identify a *wall core* that is much more than a layer of material. The core influences the behavior of the wall and how the wall interacts with other elements in the model. Every wall type in Revit has a core material with a boundary on either side of it. You can dimension to these core boundaries, designating the location of structural wall components rather than finish materials. The core boundary can also be used when drawing host elements (walls, floors, ceilings, roofs). For example, you can constrain a floor sketch to the structural stud layer of walls by using the wall-core boundary to create the sketch. If walls change size or are swapped, the floor sketch maintains its relationship to the core boundary and will auto-adjust to the new wall.

To access and edit wall-core boundaries and material layers, select a wall and choose Element Properties ➢ Edit/New. In the Type Properties dialog, select Structure as the parameter to edit. This will open a new Edit Assembly dialog. From here you can define materials, move layers in and out of the core boundary, and assign functions to each layer (see Figure 11.1).

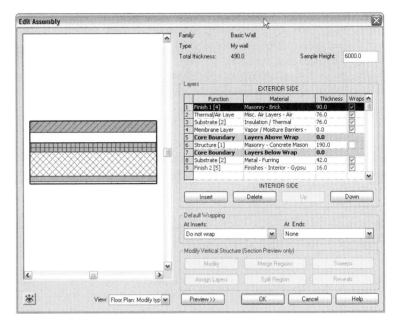

To get a feel for how core layers are used in relation to a floor, start a new session of Revit and follow these steps:

1. Open a new project, and draw a simple floor plan using walls. Select a multilayered wall type in order to understand the value of the exercise—the Brick on CMU wall type works well. Draw at least four connected walls that represent a simple floor plan.

2. Use the View Control bar to switch to fine or medium detail view so you can see the wall layers. (In coarse views, wall layers are never displayed.)

3. From the modeling Design bar, select the Floor tool, keep the default Pick Walls option, and in the Options bar, check the "Extend into wall (to core)" option.

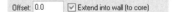

4. Position your cursor over an edge of the wall (do not click the mouse button yet), press Tab to highlight all the walls, and then click to select and zoom in. A sketch line indicating the shape of the floor will be created. This sketch line indicates the position of the floor relative to the wall—it's drawn at the exterior edge of the wall core. Make sure you've selected all walls as a reference to create the floor and click Finish Sketch.

5. Create a section through the wall and open the section view. Again, make sure your view is set to medium or fine. You'll see the edge of the floor and how it aligns with the wall construction. Figure 11.2 shows the sketch in plan and how the floor looks when finished in section.

FIGURE 11.2
The floor sketch in
plan view and in
section

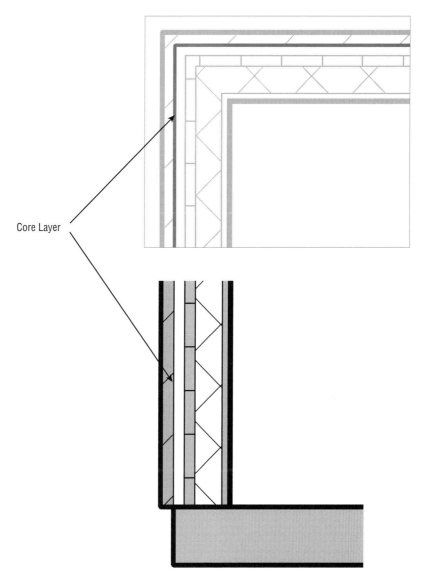

Core Layer

If you change the wall type, or move it, the floor will update to match.

Layer Join Cleanup

Having clean and legible drawings is important when representing construction design intent. To this end, Revit provides a wall-layer priority system that intelligently manages the cleanup of internal wall layers. Revit provides six functions (levels of priority), with *Structure* having the highest priority (Figure 11.3).

FIGURE 11.3

Wall layers and function

When you create a new wall type and begin adding layers to the wall, you need to assign a material, thickness, and priority to the layers. When you're assigning a priority, think about the function of the layer in the wall—is it finish? Substrate? Structure? This decision will help clean up your walls down the road.

Editing Wall Joins

If you encounter situations in which the automated wall cleanup doesn't correspond to your expectations, Revit will let you cycle through a range of possible layer configurations using the Edit Wall Joins tool, located in the Options bar.

With the Edit Wall Joins tool, you can edit wall-join configurations. The default wall join is set to butt join. Activate the Edit Wall Joins tool, and place your cursor over a wall join. (This can be a corner where two walls meet.) The Options bar shows some alternative configuration options: Miter and Square. A Miter join is shown in Figure 11.4.

FIGURE 11.4

Mitered wall join

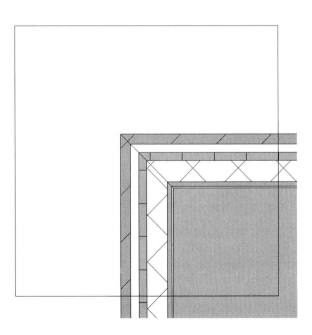

Disjoining Walls

In some cases, you will want to override the intelligent wall cleanup that Revit provides. For example, a nonrated partition should not interrupt the gypsum board in a fire-rated wall. The Disallow Join option will allow you create this condition. To access this command, right-click the blue control dot at the end of any wall and select Disallow Join from the context menu. Doing so breaks the auto-join cleanup. Figure 11.5 shows the default cleanup (left) and the same join after disallowing the join and adjusting the wall end (right).

FIGURE 11.5
The Disallow Join option provides extra flexibility.

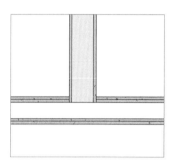
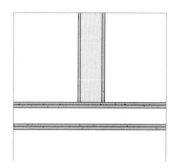

Stacked Walls

Walls in a building, especially exterior walls, are often composed of different wall types that stack one on top of another over the height of the façade. At the very least, most walls sit on top of a foundation wall. If the foundation wall moves and you expect walls on top of the foundation to also move, a *stacked wall* might be a good way to go. Stacked walls allow you to create a single wall entity composed of different wall types vertically stacked. The wall types used in a stacked wall need to be existing types already defined in your project. To understand how stacked walls work and how to modify one, follow these steps:

1. Open a new session of Revit, and make sure three levels are defined (if you don't have three levels defined, switch to an elevation view, add a third level, and then go back to your floor plan view).

2. Pick the Wall tool and select Stacked Wall: Exterior - Brick Over CMU w Metal Stud (located at the bottom of the list in the Type Selector). In the element properties, click the Edit/New button and then duplicate the wall type to create a new stacked wall.

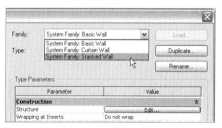

3. Edit the structure parameter and click the Preview button to see the wall in section (Figure 11.6). When you're editing the Stacked wall type, you'll notice that the UI is slightly different than when you're working with a basic wall. Rather than editing individual wall layers, in this dialog you are editing stack predefined wall types.

FIGURE 11.6
Sectional preview
of stacked wall type

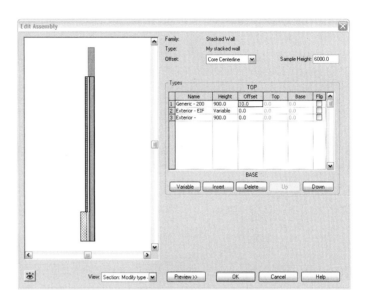

4. Click the Insert button to add a new wall. A new row appears in the list and allows you to define a new wall. Select the Generic wall type from the Name list, and set the Height value. With a new row selected, click the Variable button. This will allow the wall to vary in height to adjust with level heights.

5. Go back to your plan view and draw the new wall, setting its top constraint to Level 3.

6. Cut a section through the model and change the heights of Level 1 and Level 3 to see the effect this has on the wall. (Make sure the level of detail is set to medium/fine so you can see the wall layers.) You'll see that changing Level 2 does not change the bottom walls because they are fixed in height. However, changing the height of Level 3 will change the height of the variable wall (Figure 11.7).

FIGURE 11.7
The middle section
of this stacked wall
varies on a per
instance basis.

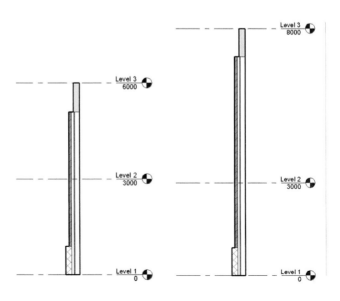

Adding Wall Articulation

Walls are often complex and articulated in their composition. Cornices, reveals, corrugated metal finish, and other projections are used all the time. Some wall finishes have more than one material on them and they can be flush or of different thickness. Revit can accommodate any of these types of design articulation. Some examples of compound walls are shown in Figure 11.8.

FIGURE 11.8
Compound vertical walls: (A) brick wall with horizontal sweeps, reveals and a top finish; (B) compound wall with aluminum corrugated finish, trapeze-shaped; (C) compound wall with aluminum corrugated finish curved; (D) compound wall with slanting wall finish.

From the Edit Assembly dialog of any Basic Wall Type, you can enable a preview of the wall. This preview allows you to view the wall in either plan or section. When the section preview is active, additional tools also become active and allow you to place geometric sweep/reveal components on the wall (Figure 11.9).

FIGURE 11.9
With section view active, tools for modifying the vertical structure become active.

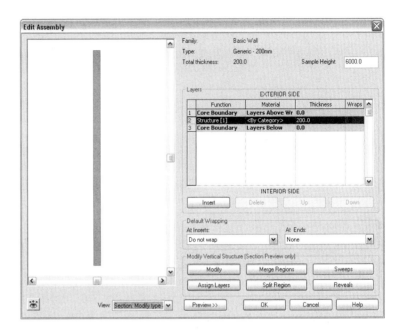

EXAMPLE: ASSIGNING TWO DIFFERENT MATERIALS ON THE FINAL FINISH OF A WALL

Let's start with a case where you need to create a wall that has two different material finishes that are flush aligned (Figure 11.10).

FIGURE 11.10
Exterior wall layer built of two different materials in the height

1. Select a multilayered wall as a base and duplicate it to create a new wall type

2. In the Wall Edit Assembly dialog, switch the view to show a section view of the wall.

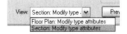

In this exercise, the exterior wall layer is plaster, but what we need is the lower 4 inches (1.20m) to be brick and to keep the walls flush with one another.

3. Place your cursor at the beginning of the exterior finish layer. This will highlight the wall component in the section preview. Select the Split Region tool and split the layer at 4″ (1.20m) height (Figure 11.11).

FIGURE 11.11
Split Region applied
to the exterior
component

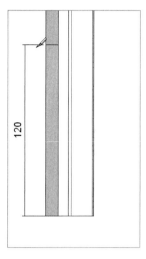

4. The moment you split the layer, you will notice that the Finish layer reports a reports a thickness of 0.00, meaning that it is variable.

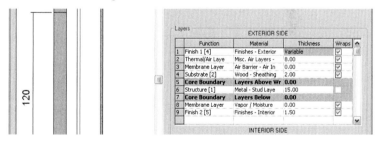

	Function	Material	Thickness	Wraps
	EXTERIOR SIDE			
1	Finish 1 [4]	Finishes - Exterior	Variable	☑
2	Thermal/Air Laye	Misc. Air Layers -	8.00	☑
3	Membrane Layer	Air Barrier - Air In	0.00	☑
4	Substrate [2]	Wood - Sheathing	2.00	☑
5	**Core Boundary**	**Layers Above Wr**	**0.00**	
6	Structure [1]	Metal - Stud Laye	15.00	☐
7	**Core Boundary**	**Layers Below**	**0.00**	
8	Membrane Layer	Vapor / Moisture	0.00	☑
9	Finish 2 [5]	Finishes - Interior	1.50	☑
	INTERIOR SIDE			

5. You will now need to add one additional layer. To do so, use the Insert button and add that component right after the first exterior finish. Change its function to Finish 1, its material to Brick, and its thickness to zero.

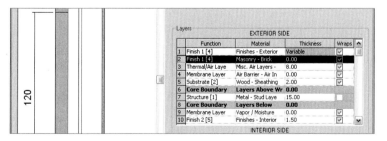

	Function	Material	Thickness	Wraps
	EXTERIOR SIDE			
1	Finish 1 [4]	Finishes - Exterior	Variable	☑
2	Finish 1 [4]	Masonry - Brick	0.00	☑
3	Thermal/Air Laye	Misc. Air Layers -	8.00	☑
4	Membrane Layer	Air Barrier - Air In	0.00	☑
5	Substrate [2]	Wood - Sheathing	2.00	☑
6	**Core Boundary**	**Layers Above Wr**	**0.00**	
7	Structure [1]	Metal - Stud Laye	15.00	☐
8	**Core Boundary**	**Layers Below**	**0.00**	
9	Membrane Layer	Vapor / Moisture	0.00	☑
10	Finish 2 [5]	Finishes - Interior	1.50	☑
	INTERIOR SIDE			

6. Place the cursor at the front of the row of the new material and select it. This will highlight the material and show a thin red line in the section view (Figure 11.12).

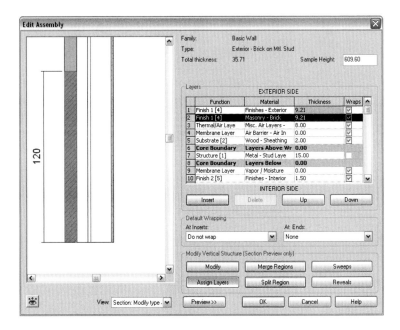

7. After having added that layer, click the Assign Layer button and pick the portion of the wall that you wish to assign the zero thickness layer to (in this example, the lower portion).

The result will be that the picked portion of the wall will have the new layer assigned and your wall exterior face will show two different materials.

While working on a complex compound wall, you might have a situation where you need to merge horizontal or vertical wall layers that already exist in the wall. For that, use the Merge button and pick on the line between two layers. Once the cursor is over a line between two layers, an arrow indicating which layer will override the other one during the merging will show up, as shown in Figure 11.13.

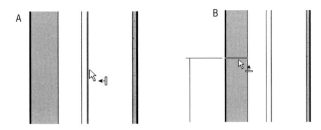

Wall Wrapping

The way materials are detailed at insert conditions (doors, windows, and openings) varies depending on the construction type, building conventions, and aesthetics. Layer wrapping options are available in the wall Edit Assembly dialog; however, they aren't sufficient to accommodate a complex wrapping situation specific to a particular door or window. To achieve more control over these construction conditions, you need to set parameters in the window or door family itself.

In the Family Editor, you can assign a *Wall Closure* property to reference planes; it defines a plane that wall layers that have wrapping assigned to them will wrap to.

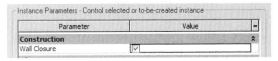

In the Element Properties dialog for the reference plane, check the option Wall Closure. This means that the exterior wall layers that have wraps assigned will terminate at this reference plane. The effect can be seen in Figure 11.14.

FIGURE 11.14

(A) The reference plane in the Family Editor and (B) its effect when set to Close

A 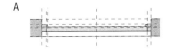 B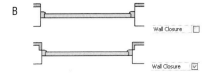

Sweeps and Reveals

Many walls have linear embellishments that are attached or embedded in the construction. Cornices, brick soldier courses, and reveals are all examples. Using Basic Walls, you can add these elements directly into wall types.

Clicking the Sweeps or Reveals button in the Edit Assembly dialog opens a new dialog where you can define profile families to use as sweeps or reveals.

These profiles, which are 2D shapes made out of simple lines, are then swept along the length of the wall at a specified height. Many profiles representing cornices, skirting, and chair rails ship with Revit, but if you need to create a custom profile, you can use the Profile Family template. Choose File ➢ New Family ➢ Profile to access the Revit Family Editor. From here, you draw a closed loop of lines at the desired real-world scale and load the profile back into your project. Follow these steps to get a feel for the workflow:

1. Click the Wall tool and select Generic Wall and duplicate it.

2. Open the wall assembly dialog.

3. In the preview view, switch to section view. The six Modify Vertical Structure options become active at the bottom of the dialog.

4. Click the Sweeps button to bring up the Wall Sweeps dialog, shown in Figure 11.15.

FIGURE 11.15
The Wall Sweeps
dialog before inserting
any profiles

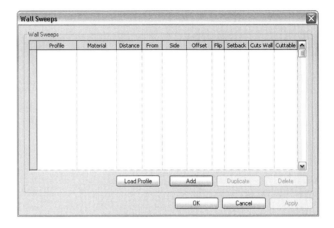

5. Click the Load Profile button, browse to the Profiles folder, and load the two profiles as shown here:

◆ Cornice profile: Traditional (1)

◆ Skirting profile: (Base 2, Ogee or similar)

6. Click the Add button. This adds a row in the dialog that lets you select one of the loaded profiles and set its position relative to the wall geometry.

7. Add both profiles. Set the Traditional profile's From value to Top and the Ogee profile's From value to Base. Doing so attaches the profiles to the top and bottom of your wall. Figure 11.16 shows the profiles attached to the top and bottom of the wall.

8. Click OK. Draw a segment of this wall in the drawing area. Check out the wall in section and 3D views to see the result.

Using the same principles outlined for adding traditional elements, you can get creative and add any type or profile you want. Figure 11.17 shows a wall with a corrugated siding added as an integrated wall sweep.

REVEALS

Reveals can be added to a wall using the same workflow you use with sweeps; the only difference is that the profile is *subtractive* rather than additive.

FIGURE 11.16
Profiles attached to
wall top and base

FIGURE 11.17
Wall with integrated
wall sweep for
corrugated siding.

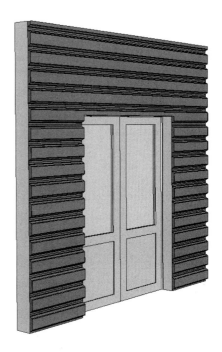

WALL SWEEP RETURNS

When you're working on traditional architectural projects, the wall sweeps usually wrap around door openings in thick walls. Revit can accommodate that using the Change Sweep Return command. To understand this feature, follow this simple exercise:

1. Open a new session of Revit and place a generic wall.

2. Rather than placing a sweep in the wall type (as we just did), we can use another method for placing sweeps: the Host Sweep tool in the Modeling tab of the Design bar.. Choose Wall Sweep, and then select a wall sweep from the Type Selector.

These sweeps can be placed either vertically or horizontally using options in the Options bar.

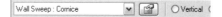

3. Add a horizontal sweep to the middle of the wall. Use the temporary dimensions to place the sweep at the desired height.

4. Choose the Opening tool, also located in the Modeling tab.

Using this tool, draw an opening that intersects the sweep (Figure 11.18).

5. Select the sweep—it will display a blue grip at the end (edge of the opening). Click the Change Sweep Return button in the Options bar. The mouse pointer turns into a knife symbol, and when you click somewhere on the profile it creates a new segment that wraps around the edge of the opening. Press Esc or use the Modify tool to exit the command. You will need to zoom in close to the end of the sweep to really see the effect. (If you zoom very closely, the lines might become very thick and ugly—in that case, click the Thin Line Mode button in the toolbar.)

6. Select the sweep again, and drag the control to adjust the length of the sweep. Figure 11.19 shows how the return can be modified.

FIGURE 11.18
A manually placed
wall sweep intersect-
ed by a wall opening
shown in (a) perspec-
tive, and (b) elevation.

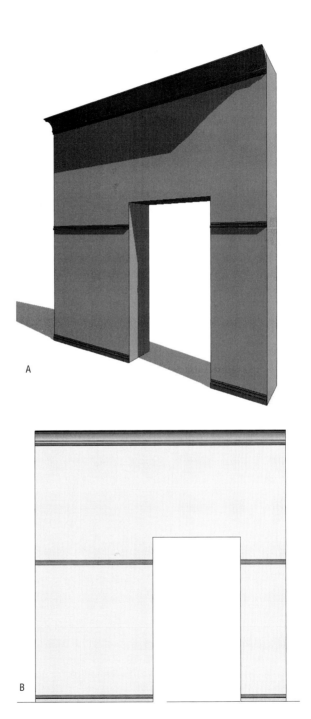

FIGURE 11.19
Host sweep returns

Creating Custom In-Place Walls

When you're working on traditional architecture or restoration of historic buildings, you'll often need to create walls that are irregular in shape. The *Create* tool, found under the Modeling Design tab, lets you address such wall styles. Figure 11.20 shows an example. This tool allows you to draw solid geometry using one of four modeling methods. Each created form is assigned a specific category that is later used to control visibility and behavior in the model. For example, assigning a sweep to the category Wall allows the wall to host inserts such as windows and doors.

FIGURE 11.20
Manually constructed wall used to create nonvertical wall surfaces (Image courtesy of Architect S. Cappochin)

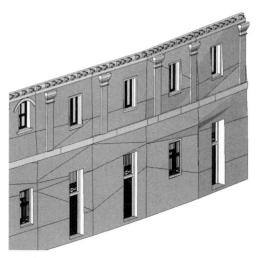

The finished wall

A series of connected blends form the complex shaped wall

The wall in Figure 11.21 was created using a series of blends assigned to the category Wall using the manual creation method (also referred to as "in-place" components). It still behaves as a wall: You can make doors and windows, and they cut through the geometry of the wall as with standard walls—very slick! Various wall types can be created using this method. Consider the form-making tools we've covered and how you can use them to generate unique wall profiles.

Curtain Walls: Advanced Design Techniques

The Curtain Wall tool is designed with flexibility in mind. You can use it to generate anything from simple storefronts to highly articulated structural glass façades. In this section, we'll look at the basic principles and how to extend these principles to create a range of designs. The composition of a curtain wall is divided into four primary elements, shown in Figure 11.21:

◆ The wall and its geometric extents

◆ Curtain grids

◆ Mullions

◆ Curtain panels

FIGURE 11.21
Curtain wall parts

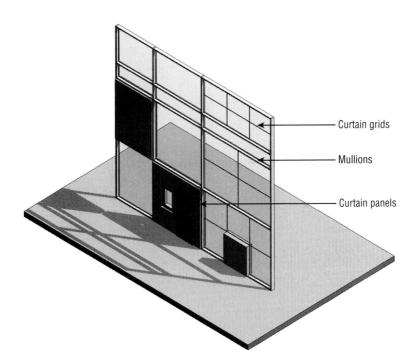

Curtain grids

Mullions

Curtain panels

The wall   A curtain wall is drawn like a basic wall and is available in the Type Selector when the Wall tool is active. It has top and bottom constraints, can be attached to roofs, can have its elevation profile sketch-edited, and is scheduled as a wall type.

Curtain grids   These are used to lay out a grid that defines the physical divisions of the curtain wall. The layout grid can be designed freely as a combination of horizontal and vertical segments or can be a type with embedded rules that specify regular divisions. Figure 11.22 shows a typical grid division and expressive curtain panels in between.

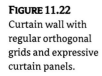

FIGURE 11.22
Curtain wall with regular orthogonal grids and expressive curtain panels.

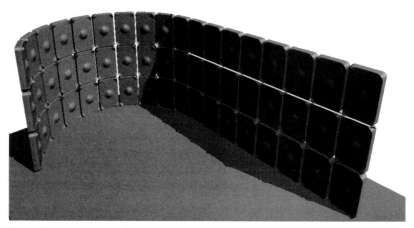

IMAGE COURTESY OF PHIL READ

Mullions These represent the metal profiles on a glass façade, and in Revit they follow the geometry of the grid. They can have any shape that is based on a mullion profile family.

Curtain panels These fill in the space between gridlines and are always one of the following:

Empty panels No panel is placed between the grids.

Glazed panels These can be made out of different types of glass that can have any color or transparency.

Solid panels and panels with wall types These can take on any geometry you wish and thus create most interesting structures, like the one shown in Figure 11.23.

Wall types as infill From the type selector you can also choose a wall type to fill the space between the gridlines (mullions). All wall types in the project will be available for your selection. Adding a wall type is usually a typical case in office partitions where the lower portion is a parapet wall and glass fills the upper portion of the metal stud wall.

Designing a Curtain Wall

In this simple exercise, we'll walk through the creation of a simple curtain wall. To draw a curtain wall, you can either draw a standard wall and then change its type to Curtain Wall or select a Curtain Wall type from the Wall Type Selector first. Follow these steps:

1. Select the Wall tool.

2. From the Type Selector, select Curtain Wall.

3. In the Level 1 plan view, draw a simple curtain wall (Figure 11.24). Use the wall type Curtain Wall 1.

4. Toggle the view to see the result in 3D.

FIGURE 11.23
Customized curtain panels

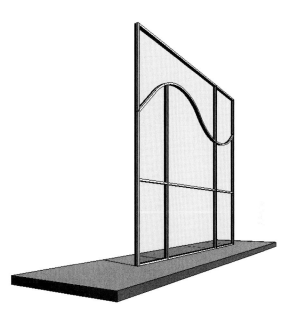

FIGURE 11.24
A generic curtain wall before adding any grids or mullions looks like a simple glass wall.

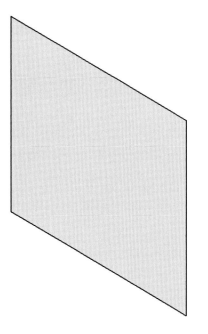

   5. Divide the wall into panels using the Curtain Grid tool on the Modeling tab in the Design bar. Mouse over the edges of the wall to get a preview of where the grid will be placed. Revit has some intelligent snapping built into grid placement that looks for midpoints and points that will divide the panel into thirds. Place the grid so that you get something like Figure 11.25.

FIGURE 11.25
Curtain wall with a
few added grids

FIGURE 11.25
Curtain wall with a
few added grids

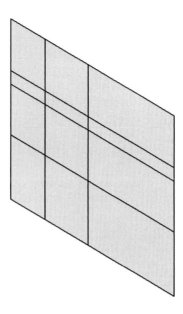

6. Place mullions on the wall. You can place one mullion at a time by selecting separate grid segments. If you want to apply the same mullion on all segments, hold the Ctrl key and click a gridline to select all segments and apply the mullions. With mullions placed, your wall should look like Figure 11.26.

FIGURE 11.26
Mullions applied to
the grids on a
curtain wall

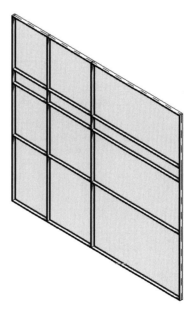

7. Let's say you want to add more mullions, but this time you don't want them to extend the entire height of the curtain wall. Select the Curtain Grid Line tool, and place new grids (Figure 11.27).

FIGURE 11.27
To add more mullions, you will need to add another grid.

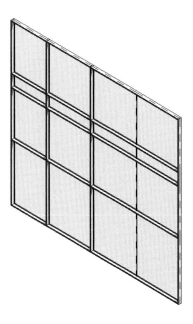

8. Before applying a mullion to the new gridline, delete the segments of the gridline where you don't wish the mullion to occur. Exit the Curtain Grid tool, and select the newly created gridline. Click the Add Or Remove Segments button in the Options bar, and click the segment you want removed.

Add or Remove Segments

Remove the top and bottom segments, and then add mullions (Figure 11.28).

FIGURE 11.28
Removing portions of the grid and applying a mullion on the remaining segment of the grid

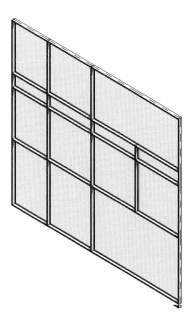

Curtain Panels

Curtain panels fill the space between the curtain grids and mullions. These elements are created in the Family Editor using the Curtain Panels family template. They can be found under File ➢ New Family ➢ Curtain Wall Panel.rft. The Revit default template has a couple of curtain panels preloaded: System Panel Glazed and System Panel Solid. You can duplicate different types of these families and change the material, thickness, and offset to customize the appearance. Figure 11.22 shows some very creative curtain panels.

SELECTING THE ELEMENTS WITHIN THE CURTAIN WALL

Revit provides specially tailored selection options in the context menu to aid with workflow and interaction when you're working with curtain walls.

When you hover the cursor over or pick an element in a curtain wall, take note of the Status bar in the lower-left corner of the screen: It tells you exactly the type of element you're about to select or have already selected. Depending on what the cursor is hovering over, various selection options are available. The elements you can select include the following:

♦ The entire curtain wall entity (indicated by a green dashed line surrounding the curtain wall)

♦ A gridline

♦ A mullion

♦ A curtain panel

To select the element you want, use the Tab key until that element is highlighted.

Curtain Wall Doors and Windows

Curtain walls can host specially designed doors and windows. Keep in mind that standard doors and windows cannot be hosted by a curtain wall. These specially designed elements are recognizable by a name that indicates they are curtain wall doors/ windows. Revit schedules them as doors and windows, but their behavior is dependent on the curtain wall. Curtain wall doors and windows adapt their width and height to fill in grid cells. Essentially, they behave exactly like panels—they've just been made to appear and schedule as doors or windows. To insert a door within a curtain wall, choose File ➢ Load Library ➢ Load Family. Navigate to the Doors folder, and select a curtain wall door (single or double). Figure 11.29 shows a curtain door panel has been swapped with a glazing panel.

Complex Curtain Wall Panels

Look at the complex-shaped curtain panels in Figure 11.30. You may think, "Oh, I can *never* do that!" Well, Revit can help you do it—and do it easily. The creation principle behind any of these types of curtain walls is the same as you learned in Chapter 10. By being smart about nesting and linking parameters, it is possible to build some very sophisticated curtain panel families.

FIGURE 11.29
Curtain door panel
in the example
curtain wall

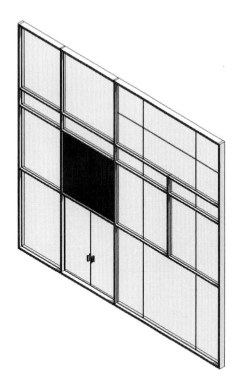

FIGURE 11.30
Complex curtain wall
panel example using
a series of nested
components

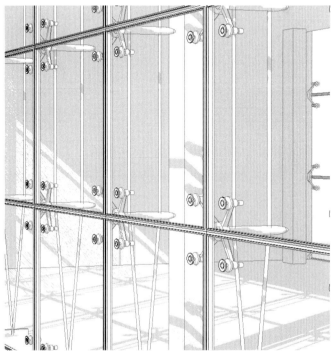

Roofs

Roofs can come in many shapes, sizes, and degrees of complexity. They can be as simple as a single-pitch shed roof, or they can involve complex sine curves or intersecting vaults. One can surely say that all of these shapes are possible within Revit. Once you have understood the primary concepts, logic, and tools, you will be able to design any roof shape.

In general, roofs in Revit can be constructed in three different ways:

◆ Roof by footprint: Use this method to create any standard roof that more or less follows the shape of the building footprint and is a simple combination of roof pitches.

◆ Roof by extrusion: This method is best applied for roof shapes that are generated by extrusion of a profile, such as saw-tooth roofs, barrel vaults, and waveform roofs.

◆ In-place roof: This technique will be used to accommodate roof shapes that cannot be achieved with either the footprint or extrusion methods.

The following sections provide a close look at all three approaches and review their application to real-world scenarios.

Footprint Roofs

As previously stated, use the roof by footprint method to create any standard roof that more or less follows the shape of the footprint of the building and is a simple combination of roof pitches (Figure 11.31).

FIGURE 11.31
Simple roof created using the "by footprint" method

These roofs are based on a sketched shape that you define in plan view at the soffit level and can be edited in plan and axon 3D views only. The shape can be drawn using the Line tool or can be created using the Pick Walls method. The best way to conceptualize this method is to understand that the sketched shape defining the main shape of the roof is really just a closed loop of lines, nothing more than that, regardless of whether it's drawn or picked.

The Pick Walls method provides an intelligent selection method, so if you pick walls as references to generate the sketch lines, the lines will maintain a smart relationship with the walls. The Pick Walls method is the suggested approach for creating roofs by footprint. By picking the walls to generate the sketch for the roof, you are creating an exclusive relationship between the walls and the roof so that if the design of your building later changes (wall position, level height, etc.), the roof will follow that change and adjust to the new wall position (Figure 11.32). Like any change in Revit, this happens everywhere in all views (plan, section, 3D).

FIGURE 11.32

Using the Pick method:
(A) original roof;
(B) entrance wall position changed, roof
updates automatically;
(C) the angle of the
wall right from
the entrance changed,
the roof changes to a
new shape.

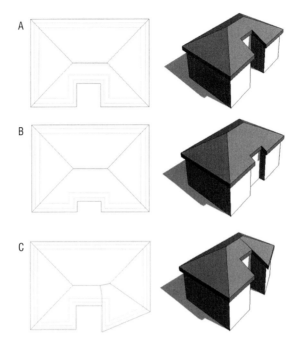

A

B

C

To guide you through the creation of roof by footprint and explain some of the main principles and tools, here is a brief exercise demonstrating the steps:

1. Open a plan view and create a building footprint similar to Figure 11.33.

FIGURE 11.33

Draw a simple set of walls.

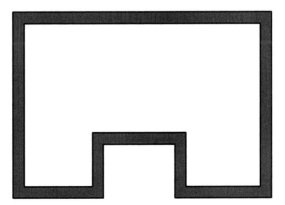

2. From the Design bar, click the Roof tool and choose Roof By Footprint.

3. Select the Pick Walls tools.

4. To define whether you want a sloped or flat roof, you will use the Defines Slope check box in the Options bar. The Overhang parameter allows you to define the value of the roof overhang beyond the wall. When the "Extend into wall (to core)" option is checked, the overhang

is measured from the wall core. If the option is unchecked, the overhang is measured from the exterior face of the wall. When you've chosen to create a roof by footprint, the Options bar makes these tools available.

Overhang: 300.00 ☑ Defines Slope ☑ Extend into wall (to core)

5. After defining these settings, place your cursor over one of the walls (don't click), and using the Tab key, pick all connected walls. Your display should look like Figure 11.34.

FIGURE 11.34
Roof sketch lines are automatically drawn after Tab-selecting the bounding walls and entering the command, and they are offset from the walls by the value of Offset as defined in the Options bar.

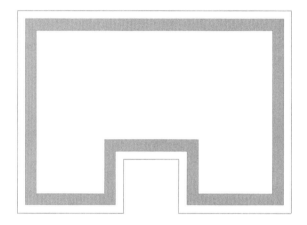

6. Click the Finish Roof button.

If the shape of the roof doesn't respond to your expectations, at any time you can select the roof and select Edit from the Options bar to change the shape of the roof sketch lines or their slope. To change the slope definition or angle of individual portions of the roof, select the sketch line and toggle the Defines Slope button in the Options bar, or click on the slope value that is displayed when you select the sketch line.

Here are some of the important instance properties you should be aware of and need to set properly; all are found in the dialog shown in Figure 11.35.

Base Level As in other Revit elements, this is the level at which the roof will be placed. The roof will move with this level if it changes height.

Room Bounding When this is checked, the roof geometry will have an effect on calculating room area and volume.

Related to Mass This property will be active only if a roof has been created with the By Face method (Massing tools).

Base Offset From Level This option will lower or elevate the base of the roof relative to the base level.

Cutoff Level Many roof shapes require a combination of several roofs on top of each other—for this you would need to cut off the top of a lower roof to accommodate space and the creation of the next roof in the sequence. Figure 11.36 shows an excellent example of this technique.

Cutoff Offset When the Cutoff tool is applied, the Cutoff Offset value also becomes active and allows for setting cutoff distance from the level indicated in the Cutoff Level parameter.

FIGURE 11.35

Roof Properties dialog

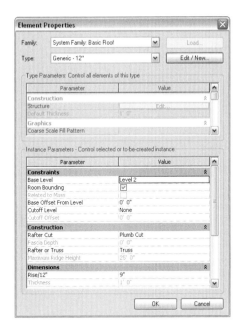

FIGURE 11.36

Cutoff level applied to the main roof, and a secondary roof built on top of the main roof using the cutoff level as a base

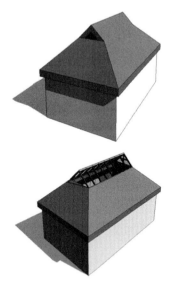

Rafter Cut This defines the eave shape. You can select from Plumb Cut, Two Plumb Cut, Two Plumb Square. When Two Plumb Square is selected as a choice, the Fascia Depth parameter is activated and you can set the value for the depth.

Rafter or Truss With Rafter, the offset of the base is measured from the inside of the wall. If you choose Truss, the plate offset from the base is measured from the outside of the wall. Figure 11.37 is a typical example of a roof by rafter cut.

FIGURE 11.37
Construction drawing
of rafter detail

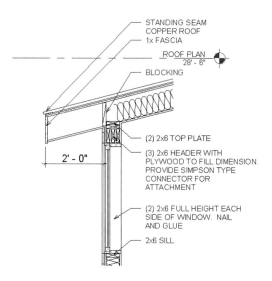

STANDING SEAM
COPPER ROOF

1x FASCIA

ROOF PLAN
28' - 6"

BLOCKING

(2) 2x6 TOP PLATE

(3) 2x6 HEADER WITH
PLYWOOD TO FILL DIMENSION.
PROVIDE SIMPSON TYPE
CONNECTOR FOR
ATTACHMENT

(2) 2x6 FULL HEIGHT EACH
SIDE OF WINDOW. NAIL
AND GLUE

2x6 SILL

2' - 0"

Roof by Extrusion

This method is best applied for roof shapes that are generated by extrusion of a profile, such as saw-tooth roofs, barrel vaults, and waveform roofs. Like the by footprint method, it is based on a sketch; however, the sketch that defines the shape of the roof is drawn in elevation/section view (not in plan view) and is then extruded along the plan of the building (Figure 11.38).

FIGURE 11.38
Barrel-shaped roof
extended with sun
shades. The main roof
is an extruded arch
sketch.

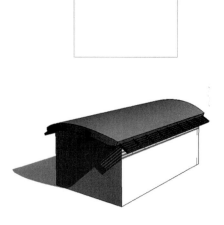

The Roof By Extrusion tool offers additional settings in the Options bar when selected.

[Edit] [Cut Plan Profile]   [Edit Work Plane...]   [Rehost]

Roofs by extrusion do not have an option to follow the building footprint, but that is often needed to complete the design. To accommodate this, use the Cut Plan Profile tool, available only when Roof by Extrusion is selected.

Briefly, you create your roof by extrusion by defining a profile in elevation that is then extruded above the building. The extrusion is along a straight path, which is not necessarily the same as to the building footprint. If the shape of the building is nonrectangular in footprint or the shape of the roof is not regular, the use of this tool allows you to shape the roof profile to match the footprint.

Recall that with sketch-based design, any closed loop of lines creates a positive shape, every next loop inside it is negative, and so on. In Figure 11.39, a roof by extrusion is drawn at an angle to the walls. To clip the roof to meet the walls, the Cut Plan Profile tool is used to draw a negative shape.

FIGURE 11.39

Cut Plan Profile applied to extruded roof to follow the exterior shape of the building

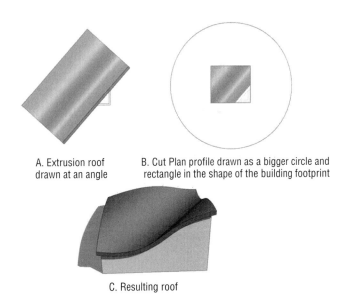

A. Extrusion roof drawn at an angle

B. Cut Plan profile drawn as a bigger circle and rectangle in the shape of the building footprint

C. Resulting roof

In-Place Roofs

The in-place roof technique will be used to accommodate roof shapes that cannot be achieved with either of the previously mentioned methods, usually being modeled with historic shapes or challenging geometry such as domes and onion domed roofs (Figure 11.40).

FIGURE 11.40
Manually constructed
"In-place" roofs

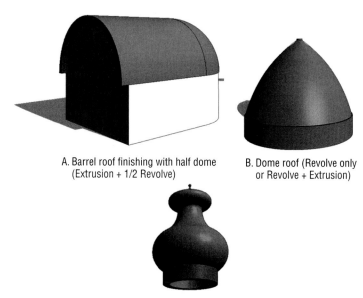

A. Barrel roof finishing with half dome
(Extrusion + 1/2 Revolve)

B. Dome roof (Revolve only
or Revolve + Extrusion)

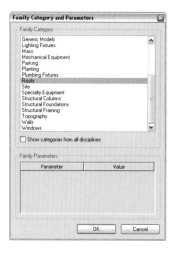

C. Traditional Russian onion dome (Revolve)

To start an in-place roof family, from the Modeling tab, click the Create button. Select Roofs from the Family Category list (Figure 11.41) and click OK. This list allows Revit to schedule the new element as a roof.

FIGURE 11.41
Set the category for an
in-place roof.

You can create any roof shape using the modeling techniques of Extrusion, Sweep, Revolve and Blend or any combination of them. You can, using the Edit shape tools, edit any roof shape manually, adding points and slopes. There will be more about advanced shape editing later in this chapter, in the section "Roof and Slabs."

Sloped Glazing

You saw earlier that a curtain wall is just another wall type made out of panels and mullions organized in a grid system. Similarly, sloped glazing is a type of a roof that has glass as material and mullions for divisions. Using sloped glazing, you can make roof lights and shed lights and also use them to design simple framing structures.

To create sloped glazing, make a simple pitch roof and select a sloped glazing type. Once you have done that, start applying grids that will define the panel sizes and apply mullions. Figure 11.42 demonstrates the process of converting a standard roof into sloped glazing.

FIGURE 11.42
(A) standard roof,
(B) Convert a standard roof into sloped glazing, (c) divide with curtain grid, (D) add mullions to the grid, (E) finished all mullions applied to the grid, (F) change curtain panel from glass to empty, (G) finished rafters

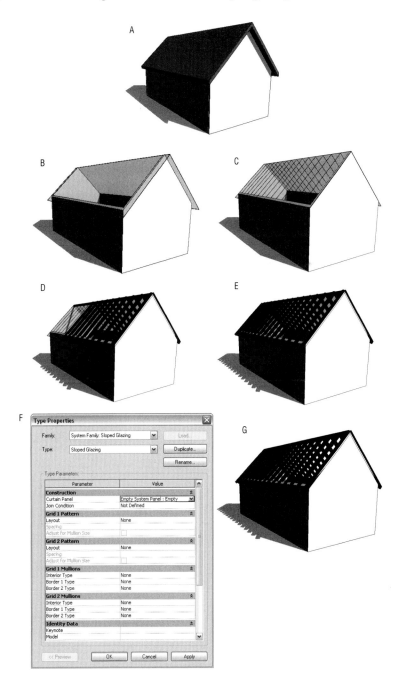

Using the knowledge and the principles mentioned, you will be able to create any of the roofs shown in the typology that follows the real world scenario.

Real World Scenario

CREATING A RIDGE SKYLIGHT ROOF

Suppose we are planning a factory whose roof needs to be a ridge skylight on a pitch.

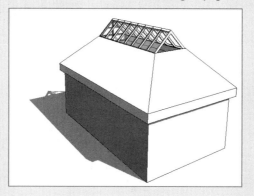

Here's how we make this roof:

1. In Level 1, draw the floor plan of the building. For the simplicity of the exercise, we will assume that the floor plan is a rectangle shape.

2. Define three levels in the drawing, Level 2 being 4m, Level 3 6m.

3. Switch to Level 2 and select the Roof tool.

4. Select Roof By Footprint.

5. Click on the Pick Walls option in the Design bar.

6. Define offset of 1´-6˝ (50cm), and check Defines Slope.

7. Click Finish Roof in the Design Bar

After having completed these steps, this is the resulting roof.

We now need to cut the top of this roof at Level 3.

1. Select the roof, and in its instance properties, select Level 3 under Cutoff Level and –1′8″ (–57cm) for Cutoff Offset (the roof thickness value) and Finish Roof. The result will look like this.

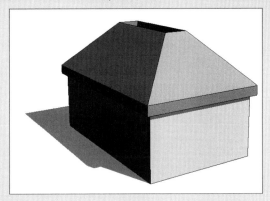

We will now create the second roof and use the opening in the first roof as a reference for the sketch lines defining the new roof.

1. Switch to Level 3, and select the Roof By Footprint tool. Instead of picking walls, select the Line tool, and in the Options bar, change from the Draw option to Pick. Pick the four edges of the opening of the first roof and lock all padlocks that appear when the four pink sketch lines are selected.

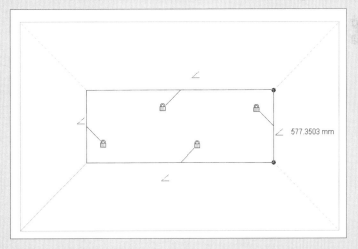

By doing this, you are creating a relationship between the two roofs so that if you later change the cutoff level or the geometry, the second roof will change to match.

Select the second roof, and from the Type Selector, pick Sloped Glazing to get the following configuration.

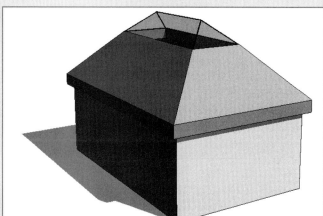

If the slope of the second roof isn't what you desire, you can change it at any time. Select the roof, click Edit on the Options bar, click on each of the sketch lines, and type in a new value over the slope value displayed. In this example, we have set 40 degrees for the second roof (the skylight).

Tip: In the Project Units dialog box, the Slope setting defines how the slope of a roof is measured.

Slope has these possible settings:

Slope Angle   The value of the slope is described as an angle.

Rise/1000   If this is the selected option, when you select a roof sketch line to define the slope, you will be putting in the height value between the pitch of the roof and its base (that is, you'll enter the Height Offset at Head property of a slope arrow). By default, when the project units are set to Imperial, the default slope is set to Slope Angle. For metric, it's Rise/1000. Of course, you can change that to your liking throughout the course of the project.

The last thing to do is to divide the sloped glazing into segments and apply mullions. For that you will use the Curtain Grid tool and start dividing the glazing.

At the end, add mullions by selecting the Mullion tool and picking the grid lines on the glazing. The final outcome should be similar to this.

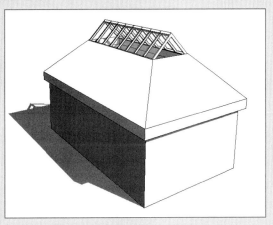

Sloped Arrows

Another way to slope a roof is by manually adding slope arrows to flat roof slabs. This can be useful for unusual shapes, especially if the roof edges are not straight.

First create the sketch lines to define the shape of a roof, and do not check Defines Slope on the Option bar. Instead, choose the Slope Arrow tool. Draw the slope arrow in the direction you wish your roof to pitch and at the intended height between the base of the roof and sloped end (Figure 11.43).

FIGURE 11.43
Slope-defining arrow added to sketch in roof by footprint

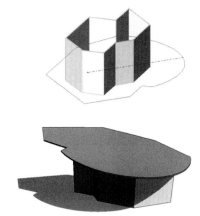

Once you've drawn the Slope Arrow, you can select it, and in the element properties, you can set any of the parameters shown in Figure 11.44. The most critical parameter to check is Height Offset At Head. This defines the height of the roof slab from the base to the top of its slope.

FIGURE 11.44
Slope arrow
properties

To create a shed roof you can draw a roof without any slope-defining sides and then apply a slope arrow that defines the exact sloping (Figures 11.45 and 11.46).

FIGURE 11.45
Shed roof defined
using slope arrow tool

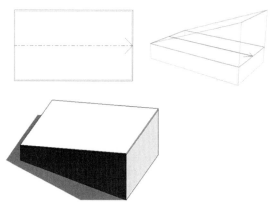

FIGURE 11.46
The same roof, with
the slop arrow short-
ened. Note that the
roof became much
steeper.

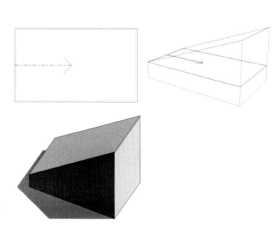

Roof Typologies

The following section demonstrates a series of typical roof conditions and the appropriate strategy to use in Revit to create these roofs. For any roof, there can many ways to solve it; use this as a guide and to shore up your skills with the roof tools. Each roof in the typology is represented with Roof Plan View, Sketch Plan and 3D view of the roof.

FLAT ROOF

This flat roof was created using roof by footprint and the Pick Walls method, checking Defines Slope.

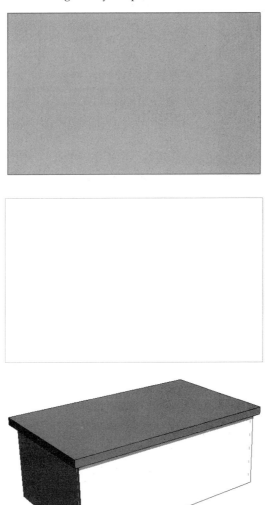

GABLE ROOF WITH ASYMMETRIC SLOPES

This roof is also created using roof by footprint and the Pick Walls method, but in this case Defines Slope is checked only for the shorter sides of the roof, with slope angles that are not identical.

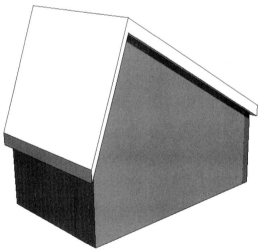

SHED ROOF

This roof by footprint was created using the Pick Walls method with Defines Slope checked only for the one of the short sides of the roof.

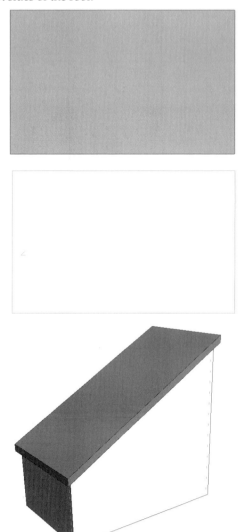

Note that you could also make this same roof by adding a slope-defining line to a flat roof:

HIPPED ROOF

This roof by footprint was created using the Pick Walls method, and Defines Slope was checked for all sides of the roof.

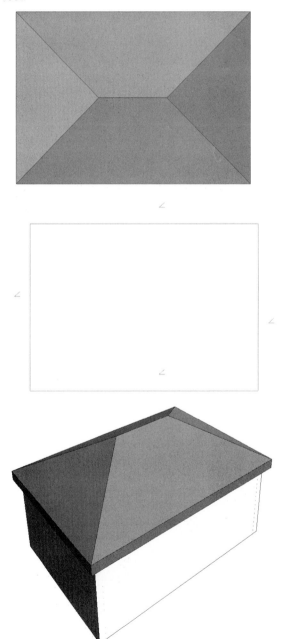

HIP ROOF FOLLOWING RECESSED WALLS

This roof by footprint was created using the Pick Walls method. Defines Slope was checked for all sides of the roof except the three walls that recess toward the inside.

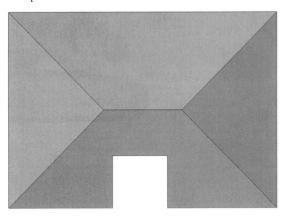

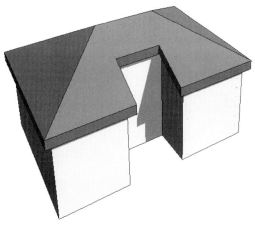

GABLE ROOF

This roof by footprint was created using the Pick Walls method with Defines Slope checked for all sides of the roof but the one that recesses toward the interior of the building.

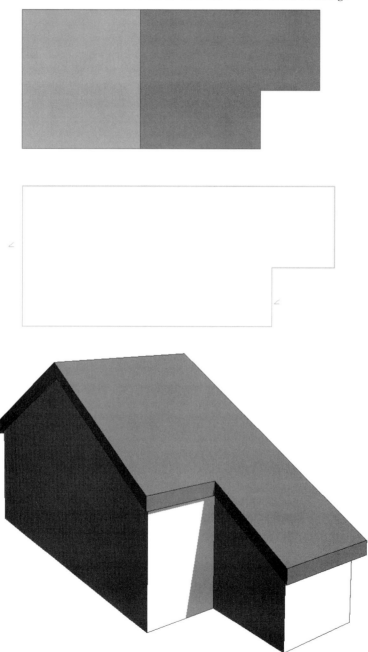

Gable Roof with Extending Pergola

This roof by footprint was created over a rectangular floor plan using the Pick Walls method. Its sketch was then edited and additional sketch lines added to shape up the extension. Slope is defined only for the sides indicated in the sketch.

HIP AND GABLE HYBRID ROOF

This roof by footprint was created with the Pick Walls method with Defines Slope defined for all sides.

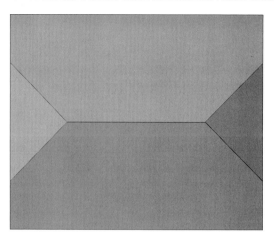

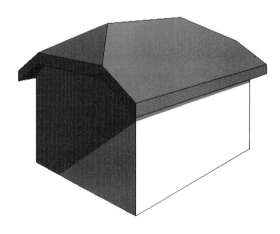

Notice that the sketch lines of the shorter sides have been split in thirds and Defines Slope is checked *only* for the middle portion of the line, as shown here.

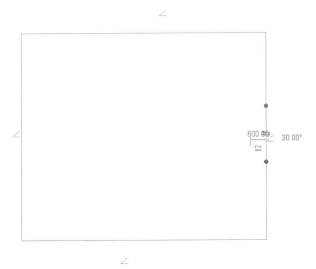

GAMBREL ROOF

This roof by footprint was created using the Pick Walls method. Defines Slope was checked for the two long sides of the roof only. The roof is cut off at a certain height (cutoff level), and a second roof has been created using as a sketch the cutoff shape of the first roof. The second roof also has Defines Slope Option checked for its two longer sides.

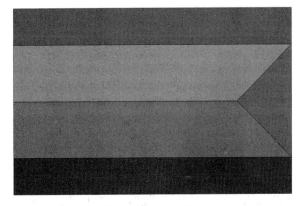

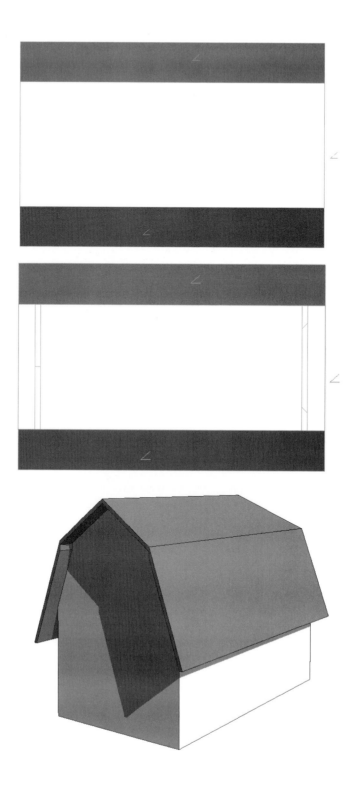

DUTCH GABLE WITH GLAZED ROOF

This roof by footprint was created with the Pick Walls method with Defines Slope checked for all sides of the roof. The roof is cut off at a certain height (Cutoff level), and a second roof has been created using as a sketch the cutoff shape of the first roof. The Type value of the second roof is set to Sloped Glazing. The second roof also has Defines Slope checked for all sides of the roof, but the slope of the second roof is slightly steeper than the one of the first roof. Curtain grid and mullions are applied to the sloped glazing. (See "Real World Scenario: Creating a Ridge Skylight Roof" for a full step-by-step procedure for this example.)

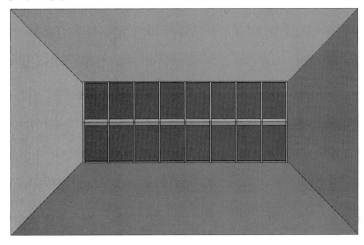

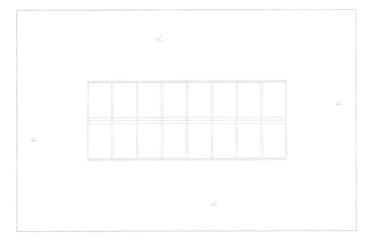

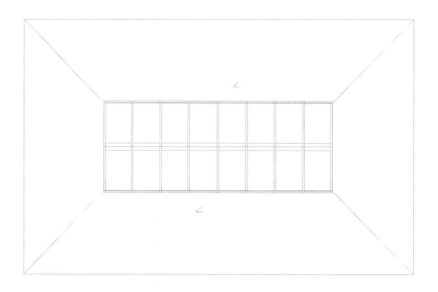

DUTCH GABLE

This roof by footprint was created with the Pick Walls method with Defines Slope checked for all sides of the roof. The roof is cut off at a certain height (Cutoff level), and a second roof has been created using as a sketch the cutoff shape of the first roof. Defines Slope is also checked for all sides of the second roof; the slope of the second roof is slightly steeper than the slope of the first roof.

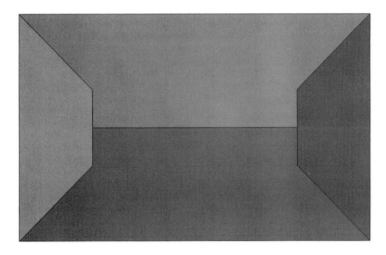

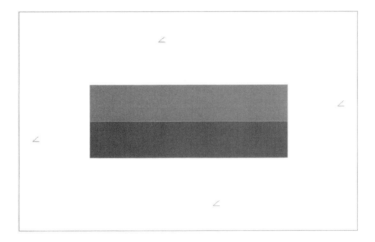

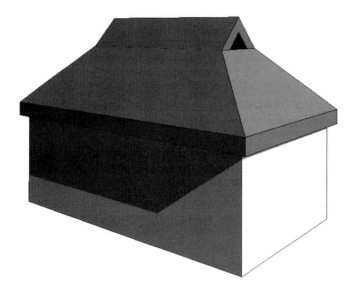

Hipped Roof with Sloped Arrow Dormer

This roof by footprint was created by using the Pick Walls method with Defines Slope checked for all sides of the roof. The sketch line on the south of the building is split into four segments to allow for the dormer creation. Sloped arrows facing each other and meeting in one point have been added to the middle two segments of the split sketch line.

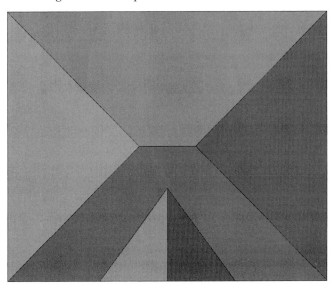

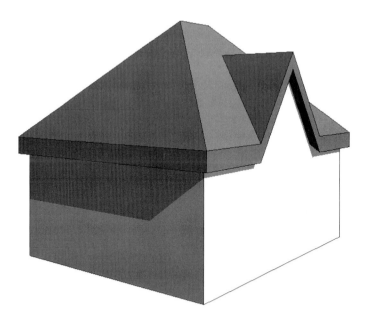

HIPPED ROOF WITH TWO DORMERS

This roof by footprint was created using Pick Walls method with Defines Slope checked for all sides of the roof. The two dormers are also separate roofs created by the footprint of the walls defining the sides of the dormer. The roofs are then joined. The opening in the roof slab is made up of two simple closed loops of lines (this can be done directly in the sketch or with the opening tool later).

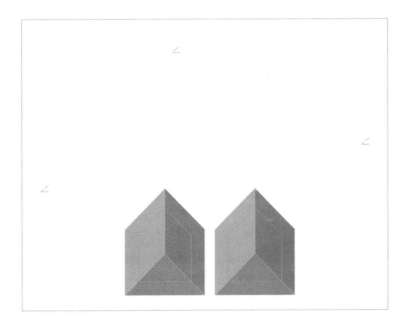

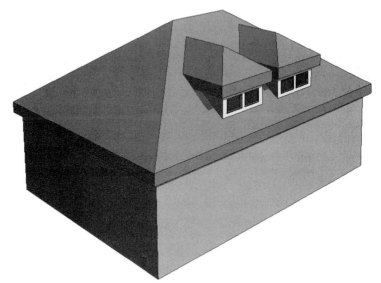

FOUR-SIDED GABLE

This roof by footprint was created using the Line Draw method in the shape indicated in the sketch. Defines Slope is checked for all four corners (see the blowups of the corner and middle roof edge).

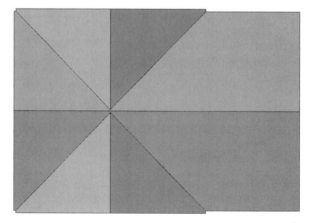

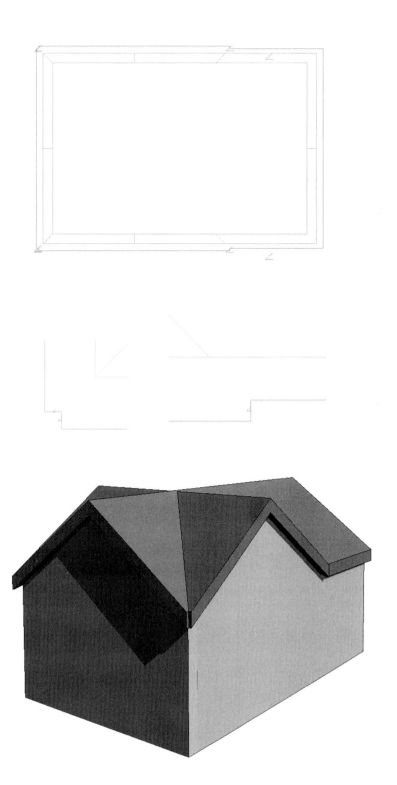

HIPPED ROOF WITH EXTRUDED ROOF DORMER

This roof by footprint was created using the Pick Walls method with Defines Slope checked for all sides of the roof. The dormer roof is created as a roof by extrusion using the wall face as a work plane and then joined with the other roof in the sketch or with the opening tool later.

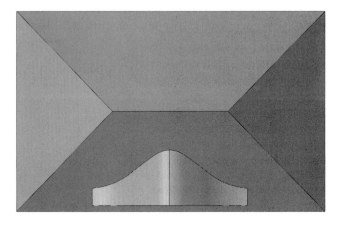

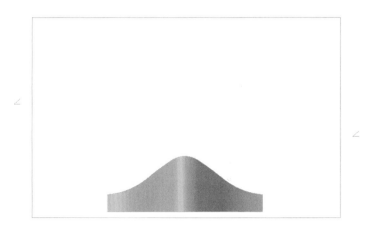

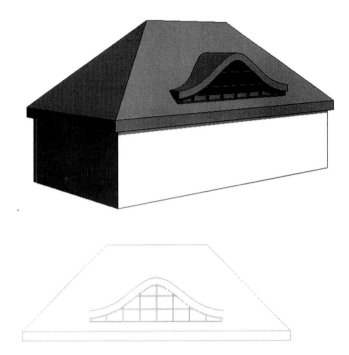

CONE ROOF

This is an in-place roof, created using the Create tool from the modeling Design bar with Roof as the category assigned to it. A simple closed line loop sketch is revolving around an axis.

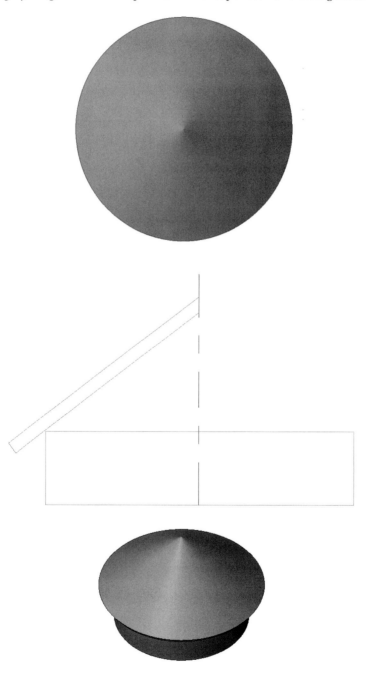

DOME

The dome was created using the revolve modeling technique. You will first need to draw a reference line in plan view that crosses the center of the circle describing the exterior walls, and then in section view, you will draw the revolving shape and also the axis of rotation.

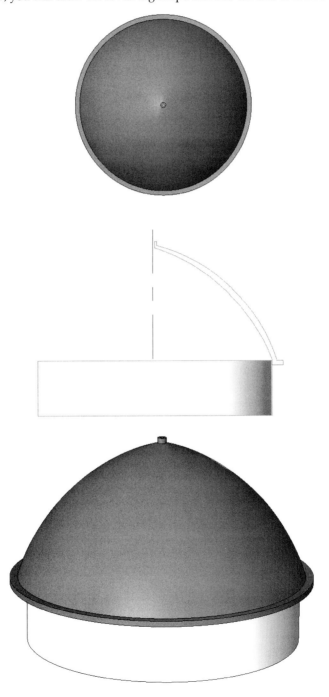

BARREL ROOF

This was created using the Roof by Extrusion method. A simple line in arc shape defines the main shape of the roof extruded over the building Footprint. In this particular example additional Roof by extrusion is added, converted into Sloped glazing, The Sloped Glazing Curtain Panel type is set to Empty glazing allowing for the mullion structure to create a sun shade.

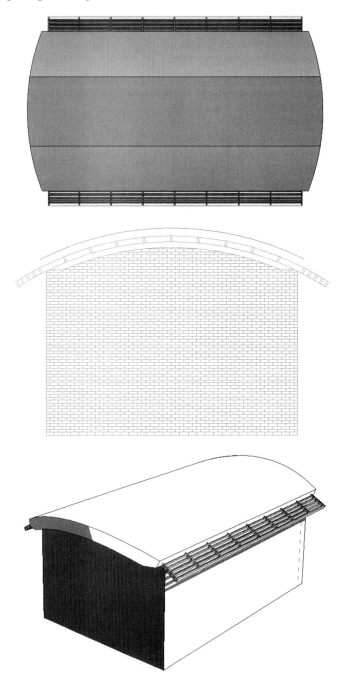

MULTIPITCH ROOF

This roof by footprint was created using the Pick Walls method with Defines Slope checked for all sides of the roof. Regardless of how complicated the underlying footprint, Revit will correctly calculate the ridges as long as the eaves are aligned.

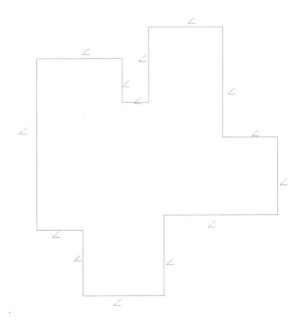

Roofs and Slabs: Advanced Shape Editing

No flat roof is ever really flat! Creating tapered insulation over a flat roof is no longer a challenge with the new Shape Editing tools for roofs and slabs introduced in the 2008 version of Revit. These powerful tools are modifiers that are applicable to roofs and floors with straight edges and offers the ability to model concrete slabs with multiple slopes, often referred to as warped slabs (Figure 11.47).

FIGURE 11.47
Sloped roof with
drainage

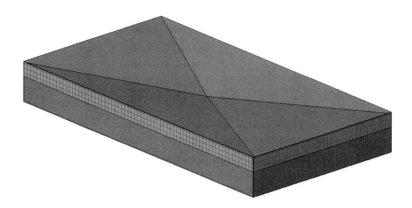

The modification tools appear in the Options bar when a roof or floor is selected.

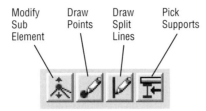

Here is what each tool is for (left to right):

The Direct Editing tool (Modify Sub Elements) This allows you to edit element geometry using selection and modification of points (vertices) and edges.

The Draw Points tool This allows you to add points on the top face of a roof or floor. Points can be added on edges or surfaces.

The Draw Split Lines tool This allows you to sketch directly on the top face of the element, which adds split lines to the floor and roof so that hips and valleys can be created.

The Pick Supports tool This allows you to pick linear beams and walls to create new split edges at the correct elevation automatically.

As you can see, there is also a Reset Shape button. This button will remove all modifiers applied to the floor/roof that is selected.

Sloped Roofs

Let's do a short exercise that shows how to make a sloped roof like the one in Figure 11.48 (shown in plan view).

FIGURE 11.48

A roof plan showing a roof divided in segments with drainage points

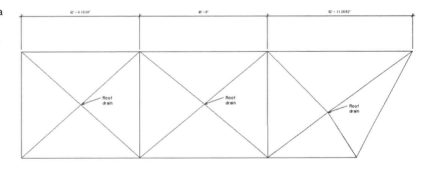

Follow these steps:

1. Open Modifying Roof Shape start.rvt from the website for this book (www.sybex.com/go/ masteringrevit2008).

2. Select the roof that has been already prepared for you.

3. Activate the Draw Split Lines tool (note that the color of the rest of the model grays out).

4. Sketch ridge lines to divide the roof into areas that will be independently drained.

5. Using the same tool, draw diagonal lines within those areas to create the valleys.

What you have done is split the roof surfaces into many subslabs, but they are still all at the same height/inclination. You should have a roof that looks like Figure 11.49.

FIGURE 11.49
Using the Draw Split Lines tool, ridges and valleys are created.

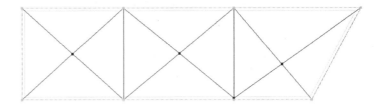

6. Switch to a 3D view.

7. To add a slope, you need to edit the height of the drainage points. Tab-select the crossing point of the diagonals. New controls that allow you to edit the text appear, and you can either move the arrows up and down or type in a value for the point height. As shown in Figure 11.50, type in **-0′ 5″** (-13cm):

FIGURE 11.50
Edit points to change height.

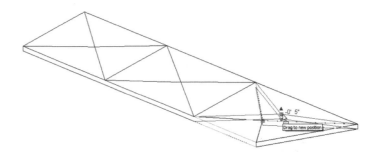

8. Repeat steps 1-7 for all three drainage points.

9. If you need to move the point to another position (as often happens to accommodate what's happening in the room below the roof), it is easily done by a simple select and drag-and-drop of the point.

10. Make a section through the roof—if possible, somewhere through the drainage point. Open the section; change the detail level to Fine view to see all layers. What you will see is that the entire roof structure is sloped toward the drainage point.

What if you wanted the insulation to be tapered but not the structure? For that, the layers of the roofs can now have variable thickness. Let us see how we can apply a variable thickness to a Layer.

1. Select the roof, and navigate to its type properties to edit its structure.

2. Activate the preview. You will notice that in the roof-structure preview, you do not see any slopes. That is correct and will not change. This preview is just a theoretical preview of the´ structure and will not show the exact sloping. You'll now see a Variable column under Layers (Figure 11.51). This allows layers of the roof to vary in thickness when slopes are present. Check Variable for the insulation material.

FIGURE 11.51
The Edit Roof
Structure dialog

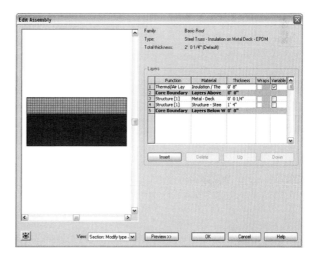

3. Go back to the section view and take a look at the difference that this change provoked. As you will see, only the insulation is tapered now, while the structure remains flat.

Currently this modifier cannot be applied to any floor or roof that has a *nonstraight* segment. However, you can work around that by using a vertical opening (Figure 11.52). You need to start with a simplified straight segment floor/roof shape that contains no arcs. You add the arc as a subtraction in the form of an opening. By using the Opening tool in the Modeling tab and choosing the Vertical option, you can then sketch the arcs you need.

FIGURE 11.52
Roof Opening can be used to make non-straight roofs with the new slope options.

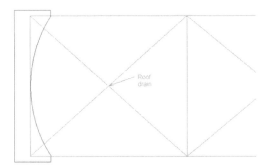

Warped Surfaces

Warped surfaces can also be created using this tool. Draw a flat roof (no slopes) and then select the roof. Using the Modify tool in the Options bar, you can start moving edge points up and down (Figure 11.53).

Railings and Fences

Railings and fences can range from very simple shapes to quite complex ones, as you can see by looking at the examples in the Revit help system (Figure 11.54). They can be represented as simple walls that follow the sides of a stair flight, balcony, or your garden; you can also create glass frameless railings or quite complex combinations of balusters and posts with combinations of materials. Revit allows most combinations of railings to be built, but this does require a thorough understanding of one of the more complicated systems in Revit.

FIGURE 11.53
Warped roof

FIGURE 11.54
From the Revit help system, a variety of possible railings and fences that can be created with Revit.

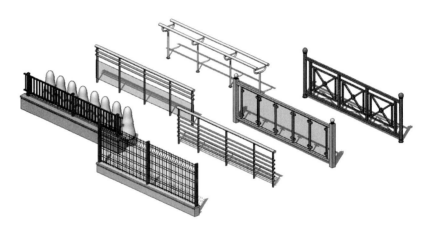

We will attempt to cover some of the main principles used to create different types of railings in Revit.

Railings

Railings are sketch based, and you define their position and length by drawing a simple base line (Figure 11.55).

FIGURE 11.55
Define the position
and length of a railing
by drawing a base line.

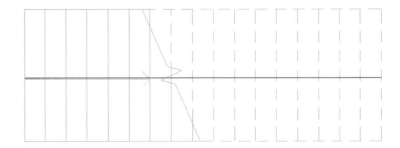

Railings must be placed on a host. A valid host for railings is a slab, a stair, a ramp, or a level.

So, the principle is as follows: If you draw a railing sketch line without setting a specific host, it will be drawn on the level and you will get a horizontal railing. If you want to add a railing to a stair that doesn't have any, you will need to select the Railing tool and then use the Set Host option from the Design bar to select the stair, and only then you draw the railing.

✥ Set Host

If you forget to set the host prior to drawing the railing, the railing will be placed on the floor/level at which the stair starts, beneath the stair. But no worries—you can rehost it later. Select the railing, edit its sketch from the Options bar, select Set Host, and pick the stair as a host.

Since a railing is based on a sketch line, you can have your railing follow just about any path (Figure 11.56).

FIGURE 11.56
A free-standing railing and a railing hosted by a stair, both following the sketchline shape

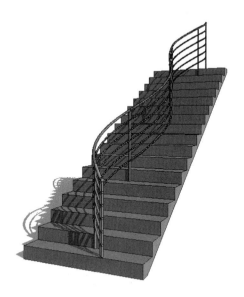

Sub-elements and Principles of the Railing Element

A railing element consists of the sub-elements shown in Figure 11.57.

FIGURE 11.57

Railing components

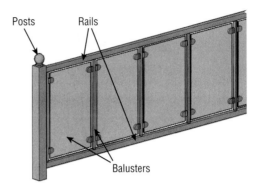

Balusters   These can be any shape or form, and they can be represented by just about any geometry that will repeat itself in a railing (balusters are anything between posts). You create the baluster families in the Family Editor using one of the three available family templates: `Baluster.rte`, `Baluster-Panel.rte`, or `Baluster Post.rte`. Using the basic modeling tools explained in Chapter 6, you can make balusters such as those shown in Figure 11.58.

FIGURE 11.58

Balusters can have any shape and size.

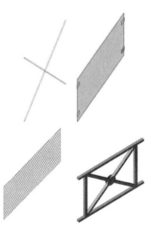

Posts   Posts can have any shape, as shown on Figure 11.59. They are created using the `Baluster-Post.rfa` template in the Family Editor.

FIGURE 11.59
Various post types
created using
`Baluster-Post.rte`

Rails   These are horizontal elements that connect posts (should there be any). The geometry of the rails is defined by profile families that you create in the Family Editor using the Profile Rail family template. Here are some examples of typical rail profiles.

Rails can appear attached to a wall as a handrail, as shown in Figure 11.60. In this case, no posts are used and the wall mount brackets are custom-designed balusters. The rail is following the stair and is given an appropriate offset from the wall.

FIGURE 11.60
Handrail seemingly
attached to wall

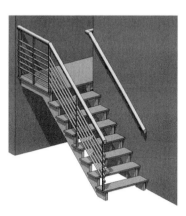

Railing Construction

The order and combination of these subelements of the railing element can create unlimited varia-tions of railings. In the type properties of the railing, under the Rail Structure and Baluster placement options (Figure 11.61), you can set any combination.

FIGURE 11.61

Type properties of a railing element with embedded editors for rail and baluster placement

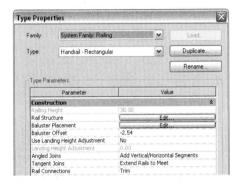

Setting Up Rail Structure

Choosing Rail Structure ➤ Edit Rails displays the dialog shown in Figure 11.62, where you define the number, shape, and position of the rails in your railing. Figure 11.63 shows a railing with two rails: one set to 6″ (15cm) height and the upper one set at 4′ (120cm). Both of them use the profile Rectangular Handrail. The 1″ (2.5cm) offset pushes the rail away from the sketch line, as you can see in the front elevation.

FIGURE 11.62

The Edit Rails dialog

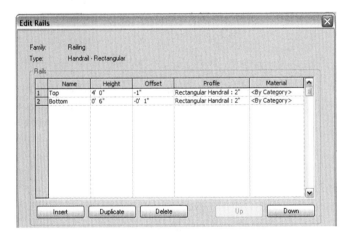

FIGURE 11.63

(Left) Elevation of a railing with two rails (lower and upper); (right) the rails are placed with an offset to the mid-axis of the rail sketch line (balusters have no offset).

To define posts and baluster patterns, click the Edit button for Baluster Placement in the type properties of the railing. You'll see the window shown in Figure 11.64.

OPTIONS IN THE POSTS GROUP

Depending on their position in the railing, posts can be start , corner, or end posts. You can choose to have different families for the three types and thus select a different baluster-post family for all three, or you can keep it simple and use the same family. You also don't have to have them all—you can set None for the post placement for any of them (for example, you can have start and end and no corner). Figure 11.65 shows various possibilities for the placement of posts.

FIGURE 11.64

The Edit Baluster Placement dialog

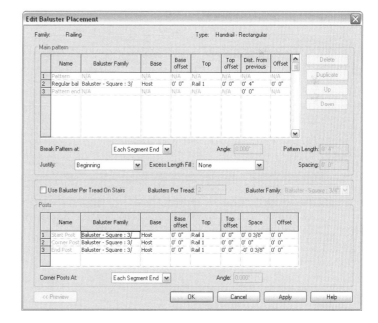

FIGURE 11.65

(Left) Railing with start, corner, and end posts using the same post family. (Right) Railing with corner post set to None and different post families used for start and end posts.

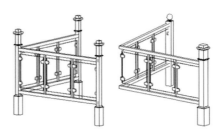

You can define corner posts to be dependent on the angle of the railing or to only appear under certain conditions, or you can not use them at all.

The option Angles Greater Than allows for visibility control dependent on the set angle. This means that if the individual segments of sketch lines of a railing turn into angles greater than 70 degrees (for example), a corner post will be placed. If smaller, none will be placed (Figure 11.66).

FIGURE 11.66

When the sketch lines of a railing meet at an angle greater than the angle defined for corner posts, a corner post will be placed.

As mentioned, railings and their subelements can be hosted only on floors, levels, and stairs. So their placement is usually defined as an offset from the host. In the Edit Baluster Placement dialog, you will find that you can also define the position of a rail as an offset from another rail that exists in the structure.

	Name	Baluster Family	Base	Base offset	Top	Top offset	Space	Offset
1	Start Post	Baluster - Round : 2"	Host	0' 0"	Rail 1	0' 0"	0' 0 3/8"	0' 0"
2	Corner Post	Baluster - Square : 3/	Host	0' 0"	Rail 1	0' 0"	0' 0"	0' 0"
3	End Post	Baluster - Square : 3/	Host	0' 0"	Host	0' 0"	-0' 0 3/8"	0' 0"
					Rail 1			

That is what the Top parameter means—here you can either select the host of the entire railing or choose from a list of existing rails in the railing as a top reference. The top offset can be a positive or negative value.

The Space parameter defines the distance of the post center line to the railing viewed in a longitudinal direction, as shown in Figure 11.67. This value can be positive or negative.

FIGURE 11.67
Space parameters define the longitudinal position of the rail.

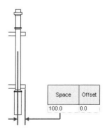

DESIGNING THE MAIN PATTERN

The Main Pattern section of the Edit Baluster Placement window is where you define the pattern of the railing between the posts to generate a complex railing, such as Figure 11.68. The options (Figure 11.9) are similar to those just discussed for the rails.

FIGURE 11.68
Baluster main pattern

FIGURE 11.69
The Main Pattern options

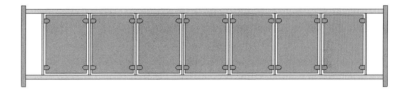

Note that all parameters that define position (such as Dist. from Previous or Offset) are calculated from the midpoints of the baluster families.

The Dist. from Previous setting allows placement of balusters at a specific set distance from one another. You will have to know the actual dimensions of your different balusters prior to defining this (Figure 11.70).

FIGURE 11.70

The baluster position is always measured to the mid-axis for all positioning parameters.

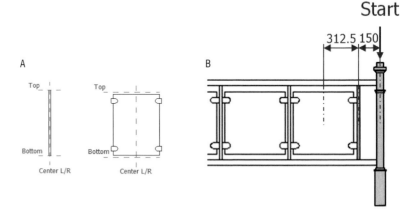

As you can imagine, the railing length will not always fit an even number of panels or balusters based on the pattern length. How do we deal with that?

Revit provides four different justifications for the pattern fit: Beginning, End, Center, and Spread Pattern To Fit.

Their names explain the usage, but Figure 11.71 shows the different justifications and their implications on a design.

The justification you select will obviously depend on your design, but you may also be using prefab standard railing patterns that come only in certain dimensions.

FIGURE 11.71
Pattern options

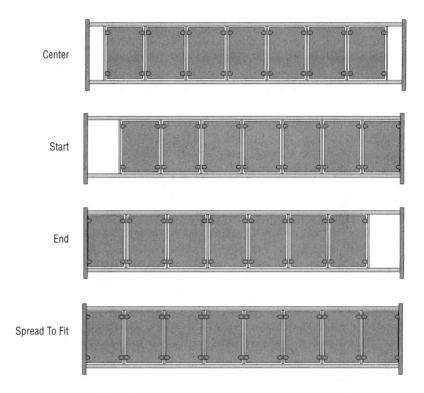

Center

Start

End

Spread To Fit

BALUSTERS PER TREAD

Revit allows you to set specific number of balusters per tread on stairs.

If you want to control the number fo the balusters per tread, you will check the first option: Use Baluster Per Tread On Stairs. This will make the next option active and you can then type in the number of balusters you wish to have per tread. You will also be able to change the baluster family by clicking the Baluster Family option to display a list of all loaded baluster families available in the project.

Figure 11.72 shows a railing with a two balusters/tread setting, a one baluster/tread, and then one with a changed baluster family (when the Use Baluster Per Tread On Stairs option is not activated, the effect is to change the baluster family).

FIGURE 11.72
Spiral stairs with different settings: (A) two balusters per tread; (B) one baluster per tread; (C) Use Baluster Per Tread On Stairs is not activated, so the railing will follow the main pattern.

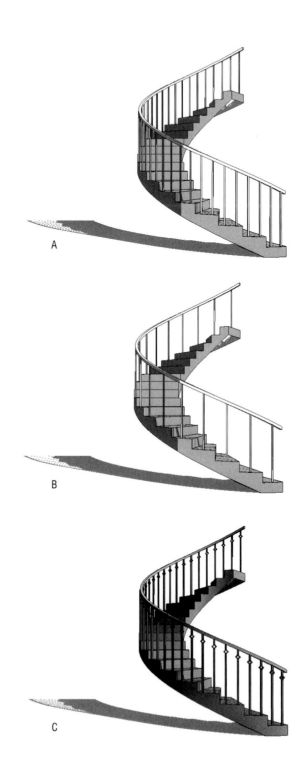

As you will notice, the moment you use the Use Baluster Per Tread On Stairs option, the Baluster Family selection overrides the one set in the Main Pattern section.

ADDITIONAL CONTROLS

Landings can be difficult to work with when designing railings. Revit has a set of additional tools and type parameters to control them (Figure 11.73).

FIGURE 11.73
Landing parameters:
Use Landing Height
Adjustment

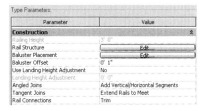

By default, each railing in Revit will follow the stair flight and the landing and will create the most logical solution. Often, however, the height of the railing on a landing is not calculated according to your design intent. With the Use Landing Height Adjustment parameter, you will be able to change the railing at the landing to a specific height.

Landings can also generate unresolved situations where segments of the railings meet. By default, the joins at the angles are unresolved and the segments are not connected. You can fix that by adding vertical/horizontal segments and refine it further by setting the rail connections to Trim or Weld (see Figure 11.74). All these settings are also part of the type properties dialog for the railing.

FIGURE 11.74
Angled joins: (A) no
connector; (B) add
vertical/horizontal
segments; (C) with
Rail parameter set to
Trim/Weld

The Tangent Joins tool does a similar job but affects connections of different segments of the railing that are on a continuous tangent. The options are located in the type properties of a rail.

The effects can be seen in Figure 11.75.

FIGURE 11.75
Mid-landing railing segments cleanup: (A) No Connector; (B) Add Vertical Segments; (C) Extend Rails to Meet

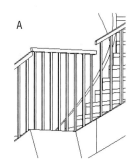
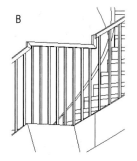
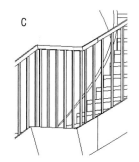

Finally, there are a few more adjustment tools needed to refine the railing and bring it closer to your design goals. These last tools are available in sketch mode of the railing tool only.

Edit Joins   Use this tool to clean up segment joints while in the railing sketch. Once you're in a sketch mode, this option appears in the sketch Design bar.

Click the Edit Joins button, hover the mouse pointer over the sketch line joins, and then click the join (Figure 11.76) to activate options in the Options bar. These provide the same controls you saw in the previous example.

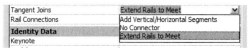

FIGURE 11.76
Edit joins by clicking on the end join of sketch lines.

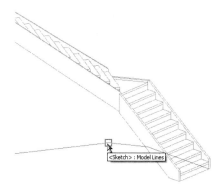

In sketch mode, after you select one of the railing sketch lines, the following Options bar tools appear.

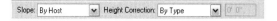

What these tools will let you do is manipulate the sketch lines in order to adjust the slope of the railing or correct the height connection.

The Slope tool will offer you three possibilities:

By Host   Follows the slope of the host, which is what you would most probably need in the majority of the cases.

Flat   This option keeps the railing flat, regardless the slope of the host.

Slope   This option defines a completely custom-chosen slope to your railing that ensures uninterrupted connection between adjacent segments.

Similar to what we have shown about the height adjustement on the landing, there is an additional adjustment of the height of a railing useful for controling the extension of a railing. This is also available when in sketch mode only and offers two options:

By Type   The railing height for the selected segment depends on the properties of the railing type.

Custom   The railing height for the selected segment can be forced to a different custom value. Figure 11.77 demonstrates both situtations.

FIGURE 11.77
Railing height adjusted By Type or forced to a new height value (custom)

Real World Scenario

ADDING A RAIL ONTO A WALL

Adding a rail to stairs is easy, but adding a rail on top of a wall is more difficult. Shown here is a railing design consisting of a base wall and a railing element on top of it. This is a common type of railing in institutional buildings or outdoor stairs, so let's see how it is made.

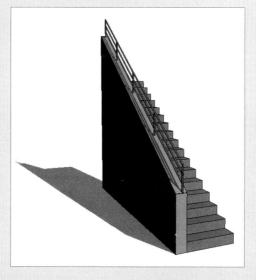

The challenge we face is that a wall is not considered a host for a railing element, so we have to find a workaround for how to place a railing that will follow the stair angle and is based on the wall.

Start by creating a stair without any railings (or delete the default railings later) and create a wall next to it with an edited elevation profile.

You then create a very thin floor on top of the wall that will play the role of hosting for the railing:

1. Create a floor type that is very thin.

2. Switch to elevation view. Using the Dimension tool, measure the height of the top of the wall at the beginning and end of the stair. You will need these values when you slope the floor to match the stair.

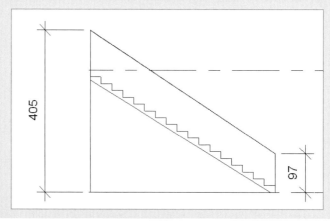

3. Define the floor shape by switching to plan view and drawing a floor. Use the Pick method and pick the four lines representing the top of the wall.

4. While still in floor sketch mode, click on the Slope Arrow tool and set the properties as shown:

For Specify, choose Height At Tail.

For Height offset at Tail, set the value of the lower height of the wall to 3´-0˝ (97cm).

For Height offset at Head, set the higher value of 12´-0˝ (405cm)

Draw the slope arrow in the middle of the floor starting at the beginning of the stair and finishing toward the end of the stair. By doing this, you have added a sloping to the floor that matches the sloping of the wall.

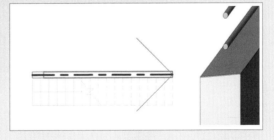

5. Select the Railing tool, click on Set Host, pick the floor, and draw the railing in the middle of the floor.

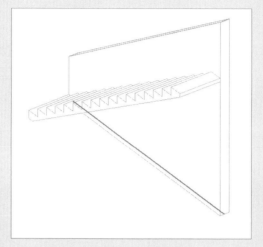

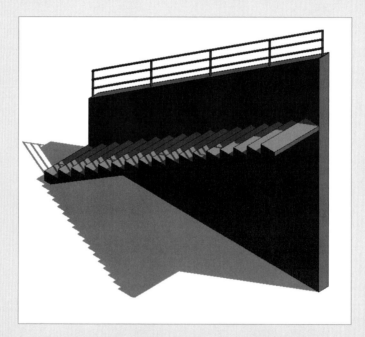

This workaround proves to be quite practical when dealing with railings in big auditoriums. Auditoriums are rarely done using huge stairs but rather stairs divided into many floors, and a railing can only have one host, so it won't be possible to host the railing on many floors at the same time. Using this workaround, you will be able to create a railing that runs through many auditorium levels and is still hosted.

The Bottom Line

Revit provides extensive tools for modeling basic elements such as walls, roofs, and railings, allowing for tremendous flexibility.

Take advantage of advanced wall features   Many design situations require more than just the basic wall features; learn to use the more advanced Revit tools.

> **Master It**   A design calls for a horizontal soldier course in a brick wall every 12′ on the façade. Using Revit, how would you build this into a wall element?

Work with advanced roofs and slab editing   Roofs are another seemingly simple element that present architectural challenges, and Revit has tools for them.

> **Master It**   You are working on a flat roof retail project, but of course the roof is not really flat and will need to drain. Using Revit roof tools, how would you go about modeling this?

Work with railings   Railings are another bread-and-butter architectural element whose design can be streamlined with Revit.

> **Master It**   You've found some nice-looking railing panels and balusters while scouring the Web for interesting rail designs. How do you go about building the railing in Revit?

Chapter 12

Presenting Your Design

As design professionals, we are deeply rooted in the art of representation and expression. Our drawings are not just communication methods, they gain personal expression at our hands: Color, contrast, light, and shadow are manipulated to give a drawing life and dramatic poise. From the loose napkin sketch to the photorealistic rendering, we imbue our designs with a sense of purpose and intent. This intent is a driving force in architecture and critical to its progression. Without models and drawings that challenge the senses, that make us imagine the otherwise unimaginable, where would we be today? For a moment, consider the drawings of Piranesi, Boullée, Wright, Woods, and Hadid. Each is distinct, thoughtful, evocative—at times utopian. Consider your own practice and your techniques—your role in shaping the built environment.

Think about how your drawings are interpreted, received, and understood. How do they shape the evolution of a design? How have digital tools changed the way you present and evaluate a design? Keep these questions in the back of your mind as we move through this chapter. Consider how the techniques we look at can help you, and also think of how you might push some boundaries and extend your creativity using the tools available in Revit.

You've seen with Revit that many traditional documentation drawing types are generated on the fly with little or no effort. With a few clicks of the mouse, you can generate entire building sections and elevations. A perspective view takes a few seconds to generate. Revit does a fairly good job of producing these drawings, but it can't fully replace the skill and decision-making process of an artist--design intent and the message still need to be considered by the designer, despite the afforadaces provided by technology. Knowing this, Revit provides some tools to help you make your drawings more legible and expressive. If need be, you can export a drawing as vector lines (`.dwg`, `.pdf`) or as pixels (`.jpg`, `.png`, and so on) and further refined to meet your design requirements.

In this chapter you'll learn the following techniques:

◆   Using shadows for presentation purposes

◆   Creating quality presentation plans and sections

◆   Creating elevations that convey depth

◆   Creating quality rendered perspective views

Drawings with Shadows

Shadows tend to be used for two purposes: analytical (Figure 12.1) and expressive (Figure 12.2). For analysis, shadows are used to see how a building will be affected by its environment and real-world sun angles based on the location of the site. This analytic use is explored in depth in Chapter 14 and is covered here primarily to introduce the shadowing tools. The expressive use of shadow, our focus in this discussion of presentation issues, conveys depth in drawings and gives them more character; it may or may not be tied to real-world sun positions.

Revit provides a tool for both use cases, and you'll see how to use each of these. The nice thing about shadows in Revit is that it's easy to enable them, and voila!—shadows are there.

FIGURE 12.1
Analytical use of shadows in a site plan shows the effect of buildings on their environment.

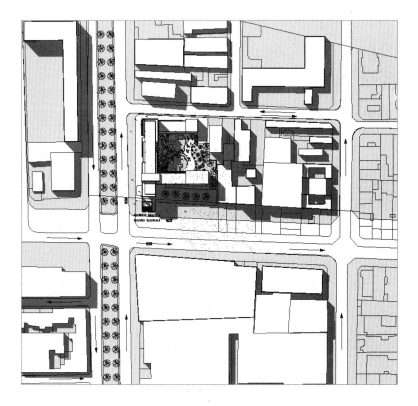

FIGURE 12.2
A more expressive view using shadows in a shaded view without edges

IMAGES COURTESY OF FELIPE MANRIQUE DIAZ

Analytical Drawings: Sun and Shadow Studies

Using shadows analytically allows you to see (and demonstrate) the effect of a building on its environment and, likewise, the effect of the environment on your building. Using real-world sun and building positions, you can evaluate the design impact on its surroundings. You need to know whether the building will have a negative impact and make sure building codes are satisfied. You'll also want to see the effect of the sun on the building itself, to study light penetration and how other buildings will affect light and shadow. Figure 12.1 showes a site plan view with shadows turned on.

To get accurate sun shadows, you need to establish where the building is on the planet, and the date and time that you wish to analyze. For example, it's common practice all over the world to represent the extreme sun angles at both the summer and winter solstices—both are provided in the default template. Depending on the city you're in, these angles vary based on the latitude and longitude. In Revit, every project has a location that is defined in the Settings ➢ Manage Place And Locations dialog, which has a direct influence on sun position (Figure 12.3). In the Place tab, choose from a list of cities; the latitude and longitude are set for you automatically. If you don't find your city in the list, choose a nearby city, and then edit the latitude and longitude to match your location.

FIGURE 12.3

Set your building location using the Manage Place And Locations dialog.

You need to set your location only once in a project. This will affect all sun angle calculations.

To turn on shadows and see the effect of date, time, and location, choose the Shadows On option from the view controls at the bottom of any view:

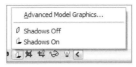

ENABLING SHADOWS

Shadows are view specific. They appear in the view—but how are the shadows being drawn? Where is the sun defined? To see how the light is being cast, you need to click the Advanced Model Graphics option (Figure 12.4) where all the shadow settings are defined, including a direct link back to the Manage Place And Locations dialog. From this dialog, you can access the Sun And

Shadows Settings, play with the brightness and darkness of the sun and shadows, and override silhouette edges.

FIGURE 12.4
The Advanced Model
Graphics dialog

SUN AND SHADOW SETTINGS

Clicking on the ellipsis button (…) next to the Sun And Shadows Settings opens a dialog where you set the angle of the sun. For analytical views, choose meaningful times and dates. Revit ships with the presets shown in Figure 12.5.

FIGURE 12.5
The Sun And Shadows
Settings dialog for still
images

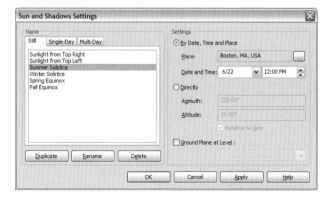

There are two methods for setting the sun angle: By Date, Time, and Place; and Directly. Be careful in this dialog not to change the radio buttons for a given named setting—doing so could cause problems later. For example, if you set Summer Solstice to a manually set azimuth and altitude that aren't accurate, you can create misleading settings. If you need to create a unique setting, *duplicate an existing setting* and go from there, rather than editing the preset options. Or, if you really intend to change the setting, go ahead and rename it to an appropriate and meaningful name.

INTENSITY

To get different graphic results, try experimenting with the Sun and Shadow intensities in the Advanced Model Graphics dialog:

If you give the sun 100% intensity, the model appears brightly lit, and shadows appear more subdued. Figure 12.6 shows the different effects that can be achieved by adjusting the intensity values. The sun only affects views set to Shading or Shading With Edges. In other words, for Hidden Line views, you can only change the darkness of the shadows but not the intensity of the sun.

FIGURE 12.6
Adjust intensity to get different graphic results

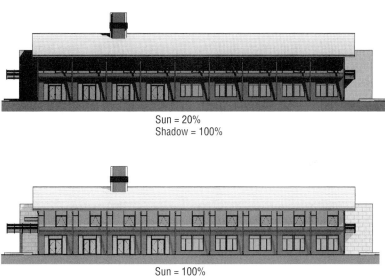

Sun = 20%
Shadow = 100%

Sun = 100%
Shadow = 20%

To apply different settings to the same type of view, you need to duplicate the view and apply different Sun settings using the Advanced Model Graphics dialog. Be aware that Sun settings (shadows and intensity) *are not* retained when you duplicate views—you must manually set the Sun settings for each view you duplicate.

Expressive Drawings with Shadows

When you use shadows expressively, the need for accurate lighting conditions is not as important as the need to define consistent angles so that your drawings express depth. Without shadows, a façade appears flat and difficult to interpret. By adding shadows and setting them to be Relative To View, you can establish a shadow angle that suits your needs and reuse those settings for multiple views. The default template includes two presets for this in the Sun And Shadows Settings dialog: Sunlight From Top Right and Sunlight From Top Left (Figure 12.7).

FIGURE 12.7
Sun locations in the
default template

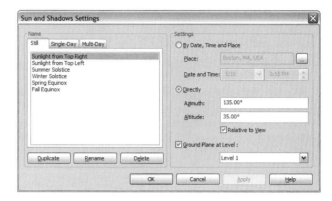

The combination of Azimuth and Altitude with these presets produces 45° shadows on an elevation.

HIGH-CONTRAST BLACK AND WHITE EFFECTS

Using Hidden Line display and increasing the shadows to 80–90 percent produces nice, high-contrast elevations. As you can see in Figure 12.8, this is a great way to create visuals that will read from far away.

FIGURE 12.8
High-contrast black
and white elevation

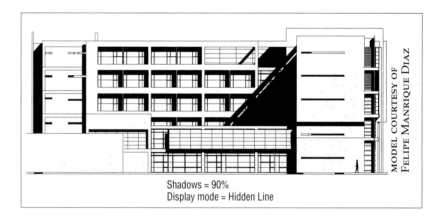

Shadows = 90%
Display mode = Hidden Line

SOFT SHADOWS

For a softer appearance, try using a Shading view (without edges) and setting Shadows to 30 percent and Sun to 70 percent. You'll get a very even-colored, washed-out feel (Figure 12.9).

FIGURE 12.9
Soft edges and low-contrast shadows

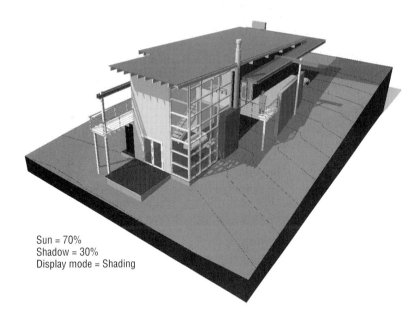

Sun = 70%
Shadow = 30%
Display mode = Shading

Performance

As you'll discover when working in views with shadows enabled, the speed of panning and zooming in the model degrades when shadows are on. So, as you start to use shadows, keep this in mind: *Turning off shadows is always two clicks away*. If you want to start panning and zooming around the view, turn off the shadows for a while. When you're done zooming about, turn them back on. Remember that the settings are persistent, and turning off shadows is just a simple way to improve performance while working with your model.

Color-Coded Plans and Sections

Color, when associated with a key, is an effective way to signify meaning. In the context of architectural expression, the use of color is often used to convey how space is used, or intended to be used. With Revit, you can use color to differentiate one object from another to communicate ideas about usage, size, importance, and cost—to name a few. By assigning parameter values to colors and patterns, you can quickly make views that show how a building is spatially organized (Figure 12.10). For example, you can create a department floor plan by assigning departments to all your rooms and then apply a color fill scheme to the view that changes the color of rooms based on what department they're assigned to.

FIGURE 12.10
Use color and
parameters
to generate
color-fill plans.

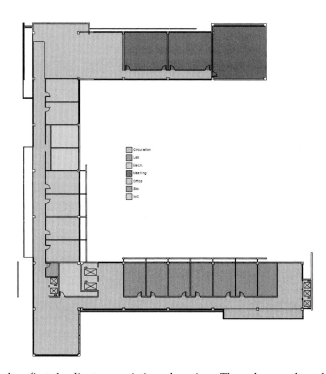

To make a color-coded plan, first duplicate an existing plan view. The colors are based on the room element, so you need to place rooms in the plan before you can create a room color scheme. You can also create new area plans, and use area separation lines to divide space at a more macro scale, and then assign values to each area that can then be colored with a color fill scheme. You can select any room and access its element properties. All of the properties in the Identity group can be color-coded. Using project parameters, you can also add custom parameters to rooms. In the View Properties dialog of the plan view, you can assign a color-fill scheme to the view. Clicking that parameter takes you to the Color Fill Schemes dialog, where you can set up various schemes. Whatever is selected in that dialog is applied to the view, and the rooms become colored.

Color Fill Schemes

Color fill schemes are applied to views on a per-view basis, and are exposed as an instance property of plan and area plan views. To access and create color fill schemes, choose Settings ➢ Color Fill Schemes (Figure 12.11), or you can get to the same dialog from the View Properties dialog. In the resulting dialog, you see a list of schemes on the left and all the rules and colors for those schemes on the right. Each scheme colors one parameter and all its values. For each unique value, a unique color and/or hatch pattern can be assigned. For example, if you choose to color by name, the table fills with all the room names in the project and assigns a color to each. Clicking the button in the Color column allows you to choose your own colors. While Revit will create new colors for you automatically with each new value, you are free to define your own colors, and can even save these into a template for use in other projects.

FIGURE 12.11
The Edit Color
Scheme dialog

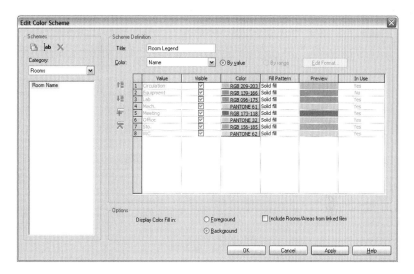

Information in this dialog is also used to fill out color-fill legends, which are essentially graphical tags of the color scheme and are placed next to the plans to explain the color coding. The legend shows the title, values, and color swatches for the scheme applied to a view. To place a legend in a view, use the Color Scheme Legend command in the Drafting tab of the Design bar.

The color-scheme legend allows you to edit its type properties to control the visibility of the title, swatch size, fonts, and color (Figure 12.12).

FIGURE 12.12
Color-scheme legend
properties

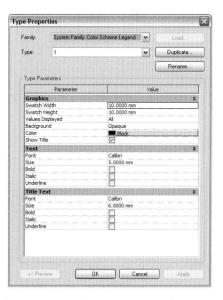

Note that the order of the values in the legend coincides with the order set up in the Edit Color Scheme dialog. The default behavior lists each entry alphabetically, but you're free to change that by using the Move Up/Move Down buttons when a row is selected. Doing so simultaneously updates the color-scheme legend:

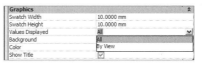

Another important graphical control of the legend is the Values Displayed parameter. This gives you the option to show only values in the legend that are also in the view (By View). In a project where the number of departments and room names can be large, and they aren't used in all floor plans, this is a great way to focus the legend on what is important to that view. Many designers do not want to display all the color swatches, but this is ultimately up to your own personal taste, and what the drawings are intended to convey. Choosing the All option shows all values used in the project, whether used in the view or not.

Graphics	
Swatch Width	10.0000 mm
Swatch Height	10.0000 mm
Values Displayed	All
Background	All
Color	By View
Show Title	☑

CREATING PREDEFINED COLOR SCHEMES

If you've created a list of room names, departments, and a carefully chosen color palette of colors that are likely to be reused in future projects, you can transfer the color scheme from project to project and into your office template. This transfers all the values and colors, even if the project you're transferring to doesn't contain that value.

🌐 Real World Scenario

TRANSFERRING COLOR FILL SCHEMES BETWEEN PROJECTS

In an existing project, you can add room names and departments and assign them colors in the Color Fill Scheme dialog. To reuse the same values and colors from the project in other projects, use the following strategy:

1. Open the source project, and then open the project into which you want to transfer.

2. Choose File ➤ Transfer Project Standards. Select Color Fill Schemes in the Select Items To Copy dialog:

3. Values are transferred into the project. You can then access the list of values from the room's Element Properties dialog:

This saves you from having to manually retype all these commonly used values, and the colors will be consistent from project to project.

COLORED SECTIONS

In architectural practice, section views are often color-coded as well, showing the stacking of various functional zones (Figure 12.13). In Revit, you can't get automated coloring of the rooms in section as you can in plan, so you need to use more traditional, methods to manually draw colored filled regions and assign color to each region. Follow these steps:

1. Open a section view.

2. From the Drafting tab, choose the Filled Region tool (Revit's definition for Hatch), and click the Region Properties button on the Design bar. Select Edit/New, and then duplicate the type—give it a name like **Transparent Fill**. Change the Fill Pattern setting to Solid Fill and Background to Transparent, and choose a color.

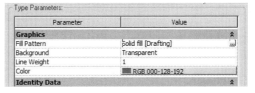

3. In the view, create the filled region boundary by tracing model elements.

4. Finish the sketch.

5. Continue adding filled regions to the view. If you don't want to make a new type of region for each and every color you use, you can use element overrides to change the color of each region:

Creating Presentation Plans and Sections

Not all plans and sections end up as drawings full of dimensions, tags, notes, and layers of construction information. Easy to read, graphically clean drawings are used all the time in marketing collateral, on project websites, in print magazines, for competition boards, and for client presentations. A great way to create presentation-quality plans and sections is to clear out most of the textual information and fill in walls, floor, and roofs with a solid fill when they're cut. This creates views that are easier to read and that convey solid and void effectively (Figure 12.14). With Revit, this kind of representation is a few clicks away, and the fill hatch is tied directly to the element. You don't need a paint-bucket tool or special hatch tool to get results.

FIGURE 12.13
Use transparent filled
regions with solid
color to color
section views.

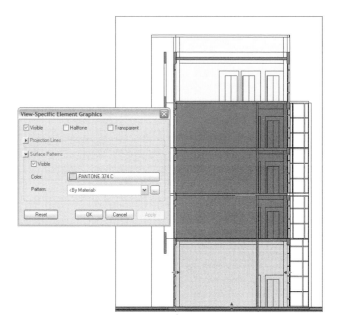

FIGURE 12.14
Plan view with walls
and columns filled
with solid black

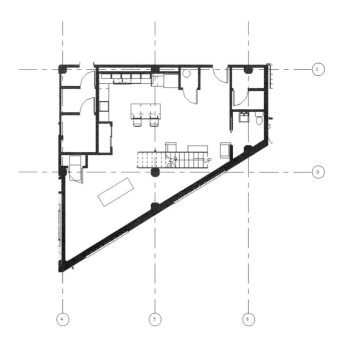

There are two strategies for dealing with solid fill for elements that are cut: as a property of the element, or as a property of the view. Each strategy has its own merits. Let's review the options:

COARSE SCALE FILL PATTERNS

Walls, floors, roofs, ceilings, and columns all have a Coarse Scale Fill type parameter. This allows you to define how the element will appear when cut in the view if the view detail level is set to Coarse.

The downside is that the property is stored with each type, so making all walls have the same hatch requires you to edit every wall type—the same goes for floors and roofs. And if you decide to change the color of the fill, you have to again edit every type.

Also, not all elements have this property. For example, in-place family walls, floors, and roofs don't have this parameter, so you'd have to go a separate route to get correct graphics if you chose to use this type of element.

GRAPHIC OVERRIDES AND VIEW TEMPLATES

The other way to think of this problem isn't as a property of the element but as a property of the view that can be re-used in other views. Think of a view as a multidimensional lens through which you look at the model. Once you've set up the right lens, you can apply it to any number of views and get the right results using view templates. We recommend this direction for graphic overrides, as it makes for an easier way to deal with entire categories of elements. For example, most Revit categories can have their cut pattern overridden with a hatch or solid fill. If you go to the Visibility/ Graphic Overrides dialog and select the Wall, Floor, Roof, and Column categories (by holding Ctrl with each row selection), you can then click the Fill Override button and apply a solid fill hatch (Figure 12.15). This applies to elements in your active view but isn't stored with the element. These overrides are stored on a per-view basis and are distinct from the Object Styles dialog.

FIGURE 12.15
Use pattern overrides to apply a solid fill to categories.

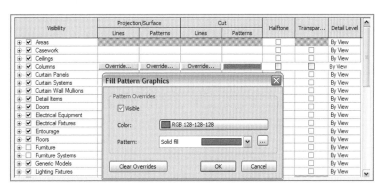

This view setting is great—but what if you want to apply the same graphics to other views? Follow these steps:

1. Once you have the overrides set up, choose View ➤ Create ➤ New View Template from View.

2. Name the view **Cut Overrides**.

3. Right-click the view name you want to apply the overrides to in the Project Browser, and choose Apply View Template. Choose the View template you just created.

You need to be aware of one thing when you go this route: All parameters are applied to the view, including Scale, so be prepared to change Scale back. Also, the view display style is affected, so a view may jump from Shading with Edges to Hidden Line.

Elevations That Convey Depth

Revit applies the same line style to all edges based on the cut or projection settings in the Object Styles dialog. This can lead to elevations that appear flat and lack depth. Strategies for dealing with this issue range from highly parametric to using lines and drafting right on the view. In Figure 12.16, the Linework tool and some graphic overrides were used to punch out the building elements in the foreground and halftone elements in the background.

FIGURE 12.16
Edges can be made thicker with the Linework tool.

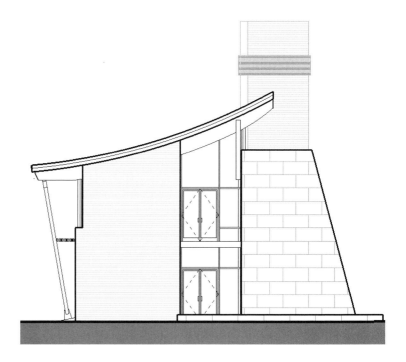

Linework

The Linework tool allows you to select a line style and then apply it to edges of the model as an override. Any edge can be overridden by this tool in order to change the line's graphic appearance. When activated, the Type Selector displays a list of available line styles in your project:

The cursor changes to a pencil and highlights edges of the model as you move the mouse around the view. With each click, the override is applied to the edge. This override is associated with the element; if you move the element, the linework moves with it. The line style applies to the entire edge of an element by default, but this can be adjusted. For example, if you need to make the diagonal line of this wall with a thicker line style, you select the Linework tool, choose the Wide line style, and then pick the edge of the wall. The line goes the entire length of the wall (Figure 12.17a). While still in the Linework command, click and drag the blue control dot to adjust the length of the Linework override (Figures 12.17b-c). Note that if you have your view set to thin line display, you will not see the effects of using linework.

FIGURE 12.17
A) Initial condition;
B) Linework applied;
C) Cleaning up the line
by dragging the
control

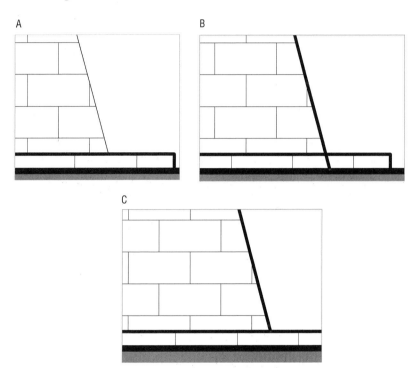

To re-edit the length of Linework, you need to activate the tool and then again pick the edge you're concerned with. The same blue controls appear, allowing you to adjust the length of the line.

If you need to remove a Linework override, the same principle applies: Activate the tool, choose By Category in the Type Selector, and then pick edges in the model that you don't want overridden.

Drafting Lines

The other way to punch out the elevation is to use drafting lines and draw directly over the model in the view. This means you are not changing the appearance of a line in a view but adding new lines on top of the model. With this method, you also choose a line style, and you can even use the Pick tool to get the same behavior you would with the Linework tool. The only difference is that the lines aren't automatically associated with the element you draw on. Depending on your workflow and where you are in the process, this may be the best way to create a final elevation drawing. A nice benefit to this method is that you have access to all the familiar, time-saving tools such as Trim, Align, and Multi-select.

True-Color Elevations

Every material in Revit has a shading color and transparency—this is the color you see when the display mode is set to Shading or Shading With Edges. Be aware that the transparency is graphically visible only in 3D views—in elevation, a glass window will not appear as transparent so as to keep drawings clear of unwanted visual noise. After all, who wants to see interior furniture showing through the glass of a hotel façade in an elevation? The color you select in the Materials dialog is an RGB or Pantone color (Figure 12.18), but it often doesn't look like that color in shaded elevation views. The reason is that shaded views use a hidden light source to light the scene, which causes the color to appear washed out or brighter.

FIGURE 12.18

Every material has a shading color.

To overcome this limitation, you can control where the light comes from by using the Sun And Shadows Settings dialog. You can also force the light to come from directly above the model so it doesn't affect any vertical surfaces. To do this, follow these steps:

1. Open the Sun And Shadows Settings dialog, and duplicate the Sun From Top Right setting—give it a name like **True Color Shading**.

2. Change Azimuth to 0 and Altitude to 90 (Figure 12.19)

3. Open an elevation view, and go to the Advanced Model Graphics dialog from the view frame. Set the Sun And Shadows Settings to True Color Shading. Set Shadow Intensity to 0. Set Sun Intensity to 80.

Be sure to enable shadows in the view. The effect should be immediately obvious.

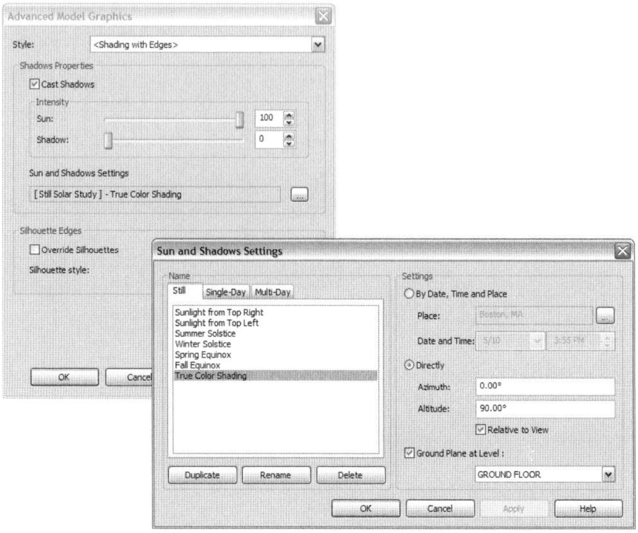

FIGURE 12.19

Use these settings to get accurate RGB colors in elevation.

Elevations with Transparent Materials

Using the standard Revit elevation views, transparent surfaces are always rendered as opaque surfaces. This generally produces the right quality and meets most expectations, but it can also seem limiting. Luckily, creating an elevation view with transparency enabled is easy using the default 3D view. Follow these steps:

1. Open the default 3D view.

2. Choose View ➤ Orient ➤ South (or any other elevation view):

3. The camera swings around so it's lined up with the elevation view, and transparent surfaces appear transparent.

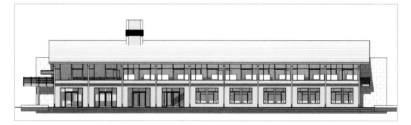

Using Images in Elevation Views

You can import image files (File ➤ Import/Link ➤ Image) into a Revit view to create effects such as gradient fills, add a backdrop to the view, or add a photo-style entourage to a non-rendered view. By taking advantage of the draw-order options for images when placed in a view, you can position the image either in front of or behind the model. When you select an image, the Options bar gives you the ability to position the image in the foreground or background.

To add a gradient fill to the background of an elevation, follow these steps:

1. Import a gradient image file into an elevation view.

2. Select the image, and send it to the background.

3. Stretch the image to fit using the grip controls. You can unlock the proportional scaling using the Options bar (Figure 12.20).

FIGURE 12.20
Elevation with gradient JPEG import set to Background

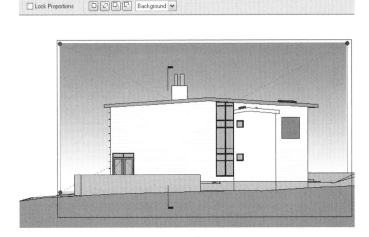

Another great technique is to use the transparency channel available in PNG formatted images. By making a color transparent and pushing images to the foreground and background, you can add trees, people, and cars, and the image won't mask the model. In Figure 12.21, the tree image was imported into an elevation view and then copied and scaled. The copy on the right is set to Foreground, and the copy on the left is set to Background.

FIGURE 12.21
Imported PNG file of one tree set to Foreground and another to Background—note that the transparency channel is preserved

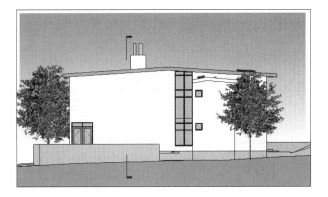

Working with Perspective Views

Open any Revit project and you'll find dozens of perspective views. Although most of these views will never make it onto sheets, it's becoming standard practice to include one or two exterior perspectives on the cover sheet. Sheets aside, these views are critical for understanding your design from a human point of view and are used consistently for client meetings and internally when fleshing out a design. In many cases, a Hidden Line view with shadows enabled provides an excellent graphical representation of your model. You can also take the visualization up a notch and produce some semi–photo realistic renderings.

For perspective views, a good exterior shot typically shows a corner of the building from a human vantage point (Figure 12.22).

Revit puts the camera at eye level by default when you place new camera in a plan view. This is usually fine, but you're free to adjust the camera dynamically or by manipulating the elevation of the eye level and target level. To adjust your camera dynamically, enable the Dynamic View dialog from the tool bar.

Use this dialog to pan, zoom, and spin your camera. You can also use the tabs to move the camera (Walkthrough) and change your field of view. The Walkthrough options are self-explanatory and include Dolly, Forward/Backward, and Turn. The Field of View control is used to set the focal length of the camera; it acts as if you're zooming your lens in and out, while keeping the camera stationary—not to be confused with walking the camera closer to the building.

Currently, perspective views are used only for visualization purposes. You can select elements and change their properties from a perspective view, but you aren't able to interactively edit any of the model using grips or edit commands.

To see a 3D view camera from the context of other views, right-click the view name in the Project Browser and choose Show Camera. The camera appears in all views as a camera icon with the view extents shows as red lines (Figure 12.23); you can visualize where the camera is relative to your model. At this point, the camera is selected; you can move it to a new location, and the view updates automatically to reflect the change. Clicking anything else (including nothing) deselects the camera, which graphically disappears from view.

FIGURE 12.22
Street-level perspective view

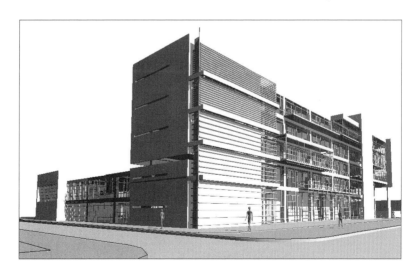

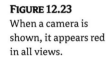

FIGURE 12.23
When a camera is
shown, it appears red
in all views.

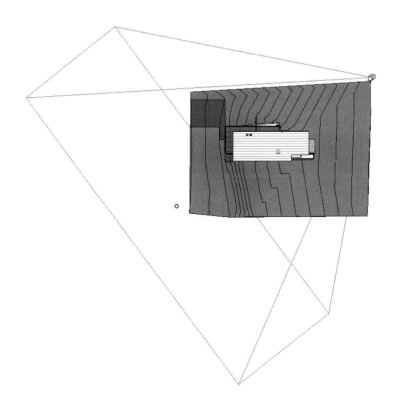

Silhouetted Edge Display

As you saw when we discussed elevations, overriding the edges of elements can help make a drawing more legible and graphically clear. In addition to using linework, you can use a more dynamic
feature built into Revit that accounts for the fact that perspective views are more likely to be spun
around and reoriented (and thus make the Linework tool obsolete). At the bottom of the Advanced
Model Graphics dialog is a control for setting a line style for *silhouette edges*.

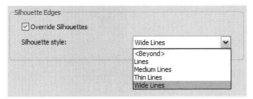

By choosing a line style with a thicker line weight, you'll see the effect of this feature. The line
style isn't applied to specific edges of the model but is dynamically redrawn depending on your
point of view. Revit applies the line style to the outer edges of elements visible in the view, giving
the model a bold outline. The effect can be subtle but nice, as shown in Figure 12.24.

FIGURE 12.24
Top: No silhouette edges applied.
Bottom: Silhouette edges applied with a line style using a line weight of 6

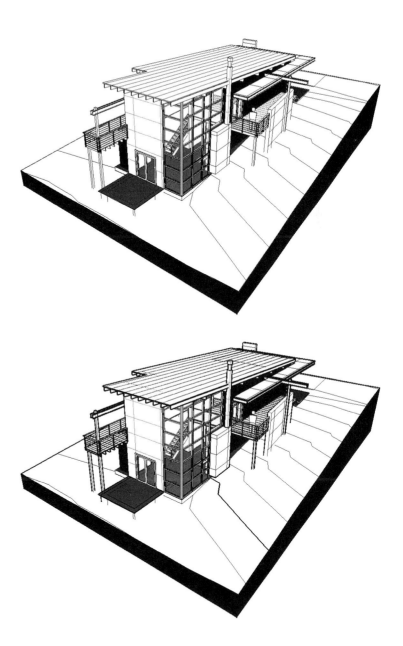

Rendering

Revit has an integrated rendering engine (AccuRender) that lets you visualize the model with material texture maps and more realistic lighting effects. With some quality material images, good composition, and reasonable lighting, you can produce nice imagery.

Rendering can be time consuming, and the results can be mixed. Be realistic in your expectations when approaching rendering, because there is no quick way to get high quality, especially if you are not familiar with the rendering engine in question. Clicking the Raytrace button won't give you a striking image right out of the box. You may find that a shaded view with shadows is sufficient to convey your design ideas without getting heavily invested in producing a photo-realistic image. Nonetheless, you should be familiar with what is possible.

The Rendering Design Bar

To render a view, enable the Rendering tab on the Design bar by right-clicking the Design bar and selecting Rendering. Once the tab is open, you'll see commands specific to a rendering workflow. The most important button in the tab is *Settings*, which opens the Render Scene Settings dialog. This dialog (Figure 12.25) contains all the variables used to raytrace a view, such as lighting, background, view culling, and quality options:

FIGURE 12.25

The Render Scene Settings dialog

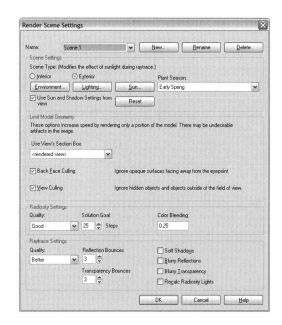

Let's look at these settings in more detail, because they affect the overall look and feel of your renderings.

LIGHTING THE SCENE

The options in the Scene Settings group control lighting parameters. Let's look at them.

Sunlight

For renderings, AccuRender will, by default, use the Sun And Shadows Settings set up in your view for the sun position. Keep this in mind: Even if your view doesn't have shadows enabled, when rendered it will use the setting associated with the view. You can check what sun position the view is using by accessing the Advanced Model Graphics dialog. You can choose to override this behavior and use AccuRender features for setting the sun angles; do this by deselecting the "Use Sun and Shadow Settings from view" check box. When you do so and click the Sun button, you get the same functionality as the Revit Sun And Shadows Settings, but presented in a more graphical manner (Figure 12.26).

Figure 12.26
Sun and Sky
Settings dialog

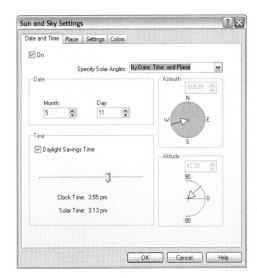

As you can see, the controls for setting Azimuth and Altitude are graphical and give you a better idea of the sun angle with respect to North, South, East, and West, as well as the height of the sun.

Interior Lights

Revit renders a scene with artificial lights (lighting families), which are good for studying interior views. Light families are set to be on by default, but you can turn them off if you desire. If you're doing an exterior rendering, Revit prompts you to turn off the interior lights prior to raytracing the view:

We recommend selecting Yes to improve rendering performance. You'll only want lighting families "On" for exterior renderings if you're doing a nighttime or dusk shot where you definitely want to see the effect of artificial lights. Otherwise, keep the lights off, because they slow down the calculation and don't add anything meaningful to the view when the Sun is on.

All Revit lighting families have the ability to cast light when rendered. You can turn off lights in a view and also dim them using the Lighting button in the Render Scene Settings dialog or from the Rendering tab. You should turn off lights for these reasons:

◆ To create desired effect in the rendered view

◆ To limit the number of lighting calculations AccuRender must perform

Click the Lighting button, and you're taken to the Scene Lighting dialog (Figure 12.27). Here, each light in the model is listed and can be turned on and off. When you select a light in this dialog, it turns red in the view, indicating its location.

It's possible to group lights together for better control if collections of lights are turned on/off in a view. Clicking the Groups button prompts you to give a name to the group, after which you can interactively pick lights and add them to the light group. Each click adds or removes lights to the named group. Note that this is a specific type of workflow geared for lights only: Don't confuse it with Groups functionality.

FIGURE 12.27
Lights can be turned on and off in the scene.

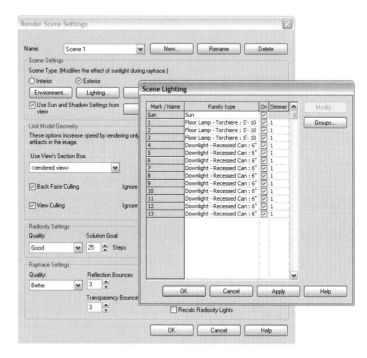

Figure 12.28 shows the Scene Lighting dialog after selecting four lights and adding them to a group named Interior Lights.

FIGURE 12.28
The Scene Lighting dialog controls which lights are on and off in the view when rendered.

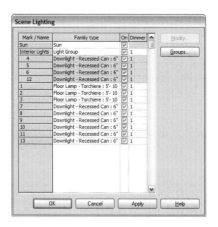

To re-edit a light group, click the Light Group button in the Rendering tab. This allows you to make new groups, edit existing groups, or delete groups using the Options bar:

When you're editing a light group, lights in the group are shown in red.

BACKGROUND

The background helps give your model some context by using an image, color, color gradients, or procedural sky. If you intend to add your own background and effect using an image editor like Photoshop, set the background to a solid color to make it easy to key out later. This is a common practice, and it's recommended to get the best results. Nearly every good rendering we've seen has gone through some post-processing in Photoshop. The AccuRender automatic skies aren't convincing and tend to be too bright, so try to avoid the temptation to use them.

To set up a background for the rendered image, click the Environment button in the Render Scene Settings dialog. In this dialog, you can choose from several different sky options. Selecting Background Image in the Advanced section enables a new tab in the dialog, from which you can browse to an image on disk to use for the background (Figure 12.29). This can work out nicely if you've taken a digital photo of the site, and you know the position of your camera in the model is relatively close to the position where you took the photo. For that scenario, you have to eyeball the camera placement and focal length, because Revit doesn't have a built-in method for exactly matching a photograph with a camera in the model.

FIGURE 12.29

The Environment dialog allows you to define the background of the rendered image.

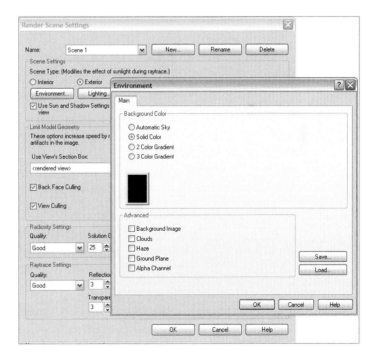

Materials

In addition to good lighting, you need convincing materials to produce a good rendering. Materials should convey characteristics of texture, color, reflectivity, and transparency that you expect to see in reality. If you don't have good rendering materials, your rendering will look flat, unconvincing, and even amateurish—so this becomes a critical part of the workflow.

For rendering purposes, you assign AccuRender materials to Revit materials. These special materials are visible only when you raytrace a 3D view. All elements in Revit have a material, but not all materials have rendering attributes assigned to them. To assign a rendering material, use the AccuRender field in the Materials dialog, as shown in Figure 12.30.

FIGURE 12.30
The AccuRender library has many premade materials, good for glass and solid colors.

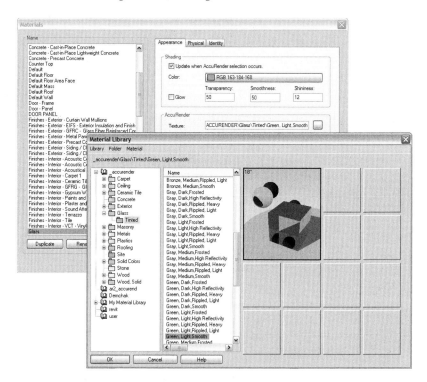

This takes you to the Material Library dialog, where you can choose a rendering appearance for your material. In Figure 12.30, the Revit material Glass is assigned to the AccuRender material Green, Light, Smooth. On the right, you can see a visual preview of what the glass might look like when rendered. Clicking other materials shows their preview. Click OK to assign the AccuRender material to the Revit material.

EDITING AN ACCURENDER MATERIAL

AccuRender provides a set of tools for creating and editing materials (Figure 12.31). You can choose materials from a predefined library, edit existing materials, and make new libraries and materials from this interface. To get a feel for the interface, spend some time browsing through existing materials, and look at how they're defined. To access a material definition, right-click the name or the preview swatch, and choose Edit. A new dialog pops up with all the parameters used to define the material. Here, you'll find controls for color, transparency, reflectivity, shininess, and texture-map assignment.

ADDING A TEXTURE MAP TO A MATERIAL

Many good-looking materials use digital images that are scaled to match the building model. These images are often professionally produced and edited so as to not tile in an obvious manner when repeated over a surface in the model. You'll notice a bad image map if you can see where each image begins to repeat. We don't recommend making your own texture maps, because this tiling effect is difficult to manipulate on your own. Go to a website such as www.turbosquid.com or do image searches for materials.

To assign an image map, follow these steps:

1. Select the Map tab, and then click the Browse button.

2. Browse to an image, and click OK.

3. In the main tab, change the X scale to a real-world unit such as 20.

    This number sets the dimensions of the image in decimal feet. By setting X equal to 20, you're saying that the image repeats every 20 feet (Figure 12.32). You'll likely need to play around with these numbers by looking at the preview cube and then making adjustments until the image looks to be the right scale. The image on the preview cube will update with each change to the X or Y tile values.

4. On the Map tab, you see a preview of the texture map and can browse to a new image if need be (Figure 12.33).

FIGURE 12.31
The AccuRender Materials Editor

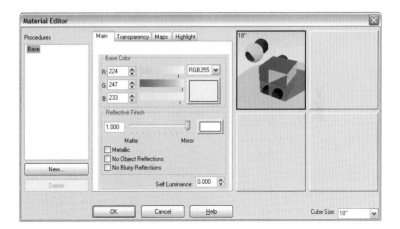

FIGURE 12.32
Setting tile size is critical to getting believable results.

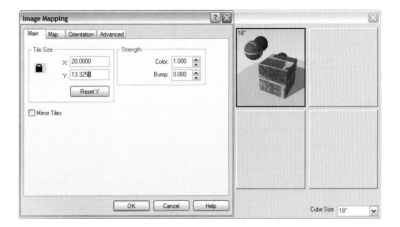

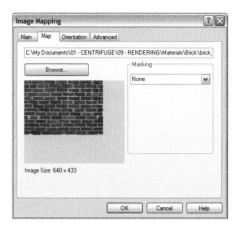

NON–IMAGE BASED MATERIALS

For materials such as glass, where an image isn't needed, you can choose from the default material libraries that ship with Revit. Browse through the AccuRender library, and you'll find a set of glass options as well as a host of other materials to choose from (see Figure 12.34).

FIGURE 12.34
AccuRender materials
are good for glass.

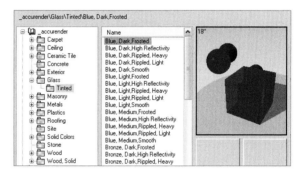

Raytracing the View

Once you've assigned materials and set up a camera view, you're ready to make a rendering. To start a raytrace, follow these steps:

1. Open a perspective view, and then open the Rendering design tab. Click the Raytrace button.

2. Choose an appropriate scene type (exterior/interior).

3. On the Options bar is a green button labeled Go. Click Go to start the raytrace process.

4. When it's complete, evaluate the image, and make changes to the camera, model, environment, and materials. Repeat this process until you're satisfied.

5. When you like what you're seeing, bump up the view size and increase the quality settings in the scene. The render will take longer, but the quality should be noticeably better.

6. To keep the rendered image, export the image, and/or capture the rendering using the options in the Rendering design tab. Capture adds the image to your project file, and Export lets you save it as a file on disk.

Rendering Best Practices

Here are some guidelines for rendering efficiently:

◆ Don't set raytrace quality settings to Best when iterating through materials; doing so only slows down the time it takes to raytrace. Keep Quality set to Good until you're ready for a final pass.

◆ Set image size to approximately 8.5″ × 11″ for initial rendering passes to keep rendering time down. You should be able to see enough detail in the rendering at this size to make judgments about lighting and material quality. Bump the size to final output size only when you're ready to run a final pass.

◆ Turn off lights that aren't visible in your view using the Light dialog and light groups. This will speed up your renderings.

◆ Don't use the Soft Shadows, Blurry Reflections, Blurry Transparency, or Recalc Radiosity Lights options (Figure 12.35). They only slow down the raytrace, and the effects aren't convincing or worth the extra wait time.

FIGURE 12.35
Recommended
raytrace settings

◆ Keep Reflection Bounces and Transparency Bounces set at 3. Increasing this number will slow down rendering and not add any significant quality to the final output.

Creating Animated Walkthroughs

Moving through a building in a virtual manner is a great way to experience a design before it gets built. Static images are nice, but it's becoming common to create animation sequences that showcase key aspects of the design. Revit provides tools for creating walkthrough sequences for the model, which you can then export as an AVI file.

To make a walkthrough in Revit, the process is as follows:

1. Create a path through the model by starting the Walkthrough tool.

You're put into a sketch mode where each click creates a keyframe that lets you change the direction of the camera. Think about how a camera would move through or around a building. When you're finished sketching, click the Finish button on the Options bar.

2. Edit the keyframes along the path so the camera looks in the proper direction, by clicking the Edit Walkthrough button in the Options bar.

In this mode, you can edit the camera and path. The default setting allows you to step through each keyframe using the VCR-style controls and adjust the camera direction in the view. You can only edit the camera direction at keyframes. To see what the camera sees, click the Open button. Keep stepping through keyframes and adjusting the camera. In the camera view, you can enable the Dynamic View controls and change the direction the camera is looking just as you can in a 3D perspective view.

3. With the walkthrough view open, export the walkthrough to .avi format by choosing File ➢ Export ➢ Walkthrough. Figure 12.36 shows the resulting Save As dialog.

FIGURE 12.36

The File ➢ Export ➢ Walkthrough dialog will let you save your walkthrough in AVI format

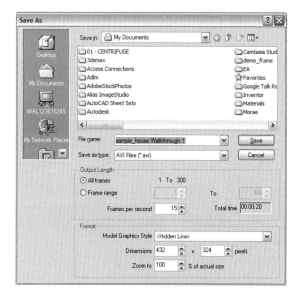

Exporting to Other Formats

If you have established ways of working with vector- or pixel-based artwork, you can always export Revit views and use them as backdrops for your artistry. On the Export menu, you'll find CAD .dwg, .dxf, .dgn, and .sat formats. You can also export any view as an image file using the Export Image option. Supported formats include .bmp, .jpeg, .png, .targa, and .tiff.

Once you've made edits to the exports in applications such as Photoshop, Illustrator, and Piranasi, feel free to re-import the artwork and place it on sheets with your other views.

For rendering purposes, you can export a Revit file to .dwg format and link it into 3ds Max. In addition to the geometry, the DWG file also contains information about the materials in the model and to what elements the materials are applied. This information is available only if you *link* the DWG file into 3ds Max. All the materials and their applications in the model are stored in an XML data schema that 3ds Max can read. Figure 12.37 shows a model that started in Revit, was exported to a DWG file, and was finally linked into 3ds Max.

FIGURE 12.37
Rendered model using
3ds Max.

IMAGE COURTESY OF ANDREA SADER AND INES MAGRI

The Bottom Line

Revit is a complete solution that allows you to generate construction documentation while also providing powerful presentation tools. Using some automated routines to render shadows, depth, color, lighting, and materiality, you can create compelling graphics directly in Revit. The value of doing this is that as the model changes, so will your presentation views—you won't have to re-model anything to maintain the nice-looking plans, sections, elevations, and perspective views you've set up.

Using shadows for analytical and presentation purposes   Presenting your design to stakeholders is a critical part of your workflow and allows you to sell your ideas. Having tools that make this process easier without compromising your creativity is essential to being successful.

Master It   You've been asked to show the effect of your building's shadow on its surrounding site during the winter solstice. How would you do this with Revit?

Creating elevations that convey depth   2D drawings can be hard for clients to read, which makes shadows a useful mechanism for illustrating recesses and projections.

Master It   You need to give your elevation view more variation in line weight to convey depth beyond the default line styles established in the Object Styles dialog. How do you do this?

Creating plans and sections for a print publication   Creating clean, easy-to-read plan and section views using Revit is a huge time saver.

Master It   Your latest design is all the rage, and you've been asked to publish the plans and sections in a magazine. How do you make these?

Creating photo-realistic renderings of your building   You know those signs that are put up at the site before and during construction—the ones with the nice rendering showing the final product? Well, you can generate those directly in Revit!

Master It   You've been asked to produce an exterior rendering of the building. Can you do this in Revit? Can you tweak the results in Photoshop?

Chapter 13

Fine-Tuning Your Preliminary Design

The next step is to take the preliminary building design and begin some basic spatial analysis on the Revit model. You'll see how creating some simple schedules of building and room areas can be used to verify program data and start some preliminary cost analysis.

In this chapter you learn about verifying program data and evaluating a project's initial feasibility. You'll learn how to do the following:

♦ Create your own dynamic area plans

♦ Perform an initial cost estimate for the project

♦ Create a schedule of materials from the model

Preliminary Design Tools

At this point, we are going to introduce a scenario we will be building upon for the next several chapters. As this is a Mastering book, we will not go into significant detail about how to perform some of the more basic skills in Revit, such as how to make simple walls, floors, and roofs. Instead, we will work off of an existing design that is more developed and build skills by adding and extracting information from this base model. In this and the following chapters, we will take the design and push it from a preliminary design level into a set of design documents with many of the common architectural requirements that occur in a typical project workflow.

The Foundation Model

The model we will be using for the next several chapters can be downloaded from www.sybex.com/go/masteringrevit2008. Called the Foundation, it was part of a design competition for a university alumni facility and was created by BNIM Architects. The building is approximately 46,000 sq. ft. and comprises office space, meeting areas, and multipurpose space spread out over three floors of the building. It is located at a major university in the Midwestern United States (Figures 13.1, 13.2).

FIGURE 13.1
Perspective view of
the Foundation model

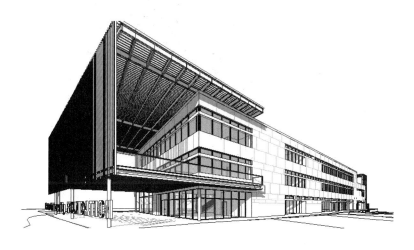

FIGURE 13.2
Another view of the
Foundation model

To get familiar with this model, we recommend doing a few things:

◆ Open the project, and in the Project Browser, choose View (All). This will give you a list of all the views in the model and give you an opportunity to browse through them and see what has been given focus and importance.

◆ Take a look at the generic 3D view. Spin it around a bit and kick the tires, so to speak. Take a look at the overall building form and geometry to help acclimate yourself to the overall design so you have a sense of direction within the building.

◆ Browse through any sheets that have been set up. This will not only give you an idea of what the building looks like, it will tell you what stage the project is in and where the focus has been given to date.

In the Foundation model, you will find many preestablished 3D views as well as some sections and generic plan views. A set of sheets have been started, and views placed on those sheets. A structural grid, elevations, and primary building materials have all been defined. Based on the plans, you can get a fairly clear idea of what the building program is and how the spaces are organized. At this stage in a project workflow, we need to take a short time out of design and do some program verification and evaluation. Our goal is to make an initial cost per sq. ft. assessment. To do that, we will first create area plans for the Foundation's total and rentable areas and then create schedules of materials so we can check our costs against some sq. ft. assumptions. (Under a leaseback agreement, the building will be owned by its builder rather than the university, hence the need to calculate rentable area.) This is where we are going to begin with this model.

Calculating Areas

For the purpose of program verification, we will need to have a sense of the area values. There are several different area calculations you can perform within Revit, each providing a slightly different result. The simplest method is to use room tags, but you'll quickly see the limitations of that approach. For the feasibility study in this chapter's example, we need to create area plans for both total area and rentable area. Then you'll see how to add areas and area tags manually.

Room Tags

The room tag shown in Figure 13.3 has been placed in the model and is tagging a room. This is used to label the rooms and its area. The surface value or the value expressed in SF on the room tag is the usable area within the room, sometimes referred to as the "carpet area."

FIGURE 13.3
Room area as a property reported in the room tag

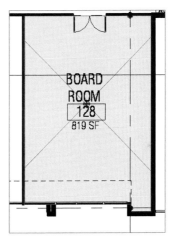

Revit will calculate this area by finding all of the entities that touch the floor bounding a space and report back that square footage. As you can see in Figure 13.4, it will not include things like columns or other objects that penetrate the space, giving you a truly usable floor area. Later in this chapter, we will discuss how to schedule those areas so you can report them in a way that they are all visible at the same time.

FIGURE 13.4
By default, Room areas do not include columns

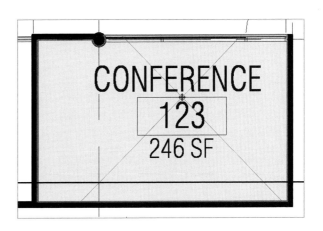

While this is certainly a useful feature, it does not accommodate calculation of the precise areas you will need to verify your program or perform any cost takeoffs.

Area Plans

Area plans are views of the model used to calculate the areas of rooms according to various calculation standards. Some of the standards for area calculations are as follows:

Gross area   This is the overall area of a floor or footprint of the building.

Rentable area   Different developers and leasing companies have different standards for rentable areas. For example, it may include all the spaces in a building except egress corridors, vertical transportation, and mechanical spaces. However, this includes the floor area taken up by columns and some walls.

Usable area   This area defines only the usable space in a plan. It doesn't count areas taken up by columns, walls, mechanical rooms, and shafts and other nonusable space.

BOMA area   BOMA is the Building Owners and Managers Association. Widely used in the United States by architects, developers, and facilities managers alike, it was created to help standardize office-building development. BOMA has its own set of standards used to calculate areas. More information on BOMA standards can be found at www.boma.org.

Revit allows you to choose from two predefined area schemes or it gives you the option to create your own scheme based on standard area calculation variables. To add or modify the area settings, choose Settings ➤ Room and Area Settings.

FIGURE 13.5

The Room and Area
Settings dialog

The Room Calculations tab allows you to change how the areas are calculated for each area scheme. You can set the calculation height and boundary type that Revit uses to autogenerate room areas.

The Area Schemes tab, shown in Figure 13.6, lets you add different schemes to calculate room areas, allowing you to calculate multiple area types.

FIGURE 13.6

FIGURE 13.6

Area Schemes tab of
the Room and Area
Settings dialog

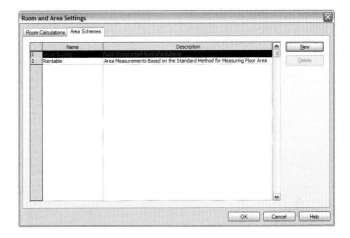

For our use in the Foundation model, we will first need to establish the gross area per floor of the building. To do this, we will start by adding an area plan to the model.

MAKING A GROSS AREA PLAN

Take the following steps to begin creating a gross area plan:

1. Open the Foundation model located on the website in the folder for this chapter.

2. Select the Room and Area tab in the Design bar, and click the Area Plan button. This opens the New Area Plan dialog box (Figure 13.7), where you select the area scheme, level, and drawing scale. Select Gross Building from the drop-down menu at the top. Using Ctrl-pick, select the floor plans for Level 1, Level 2, and Level 3. Leave the scale at 1/8″ = 1′-0″ (1:100) (the default setting) and click OK.

FIGURE 13.7

Creating area
plan views

Area Plan...

3. Revit automatically adds a new folder called Area Plans to the Project Browser and adds plans for each level you selected.

4. In the View window, you'll see a duplicate plan view of the level you selected with purple lines defining the area boundaries, as shown in Figure 13.8. These lines are placed on the walls according to the type of area plan you selected. You can move or delete the lines if they don't appear where you want them.

FIGURE 13.8
Area boundary lines
for gross area

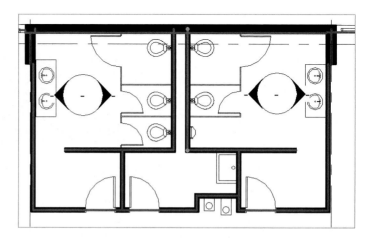

🔲 Area Boundary

To add additional area boundary lines, use the Area Boundary tool available in the Room and Areas tab. Area boundaries must be closed loops of lines in order for Revit to be able to calculate the area. Any breaks or gaps in the area lines, or lines that don't intersect, will result in Revit returning a Not Enclosed value for the area. (Should you get that error message, try trimming the corners.)

5. Now that the areas have been defined for each floor, you can drop in area tags and get an idea of what your floorplate areas are for this project. As you can see, you have about 22,800 sq. ft. (ca -7,000 m²) of area for the first floor.

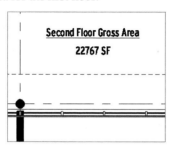

Note that it is not possible to add area lines to anything but an area plan. That option will be grayed out in all other views.

Making a Rentable Area Plan

Now that we have our gross area defined and we have a good idea of what our floorplate sizes are, we can move on to getting a better understanding of our building program. For our program verification, we will need to figure out the rentable area for each of the spaces so we can see how well we fared against the program supplied by the client for this project. Using the same process we described earlier for the gross areas, we can make rentable area plans for the building. Repeating the technique described earlier and selecting Rentable Area this time, we will get a new view in the Project Browser—Area Plans (Rentable), as seen here.

You will notice that in displaying rentable areas, Revit will draw the area boundary on the inside of the exterior walls (unlike with the gross area, where the lines were drawn on the exterior of the exterior walls), but it will also draw boundaries down the centerline of the interior walls. All of this happens automatically—all that is left for you to do is to verify the lines and make sure you have them where you need them.

For this exercise, we want to modify the results slightly from what Revit has provided by default. For our program and client on this project, we are not going to calculate core areas (areas around the elevator and stair cores) as part of the rentable area, so we will need to adjust the area boundary lines around the core walls to reflect our needs and turn the many spaces into one area.

AUTOMATING AREA CALCULATIONS DURING DESIGN

When Revit creates area boundary lines, those lines by default are locked to the walls on which they are created. This is to aid you so as your design changes and walls are relocated, the area boundaries will automatically update as well, keeping your area plans always up-to-date.

In the case of our restroom core, we can start by deleting the lines that separate the restrooms from the janitorial closet (see Figure13.9).

FIGURE 13.9
Modifying an area plan

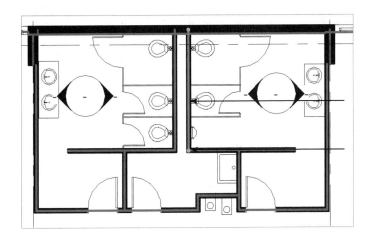

As we are deleting these area lines, we will more than likely get the warning message shown in Figure 13.10. What this message is telling us is that we have removed the boundary between two areas, and Revit is asking what we would like to do with them. Before we answer this question, let's discuss what areas are in Revit.

FIGURE 13.10
Area warning message

In the context of Revit, areas are elements, similar to walls, doors, or furniture. They are selectable, have properties, and can be scheduled. When selected, they will highlight in yellow and appear within the space as a box with an *x* through it, as seen in Figure 13.11.

FIGURE 13.11
Areas are selectable
elements with
properties

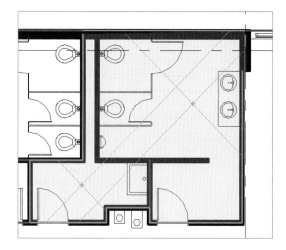

Because areas are elements, you can tag them. An area tag will reflect the properties of the element it is tagging. The tag itself is only an annotation.

At this point, you might be asking yourself, "Where did those areas come from? I didn't insert them." Revit generated them automatically when you created the area plans. By default, when you create a new area plan, it will create an area element within all of the closed area boundaries, so provided there are no adjustments for you to make, it is only necessary for you to tag and label the areas.

In our case, however, we needed to make some changes and we now have more areas than we have spaces. So let's jump back to the warning dialog: We have been given two choices. We can delete all but one of the areas or click OK and accept having multiple areas in the space. Both of these options have viable workflows. If, as in our case, we do not plan to subdivide the room again, we can click Delete Area(s) to delete the extra areas and continue with our work. If we had deleted these lines with the intent of drawing new ones in a different location within this boundary, we could click OK knowing we would have redundant areas for a short time until we finish this area of the model.

Clicking OK will delete the redundant areas and give us a single core area for the restrooms shown in Figure 13.12.

FIGURE 13.12
One area is used for the restroom core.

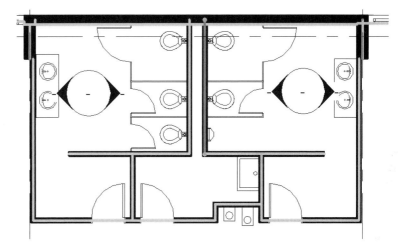

Since we do not want to count any of the core areas, we will need to move the boundary lines from the centerlines of the walls to the inside face of those walls. Because the area boundaries surrounding the restrooms are locked to the walls themselves, we will need to delete those lines and redraw them in their desired locations. We will be expecting a warning message about redundant areas, but we will know in this case we want to keep the areas and simply click OK in lieu of the Delete Areas button.

To draw the new area boundary lines in, we can use the Area Boundary tool described earlier in this chapter and, using the Draw tool, add the new area lines to surround the core. If you choose the Pick option, it will automatically choose the line location based on the rules established for that area plan type. Since we specifically want the area lines on the outside of the core, it is best to draw them manually. So, very quickly, our new core boundary will look like Figure 13.13.

FIGURE 13.13
Revised Core Boundary

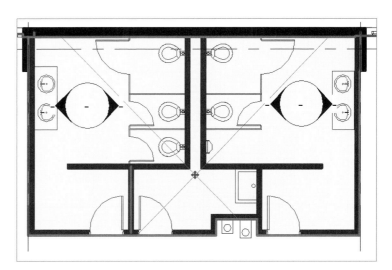

Adding Areas and Tags

As we mentioned earlier, areas are actually elements within the model. When we made our area plans, Revit automatically populated the plan with areas for us. However, we might want to create areas if we want to define spaces that Revit cannot automatically populate. This might be units in a condominium building, for example. To add them manually, we can use the Area button in the Room and Area tab on the Design bar. This will add an area and a tag at the same time to your area plan.

To tag an existing area element, use the Area Tag button located directly below the Area tool.

DON'T DRAW MORE THAN NECESSARY

When designing office buildings, you will probably have your building cores as a repeating element on each floor of the building. In many cases, these cores will be identical. If that is the case, there is no need to redraw your area lines. You can simply copy those elements between floors.

To copy the area boundaries between floors, select them and copy them to the Clipboard.

1. To select area boundaries, you have several options:

   ◆ Ctrl-select each line individually.

   ◆ Highlight one line by mousing over it and press the Tab key. This will highlight the chain of all the connected lines and you can then left-click to select them.

   ◆ Drag a selection window around all of the lines, and using the Filter tool in the Options bar, filter out all but the <Area Boundary> lines, as shown in Figure 13.14.

FIGURE 13.14
Filtering your selection

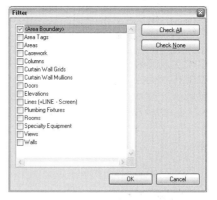

2. Once they are selected, you can use Ctrl-C or Edit ➢ Copy to copy them to the Clipboard. Now, by choosing File➢ Edit ➢ Paste Aligned ➢ Select Views by Name (see Figure 13.15), you can paste your copied area boundaries directly into the same location on other floor, ensuring consistency in your area calculations.

FIGURE 13.15

Pasting into selected views

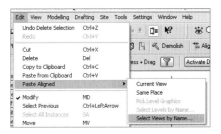

3. Now that you have all the areas defined, you can present them by printing the individual views to see graphically how our spaces are assembled (see Figure 13.16).

FIGURE 13.16

Area and tag graphics

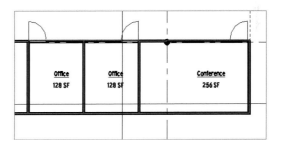

But what happens if we want to show this information in a tabular, spreadsheet format? Often we will need to share it in this kind of summary format. If changes were to happen to the drawings, we would need to go back through the areas and manually verify sizes and recalculate. Because Revit is based on a bidirectional concept, it can do all of these tasks for us, simultaneously. All we need to do is set up a particular view type within the model that allows us to look at the data in a list format in lieu of showing the information graphically. For this, we will use schedules.

Schedules

Schedules are lists of entities and objects within the model. They enumerate items, including building objects such as walls, doors, and windows; calculate material quantities or areas and volumes; and list the number of sheets, textnotes, keynotes, and so on. Giving you the ability to dynamically create and update schedules is a core aspect of BIM and Revit.

Creating schedules of objects, areas, or material quantities in a project is usually one of the most painful (if not boring) but necessary evils for architects. Needless to say, performing a manual calculation takes a long time and can result in errors. Using CAD tools can partly automate this process, but when it comes to calculating numbers of objects, the calculation can only count the number of blocks that are predefined in a file. In Revit, all elements have information about their physical properties, and you can add information to individual elements. For example, doors can have properties like size as well as material, color, fire rating, and exterior/interior.

Revit lets you schedule any element based on properties of the element. In effect, this means that almost anything placed in a Revit model can be scheduled and quantified. Additionally, because the schedule is linked to the objects in the model, you can use the schedule to locate objects within the model or to change their types and properties. This ensures that in any view, regardless of type, the count and properties of all elements are always synchronized. As we often state, the view in which you add or change something doesn't matter. The changes will be reflected in all the views.

If you're unfamiliar with database concepts, don't worry; we'll explain the options in the New Schedule dialog box. The following types of elements can be scheduled:

Casework	Gutters	Rooms
Ceilings	Lighting Fixtures	Site
Curtain Panels	Mass	Slab Edges
Curtain Systems	Mechanical Equipment	Specialty Equipment
Curtain Wall Mullions	Parking	Stairs
Doors	Planting	Structural Columns
Electrical Equipment	Plumbing Fixtures	Structural Foundations
Electrical Fixtures	Property Line Segment	Structural Framing
Fascias	Property Lines	Structural Trusses
Floors	Railings	Topography
Furniture	Ramps	Walls
Furniture Systems	Roofs	Windows

There are also some other schedules you can create that are not limited to specific types of elements:

Multicategory This type of schedule is for objects that don't normally share family types or categories. For example, you may want to create a list of windows and doors in the same schedule. You may also want a schedule showing all the casework and furniture in a project. A multicategory schedule allows you to combine a number of different items in separate categories into one schedule.

Area (gross building) This schedule lists the gross building areas created with the area plans.

Areas (rentable) This type can be created with a rentable plans schedule. Later in this chapter, we'll walk through an exercise demonstrating how to create a simple schedule showing the program areas we created in our area plans.

Although we've listed quite a few, we haven't included all the schedules available in Revit. There are still a few more worth mentioning. These schedules can be accessed only from View ➤ New.

Material takeoff This type of schedule can list all the materials and subcomponents of any Revit family and allow an enhanced level of detail for each assembly. You can use a material takeoff to schedule any material that is placed in a component. For example, you might want to know the cubic yardage of concrete within the model. Regardless of whether the concrete is in a wall or floor or column, you can tell the schedule to report the total amount of that material in the project. As we will show later, you can use this schedule type to make some preliminary sustainable calculations around the use of recycled materials in the project.

View list This schedule shows a list of all the views and their properties in the Project Browser.

Drawing list This schedule shows a list of all the sheets in the project, sorted alphabetically.

Note block   This schedule lists the notes that are applied to elements and assemblies in your project. You can also use a note block to list the annotation symbols (centerlines, north arrows) used in a project.

Keynote legend   This schedule lists all the keynotes that have been applied to materials and objects in the model. You can either use this list as a complete index of all the notes in the drawing set or filter it by sheet. The legend can then be placed on multiple sheets.

These schedules are separated from the main list of schedules because they aren't commonly used in building documentation. They are primarily for data coordination that happens outside of the project documentation.

STANDARDIZE YOUR SCHEDULES

You will find yourself making the same schedules for each and every project. Take the ones you find the most universal and make them a part of your default template.

Making a Simple Schedule (Rentable Area)

[Schedule/Quantities...] You can begin making a new schedule by selecting the View tab on the Design bar, choosing View ➤ New ➤ Schedule/Quantities or clicking the Schedule/Quantities button. When you begin a new schedule, you're presented with a number of format and selection options. These will help you set the font style and text alignment as well as organize and filter the data shown in the schedule. Remember that Revit at its core is a database, so many of the same functionalities that are available in database queries are also available in Revit.

SORTING YOUR DRAWING LIST

The drawing list can also be used as a sheet index to the documents. Because Revit sorts sheets alphabetically, it's typically not desirable to prepare the sheet index in the traditional fashion, with civil sheets first, then architectural, and so on. One way to customize sheet sorting is to add a field to the schedule and number the sheets so civil is 1, architectural 2, and so on. You can then sort by that numbered column.

The process of creating a new area schedule is best demonstrated with an example. Take the following steps to create a new rentable area schedule for the Foundation model:

1. Open the Foundation.rvt file for Chapter 13, found on the website.

2. Navigate to View ➤ Schedule/Quantities or click the Schedules/Quantities button on the View tab.

3. Choose Areas (Rentable) from the Category menu, name the schedule Rentable Area Schedule, and confirm with OK.

   You will see a series of tabs that allow you to specify the schedule's graphic appearance and choose exactly what data you would like to show. Figure 13.17 shows you the dialog box for the rentable area schedule. As each grouping of elements within Revit is somewhat unique, the list of possible schedule values will change accordingly.

FIGURE 13.17

Rentable area scheduling options

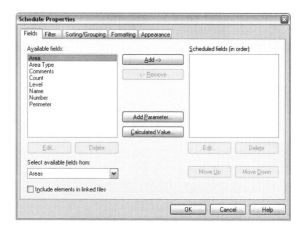

Each tab controls different ways to sort and view the data within a schedule. Here is a basic understanding of their functions.

Fields   The Fields tab lets you select the data that will appear in your schedule. For the wall schedule, it shows all the properties available in the wall family.

Filter   On the Filter tab, you can filter out the data you don't wish to show. You'll use this tab, for example, to restrict displayed data so that only information about the concrete walls in the project appears in the schedule.

Sorting/Grouping   This tab lets you control the order in which information is displayed. You can also decide whether you want to show every instance of an item or only the totals for a given family.

Formatting   The Formatting tab controls the display heading for each field and whether the field is visible on the schedule. It's possible to add fields that are necessary for calculations or sorting but don't show on the printed copy of the schedule. Additionally, this tab can tell Revit to calculate the totals for certain fields.

Appearance   The Appearance tab controls the graphical aspects of the schedule, including the font size and type of text for each of the columns and headers in the schedule. It also allows you to turn the grids on and off or modify the line thickness for the grid and boundary lines. The following example walks through the different options in the New Schedule dialog box while you create a new wall schedule.

In this example, you'll create the schedule, filter out all but the concrete walls, and calculate the volume of recycled content in the walls based on the assumption that you're using 15 percent recycled content in all the concrete you pour on this project.

4. For our schedule, let's choose the following fields from the Fields tab and sort them in this order:

Level

Name

Area

5. Moving to the Sorting/Grouping tab, we want to give the schedule some parameters to sort by. First, let's sort by level so we can see which floors we have the areas on, and then let's sort by area name. We will also want to see a total of the areas by floor, so let's include a footer showing totals only for the levels. Also check the Header check box so we can tell which floor we are on in each grouping. Finally, we want to see a grand total of all the areas in the building. Your dialog should look like Figure 13.18.

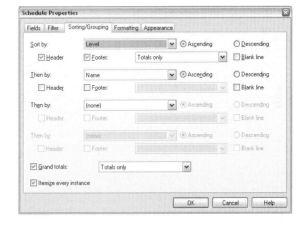

6. Now, on the Formatting tab, we will also want to make a couple of changes. Highlight the Level parameter and select the Hidden Field check box. We don't need to see a level heading for each item in the list, especially since we have one established already as a header for each floor. We also want to select the Area field and make two changes. First, right-justify the areas so they align properly, and then check the box to have the schedule calculate totals as shown in Figure 13.19.

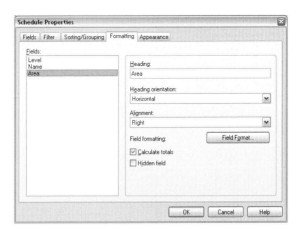

7. Hitting OK at this point will give us a schedule broken out by level and totaling each floor's areas. Your schedule should look something like Figure 13.20.

FIGURE 13.20

The area schedule

8. For our areas, we are concerned only with the rentable spaces and we don't need to see how much area the cores take up in the building. By right-clicking on the schedule, you can view its properties and make some modifications. Choose the Filter tab this time, filter out any name that does not contain the word *Core* (with a capital C), as shown in Figure 13.21, and click OK.

FIGURE 13.21

Filter the areas to remove the word Core.

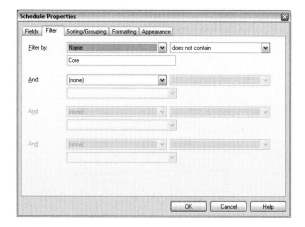

9. Pan down to the bottom of the list and you will notice that we still have the name Restroom core in the list (see Figure13.22).

FIGURE 13.22

Check the schedule to see the effect of the filter.

Level 2	
Conference Rm	608 SF
Office	125 SF
Office	125 SF
Office	125 SF
Office	125 SF
Open Office	17989 SF
	19097 SF
Level 3	
Open Office	16215 SF
Restroom core	513 SF
	16728 SF
	54350 SF

Project Gallery

This gallery of projects comes from architects from all around the globe who have embraced the move to a smarter way of working on projects and use BIM as their main methodology. Each has a different approach to how they start a project, from using conceptual massing or legacy CAD files to hand sketching and importing from other modeling applications. All have different skill levels with Revit, but what ties them all together is that they have produced beautiful architectural examples using BIM. They have all adapted their workflows and offer a competitive advantage as a result.

All projects shown have been modeled in Revit using many of the concepts, principles, and techniques explained throughout the book. The renderings vary—some are done within Revit, using the embedded rendering engine Accurender. The majority, however, have been made using 3ds Max and Vray, producing some stunning visuals.

BIM is not a myth. These are real people, real projects, and real sources of inspiration. And don't forget, it's technology, it's digital, but still, what really matters is that it's good architecture.

We would like to express our sincerest gratitude to all architects who generously shared their work, allowing us to inspire you with it: Little Diversified; Kubik-Nemeth-Vlkovic; Atelier G. Cappochine; Arch. A. Torre; A. Sadder; I. Magri; F.M. Diaz; H.L. Stewart; RMJM Hillier; Gensler, HOK; Arch. S. Pfundt; Arch. A. Lillystone.

Enjoy!

Hotel and Wellness center, Kubik-Nemeth-Vlkovic

Andrea Torre

Italy

Residential design

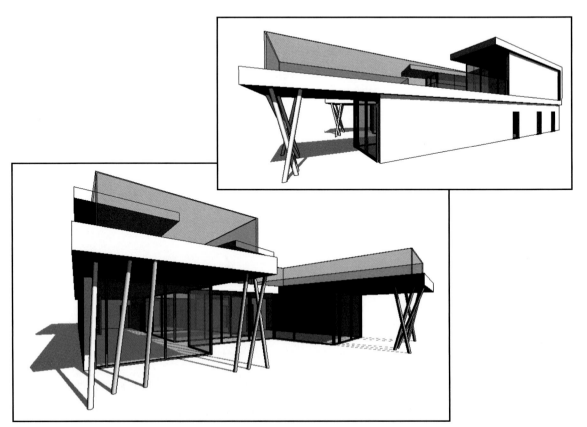

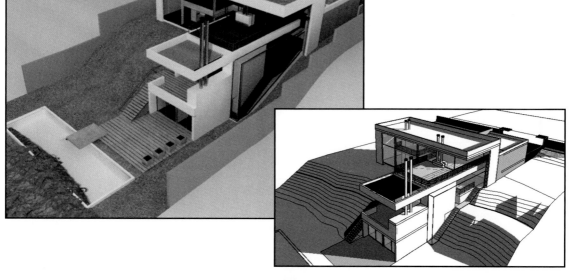

Andrea Sader
and Ines Magri
Uruguay
Residential design

Hector Lira Stewart
Chile

Student project, Universidad de las Americas
Centre for children with cancer

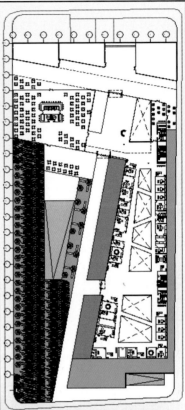

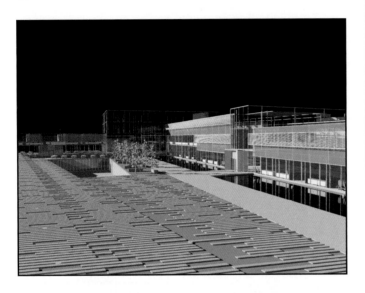

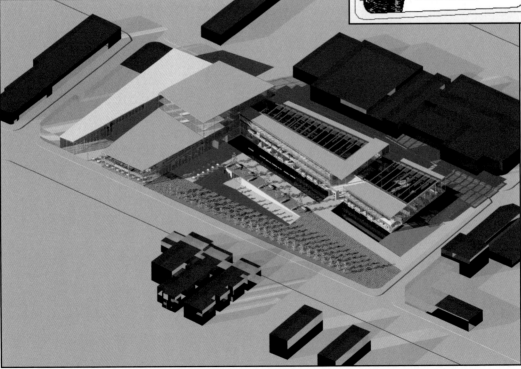

Felipe Manrique Diaz
Chile

Student project, Universidad de las Americas
Centre for children with cancer

RMJM Hillier

USA

Glass-encased addition to the Carnegie-era St. Louis Public Library

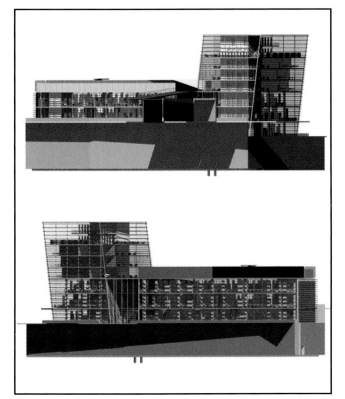

Gensler
USA
American University of Beirut,
School of Engineering

Gensler
USA

Government
Office Building

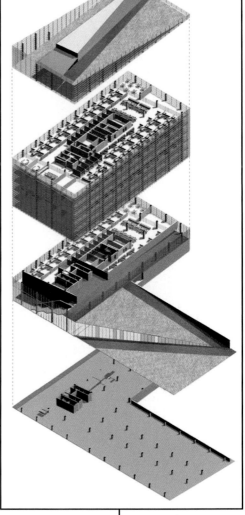

Rand Corporation Headquarters

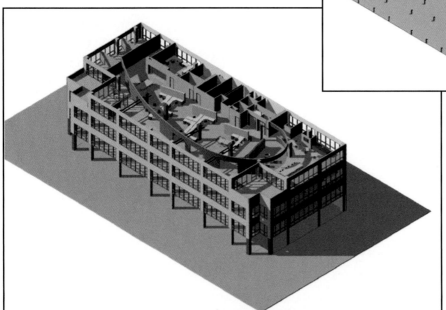

Gensler
USA
Hotel and residence,
Los Angeles

HOK
USA, UK, Canada, Mexico

School project,
Kazakhstan

HOK
USA, UK, Canada, Mexico
Edmonton clinic, Canada

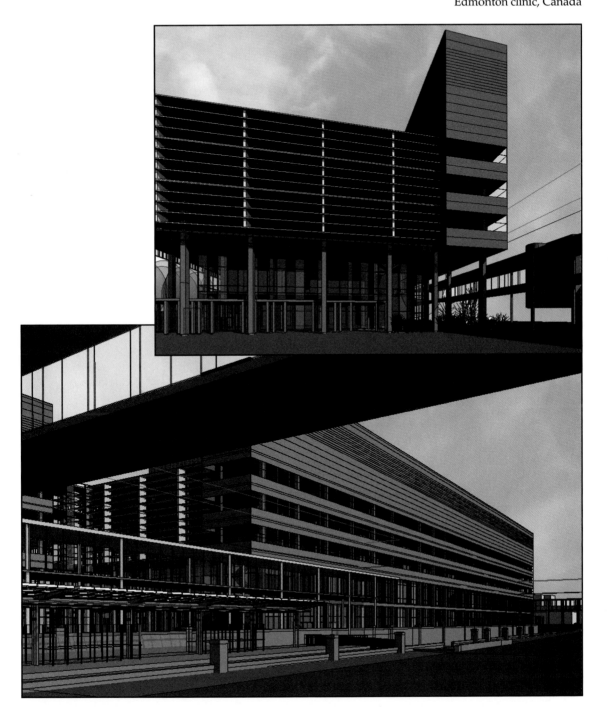

HOK
USA, UK, Canada, Mexico
Tower designs

Skyscraper3d/Little
USA
Phipps Tower, Crescent Resources LLC Atlanta

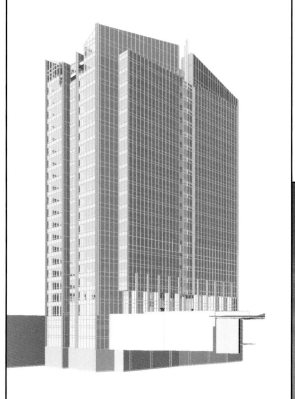

Siggi Pfundt

Germany

Weekend home, Slovakia

- abstellraum
- bad wc
- galerie
- steg
- technik
- wf
- wohnen kochen
- zimmer

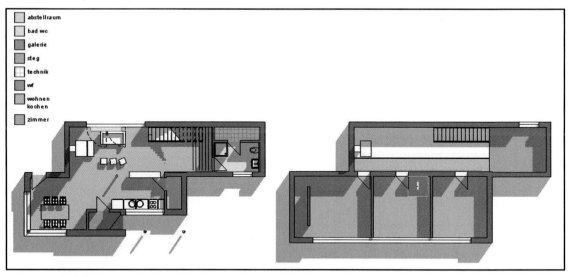

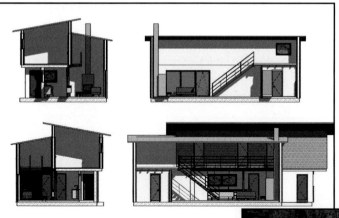

Atelier Giuseppe Cappochin
Italy
Multifamily housing, Italy

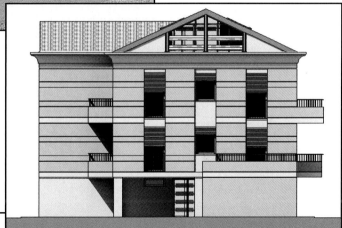

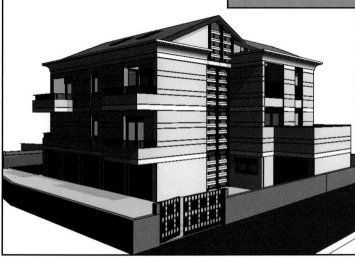

Alistair Lillystone
UK
Weekend experiments with office tower designs

10. The name *Restroom core* is still in the list because the filter and fields in the schedules and families within Revit are case sensitive. *The fields need to match exactly.* However, there is an easy fix. By simply clicking within the cell itself, as you would do in Excel, you can modify the word *core* so it has a capital *C* and the name will then be filtered from the list. Our finished schedule look like Figure 13.23.

FIGURE 13.23

The finished area schedule

Rentable Area Schedule	
Name	Area
Conference	256 SF
Conference	256 SF
Daycare	2054 SF
Electrical	233 SF
Entry	214 SF
Mechanical	674 SF
Multi-purpose space	2695 SF
Office	104 SF
Office	163 SF
Office	128 SF
Office	128 SF
Open Office	8872 SF
Restroom	48 SF
Restroom	48 SF
Restroom	48 SF
Restroom	48 SF
Storage	252 SF
Telefund	838 SF
Vestibule 1	237 SF
Vestibule 2	70 SF
	18525 SF
Level 2	
Conference Rm	608 SF
Office	125 SF
Office	125 SF
Office	125 SF
Office	125 SF
Open Office	17989 SF
	19097 SF
Level 3	
Open Office	16215 SF
	16215 SF
	53837 SF

 Real World Scenario

KEEPING BUILDING AREA SCHEDULES UPDATED

To most clients, building areas are a critical part to the development pro forma (the pro forma is typically a spreadsheet that outlines the financial goals of the project or development). In practice, you will create area plans that coincide with how the owner needs areas computed for their calculations. You keep these in a schedule allowing the owner regular updates to the building areas so they can compare those to the current pro forma. Since you can keep the schedules dynamically updated, you can set this up once and know that the areas will always be up-to-date.

Placing the Schedule on a Sheet

Now that we've created the schedule for our program, we need to put it on a sheet. As we've mentioned, schedules work like any other view. To place the schedule on a sheet, simply drag and drop it from the Project Browser onto the sheet you wish to place it on. One of the nice things about schedules is that you can actually place them on multiple sheets and they will always provide the most current information.

What we want to create is a set of sheets we can provide to our client that demonstrate our program for each floor graphically and in list form. When we are finished, we will have an 11 × 17 presentation sheet that looks like Figure 13.24, with a floor plan and schedule for each floor.

FIGURE 13.24

Finished presentation sheet with area plan and schedule on it

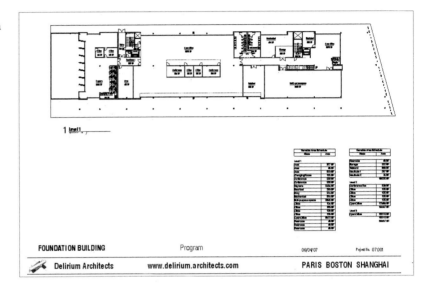

1. Expand the sheets in the Project Browser and find the sheet 01 – First Floor Program.

2. Expand the rentable area plans and drag and drop the Level 1 Plan onto the sheet.

3. You will notice that the plan will be much larger than the sheet since we made the area plan at 1/8 scale originally. Right-click on the plan and choose Activate View from the context menu. In this view, you want to do two things: Change the scale, and turn off some of the unnecessary annotations. So, first, adjust the scale of the drawing to be 1/16″ = 1′-0″ (1:200). Second, open the Visibility Graphics dialog (by typing **VG** on the keyboard or choosing View ➤ Visibility/Graphics). On the Annotations tab, turn off visibility for the following categories:

   ◆ Elevation tags

   ◆ Grids

   ◆ Reference planes

   ◆ Section tags

   Once the view is resized and the display reconfigured, place the plan at the upper portion of the sheet.

4. Drag and drop the rentable area schedule onto the same sheet. When it first appears, it will look something like Figure 13.25. We will need to do a bit of rearranging to get the schedule to fit the sheet properly.

Figure 13.25
Unformatted
schedule placed
on sheet

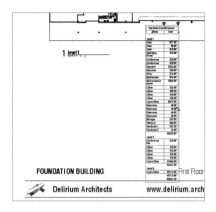

FOUNDATION BUILDING

Delirium Architects   www.delirium.arch

5. There are two different ways to modify the schedule directly from the sheet. On the upper
    portion of the schedule header, there is one blue triangle for each column. By simply drag-
    ging them left or right, you can resize the width of each column. You will notice some of our
    longer room names have wrapped to the next line. Grab the left triangle and drag it to the
    right to lengthen the Name field. Note that this will also shorten the schedule by removing
    the wrapped lines.

6. The other tool you can use to modify how the schedule fits on the sheet is the squiggle,
    located in the center of the schedule. Clicking this tool will split the schedule into two col-
    umns. It is important to note that you cannot choose where this split occurs. However, it will
    give you two separate columns that you can now drag independently of each other. Now
    that the columns fit within the space we have remaining, we can locate them to the right-
    hand portion of the sheet. The sections of the schedules can be subdivided as many times as
    you need and each section will subdivide independent of the others. Your final sheet will
    look like Figure 13.24.

Additional Schedule Capabilities

Now that we have made a schedule of our spaces, let's look at some of the other advantages of using
schedules in the design process. Since Revit is a parametric modeler, all of these labels are linked
to elements within the model. You might notice that at the top of our schedule, we seem to have
missed the labels for three of the areas; they are simply labeled Area.

Rentable Area Schedule	
Name	Area
Level 1	
Area	377 SF
Area	48 SF
Area	613 SF
Changing Room	120 SF

If we were not using BIM as a modeler, it would become very tedious to locate these areas so they can be properly labeled. In Revit, it is quite simple. We have two options to rename these spaces. First, if we know what the areas are supposed to be, we can either type the name in or select it from the list of already used names. However, what happens when we need to locate the room on the plan before we can figure out what room it is? This is also easily possible within Revit. By selecting the area name, we will get a few tools in the Options bar.

Click the Show button repeatedly. This will cycle through all of the existing views within Revit and zoom into the one that would best show the area in question. Clicking the button will give you a view similar to what you see in Figure 13.26. As you can see, we missed the label of one of the restrooms as it is shown highlighted in the view.

FIGURE 13.26
Showing the elements from the context of a schedule

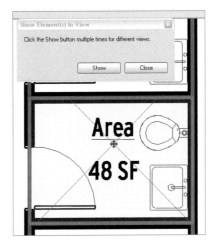

This is a very powerful tool because it can be used to locate any of the elements within the Revit model directly from any schedule. Not only do Revit schedules report information about elements in the project, they can also be used to control elements. If you decide to exchange one wall type for another, you can do so by clicking in the schedule—under wall types, for example. A drop-down menu appears, listing all available types currently in the model, and you can choose the type you want. Again, this automatically changes the instance of the wall to another wall type in all views in which the wall is present.

Using Schedules for Preliminary Cost Estimates

Since we are in still in preliminary design for this project, we have probably not gone through the rigor of cost estimating the project yet. Nonetheless, we can use some of the scheduling tools to help us calculate a rough cost of the building based on a cost per sq. ft. assessment. The disclaimer here is that Revit is not a cost-estimating package. It is a database that can count, total, and tally the number of items, areas, or other properties within the model. Cost estimating itself is part counting and part experience; we can work on the counting part with the BIM model.

Since we have already created gross area plans earlier, let's go ahead and create a new schedule to analyze the area plans and give us a rudimentary cost estimate based on the building square footage. Let's only include the Level and Area fields, but in the Fields tab. Next, we need to add a parameter for Cost. That parameter is *not* a standard property of the areas so we will need to add it to the list.

1. To add the Cost parameter, use the Add Parameter button on the Fields tab. What this allows you to do is to add a new custom parameter to the Areas field. We need to add one for Cost and we need the parameter type to be a number so we can get a cost per sq. ft. See Figure 13.27 for the dialog box properties.

FIGURE 13.27
Adding a new parameter

2. We are now going to use the Calculated Value button to add a new field to the schedule. The button will display a new dialog box (Figure 13.28) where you can create new fields that are basically custom formulas defined by combining numerical values with other fields.

In our example, we want Revit to calculate a total cost for our project based on a cost per square foot we consider close to accurate based on previous experience.

FIGURE 13.28
Calculated value fields

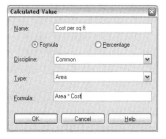

1. For our Type setting we made the type an Area. In Revit, you need to make sure the types of fields are compatible so you are not multiplying length times something like material. Also, as we mentioned before, the fields are case sensitive. In the formula line, you will need to type in **Area * Cost** to get the total project cost. Click OK to exit the dialog box.

2. Finally, on the Sorting tab, check the box for Grand totals, and on the Formatting tab, highlight the Cost per sq. ft. field we just created and check the box to calculate totals. Once you enter an estimated cost of $169.00 for each floor, the final schedule will look like Figure 13.29.

FIGURE 13.29
Building cost
per sq. ft.

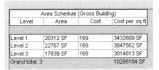

Now we have a constantly updated area of each floor of the building multiplied by our estimated cost per sq. ft. for a continuously accurate total, based on those metrics. However, the costs are being reported as SF values and not dollar amounts. We can fix that problem in the Schedule Properties dialog box.

Editing the Graphic Appearance of a Schedule

When you create a new schedule, you're presented with a number of format and selection options on the Appearance tab of the Schedule Properties dialog. These let you set the font style and text alignment and decide how to organize and filter the data for display in the schedule. Let's explore the options in the Schedule Properties dialog box.

Under the Appearance tab (see Figure 13.30), we have the options to change the font styles, grid line visibility, and other variables for header and body text of the schedule.

FIGURE 13.30
In the Appearance
tab, you can control
font, size, and header
visibility.

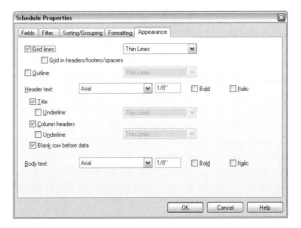

However, the change we need to make to the appearance of the data in the schedule is found in the Formatting tab of Schedule Properties. For our purposes in our Cost per sq. ft. schedule, let's highlight Cost per sq ft and make some adjustments.

1. Change the alignment to right justified, which is conventional for money totals.

2. Select the Field Format button and uncheck the box Use Project Settings. Here is where you can choose to change the Unit suffix and remove SF from the cost per square foot values (see Figure 13.31). Select OK to close all the dialog boxes and return to our schedule.

FIGURE 13.31
The Format dialog

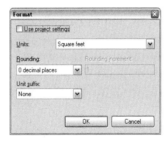

We also have the ability to add headers to our schedule. By selecting the Headers check box, we can group them under another title.

1. Select Level and Area by clicking in one of them and dragging the mouse to the other one (see Figure 13.32). They will show as highlighted. While Level does not look selected, it currently is.

FIGURE 13.32
Selecting headers

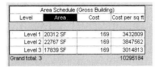

2. Doing this will activate some of the different tools on the Options bar above. We now have the option to group (or ungroup) these headers. Choose the Group button.

3. We now have a header that spans the two headers selected and we can add some more descriptive information in there to help clarify the schedule a bit. In this example, we have added the text "Preliminary Design Plan" to the header (see Figure 13.33).

FIGURE 13.33
Grouped headers

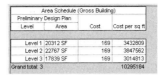

The Bottom Line

Remember that area plans and schedules are nothing more than different ways to view your model and the parametric data inside it. Learning how to leverage these view types can be a huge time-saver for your project. In this chapter we created some area plans and schedules, but remember that this data will be constantly updating itself to reflect the most current status of your project. Set it up once and you have a tool you can regularly refer back to for project metrics.

Create your own dynamic area plans   Once your plans are established, create your own area plans to dynamically track changes in the project.

NOT ALL SCHEDULES NEED TO APPEAR ON SHEETS

You can use schedules to document used objects in your project (number of doors or windows, furniture pieces, material quantity, areas of rooms, etc.), but you can also use it to look for inconsistencies within your model. For instance, you can keep a schedule of textnotes only within a model and not use them on sheets. This schedule can then be used to look for odd items inserted into the model. For example, you can schedule the textnote name and the number of times it appears in the model. Perhaps the schedule indicates that a particular note is used only one or two times in the model. You can then decide if the note was inserted incorrectly into the project and determine whether it's inconsistent with the other notes in the model. The same thing can be done for wall types or anything else in the model.

> **Master It** Establish your preliminary design, and then create area plans so you can keep up-to-date with space sizes, allocations, and your project program.

Perform an initial cost estimate for the project Create a schedule that tracks project costs based on an estimated sq. ft. cost.

> **Master It** Many developers and facilities managers use BOMA calculations for figuring rentable area, gross area, and R/U (rentable/usable) ratios. Establishing area plans and schedules can help you find these numbers much quicker than a legacy CAD system would have allowed.

Create a schedule of materials from the model One of the benefits of Revit is the ability to manage not only your drawings, but also other information about the project. Create schedules for your project templates to manage the materials within the project.

> **Master It** Schedules have a multitude of uses and value at all levels of the project. Explore a variety of schedules to optimize your workflow and maximize what you can get from the model.

Chapter 14

Evaluating Your Preliminary Design: Sustainability

In this chapter, we will take our preliminary building model and investigate sustainable design strategies using the building information model.

There are a number of things Revit does to support a sustainable design process and workflow that range from accurate material takeoffs to full-blown energy analysis. As you move to Revit from a more traditional drafting approach you will begin to see more opportunities to engage in model-based simulation. This represents a shift in office workflow and culture. Revit changes how teams communicate since everyone works within the same file instead of multiple files. This reality extends to the rest of the project team, including structural, mechanical, engineering, and plumbing (MEP) consultants using Revit. This close integration allows team members to better understand the overall direction of the project from many vantage points. This ability to see the model from different points of view makes a BIM project perfect for exploring sustainable design strategies.

In this chapter, we will explore how Revit can help support those strategies. You'll learn to do the following:

- Incorporate a sustainable approach from project inception

- Use Revit to track sun and shade patterns

- Track recycled materials and other sustainable strategies using schedules

Sustainability in Architecture

Sustainable design has been a long-standing practice among the architectural profession, but it has recently received mainstream recognition and grown in popularity. Sustainable design can address many issues, such as energy use, access to natural light, human health and productivity, water conservation, use of recycled materials—the list goes on. The goal of sustainable design is to reduce a building's *carbon footprint* (the amount of carbon dioxide a building and its energy demands uses) to a net of zero. This means the building uses no more energy than it can produce or offset.

An important factor in sustainable design is the huge effect that U.S. construction has on the environment. The United States uses 25 percent of the world's energy, and the U.S. building industry uses 40 percent of the global resources. Buildings are the largest single resource consumer in the world. In order to solve the problem of global warming, we need to look at the low-hanging fruit of the Architecture, Engineering, Construction (AEC) industry and work toward a more efficient, more sustainable building practice.

Preliminary Design Tools

In the preceding chapter, we introduced the Foundation model by working with the preliminary design and verifying program and area information by creating area plans and schedules. We will be building upon the same model in this chapter to investigate sustainable strategies.

Since we have a digital building model, we can also rapidly iterate different variations of the design using sustainable strategies. When designing for sustainability, the important thing is to understand which questions to ask—and to ask them early enough in the process that you can make appropriate changes. There are five simple things you can do to help make any project more sustainable:

- Optimize the building mass.

- Create good site orientation by maximizing north/south exposure and minimizing east/west exposure.

- Optimize the use of daylight and sun shading.

- Optimize the building envelope assembly.

- Optimize the use of "free" resources such as sunlight, wind, and rain.

Although it's not designed primarily as a sustainable design tool, Revit does provide an integrated 3D model that can be consumed by other applications for the purpose of running analysis. This saves you the time of having to remodel geometry in these applications and thus reduces the amount of time and money spent on analytical modeling. With Revit, you are building a 3D model by default—so testing a number of simple but effective sustainable strategies early on only makes sense and will not require you to remodel anything.

The LEED Rating System

One widely used tool for sustainable design within the building industry is the LEED rating system. Created by the U.S. Green Building Council (USGBC), the Leadership in Environmental and Energy Design (LEED) system is a nationally recognized benchmark for high efficiency design and construction. The LEED rating system consists of five key areas:

- sustainable site development

- water savings

- energy efficiency

- material selection

- indoor environmental quality

Each of these areas has point values assigned to a variety of methods and processes of sustainable design. The goal of the ranking system is the ability to determine and rank a building's sustainability. For more information on the USGBC and LEED, visit www.usgbc.org.

Sun Studies

Chapter 12, "Presenting Your Design," introduced Revit's tools for adding physically accurate shadows to a drawing and showed how to enable and control them. Here we will take a closer look at using these features analytically.

Good sustainable design will optimize use of natural daylight within a building and thereby minimize the need for heavy use of electrical (artificial) lighting. The design should be cognizant of the direction the daylight is coming from because this will dictate the amount of solar gain the building takes in during the course of the day. East and west daylight is much harder to control, while north elevations (in the Northern Hemisphere) provide a great amount of indirect lighting and the southern elevations get a great deal of direct exposure, which can be mediated with the proper use of sun shading devices (see Figure 14.1).

Sun shading devices are specific to the local climatic conditions; however, there are some fairly typical rules of thumb. North and south sunlight is the easiest to control since the angles of exposure are not nearly as dramatic as the east and west façades. Because of this, sun shading on the south side is typically horizontal to allow more sun exposure to the interiors during winter months when the sun is lower in the sky and less exposure in the summer months when the sun is higher. Conversely, sunlight affecting the east and west façades is more difficult to control and sun shading is typically vertical in nature.

FIGURE 14.1
Sun shades and
natural ventilation

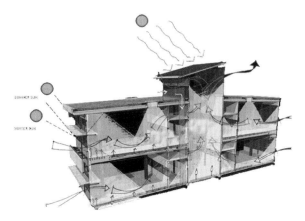

Working directly with a mechanical engineer early on who is knowledgeable about sustainable principles and approaches can help direct and maximize the use of natural light and heat in your design. However, even without an expert, a simple daylighting view can help a design team make good decisions regarding daylighting.

Sun studies are views (they can be still or animated) that you can generate to reflect the solar conditions during specific times of the year to visually gauge light and shadow conditions. By creating camera views at key locations within the model, you can see the resulting shadows based on the location of the model on the planet and the date and time. In Figure 14.2, you can see the effect of sun on the Foundation model during four peak times of the year: the summer solstice (6/12), the spring and fall equinox (3/21 and 9/21), and the winter solstice (12/21). We will be using these same dates as we study the model from other angles.

Remember, once we establish these views, they will be constantly updated as we make modifications or design changes to the model.

FIGURE 14.2
Sun studies at various times of the year

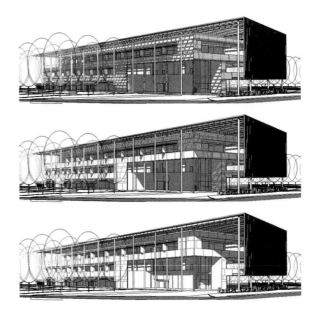

MAKING A SUN STUDY

Open the Foundation model in the Chapter 14 folder on the book's website (www.sybex.com/go/masteringrevit2008), and let's establish a few views from different locations. We'd like a better understanding of the play of sun and shadow within the model from these locations. To do this, we are going to set up some sun studies in these spaces.

1. Set up the following camera views:

    1. From the second floor, place a camera from the view design tab looking at the southern elevation of the building, eastern half (because of the building's length, we will not be able to see sufficient detail if we look at the entire façade at once). Name it Sun Study-South E façade (Figure 14.3).

FIGURE 14.3
Exterior camera
placement looking
at south façade

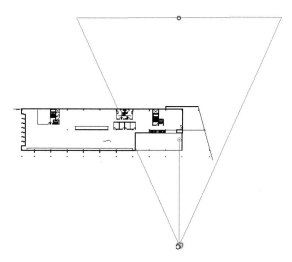

2. From the second floor, place a camera looking at the western elevation of the building, east half. Name it Sun Study-West façade (Figure 14.4).

FIGURE 14.4
Exterior camera
placement looking
at west façade

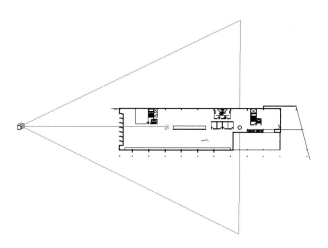

3. From the interior third floor office space, place a camera looking to the southwest. Name it Sun Study-3rd floor Interior (Figure 14.5).

FIGURE 14.5
Exterior camera place-
ment looking at the
third floor interior

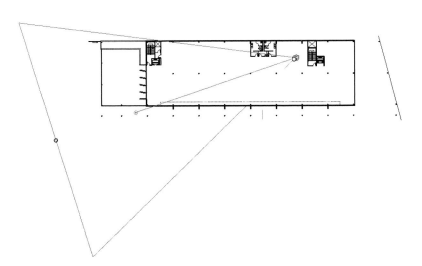

2. Now if you go back to the first view, the *Sun Study-South E façade*, the view by default will look like a colorless perspective of the south façade (see Figure 14.6). You can choose to either accept the way this view looks or choose Shaded Lines or Shaded Lines With Edges from the View Control bar at the bottom of the view window.

3. We need to turn on the sun and cast some shadows.

4. In the View Control bar, the third button from the left is the Shadows button. Clicking this button will toggle the shadows on and off. It will also give you the option to go to the Advanced Model Graphics dialog box where you can then set the parameters for what time of day to show the shadows. Choose Advanced Model Graphics from the menu.

FIGURE 14.6
Default appearance of
perspective view

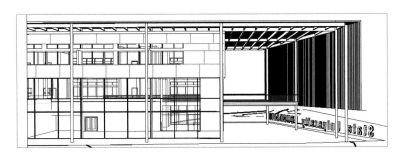

5. In the Advanced Model Graphics dialog box, select the Cast Shadows check box. (Figure 14.7)

This will activate the browse button for the Sun And Shadows Settings dialog. Click it to access the dialog box.

FIGURE 14.7
The Advanced Model
Graphics dialog box

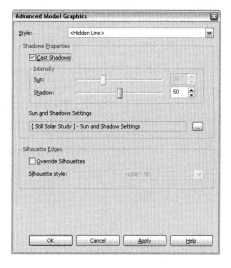

6. In the Sun And Shadows Settings dialog, you have three options.

Still will cast the sun at a specific time of day based on the parameters you choose.

Single-Day will allow you to animate the sun and export the animation to an AVI file to show it over the course of a single day.

Multi-Day will cast the sun in the same position (same time of day) over the course of multiple days.

For the sake of our current investigation, choose Still (see Figure 14.8).

FIGURE 14.8
Sun And Shadows Settings dialog.

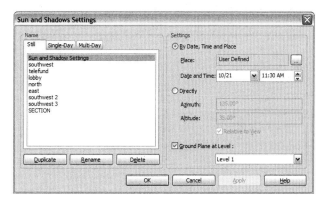

7. Here we need to start by setting the location for our investigation. Choosing the By Date, Time And Place option, we can give our building a geographical location.

8. Click the browse button to open the Manage Place And Location dialog box. Here you'll find a long list of choices available. Choose Kansas City, MO and click OK. For the date, choose 6/21 because we want to see the sun during the summer solstice. Set the time to 10:30 am. Finally, make sure the Ground Plane At Level button is checked and set to Level 1. This will allow Revit to cast shadows against the ground.

9. Before you click OK and let Revit calculate the effect of the sun for the location you have selected, we need to name our settings. Choose Rename from the buttons on the left of this dialog box and rename Sun And Shadows Settings to 6/21, 10:30 am.

10. Click OK twice to exit the dialog boxes. It will take a moment for Revit to calculate all the shadows. The finished view should look like Figure 14.9. It looks like the sun canopy extends far enough to reach all the floors at this time of day in the summer and it will give us an interesting play of light on the façade.

In Figure 14.9, you can see the results of the sunshades on the southern façade. Both solar studies were done at the same time of day, but there is an obvious impact of the shading devices on the second elevation over the first. Later in this chapter, we will discuss different energy modeling strategies that are designed to report the actual load differences the building will have with or without the shades.

FIGURE 14.9
How the sun affects the south façade on a summer day

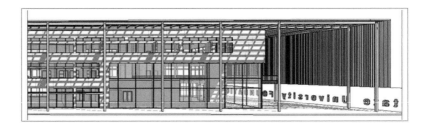

ANIMATED SUN STUDIES

A great feature in Revit is the ability to create animated solar studies. This allows you to see the effect of sun and shadow over the course of time. For example, it is possible to animate the sun over the course of an entire year to see the extent of light penetration and shadow cast by your building and other buildings in its context. This is an excellent communication tool for explaining the impact of your building on the site and can be used very early on in massing studies to make adjustments to orientation, placement, and form.

SUN STUDIES THROUGHOUT THE YEAR

By going back to the Sun And Shadows Settings dialog box, you can duplicate the settings and modify only the date or time of day to include a sun study for the equinox and the winter solstice. You can then export each view using the Export image option. Choose File ➢ Export Image and export each view to keep a record of the sun at different times of the year. Here are some examples of how shadows are cast on the building: The top is winter; the middle is spring/fall; the bottom is summer.

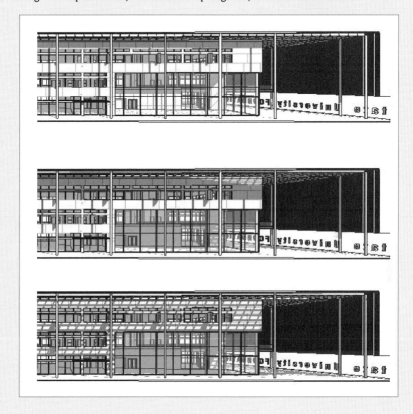

Any view can be animated to show the effects of sun. To access this feature, use the Advanced Model Graphics dialog and navigate to the Sun And Shadows Settings dialog. There you will find three tabs: Still, Single-Day, and Multi-Day. The default tab is Still, and the settings on this tab affect static views. The other two tabs are specifically designed for creating multi-image representations of the model over time (Figure 14.10).

FIGURE 14.10

Use the Single-Day and Multi-Day tabs to define time and time intervals for the animation.

Single-day studies Create single-day studies with the settings on the Single-Day tab. These settings will show the effect of sun on a specific day at various intervals (15, 30, 45, 60 minutes). By setting Date and checking the Sunrise To Sunset box, you'll be able to animate the effect of sun on your model.

Multi-day studies The settings on the Multi-Day tab (Figure 14.11) are just like the settings on the Single-Day tab, but the interval is days, weeks, or months, and you can see the effect of sun over the course of an entire year.

Once you select either a Single-Day or Multi-Day setting, a new control will become available in the View shadow fly-out menu to help facilitate visualizing and generating the animation.

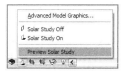

FIGURE 14.11

Sun And Shadows Settings for a multi-day sun study

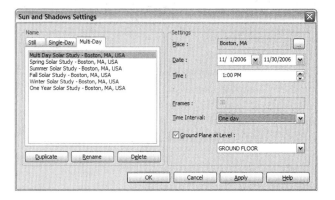

Previewing a Solar Study

To preview the solar study, click the option, and controls will appear in the Options bar:

Frame number   Access Sun and   VCR-style controls
Shadows Settings
dialog box

You can use the controls to step through the frames of the animation and access the Sun And Shadows Settings dialog. The animation will play slowly because the frames have to be redrawn one by one to recalculate the shadows. We do not recommend playing the animation using these controls. To get a feel for the final output, you really need to export the view and see it play back at real-time speed in a video viewer.

Exporting the Animation

Once you've set the correct values for the solar study, you can export it and play it in a media player. To do so, choose File ➤ Export➤ Animated Solar Study. The Save As dialog includes options to set file type, duration, size, and model graphics style (Figure 14.12). For better performance, drop the image size to something reasonable for a monitor (800×600, for example). As with the interactive preview, it will take Revit some time to process all the frames. The more frames, the longer the export will take, but the final result makes for compelling demonstration media. To maintain decent quality, keep it at 100 percent when the compression dialog appears. Dropping quality will result in blurry results that don't present well. The only downside to not compressing the file is the resulting larger file size.

FIGURE 14.12
Set the values for your
animation.

 **Real World Scenario**

ANIMATED SOLAR STUDIES

Animated solar studies can track the course of the sun over the period of a day or at one time of day over a period of many days or months in an animated video format. This helps to better understand the implications of the sun on the building and of the building on the surrounding context. To set up an animated solar study, follow these steps:

1. Open our second perspective, Sun Study-West façade.

2. Using the View Control bar at the bottom of the screen, or by navigating to View ➢ Advanced Model Graphics, open the Sun And Shadows Settings dialog.

3. Choose the Multi-Day tab. You will notice that since we have set our location previously for the Still study we did earlier, we don't need to set a new location for the project. Set the start date to 1/2/2007, the end date to 12/28/2007, the time interval to one day, and the time of day to 3:30 p.m. The dialog box should look like this.

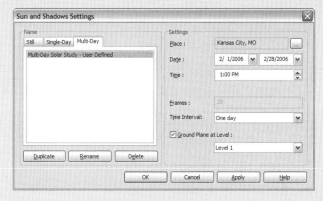

4. Clicking OK to exit the dialog will give you a perspective with the sun located in a position to support the first date (1/2/2007) at the 3:30 time. If you go to the View Control bar and click again on the shadow button, you will notice a new option: Preview Solar Study.

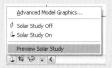

5. Choosing this tool will highlight the view window and give you a new set of tools in the Options bar, as shown here.

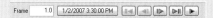

6. The controls work the same as they do on your DVD player. Pressing the time and date will take you back to the Sun And Shadows Settings dialog. The other controls are there to set the frame rate and initiate playback. Playback time will vary depending on the size and complexity of your model and your processor speed.

7. You also have the ability to export this animation to an AVI file. Choose File ➢ Export ➢ Animated Solar Study and you can set the dimensions of the image, the model graphic style, and the frame rate for your AVI. You can play around with the settings until you get the right proportion of size and time for each slide.

8. Once you have begun the export, you can view the progress of the AVI at the bottom of the View window.

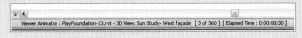

These types of sun and shadows studies are not designed to provide you with quantifiable metrics for the amount of daylight in a given space. However, they are a good, quick tool during the earliest design decisions phase to help check your design assumptions regarding where, when, and how the daylight enters the space.

Tracking Recycled Materials

In Chapter 13, "Fine-Tuning Your Preliminary Design," we discussed maximizing the power of schedules by adding custom variables to the calculations. We did this by doing a basic cost analysis on the Revit model and calculating a square foot cost against the gross square footage of the building. It is possible to use this same method to track the amount of recycled materials used in the project.

In our project, we have decided to substitute a percentage of Portland cement with fly ash in all of the cast-in-place concrete. As a by-product of burning coal, fly ash will help count toward the recycled materials points we need for LEED accreditation. Based on a number of concerns, we have chosen to use 21 percent fly ash in our concrete. We can calculate this very quickly using a simple schedule:

1. Navigate to View ➢ New ➢ Material Takeoff and choose <Multi-Category> from the list.

2. In the next dialog box, you will be asked to choose fields for the schedule. Choose the following fields and place them in this order:

   Material: Name

   Material: Volume

3. Clicking OK at this point would give us a list of all the materials in the project. Since we want only the concrete, select the Filter tab. Choose Material: Name and then Contains from the Filter By drop-down menu and type **Concrete** in the Filter field (see Figure 14.14).

4. Now, we need to add another calculated value to tabulate our percentage of fly ash in the project. Click the Calculated Value button. Name the field Volume Of Fly Ash. Change Type to Volume and enter the following formula: **Material: Volume *0.21**.

   Remember, it is all case sensitive, so make sure you type it right. The finished dialog box should look like Figure 14.13. Click OK.

FIGURE 14.13
Use a formula to
calculate a value for
fly ash.

FIGURE 14.14
Set the schedule so
that it filters for
concrete materials.

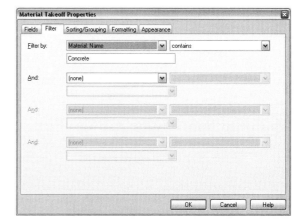

5. On the Sorting/Grouping tab, check the Grand Totals check box.

6. Finally, on the Formatting tab, select Volume and change the alignment to right. Select Volume Of Fly Ash and change the alignment to right. Also, check the Calculate totals box. Click OK.

When the schedule is complete, you will get an up-to-date list containing all the instances of concrete in the building and a calculation showing how many cubic feet of fly ash each contains. This will all be totaled at the bottom of the schedule. As you can see, we have 6,898 cubic feet (CF) of fly ash so far in our project if we are using 21 percent recycled content (Figure 14.15).

Each of these schedules can be added to a template. Even if the percent of fly ash varies from project to project, you will have the basis for the schedule already created.

FINDING "CONCRETE" IN THE MODEL

Remember, by scheduling things within Revit, you can easily use the schedule to locate them. Simply highlight the element within the schedule view. The Options bar will provide a button labeled Show. Clicking this button will cycle you through all of the relevant views showing the element highlighted. This is true for any schedule.

FIGURE 14.15
You can see the total amount of fly ash in the schedule.

Multi-Category Material Takeoff		
Material: Name	Material: Volume	Volume of Fly Ash
Concrete - Cast-in-Place Concrete	258.04 CF	54.19 CF
Concrete - Cast-in-Place Concrete	210.28 CF	44.16 CF
Concrete - Cast-in-Place Concrete	239.44 CF	50.28 CF
Concrete - Cast-in-Place Concrete	66.89 CF	14.05 CF
Concrete - Cast-in-Place Concrete	804.91 CF	169.03 CF
Concrete - Cast-in-Place Concrete	230.04 CF	48.31 CF
Concrete - Cast-in-Place Concrete	699.80 CF	146.96 CF
Concrete - Cast-in-Place Concrete	86.00 CF	18.06 CF
Concrete - Cast-in-Place Concrete	272.33 CF	57.19 CF
Concrete - Cast-in-Place Concrete	4286.33 CF	900.13 CF
Concrete - Cast-in-Place Concrete	476.81 CF	100.13 CF
Concrete - Cast-in-Place Concrete	230.70 CF	48.45 CF
Concrete - Cast-in-Place Concrete	191.17 CF	40.14 CF
Concrete - Cast-in-Place Concrete	258.04 CF	54.19 CF
Concrete - Cast-in-Place Concrete	5109.22 CF	1072.94 CF
Concrete - Cast-in-Place Concrete	0.00 CF	0.00 CF
Concrete - Cast-in-Place Concrete	537.35 CF	112.84 CF
Concrete - Cast-in-Place Concrete	13.70 CF	2.88 CF
Concrete - Cast-in-Place Concrete	13.88 CF	2.91 CF
Concrete - Cast-in-Place Concrete	13.88 CF	2.91 CF
Concrete - Cast-in-Place Concrete	12.33 CF	2.59 CF
Concrete - Cast-in-Place Concrete	211.37 CF	44.39 CF
Concrete - Cast-in-Place Concrete	19.87 CF	4.17 CF
Concrete - Cast-in-Place Concrete	12.89 CF	2.71 CF
Concrete - Cast-in-Place Concrete	10.96 CF	2.30 CF
Concrete - Cast-in-Place Concrete	10.96 CF	2.30 CF
Concrete - Cast-in-Place Concrete	10.96 CF	2.30 CF
Concrete - Cast-in-Place Concrete	10.96 CF	2.30 CF
Concrete - Cast-in-Place Concrete	10.96 CF	2.30 CF
Concrete - Cast-in-Place Concrete	10.96 CF	2.30 CF
Concrete - Cast-in-Place Concrete	18527.22 CF	3890.72 CF
Grand total: 31		6898.13 CF

Window Surface Percentage vs. Room Area

We discussed concepts of sustainability early on in this chapter and specifically the use of sun shading devices to allow natural daylight into spaces but minimize the effects of solar gain at unwanted times of the day or year. Another way to keep out the sun is to simply minimize the amount of glazing on a given façade. There is a balance to be had between the amount of glazing on a façade and the amount of daylight into the space. In the ideal design, we want to maximize daylight but still be efficient with glazing. Again, north and south light is easier to control, the north particularly because it includes no direct sunlight. East and west light can be more challenging. One way to work toward the most efficient amount of glazing is to work directly with your mechanical engineer or energy modeler to calculate the ideal percentages of glazing for a given façade or cardinal direction. Once you have these goals, you will want to quickly calculate the percent of glazing versus wall area or room area. Revit can help you do this with the Room/Area Report (Figure 14.16).

One of the export commands available within Revit is Room/Area Report. (File ➢ Export ➢ Room/Area Report). If all the room objects are placed within a given floor in the model, this report will create an HTML file detailing how the areas for the rooms were calculated. The report will list in graphic and table format each room, its perimeter, and the triangulated areas within the room that generate the areas. If you choose the Settings option before you export the table, you can check a box to additionally report window area as a percentage of the room. This will give you the square footage of window area within the room as a percentage of the overall area of the room. This square footage percentage can also assist in the documentation you will need for LEED credit EQ 8.1 (for more information, see www.usgbc.org/leed).

FIGURE 14.16

Analytical views
of room area and
window area

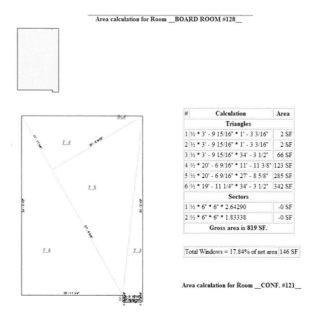

Area calculation for Room __BOARD ROOM #128__

#	Calculation	Area
	Triangles	
1	½ * 3' - 9 15/16" * 1' - 3 3/16"	2 SF
2	½ * 3' - 9 15/16" * 1' - 3 3/16"	2 SF
3	½ * 3' - 9 15/16" * 34' - 3 1/2"	66 SF
4	½ * 20' - 6 9/16" * 11' - 11 3/8"	123 SF
5	½ * 20' - 6 9/16" * 27' - 8 5/8"	285 SF
6	½ * 19' - 11 1/4" * 34' - 3 1/2"	342 SF
	Sectors	
1	½ * 6" * 6" * 2.64290	-0 SF
2	½ * 6" * 6" * 1.83338	-0 SF
	Gross area is 819 SF.	

Total Windows = 17.84% of net area	146 SF

Area calculation for Room __CONF. #121__

Energy Analysis

Energy analysis is a very useful tool in estimating building life cycle costs and is becoming more and more important to facility managers and owners early on in the design process. The tool gives us the ability to predict building energy use. By making design changes to the model and running a series of energy analyses based on the various design iterations, we are able to estimate the building's loads based on the design schemes, thereby helping to minimize energy use and overall life cycle costs.

In its current incarnation, Revit Architecture will not provide energy analysis. The software is primarily created for architects to model and document their designs; you'll need to use one of the third-party applications discussed in the following pages. At the same time, the design of a building involves not only its function, but also its aesthetic and social implications as well as its environmental impact. Today, the focus on energy efficiency is becoming more and more important to stakeholders involved with architecture. Owners and facilities managers alike are increasingly looking to get up-front data on predicted energy footprint and short-term and long-term costs and other information at the early stages of design.

Energy modeling can involve a complex set of analytical calculations, and entire careers are based on deriving accurate and predictable results. This type of analysis can encompass building energy use, daylighting, alternative power sources, computational fluid dynamics, thermal gain, and carbon footprint, to name a few. Essentially, energy modeling allows you to understand the building from a more holistic, ecological point of view.

It is important to keep in mind that any value you get out of the Revit model with respect to energy analysis will be only as useful as the information you have been able to put into the model. Good input will lead to good output.

There are a couple of applications that can be used in unison with the Revit architectural model for additional energy analysis data.

IES <VE>

IES <Virtual Environment> (www.iesve.com) is one application that provides a direct link to Revit Systems (Revit application for MEP). IES <VE> is advanced simulation software that provides analytical tools for energy, daylighting, computational fluid dynamics (CFDs), and a variety of other analysis features. Opening a Revit Architecture model in Revit Systems, you can link to IES with a single-click and get an estimation of the building's energy consumption based on rooms, location, and construction type (Figure 14.17). Revit Systems allows you to export the whole model to IES so that a full-blown analysis can be performed.

FIGURE 14.17
The Foundation model as seen in Revit MEP heating and cooling interface

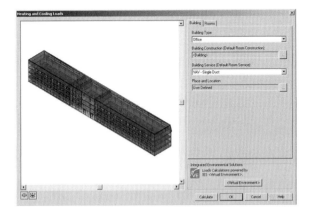

If you do not have Revit Systems, you can still use the Revit Architecture model and analyze it without remaking the building model in IES by exporting to gbXML and importing it in IES.

gbXML

gbXML, or Green Building xml (www.gbxml.org), was designed as a neutral file format to transfer the data required for an energy model into various analysis applications from a Revit model. This file format, while not quite an industry standard, has been quickly adopted by a number of leading CAD vendors and is one way to transfer design intent into an energy modeler without having to re-create the building form in another application. IES <VE>, for example, will import a gbXML file, but it will not have all the geometric and spatial data that you will have if you imported directly from Revit Systems.

EXPORTING TO GBXML

Exporting to gbXML is a very simple, fluid process, and one of the primary benefits of using this file format as a basis for your energy analysis is that it is easy to create. To begin, you need to set one variable before you start the export.

1. There is a location in the Revit file to set the zip code of the project specifically for the energy analysis. Navigate to Settings ➤ Project Information. Click the Energy Data button. In this very simple dialog box, you will need to define the project type from the drop-down menu and type in the postal zip code (Figure 14.18). There is a host of different options for project

type that cover most of the building types out there. The drawback of this system is that it does not currently accommodate for mixed-use building types. For our Foundation project, let's make it an office building with a 64105 zip code (Kansas City).

2. Now that you have set those variables, exporting is a simple process. Choose File ➢ Export ➢ gbXML. It will automatically begin calculating the export before you are given the option to save the file. The export will take a little time, depending on the speed of your computer. Once it's created, you'll have a small, compact file you can easily share with your mechanical consultant or upload directly into your energy analysis application.

FIGURE 14.18
Set building type and postal code to establish some assumptions about the energy requirements for your building.

Green Building Studio

Green Building Studio (www.greenbuildingstudio.com) is an online service that will provide you with a simple energy analysis based on your gbXML file and some basic energy demand assumptions you provide. The results are reported in an easy-to-interpret Web format with a lot of visual cues and graphics. The report takes into account TMY2 (Typical Meteorological Year 2) data (historical data of sunny vs. overcast days), regional utility demands and costs, and climatic data. It will return information such as the predicted annual utility costs, building life cycle costs, and carbon footprint (see figure 14.19).

This is a free service for basic energy calculations and there is a very nominal charge for more developed results. There is a small client application to download that will help coordinate the uploading and calculations of the gbXML files. You can download it from www.greenbuildingstudio.com/Tutorial.aspx.

Figure 14.19

Example from Green Building Studio showing the estimated energy cost of the building

General Information	Location Information
Project Title: Foundation	Building: KANSAS CITY, MO 64105
Run Title: Foundation-13.xml	Electric Cost: $0.057/kWh
Building Type: Office	Fuel Cost: $1.286/Therm
Floor Area: 52,697 ft²	Weather: TMY2 weather for Kansascity, MO

Estimated Energy & Cost Summary

Annual Energy Cost	$35,642
Lifecycle* Cost	$485,441

Annual CO_2 Emissions

Electric†	743,613 lbs
Onsite Fuel	167,846 lbs
H3 Hummer Equivalent	41.4 hummers

Electric Power Plant Sources‡

Fossil:	80%
Nuclear:	19%
Hydroelectric:	0%
Renewable:	1%
Other:	0%

‡ Based on US EPA EGRID 2006 Data (2004 Plant Level Data).

The Bottom Line

Sustainability is an increasingly important goal for your clients. Revit, thanks to its BIM database of project information, provides tools that greatly simplify sustainability analysis.

Incorporate a sustainable approach from project inception   Sustainability is quickly becoming a core approach to any design. Learn to leverage the Revit model for a more holistic approach to sustainability.

Master It   BIM is also a computational database that can report information about the virtual building. The important thing about a sustainable approach is to know which questions to ask and to ask them at the right time.

Use Revit to track sun and shade patterns   Understanding the sun's effect on a building is paramount to sustainable design.

Master It   Use the tools within Revit to produce still and animated solar studies from interior and exterior views in order to understand shading and the sun's effect on the building and space.

Track recycled materials and other sustainable strategies using schedules   Keeping track of project goals is an important part of any project process. By using the schedules and other tools in Revit, you can also track key sustainability goals.

Master It   Tracking recycled material usage is key to LEED credits and sustainability. Create a material schedule that tracks recycled content volume for concrete.

Chapter 15

Annotating Your Model

In this chapter, you will learn how to add annotations to your views to begin noting information for presentation and construction documents. No set of documents is complete without annotations to describe the drawings. Even in a parametric model, you will need to supply dimensions, tags, text, and notes to aid in the communication of the design to the owner, contractor, and design team.

In this chapter you'll learn to do the following:

- ◆ Create rooms and tag them
- ◆ Combine rooms and tags with schedules
- ◆ Understand the different ways to annotate a project
- ◆ Create and modify keynotes

Annotating Your Views

In any set of documents, showing geometry alone isn't sufficient to communicate all the information a builder or fabricator needs to construct the building. Annotations assist in clearly documenting your model for others to read and understand. Tags, dimensions, text, and keynotes all need to be added to the drawing in order to clearly and concisely guide construction. Revit provides a rich set of tools for accomplishing these tasks.

Annotations, dimensions, and tags are placed in the views, in relation to real elements, not on the sheet. This allows you to annotate a view at any point in the process, before or after the final (sheet) document has been created. See Figure 15.1.

FIGURE 15.1
The annotated floor plan

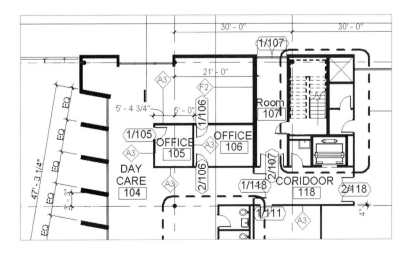

Displaying Information about Rooms

Rooms help define areas and spaces within the Revit model. Even if a room represents "empty space between boundaries of physical elements," it is still considered an *element* in Revit, similar to a door, window, or wall. Rooms have properties and can be added, deleted, modified, and scheduled like every other element in Revit. Rooms can also be used for energy calculations and are critical to gbXML exports. For more information on this feature, see Chapter 14.

Placing and Tagging Rooms

You need bounding elements to be able to calculate the area and volume of a room. Bounding elements for rooms are roof, and room separation lines.

These elements all have a property called Room Bounding that determines if the element participates in calculating room extents. By default, all these elements are set as Room Bounding. If you do not want an element to affect how rooms are calculated (for example, toilet partitions), select it and uncheck the option Room Bounding in the element properties (shown checked in Figure 15.2).

FIGURE 15.2
Making a wall
bounding

Every model element in Revit can be tagged, including rooms. These tags report information stored in the room element properties. This means you can have the tags tell you anything about the room based on parameters of the room: name, number, area, finish, and so on. Rooms are separate elements from room tags, which, like all other tags used in Revit, report information stored in the building elements they are tagging. Door and wall tags report values within the door or wall elements. Room tags do the same.

Room elements are not visible in a view by default, so it can be easy to confuse the tag with the element. As with other elements in Revit, the tag can be placed automatically when adding a room using the "Tag on placement" button in the Options bar. Unchecking this box will still create rooms, just without the tags.

Rooms can be inserted from either the Basics tab or the Room And Area tab. To insert a room, choose one of the plan views of your project and choose the Room tool from the Design bar. When you select this tool, all of the rooms already placed within that view will highlight blue and an X will be shown across the area that bounds that room (see Figure 15.3).

This is an aid to show you where room elements already exist within the model. As you can see in Figure 15.3, we are missing a room element in Room 120. To place that room, mouse over the white area and click to place a room element. A blue box will appear and a room tag will automatically be placed within the room. The Room tool will remain active after the placement of each room and will allow you to keep placing rooms in sequence. You'll notice that Revit auto-increments each room tag as you place the rooms. If you change a room number, the number of the room you place next will base on the number of the last room you placed.

FIGURE 15.3

Placing a room

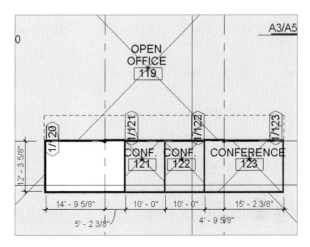

Once a room is placed, it becomes an object in the model. As we mentioned, the room tag is a separate element and can be removed without compromising the room element itself or any of the information you might have added to the room element. In fact, deleting the tag from a room will prompt a warning message alerting you that the room element still exists (Figure 15.4). In a schedule, these rooms will continue to all show up with their proper room names and any other information you've added, regardless of whether they have been tagged.

FIGURE 15.4

Deleting a room tag

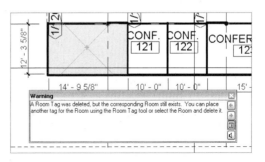

Once the tag has been removed, you can still select the room element. By default, the element is not visible within Revit. This is intentionally done to avoid cluttering up precious space in a view. To select a room to edit, simply drag the mouse through the room and left-click when the room element highlights (shown by the crossing lines).

There are a couple more features critical to rooms that you will want to be aware of as you begin placing them within your model:

♦ **Room elements need to be bounded in plan.** Room elements need to be in an enclosed area in order to be properly placed. Placing a room in a non-enclosed area will generate an error message like the one shown in Figure 15.5:

FIGURE 15.5

An unenclosed
room error

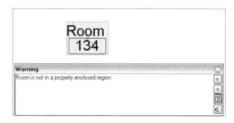

If this room is left unbound, it will not properly report in any schedules. There are a few
ways to resolve an unbounded room:

◆ If you are still in the midst of design, simply finishing the design may give you the walls
or other bounding elements you need to complete the enclosure. The room element will
recognize that and dynamically stretch to fill the room.

◆ You can delete the room if it has been incorrectly placed. If you decide to remove a room,
you must delete the room element itself, not just the room tag. (To toggle between the
room and room tag selection, use the Tab key.)

◆ You can use Room Separation lines (in the Room/Area design tab), which create room
boundaries to define the edges of the space and close the areas where the rooms "leak"
and thus cannot be generated.

◆ **Rooms do not like to overlap.** You may come across this issue in any of three ways:

◆ First, you can place a room in a space that already has a room element. If this occurs,
Revit will alert you to the issue by showing you both room elements in the space and an
error message asking what you'd like to do (see Figure 15.6). Clicking OK in this dialog
box will leave both rooms in place. Clicking the Delete Room(s) button will remove the
most recently placed room element.

FIGURE 15.6

Placing one room
within another

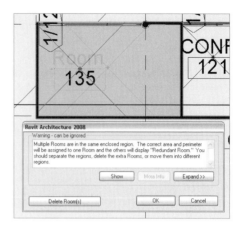

◆ The second way this can occur is if you remove a wall or other bounding element between
two rooms. Revit will give you the same warning and ask how you would like to resolve
the problem (see Figure 15.7).

FIGURE 15.7
Overlapping rooms

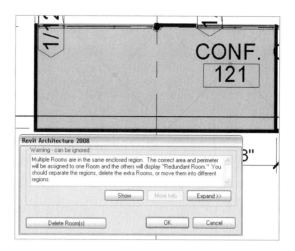

♦ A third way to get overlapping rooms is when the heights of rooms overlap. If a room extends vertically into a room on the next floor, a similar warning message will occur. It is important to understand that rooms are volumes with 3D dimensions. Room volumes are covered in more detail in the section "Rooms Settings" later in this chapter.

Room Separation Lines

So, what happens when you need one room to "end" and another to "begin" and you don't want to add a wall? For example, you might want a room to end at the end of a corridor that opens to an entry space, or you may have an open living room and dining room connected to a great room.

For these conditions, use the Room Separation tool found on the Room And Area tab. This tool allows you to draw lines in plan that will act as bounding elements.

Room separation lines show in plan views as distinctive green lines (Figure 15.8). These lines can be turned on or off in the Visibility/Graphic Overrides dialog box.

FIGURE 15.8
Room separation lines

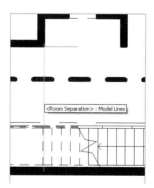

Room separation lines will print with the plans if left visible. If they are turned off, they will still maintain their room boundaries—but just remember they are there! "Out of sight, out of mind" can cause problems later when you move walls and the rooms seem to react in strange ways.

Real World Scenario

ADDING A ROOM SEPARATION LINE

In the Foundation project, there was a room named Corridor 127 that needed to be separated into a corridor and an entry area because have slightly different finishes in the finish schedule.

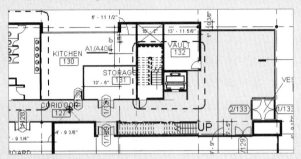

The Room Separation tool was used to divide the spaces.

Drawing a room separation line from the stairwell across to the wall created a boundary, allowing a new room to be added named Entry 139. In the following view, you can see where the room element ends without requiring us to create a wall to divide the space.

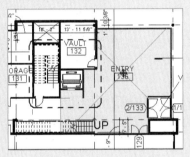

Selecting Rooms

You can select rooms in one of two ways: graphically and from a schedule table. To select rooms from a schedule table, simply highlight the room within the schedule in the schedule view and click the Show button on the Options bar.

GRAPHICAL SELECTION

You must have noticed by now that Rooms are represented with two diagonal crossing lines when selected (Figure 15.9).

These are selection helpers. Without them, the room element could be selected only at an edge of a room—but at the edges of rooms there are always many other elements (walls, floors, windows, etc.) and the selection isn't easy. These diagonal lines facilitate easier selection and will highlight when the cursor moves over them so that you can pick the room (Figure 15.10). When the "Tag on

placement" option is checked, your room tag is always placed at the intersection of these two diagonal lines. These lines are a subcategory of the Room element and if you wish to see them all the time
in the view, you can turn on the Reference subcategory using Visibility/Graphic Overrides dialog.

FIGURE 15.9
The graphic represen-
tation of the Room
object

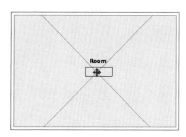

FIGURE 15.10
A highlighted room
element

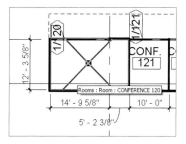

Once a room element is selected, your mouse will turn into a move sign and let you move the
entire room somewhere else if needed. When a room is selected and you move it, you are displacing
the room information and assigning it to another space. Moving a room allows you to take all of the
data you've entered for the room (wall finishes, ceiling, floors, and so on) and relocate rather than
retype it. The same is true for copying a room into a new space.

There is a difference between using the Move tool when a room is selected and when a room tag
is selected.

When you select a room tag, you are moving the tag around in the room or outside the room:
with small spaces, tags often need to be taken out of the space the room describes because they
don't fit. When you attempt to do that and move the tag outside of the building, the tag will display
a question mark and you will get this warning message.

If you select the tag that is outside of the room, a new button appears in the Options bar called

Explain Error. It gives anyone who later joins the design team and isn't aware of why the tag shows
a ? sign the ability to understand the error.

To fix the error and clarify which room the tag is tagging, you can use the Leader option in
the Options bar. This will connect the room and the tag with a line and help you understand the
relationship between the tag and the room. Figure 15.11 shows the room tag with the leader line
checked.

FIGURE 15.11
A highlighted room
element. Notice that
the tooltip that
appears when the
room is highlighted
shows the room name
and number.

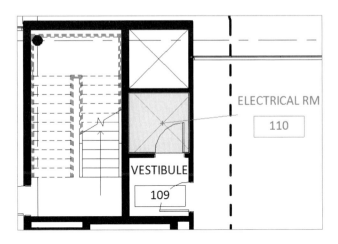

Rooms in Section Views

While you can tag rooms also in a section view, you will not be able to make new room elements in section. You can create and select rooms only in plan views. Even though you'll be able to tag a room in section view, you will not be able to select the room and access any of its properties.

The graphic representation of a room in section does not reflect the true room boundaries defined in Room Area Settings. Room areas are calculated using the Area Settings rules, despite the representation. This might be confusing, especially when you calculate room volumes. As an example, if the room in section shows a 10′ ceiling height and the Room Area Settings are set to calculate a room height of 8′, the room volume will reflect the 8′ calculated area, not the 10′ actual area.

Room Properties

Like all other elements in Revit, rooms have properties. By selecting the room element and clicking the Properties button, you can see the room properties that are available. These properties can be scheduled, displayed in room tags, or used to color-code a floor plan with a color fill scheme. The parameters are divided into sections to help organize the information:

Level reports the level on which the room has been placed.

Upper Limit defines the top level of the room. For example, if you have a double-height space, you might want the upper limit to be more than one floor high so the entire space is treated and scheduled as one element. By default this is set to be the same as the level on which the room is placed so that you define the actual room height as an offset of Level.

Limit Offset defines the height of the upper limit of the room relative to the Upper Limit setting. This function is critical for volume calculations and gbXML exports. There are some settings that need to be addressed to get accurate results from gbXML exports:

- Limit Offset needs to coincide with the bottom of the ceiling plane above for any given room on floors below the roof line.

- Limit Offset can exceed the top of the roof for rooms that are on the uppermost floor.

- Rooms cannot overlap vertically for accurate gbXML exports. This means the upper limit of a room cannot encroach into the bottom of the room above it.

Area, Perimeter, Unbounded Height, and **Volume** are noneditable fields that report the metrics of the room element. We will review how these numbers are calculated in the next section.

The **Identity Data** section includes identity information about the room. You can manually add data using these parameters and it will show up in tags. If you're using a color fill scheme, it will also be used to color-code the plan.

Phase is a noneditable field that reports the phase the room was created in.

Room Area and Volume

There are rules that dictate the automated calculations of area and volume for room elements. They can be found under Settings ➢ Room and Area Settings. The dialog (Figure 15.12) gives you the option to select from a number of area calculation schemes by relocating the boundary element of the rooms.

It is important to note the difference between room areas and area plans. *Area plans* follow different rules and will treat exterior and interior walls differently. The rules that apply to rooms will apply to all the walls regardless of location relative to the exterior wall. You can choose between the following area calculation options:

- ◆ At wall finish

- ◆ At wall center

- ◆ At wall core layer

- ◆ At wall core center

FIGURE 15.12
Room And Area
Settings dialog

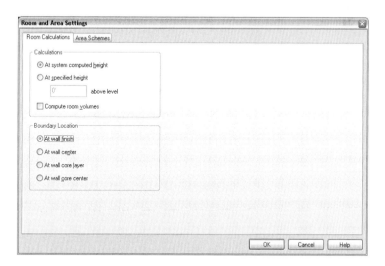

In addition to calculating room areas, Revit will calculate room volumes. This feature is not enabled by default and must be turned on in the Room And Area Settings dialog box. Simply check the box to calculate the volumes. It should be noted that depending on the size and complexity of your model and your processor speed, calculating volumes in Revit can negatively impact file performance.

There are some rules that you should be aware of when activating room calculations:

1. Every room can have an independent theoretical room height that you define using the Limit Offset room property. This is the height the room will use for calculating volume if the actual height of the ceiling, floor, or roof above it is higher than the applied height of the room (Figure 15.13).

2. If the room height is above the existing ceiling, floor, or roof, it will be the height to the first architectural element the room object "hits" (Figure 15.14). Note that, as we mentioned earlier, the room height can begin to cause other problems if it extends into the room on a floor above or below (Figure 15.15).

FIGURE 15.13
Room Offset (bounding box) is set to lower than the ceiling height, and the room displays 214.72m³.

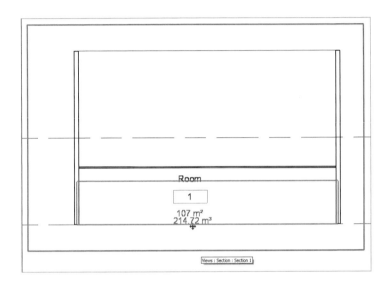

FIGURE 15.14
Bounding box is set to 4100mm (above the ceiling). The tag displays 279.14m³, which means that the volume was calculated taking a room height only up to the ceiling as a value.

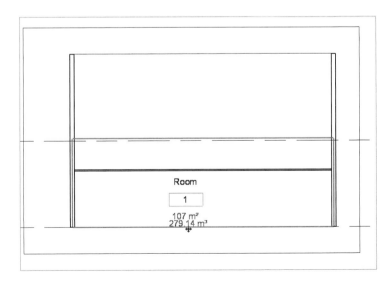

FIGURE 15.15
A change in the offset height doesn't have any effect on the room volume calculation unless it "hits" the next floor, ceiling, and so on.

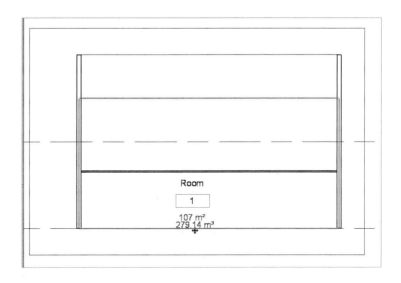

Schedule Keys

Once you have populated your model with rooms and begin adding information to each room about its department and finishes, you'll most likely discover that information about rooms tends to repeat. Representing this information will be useful when you're generating room and finish schedules. In previous chapters, we discussed ways to report the information in those elements using the schedule functionality. But what if you want to define a common set of parameter values that can be shared across many rooms? For instance, if you are working on a large office project, doing a room finish schedule that lists individual rooms might be a bit unnecessary if many of the rooms share identical finishes. For these situations, a specialized schedule called a *schedule key* can be handy and save time. Schedule keys can report any number of values that repeat across similar elements.

Creating a Schedule Key

Since we have already added rooms to the Foundation model, let's make a room finish schedule using a schedule key for the project. To do this, we will need to generate two schedules. The first one will define the *room styles* by using what is called a key name. The second schedule will link our room styles to the rooms themselves.

Let's begin with the room style schedule. On the View tab in the Design bar, choose Schedule/Quantities, or from the menu choose View ➤ New ➤ Schedule/Quantities. The same dialog box you use when making any schedule will appear. This time, however, we are going to choose some different values.

Choose Rooms from the list on the left, select the Schedule Keys radio button (see Figure 15.16), and click OK.

FIGURE 15.16

Selecting a
schedule key

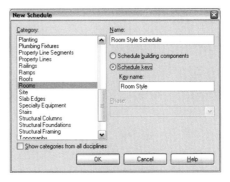

The next dialog should look very familiar (Figure 15.17). It is basically identical to the Schedule Properties dialog (in fact, it is named the same), but one tab is not included in the dialog: the Filter tab.

FIGURE 15.17

Making a schedule key

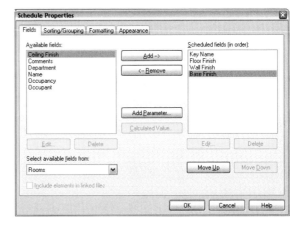

Upon opening the Fields tab, you will notice that one of the values is already on the right side to be included in our schedule: Key Name. Now, we want to move the following values from the left to the right (they've already been moved in Figure 15.17):

◆ Floor Finish

◆ Wall Finish

◆ Base Finish

The remaining tabs in this dialog box are identical to the dialog box for other schedule types. For more information on formatting or changing the appearance of a standard schedule, see Chapter 13.

Once you have these values selected, click OK. A blank schedule appears and needs to be filled in with finish values.

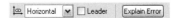

Select the New button in the Options bar to begin to add standard room finishes to the schedule. In this table, the key name is important because it will be the link between the two schedules. Using the New button, add the following room styles to your table: Key Name, Floor Finish, Wall Finish, Base Finish.

Once the schedule is complete (you can always add to it or modify it later), you need to create the finish schedule to be used in the construction document sheets. Again, select Schedule/Quantities from the View tab and select Rooms from the list. This time, leave the default value Schedule Building Components selected (Figure 15.18) and click OK.

FIGURE 15.18
Making the finish schedule

Again, you'll see the standard Schedule Properties dialog. Add the following fields to the Schedule fields list (the right side) in this order and click OK:

Number

Name

Room Style

Floor Finish

Base Finish

Wall Finish

Area

The schedule that shows up will be a list of the Rooms in the project, sorted by room number with (none) set as the value for Room Style. The Floor, Base, and Wall Finish columns will all be blank. Some sample lines are shown in Figure 15.19.

FIGURE 15.19
The finish schedule

From here, adding values and finishes to the rooms by room style is fairly easy. Once you select the (none) value in the Room Style column, you will be given the option to select from the list of values we defined in the room style table (Figure 15.20).

FIGURE 15.20

Selecting a room style

Selecting a value from this list will automatically fill in the values for the Floor Finish, Base Finish, and Wall Finish columns to match the values we defined in the previous schedule. As you modify values in the room style schedule, they will be dynamically updated in this schedule, adding consistency and predictability to your workflow.

FIGURE 15.21

Adding values to the schedule

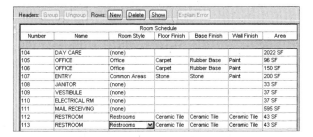

Imagine the time it would take if you had to manually enter all these finishes in each schedule in each project! Key schedules are a big time-saver and ensure consistency.

Tags

Tags are textual labels for doors, walls, windows, rooms, and a host of other objects that architects typically need to reference in a set of drawings. In Revit, tags are intelligent, bidirectional symbols that report information stored in the properties of an element. A value can be directly edited from the tag; likewise, editing an element's properties affects the tag.

Selecting a wall tag, for example (Figure 15.22), returns the wall type that is set in the properties of the wall itself; but it can show much more information, such as the wall's fire rating or area.

FIGURE 15.22

A wall tag

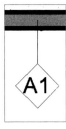

Loading Tags

Revit comes with a variety of tags that can be customized to meet your office's graphics requirements. The preloaded tags loaded into the default templates cover many common requirements but
are by no means exhaustive.

Every category of a family can be tagged, and you can load multiple types of tags for each category. Tags are loaded like any other family or component in Revit. Navigate to File ➢ Load from
Library ➢ Load Family, and navigate to the tag you want to add to the project.

Tags that you design and use frequently in your project should be loaded in your office template.

Placing Tags

Tags can be placed during the creation of an element (using the Options bar option) or can be
placed later. As a best practice workflow, it is easier to model your project first and then document.

You can insert tags from the Tag button on the Drafting tab (see Figure 15.23).

FIGURE 15.23

Tagging by material

During tag placement, the Options bar lets you position a tag in several ways.

Should you not find any appropriate tag, the Tag button allows you to load on-the-fly additional
tags without having to cancel the command and go back to the Load Families tool. If you click this
button but don't have a tag loaded, you're prompted to do so.

Tags can have a horizontal or vertical orientation and can include or omit a leader line. In the
case of a wall tag, you typically have a leader coming from the wall, whereas you probably would
not use a leader with a door or window tag. The Tag button presents three options:

By Category This option allows you to tag elements in the model by category or type. Examples
are doors, walls, windows, and other commonly tagged elements. After you choose By Category,
the elements you can tag highlight as you mouse over them in your view. Revit also displays a
ghost image of the tag you're inserting and the value in that tag.

Multi-Category Use the Multi-Category tag when you want to tag an element across different
family types—for instance, when you're using a similar glazing type in your windows and exterior doors and you want to be able to tag the glazing consistently. The Multi-Category tag allows
you to have the same tag and tag value for the glazing in both families. (Fire rating is another
common application of this tag.)

Material   The Material tag lets you tag the materials in a given family. Tagging a wall by material exposes materials used in the wall assembly. This allows you, for example, to tag the gypsum board, sheathing, and studs separately.

Changing a Tag Value

There are two ways to modify text in a tag. Selecting the tag makes the text an active control and turns it blue; just click the blue text and start typing. The second option is to access the properties of the element being tagged. Using a wall example again, if you select the wall, navigate to its properties, and change the Type Mark field, the wall tag updates to reflect this. See Figure 15.24 for examples of each location.

FIGURE 15.24

Changing a tag value

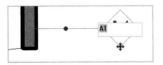

URL	
Description	
Assembly Description	Exterior Walls
Assembly Code	B2010
Type Mark	A1
Fire Rating	
Cost	

Whichever way you choose, you change the symbol text for every instance of that tag type. Therefore, if you change a wall type from A1 to A2, you change every instance of that wall family that was previously tagged A1.

Some tags only report instance values—values that are unique to the individual element. A room tag or door tag is a common example. The room tag graphics are consistent, but the room name varies from room to room. Doors are often tagged like this, with a unique numeric value for each door. With these types of tags, Revit detects if you enter duplicate values and warns you when that happens.

Tagging Untagged Elements

You can tag many elements at once using the Tag All Not Tagged tool in the Drafting tab of the Design bar. This time-saving feature lets you tag all the elements in a view simultaneously. During early phases of design, you often are not concerned with tags and annotations but are more focused on the model. Tags can become graphic clutter that obscures the design at times.

Later in the process, when the design is more complete, you may want to annotate the drawing quickly. This is where the Tag All Not Tagged tool is helpful. When you select this tool, the dialog shown in Figure 15.25 appears. You can orient your tag or add a leader to it before tagging all the listed elements in your current view.

FIGURE 15.25

The Tag All Not
Tagged dialog box

If you have elements selected, you can choose to tag only the selected elements. Note that this option is grayed out in the sample dialog box in Figure 15.25 because nothing in the model is selected.

TAGGING ELEMENTS IN PLAN: DOORS

Try the following exercise: In the Foundation file we have been using, open the view called Level 1. You'll notice in this file we've moved the documents forward a bit by defining the views we'll be using in our callouts. In this view, using the tools mentioned, let's add tags for the doors and walls, From the Drafting Tab, choose Tag ➢ By Category. Make sure your leaders are turned off in the Options bar before adding any tags to the plans.

Mouse over the door, and click when it highlights. This will insert a tag for the door centered on the door opening. By choosing Horizontal or Vertical for the tag orientation from the Options bar, you can quickly run through the plan placing door tags.

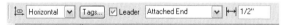

These tags might not be ideally located. As we've mentioned, the tag will come in centered on the door. However, it is a simple process to drag the tag to a more appropriate location if needed.

Now that you have placed the door tags, you can see how each door is tagged and change the tags if appropriate. As we mentioned earlier, to change the value for any of the tags, simply highlight the tag and select the blue text. This will allow you to enter a new value in that field. For our drawing set, you are going to number the doors with a door number / room number system as shown in Figure 15.26. You can also change these values directly in the door schedule.

(Note that another way to quickly tag the doors in this plan would be to use the Tag All Not Tagged function shown in Figure 15.25. This feature will apply all the tags of a given family type at one time within the model. It's a quick way to populate a view with tags.)

Figure 15.26
Numbering doors
in plan

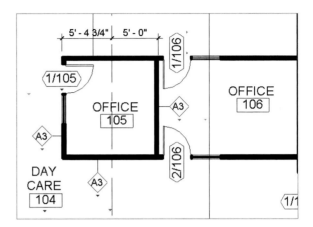

Using the Tag ➤ By Category tool in the Design bar again, highlight and select the interior walls. For wall tags, make sure to turn on your leaders, but adjust the leader size in the Options bar to ¼″ rather than ½″. The finished floor plan looks like Figure 15.27.

Figure 15.27
Adding wall tags

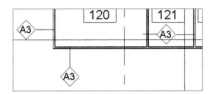

The number of annotations possible in any given view can be rather large, so it's typically a good idea to conserve the available white space on the sheet by not duplicating notes and tags. As Revit is designed to annotate only single items, avoiding duplication in a given view can be a challenge using only the standard tools. In Figure 15.27, you'll notice that in Room 121, the wall tag A3 has a leader going left and right to each wall. The "leader" on the left is simply a drafting line (see Figure 15.28). While this eliminates the parametric value for that single wall condition, in many cases adjacent interior walls will have the same type. It is recommended that you weigh accuracy for your wall types against workflow and the space available in your documents for this kind of approach.

Figure 15.28
Adding leaders to a
wall tag

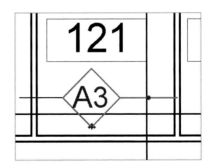

Shared Parameters

Each Revit element has a set of default defined parameters that can consist of materials, lengths, areas, or other characteristics that describe the element. Often, however, you need to add your own parameters to elements and schedule or tag those parameters. There are a couple of ways to add a custom parameter, depending on where you want it to appear in a project:

- If all you intend to do with your custom parameter is to schedule it (for example, if a door has a lock or not), you cam take two approaches:

    - Add that parameter directly in a schedule using the Add Parameter function (this will add that new parameter only to the element that you create the schedule for, such as doors, for example).

    - Create a new project parameter and assign it to one or more element categories—the difference is that this method allows you to assign the same custom parameter to more than one element (doors and windows, for example).

- If however you wish to be able to both schedule *and* tag your custom parameter, you will need to use *shared parameters*.

Shared parameters in Revit are parameters that can be shared between families and projects. This allows you to add information to your elements that can be both scheduled and tagged in your project.

In the following sections, we'll use a detailed example to present the whole process of creating and using a shared parameter, but first we'll present a basic procedure for creating a custom parameter that doesn't need to be shared.

Creating a Custom Project Parameter

You can create a custom project parameter at any time in the project cycle. You can then assign it to any element and it can be scheduled later. In the following example, we want to record whether materials are recyclable.

1. To add a new project parameter, choose Settings ➢ Project Parameters and click the Add button. See Figure 15.29.

FIGURE 15.29

Adding a project parameter

2. In the next dialog box, give the new parameter a few definitions (see Figure 15.30):

- Name, used for describing the parameter.

◆ The group the parameter will belong to. This is specifically for sorting the parameter within the element properties.

◆ The discipline. This is also used as a method to help organize the parameters.

◆ Whether it is an instance or type parameter.

Instance parameters will be specific to any instance or insertion. So if you insert three doors, they can each have different instance parameters. An example might be the door number.

Type parameters will remain consistent for the family type. So, in the door example, this might be the door width, and you'd create a separate type for each door style (36″, 34″, 32″, etc.) within the project.

◆ What type will it be (text, integer, yes/no).

◆ You will be asked to choose the Revit element to which this new parameter will be applied.

FIGURE 15.30

Parameter Properties dialog

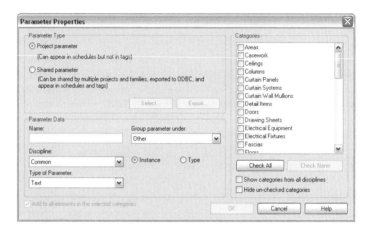

3. Following a scenario in which we are adding a "recyclable" parameter to the materials, we will name the parameter Recyclable and assign it to the category Materials. We will also choose that it will be an instance parameter of the yes/no type (see Figure 15.31).

FIGURE 15.31

Creating a custom project parameter

4. Navigate to the Materials dialog under Settings ≻ Materials and select the Identity tab. You will find the parameter you just created (Figure 15.32).

FIGURE 15.32
Locating the new parameter

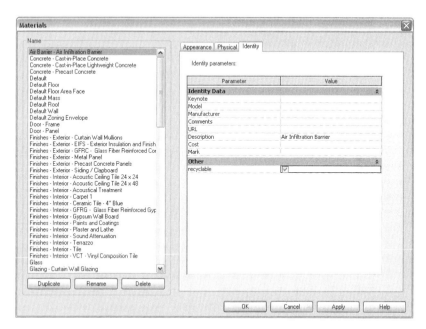

You can later make a schedule of your materials and sort or filter them with this new parameter.

Note that you *cannot* tag a value of a project parameter with a default tag. A tag does not recognize a custom parameter that you create on-the-fly in a project and has no label attached to it. Tagging a project parameter is possible, but it can only be done when using shared parameters.

Creating Shared Parameters

When you want to schedule and tag a custom parameter you have created, you will need to use shared parameters. For example, you might wish to tag the hardware set in a door or window, tag the level of radioactivity of medical equipment, or tag whether a door has a lock. None of these parameters exist by default in any of the families, so you will need to add them to the families if you want to use them. They also don't exist in any of the family tags, so to tag them, you will need to add the same parameters to the tag families as well.

The concept seems complicated, but it's actually straightforward. Imagine this: You have a set of chairs, some that are original Tonet chairs and some that are fake. You want to tag the originals with a special parameter called original. To do this, you need to add that parameter in the tag (by creating a label and calling it out), and you then need to add the parameter to the chairs that are the originals. Now, if you created the original parameter as a project parameter, that parameter will only exist in the project you created and not the chair family or tag family. That is where shared parameters come in handy—they allow you to reference the same parameter between project and family.

Let's look at the workflow behind creating these using the example of a hardware set for doors and windows.

CREATING A CUSTOM PARAMETER WHILE SCHEDULING

When scheduling, you can add a custom parameter to any schedule on-the-fly. This parameter will be assigned only to the category of elements that you are scheduling. To create such a custom parameter, click Add Parameter in the Schedule Properties dialog box.

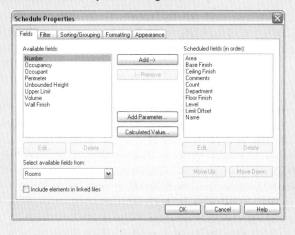

1. You create a new shared parameter file. At this stage, it doesn't matter if you are in a project or the Family Editor. In both environments, you can choose File ➢ Shared Parameters. This will open the Edit Shared Parameters dialog.

2. Select the Create option and enter a shared parameter file directory path and name. This will be the place where you will store all your custom created shared parameters.

3. Next, create a group by clicking the Groups ➢ New button that is now activated. Name this group Hardware. Revit requires you to create groups for your shared parameters because you might end up having many shared parameters and this will help you sort them and organize them easily.

4. Once you have created the group, you can create the shared parameter by clicking the New button. Name it Hardware Set. This is the shared parameter that we wish to have visible in our schedules—and more important, that we wish to tag.

The shared parameter file you've just created is nothing more than a simple text (.txt) file that you will find in the directory you created at the beginning of the exercise. Now that you have this parameter, you can add it to any of the following:

◆ The tag family

◆ The project (as a project parameter)

◆ The categories of elements you wish to have that parameter

For this exercise, we will use the Foundation.rvt file located in the Chapter 15 folder on the book's website (www.sybex.com/go/masteringrevit2008) to create a shared parameter file.

CREATE THE SHARED PARAMETER FILE

In the following steps we will first create the shared parameter file:

1. From the File menu, choose Shared Parameters.

2. In the Edit Shared Parameters dialog, click Create (Figure 15.33).

FIGURE 15.33
The Shared
Parameters dialog

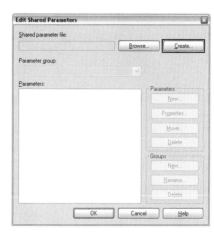

3. Here you will need to specify the directory path and name of the new file; then click Save.

Again, the name you assign here is not as important as the fact that this file will need to be accessible in Read mode for all team members. Do not give the filename an extension because the .txt extension will be appended automatically.

CREATE A GROUP OF PARAMETERS

Revit requires that you create a group before you can create a shared parameter.

1. In the Edit Shared Parameters dialog, under Groups, click New to create a new parameter group (Figure 15.34).

FIGURE 15.34
Making a new group

2. Give the new group the name Doors. To help you organize your shared parameters, you will want to name the group logically.

CREATE THE SHARED PARAMETER

Now that we've created the backbone for the shared parameters, let's create the parameters themselves.

1. Still in the Edit Shared Parameters dialog, click the New button in the Parameters section (Figure 15.35).

FIGURE 15.35
Adding a new parameter

2. In the Parameter Properties dialog, do the following:

◆ Enter a name for the new shared parameter: Lockable Door.

◆ Under Discipline, keep the default, Common.

◆ In the drop-down list under Type of Parameter, select Yes/No.

◆ Confirm with OK.

And that's it! We have just created the shared parameter and we are ready to use it in the Family Editor (to add it in a door tag) and in the Project, to assign it to the category Doors. As explained earlier, you can only tag a custom property that you define if you share it across the families and the project.

CREATE A NEW PROJECT PARAMETER USING THE SHARED PARAMETER AND ASSIGN IT TO A CATEGORY

In the following steps we'll make our shared parameter a project parameter and assign it to the Door category.

1. Open the file Foundation.rvt.

2. Open the plan view Level 1.

3. From the Settings menu, choose Project Parameters. A list of parameters will appear. Our shared parameter is *not* among them, so you will need to click the Add button (Figure 15.36).

FIGURE 15.36
Adding the parameter

4. In the Parameter Properties dialog, in the Parameter Type group you will see a Shared Parameter option. Check it and click Select.

5. The Shared Parameters dialog opens and there you will find the shared parameter you have just created, automatically selected. Click OK (Figure 15.37).

FIGURE 15.37
Linking the shared
parameter

6. In the Parameter Properties dialog, set the Group parameter to Identity Data. Make sure you select the Instance radio button.

7. All that is left to do is to select the category to which this shared parameter will apply. In the Categories list, select Doors (Figure 15.38). You can assign a parameter to as many categories as you wish.

FIGURE 15.38
Assigning categories

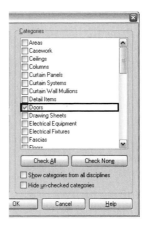

8. Confirm all that you have done by clicking the OK button.

SET THE SHARED PARAMETER IN THE OBJECTS THAT BELONG TO THE SELECTED CATEGORY (DOORS)

Now that we have created a shared parameter, we need to add the tags to show the lockable and non-lockable doors.

1. In plan view, select a door (let's say the door belonging to Room 131-Storage) and open its properties (Figure 15.39).

FIGURE 15.39
Selecting a door
in plan

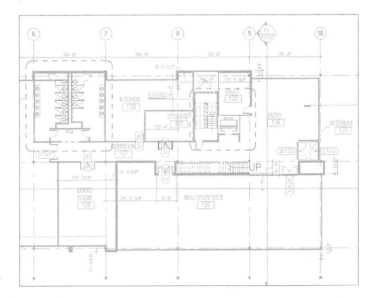

2. You will notice that the newly created parameter appears in the group Identity Data, just as we wanted it to. Note that the value is gray, meaning that it has not been set.

Identity Data		≽
Comments		
Mark	1/131	
Lockable Door	✓	

3. To set the parameter to Lockable or not, click on the check box and it will become black, indicating that it is checked. If you want it unchecked, click again and it will void the selection.

Identity Data		≽
Comments		
Mark	1/131	
Lockable Door	✓	

You don't have to do this one by one for each door. You can select multiple doors that will have a lock and check the box using the same method.

ADD A SHARED PARAMETER TO A DOOR TAG

If you only wanted to add a new parameter to a category and schedule it, you could have done so by using a simple project parameter. The point of making a shared parameter is that you will be able to also tag the door and display the value of the shared parameter in a tag. We will now add this shared parameter to the door tag family so that the tag understands the shared parameter value and displays it. If we simply added a new label for the shared parameter and the door is lockable, the door tag for a lockable door would simply display Yes—which is not very helpful. So you'll need to add a static text note next to the label: Lock= (see Figure 15.40).

FIGURE 15.40
The tag with fixed text

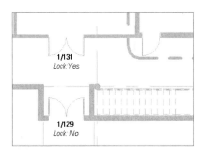

1. There are two approaches to re-create the new tag. You can take an existing Door Tag, dupli-cate it, and then add the shared parameter. The second approach is to make a tag from scratch. For this exercise, we will make a new one from scratch.

   From the File menu, select New ➤ Family. Choose the Annotation folder.

2. In the New dialog, select the family template Door Tag.rft and click Open.

3. The Family Editor opens in plan view, showing two crossing reference planes. The intersec-tion of the two reference planes represents the insertion point of the tag. In the tag, we would like the following information to be displayed: the door mark and whether it has a lock.

4. Click the Label button in the Design bar. Click with the mouse somewhere close to the cross-ing point of the two references.

5. In the Select Parameter dialog, select Mark and click OK (Figure 15.41).

FIGURE 15.41
Selecting the mark
parameter

6. The Mark text is set to ⅛″ (3mm) by default, and this might be a bit big if we want to add a mark and a lockable parameter, so we need to make the font size smaller. In the Element Properties dialog of the mark, click Edit/New. Click Rename in the Type Properties dialog box and enter a new name, indicating the size of the mark, ³⁄₃₂″ (1.5mm) bold. Click OK.

7. In the type properties dialog, set the properties of the mark as shown here.

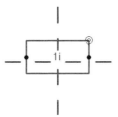

8. Confirm with multiple OKs when finished. What you see should be similar to what is shown here.

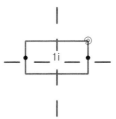

Note that 1i is just a symbolic representation of the label. Once placed in the project environment, it will read and display the mark of the door.

9. Click again on Label in the Design bar and position this second label below the first, also centered in the tag.

10. We will now add the shared parameter we just created. Click Select A Parameter and then select Add. In the Parameter Properties dialog, click Select. The shared parameter list opens and here you will find the Lockable Door parameter. Select it and click OK in all remaining open dialog boxes.

11. You can also select the Shared Parameter label, click Modify to access its element properties, and set sample text to Yes.

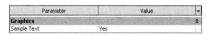

12. You will probably want to change the size of the text here as well, to ³⁄₃₂″ (1.5mm), so navigate to Edit/New and under Type Properties, select Duplicate. In the Name dialog, enter ³⁄₃₂″ (1.5mm). Confirm with OK.

13. Uncheck the Bold parameter and click OK in all remaining dialogs.

14. Adjust the position or the size of the label if needed.

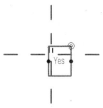

All that remains for us to do is to add the fixed text that will read Lock: and position it just in the front of the shared parameter label.

15. Click Text in the property dialog, and in the drawing area, click somewhere in the front of the label Yes.

16. Enter the text **Lock:**, and in the Options bar, select Properties. Repeat the steps 6 and 7 of this exercise to adjust the size and name of the new text type to match the label we added. Click OK in all remaining open dialogs.

The tag is ready. Save it and load it in the project Foundation.rvt. If you have already placed door tags, you can select them all and exchange them with the new tag that contains the shared parameter by simply selecting it in the Type Selector. You will notice that now all your door tags will display the mark on the top and the word *Lock* at the bottom. For doors that you previously defined as lockable, it will also show *Yes*. You will see that many doors have nothing shown in the tag after *Lock:*. Those are the doors that haven't been marked Yes or No, like the one in Figure 15.42.

FIGURE 15.42
A door without a Yes
or No value for Lock

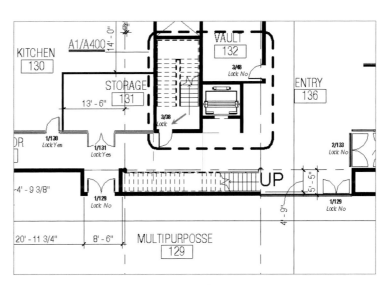

Shared Parameter Notes and Cautions

Keep the following points in mind when you create shared parameters:

◆ Once you have added a shared parameter to your project, you will not be able to change any of the properties. If you forgot to set the Yes/No parameter, or if you mistakenly selected Type instead of Instance, you will not be able to change this setting. To fix that, you will need to create a new project parameter using the same shared parameter and be more careful the next time.

◆ Shared parameters are based on globally unique identifiers (GUIDs). Each GUID is unique and they cannot be renamed. If you do so, or if you delete them, you will not be able to continue using the tags to tag the parameters described in the project.

Make sure you keep these tips in mind when working with shared parameters and store the shared parameters in safe locations where they cannot be easily deleted or moved.

Text and Keynotes

Notes are a critical part of communicating design and construction intent to contractors, subs, and owners. No drawing set would be complete without textual definitions and instructions on how to assemble the building. Revit has two primary ways of adding this information to the sheets. One way is through text. Text in Revit consists of words arranged in paragraphs with or without a leader. Text can be used for specialized annotations, sheet notes, legends, and similar applications. Keynotes, the other tool for annotating a drawing, are element specific and can be scheduled and standardized in the Revit database. Chapter 4 briefly introduced text and keynotes as elements you can include in customizing your template. In the following sections, we'll explore the use and function of both tools in more detail.

Text

Text is easy to add to any view. However, it's important to understand that text is nothing more than a view-specific label. Specific text families will maintain a parametric relationship throughout the project, and changing one text family type will change each type through out the project. However, it is important to recognize that while text is a family within Revit, it is not directly tied to values of other families like keynotes or tags. Text is only text, and it will not dynamically report properties from elements it is pointing to.

You can access the Text tool from both the Basics and Drafting tabs in Revit. Text can be added to any view, including a 3D view. To begin adding text, click the Text button after you've opened the view of your choice, select where in the view you wish to place text, and begin typing. To edit text you've already placed, click the text to highlight it, and then click it again to activate the text box. To move text once you've located it, select it and drag it, or use the Move command.

As with all the elements in Revit, there are ways to change the look and feel of the object being created. Once you've selected the Text tool, the Type Selector and Options bar provide formatting choices.

The Type Selector allows you to choose a style for the text you're about to create. Each text style is managed through the Properties dialog, where you can modify parameters such as font and size. To create a new text style from an existing one, click the Properties button in the Type Selector, choose Edit/New in the properties, and then duplicate the type and make adjustments to the properties (see Chapter 4). You can also choose to add a leader to the text note before placing the note.

There are four options for leaders: None, a one-segment leader, a multi-segment leader, and an arced leader. Once you've placed the text, highlighting the note itself provides additional options. You can add or remove additional leaders and rejustify the placed text.

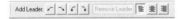

After selecting text, click the blue letters to edit it. When you're editing the text, you're given additional formatting in the Options bar for bold, italic, and underline. These apply to whatever text you've selected in the note.

When you use the Move command, you move both the text and the leader. When you move text by dragging the arrow icon, you move only the text box, leaving the leader anchored in its original position.

One of the biggest limitations of Revit is the fact that one cannot apply changes in text style to multiple elements (tags, schedules, title blocks, keynotes, or dimensions, for example). If you want to make all text in Revit use a particular font, you will not be able to change a global project setting. You need to edit each element type individually. A good way to avoid this type of change is to standardize the fonts in your project templates, as covered in Chapter 4.

Keynotes and Textnotes

Keynotes and *textnotes* are textual annotations that relate text strings to specific elements in the model using an external file. You can format font style, size, and justification in the same manner you can format standard text, but keynotes and textnotes behave like a Revit family. This means you can insert different family types of text in Revit, just as you would door or window families. Changing one instance of the family type changes all the instances in the project. Because keynotes and textnotes act as families in Revit, they can also be scheduled. It is important to understand the difference between a keynote and a textnote.

A keynote is a short reference, typically a number followed by a letter. An example would be 03300.AA, which might point to a cast-in-place concrete wall. The 03300 portion of the note refers to the specification section the note is generated from, and the AA portion is a sorting mechanism used to differentiate cast-in-place concrete from another note in Division 3 of the specifications.

All of the notes on a given sheet are keyed back to a legend that is typically placed on the right side of a sheet. This reference is an aid to add more detail and understanding to the keynote without having to directly reference the specifications. See Figure 15.47 later in this section for an example of a keynote and legend. Textnotes are very similar to keynotes, but they combine the text and the key into one note. This saves you from having to coordinate the legend on the sheet and puts the note right next to the item you are pointing to. See Figure15.44 for an example of text notes. No matter which style you prefer, both the keynote and textnote can be created with the same command within Revit. Since the command is called Keynote within Revit, we will refer to the process from here on out as *Keynoting* regardless of the style of keynote (or textnote) you choose to use. See Figure 15.43.

FIGURE 15.43
Keynotes and textnotes

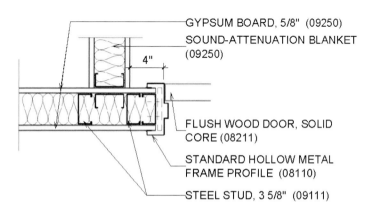

GYPSUM BOARD, 5/8" (09250)

SOUND-ATTENUATION BLANKET (09250)

4"

FLUSH WOOD DOOR, SOLID CORE (08211)

STANDARD HOLLOW METAL FRAME PROFILE (08110)

STEEL STUD, 3 5/8" (09111)

The Keynote command is located on the Drafting tab of the Design bar. When you add keynotes in Revit, you have three options:

Element allows you to note an element in the model, such as a wall or a floor. This type of note is typically used if you want to note an entire assembly, such as a wall assembly. You can find this value in the family properties of that element.

Material allows you to note a specific material in Revit. You can add a note to concrete, gypsum board, or acoustical tile.

User allows you to select any model-based component in Revit and define a custom keynote for it. Notes defined this way differ from those defined as element or material because they're unique to the particular object selected. They can be used in conjunction with element and material notes.

Keynote Behavior and Editing

A core concept in keynoting is how the notes react in the model. Keynotes are integrated into Revit just like any model element. Keynoting an object in Revit lets you associate a text value with that family's keynote parameter. This value is consistent for every identical element in the model. For example, all doors have a type parameter that lets you set the keynote value. If you keynote a door—anywhere in the model—the keynote will show that value. Likewise, if you ever change the value of the keynote for the door type, all keynotes will update automatically.

Keynotes are special in that you cannot *edit the text of a keynote directly in Revit*. All the keynotes in Revit are tied to an external text file, which is the only location they can be edited. This file can be modified at any point to add or remove values and notes. A sample list looks like this:

```
03100   Concrete Forms and Accessories       03000
03200   Concrete Reinforcement               03000
03300   Cast-in-Place Concrete               03000
03400   Precast Concrete                     03000
03500   Cementitious Decks and Underlayment  03000
```

This external text file is designed to keep annotations consistent by storing all of them in one repository. Every time you add or change the text of an annotation and reload the text file, it dynamically updates all the keynotes of that type used in the project.

You can edit a keynote text file (.txt) or add one to a project at any time. You can have multiple text files for various projects, but you can have only one text file per project at a time. The text file works just like any other Revit family. Since all the notes are parametric, changing a note in the text file will change all of the notes in the project when the text file is updated.

A powerful way to ensure consistent use of notes throughout your office is to create a master text file for your various project types. These master note lists can be "prelinked" to materials or assemblies within your project template so that you can immediately begin inserting common notes into any project. To prelink, choose Settings ➢ Materials and select the Identity tab. In the Keynote field, a predefined note can be added to any material.

Since the keynote text file is separate from the Revit file, if you send a project file to someone and don't send `keynote.txt`, they will be able to see all the keynotes you've added to the views but they won't be able to add or edit the notes without the text file.

Keynote Filenaming Conventions

The default text file in Revit is found in the following folder:

```
C:\Documents and Settings\All Users\Application Data\Autodesk\RAC 2008\Imperial
Library (or Metric)
```

To edit this file, open it in Notepad or Excel and follow the format already established in the file. Let's look at that format to get a better understanding of how to customize keynotes.

The first few rows designate the groupings. They consist of a label (in this case, a number) followed by a tab and then a description. An example grouping looks like this:

```
03000 Division 03 - Concrete
```

Below the groupings, with no empty lines in the file, are the contents of the groupings. These are shown with a minor heading, a tab, a description, a tab, and the original grouping header. Here's an example:

```
03200 Concrete Reinforcement 03000
```

Here, 03200 is the subheading, Concrete Reinforcement is the description, and it all falls under the 03000 grouping from the previous example.

Using this method, you can add or edit notes and groups of notes to the keynote file. It might seem horribly inefficient at the beginning of the process to have to constantly go to the keynote text file to edit or add notes. While this might seem like a burden, it can be a blessing as well. Accessing this file ensures a global level of consistency within the keynotes on a project that is unattainable in most drafting applications. If you are feeling frustrated with having to access this file to make changes, think about all of the time you are saving *not* having to check your set sheet by sheet to verify that all of the notes pointing to a material are the same.

Keynote Settings

Once you change a keynote text file, you need to reload the file into Revit to update the keynotes. You can locate the dialog box to change or update the text file by choosing Settings ➢ Keynoting Settings (Figure 15.44).

FIGURE 15.44
Keynote Settings
dialog box

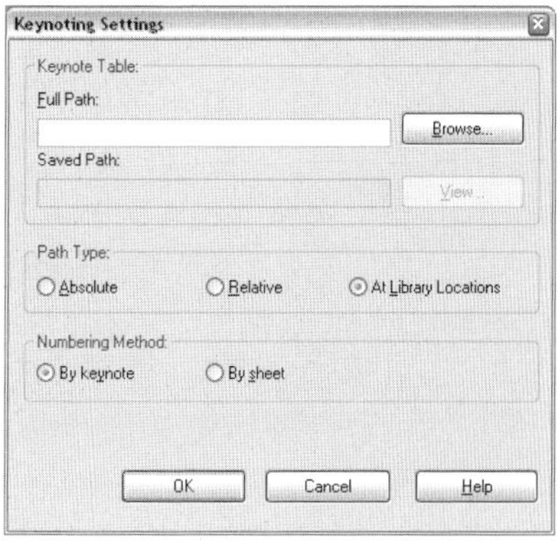

In the Keynote Table group, you define the path to the text file used for keynoting:

Path Type Defines how Revit looks for your text file using one of three methods:

> **Absolute** This option follows the UNC naming conventions and searches across your network or workstation for a specified location.

> **Relative** This option locates the text file relative to the Revit project file. If you move the Revit file and the text file and maintain the same folder structure, Revit knows where to look for them.

> **At Library Locations** This option lets you put the text file in the default library location defined in the Settings ➤ Options ➤ File Locations tab.

Numbering Method Defines how the keynotes are numbered:

> **By Keynote** Allows you to number keynotes as they come from the associated text file.

> **By Sheet** Numbers the keynotes sequentially on a per-sheet basis.

Adding Keynotes to a View

To add keynotes to a Revit model, choose one of the three keynote types from the Drafting tab in the Design bar. In your view, mouse over the various model objects until you find the one you wish to note, and click to add the keynote. Once you've placed the note on the sheet, you'll see a dialog box (Figure 15.45) asking you to identify the element you're trying to note.

FIGURE 15.45
Selecting a keynote

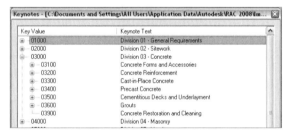

Expand the plus signs until you find your desired keynote and double-click it. Doing so associates that particular note with the element or material in the model. As mentioned previously, you only need to make this association once. For example, if you keynote a material called Concrete, then every time you hover the cursor over that material anywhere else in the model with a keynote tag, you'll see the preview graphic of the tag showing Concrete. This way, you can define the materials and assemblies in the model and begin your documentation process.

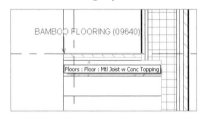

With the exception of detail components (covered later in this chapter), you can't keynote lines or other 2D information.

Keynote Legends

Depending on your workflow and style of annotation, you may want to create a legend for your keynotes that appears on each sheet so that the legend shows only the keynotes used on the sheet you're currently viewing. Or you may wish to have one legend for the entire project that will show all keynotes used in the project. The legends allow the builder to reference the note number with the text quickly and easily (Figure 15.46). These lists usually reside on the side of the drawing near the title block information and can take either of two forms. The first type is all inclusive and will show every note within the project. This style has the benefit of consistency between each sheet in the set. The same note will always be in the same location in the list. The other type of keynote list includes only the notes that are present on a particular sheet. This has the advantage of supplying a list of notes customized for each sheet without extraneous information. As you can imagine, this second list can be very labor intensive and fraught with opportunities for human error. One of the beauties of Revit is its ability to accurately manage this kind of information for you. We will review how to create both styles of lists.

FIGURE 15.46

A keynote legend

KEYNOTE LEGEND	
Key Value	**Keynote Text**
03300.AO	CIP CONC FLOOR SLAB (03300)
04810.BF	STONE CLADDING (04810)
05120.AC	STEEL BEAM (05120)
05310.AH	COMPOSITE FLOOR DECK (05310)
05500.BB	STEEL COLUMN (05500)
05500.BU	STEEL ANGLE (05500)
06105.AB	WOOD FURRING (06105)
06105.AC	PLYWOOD (06105)
06105.AD	1X IPE WOOD SUNSCREEN (06105)
07210.AB	RIGID INSULATION (07210)
08411.AA	EXTERIOR ALUMINUM-FRAMED STOREFRONT (08411)
09111.AO	HAT-SHAPED, RIGID FURRING CHANNEL (09111)
09250.AC	GYPSUM BOARD, TYPE X (09250)
09640.AA	BAMBOO FLOORING (09640)

Creating a legend in Revit is simple: Choose View ➢ New ➢ Keynote Legend. You'll be prompted to name the legend; enter a name and click OK.

There are only two fields available in a keynote legend, and by default, they are both loaded into the scheduled fields side of the Fields tab. Those fields are as follows:

Key Value: The numeric value of the keynote

Keynote Text: The text value for the keynote

A keynote legend works very much like any other schedule as far as formatting and appearance. By default, the sorting/grouping is already established because the key value is used to sort. The one special item to note is located on the Filter tab. At the bottom of this tab is a feature unique to this type of schedule: a "Filter by sheet" check box (Figure 15.47) is available. Checking this box will give you the ability to filter the list specifically for each sheet set.

Either legend style you make can be placed again and again on every sheet in the project. The filtered legend style will dynamically modify the note list based on each sheet and the contents on each sheet. As views are added or removed from a sheet or notes are added to the project, the keynote legend will update accordingly. If the keynote is not used in the view placed on the sheet, it will not show up in the legend.

FIGURE 15.47

"Filter by sheet" check box

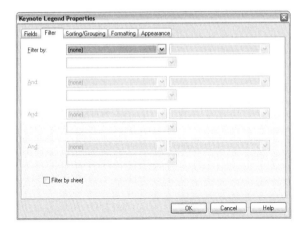

A SCHEDULE FOR KEYNOTES

Creating a schedule for keynotes is a great way to find rogue notes and typos in a project. If you are working on a project team of any size, there's always a chance that someone could be inserting an incorrect textnote into the project. Scheduling the notes is a great way to help manage this process and give you the tools to verify consistency. Scheduling textnotes allows you to do two things:

◆ List all of the notes within a project and verify their spelling and accuracy

◆ Find the "odd" note, instances of notes that show up only once or twice.

The Keynote Family

Revit comes with a keynote family that allows you to produce both keynotes and textnotes. If it is not loaded into your project, you can find it under the Annotations folder in the Imperial or Metric library. The family name is `Keynote Tag.rfa`. This family has three family types that allow you to change note styles within the project. You can see the three note styles in Figure 15.48.

FIGURE 15.48

Note styles available in the default Revit keynote tag

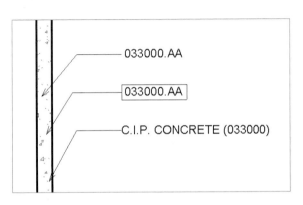

The three styles are Keynote Number, Keynote Number—Boxed, and Keynote Text. Each of these notes pulls information from the text file we discussed earlier in this chapter. We are simply using the flexibility of family types to report different values within the model from the same note. Like any other family, this family can be edited to change the note length, font style, or other attributes to match your office standards.

Adding Notes to a Wall Section by Material

As we discussed earlier in this chapter, there are three styles of keynotes: element, material, and user. With all of these styles, there are limits to what you can note within Revit. Understanding this is critical to successfully using the keynote system within Revit so you can optimize the value of your predefined notes.

These three note styles can annotate only objects within Revit. This means you can add notes to elements such as walls, roofs, floors, and families that are a combination of materials or elements; you can add notes to the individual materials themselves or any element that can be given a material; and you can add notes to detail groups and detail components. While this is an extensive list and covers most of what happens in Revit, there are a couple of things you cannot tag with the Keynote tool: detail lines and groups (although you can tag elements within groups).

This becomes a critical issue when you begin embellishing details within a model. As a best practice, it is recommended that you optimize the use of detail components and embed them into the project families. Detail components are families created with 2D linework that can be dropped into any view to represent elements that are not directly modeled. For example, blocking that would appear over a window head is not something you would create as a model element, but it is still necessary to show in a section or detail (see Figure 15.49). We will cover the technique of creating and noting detail components in Chapter 17.

Figure 15.49

Detail components

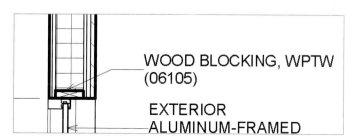

Once you've established your keynote style and made your adjustments to font size and type, you can add some notes to the drawing. Adding notes to a drawing from this point is quite simple.

1. On the Drafting tab, click the Keynote button.

2. Select Element, Material, or User from the list. In our example, we've selected Material.

3. When you mouse over the material, Revit will try to identify it. If the material already has a note value defined, Revit will show you a floating note identifying the material.

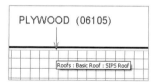

From here, click to place the arrowhead of the note, click again to locate the joint in the leader, then a last click to locate the text. If the material is unknown, Revit will show a question mark to tell you this material has not yet been identified in the project.

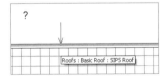

Locate the note using the same method for materials that are already defined (Figure 15.50), but after you set the text location, Revit will prompt you to select a value from the Keynotes table.

FIGURE 15.50

Adding notes to a material

Once you've selected the note for a material, that same note will be applied every time you select that material with a keynote in every other view within the project.

By default, Revit does not include an arrowhead with any of the keynotes. There isn't a way within Revit to preset arrowhead styles for notes. After you first insert a note into Revit, you will need to select it to add an arrowhead. To do this, select the note and navigate to its properties, and then select Edit/New. Here you can globally set an arrowhead style for any of the keynote family types. Most of the common arrowhead styles can be found in this properties box. Selecting one from the list will change the arrowheads for all of the notes of that type within the project.

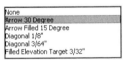

Once you've added a couple of notes, it's an easy process to continue noting the remaining materials in the wall section. The completed section with keynotes looks like Figure 15.51.

FIGURE 15.51

A wall section
annotated by material

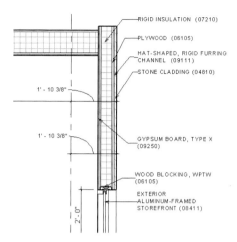

FIGURE 15.51

A wall section
annotated by material

ADDING NOTES TO A WALL SECTION BY ELEMENT

Another way to keynote a drawing is to note by assembly, or within Revit, by element. Keynoting
by element means that you are not noting the individual materials as we did in the previous example
but the entire assembly at once. So, in lieu of noting plywood and gypsum board, you are noting
the entire wall assembly at once. The process to add the notes is very similar.

1. On the Drafting tab, click the Keynote button.

2. Select Element, Material, or User from the list. In our example, we've selected Element.

3. When you mouse over the element or assembly, Revit will try to identify it. If the element
   already has a note value defined, Revit will show you a floating note identifying the material. From here, click to place the arrowhead of the note, click again to locate the joint in the
   leader, and finally, click to locate the text. If the material is unknown, Revit will show a question mark to tell you this element has not yet been identified in the project. Locate the note
   using the same method you used for elements that are already defined, but after you set the
   text location, Revit will prompt you to select a value from the keynotes table.

A wall section noted by element looks like Figure 15.52.

FIGURE 15.52

A wall section noted
by element

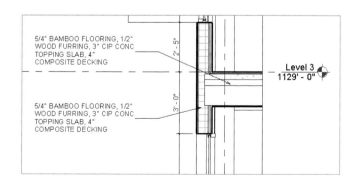

Remember that element, material, and user notes in Revit are different entities and are allowed their own, unique notes. You can note by material, by element, and by user within the same project.

Predefining Keynotes

There are a variety of other ways to add notes to a project without adding them directly in a view. Within the properties of elements and materials is a field to predefine a keynote. By putting a value in this field before noting the drawings, you can avoid selecting notes from the keynote list when you are actually annotating a view. All of the notes would be preselected. Depending on the note type, the location for these settings varies.

Element This value can be set in the properties of the various families in a Revit project. By selecting a wall, for example, you can select this wall's properties, and then click Edit/New to reach the wall type properties. Under Identity Data, you can then define a keynote (see Figure 15.53). Selecting this field, you will be presented with the same keynote table that you'd receive if you were noting this element in a view. If the note is incorrect for this project or element, you have the option to change the note here as well.

FIGURE 15.53

The type properties of the wall showing the predefined Keynote field

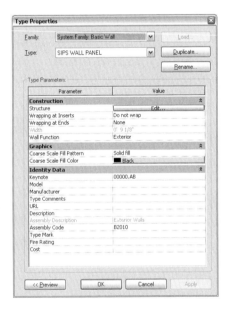

Material This value can also be set by choosing Settings ➤ Materials. By selecting a material from this list, and then selecting the Identity tab, you can add keynote values directly to your materials (see Figure 15.54). You will again be presented with the familiar keynote dialog box to select your materials.

User User notes are view specific and cannot be predefined. While it is still possible to annotate only model elements and detail components with user notes, this tool will allow you to note the same element with different notes in separate views. This can be dangerous to the consistency of your notes in your drawings if used inappropriately. The advantage of this note type, however, is if you need to note something differently in one view based on a unique condition. For example, you might need to note a material or color change in a special location or a special flashing or sealant issue around a unique window condition. This will spare you from having to re-create a new family type simply to add a different note.

FIGURE 15.54
Defining keynotes
for materials

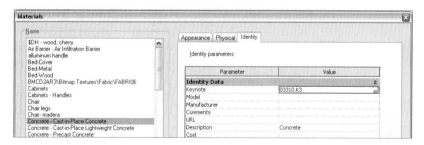

Revit does not support more than one `keynote.txt` file per project, so if you wish to include keynotes from different standards, you can simply add more text entries to the oneZz text file that you have and they will all be available to be used.

The Bottom Line

Create rooms and tag them   Room elements are highly useful tools for a number of different applications in a set of documents. Learning how to use them and tag them will help you find areas, create finish schedules, and identify spaces.

Master It   Once the model has been largely built out, you need to start adding information about rooms and finishes. What tools would you use?

Combine rooms and tags with schedules   Adding information to the room elements is only part of the documentation and design process. Knowing how to schedule that information allows you to communicate effectively with owners and contractors.

Master It   Tags are used to report information about an element. How do tags work in Revit so that they always report accurate and consistent information about the elements they tag?

Understand the different ways to note a project   Revit supplies you with three ways to annotate your model and the project. Knowing when to use each and planning for them early in the documentation phase saves time and frustration.

Master It   It is important to understand the relationships between elements and materials in Revit early. How does this help streamline the process of keynoting your project when you reach the documentation phase?

Create and modify keynotes   No set of drawings is complete without keynotes or textnotes. Understand how to create and modify them for a complete set of documents.

Master It   You will need to add notes in every stage of design to communicate your design intent on a project. How do you create and modify the notes to ensure accuracy through out all the sheets in the set?

Chapter 16

Developing the Design with Smart Workflows

In this chapter, we will explore scenarios in which building elements repeat, and you'll learn how to take advantage of some tools in Revit to help your workflow be more efficient and less prone to error. Groups and Links are tools in Revit specifically designed to support such workflows and allow for design and propagation of repetitive entities that can range from entire buildings, to individual rooms, and even to furniture arrangements.

Both of these tools require an understanding of some basic principles that will help you make decisions about when and where to engage these features in a design. We will introduce the concept behind each tool and present a series of use cases in which groups or links provide a useful solution to a design problem.

Here's what you'll learn in this chapter:

◆ Gain understanding of the principles of groups

◆ Understand workflows where groups can be used

◆ Gain understanding of the principles of links

◆ Understand workflows where links are best applied

Working with Repetitive Elements

Many architectural projects deal with the design and organization of repetitive elements. The concept of a modular unit that is repeatable has been one of the more important experiments of modern architecture and continues today in the form of housing, hospitals, schools, and office buildings. A repetitive element can be found at nearly every scale: from repeating buildings to housing units, repeating hotel rooms, classrooms, hospital rooms to bathrooms, closets, and furniture layout. In each case, the basic requirement is to group a collection of elements that is repeatable so that later in the process any change to the module will be propagated to all the other instances (copies) of the module. This propagation results in huge time savings, as you don't have to manually update the model, element by element. This also guarantees consistency, and less red-lines to pick up as documents are reviewed. At the same time, there needs to be some flexibility built into the tool to account for edge conditions (where the repetitive unit needs to stray away from base) without breaking its relationship to the essential nature of the module. Revit is remarkably well suited to support a diverse set of design requirements.

Groups

Groups will significantly improve your workflow when you are working with collections of elements that need to be repeated throughout a project.

When a collection of related elements are made into a *group*, it becomes possible to manage and change *any* single instance of the group and then have the changes propagate throughout the entire model—all in one interaction. It is also possible to execute a change on one group instance only and *not* have that change propagate; as you will see, Revit was designed to be flexible.

Revit Architecture 2008 introduced significant improvements to groups, making them an excellent solution when working with projects with many repetitive design elements. You can group elements in a project or even inside a family and use them to quickly lay out entire floor plans. You can also save groups and reuse them in other projects, making them quite versatile.

As we've discussed previously, Revit categorization is intelligent—objects know what they are and in what views they are visible. This directly impacts how groups are created and organized. For example, model elements (walls, floors, furniture, etc.) are grouped as *model groups*, and 2D, view-specific elements (dimensions, annotations, etc.), are grouped as *detail groups*. There is also a hybrid category called *attached detail groups*, which relates grouped details to a specific model group. If you create a group that contains both types of elements (model + annotations), Revit will automatically store this group as a model group with an attached detail group for the view-specific information. Keeping tags and keynotes associated with a model element in a group would be an example of this. That said, there are certain conditions where information *cannot* be attached within a group. For example, if a dimension between two walls is added to a group but only one of the walls is in the group, Revit would not be able to attach the dimension. The reason behind this is simple: when new instances of the group are placed, where should the dimension go in the absence of the original, ungrouped wall? Remember, dimensions, tags, and keynotes are referencing real model elements and cannot exist without their references (hosts).

Some other important features that were addressed in Revit Architecture 2008 have to do with modifying the origin of the group, and some great enhancements have been made to group editing, which have improved the usability and the workflow of working with groups tremendously.

Using Groups for Repetitive Rooms

Most architectural firms have projects where repetitive units are used throughout the design. In our first example, we will work on a day care center for children with cancer project (Figure 16.1). The design calls for many typical bedrooms, most of which will be the same size and have the same accommodations (beds, bathrooms, furniture). The ability to design, iterate, and manage all these bedrooms will be a major part of the project, which also needs to be easy to maintain, schedule, and update.

We will work with groups to solve this design challenge and then later look at the same issue from the vantage point of using links and compare the differences. As you will see, each method will lead to different results.

FIGURE 16.1
Repetitive elements
sample model. Model
Courtesy of Felipe
Manriquez, Univer-
sidad de Las Americas.

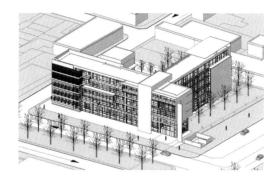

Creating and Managing Groups

As soon as the building design is roughly oriented on the site and you start laying out the modules inside the project, you can immediately take advantage of group functionality by defining the basic room unit(s) that will repeat. Later, you can build more content in one instance of the group, which then populates into other instances of the group placed in the project.

Early on, you work with walls and rooms to begin creating reliable area schedules in order to see how the design is stacking up against program requirements. You'd also like to take full advantage of the BIM by keeping all information centralized in one file. Using links (external file references), you would not get these benefits.

Creating and Placing Repetitive Units Using Groups

Let's step through a workflow using groups to lay out bedroom units.

1. Open the `Model_groups_01.rvt` file from the book's website (`www.sybex.com/go/masteringrevit2008`). The project should open with the plan view shown in Figure 16.2.

FIGURE 16.2
Floor plan showing just
the exterior skin and
core—interior has not
yet been designed

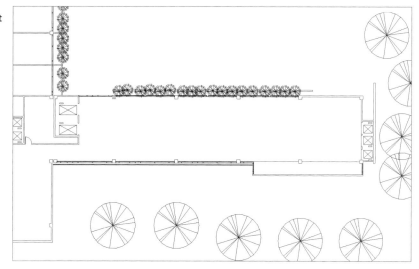

Group

2. Create a room and add a door as shown in Figure 16.3. Select the front wall with the door and one perpendicular wall and make a group by clicking the Group button in the toolbar at the top of the screen.

   When creating the group, we only chose one of the perpendicular walls (the one on the right side) because we will repeat the module along the length of the space. If you added *both* perpendicular walls to the group, you would end up with *overlapping walls* as the unit is copied along the length of the building. This would result in lots of warning messages to deal with. Not taking these warnings into account would later affect the scheduling of walls, so you need to be smart about how groups are made.

3. Once the Group tool is activated, you'll be asked to name the group. As soon as this task is finished, the new group will appear in the Project Browser under Groups ➢ Model Node. The group is listed as a model group because all elements we selected to become a part of the group were model elements.

4. Before making any changes to the group, take a look at a symbol showing the group origin (Figure 16.4).

FIGURE 16.3
Model group created out of the elements of the first room you created

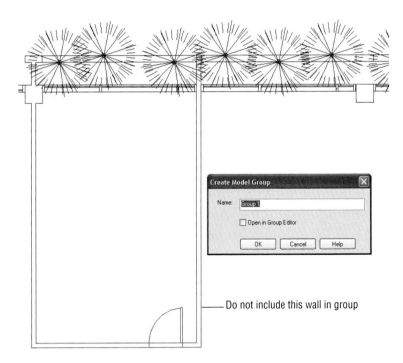

Do not include this wall in group

FIGURE 16.4
(Left) Group Origin default location.
(Right) Origin moved to new location.

The group origin symbol (insertion point) is placed at the middle of group geometry by default—but you can change it to what you feel will be the most appropriate and practical point of insertion when you pick the group to reuse and place again in the project. Move the origin to the intersection of two walls, which will help when placing new instances of the group. To do so, simply place the mouse over the crossing of x and y and drag it to a new position or use the Move tool.

There are many possible ways to proceed in the group placement process, one being to insert more instances of this group along this wing of the building using the Copy Multiple Instances or the Array tool. An alternate approach is to use the Project Browser and drag and drop the group instances into the view (Figure 16.5).

FIGURE 16.5
The group can be placed from the Project Browser.

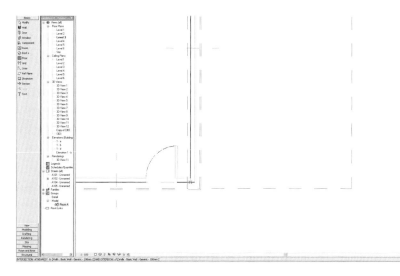

1. For this exercise, let's try the drag and drop from the Project Browser approach and place new instances of the group in the floor plan (you can place groups in 3D views as well, but the common use case is in plan). Once you drag the group from the Project Browser into the view, release the button and take your time zooming in to the insertion point in order to get the correct snap without stressing out your hand.

   After choosing the insertion point, you'll see that the walls belonging to the group clean up with other walls that do not belong to the group. This is perhaps the most profound difference in behavior between groups and links, which we'll get into a bit later, but essentially, linked elements cannot interact with elements in the model they are linked to: walls belonging to a group will clean up with walls from the main model, while walls from a linked model will not.

2. Continue to place groups, until you arrive at a more developed floor plan (Figure 16.6).

FIGURE 16.6
More groups added to the floor plan

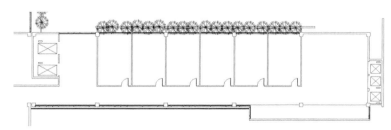

3. With the basic unit established, you can start adding more complexity and really see the power of groups. Because all the groups are instances of the original model group, any changes to this group will affect the others. Select any one of the groups in the floor plan, and take a look at the Options bar.

4. To change a group during the process of design, you will select the Edit Group option. This will take you to the Group Edit mode, where a new floating toolbar will appear.

The screen will turn a washed-out yellow, indicating that you are now in a special Group Edit mode (Figure 16.7).

The Group Editor in 2008 has some significant enhancements when compared to previous versions of Revit; namely, the ability to add/create new elements in a group on the fly. This happens in the Group Edit mode and is facilitated by the introduction of the floating toolbar.

FIGURE 16.7

The Group Edit Mode is indicated with a pale yellow coloring of the drawing area, indicating the special mode. The floating group editing bar offers group specific tools.

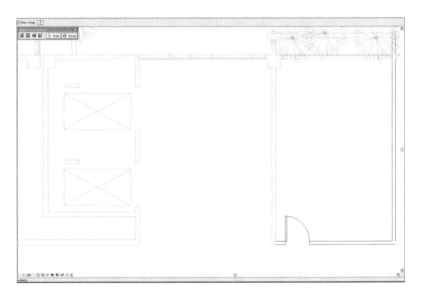

The need to change the design is quite common throughout the lifecycle of a project, where the process is such that ideas evolve over time and are not complete with the first iteration. In previous versions of Revit, working with groups did not support a seamless creation workflow where you could place new elements into the group on-the-fly. Now, however, you can make changes and add new elements to a group while in Group Edit mode seamlessly and at any point of the design process. You can now access the modeling commands while editing the group (in previous versions, all the modeling tools became disabled as soon as you entered Group Edit mode). If you need a new component added to the group, it's just a matter of creating it while in Group Edit mode.

The Group Edit toolbar provides the following features:

Add to Group   This allows you to add any element from the project as the current objects in the group.

Remove from Group   This allows you to remove elements from the group.

Attach Detail   This allows you to add view-specific annotations, which will become attached details and will be displayed as a subcategory of the model group in the Project Browser.

Group Properties   This provides access to the Group Properties dialog, where you can edit the group's name. The level the Group is attached to and its offset from that level are presented but not editable.

While in Group Edit mode, move the door to other side of room. When you click Finish, all the other group instances update with the new door location (Figure 16.8).

FIGURE 16.8
Editing one group propagates changes to all other instances of the group.

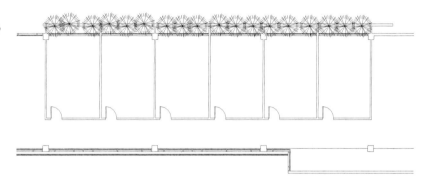

At this stage, you can generate an area report to check the requirements, and the design can continue to evolve. We will now add the bathroom and some furniture. Both of these will expand on the concept of groups by making new groups and nesting them inside of the unit group. We will also add some details (dimensioning) to create an attached detail group. Then, to conclude, we are going to explore alternatives in the room's layout.

Adding Rooms to a Group

The next step involves adding rooms so that you can schedule the room units by areas or by room type.

1. Select the unit group, and then click Edit Group in the Options bar. Once in Group Edit mode, use the Room tool to place the room. It will automatically be added to the group (Figure 16.9).

FIGURE 16.9
While in Group Edit
mode, place a room.

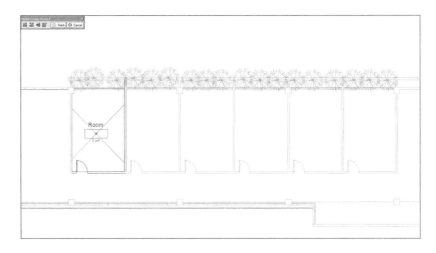

FIGURE 16.9
While in Group Edit
mode, place a room.

2. Click the Finish button on the Group toolbar to finish the change to this group and populate the change into all other instances of this group.

3. To verify that the rooms now exist, tag them as shown in Figure 16.10. Note that when updating a group with a room and room tag, only the room gets propagated but not the tag. You will still need to tag the rooms.

4. To see how many rooms you have, and their areas, create a room schedule that includes name, number, and area (Figure 16.11). This can be useful for making decisions about the composition of a floor plan and seeing if you are meeting program requirements as you make changes to the design.

FIGURE 16.10
Tag the rooms.

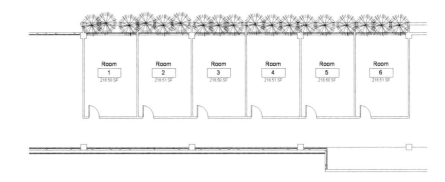

FIGURE 16.11
Room schedule
showing areas

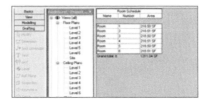

Nesting a Group into Another Group

Often, repetitive units can be a part of other repetitive units. For example, a typical bathroom unit will repeat throughout many typical hotel rooms. To support this in an intelligent way, Revit offers a methodology of nesting a group into a group so that the intelligence of the unit is maintained. The bedroom group we just created can be completed with the addition of a bathroom group and furniture group that can be nested in it. The nested group/s will appear in the Project Browser as a subnode of its host group in the Project Browser.

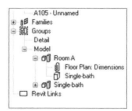

We will follow a natural workflow and start designing the bathroom by adding walls and plumbing fixtures. As these elements will need to repeat in many bedroom units, we will make a bathroom group by selecting the new walls and plumbing fixtures (Figure16.12). You'll notice that walls in groups clean up with walls outside of the group, making the grouped wall interaction with walls outside of the group seamless.

FIGURE 16.12

Build out the bathroom with walls and fixtures; then group them as new group.

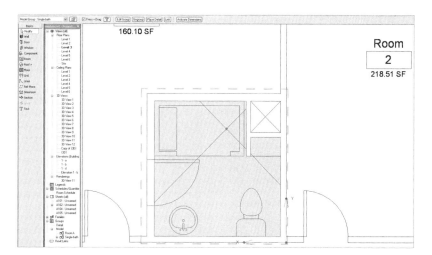

To add the bathroom group that you just created to the bedroom unit group, select the group, click Edit Group, and use the Add To Group button (at the far left of the floating toolbar). By selecting the bathroom group, you have added it as a nested group in the Bedroom unit group. You will notice that a new entry will appear in the Project Browser under the Bedroom Unitnode.

Finish the Group Edit mode by clicking on the Finish button on the floating toolbar and the bathroom will be propagated to all other instances of the Group (Figure 16.13).

FIGURE 16.13
All the instances of the group are updated.

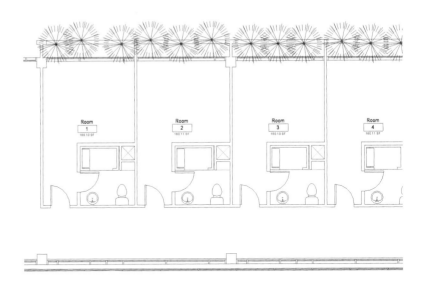

Adding Detail Elements to Groups

Now that the unit is more or less complete, you can start adding some annotations and dimensions to the plan in order to better communicate the design. Begin by dimensioning and adding text or tags in one of the units. To repeat the dimensions in other units, you can again take advantage of group functionality.

With the unit group selected, click Edit Group, and then add your dimensions to the group using the Add To Group button. Because the dimensions are not model elements, you will be prompted to make a new detail group. This will be attached to the unit group as an *attached detail group.*

Once you have a detail group, you can attach it to other instances of the group with relative ease. To do so, select a group and then use the Options bar to attach the detail group. The details will be added to the group (Figure 16.14).

FIGURE 16.14
Details can be attached to group instances.

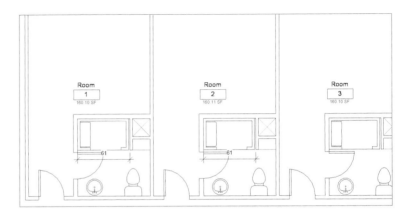

Nesting a Group from a Previous Project

To continue the design of the unit, add furniture to one of the units. You can place the beds, dressers, and chairs and then group them and nest them just as you did with the bathroom. But suppose you already have a similar grouping of furniture from a previous project that you'd like to use in this project. To use a group from another project, open the other project, right-click on the group in the Project Browser, and choose to save the group to file. This will create an RVT file of that group only and that new file can be reused in other projects as a group.

To reuse a saved RVT file as a group, use the option Load From Library ➢ Load File As Group (Figure 16.15). The dialog that appears has some special options that let you choose whether to include attached details and/or levels and grids when loading. With the Attached Details option checked, you will import any details attached to the file, such as dimensions and tags. Levels or Grids can also be imported with the group, if necessary, but don't bring in levels and grids if you don't need them.

Load the file `furniture.rvt` to use it in this project.

The group will appear in the Project Browser and can be dragged into the view like any other group. Drag the group into the view and add it to the unit group. Once you do that, it will propagate to all the other units, as shown in Figure 16.16.

FIGURE 16.15
The Load File as Group option

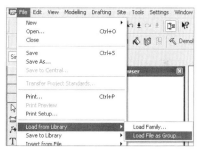

FIGURE 16.16
Furniture group nested into the room group

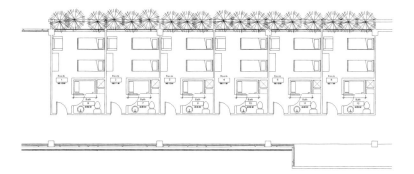

Making Variations to a Group Instance

In just a few steps, you've developed quite a complex structure with extreme flexibility. Not only can Revit manage model and detail groups, it can also work with different levels of nested groups within the main group. For example, if an alternative layout is needed, Revit provides tools that can facilitate a smart workflow. By right-clicking on the group's name in the Project Browser, you'll get a better picture of the possibilities (Figure 16.17).

FIGURE 16.17

The context menu for groups

The options displayed here provide the following functionalities:

Duplicate   Creates a copy of the group with a new name. This will allow you to edit a copy of the group without disturbing the original and affecting all other instances of the group. This is helpful when you need a significant geometric variation in design from the first group. You can then at any point swap groups using the Type Selector.

Copy to Clipboard   Provides an easy way to choose a group and copy it to other levels.

Select All Instances   Selects all instances of the group in the entire model. Use this to quickly make selections for the purpose of deletion or swapping.

Create Instance   An alternative means of placing a group—it's as if you were dragging the group from the Project Browser into a view.

Match   Same as the Match Type tool. Enable the tool by selecting it. By first clicking Room Type A and then clicking a room of type B, you can change room B into a room of Type A. Another way of doing this would be to just select a group in the view and change the type directly using the Type Selector.

Edit   Opens the group for editing in an independent session, not the active project. This allows you to see and edit the group in isolation without the clutter of the project.

Save Group   Allows you to save the group as an RVT file and reuse it later in other projects. This option leads to a dialog where the new file's name is by default the same as the group's name, and you decide whether or not to include the attached detail groups as views.

Reload   Lets you reload a group if you edited the group as a separate file, saved the changes, and then need to reload it to get the most up-to-date version. Reload is not automatic; you'll be prompted to locate the file on disk to do this.

In our example, you can duplicate the unit group, giving it a new name, and then make edits to the newly created group. You can then swap entire groups just as you would any other component in Revit (Figures 16.18 and 16.19). With just a few clicks, you can explore design variations and propagate changes quickly and reliably.

If you create a furniture schedule, you will be able to see easily how the changes to the design affect the quantities (Figure 16.20).

FIGURE 16.18
Groups before
changing types

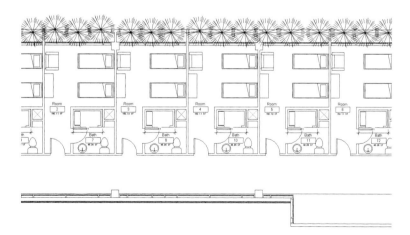

FIGURE 16.19
Groups after
changing type

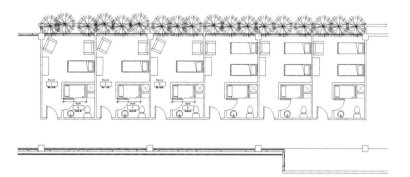

FIGURE 16.20
Schedules update as
groups are swapped in
and out.

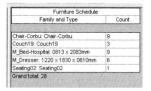

There are some other options you need to be aware of to understand the full potential of Revit groups. Let's consider a practical example. What would happen if we need just one of the "Room A" groups to have, say, eight pieces of furniture instead of nine? The intuitive answer would be to duplicate the group and just take away the chair while in the Group Editor. Although this option would work, it is generating an additional new group and thus additional information for the project to handle, thereby adding more complexity, which always makes the project more prone to user error.

Revit 2008 has a new feature called *Exclude*, which basically takes away selected objects from selected instances of a group without altering the rest of the group instances. The object is not actually deleted (you have the option to restore excluded objects), it is just "deactivated" in that group, and removed from the schedule. This option is more powerful than just overriding the view (by hiding individual elements using the Hide Graphics in View By Element feature) because overriding the view would not update the schedule while this method will remove the deactivated element from the schedule and guarantees accurate documentation.

To access this option, Tab-select an element within a group to see the exclude icon (Figure 16.21).

Clicking the icon will exclude the element, and it will no longer be counted in the schedule (Figure 16.22). You can always add the element back to the group by right-clicking and choosing Restore All Excluded or clicking the icon again. Note that the icon will only show up when you are not in group edit mode.

FIGURE 16.21
The exclude icon appears when you select an element inside of a group.

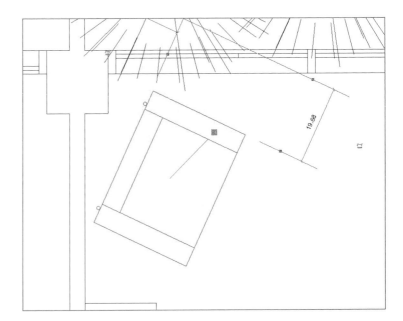

FIGURE 16.22
The schedule updates to reflect that furniture was excluded.

Furniture Schedule	
Family and Type	Count
Chair-Corbu: Chair-Corbu	8
Couch19: Couch19	3
M_Bed-Hospital: 0813 x 2083mm	9
M_Dresser: 1220 x 1830 x 0610mm	6
Seating02: Seating02	1
Grand total: 27	

Repeating Groups to Other Levels

If parts of the whole floor plan need to be repeated in other levels, you can make a group out of many groups, generating a new high-level group in the Project Browser. For example, you can select the six unit groups (also containing nested groups and attached detail groups) and make a new "master" group, which we have called Complete Level Group (Figure 16.23). The result of this action is represented in the Project Browser, seen in Figure 16.24.

FIGURE 16.23
A master group for the entire floor layout

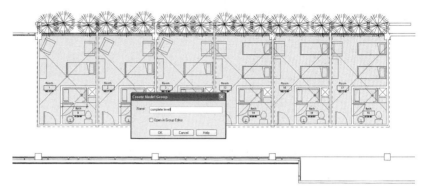

FIGURE 16.24
Complete level group

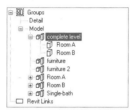

With the entire collection of rooms on the floor now grouped, you can select it and copy it to the Clipboard. Choose Edit ➢ Paste Aligned ➢ Select Levels by Name and choose which levels you want the bedrooms copied into. In a few clicks, you can have several floors filled with bedrooms (Figure 16.25)!

So to recap, we chose to leave the exterior wall outside of the group to treat it as a single element in the project that spans many levels in the project. We proceeded to make a rough definition of the room unit, which was necessary to fill out the building's wing. If we had instead added a portion of the exterior wall to the group, our exterior wall would have consisted of many separate walls, which would violate typical workflows and expectations. By placing just the initial module, we were able to quickly evaluate the needs of circulation and elevator locations, generate area calculations, and evaluate the design.

Then, by nesting groups, we solved the whole bathroom design and propagated it to the other rooms in one interaction, and likewise the furniture layout. If we had wanted alternatives in the room's layout, a new group made from the previous group could have been created, modified, and swapped out. For more granular changes, such as removing a seat from one single instance of a group, we used the Exclude option to avoid making unnecessary new group types.

Making the Group a Part of the Project

The ability to make the group a part of the project is also new to the 2008 release. If there is a slight variation in an instance of a group that requires moving one or more objects, you can select the desired element, and by right-clicking on it, choose Move To Project. This option excludes the object from that specific instance of the group and puts it into the model, where it can be freely edited without editing the group. For AutoCAD users, the closest analogy to this is exploding a block.

FIGURE 16.25
The bedroom group can be copied and pasted into other levels with a few clicks.

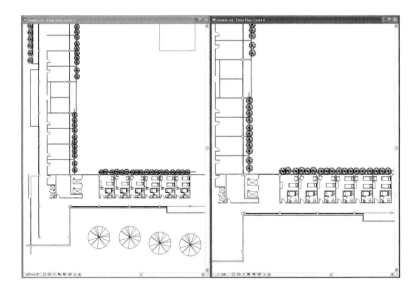

 Real World Scenario

MOVING AN ELEMENT IN A GROUP TO A NEW LOCATION

In the bedroom design, the dresser needed to be repositioned in the last unit in the layout without making a brand-new group for such a slight variation. By tabbing into the dresser and selecting it, the designer was able to move it to the project using the context menu.

This action moved the element out of the group, allowing it to be relocated to a new position:

The left image shows the dresser before being moved to project. The right shows the dresser moved to project and then repositioned.

In terms of workflow, before deciding whether to move or exclude an element, the main question to ask is whether that change will be reused or not. Exclude and Move To Project are solutions for specific problems in an instance of the group, but that's where their whole power resides. Always remember that when you exclude an object, it also disappears from the schedule, whereas Move To Project does not affect scheduling at all since the object is still around.

Editing a Group in a Separate File

When working on a large file, it can be difficult to isolate a group for the sake of editing it. For example, when working in a complex building where you don't want to be burdened with hiding unwanted elements to get a clear view of the group (Figure 16.26), you can use a feature that allows you to edit the group as a separate file. Since this option isolates the group in a single file, you can work from there and then save the file and use the Reload option explained previously. The Edit option that appears when right-clicking a group in the Project Browser will open the group as an independent file outside the project environment, similar to the way you can edit families independently of the project. You can have both the whole project and the single file open at the same time, working with changes that are reflected immediately after saving and reloading.

After editing the group, save it and then go back to the project and reload it from the Project Browser using the right-click context menu. All groups of that type will then be updated.

FIGURE 16.26
Opening a group for editing in a separate RVT file

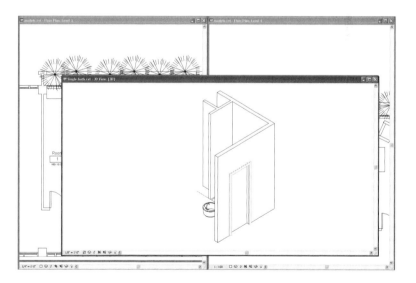

Detail Groups

We have touched on detail groups, but let's look at them a bit closer. We can create annotations to add textual descriptions, add dimensions to measure elements in a group, and then group them in what is called a detail group. The detail group can then be attached to instances of the model group.

With a detail group, once it's created, it can be attached to a model group by using the Options bar when a model group is selected. This is a quick way to apply consistent annotations to many groups.

In Figure 16.27, a room is annotated, and then the annotations are grouped.

By multi-selecting all the unit groups and clicking the Add Detail button, your recently created detail group will be applied to all your groups in one interaction (Figure 16.28).

FIGURE 16.27
Annotations can be made into a group.

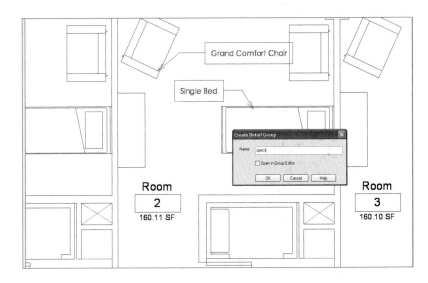

FIGURE 16.28
The annotation group is then attached to a model group.

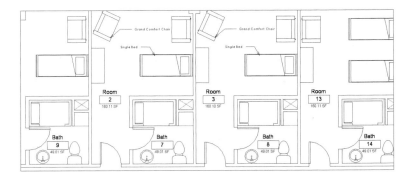

Best Practices for Grouping

Here are some aspects to consider when working with groups:

◆ When using groups on multiple floors (levels), the levels have to have the same floor to floor height for groups to work effectively. Currently, there is no way to make walls in a group taller from one floor to the next, so just be aware of that. Always remember that although you are working in a seemingly 2D floor plan, everything is 3D.

♦ Placing multiple instances of a group affects the file size. The group is not a link but an element repeated inside the project, what is called *instantiated*. Once you load a file as a group, it is part of the project and will add to the file size as often as it is used.

♦ If you need to have reduced file sizes, using links instead of groups might be a solution, although it depends on the applicability of the scenario in which you wish to use them, and most important, you need to be aware of the consequences of using links.

Links

You've seen that Revit groups can be a powerful tool for streamlining the design workflow, but the performance hit you take from increased file size can be significant. Revit provides another tool that allows you to work with repeating elements and avoid the file size problem: links. Be aware that there are limitations that you might not be comfortable with so make sure you understand these before deciding to go with the linking method.

To see how links work, we'll continue with our example project. When you select a group, you will notice that the Link button will appear in the Options bar.

When you select the Link button, a dialog appears with some options you should understand (Figure 16.29). Is the information contained in the link going to a new file, or will it be added to an existing file? In this particular case, we are creating a new file, so Revit will automatically create a new file in the folder of the project (by default) and replaces the group with a link in the exact same place (Figure 16.30). The process does not involve any user action at all apart from selecting the Link option. This might look like the ultimate solution for managing file size, no? Yes, in certain cases this may be true, but let's look closely at the implications.

FIGURE 16.29

Converting groups into links

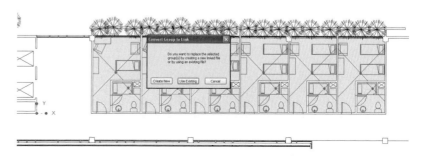

The first thing you will notice once you converted the group into a link is that the walls belonging to the link do not clean up with walls belonging to the active "host" model, because joining between elements in a link and those of the project isn't possible. When we talked about the interactivity of the group with its surrounding context, this was one of the points mentioned as an intelligent behavior specific to the groups. Walls in a linked file will not create clean wall join conditions with the host file, which can make scheduling of rooms particularly difficult, if not impossible.

If wall cleanups or definition of rooms are not a serious issue in your workflow, this could be a good solution to help manage file size. Even so, it is nice to know that as soon as you *bind* the link (convert it back into a group), you'll get wall cleanup and valid rooms again

Note that binding links will work on any instance of a linked Revit file. This brings the link file completely into the project file and severs the link to the external file. For AutoCAD users, the closest analogy is binding of Xrefs.

FIGURE 16.30

A group converted into a link on-the-fly. Note the rooms no longer find boundaries.

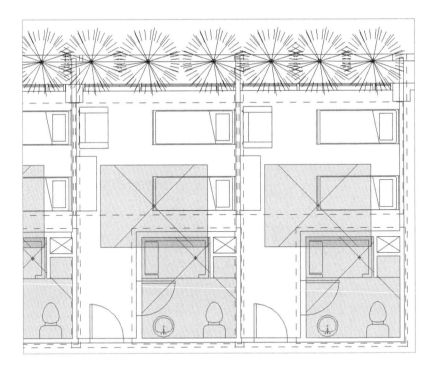

Common Link Use Cases

Links are well suited for workflows where you don't need a tight connection between elements, such as linking entire buildings or site plans into your project file. Links are commonly used when working with the following kinds of projects:

◆ Separate buildings on a shared site plan

◆ A site plan and contextual masses

◆ Large-scale divisions in building mass and program

◆ Other disciplines (Structure and MEP)

In the following examples, you'll see various situations when linking files can be really useful.

MULTIPLE BUILDINGS ON SHARED SITE PLAN

At Koolhaas's station complex in Lille (Figure 16.31), there are buildings designed by other architects directly over the station's roof. Interaction between the models is important in order to know heights and possible restrictions between the buildings. This interaction can easily be created by linking the buildings for coordination, with each model residing in a separate file. What's more, each building could also use nested links or groups. For example, when working on the building over the station, you could link the train station into your model. Within the train station could be links to mechanical system files. All of these elements would be visible in the main host file. This form of nesting keeps file size down and makes working manageable.

FIGURE 16.31

Rem Koolhaas's train station would be a good candidate for links. Photograph by Guillermo Melantoni.

IDENTICAL BUILDINGS ON SHARED SITE

Another use would be a project where a housing unit is duplicated many times on a site. For example, if you have three identical buildings, you would model it once, then link it into a site file, and then make two additional copies. If you then edit the original housing file and update the link, all three instances of the linked file will update in the site file.

COORDINATION WITH OTHER DISCIPLINES

The Linking method is not only applicable to buildings with repeating units but can also be used as methodology for working in a highly coordinated way with other engineers and consultants using Revit Structure or Revit MEP. This workflow is designed as a fully collaborative use of BIM for all the disciplines. Using links, you can integrate structural framing, ductwork, and mechanical systems into your base architectural project for coordination. In a traditional process, this coordination was based on endless revisions, miscommunication, and colliding systems that ended up being resolved on-site during construction at tremendous cost. The Revit BIM platform provides transparent connections between Revit Architecture, Revit Structure, and Revit MEP. In fact, you can open a Revit MEP or Structure file in Revit Architecture because they are all based on the same technology. The only difference will be the available tools; with one of these files you'd be able to select and modify ductwork, but you would not be able to make new ducts.

Linking different disciplines in Revit provides better coordination and even allows for collision detection. This toolset will not be covered now, but you should be aware that it is all possible in Revit using what are called Copy/Monitor and Interference Checking. For further reading on these subjects, consult the Revit help documentation.

Linking Files

To link a RVT file, choose File ➤ Import/Link ➤ Revit. The dialog involves some decisions in terms of how to position the linked model in a project and which worksets to open (Figure 16.32).

FIGURE 16.32
The Revit Add
Link dialog

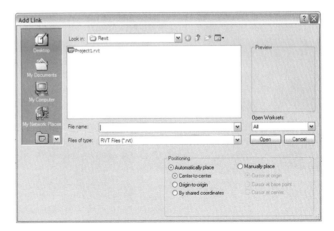

The positioning defines the location of the linked model inside the project and can be manually or automatically done. Automatic positioning of the link provides these options:

Center-to-center This aligns the 3D center points of both models.

Origin-to-origin This places the world origin of the linked file at the model's origin point. If the linked model was created far away from the origin point, linking with this option may put the linked file far away from the main model.

By shared coordinates This places the linked file geometry according to the shared coordinate system created between the two files. If no shared coordinate file has been created, Revit will alert you. These Shared Coordinates settings can be found in the Tools drop-down menu:

Acquire Coordinates This allows taking coordinates of the linked file into the host model. There is no change to the host model's internal coordinates, but it acquires the true north of the linked model and its origin point.

Publish Coordinates This allows publishing the origin and true north settings into the linked model. Revit understands that there may be other things in the linked file and that you may not want this to be a global change to the linked file. An additional dialog box appears, giving the option to name separate locations for each set of coordinates.

Specify Coordinates at a Point This allows you to manually key in x-, y-, and z-coordinates relative to the origin point or define where the 0,0,0 will be.

Report Shared Coordinates This shows the E/W (East/West, x-), N/S (North/South, y-), and Elevation (z-) coordinates of any point in the model.

Special Link Features

As you use links, keep these concepts in mind because they can aid in your workflow and set proper expectations:

Schedule elements in links You can schedule elements in link files without any trouble by choosing the option "Include elements in linked files" located in the Schedule dialog.

☑ Include elements in linked files

Display nested links in the host file   This is another big feature because you can have two different states: Attach and Overlay. As with AutoCAD's XREFs, if a file has a nested link set to Attachment, when you link it into another one, you will see both files. If the nested link is set to Overlay, it will not show up in other files. This setting is located in the File ➢ Manage Links dialog.

Using nested links in the Project Browser   The Project Browser provides the same kind of interaction for links as it does for groups: dragging and dropping will place the link into the view. By right-clicking on the Link, you'll get nearly all the options available in the Manage Links dialog (Reload, Unload, Open, Reload From).

Make areas and area boundaries in linked file visible and schedulable   In Revit Architecture 2008, you can now show areas from linked files, and this includes the ability to create color fill plans that color linked rooms and/or areas.

Dimension to and from elements in a linked file and establish constraints   You can align and dimension to elements in linked files.

Copy and paste elements from the link into the parent file   By Tab-selecting an element embedded in a link file, you can copy it to the Clipboard and paste it into the host file.

Control and change the visibility properties of linked file and nested links as well   You can turn on and off categories of linked files, giving you total flexibility in controlling the display of information.

Bind a Revit link within the parent model   This option creates a group inside the parent file, fully integrated to the project. More on binding later in the chapter.

UNLOAD AND RELOAD LINKS

If you link a Revit file into the model, you cannot open the link without unloading it from the project. In that case, you will unload the link, make the necessary changes, and then reload the link after saving what you've done, or open a second session of Revit (you can run multiple instances of the Revit application at the same time) and open the link there. This way, you have direct feedback on any changes made in the link by just reloading in the session with the parent file.

Controlling the Visibility of Links

The linked model will display levels, grids, and any annotation they have because by default their visibility is defined by the model's visibility. In an elevation, you will see not only the model's levels, but also the linked levels, which may become a problem. To solve this, apply custom visibility settings that override the link in the view. In the Visibility/Graphic Overrides dialog, choose the Revit Links tab, and override visibility by selecting the Custom radio button.

This will allow you to turn off visibility of categories in the link file. To hide levels, choose the Annotations tab and turn them off (Figure 16.33).

You can control the visibility of all categories in a linked file by using this custom setting, giving you practically unlimited flexibility for what you can display.

FIGURE 16.33
You can turn off visibility of categories in a linked file independently of the host file.

Groups, Links, or Both?

So, is it better to use links or groups to handle repetitive content? Or is there a way to capture the advantages of both groups and links without their disadvantages?

The answer depends on the project and definitely on the workflow—the interactivity you need between the elements in the link and the ones in the project. For smaller projects, where file size and performance are not an issue, groups should work fine. If you have a huge project with many instances of repeating elements, linking will reduce file size and make working on the model faster. But if you need control over rooms and cleanups, groups are a better solution.

Had we worked with links for the room units in the previous example, the rooms' file size would not have been a major issue since we are working with instances of a link whose information (and file size) resides outside the project file. If you have a massive repetition of something modular, you might want to consider using links over groups.

If you do go with links but later change your mind, no problem: it is possible to convert the link into a group by *binding the link*, which transforms it into a group and thus adds it to the project. An example would be linking an entire floor plate full of hundreds of rooms.

In our example, we could have linked the furniture since there is not much interaction with anything else in the project. Since models of furniture can increase the file size, this approach could be a smart way of managing size. We can start working with the furniture as simple components in the floor plan and, as soon as we have something, group and afterward link them. As soon as we have the link, we can just copy it around the whole floor plan, resulting in a marginal file size (we don't have 100 beds, but 1 bed repeated in 100 instances). Keep in mind that there is no way of excluding objects from the link without affecting the rest.

If you need to work with the group as a link to reduce file size during the project, you can link it (thus losing room definitions and wall cleanups) and then later bind it back for final construction documentation. Be careful: when you bind the link, a dialog opens with some options to be aware of (see Figure 16.34).

FIGURE 16.34

FIGURE 16.34
When binding links,
you can choose to
include details, levels,
and grids.

If you bind levels and grids, it will create additional uniquely named levels and grids in the project, duplicating information that could result in problems.

All in all, binding links is a very smart workflow that allows working with a sensible file size while restoring the lost relationships within the project as soon as you bind. Depending on the workflow and the size of the project, this seems to be the best of both worlds. You just have to remember that while the file is linked, you lose many key value propositions of using a BIM.

Final Considerations

Having gained an understanding of the basic differences between groups and links, there are still some important things to mention. This is not about using one or the other; it's about taking full advantage of both tools' potential to solve specific problems. It is again the criteria of the user that should dictate your direction—and not getting lost between the picks and clicks.

The new relationship between groups and links is definitely good news and has greatly improved workflows.

Therefore, if you are looking for a tool for working on a massive repetition of elements with few or no inter-interactivity within the project and you want to keep file size down, and still be able to schedule its contents, think about using links. You could even have someone else on the team working on that information and eventually bind it all into the model and take advantage of how groups interact with the model.

If you want to keep elements as links but still need rooms, you could use Room Separator lines as a workaround, and therefore be able to define rooms without binding all the information into the project. This requires some manual work, but it can be a practical solution if you give some intelligence to the separators. Using the Pick Lines tool when drawing Room Separation lines will give you a chance to lock the line to model elements and thus capture design intent and keep elements connected.

So, when you're looking for a tool that maintains consistency throughout the project and enables the management of repetitive content, when file size is not an issue and interactivity with the rest of the model is crucial, groups are the way to go. And remember, you can at any point swap the group into a link and vice versa.

The Bottom Line

Most architectural projects of any size rely extensively on repeating components, with or without variations, and mastering the tools Revit provides for this kind of repetition—groups and links—will greatly simplify your workflow.

Gain understanding of the principles of groups   Groups are a powerful design tool. Anyone working with repetitive elements needs to understand how they work.

Master It   Describe a fundamental benefit of using groups.

Understand workflows where groups can be used   Many projects have repetitive elements and can benefit by using groups efficiently.

Master It   Think of a scenario in your own practice where elements repeat and how you might use Revit groups to solve the problem.

Gain understanding of the principles of links   Links are Revit's second major tool for repetitive elements, avoiding the file size and performance issues associated with groups.

Master It   Using a link paradigm means that the BIM model now depends on links to external files. Even so, the links can be scheduled, dimensioned to, and graphically altered. Despite that, there are still some limitations. What are they?

Understand workflows in which links are best applied   Knowing when to link a file can improve file performance and provides an easy way to operate on large clusters of building data. You can hide links, remove them, and work on them independently.

Master It   Knowing that links can reduce the overall file size, and thus improve performance when working in Revit, imagine a scenario in which you would most certainly want to employ links over groups.

Chapter 17

Moving from Design to Detailed Documentation

In this chapter, you'll learn how to expand the model and create details. Typically, details are created by taking the model data in section or callout and embellishing it with 2D elements. Understanding the 2D component details within Revit will allow you to quickly and easily complete a set of documents for a client or contractor without the burden of having to model every component and detail within the project.

Here's what you'll learn how to do in this chapter:

- ◆ Create drafting views
- ◆ Import CAD details
- ◆ Create 2D detail components

Advancing the Design

In the life cycle of a project, eventually it becomes necessary to add to the model detail that is then used to actually build the building. Historically, the conceptual design, schematic design, and design development project phases progressed through a series of refinements to develop the final set of construction documents. With a BIM process, these discrete phases are being redefined but the workflow remains the same. At the stage prior to adding details, the "big idea" is refined and most plans and building sections are in place. Materiality is added to the design, and the assemblies that make up walls, floors, and ceilings are refined. Creating wall sections, schedules, and enlarged plans helps to describe the project further. Eventually, the systems solidify and details are created that *really* begin to define how many of these things are put together. In this chapter, we are going to explore a few scenarios for detailing the model and creating some of the smaller-scale drawings that go into construction documents. We will look at some of the more common methods:

- ◆ Creating details from scratch
- ◆ Importing details that have already been drawn
- ◆ Creating the detail from the model and embellishing it using 2D detailing tools

Creating Drafting Views

It isn't feasible to model every construction detail in 3D in Revit. A 2D detail is often enough information for the construction in the field. To this end, Revit provides a means of drafting in views strictly used for 2D information that can be placed on sheets like any other view. These views are called *Drafting Views* and are used for drawing or importing details and creating legends, maps, text, or any of a variety of things necessary for a construction document set. When placed on a sheet, drafting views have the same intelligent referencing as all the other views within Revit. Even though drafting views present only 2D information, they are still tied parametrically to sheets so all the references are dynamic and coordinated.

To create a new drafting view, follow these steps:

1. From the View tab in the Design bar, choose the Drafting View tool.

2. In the dialog that appears, enter a name in the Name field (Figure 17.1).

FIGURE 17.1
Making a new
Drafting View

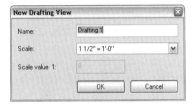

3. Using the Scale drop-down list, choose a scale.

4. Click OK. A new node, Drafting Views, is added to the Project Browser. This new Drafting View is primed for either drafting a new detail or importing existing CAD details. This essentially creates a blank sheet within Revit for you to begin drafting (or importing) 2D details.

Importing and Linking

It is common to have details from manufacturers you'd like to include in your drawing set, or you may have standard details from an office detail library that need to be included in your documents. What if all these files were created in a 2D CAD package? As we discussed earlier, you can easily import these 2D details into Revit to be used and reused across many BIM projects.

To see the types of files you can import into Revit, choose File ➤ Import/Link (Figure 17.2). The resulting submenu contains all the file types you can import into Revit:

Category of File	Typical Extensions
CAD formats	`.dwg`, `.dxf`, `.dgn`, `.sat`, and `.skp`
Images	`.jpg`, `.bmp`, and `.pgn`
Revit	`.rvt`
Link DWF Markup Set	`.dwf`
IFC	`.ifc`

FIGURE 17.2
The Import/Link
dialog

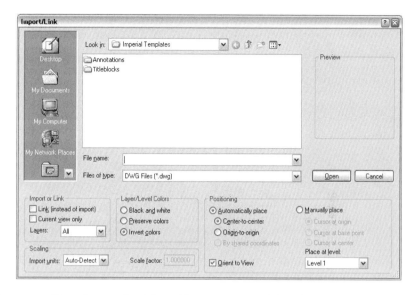

FIGURE 17.2
The Import/Link
dialog

Later in this chapter, we'll see how each of these file types are used, but first we want to make sure you understand the distinction between importing and linking.

Linking vs. Importing

Use linking when you have files on disk that will update throughout the design process. By linking the file into Revit, you ensure that the information will update as the source file changes. Linking creates a *live* connection to a file on disk. This allows you to work on the linked file and then have the Revit model update to reflect the changes in the link. This behavior is similar to an XREF in AutoCAD.

Use importing when you are looking to embed the CAD file within the project file itself. This might be a value if you plan to explode and edit the CAD file, or if it is geometry you want to embed within the project model.

LINKING CAD FORMATS

The ability to link one file into another can be helpful in a collaborative environment. Perhaps someone on your team—a person working on details within your office or an external consultant— is working in a CAD environment while you build up the project in Revit. Linking lets you have their latest work updated in your Revit model. If you import without linking, you get a static file that will not update. When you link, however, it's possible to always get the latest state of the DWG by updating the link within Revit. From File ➤ Manage Links (Figure 17.3), you can reload, unload, import, or remove a CAD link or see what is already loaded.

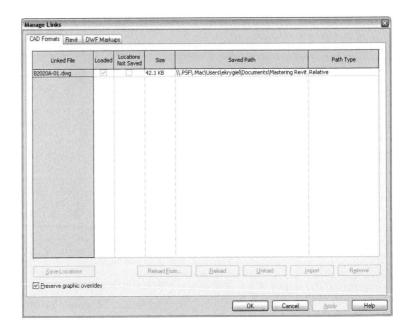

IMPORTING OR LINKING CAD FORMATS

Site plans, consultant files, and details or drawings done with CAD technologies on prior projects are all examples of information you may want to link or import into Revit. This isn't limited to 2D data; you can link 3D files as well. The data you import or link into your model can be view specific (imported in *one* view only as opposed to all views). Start by opening the view into which you want to bring data. Choose File ≻ Import/Link ≻ CAD Formats. The CAD Formats tab in the Manage Links includes additional options. You can link or import five types of CAD files in 2D or 3D in Revit:

Extension	Types of Files
.dwg	Files made from AutoCAD or other applications that can export to this standard format.
.dxf	Drawing Exchange Format files. Most software packages can write to DFX in addition to their native format.
.dgn	Microstation native files
.sat	Standard ACIS text files. Many modeling and fabrication applications can write to this file type.
.skp	SketchUp native files

The "Link (instead of import)" section of the Import / Link dialog gives you the option to import your file or link it. There are some pros and cons to each option:

Linking If you link a file, any changes made in that *original file* will be apparent in the Revit file in which it was linked. If your office or team workflow has personnel who are dedicated to working solely on details in a 2D environment, they can continue creating and changing the details in CAD and you can update the link to reflect the changes automatically. You can also manipulate the linked file through the Manage Links dialog box found under File ➢ Manage Links.

Importing   An import is not tied to an external file, which will allow you to explode the file and modify the CAD drawing directly in Revit. *You cannot explode or modify lines of a linked import.* Once an import has been exploded, the import ceases to exist and everything become lines. These lines are just that: lines, with no inherent intelligence.

Current View Only   Selecting the Current View Only check box brings the linked or imported file into *only* the view that is currently active. It's not always desirable to see your CAD files in all the views in your model. More often than not, you'll want to select this check box because you will likely want to limit the number of views in which your linked files appear. If you import with this option unchecked, the file will be visible in *all* of your views and you'll need to manage the visibility via the Visibility/Graphic Overrides dialog or View Templates.

Layers.   The Layers drop-down menu gives you the option to import or link in all the layers, only the layers that were visible at the time the CAD file was last saved, or a selected group of layers from a secondary dialog. (Layers are a DWG-based naming convention. Revit allows the same functionality with levels from DGN drawings.)

Layer/Level Colors.   The default view background in AutoCAD is usually black, so the colors used in AutoCAD are easily visible on a black background. When you import a DWG file into Revit, which has a white background, many of the colors usually used in AutoCAD (yellow, light green, magenta, cyan) are difficult to read. Revit recognizes this issue, and in the Layer/Level Colors section of the Import/Link dialog you have the option to invert these colors. You also have the option to not change the colors or to convert them to black.

Scaling.   The Scaling section of the Import/Link dialog allows you to let Revit autodetect the scale at which the imported or linked drawing was created and convert accordingly. Or, you can do the detection manually and apply a scale factor.

Importing CAD Details

The ability to communicate design intent with others is critical to any design and documentation process. With that inevitably comes the need to translate or transfer ideas, drawings, and information from one format to another to create a versatile workflow. Revit recognizes this need to share information and allows you to import and export CAD-based drawings to aid in communication.

If you're working with someone who produces details using only CAD, you can incorporate their work into your Revit model without disrupting the workflow. It's strongly recommended that you delete all the superfluous data in the CAD file before importing it into Revit. Here are some general tips to help your workflow:

- If your import contains hatches or annotations that you don't intend to use in Revit, delete them before importing.

- Import only one detail at a time so you can take better advantage of Revit's ability to manage sheet referencing. If you have a series of details organized in a single CAD file that you'd like to import into Revit, isolate each detail, save it as a separate file, and then import.

- Consider annotating in Revit and removing the annotations from CAD. This can help keep consistency in your documents.

◆ Make sure you import the CAD details using the proper line weights, colors, and styles. Check your CAD file before importing into Revit to make sure it is consistent with your office's standards.

◆ Every time you explode a CAD file in Revit, you add objects to the database. An inserted CAD file is one object. An exploded CAD file is many objects—maybe thousands of objects. For the best performance, explode CAD files as seldom as possible.

IMPORTING A CAD DETAIL

It is common to have a library of existing details that can be used for many projects. This example demonstrates the process of getting these details into a Revit project using a DWG file you can download from the book's website (www.sybex.com/go/masteringrevit2008):

1. Create a new drafting view. Under the View tab, choose Drafting View and give it a custom scale of 1:1.

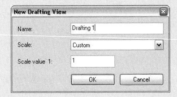

2. Import your CAD detail. In this example, we have a typical door jamb detail that is already noted and dimensioned. Choose File ➢ Import/Link ➢ CAD Formats and select the following options:

   ◆ Link (instead of import)

   ◆ Black and White

   ◆ Automatically Place Center to Center (the default)

3. Choose detail B2020A-01.dwg (located on the book's website), and click OK.

This will import your CAD file into a new Drafting View. Now you can change your view scale to match the scale in which you'd like your detail to be displayed. For our detail, we will change the scale to read 1½" = 1′-0″.

It seems that in our detail the wall tags are now unnecessary. Unfortunately, we did not delete them in CAD as recommended before we linked the file.

So, we have two options. One is to address the issue in CAD. For this exercise we'll assume that's not feasible. Our second option is to manage the layers within Revit. As mentioned earlier, you can do this using the Visibility/Graphic Overrides dialog box. You can also do it through Revit's graphical interface. Highlighting the detail will bring you some tools in the Options bar. We have already discussed the Explode options. Now let's focus on the Query tool.

Selecting this tool will turn the detail from red (highlighted) to black again and allow you to select or pick any of the lines or hatch within the CAD file. Choose the border of the wall tag. This will give you the dialog box shown here, which will tell you the entity along with its layer, block name, and style.

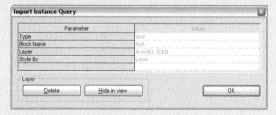

The Import Instance Query dialog will also allow you to delete the entity (which we do not want to do here) or hide the layer. Choosing "Hide in view" will turn that layer off in this view. It can be turned on again with the Visibility/Graphic Overrides dialog box.

Now, the detail is complete and we can drop the drafting view onto our sheet A350 Details. If we need more details from CAD files for our project, we will simply create more drafting views.

The finished detail is shown here. The imported detail on the printed sheet should be indistinguishable from the details created in Revit.

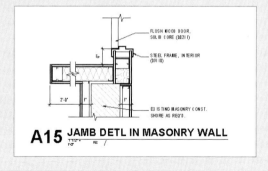

Now that we've discussed how to import details already created in CAD, let's take a closer look at how to make them from within Revit. We'll start by reviewing some of the other tools on the Drafting tab and then using those tools to create and embellish a wall section in our Foundation model.

Detail Groups

Detail groups are similar to blocks in AutoCAD. They're collections of 2D graphics (drafting lines, other detail groups, 2D content) that you'll probably want to use again and again in the same or different views. A classic example is wood studs or blocking. You can easily and quickly set up a group and use that group over and over in the model. Doing so helps control consistency throughout the drawing.

To make a detail group, create the detail elements you'd like to group and then group them using Edit ➤ Group ➤ Create Group, which prompts you for a group name. We suggest that you name the group something clear rather than accepting the default name Revit wants to give it (Group 1, Group 2, and so on).

To place a detail group, use the Detail Group button in the Drafting tab. Then use the Type Selector to choose which group you want to place.

Detail Components

Detail components are parametric 2D families. They're similar to detail groups but are created in the Family Editor and can be designed with dimensional variation built right into the family. In other words, a full range of shapes can be available in a single detail component. Because they are families, they can also be stored in your office library and shared across projects easily.

To add a detail component to your drawing, select the Detail Component button in the Drafting tab.

If you need to load a new component, click the Load button in the Options bar and browse to the Detail Components folder. Revit has a wide range of common detail components in the default library.

To make a new detail component, use the Family Editor and choose File ➤ New Family ➤ Detail Component.rft. From there you begin drawing lines, as you did in the project, and then save the file as an independent family that can be loaded into any project.

Masking Regions

A masking region is designed to hide portions of the model that you don't want to see in the view. Affectionately referred to as "whiteout," a masking region places a 2D shape on top of the model that masks elements behind it.

To add a masking region to your view, click the Masking Region button on the Drafting tab.

This takes you to sketch mode, where you can draw a closed loop of lines over the area you wish to mask. When you draw a masking region, you can assign the boundary lines different linestyles—check the Type Selector to make sure you're using the linestyle you want. One of the linestyles that is particularly useful for the Masking Region tool is the invisible linestyle. It allows you to create a borderless region, which is ideal if you want to truly mask an element in the model. A masking region is shown in Figure 17.4. Masking regions do not mask text, annotations, or leaders.

Creating a Repeating Detail Element

Repeating details are a common occurrence in architectural projects. Masonry walls, metal decking, and roof tiles all comprise a series of repeating elements. Most of these elements aren't modeled as 3D components in Revit but are represented with symbolic detail components.

You create repeating details in Revit by clicking the Repeating Detail button on the Drafting tab.

This tool takes a single Detail Component and arrays it along a straight line at regular intervals. Open the element properties of a repeating detail to get a feel for how it's laid out. Figure 17.5 shows the Type Properties dialog for a repeating brick detail. When you select a repeating detail, the Type Selector is activated so you can select any repeating detail you've already loaded in the project. Repeating details are similar to families: they have types and properties. If you don't have the repeating detail that you want loaded, it's easy enough to create one on-the-fly. All you need is a detail component that you wish to repeat.

FIGURE 17.4
(A) The detail without
a masking region
(B) portion of the
detail covered with
Masking region
(C) Masking region
with invisible line
style outline

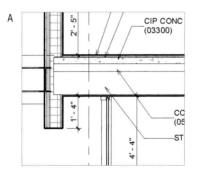

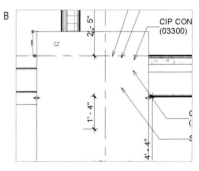

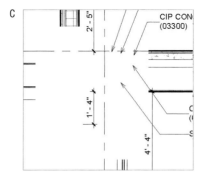

FIGURE 17.5
Repeating detail
type properties

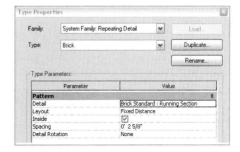

Creating a repeating detail is similar to creating a line—the repeating detail has a start point, an end point, and repeating 2D geometry in between. Take these steps to make a repeating detail:

1. Click the Repeating Detail tool on the Drafting bar.

2. Click the Properties button next to the Type Selector.

3. Click Edit/New.

4. Click Duplicate.

5. Give your new repeating detail a name.

6. Select a detail component to repeat.

The default repeating detail in Revit is a running brick pattern. If you look at it in detail, it consists of a brick detail component and a mortar joint (Figure 17.6).

FIGURE 17.6
Single brick detail
component

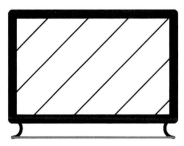

When you create a repeating detail layout, measure the distance between the beginning of the brick and the end of the mortar joint to understand the module on which the detail will repeat. When the detail component is inserted, it acts like a Line tool and allows you to pull a line of brick, as shown in Figure 17.7. This line can be lengthened, shortened, or rotated like any other line.

FIGURE 17.7
A repeating
brick detail

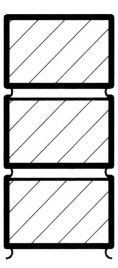

Detail Component Properties

If you're making a repeating detail from a component that isn't loaded in your project, you won't find it listed next to the detail item in the Properties dialog. You first need to load it in your project and then make it a repeating detail component. The Properties window will then look like Figure 17.8.

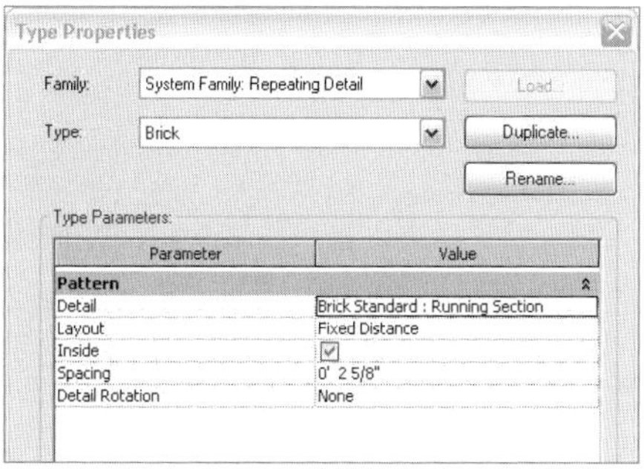

FIGURE 17.8
Repeating detail type
properties

Detail   This allows you to select the detail component to be repeated.

Layout   This offers four different modes:

Fixed Distance   The path drawn between the start and end point when the repeating detail is the length at which your component repeats at a distance of the value set for spacing.

Fixed Number   This mode sets the number of times a component repeats itself in the space between the start and end point (the length of the path).

Fill Available Space   Regardless of the value you choose for Spacing, the detail component is repeated on the path using its actual width as the Spacing value.

Maximum Spacing   The detail component is repeated using the set spacing, and the number of repeated components is set so that only complete components are drawn. Revit creates as many copies of the component as will fit on the path.

Inside   This option adjusts the start point and end point of the detail components that make up the repeating detail.

Spacing   This option is active only when Fixed Distance or Maximum Spacing is selected as the method of repetition. It represents the distance at which you want the repeating detail component to repeat. It doesn't have to be the actual width of the detail component.

Detail Rotation   This allows you to rotate the detail component in the repeating detail.

Creating Custom Line Types Using Repeating Details

You can use the Detail Component tool to create custom line types (lines with letters or numbers for various services such as fireproofing, rated walls, fencing, and so on). Note that when you create a detail component, you can't use text for the letters; you need to draw them using lines. Figure 17.9 shows the creation of a detail component in the Family Editor and the final result used as a repeating detail in the project environment.

FIGURE 17.9
Repeating detail:
(A) in Family Editor;
(B) used in project

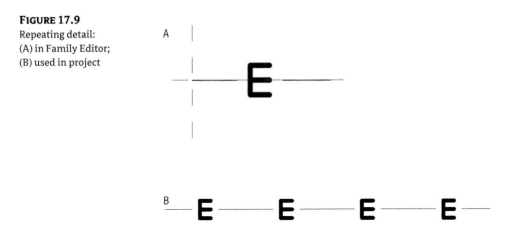

Miscellaneous Line Tools

The Insulation tool, Filled Region tool, and Show/Remove Hidden Lines tool serve important specific purposes in your drawings.

Insulation

Designed as a symbolic representation for batt insulation, the Insulation tool works just like any other line type. When it's selected, two blue grips appear at the ends and let you change the length. The element properties of the insulation include two editable parameters:

Width   This parameter is used to control the width of the insulation that is used. The Width parameter is also available in the Options bar when Insulation is selected (see Figure 17.10).

FIGURE 17.10
Insulation

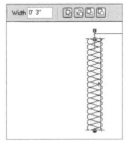

Insulation Bulge to Width Ratio   This parameter is used to control the density of the circles used in the insulation line and can be set in the Options bar when the tool is selected. In most cases, you'll have two lines representing the space in the wall where the insulation needs to fit. Revit allows you to place the insulation using the center line of the insulation as a location line.

Filled Region

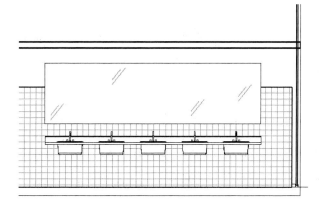

The Filled Region tool is a drafting tool for making 2D hatch and solid fill shapes. It can help you color surfaces or areas for graphic representations during the conceptual or design-development phase, as we discussed earlier in this book. It is also a useful tool for showing materials at finer levels of detail.

A filled region consists of a boundary, which can be created using any linestyle, and a fill pattern that fills the area defined in the boundary. Figure 17.11 shows a filled region with a tile hatch pattern used to show tile in an interior elevation. In lieu of a complex stacked wall condition for bathroom walls, a filled region with a 4″ square model pattern to represent tile on the restroom wall. While this will not be reflected in any material takeoffs, it is a quick way to create interior elevations.

FIGURE 17.11
Filled regions as representation of tile wall finish

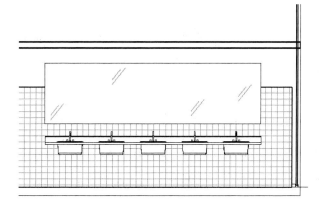

Filled regions can be either transparent or opaque to show or hide what is behind them. Figure 17.12 shows two filled regions: The left one is opaque, and the right one is transparent.

FIGURE 17.12
Transparent and opaque filled regions

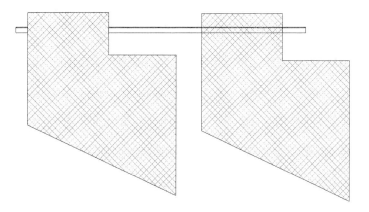

FILLED REGION TYPE PROPERTIES

Filled region type properties define how a fill appears, including pattern, pattern color, and transparency (Figure 17.13). Notice that the boundary lines of the region are not part of the type properties and are defined independently when the sketch is edited.

FIGURE 17.13
Filled region type properties

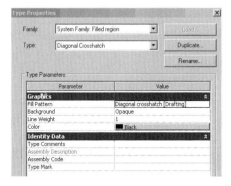

For each filled region that has a different pattern, transparency, or other variation in appearance, you need to make a new type. Remember that type properties propagate to all instances of the type, so making a change to one type may affect many instances in many different views. If you want to make a filled region that uses a new pattern, be sure to duplicate an existing type before you start changing type parameters.

Filled regions can use both drafting and model patterns, making them a very flexible and handy tool for 2D workflows. Just keep in mind that these are truly just 2D shapes with no 3D BIM characteristics.

Show Hidden Lines

In visual communications between architects and engineers, when one element obscures another, the hidden element is usually graphically represented with dashed lines. Often, just a portion of an element is hidden. In the CAD world, it can take a lot of work to explode a block, split lines, and change many of the linestyles to a hidden line type.

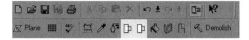

Revit has a special tool, Show Hidden Lines, for recognizing obscured elements and representing the portion that is hidden with dashed lines while still maintaining the complete object.

1. Select the Show Hidden Lines tool in the toolbar.

2. Click the element that obscures the object.

3. Click the element that is obscured. The hidden portion of the element becomes dashed. If an element is obscured with more than one element, keep repeating this operation until you get the desired look.

When you relocate or delete the obscuring element, the hidden element responds intelligently to those changes. Figure 17.14 shows an I-beam hidden by another beam. Figure 17.15 shows the results after using the Show Hidden Lines tool when the second beam is selected as an obscuring element and the I-beam is selected as an obscured element.

FIGURE 17.14
An I-beam hidden by another element

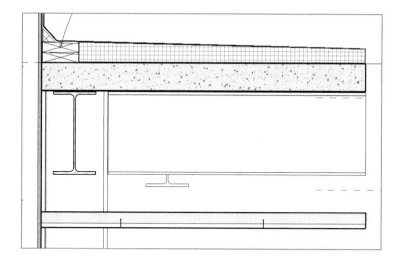

FIGURE 17.15
The I-beam after using the Show Hidden Lines tool

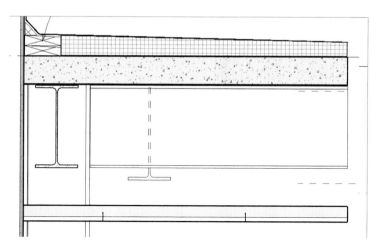

The Show Hidden Lines tool applies to 2D and 3D elements in all possible combinations: detail over detail, detail over model, model over detail, model over model. Right next to the Show Hidden Lines tool is the Remove Hidden Lines tool, which resets the graphical display of the elements so they look as they did before you applied the hidden line behavior.

Linework

While Revit does a lot to help you manage your views and line weights automatically, it does not cover all requirements all the time. This is where the Linework tool comes into play; it allows you to choose any existing linestyle and apply it to individual edges of elements with a few clicks of the mouse.

To use this tool, click the Linework button in the toolbar, choose a linestyle from the Type Selector, and begin picking lines in your elevation or any other view. Once a linestyle is selected, you can continue selecting lines to override, and you can change the length of the new Linework that has been applied over the existing model element using the blue grip controls. Figure 17.16 shows an unaltered elevation of a window and the finished view.

FIGURE 17.16

The outer boundary of the window with Linework applied.

Before...

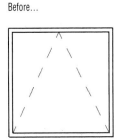

After...

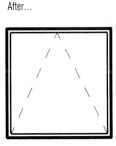

Using Callouts

Callouts are one of the various view types in Revit. They are used extensively in plans and sections to drill down to a more detailed view of various conditions in any type of construction document package. Figure 17.17 shows two callouts in a wall section.

FIGURE 17.17

Callouts in a wall section

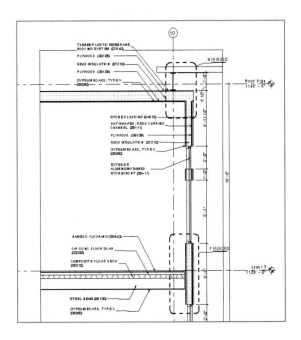

In Revit, there are two types of callouts you can choose when creating new details, one for floor plans and one for details.

Depending on which callout type you use, it will appear in different areas of the Project Browser. Choosing a floor plan callout will add a new view under Floor Plans in the Project Browser called Callout of …*View name*.

Choosing Detail Callout will add a new view under the Detail Views (Detail) heading. The subsequent view will be by default named Detail 0, Detail 1, Detail 2, and so on (Figure 17.18). For the ease of finding and organizing your views, make sure to choose the correct view type when creating a new view.

FIGURE 17.18
The new Detail Views in the Project Browser

Adding Information to Your Details

Now that we have discussed many of the tools used for detailing within Revit, let's step through a detail and see how these tools can be put to practical use. For this exercise, a detailed wall section will be used to illustrate a workflow. In the Foundation file, Detail A14 on Sheet A301 (Figure 17.19) is a wall section at the east entry. Since we have already discussed dimensioning and keynoting (Chapter 15), those items have already been added to the view.

In this view, the only thing that has been added is text notes and dimensions. The rest of the model graphics came for free the moment the section was placed in plan view. To add more detail, start by adding callout detail bubbles at each major construction joint, as shown in Figure 17.20. In this wall section we need four 1″ = 1′-0″ callouts:

◆ The roof/wall condition (Roof Detl, Typ.)

◆ The wall/floor condition capturing window heads and sills (Floor Detl, Typ)

◆ The exterior storefront (Head @ Storefront, typ)

◆ The interior storefront (Storefront Head Detl)

FIGURE 17.19
Wall detail with
callouts

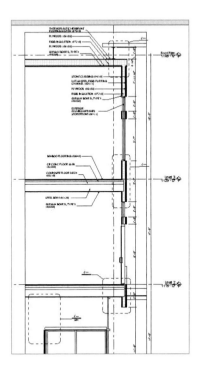

FIGURE 17.20
Detail A14/A301

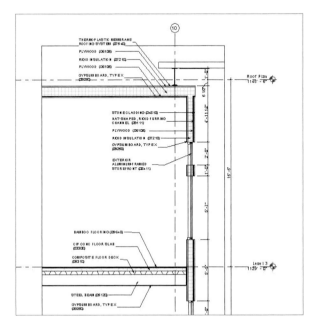

Using the Callout tool in the Detail tab of the Design bar, create callouts in those locations. The first three callouts can be made by choosing the Callout tool and drawing a rectangle around the detail condition. New views are automatically generated and can be renamed as shown in Figure 17.20. For the interior storefront, a different method will be used that takes advantage of an existing CAD drawing by referencing it rather than making a new view of the model.

To do this, follow these steps:

1. Create a new drafting view. Under the View tab in the Design bar, choose Drafting View and give it a custom scale of 1:1.

2. Import your CAD detail. In our example, we have a typical door jamb detail that is already noted and dimensioned. Choose File ➤ Import /Link ➤ CAD Formats. Choose the detail B2020A-02.dwg found in the project directory and select the following options in the dialog:

   ◆ Link (instead of import)

   ◆ Black and White

   ◆ Automatically Place Center to Center (the default)

   Click OK to link the file into the view.

3. Change the view scale to match the scale in which you'd like your detail to be displayed. For this detail, set the scale to 1″ = 1′-0″.

4. Right-click the view in the Project Browser (in the Drafting Views node) and rename it Storefront Head Detl.

5. With the drafting view for our detail created, you can now reference that detail when making new callouts. Choose the Callout tool from the View tab, but do not draw a rectangle in the view yet. First go to the Options bar and check the Reference Other View box. This will activate a drop-down menu from which you can choose the detail named Storefront Head Detl (Figure 17.21).

FIGURE 17.21

Choosing the Store-
front Head Detl from
the drop-down menu

6. Once the reference view is selected, draw the callout at the interior storefront head condition.

7. Keep the views related by dropping them onto sheet A350.

Embellishing the Wall Section: The SIM (Similar) Condition

With the four details identified, we can begin to add embellishment to the wall section. Beginning with the most recent detail we cut, the Storefront Head Detail condition, we need to do a little work in the section to match the CAD detail we plan to use for this condition. Because this is a unique condition we will see in only this one detail, we have decided not to model the assembly but to create it using the Drafting tools. In Figure 17.22, you can see the current condition of the modeled wall section (A) and what we have imported as a similar condition (B) for our CAD detail.

FIGURE 17.22

The callout (A) and its reference 2-D detail (B)

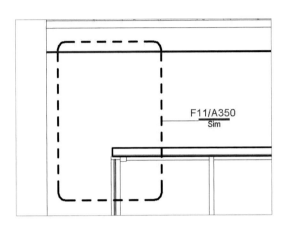

A

F11/A350
Sim

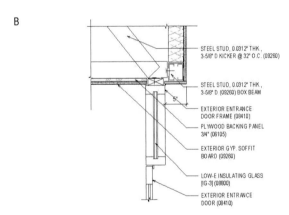

B

STEEL STUD, 0.0312" THK., 3-5/8" D KICKER @ 32" O.C. (09260)

STEEL STUD, 0.0312" THK., 3-5/8" D (09260) BOX BEAM

5"

EXTERIOR ENTRANCE DOOR FRAME (08410)

PLYWOOD BACKING PANEL 3/4" (06105)

EXTERIOR GYP. SOFFIT BOARD (09260)

LOW-E INSULATING GLASS [IG-3] (08800)

EXTERIOR ENTRANCE DOOR (08410)

F11 Storefront Head Detail

1" = 1'-0"   REA14/A301

We need to show the soffit and head condition at a lower level of detail within the wall section to make the detail work. As you can see in the detail and wall section shown in Figure 17.22, the ceiling's condition above the window head does not coincide. The wall section needs to be edited to match the detail by extending the ceiling so that it overhangs 5″ (13cm).

1. In the section view, select the ceiling and choose Edit from the Options bar. Revit will alert you to the fact that the ceiling cannot be edited in the section view and let you switch views (Figure 17.23). Choose Reflected Ceiling Plan: Level 1.

FIGURE 17.23
Choosing a new view to edit the ceiling

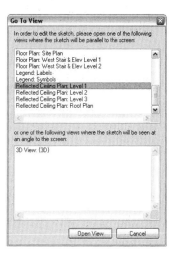

2. The RCP (Reflected Ceiling Plan) view will open, and you'll be placed in sketch mode to modify the ceiling over the entry. According to the detail, we need a 5″ (13cm) projection past the head of the door for our design (Figure 17.24).

3. Finish the sketch and return to the section view to see the effect (Figure 17.25).

FIGURE 17.24
Editing the ceiling in plan view

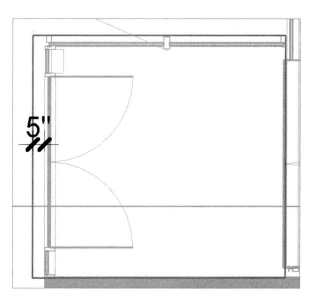

FIGURE 17.25

The edited ceiling in section

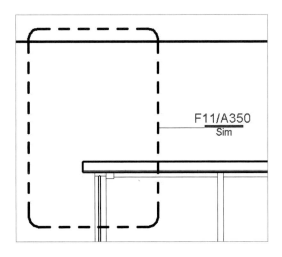

ADDING DETAIL COMPONENTS

Looking at the detail, we need to add some blocking and $3\frac{1}{2}''$ (8cm) studs. This type of element is likely to be used throughout the model, so it makes sense to use a detail component rather than draw them as individual 2D lines. There will be some strictly 2D drafting lines to add later to this wall section for sealant and flashing, but first we add architectural elements like blocking.

To represent the blocking we need above the window head, we'll use a pre-made detail component from the Revit library and load it in the project.

1. Navigate to File ➤ Load from Library ➤ Load Family, browse to Detail Components ➤ Div 06-Wood and Plastic ➤ 06100-Rough Carpentry ➤ 06110-Wood Framing, and choose `Nominal Cut Lumber-Section.rfa`.

2. A list of predefined types will show up at the bottom of the dialog. Since we are not sure which type we want right now, select a few of them by holding down the Ctrl key and selecting 2×4, 2×6, and 2×8 from the menu (Figure 17.26).

FIGURE 17.26

Choosing detail components

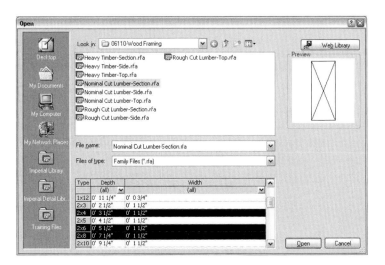

3. This loads the family and the types into the project. Click the Detail Component button and choose the 2×4 from the Type Selector. Insert it in the general location shown in Figure 17.27. We can then rotate it and move it into place.

FIGURE 17.27
The finished detail
component

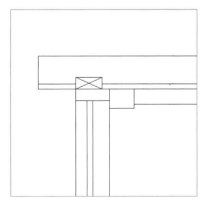

DETAIL COMPONENTS AND PROJECT TEMPLATES

If you find you are inserting the same detail components over and over again, load them into your project templates and make them readily available when you begin any new project.

EDITING A DETAIL COMPONENT

For printing purposes, the line weight for the default 2× detail components is too thick and needs to be adjusted. Because elements are so simple to modify, you will find yourself changing stock components to better meet the needs of your office.

1. For the 2×4 we just inserted, the line weight of the border can be changed by selecting the component and clicking the Edit Family button in the Options bar. You'll get a confirmation dialog before going directly to the Family Editor to change the component. Click Yes.

2. To change the thickness of the border, first hover the cursor over the element to see what it is. You'll see that this component is made of a masking region and some detail lines. Select the masking region (Figure 17.28) and click Edit in the Options bar.

FIGURE 17.28
The masking region

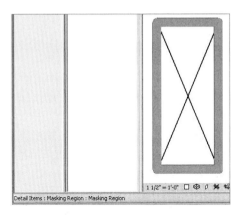

3. This opens the sketch mode of the masking region. Select the boundary lines and use the Type Selector to change them from Heavy lines to Medium lines. These linestyles are actually subcategories of the Detail Items category, which you can access from the Settings ➤ Object Styles dialog (Figure 17.29).

FIGURE 17.29
Viewing the line
object styles

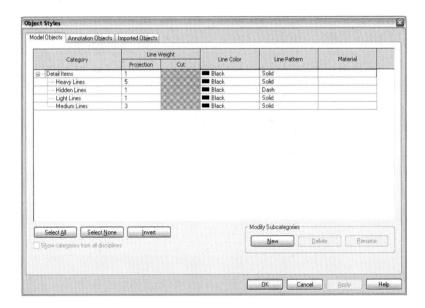

4. Clicking Finish Sketch completes the Masking Region. Clicking Load Into Projects will load the changes back into the model. You will be prompted to override parameters values of existing types. Click Yes, as we have not modified any of the values for this type.

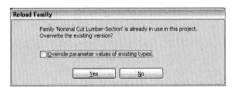

The blocking displays much better, as you can see in Figure 17.30.

FIGURE 17.30
(A) Before changing the detail component line weight. (B) After changing the detail component line weight.

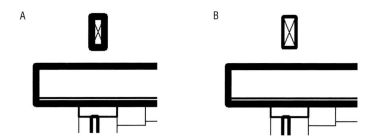

5. Moving the component into place, we use the fact that it was created as a masking region to cover some unwanted gypsum board above the door head.

   Don't forget that you have the ability to see multiple views at once. By closing all views but the detail and the wall section, you can choose Window ➤ Tile View and see both views side by side (Figure 17.31).

FIGURE 17.31
Callout view (left); drafting view (right)

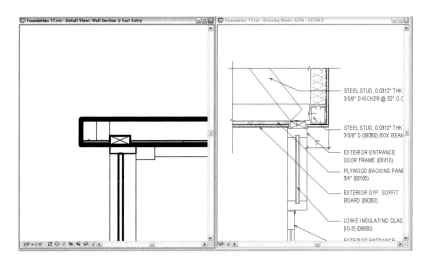

6. The same procedure can be followed to place metal studs in this detail by loading them from Detail Components ➤ Div 09-Finishes ➤ 09100-Metal Support Assemblies ➤ 09110-Non-Load Bearing Wall Framing ➤ Interior Metal Studs-Section.rfa. Place them in a similar location to what is shown in the drafting detail view.

There is one more element to add before we begin drafting lines to finish the detail. There is a ¾″ piece of plywood backing over the entry way in our detail that does not appear in our wall section. We can represent that with a filled region.

1. Select the Filled Region tool from the Drafting tab.

2. Set the boundary lines to thin lines using the Type Selector and draw a box ¾″ tall on top of the gypsum board that will represent our plywood.

3. Choose Region Properties in the Sketch tab in the Design bar, and select Edit/New and then Duplicate. Name it Plywood.

4. Change the background to opaque.

5. Set the fill pattern to Wood_Glu-LamBeam pattern (Figure 17.32).

6. Click OK to complete the new type; then finish the sketch of the filled region.

FIGURE 17.32
Select a plywood-style fill pattern.

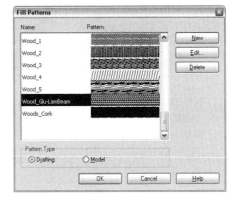

FINISHING THE DETAIL

To complete the detail, use Detail Lines from the Drafting tab. These lines are similar in nature to most drafting applications. Choose the Detail Lines tool, choose the desired line type from the Type Selector, and start drafting. By using some thin, medium, and hidden lines, you'll be able to quickly complete this detail (Figure 17.33).

FIGURE 17.33
The finished ceiling detail

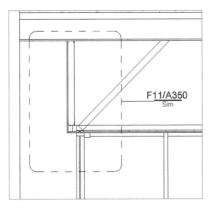

Embellishing the Wall Section: The Model Details

Now that we have explored the use of some of the drafting tools on an atypical detail, let's look at some of the more common detail types when there is no SIM (Similar) condition and only the model

Real World Scenario

REUSING DRAFTING LINES

Design is cyclical in nature. Just because you think that in one phase you won't need more than one detail of a condition doesn't mean it will remain like that throughout the rest of the project. What we have found useful is using the Copy-Paste and filtered selections together.

For instance, if we needed to make another detail similar to the drafting lines we just drew in this exercise, we can make a make a selection box over a large portion of the detail and then use the Filter button in the Options bar to filter out all but the drafting lines and detail components, basically taking the detail with us when we click OK and add a simple Ctrl-C to copy.

data. We will begin this exercise by working on the detail in the same wall section at the floor level of Level 3. This will allow us to work on the head and sill conditions of the windows at the same time. The detail right out of the model looks like Figure 17.34 (again, using the tiled views to see both conditions at same time). Since Revit is parametric, we can actually work in either the detail or wall section as the model changes will occur everywhere. For our purposes, we will be working directly in the detail with the understanding that the wall section will also be updated. The finished detail looks like Figure 17.35.

The first thing we will need to modify for this detail is the floor condition. Since we are using a structurally insulated panel (SIP) for the skin , we cannot have the floor slab bearing on the insulation inside the panel. In reality, the panel will be clipped and hung from the side of the floor system. We need to pull the edge of the floor back to $1\frac{1}{2}''$ from the inside face of the wall. We can do this the same way we fixed the ceiling in the detail earlier.

1. Select the floor and choose Edit from the Options bar.

2. When prompted for a view to edit the floor in, choose Floor Plan: Level 3.

3. Move the slab edge on that wall $1\frac{1}{2}''$ from the inside face of the wall and click Finish Sketch.

FIGURE 17.34
The detail and the related wall section

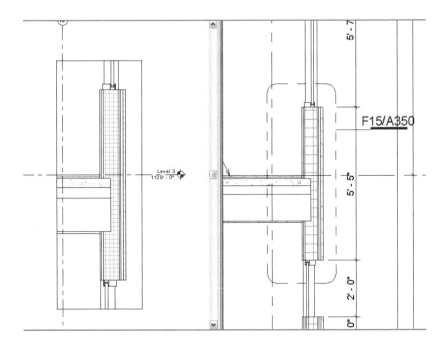

FIGURE 17.35
The finished detail

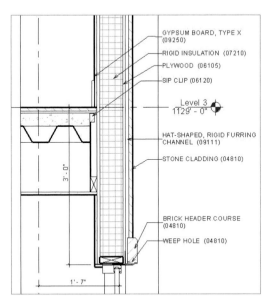

The revised detail should look like Figure 17.36.

FIGURE 17.36
The modified floor

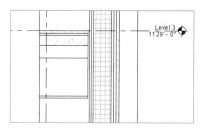

Obviously, we can't run gypsum board back behind the slab and we still don't have a clip to hold up our SIP panel. However, based on all the wall sections and details we have, it doesn't make sense to create this out of detail lines, and there is no default Revit detail component for this condition. So we will make our own detail component to reuse when we encounter this condition.

1. Navigate to File ➤ New ➤ Family ➤ Detail Component.rfa. Here in the Family Editor, we will make a quick and simple detail component.

   Detail components are like any other family in Revit. Once we add them to the drawing, we can always re-edit and update them with new information.

2. Let's start with a masking region to hide the gypsum board on the SIP wall system. Select the Masking Region tool from the Family toolbar.

We want to create a masking region ⅞″ wide × 1′ 8″ long to hide that run of gypsum board. We also want to make three sides (top, bottom, and right) Medium Lines because they will represent cut material and the left line an <Invisible Lines> type to keep it hidden. Invisible lines will show as gray when drawn in sketch mode but will not appear at all and hide other lines (if on top) in model views. Since we have overextended the masking region, we need to cut the top and bottom lines. Notice in Figure 17.37 that the left line of the rectangle appears as gray because it is an Invisible Line.

Masking regions are very precisely shaped elements. The reason this masking region is ⅞″ wide is to cover the ⅝″ gypsum board, taking into account that the line weight of the gypsum adds thickness to the line; this needs to be covered by the masking region.

FIGURE 17.37
Creating the masking region

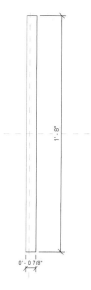

1. Now we need to draw our clip. For the moment, our clip can be represented by a simple filled region box 2″ high and 1″ wide, located 1½″ down from the top of the finished floor on the right side of our masking region. Using Medium Lines, create the box as shown in Figure 17.38.

FIGURE 17.38
Creating the filled region

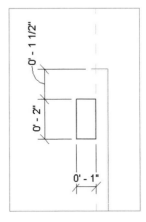

2. Before finishing the sketch, choose Region Properties and select the Aluminum pattern. Click OK and then choose Finish Sketch. The finished component should look like Figure 17.39.

FIGURE 17.39
The component

3. If you choose Load Into Projects right now, it will load with a default name of Family1, which is not highly descriptive and not easy to relocate when you want to use it again. Take a moment and save the detail component to your project directory or library as SIP Clip.rfa. Now load it into your project, as shown in Figure 17.40.

FIGURE 17.40

The component placed in the view

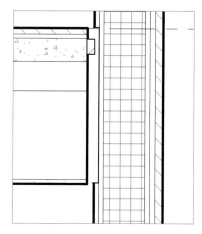

4. Because we have chosen a detail component, we have the added benefit of being able to key-note it, which we will need for our detail. Because this is a 2D, view-specific element, we use the User keynote.

A NOTE ON ANNOTATIONS

New to Revit this version is the Annotation crop region. This is designed to allow you to crop annotations separately from model elements. Be aware that if your annotations extend past the annotation crop region in any way, they will not appear in the view. The annotation crop box needs to be outside the entire keynote or other annotation for it to appear in the view.

Let's finish cleaning up this floor condition with a few more items by adding some base moulding around the floor/wall condition and then bring the ceiling finish of the second floor to meet the wall and the floor finish to meet the wall.

ADDING THE BASE MOULDING

For this detail, it is easiest to make a simple detail component. This will make it reusable and taggable—something you'd not get with mere lines.

1. Choose File ➤ New ➤ Family ➤ Detail Component.rft.

2. Draw a simple 6″ × ½″ rectangle using a masking region and thin lines.

3. This time, add a parameter to the base in case we want to change the height later in the design. Add a dimension to the base from top to bottom (Figure 17.41). Selecting the dimension, choose the Label drop-down from the Options bar and choose <Add Parameter...>

FIGURE 17.41

Adding a dimension to the baseboard

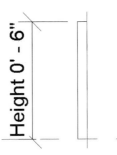

4. In the Parameter Properties dialog box, name it Height and choose Dimensions from the categories (Figure 17.42).

FIGURE 17.42

Creating the filled region

If we choose to change the height of the base later in the project, we don't have to re-edit the family. It is simply a matter of changing the parameter.

1. Save the file to your project director or library as 6in base.rfa and load it into the project.

2. Place it in the model (Figure 17.43).

FIGURE 17.43

Creating a parameter to control the base-board height

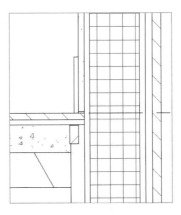

Modifying the Floor and Ceiling Connections and Details

In Revit, there are a number of ways to create any detail. There is not one solution because there is not one way to build something on site. We chose to cut the floor back from the wall and use filled regions to reextend the floor to meet the wall condition. We could have left the floor connected to the wall and simply used masking regions and filled regions to give the appearance of the floor structure being pushed back instead of the floor finish being pulled forward. We chose our particular method because our contractor had requested the use of the Revit model to do some concrete takeoffs, so we needed to make sure the volume of concrete was as accurate as possible. Before choosing a direction for a workflow, it's a good idea to understand all the uses for your model (beyond documentation) and keep those in mind when making these kind of decisions. In the following steps, you'll be walked through the techniques we used.

We cut the floor line back to make room for our clips, but now we need to finish out the subfloor and finish floor to meet the wall. To do this, we are going to create some simple filled regions.

1. Using the Filled Region tool on the Drafting tab, draw a rectangle at the ceiling of the second floor to close the gap for the gypsum board under our blocking (Figure 17.44).

FIGURE 17.44
Using a filled region to graphically clean up a detail

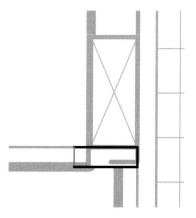

2. When drawing the rectangle, make sure to define the left line as invisible so it appears continuous with the gypsum ceiling. Make the top a thin line; the right medium, and the bottom wide. Make sure to overextend the invisible line a bit to compensate for the line thicknesses.

3. Open the Region Properties dialog, set Type to Gyp, and click OK. Verify that the filled region is opaque so we don't see the model geometry through the filled region.

After you click OK, the filled region looks like Figure 17.45. Somehow, it is not quite right. This is because the filled region and the detail components layer and can rest on top of the others. We need to resolve their order by pushing our gyp filled region to the top.

FIGURE 17.45
The filled region does
not look correct yet

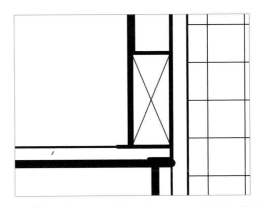

By selecting the filled region, we will be given some layering options in the Options bar. In order from left to right, these are Bring To Front, Send To Back, Bring Forward, Send Backward. Select the first button, Bring To Front, and the gyp hatch will appear correctly on top of the detail component (Figure 17.46).

FIGURE 17.46
The graphically modi-
fied condition

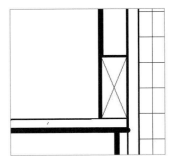

Using this same example, we can build simple filled regions for the floor extension under our base. Our floor condition looks like Figure 17.47.

FIGURE 17.47
Floor detail condition

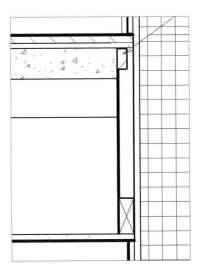

ADDING REPEATING DETAILS

To finish this portion of the detail, we need to add material definition to the floor. The concrete has been poured on top of a corrugated metal deck, but it is not possible to add a corrugated metal material pattern as part of our floor materials, so we will want to make a repeating detail in the form of our 3¾″ corrugated deck. While the structural engineer will show this in detail, we will still want to show the material architecturally in our sections and details. First, we will need to make the profile of the deck.

1. Create a new detail component using the steps described earlier. We want to make a corrugated metal deck 3¾″ tall to mimic the height we have in our model (Figure 17.48). There are a couple of ways to make the decking in the Family Editor. One option is to simply use lines. Another option would be to make it as a masking or filled region. It's a matter of personal preference, and one might be better for your project workflow than another. We only need to draw a section that can be repeated. When you're finished, save the detail component as Mtl Deck to the project folder or library.

FIGURE 17.48
Metal deck detail
component family

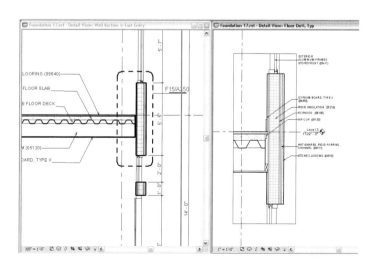

2. Once the detail component is loaded into the project, click the Repeating Detail button on the Drafting tab. We will need to make a new type, so click the Properties button next to the Type Selector, choose Edit/New, and choose Duplicate. Name the new type Metal Deck.

3. In the Detail field, choose Mtl Deck from the drop-down menu.

4. Change the Detail Rotation field to 90 Degrees Clockwise.

5. Start drawing the element as you would a line.

Since this is a 2D element, we will also want to go back to our wall section and add the corrugated deck to all of the appropriate locations. The finished deck in detail and section looks like Figure 17.49.

FIGURE 17.49
The metal deck in
section and detail

NESTING DETAIL COMPONENTS

We have a couple more conditions to address to finish this detail. Our head and sill conditions for the storefront system will probably not be affixed directly to the rigid insulation as the detail current shows. We need to add some blocking and flashing to those locations. Again, since we will want to reuse this condition in other views, we can make it with a detail component. This time, however, we are going to add a more significant level of detail to the detail component before inserting it into the model. We are going to do this by nesting detail components within each other. Let's start with the storefront head condition.

1. Start a new detail component family using the process described earlier.

2. Notice that in the Family Editor, there is a Detail Component button, similar to the one in the project environment. Click it and load a 2×6 from the same path we used earlier (Detail Components ➢ Div 06-Wood and Plastic ➢ 06100-Rough Carpentry ➢ 06110-Wood Framing and choose `Nominal Cut Lumber-Section.rft`).

3. Use the horizontal reference plane to simulate the top of the storefront. We will want to place our blocking ¼″ back from this line, centered on the vertical reference plane.

4. Using a Masking Region, draw a shim under the 2×6.

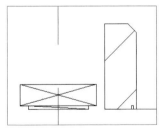

5. Once you click Finish Sketch, because this is a shim, we want to show it with a single diagonal line through it. Using the Lines button, you can add a detail line to make this condition.

To help finish the window on the exterior, we will want a stone header over the window opening. We can also create this with a filled region and make a new region type for Stone. The Stone head is 6″ high by 2¼″ wide and placed 1⅜″ from the edge of our 2×6. (This measurement isn't arbitrary: It is taken directly from our wall condition in the model.) Figure 17.50 shows our current progress.

FIGURE 17.50
Nested detail
component

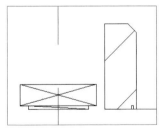

1. We need to add a steel lintel for the stone header. Revit does not provide these as default detail components, so we can create one with a filled region.

2. Save this condition as `SIP Storefront Head.rfa` and load it into the project.

Our detail component inserted into the model looks like Figure 17.51.

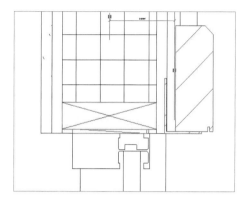

Using simple detail lines and filled regions, we can add any necessary flashing and gypsum returns to the window. Our completed head condition looks like Figure 17.52.

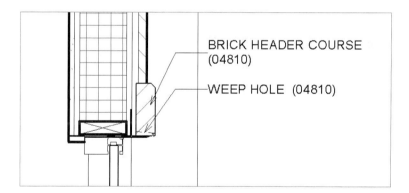

FINISHING THE DETAIL

By combining the simple tools we discussed in the previous sections, we can easily complete this detail. As we have mentioned throughout this chapter, many of the elements we imported or created we only need to make once. All of the families and detail components we built in the course of this detail are now available in the project for use in other views. The finished detail looks like Figure 17.53.

FIGURE 17.53
The completed detail with the nested component

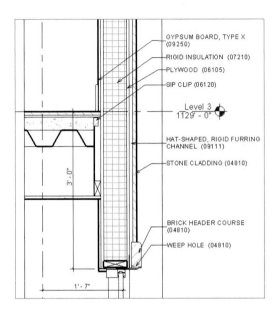

GYPSUM BOARD, TYPE X (09250)

RIGID INSULATION (07210)

PLYWOOD (06105)

SIP CLIP (06120)

Level 3
1129' - 0"

HAT-SHAPED, RIGID FURRING CHANNEL (09111)

STONE CLADDING (04810)

BRICK HEADER COURSE (04810)

WEEP HOLE (04810)

3' - 0"

1' - 7"

We can easily mimic the process went through to complete details for the other conditions.

General Tips for Detailing

When detailing, keep these ideas in mind:

- If your model is detailed to begin with, the detailing will go much faster because you will need to add fewer components. However, you need to strike a balance and not make an overly detailed model because that will negatively impact performance. When wondering what to model or what to make into a detail component, ask yourself the following questions:

    - Will I use this in other views?

    - Will it affect other aspects of the project (like material takeoffs)?

- If you insert user keynotes and in the Options bar have the end point free, you can drag the notes around anywhere on the view and add as many as you'd like. The benefit of this method is that it allows you the consistency of *always* pulling your notes from the keynote text file. And if the note is updated in the text file, it will be updated in the project.

- Remember to import only CAD files that you have cleaned up first. Only bring in what you need to reduce your overhead and keep file performance optimal.

- There is no limit to how much information you can place in a detail component. If you will be seeing similar conditions throughout the model, put in as much as you can.

- You can use detail components at every scale within the model, so it is a great way to draw the information only once.

The Bottom Line

Revit provides a full set of detailing tools to help you create finished construction documents.

Create drafting views   Not every drawing or view in Revit is created with model elements. Some of the views on sheets will be made solely with 2D drafting views. Knowing how to create and use these views is critical to any documentation package.

> **Master It**   Keeping views hyperlinked together is a key benefit to using Revit. How do you draw simple, 2D details in Revit but still keep them parametrically linked to sheets?

Import CAD details   Even if you've been using Revit for years, you will need to import 2D geometry from an old library of standards or manufacturer drawings. Understanding how to do this effectively will keep you from having performance issues with your model.

> **Master It**   Your office has a huge repository of standard details. How do you reuse details drawn in CAD in a Revit project?

Create 2D detail components   Detail components can be used again and again within a model to graphically show in 2D different typical building components. Mastering their use keeps your use of time efficient and your frustration low.

> **Master It**   Detailing is a process of adding more granular layers of information and graphics to the model and view. What tools would you use to add 2D detail?

Chapter 18

Advanced Detailing Techniques

Chapter 17 covered the transition from design to construction documentation. In this chapter, you will continue building your skills and learn some additional techniques for more detailed construction documentation. As your project experience grows, your library and detailing capacity within Revit will grow with it. This chapter is dedicated to tools and functionality that you can employ after you become comfortable with creating details in Revit. By building your library and knowledge of detailing workflows, you can cut down the time you spend detailing, leaving more time for design.

You will acquire the following skills:

◆ Create 3D details

◆ Add detail components to 3D families

◆ Export details for use in other Revit projects

Creating 3D Details

As building designs become more and more complex and the construction industry continues to specialize its assembly methods, it has become imperative that information be communicated effectively between designer and contractor. A technique for showing construction assemblies that goes way back in the history of architectural representation is the use of 3D detail drawings (Figure 18.1) that show a sectional cut through the building in a 3D format (axon or perspective). This type of drawing has been used to convey detail and constructability information rather than create a multitude of abstract sections and elevations. In recent years, this documentation technique has fallen into disuse because it has been difficult or time consuming to re-create such axonometric details in a 2D CAD-based environment.

With Revit's 3D modeling capabilities, it is easy to create such 3D details. By using the 3D views and *orienting to other views*, you can quickly generate 3D views that focus on a construction condition. These can be for constructability or to demonstrate critical building concepts. Figure 18.2 shows a detail of a sustainable solution employed on the Foundation project. In this sectional axon, we are able to demonstrate many of the green building concepts simultaneously while also showing dimensional depths of both sun-shading systems.

Creating this kind of 3D detail in Revit is quick and easy to learn. There are two methods you can use:

◆ Turning on the Section Box tool, and then adjusting the section box to focus on your detail

◆ Orienting a 3D view to an existing view, which in turn enables a section box for the view

FIGURE 18.1
Hand-drawn
perspective detail

THE ALHAMBRA, GRANADA, SPAIN.
Construction of the arcading, Court of the Lions.

FIGURE 18.2
Sectional axon
showing details of
sun-shading solution

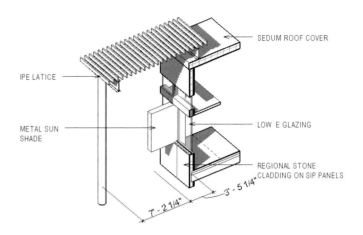

SEDUM ROOF COVER

IPE LATICE

METAL SUN
SHADE

LOW E GLAZING

REGIONAL STONE
CLADDING ON SIP PANELS

3' - 5 1/4"

7' - 2 1/4"

Enabling a Section Box in 3D View

Take the following steps to enable the Section Box tool in a 3D view.

1. Start by creating or opening a 3D axon of the building. If there is not one created, click the Default 3D View button in the toolbar at the top of the screen. Make sure to name your view something unique.

2. Open View Properties and enable the Section Box parameter. A large section box that surrounds the entire model will appear in the view. This is a 3D clipping box that will cut the model from six directions.

3. By clicking and dragging the blue arrows, you reduce the size of the box to be more precise (Figure 18.3). Manipulating a section box can take a bit of trial and error, regardless of your experience with Revit. Later in this chapter, we'll discuss some ways to make this quicker and more accurate.

FIGURE 18.3
Use the blue arrows to
size the section box

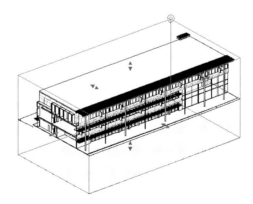

The Second Technique: Orienting to View

An alternative for creating a 3D detail is to orient the 3D view to an existing view. Do this by first creating a detail callout in a wall section (Figure 18.4). By selecting the callout and editing its properties, you can give it a recognizable name, such as Sunshade Detail. Having a recognizable name will be important because the number of details in a project can become quite large.

FIGURE 18.4
Creating a callout
detail in section

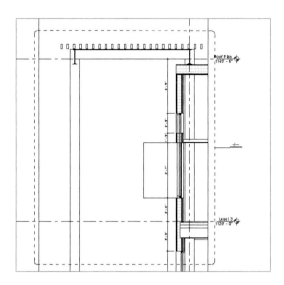

1. Open the default (3D) view and choose View ➢ Orient ➢ To Other View, and select our Sunshade Detail from the list (Figure 18.5).

FIGURE 18.5
Selecting a view from
View ➢ Orient ➢To
Other View

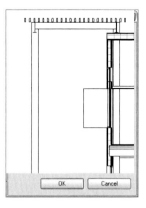

2. Once you click OK, the view will reorient and appear as a section—just like the detail callout. However, this is a 3D view. By orbiting the view (using either the Dynamically Modify View button or combining Shift and the middle mouse button), you'll be able to visualize the sectional detail in 3D (Figure 18.6).

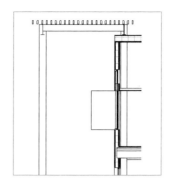

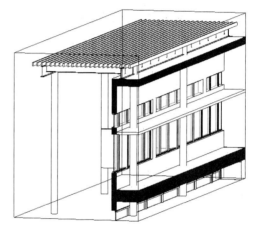

The crop boundaries of the 3D detail correlate to the boundaries of the callout, so there is no need to alter the section box. The depth of the section box in this view will be defined by the depth of the view you have used to orient. You can of course edit the section box using the grip controls. To hide the section box lines but keep it cutting the model, select it and choose Hide element in view from the context menu.

Adding Annotations to the 3D Detail

To add dimensions to a 3D view, first define the work plane the dimensions will appear on, as they can not "float" in free space and need a workplane to be drawn on. (See Chapter 6 for more on work planes.) We are showing our dimensions at Level 3 in the view. Click the Work Plane button on the toolbar and select Level 3 from the drop-down menu. Using the work plane visibility toggle, you'll be able to see what plane the dimensions will be created on, as shown in Figure 18.7. Dimensioning along this plane will be very similar to dimensioning in any plan view. By selecting parallel elements, we can apply the necessary dimensions.

You can then begin to add notes. Note that in a 3D view, you can add text and dimensions but not keynotes or tags. Also, be careful *not to rotate the axon* after you apply your notes. Text is placed perpendicular to the view you have created, and rotating the view will make the text difficult to read.

FIGURE 18.7
Setting and visualizing
the work plane in a
3-D view

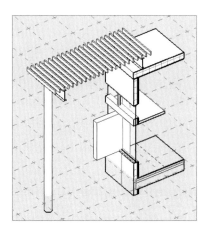

By turning on the shadows in the view, you'll be able to give the view a better sense of depth, as shown in Figure 18.2 earlier.

Be sure the ground plane is enabled in the Sun And Shadows Settings dialog for the view. A good choice is either Sun From Top Right or Sun From Top Left. See Chapter 12 for more detail on presentation techniques.

Embedding Details within Families

In the previous chapter, we investigated how to add levels of detail to a detail component by creating one detail out of a number of separate components, making it easier to replicate a detail condition across various project views. Again, this idea of "drawing it once" is a core theory in Revit. Combining these principles, we can extend this information into family creation, allowing you to turn details on or off within a family depending on a view's Level Of Detail setting.

When we explored the notion of the view detail earlier, we mentioned the ability to show different levels of detail at Coarse, Medium, and Fine settings. Combining this with detail components, we can embed details for typical conditions directly within the families themselves. Figure 18.8 shows the same window family in coarse, medium, and fine views. All of the detail has been added to the family itself, and the detail is activated by switching between View Detail settings. Note that the Fine detail level in this series shows the actual CAD detail from the manufacturer's website and is not modeled in detail in 3D. Modeling this in 3D would be a huge performance killer. Because we have created this as part of the window family, this highly detailed information will be displayed each time we cut a window in section, regardless of where the window is placed in the model.

Building this type of window family is not complicated, but it does require a bit of knowledge about how a family is created and assembled. For our purposes, we are going to assume that the window family has been created correctly and we are simply trying to apply more detail to the window itself so that it displays much more detailed information in fine view. Since we have already created the sill condition, we will now focus on creating the head detail.

Start by locating the family within the project using the Project Browser. Select it and choose Edit Family from the context menu. In the Family Editor, open a section view (or if there is no section view, create a new one). The sectional view of the window family head looks like Figure 18.9.

FIGURE 18.8

The same awning window shown in
(A) coarse,
(B) medium, and
(C) fine view

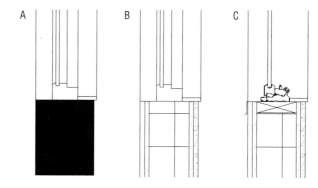

FIGURE 18.9

Sectional view of the window family head

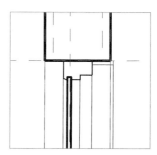

In Chapter 17, we discussed how to insert default Revit detail components. For the blocking above the window head, we can load a detail component from the Revit default library.

1. Navigate to File ➤ Load from Library ➤ Load Family. Then, once the browsing window opens, you will need to follow the path Detail Components ➤ Div 06-Wood and Plastic ➤ 06100-Rough Carpentry ➤ 06110-Wood Framing and choose `Nominal Cut Lumber-Section.rfa`.

2. Insert this component 1¼″ from the exterior face of the wall. This will ensure that it ends up in the right location relative to the wall it will be inserted into. If this window was going to be inserted into a variety of wall types, you could make the 1¼″ dimension a parametric family parameter.

3. Once this is inserted, lock it to the reference plane that is at the window head. This will ensure that as window sizes are changed, the blocking moves as well.

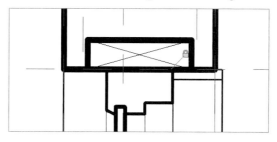

4. If we also know, based on the window type, that the blocking needs to always be set 1¼″ from the front face of the wall, we can add a constraint there as well. Add a dimension to the left edge of the blocking and the left edge of the wall and lock it into place (Figure 18.10).

FIGURE 18.10
Adding a dimension
and locking it
into place

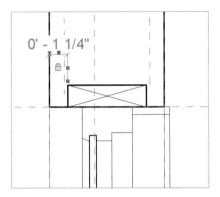

5. We want to create a new detail for the window head showing an added level of detail at the head condition. For this, we've downloaded the manufacturer's standard CAD detail and we want to incorporate it into our window. To begin with, you need to create a new detail component using this CAD detail. Choose File ➤ New ➤ Family and choose Detail Component to open the Family Editor.

6. To import our CAD detail, follow the steps we discussed in the previous chapter. Choosing File ➤ Import/Link ➤ CAD Formats will bring up the dialog to insert the CAD detail. This time, you'll want to choose slightly different options than we did last time. Accept the defaults for all but the following:

   ◆ Select the "Black and white button" in the Layer/Level Colors area.

   ◆ In the Import or Link area, change the Layers setting to Select (we want to pick the layers we will import).

   The dialog will look like Figure 18.11. Click Open.

7. A dialog similar to Figure 18.12 opens, asking you to choose the correct layers to import. Hatch is something we do not need, and typically, manufacturers are fairly good about keeping their layer management for CAD details simple and easy to understand. We want to deselect any layers that reference Hatch. Simply uncheck the box and click OK.

8. With the detail inserted, position it using the reference planes in the detail component. While you can reposition things within the Revit families fairly easily, these reference planes provide invisible lines to snap to when you import the component into the model. Because the top of the head and the face of the glass are key to this detail, use those to place the imported file, as shown in Figure 18.13.

FIGURE 18.11
Importing CAD detail into a detail component

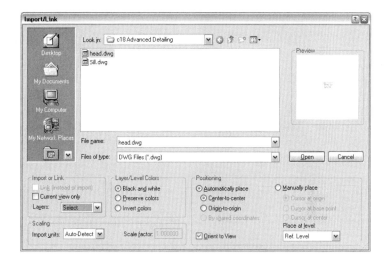

FIGURE 18.12
Selecting layers to import

FIGURE 18.13
Aligning the reference planes

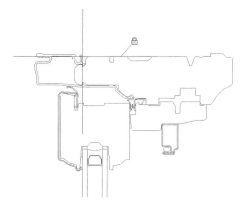

9. We are nearly done with this component. Because this detail has such a simple construction (very few lines) and we have removed the hatch, we are going to explode the detail. Select the detail and click the Full Explode button on the Options bar. This will convert the detail into Revit detail lines and allow you to modify some of the line weights and the detail geometry to better fit the family.

10. With the detail exploded, you can now remove the glazing, which is only partially drawn. We have modeled glazing in the family itself, so including it in the detail as well is a bit redundant. Select the lines shown in Figure 18.14 and delete them.

FIGURE 18.14
Select the lines for the glazing and delete them.

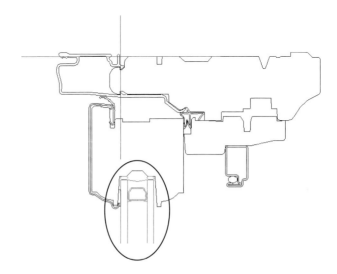

11. The last thing we need to do before we save the model is change the line weights. Select all of the lines in the detail by creating a selection box around them, and while they are selected, choose Detail Items from the Type Selector. We could keep all of the lines the way they had been imported from CAD and simply change them to the appropriate line weight using Settings ➢ Object Styles. However, this is a little cleaner for future tweaks.

12. Save the detail as Head.rfa in your project folder or library and import it into the window family using the Load Into Projects button.

13. Back in the window family, place the detail component over the existing extruded window frame and lock it to the reference plane that defines the head opening (Figure 18.15).

FIGURE 18.15
"Family element visibility settings" dialog

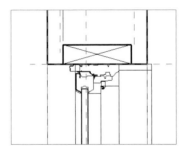

Visibility Settings

With the detail components in place, you can now establish rules for when each of them will be visible when loaded into the model. In the next steps, visibility settings will be applied to some of the model elements and detail components that will link these items to the detail level setting. For this family, we need the detail component to be visible only in fine levels of detail and the 3D solid form window frame sweep to be hidden in fine levels of detail.

1. To start, select the Detail Component. In the Options bar, click the Visibility button. Clicking this button will open the Family Element Visibility Settings dialog shown in Figure 18.16.

FIGURE 18.16
The "Family element visibility settings" window

2. This is as simple as it looks, but it's quite powerful at the same time. By deselecting any of the boxes here, you limit the visibility of components to specific detail levels. For this example, clear the Coarse and Medium check boxes and click OK.

Now you will notice that a funny thing happens—or actually, doesn't happen. If you change the visibility of detail levels, the detail component still looks the same, as if it ignores the visibility settings you just made. You can quickly confirm that you deselected those view levels by checking the visibility settings. Don't worry. You have done nothing wrong. It's just that the Family Editor always shows everything in each view detail level. Only when you load the family in the project environment will you really understand if you have modified the visibility correctly.

So, our goal was to see the highly detailed representation of the window when we switch to fine detail view. At the same time, we don't need to see the original 3D window frame because the linework of the frame will overlap with the linework of the newly inserted 2D detailing components. We need to turn off the visibility of the window frame when a section is displayed in fine view.

1. To do that, select the 3D sweep created to represent the window frame and click the Visibility button in the Options bar. The dialog that appears is the same dialog you saw previously when you selected the 2D detail component, but since this 3D element appears in more views, you now have more visibility options (Figure 18.17).

2. We still want to see the window frame in plan, reflected ceiling plan, and elevation, so leave those boxes checked for now and just uncheck the "When cut in Plan/RCP" and Fine boxes, mirroring the settings for the detail component above.

CONTROLLING VISIBILITY IN PLAN VIEWS

The same rules can be applied to plan views using this technique, so that the sweep does not show up in fine levels of detail. By unchecking the Plan/RCP check box, you turn off the visibility of the window frame in plan view as well.

FIGURE 18.17
Visibility settings for a
3D element

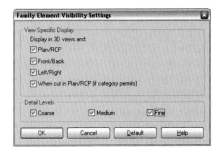

We will now add some trim. Use a masking region to cover the trim piece above the window frame on the exterior side of the glass. Because the masking region has a boundary, you don't need to have the shape previously drawn with lines. Simply create it on-the-fly (Figure 18.18). While visually scanning through the manufacturer's product information, we selected a trim piece, but we don't have any Revit or CAD details for it. So, you have two options: make a new detail family and import it or build it on the spot.

FIGURE 18.18
Draw a masking
region for trim

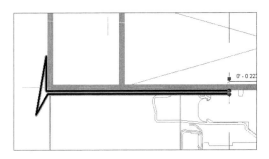

Adding Additional Information Using Symbolic Lines

At this stage of the detailing process, you need to add sealant, flashing, and trim at the window head. For that you can use symbolic lines. Symbolic lines are 2D lines that are visible *only in the view in which they were added*. An example use of symbolic lines would be to represent a door swing in elevation. The dashed lines that represent the hinge points are symbolic lines.

1. Using symbolic lines, add sealant to the detail, as shown in Figure 18.19.

FIGURE 18.19
Adding symbolic lines
for the sealant

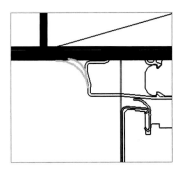

2. Before loading the detail into the project, you need to make sure the visibility of the symbolic lines and the masking region are correct. You cannot change the visibility of those elements simultaneously, so you'll need to select each one independently and set the visibility to show them only in fine detail views.

Save the family with a unique name before loading it. Once it is loaded, you can quickly cycle through the various view detail options and see the power of using visibility settings in the family, as in Figure 18.20.

FIGURE 18.20
Cycling through to different levels of detail of the window.

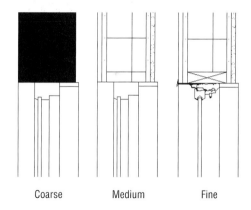

Coarse   Medium   Fine

Imagine that the door has already been modeled and you are adding the lines representing the swing. For that you add the symbolic lines in both plan and elevation to complete the element. When drawing new symbolic lines, use the Type Selector to define the subcategory of the lines.

DOORS AND SYMBOLIC LINES

Doors are typically modeled in a closed position but shown as open in plan view. To get this dual representation, turn off the visibility of the door panel (extruded solid form) in plan view and draw the 90° open door panel and its swing using symbolic lines. Symbolic lines can be controlled using the same visibility settings available for detail components and the solid model elements in the family.

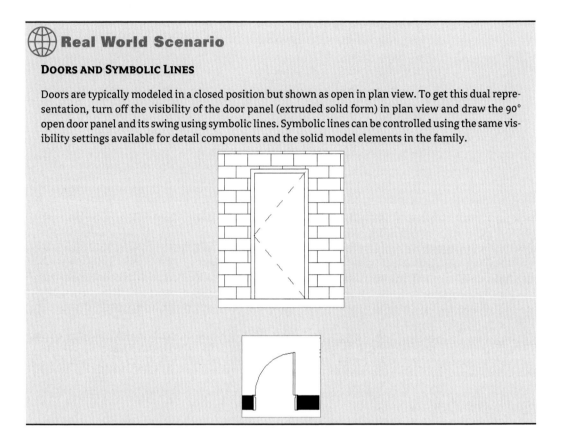

Reusing Details from Other Revit Projects

There are many times in a project workflow when you want to grab details made in other projects and reuse them. So far we have covered how to do this using CAD files from other projects and from manufacturers' websites. This workflow is also possible using details created from other Revit projects. We will also talk about how to take an active project file and export key details to the library. In this section, we will discuss how to pull details out of a Revit file and put it into our active project.

Exporting Details from Revit Projects

As you create more and more details in Revit, you will inevitably want to save some of them to your office's standard library so you can reuse them in other projects and save the work you've invested. Saving a view out of a project creates a separate RVT file that contains only that view. There are a couple of ways to do this with the same outcome. First, if you have a 3D model detail that you've embellished with 2D components and you've invested time making it and would like to save it for future projects, you can save it as a Revit file.

Right-click any view (or schedule) in the Project Browser and choose Save To New File. It might take Revit a minute to compile the view content, but you will be presented with a dialog asking you for a file location to save the view (Figure 18.21). The default file name will be the same as the view name in the project.

FIGURE 18.21
Exporting a view from Revit

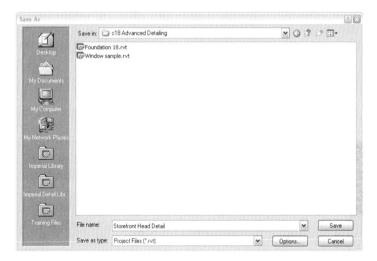

Once the view is exported, it functions like any other RVT file. Opening the view directly will allow you to edit and manipulate any of the elements you exported in the view. You will also see a streamlined version of the Project Browser (Figure 18.22) with only the related views present. These Revit files can be kept in a project library for later use.

FIGURE 18.22
Project Browser only has views appropriate to the ones for the exported view.

The second way to export a view from Revit is to navigate to File ➤ Save to Library ➤ Save Views. This will open a dialog box of all of the exportable views from the project file. Here, you can select any number of views to be simultaneously exported into separate library files (Figure 18.23). This is a great way at the end of a project to export all of the detail views you would like to keep in a project library. Select the desired views by checking the appropriate boxes and click OK.

Importing Views into Revit Projects

To import any of these files into a new project, choose File ➤ Insert from File ➤ Views with the project open. This will allow you to navigate to your library containing your exported details. When you choose the exported detail file, a dialog opens allowing you to select the view (Figure 18.24).

FIGURE 18.23
Multiple views can
be saved as separate
Revit files.

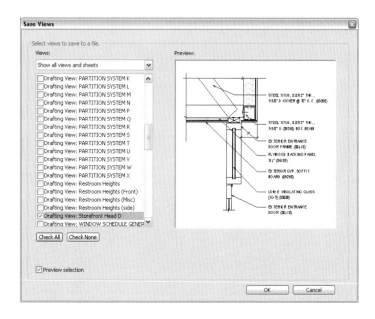

FIGURE 18.24
Selecting a file to
import into the
current project

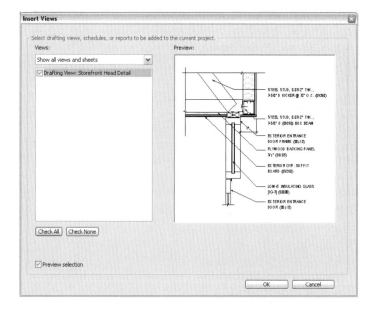

Notice that the view is described by both its location within the Project Browser (Drafting View) and its view name (Storefront Head Detail). Selecting this view and choosing OK will merge the view into your current project. The view will appear in the location called out by the view name. In this case, you can find this view in the Project Browser under Drafting Views.

Another way to insert content into Revit is to use the 2D views from exported files. For example, elements of a detail you have in your library may need to be inserted into a view you are working on to augment that view. You may only want to use a selected portion of the new view in the detail you are working on. To import the 2D content into your view, follow these steps:

1. Open the view you want to import into and navigate to File ➢ Insert from File ➢ 2D Elements. This dialog will look similar to the one for importing the full view but with some slight differences (Figure 18.25).

FIGURE 18.25
Importing 2D content

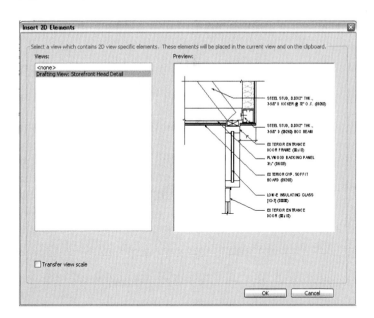

Unlike Insert Views, the Insert 2D Elements dialog allows you to choose only one view at a time to insert. There is also an option to transfer the view scale with the view elements. Checking this box will reconfigure the view you are inserting into to match the view that you have inserted.

2. Select the drafting view and click OK. This will bring all of the 2D elements in the selected view into your active view. You can repeat this command multiple times in the same view window if you need to repeat the content.

Real World Scenario

USING DETAILING TO CREATE A SHAFT OPENING

Within Revit, there are a couple of ways to create an elevator shaft. One commonly used way that we've seen discussed on the community forums is to create a door family that also contains all the elevator information (essentially, a combined door and elevator family in 3D). As a door family, it cuts a hole into a wall and gives proper representation of both the door and the elevator. This will give you your elevator, but then you need to perform a secondary task of editing the floor slab profiles to accommodate the shafts. While this method will work, it can cause a problem with making sure the floor openings stay aligned between the floors. In our practice, we use a different method, which was used in creating the Foundation model. By using the Opening tool on the Modeling tab, we can create a shaft opening.

This tool allows you to create one vertical shaft through multiple floors. This has a few benefits over the other method:

♦ The openings in the floors will always be aligned.

♦ We can extend this shaft through as many or as few floors as desired.

♦ The constraints of the shaft can be locked to reflect the manufacturer's required size.

♦ We can embed symbolic lines to represent the elevator cab.

This last point is very valuable within our office. After creating the shaft, we can add the elevator cab plan directly from the manufacturer's CAD detail as symbolic lines.

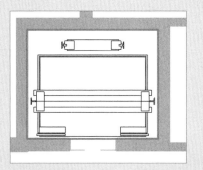
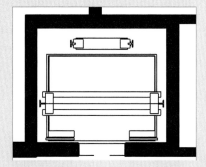

Now, anytime we cut the shaft in plan, it will display the elevator cab using these symbolic lines. If our building is complex in form and we need to move our view range up or down, we will always maintain the elevator cab in the plans.

The Bottom Line

Revit's tools for detailing can go a long way toward helping you make your construction documents read clearly and concisely. Understanding how to detail within Revit is critical to producing any set of documents.

Creating 3D details 3D axonometric details are a great way to demonstrate more complex assemblies and conditions in any document set. Know how to create them in Revit to expand the ways in which you can detail.

> **Master It** Use a 3D axonometric detail to demonstrate constructability in a unique assembly condition.

Add detail components to 3D families Adding detail components to 3D families can save time by embedding the linework of a detail within the family itself and making it instantly available throughout all the locations that family is placed.

> **Master It** Create a detail by embedding it into a family so it can be expressed by simply modifying the view detail level.

Export details for use in other Revit projects There are times when details are common between projects. Knowing how to use details from other Revit projects will cut down on your documentation time.

> **Master It** Use details you created in your other Revit projects.

Chapter 19

Tracking Changes in Your Model

Once a project is under way in the construction document phase, design changes need to be tracked. This is typically done on a per-sheet basis by adding revision clouds around elements that are changing and documenting those changes in the title block. The revision history of each sheet is then tracked in the title block with a number, description, and issue date. In this chapter, we will look at how to add new revisions, how to add clouds to sheets, how to assign a cloud to a revision, and some best practice tips and tricks. We will also look at how to use the Autodesk Design Review application to pass comments and markups back and forth.

In this chapter you'll learn to do the following:

◆ Add revisions that automatically get tracked on sheets

◆ Create revision clouds

◆ Export your designs in a lightweight file format for review

Adding Revisions to Your Project

Revisions allow designers and builders to track changes made to a set of construction documents. Typically, these changes begin getting recorded after a set of documents has been issued and permitted. Since the construction documents typically consist of many, many sheets, this methodology allows everyone on the team to track and identify which changes were made and at what time in the construction process. The purpose is not only correct construction but also creation of "as built" documentation at the end of the construction process.

In a typical workflow, the revisions will look something like Figure 19.1 when they are created in Revit and issued as part of the drawing set.

FIGURE 19.1
A revision cloud and triangle tag

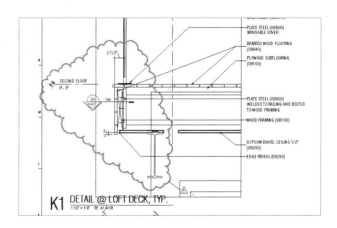

To create a Revision, choose Settings ➤ Revisions. This opens the Revisions dialog (Figure 19.2). From here you can add, delete, merge, issue, and define the behavior of revisions. Let's quickly go through the major elements of this important dialog.

FIGURE 19.2

The Revisions dialog

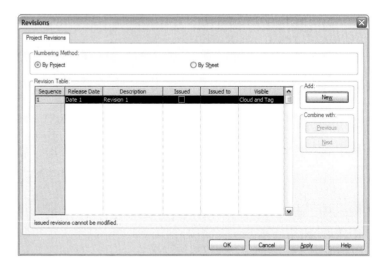

The numbering method You can choose to number revisions *By Sheet* or *By project*, and this is a global setting. Which method you choose mainly depends on how your firm tracks revisions, but most firms tend to use the By Sheet option. By Sheet allows you to have as many revisions as you want, but on each sheet, the revision numbers always start with 1. In the example shown in Figure 19.2, the tags and revision schedule are unique for each sheet, depending on what revisions are on each sheet. The revisions on each sheet are presented sequentially, depending on which revisions are on the sheet. Using By Project will tag your revision clouds based on the global sequence established within the project as a whole. In this example, all revisions with the same issue date within the model would have the same revision number. So you might skip a revision number on any given sheet.

We recommend using the By Sheet setting at the beginning of each project. You can also set this up in your default office templates.

The revision table The Revision Setting dialog starts with one default revision already in place, even though you may have not made a revision yourself. This is just so that you have a place to start—no revision will appear in your title blocks until you add revision clouds to your drawings. Each revision has a fixed number of parameters that you can fill out. As you can see in the dialog, they are fairly self-explanatory and include Release Date, Description, and an Issued check box in addition to an Issued To column and Cloud and Tag visibility options.

Creating new revisions To create a new revision, click the New button. The new revision will automatically be placed in sequential order. Only the sequence number will be automatically updated. You'll need to add your own description and date.

Issuing a revision To issue a revision, click the check box in the Issued column. This will lock the revision clouds placed on sheets or in views associated with that revision from being moved, deleted, or otherwise edited. The parameter values will gray out and become non-editable. This is to guarantee that the clouds and data do not change downstream once you issue a set of drawings. Keep this in mind: while the clouds can become fixed in the project, the model will not be. So, if you need to maintain an archive of all project phases and of each revision, be sure to export the sheets either as DWF or PDF files as a snapshot of the sheets at time of issuance.

Visibility of revision clouds and tags   The visibility of revision clouds and tags related to issued revisions is controlled from this dialog. As issues occur, you may want to hide clouds or tags of previous revisions. This is where the Visible parameter comes in handy. For example, if you've issued a revision and then have additional revisions later, and want to de-clutter your drawing, you can choose to show the issued revision as the tag only (typically a small triangle with the revision number inside it, as in Figure 19.3) or not show anything at all by using the None option (Figure 19.4).

FIGURE 19.3

A revision tag

FIGURE 19.4

Use the Visible parameter to hide clouds and tags of issued revisions on your sheets.

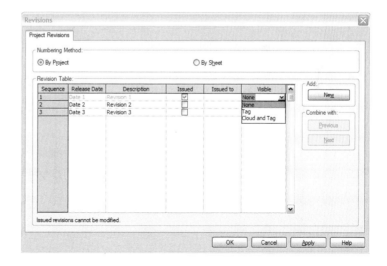

Combining revisions   If you need to combine two revisions into one, use the Combine With Previous or Combine With Next button. All associated revisions on sheets and tags will update automatically.

Placing Revision Clouds

To place a revision, open a view in which changes to the model have occurred and to use the Revision Cloud tool found in the Drafting design tab. Once you activate the tool, you will be dropped directly into sketch mode. Start drawing lines around the area you are calling out as a revision in a clockwise direction. Revit automatically creates a line that makes a "cloud" (or arc) as shown in Figure 19.5. When you're finished creating the cloud, click Finish Sketch in the Design bar.

TRACKING REVISIONS IN THE TITLE BLOCK

The revision is typically a part of the architectural sheet and is located in a prominent position in the title block to alert readers to changes made in the documents. These revisions can be incorporated into your title block design so they are parametrically read from the sheet into a revision table. To see how to add a revision schedule to a custom title block, refer to chapter 4.

Date: 2005. JULY.12		**Project No.** 04106
Proj. Architect: Designer		
Drawn By: Author		**Checked By:**

Revision	Description	Date
1	PR#1 - City Comments Addendum	Sep 02, 2005
2	PR #3	Nov 04, 2005

FIGURE 19.5
Clouds are drawn for you as you sketch.

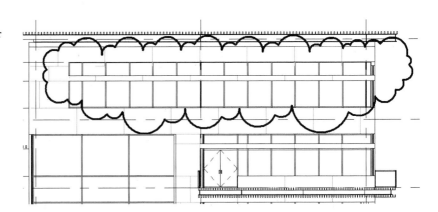

The graphics for revision clouds are controlled in the Object Styles dialog on the Annotation Objects tab, shown in Figure 19.6.

Use this dialog to make revision clouds have thicker line weights, change patterns, or colors. As we mentioned in Chapter 4, this should be set up in your office templates in advance to guarantee consistency between projects.

By default, each new revision cloud will be assigned to the last revision in the Revision Settings dialog. If you need to change what revision a cloud belongs to, select the cloud and navigate to its element properties. From there you can change the Revision parameter, as shown in Figure 19.7.

As soon as you have placed a revision cloud onto a sheet, the revision schedule in your title block will update to include revision number, description, and the date that you assigned in the Revisions dialog box earlier.

Rev. #	Description	Date Issued
1	Windows Changed	6/15/07

FIGURE 19.6

You can change the graphic appearance of revision clouds globally using the Object Styles dialog.

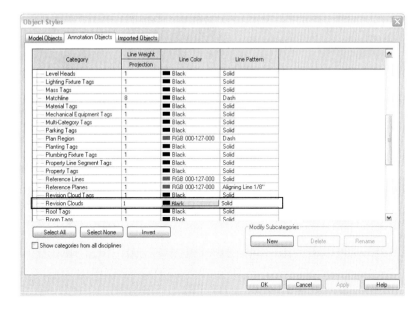

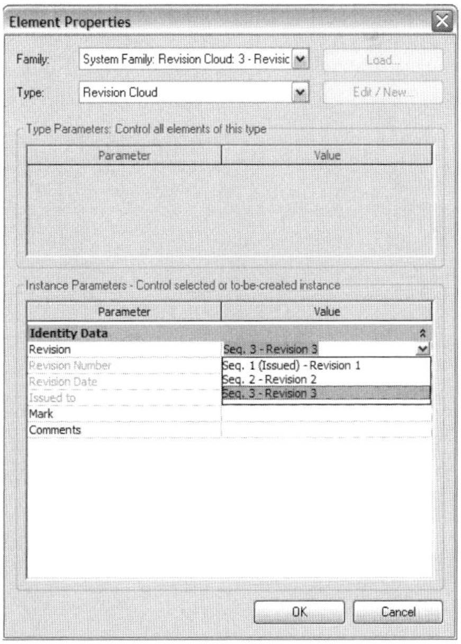

FIGURE 19.7

The revision cloud properties dialog

UPDATES IN CUSTOM TITLE BLOCKS

If you are using the default Revit title blocks, updates will happen automatically. If you are using custom title blocks, be sure you've added a revision schedule to them in the appropriate location so you can take full advantage of using a parametric model. (See Chapter 4 for how to add revision schedules to your title block families.)

Tagging a Revision Cloud

Revision clouds can be tagged like many other elements in Revit. The tags are intelligent and designed to report the revision number that has been assigned to the cloud. Place a revision tag using the Tag ➤ By Category option on the Drafting tab.

If a tag for Revisions is not in your template, you will be warned that no tag exists in your project. To continue, simply load an appropriate tag. The default Revit tag is named Revision Tag.rfa and is located in the default Annotations folder that is created with a standard installation (Figure 19.8).

FIGURE 19.8
Load a revision tag if it's not already part of your template.

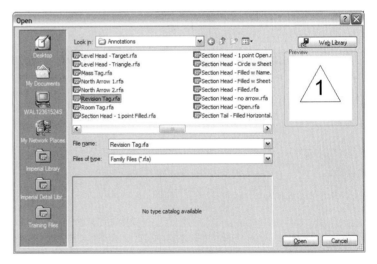

Once you have a tag loaded, you are ready to go. Simply hover the cursor over a revision cloud and click to place the tag. You will see a preview of the tag prior to placing. Once the tag is placed, you can drag it around the cloud to reposition it and it will stay associated with the cloud.

CUSTOMIZING THE TAG

If you want to customize the appearance of the default revision tag, simply select a tag already placed in the project and click the Edit Family button in the Options bar. You could also follow the steps presented in Chapter 4 to make a custom annotation tag from scratch. Editing the tag within the project will take you to the Family Editor where you can tweak its size, font, and appearance.

Once you've made your customizations, save it to your local library, then load it into your project, and swap it with the default tag using the Type Selector.

DISABLING THE LEADER

You can choose to use a leader line between the tag and the cloud or not. In many cases, the tag just needs to be near the cloud and a leader is not necessary. Disable the leader by selecting the tag and unchecking the Leader option in the Options bar (shown in Figure 19.9)

FIGURE 19.9

A revision tag can be made to have no leader by using the Options bar.

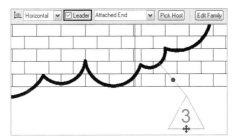

Parametric Modeling and Supplemental Drawings

The process of making supplemental drawings, or SDs, entails making a change to an existing drawing and then issuing that change as a separate package. Sometimes this can be a single $8\frac{1}{2}''\times11''$ sheet where the new detail is then pasted over the old one in the construction set in the job trailer. From a workflow perspective, this can be a little disruptive in Revit for a couple of reasons:

◆ Placing the new detail into an $8\frac{1}{2}''\times11''$ or smaller sheet to issue the individual drawing can lead to other problems. You will need to either remove the view from the sheet it was issued on temporarily (and remember to put it back) or duplicate the view and hope that you do not need to make last-minute additional changes.

◆ An SD, once issued, is like a snapshot in time. It becomes a numbered change made to the drawing set at a given date. Since the model and all the views in the model always reflect the most current state of the project, making separate SD sheets and views will show any additional changes made to that view.

As a best practice, some architects leave all of the revisions directly on the sheets where they were originally issued. The sheets are printed to PDFs and the PDFs (with the revision clouds) are imported into Illustrator where they can be properly scaled and cropped to the view or detail in question and then placed on an $8\frac{1}{2}''\times11''$ template to be issued.

Using Autodesk Design Review

Autodesk Design Review offers a fast, efficient way to view and mark up 2D and 3D designs for review. This workflow is different than what we just covered, and is more geared toward informal design review, rather than management of sheet issues. For example, if you need to have your drawings reviewed by a senior designer for quality checking and design review, this tool can streamline the process. Once a DWF is published from Revit, it can be opened in Design Review, marked up, and then linked back into the Revit file, where changes can be picked up and tracked.

🌐 Real World Scenario

TRACKING CHANGES IN THE FOUNDATION PROJECT

To see the change-tracking process in practice, you can try an example using the Foundation project. Assume that you have already submitted a CD documentation set and, after some review with the client, have decided on some additional changes. Imagine that you need to change some windows from sliders to casements.

Another team member implements this change, and now you need it to be tracked on your sheet as a revision to the original document set.

When you open the sample file, Foundation.rvt, from the Chapter 19 folder on the companion website (www.sybex.com/go/masteringrevit2008), you'll see some markup notes on the sheet indicating the desired changes, along with the revised window design itself.

You first open the Revisions dialog, click New to add a new revision, and give the revision a description: Window Modifications. Click OK and move to the Drafting tab, where you select the Revision Cloud tool, sketch a cloud around the windows, and click Finish Sketch. Then, to place a tag, you select the Tag ➤ By Category option, clear the Leader check box in the Options bar, and tag the revision cloud. Your workspace should look like this.

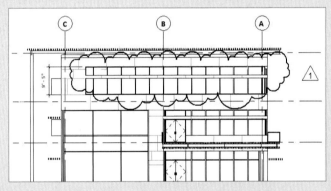

Notice the Revit revision cloud and tag. In the title block, notice that a new entry appears in the revision schedule. Your revision tag, the cloud, and the revision number are parametrically associated.

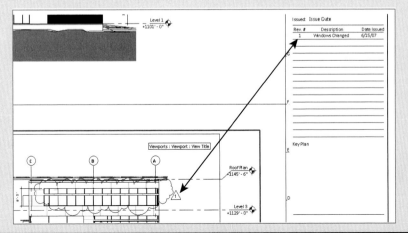

The DWF format allows you to share drawings and models with stakeholders with a lightweight and easy-to-use application. The navigation and ability to hyperlink between views works well with Revit and is easy to learn.

Design Review is a free tool that you can download from the Autodesk website: `www.autodesk.com/designreview`.

Once it's installed, you can open any DWF file produced from other Autodesk products—such as AutoCAD, Inventor, and AutoCAD Architecture—in addition to Revit.

The Design Review User Interface

The interface for Design Review is straightforward, as shown in Figure 19.10. It contains a main view window, toolbar, and a navigator pane.

FIGURE 19.10
The Autodesk Design Review interface

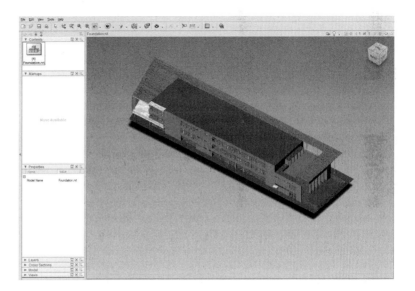

The view window   The main window shows the active view. Using the middle mouse button, you can zoom and pan. If you are looking at a 3D DWF, you'll also see the view navigation cube in the upper-right corner of the view. Use this cube to rotate the model by clicking on it, or you can hold the mouse down and rotate the cube. Before you start rotating the model, make sure the orbit method is set to Turntable in the toolbar.

This will keep your model rotating with the z-axis always pointing up. If you use the Orbit option, your model will tumble around freely in space on all axes.

The toolbar   Located at the top of the application, it contains tools for spinning, zooming, panning, cutting cross sections, moving and rotating elements, and adding markups. Feel free to experiment with all of these features.

The navigator pane Located on the left side of the application, this feature is a lot like the Project Browser in Revit: it contains lists of all the views, components, element properties, markups, and layers. Use this to move between views, check properties of objects, and show/hide elements in the view.

SELECTING ELEMENTS IN DESIGN REVIEW

This operation is very much the same as in Revit for certain types of elements. For example, when you select a wall, level, grid, or section marker, that element will highlight in other views as well—not just where your cursor is. It behaves this way because the DWF originated from Revit, where every element is a unique, model-based element and not a mere set of abstract lines. When an element is selected, check out the context menu. There are many options there that allow you to zoom, hide elements, make them transparent, and even move them (Figure 19.11).

FIGURE 19.11
The Autodesk Design Review context menu

Pubishing to Design Review

The DWF format allows others to examine your design without needing to install or license a copy of Revit. The files are also small, which makes them easy to email, something you cannot do with a large Revit file. There are two ways to share your model using Design Review: as 2D information or as 3D information. If you publish to 3D, you create a single 3D representation of your model. Publishing to 2D can create either a view or a whole collection of interconnected views and sheets all packaged as one file.

ARCHIVING WITH DWFs

A 2D DWF of all the sheets of the drawing set is a great way to keep an archive of your project. This allows you to take a snapshot in time of the state of your drawings in a single, small file that is easy to print and easy to reference back into the model should you ever need to return to a previous state in the design. Again, make sure you export sheets, not views.

3D DWF

From a 3D view, choose File ➤ Publish ➤ 3D DWF. Give your file a unique name and save. Then open the file with Design Review to see the result. When in Design Review, experiment with some of the viewing options in the toolbar (Figure 19.12). The Perspective toggle is a nice feature that lets you toggle the 3D view from isometric to perspective with a single click.

FIGURE 19.12
Options for viewing the model—note the Perspective toggle.

2D DWF

From any view, choose File ➤ Publish ➤ 2D DWF. You will be given options similar to the Print dialog, allowing you to publish the active view/sheet or a selection of views/sheets. At the bottom of this dialog, the Range group is where you choose to publish the current view or a selection of views/sheets. Press the Select button to choose from a list of views and sheets in your project. By default, all your views and sheets will be combined into a single DWF file. If you want a separate file for each view/sheet, check the option "Export each view or sheet as a single file." Let's walk through this:

1. Open the Foundation.rvt model in the Chapter 19 folder.

2. Choose File ➤ Publish to DWF ➤ 2D DWF.

3. Choose to publish selected views/sheets and click the Select button.

4. Uncheck the Views check box to show only Sheets in the list.

5. Click the Check All option. The dialog should look like Figure 19.13.

6. You'll be asked if you want to save this selection set for later use. Choose Yes and name the set "all sheets."

7. Click the Print Set Up button. In the Print Setup dialog (Figure 19.14), for Paper Size, choose <Use Sheet Size>. This will automatically detect the size of sheet being used and publish to that size. The rest of the settings should all be fine.

FIGURE 19.13
You can publish sets
of sheets into a single
DWF file.

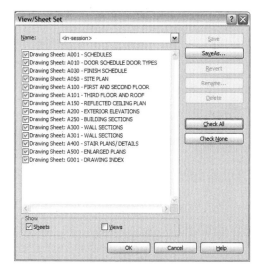

FIGURE 19.14
Set the <Use Sheet
Size> option and Revit
will autodetect the
size of your sheets
when publishing
to DWF.

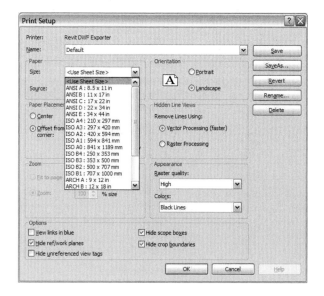

8. Save the file as `foundation_all_sheets.dwf` to a location on your hard drive.

9. This process will take some time because it is publishing all the views on all of these sheets. When the process completes, open the file with Design Review. (If you do not want to wait for the export to complete, you can open the sample DWF file provided on the website.) You'll see all the sheets displayed with previews in the navigation pane in the Contents tab (Figure 19.15).

FIGURE 19.15
Sheets are displayed
in Design Review
as previews in the
navigation pane.

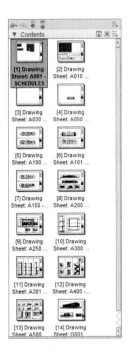

Marking Up the Model Using Design Review

Once you have published a DWF, you can open it in Design Review and add textual markups that can then be shared with your team, or even linked back into Revit. To mark up a view in Design Review, click the down arrow next to the Create Markup button and select from the array of graphic styles (Figure 19.16).

FIGURE 19.16
Design Review has a
variety of markup
graphic styles.

Draw the shape using the tool, then add your text. Figure 19.17 shows a clouded area and associated text note.

FIGURE 19.17
Type in comments and use the grips to position your mark-ups as desired.

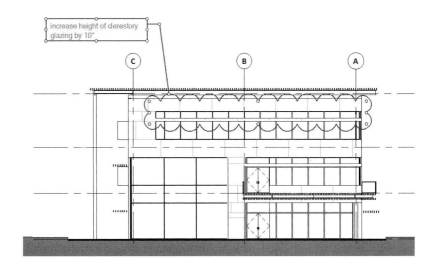

Importing a Design Review Markup

Once you've added markups in Design Review, save the file. You can then link these back into the Revit project. Choose File ➢ Import/Link ➢ Link DWF Markup Set.

When a DWF file is selected, Revit will only link and show the markups, not the entire DWF file. So if there are no markups in the DWF file, nothing will come into Revit. Markups are any textnote, markup, or stamp added in Design Review. Figure 19.18 indicates that three sheets have markups.

Note that Markups can only be linked to Sheet views. If you export a view, and mark it up, it will not show up in Revit. Always work off of sheets when using Design Review for markup transfer.

FIGURE 19.18
For each markup, there is an associated Revit view.

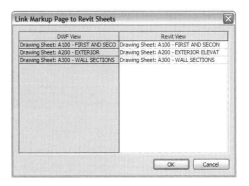

You cannot move or delete linked DWF markups—they appear with a pin when selected. You can do a number of things to graphically indicate that you've dealt with a markup:

Change its graphic appearance   Let's say you have 20 redline markups on your sheet. You need to keep track of which ones you've dealt with. One way to do this is to graphically override each one as you finish. Select the markup, then use the context menu option Override Graphics in View ➤ By Element. Choose a color to indicate "done." Yellow works well because it is reminiscent of a highlight marker.

Hide it   Similir to the graphic override, but in this case you hide the markup all together. Select the markup, and use the context menu option Hide in View ➤ Element.

Remove it   You can remove markups by choosing File ➤ Manage Links. In the Manage Links dialog, select the markup and click the Remove button. This will remove all markups associated with the link.

The Bottom Line

Add revisions to your project that automatically get tracked on sheets   You need the ability to track changes in your design after sheets have been issued. Adding revisions to a drawing is an inevitable part of your workflow.

   Master It   Add revisions to your project that automatically get tracked on your sheet.

Create revision clouds   Making an actual revision to a construction document involves adding graphics and coordinating the clouds with revisions.

   Master It   You need to cloud a design change. How would you do this using Revit?

Export your designs in a lightweight file format for review   You'll often need to allow people who don't have Revit to examine your design.

   Master It   How can you export your designs in a lightweight file format?

Chapter 20

Worksharing

Most projects involve more than one person working at any given time. It's not uncommon for many people to work together to meet deadlines and crank out a set of construction documents. Keeping with the theme of an integrated single-file building model, Revit allows for this workflow without breaking apart the model. A complex model can be edited by many people at once using what is called *worksharing*.

Linked file-sharing methodology is best applied to campus-scale projects where independent buildings are being designed for a large site. All team members work on separate files for each of the buildings, and the files are linked into a master site plan to produce a final project.

In this chapter, we'll focus on enabling the worksharing feature of Revit.

In this chapter, you'll learn to do the following:

◆ Set up a project with worksets

◆ Move elements between worksets

◆ Create a central file and local files

◆ Save to and load from the central file

◆ Request permission to use elements owned by other team members and grant others permission to use your elements

Worksharing Using the Workset Methodology

We first need to discuss some core concepts about worksharing before we can discuss how to implement it. *Worksharing* in Revit refers to the use of worksets to divide up the model for the purpose of sharing data between many people. A *workset* is a collection of building elements and components (floors, roofs, walls, windows, and so on) that can be edited by only one team member at a time. By default, worksharing is not enabled when you start a project in Revit because the software assumes you are working in a single user environment until you tell it otherwise.

WORKSHARING WARNING

Once you enable worksharing in a model, you can't undo it. We suggest that you make a copy of your file before you enable worksharing so you keep an unshared version as a backup.

You share your work by first creating a *central file*. This is the repository where all the individual work on the project is collected.

Once the central file has been established, each team member makes a local copy of it. All work is done directly in this copied—but still associated—local file. This enables all users to open their local file simultaneously (see Figure 20.1).

FIGURE 20.1

The worksharing concept

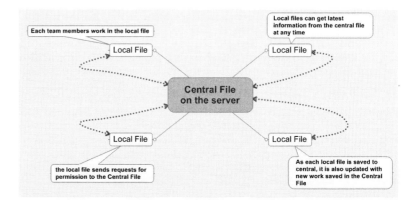

The elements in each separate file are still tied to an ownership rule linked to the central file, making it impossible to edit an element in your local file if that same element is owned by someone else in another local file. Remember, Revit is a database. In effect, you're getting permissions for one or more elements from the central database. Once you have permission for an element and modify it, no one else can make changes to that element until it is reconciled with the central file. This occurs when you use the Save To Central command (hereafter referred to as STC) and copy your work back to the network. If one user has ownership of an element, no other user can edit that element until its permissions, and any changes to it, are reconciled with the central file.

Worksets allow you to group many elements into virtual collections of objects for the purpose of managing visibility and file performance. To that end, there are a number of benefits to enabling worksets beyond allowing multiple team members to work within the same file:

◆ Turning off and on the visibility of elements that aren't being worked on or are not needed for the current tasks

◆ Unloading data heavy portions of the model to speed performance

◆ Quickly getting permission of groups of elements

When you enable worksharing, a new tab appears in the Visibility/Graphic Overrides dialog for the worksets (see Figure 20.2). You can turn on or off any workset in any view though this tab. Additionally, you can make those settings part of any of your view templates.

FIGURE 20.2

Workset visibility

Worksharing Basics

Revit's worksharing features are designed to accommodate any division of labor you see fit. There are no inherent restrictions in how you use worksharing to divide up a model. For example, you can break up a model and have one group work on the shell and one work on the interior core. You can turn worksharing on at any stage of the project, and you can create or remove worksets during the project cycle.

By default, the Worksets toolbar isn't activated in Revit. To turn on the toolbar, right-click in a blank area of the toolbars at the top of the screen and select Worksets from the flyout menu.

You can then start worksharing in *either* of two ways:

♦ Choose File ➢ Worksets from the main menu.

♦ Click the Worksets button on the Worksets toolbar. It will be the only active button on the Worksets toolbar.

Either of these actions opens a dialog box telling you that you're about to enable worksharing and that once it's enabled it can't be undone (Figure 20.3). Revit will create two worksets: Shared Levels And Grids contains the levels and gridlines from the project, and everything else in the model is placed in Workset1.

FIGURE 20.3
Activating worksets within a project

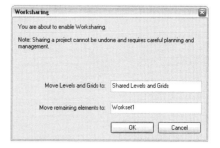

In addition to the two worksets created automatically when you initialize worksharing, there are three other types of worksets that Revit maintains in a project: view worksets, family worksets, and project standards worksets.

Views worksets   Each view in a project has a dedicated view workset. It contains the view properties and any view-specific elements (text, dimensions, tags, and so on). View-specific elements cannot be moved to another workset. You can take ownership of any view in Revit by simply right-clicking it in the Project Browser and choosing Make Workset Editable (see Figure 20.4). This will give you ownership of the view workset and all of the view-specific annotations, allowing you to easily and quickly make modifications to any of the 2D content within the view. This is a handy feature during the construction document phase when much of the work is segregated to view worksets for dimensioning and annotations.

FIGURE 20.4

Making a view
workset editable

Family worksets For each family loaded in the project, a workset is automatically created. When editing properties of a family, you will take ownership of that family unless someone else already "owns" it. You can add families to each of the views without having ownership over view worksets, but you cannot make changes to the families or their properties without having permission.

Project standards worksets This workset is dedicated to all the project settings like materials, line styles, tags, dimensions, and so on. Any time you need to edit a project-wide setting, you will be taking ownership of a workset for that setting. Something to keep in mind: you can always add new information, materials, or linestyles to a project without having to own the workset. You only need to take ownership of a workset to edit existing settings.

Once you've activated the worksets, you'll see the dialog box shown in Figure 20.5. Also note at the bottom of this dialog box that you have the option to check boxes and turn on visibility for the automatically created worksets we discussed earlier. By default, they are not activated.

FIGURE 20.5

Worksets dialog box

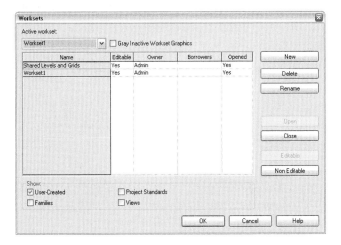

In the Worksets dialog box, you can add and remove worksets from the project. A new workset within a project does not automatically contain any model elements or components; it is simply a blank container that you can then begin to fill.

When you activate a workset, you become the owner of that workset and all the elements in it. This ownership is what the Yes value in the Editable column refers to; if you are the owner of a workset, the value in the Editable column will be Yes, but if you are not the owner, the value will be No).

WHO CONTROLS WORKSETS?

Worksets are usually activated by the team's project manager, who initially enables worksharing, creates user worksets, and assigns people and tasks for the project.

Workset Organization

It's important that you think of your project as a holistic building when dividing it into worksets. Technically speaking, you don't need any more than the initial default worksets because Revit manages ownership of elements on a per-element basis and relinquishes elements automatically when you save your changes to the central file. However, you might want to divide up the file into worksets for some of the reasons we described earlier. Some good examples of typical worksets are Shell and Core, Exterior Skin, and First Floor Interior Partitions.

THINKING WORKSETS

One of the biggest challenges facing teams new to Revit is losing the legacy of "layers." Many teams that have been drafting in 2D CAD immediately want to begin managing worksets as they would manage a CAD drawing. They make a workset for doors and one for walls and one for windows. Remember that all of your objects are in one file and you can control visibility of those objects through the Visibility/ Graphics dialog. Not only is there no need to put your doors into a separate workset, but doing so will actually make your model more difficult to manage. What happens when you have ownership of the doors, your teammate has ownership of the walls, and you want to move or add a door? You can't do so because you don't own the entire assembly. You have to own the door *and* the wall it goes into to make those changes.

Divide your project into worksets that relate to the roles and responsibilities of people working on the project. By default, you don't need more than two to three worksets per person on the job. When making new worksets, remember the old adage of Mies van der Rohe, "Less is more."

For our Foundations project, we have divided the model into four worksets (see Figure 20.6):

Interiors All of the interior walls, furniture, and other items are managed with this workset.

Shared Levels and Grids The workset *Shared Levels and Grids* contains the level and grid information from the model, as was originally established when worksharing was enabled.

Shell and Core All the exterior skin of the building as well as the elevator, stair, and toilet cores that are grouped in any typical office building are in this workset.

Site The topography (toposurface) and any site-specific elements in the project are put into this workset.

FIGURE 20.6
Workset organization

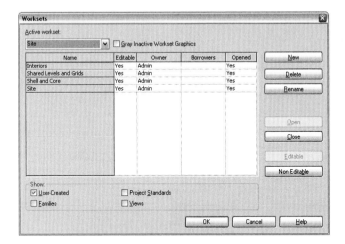

KEEPING IT SIMPLE

For our project, creating the Site workset meant renaming Workset1. Because the Shell and Core workset will have the most elements on it, renaming allowed us to forgo the additional work of moving all those objects to a blank workset.

Notice that Workset1 has been renamed. The title is not descriptive enough to be of use, so it can be deleted once all the model elements have been moved to relevant worksets. The worksets we've set up demonstrate how a typical breakdown might occur in a project of this size, but it's by no means limited to this scheme. Depending on how you structure work in your office, the worksets might be quite different.

Once in a workset environment, you can see or change an object's workset by accessing its properties. At the bottom of the dialog, you can see which workset an object or group of objects are placed in, and you can toggle between the created worksets (see Figure 20.7). Note that you can move elements to other worksets only if you own the elements. You do not need to own the entire workset to do this, just the individual elements.

Additionally, you can tell what workset an object belongs to by hovering your cursor over the object and waiting for the tooltip to appear. This tooltip will give you a host of information about the object in question. In the following example, the workset is Shell and Core, the element is also part of the Walls category, the name of the family is Basic Wall, and the family type is A3 - 4 3/4″.

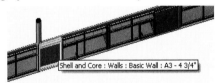

FIGURE 20.7
Change the workset
to which an element
belongs by selecting a
different workset
using the Element
properties dialog

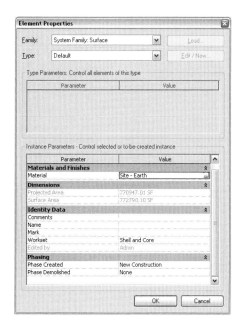

PRACTICE GOOD WORKFLOW

As a best practice, do not work directly in the central file once the worksets have been established. Working directly in the central file will change the file attributes and nullify anyone's ability to STC. Once someone has worked directly in the central file, any work by anyone else will be lost and everyone will be required to make new local copies. Working in the central file should *only* occur with full knowledge by all the team members and only if there is a file upgrade or some other historically significant event occurring.

Moving Elements between Worksets

Once the worksets are created, there are some simple steps for moving elements quickly and easily to other worksets. As mentioned, the easiest way to move the bulk of the objects is to not move them at all but simply rename Workset1. After that, it is easiest to do move elements in a subtractive method from a 3D view. The following exercise will walk you through moving elements to their new worksets using a subtractive method to locate model geometry. Note that this should be done while one person is still the solitary owner of all the worksets.

1. Open the default 3D view ({3D}) so that you can see all of your model elements within the project.

2. Open the Visibility/Graphic Overrides dialog, turn off the Site workset, and click OK. Since nothing is in the Site workset, the view should look the same when you are done.

3. Now, in the 3D view, select a comfortable number of the site elements and click the Properties button—*comfortable* meaning you don't have to try to select them all at once. In the first

image in Figure 20.8, the toposurface and some trees have been selected and are highlighted in red.

FIGURE 20.8
Moving objects
between worksets

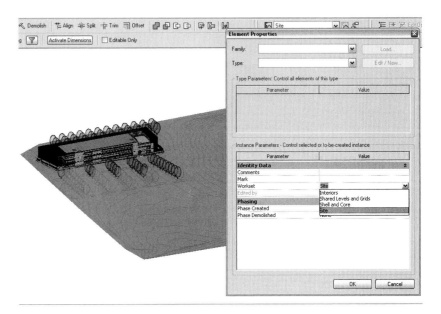

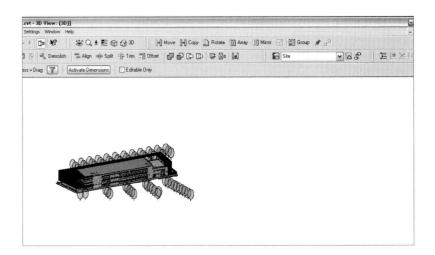

4. From the Properties dialog, select Site for the Workset value and click OK. All of the elements you selected will disappear (the second image in Figure 20.8). Not to worry: remember, you turned the Site workset off using the Visibility/Graphic Overrides!

5. Using the same technique, you can move the remainder of the site elements to the Site workset. The same procedure is repeated in order to move the Interior walls to the Interior workset.

At any point in this process, you can check your work by opening the Workset tab in the Visibility /Graphic overrides dialog and unchecking all of the boxes but one to see what is on each workset. Figure 20.9 shows the Interiors workset with all of the interior elements. As you can see, this is a great way to manage visibility without using the object categories.

FIGURE 20.9
The Interior workset

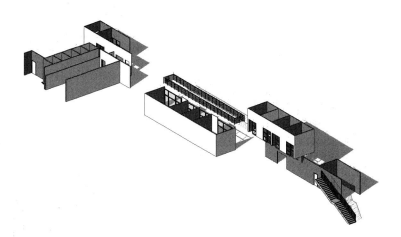

MOVING EVERY INSTANCE OF AN ELEMENT

A quick way to move every instance of a single element to a new workset is to use the Select All Instances option from the context menu. For example, select a tree in the model, then select all instance of that tree, then open the element properties. You can then change the workset for all those elements in one interaction.

Workflow

With worksharing, there is always one central file that spawns local files and manages element ownerships. This is the file that changes are saved to and from which you get updated versions of the model. Once the worksets are initialized and the model is divided into various worksets, you will need to complete a few more steps before the team can jump into the model and begin working in a multi-user environment.

To use Revit in a workset environment, you do everything any IT manager ever yelled at you for doing: You make a local copy of the central file and work directly off your C: drive. Although this approach is a bad idea for most work in an office environment, for the Revit database, there are several good things about it:

◆ It allows more than one user to make changes to the central file.

◆ Your local copy will be more responsive than a networked file because your access speed to your hard drive is much faster than it is across most networks.

◆ Should anything bad happen to your network or your central file, you will have an up-to-date backup to which you can easily apply the Save As command to make a new central file.

Making a Central File

Now that we've turned on worksharing, we need to set up the central file to be used by more than one person. To do this, we are going first make a central file located on your network; then we will make the local files to begin working on the project. To make the central file, choose File ➤ Save As and give the model a new name. Before you save, select the Options button at the bottom of the dialog box and verify that the box Make this a Central File after save is checked (see Figure 20.10).

FIGURE 20.10

Making a central file

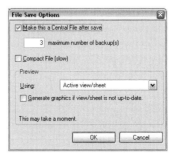

The reason for the new name is twofold. First, it gives you a backup of your old file before you made the worksets. Backups never hurt. Second, Revit sometimes does not like to have a new file saved over an active file. It can cause file corruption.

Making the Local File

Now that the central file has been created, we need to make the local files to work from:

1. Make a new, local copy of the central file by dragging the file you just made to your desktop or another location on your hard drive. Be careful not to *move* the file; you just want to make a copy of it.

2. Now, open this new, local file. The first time any local file is initialized, you will receive the warning message shown in Figure 20.11. All this means is that you've made a local file and you will be the owner of the local copy.

FIGURE 20.11

Opening the local file for the first time

Once you click OK, you are set and ready to begin working in a worksharing environment.

Now that you're in a worksharing environment, every element added to the file belongs to a workset. Try to keep model elements in a workset other than Shared Levels and Grids because these worksets may be locked down at some point to avoid accidental movement of key datums. To make sure you're placing elements in the proper workset, check the Worksets toolbar to see what the active workset is. The workset shown in this box is the workset new elements will be assigned to. Remember, you don't have to be the owner of this workset nor does the workset need to be editable to add new elements to it.

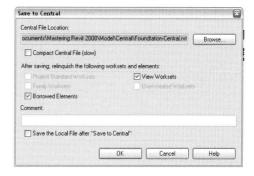

A helpful toggle in the Worksets toolbar is the Gray Inactive Workset button. It grays out all elements that aren't in the active workset, helping you identify which elements in the workset are active. This is a temporary view state and will not affect any print output.

Saving Shared Work

Once you begin working in a worksharing environment, it becomes necessary to not only save your work, but to share it with others. There are two ways to save your work when you're using a workshared file.

Save   The Save tool saves the work you've done to your local copy only; the work isn't shared or saved back to the central file. This is useful when you're in the design phase and trying out different designs or if you're not ready to share your work with others but you definitely want to save the work you've done.

Save to Central   Next to the Save tool is the Save To Central (STC) button. Use this to publish your work into the central file. When you do so, your work appears in the central file and becomes available to the entire team. Saving to central also acquires the changes that others have made (and likewise saved to the central file) and loads them into your local model. By default, a save to central will relinquish any permissions you have over objects and worksets within the model.

File ➢ Save to Central   Using the menu option for STC is a good way to save yet maintain permission over the elements you are creating. Choosing this option will open the dialog shown in Figure 20.12, which allows you to customize how you save to central. You can choose to relinquish some permissions or none of them, and you can choose to save a local copy at this time (or not). You can also add comments about this particular version you are saving. The comments are available in the History dialog box (covered later in this book).

FIGURE 20.12
Save to Central
(STC) dialog

In addition, Revit will remind you regularly to save your work. In a worksharing environment, you will receive a reminder to save to central and a separate reminder to save locally.

The reminder time shown in the dialog box can be modified across the application in the Settings ➢ Options dialog box under the General tab.

Loading Work from Other Team Members

It's possible to update your model from the central file without committing your changes to central. Think of this process as getting an update of the model. To do so, choose File ➤ Reload Latest. Revit finds the latest changes saved to the central file and brings them into your local file without publishing any of the changes you've made.

Element Ownership

While you are working in a worksharing environment, it might become necessary to see if you have ownership of an element. To do so, simply select the element. If you own it, it will be highlighted in red and can be readily moved or modified. If you do not own it, it will still be highlighted red, but you will also see an icon resembling a puzzle piece in blue. This indicates that you do not currently have ownership of that element.

You can get ownership of the element in a few ways:

◆ If you edit or move an element, Revit will grant you permission to own it provided no one else currently owns it.

◆ If you can click the puzzle piece icon, and the element is available, Revit will grant you permission to edit or change it.

◆ You can right-click the element and choose Make Elements Editable from the context menu (see Figure 20.13).

FIGURE 20.13
Making an element editable

Note that you also have the option to make worksets editable and take permission of the *entire* workset the object is assigned to.

Real World Scenario

Oops

Inevitably, with any team of people, someone is bound to make a mistake somewhere in the process. It happens; it's just human nature. The important thing is knowing how to recover when those accidents happen. On one project we worked on, someone new to the team kept accidentally deleting the west wall of the project while we were deep into CDs. Since Revit is a database and everything is tied to everything else, every time this happened, not only would the plans be messed up, but we'd lose the west elevation, the wall sections, the door and window details in those sections, and so on. You get the idea. The west wall would be deleted and the user would STC, thereby changing the central file. Fortunately, we would catch it in time and we would not have to resort to a backup from the previous night and lose a day's worth of work. Each local copy is a fully functional copy of the model. All you need to do is perform a simple File ➢ Save As. Click the Options button and then select Make this a Central File after Save. Once everyone on the team makes a new local copy, you're back in business.

Borrowing Elements

By borrowing elements, team members can take ownership of only some of the elements within a particular workset. This can typically be used if you need to modify only one or a few elements in a given workset and do not want to take ownership of the entire workset. This is also valuable if you need to edit elements in a workset and someone else already owns it.

The key idea here is that you can borrow elements individually rather than by workset. If you need to work on an element that belongs to someone else, you'll be informed of that and given the option to send a notification asking to borrow it. The owner of the element can then grant permission for you to take ownership. This is referred to as *relinquishing* permission.

Borrowing is a critical technological concept in Revit; it allows users to fluidly transfer permission of objects without having to constantly save all their work to the central file and relinquish all worksets. Let's look at this workflow in more detail.

Requesting Permission

Say you are happily working away on your model and realize that someone else is the owner of an element you need to modify. Should that occur, you will be presented with a dialog box shown in Figure 20.14. This will occur every time you are working in a model in which worksharing is enabled and you are attempting to edit an element that is already owned by someone else on the project.

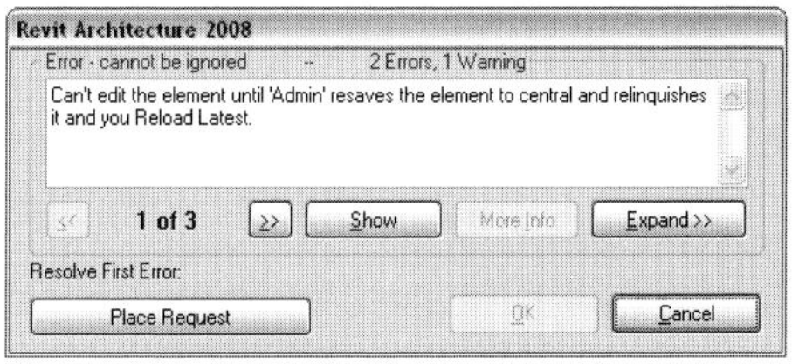

FIGURE 20.14
Placing Request for permission

You have the option to click Cancel, which will undo any edits you have made to that element, or you can click Place Request to ask the other user to relinquish permission over the element in question. If you opt to place a request, you will see the following dialog.

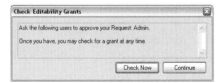

It is important to note that the other user does not receive an explicit notification that you have placed the request. Currently, there is no alert to this request that will appear on the other user's screen. You'll need to physically call or instant message that person, and get them to grant the permissions. If owning this element is critical to your task at hand, keep in mind that you will not be able to perform any more work in relation to that element until that other user grants you permission to borrow it. Once you've made your phone call, or gotten the other user to relinquish, click the Check Now button to see if you do in fact own the element. Or if you want to just keep working, click the Continue button.

GET THEIR ATTENTION!

Asking another user to grant permission to an element is a great reason to use an interoffice instant message or chat service. It is invasive enough to alert another user to the fact you are requesting permission for an element. However, the phone works well, too.

Once you've received notice from the other user that your request has been granted, click Check Now and you will receive the message shown here.

Clicking OK will apply your edits and you will then be the borrower of that element.

You can check to see who owns which worksets and who is borrowing from a workset at any time in the Worksets dialog box, as shown in Figure 20.15.

Granting Permission

Now suppose that you have been happily modeling along and you receive a phone call, IM, or tap on the shoulder from someone looking to get permission for an element you own in the model. How do you grant permission for someone else to use this element? On the Worksharing toolbar is a button called Editing Requests, which allows you to see what outstanding requests have been sent your way. Clicking this button gives you the dialog shown in Figure 20.16.

From here, you have a few options:

Grant   Gives permission for the requested element to your teammate

Deny/Retract   Denies permission to your teammate

Show Shows you exactly which element or elements have been requested to help you make an informed decision

FIGURE 20.15
Owning and borrowing worksets

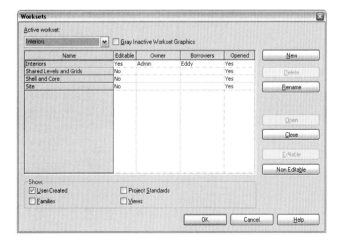

FIGURE 20.16
Editing Requests dialog

Once you are ready to grant permission, one of two things will happen. If you haven't made any changes yourself that need to be saved, you can simply grant the permission and notify your teammate that you have done so, and then both of you can continue to work. If you have been editing the requested element, you'll need to save your changes to the central file before anything else can happen. Changes of this nature are specially flagged in the Editing Requests dialog box with an asterisk before the request indicating that the element has been modified and an STC needs to occur before permission can be granted (see Figure 20.17).

FIGURE 20.17
Editing requests for changed elements

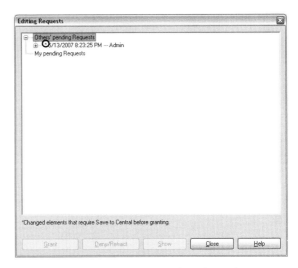

Trying to grant permission at this point will give you the dialog shown here.

In order to remedy this issue, you will need to close the dialog and perform a Save to Central using one of the methods we discussed earlier. Keep in mind that if you choose File ➢ Save to Central and uncheck the boxes for relinquishing permission, you will need to come back to the Editing Requests dialog box to grant permission for this element. Once you have saved to central and notified the other user, they can then click the Check Now button to continue to work.

The user who is requesting permission of the element will get this dialog after clicking Check Now.

This means that the object they were trying to use has been edited and they will need to choose File ➢ Reload Latest or a STC to reload the most current copy of that object before it can be edited. Unfortunately, any modifications to this element will be lost as the element is changed in the central file.

The Bottom Line

Understanding worksharing is important to any team environment or any project in which you plan to have more than one person working on the file at a time. Understanding worksharing can help support good project communication and efficient workflow across the project lifecycle.

Set up a project with worksets Knowing how to activate worksharing and set up the project file for more than one person at a time is critical in any office environment.

Master It How do you work in a single Revit file on a project team with more than one member in the file at a time?

Move elements between worksets Inevitably, you will put the right element on the wrong workset. It happens. You will need to know how to move elements quickly between worksets to keep your drawings and project organized.

> **Master It** How do you move elements between worksets?

Create a central file and local files Once you've enabled worksharing, you'll need to understand the dynamics of central and local files to fully leverage working in a worksharing environment.

> **Master It** Once you have enabled worksets to allow for multiple users, what's the best way to implement and use the file?

Save to and load from the central file Saving to and loading from the central file allows you to view other team members' work and allows them to see what changes to the project you have added.

> **Master It** How can you translate the changes you've made in your local file to the central file on the network? How do you download changes from other team members to your local file?

Request permission to use elements owned by other team members and grant others permission to use your elements Editing elements in a central file means you have sole ownership over further changes to those elements. Understanding the permissions will be critical to working in a team.

> **Master It** How do you edit an element in the model if someone has already taken permission of it in a worksharing environment?

Chapter 21

Troubleshooting and Optimizing Tips

Throughout this book, our focus has been on using Revit as an architectural design and production tool; we've shown how to use the software for all of the core BIM operations. This chapter looks at the file-management aspect of a Revit project. As we've said, a Revit project is a single database file, usually a large one. Regular file maintenance and a well-built model will keep you from having problems down the road with file performance and stability. It's worth being aware of best practices.

In this chapter, you'll find tips and tricks for keeping your file running quickly and smoothly. We've included some pointers to keep you from getting into trouble and some solutions if you do. We'll discuss performance issues, file corruption, and getting a project started and point you to some additional resources. You'll learn how to do several things to make your work more efficient:

◆ Keep your files lean and keep file performance optimized

◆ Create best practices for project workflow

◆ Repair some of the problems that can happen in Revit files

Performance

It should make sense that a small file on a good network runs the quickest. Depending on your hardware configuration, typical file sizes can vary widely.

We've seen them from 10MB to 150MB. Much of that variation depends on the level of detail you've put into your model, if you have any imported files (like other 3D files or CAD files), and the overall complexity of your model. However, there are a number of things you can do to be proactive about keeping your model's performance optimized. Here are a few we recommend:

Use the /3GB switch.   Revit now supports Microsoft XP's SP2 /3GB switch. Windows XP allows any given application access to only 2GB of RAM at a given time; if the application needs more, it get the rest from virtual memory. Microsoft's switch (which is available in XP Service Pack 2) allows you to change that 2GB limit to 3GB. To find out how to do this, visit www.autodesk.com/support, choose Revit Architecture from the menu, and read the support article on enabling the /3GB switch. Of course, you need more than 2GB of RAM on your workstation for this switch to do you any good.

More information on RAM and Virtual Memory can be found at the Autodesk knowledge website. See this link for details:

http://usa.autodesk.com/adsk/servlet/ps/item?siteID=123112&id=8018971&linkID=9243099

Don't explode imported CAD files.   A CAD file imported into Revit is a collection of objects that is managed as a single entity. If you explode a CAD file, the single object immediately becomes many—and becomes that much more data for Revit to track. If you're unfortunate enough to explode a hatch pattern, one object becomes many thousands. If you're importing DWG files, leave them unexploded as much as possible. If you need to hide lines, use the Visibility/ Graphic Overrides dialog to turn layers on and off. Explode *only* when you need to change the imported geometry, and start with a partial explode. The tools shown here are available in the Options bar when you select an imported or linked DWG file.

Using Partial Explode will break down the CAD file into subgroups; any blocks within the file will be maintained, hatch will be maintained, and so on. Using Full Explode will break each of these components down into its individual lines. If the drawing is simple and you are looking to convert an old CAD detail into a Revit drafting view, this can be a desired effect. However, remember that exploding takes one object within the database and makes many many objects from it.

Another option is to change the DWG file directly in the CAD application—delete lines and layers you don't need, then re-import.

Delete or unload unused DWGs. Often, you import a DWG as a reference but then you don't need it later in the process. It's easy to forget, but if you no longer need an import, go ahead and select it in the view and delete it. This will delete the import in all views.

Close unused views. Keeping the number of open views to a minimum helps the model's performance. Choose Window ➤ Close Hidden Windows often, because it's easy to have many views open at once, even if you're concentrating on only a few views. Once you reduce your open views to just two or three, you can take advantage of the view switch toggle: Press Ctrl-Tab, and you'll cycle through your open views. Press Ctrl-Shift-Tab to reverse the view cycle.

Calculate room volumes only when necessary. You can turn on room volume calculation by choosing Settings ➤ Room and Area Settings. Check the "Compute room volumes" box (shown in Figure 21.1) only if you need room tags or a schedule to display volumetric information. Don't forget to switch off this option after you print or view the information. Otherwise, the volumes will recalculate each time you edit something in the model, and this can affect the overall performance of your file dramatically.

FIGURE 21.1
Compute Room Volumes option should only be checked when reviewing volumes or when printing documents that display volume information.

Best Practices

Another way to improve performance is to follow some simple, best practice guidelines for your workflow. These aren't necessarily a list of do's and don'ts or a list of potential hazards, they are suggestions to make a few, simple changes or additions to your workflow and buy yourself back some time in the long run. Many users get frustrated with long load times opening views in Revit. Follow these tips and it will keep things optimally humming along.

Workshared files: Make a new local copy once a week.   Sometimes in a worksharing environment, your local copy can begin to perform poorly but others on your team don't have the same problems. If this is the case, we recommend that you make a new local file. Local files can become problematic for any of the reasons that commonly cause issues with large files in a networked environment. As a general practice, it's a good idea to make a new local copy once a week.

Use Graphics Card options to improve drawing performance.   In the Settings ➢ Options ➢ Graphics tab, make sure you have both the Use OpenGL Hardware Acceleration and "Use overlay planes to improve performance" check boxes marked (Figure 21.2). Unchecking the "Use overlay planes…" option can cause significant degradation in performance—we recommended you never uncheck it.

FIGURE 21.2
Enable video card
options for better
performance.

Import/Link DWGs in one view only.   Importing in all views can seriously affect performance. Whenever possible, import in Current View only. Exception is when you wish to create a Toposurface out of a CAD file—you will have to import the CAD file in all views. Note the "Link (instead of import)" check box in the Import or Link dialog box. Linking is better than importing if you don't need to edit the geometry.

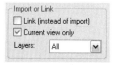

Watch out for imported geometry.   Although Revit has the ability to import files from a number of other sources, you should exercise caution when doing so. If you're importing a 60MB

NURBS-based file into your model, expect your Revit model to grow in size and react a bit slower than it did before. Delete unneeded imports to reduce file size and improve overall performance.

Purge unused elements. Revit has a built-in tool that allows you to purge unused families and content. This is a good way to reduce file size, improve performance, and minimize the list of things you need to search through when adding content in the project. Loaded but unused families can make your file grow quickly. To purge, choose File ➤ Purge Unused. If your file is very large, it may take a few minutes to run this command before you see the dialog box shown in Figure 21.3. Here, you can opt to keep or purge families individually.

FIGURE 21.3
Use the "Purge unused" dialog to reduce file size.

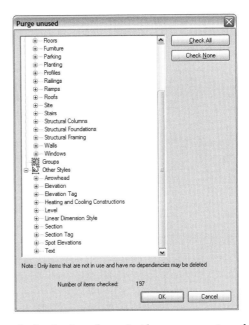

This is typically *not* a good idea at the beginning of a project because your template may contain families that you intend to use but haven't yet inserted (such as wall types).

Note that some Revit families can only be removed from the project with the Purge command. You will notice with elements such as dimensions and textnotes that there is no way to delete a family type from the Properties dialog. To get rid of unused types, use Purge Unused. Everything included in the Other Styles group falls into this category.

Manage amount of information shown in views. Learn to manage the amount of information needed in your views. Don't show more than you need to show in a view, in either the View Depth or level of detail you choose. Here are a few easy ways to keep your views opening and printing smoothly:

Minimize the level of detail. Set your detail level (in the View Control bar) relative to the scale you're viewing. For example, if you're working on a 1/32" (1:50) plan, you probably don't need Detail Level set to Fine—it will cause your view performance to suffer needlessly.

Hide elements you don't need to see. This goes along with the level of detail, but this tip is more manual than just changing a single setting such as level of detail. If you're printing a 1/32" (1:50) drawing, make sure you're showing the proper level of detail in the view. Even if Detail Level is set to Coarse, do you really need to show balusters in an elevation on your railing at that scale? They will print as a thick, black line. Turning them off in this view will help to not only improve your printing speed, but also the quality of the resulting printed sheet.

SPEEDING UP DISPLAY BY CORRECTING VIEW DETAIL LEVEL

We had a project in which it was taking upwards of 20 minutes to open plan views. As you can imagine, this was very frustrating for the users, especially when those views were opened accidentally. As it turned out, the views were set to a 1/16" scale and were set to a fine level of detail. This was completely unnecessary because none of the elements in the plan showed any significant information at this level of detail. By setting View Detail to Coarse, we were able to reduce the time it took to open those views to under 2 minutes.

We further optimized view performance by modifying complex families in the view to show less detail at a coarse level. The level of detail you need to show in a small scale view (like 1/16") is far different than what needs to be shown at a large scale (like 1/4"). We can edit the family itself to "hide" certain elements or portions of the family at different detail levels.

Minimizing View Depth. View Depth is a great tool to enhance performance. It's especially valuable in section views. A typical wall section is shown in Figure 21.4. The default behavior (top) causes Revit to regenerate all of the model geometry the full depth of that view every time you open the view. To reduce the amount of geometry that needs to be redrawn, drag the section's far clip plane (the green dashed line when you highlight the section) in close to the cutting plane (bottom).

FIGURE 21.4
Depth of a section view can affect performance.

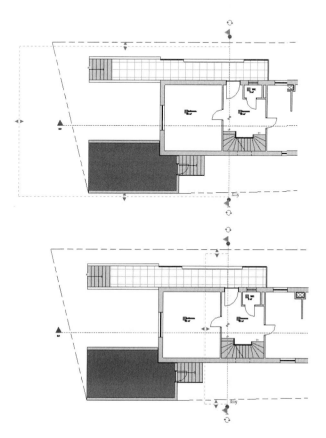

Turn off shadows. Shadows can help you make beautiful presentations, give a sense of depth in façades, and show the effect of the sun in a site-plan view. Computing shadows, however, is performance intensive and can significantly slow down printing, panning, zooming, and selection. Make sure you turn them off whenever you don't need them.

Open only what you need. One of the benefits of having worksets is that you don't have to turn them all on at once. When you open the project, open the Workset dialog box. There, you can highlight any workset you won't be working with and click the Close button (see Figure 21.5). Doing so drops that workset from active memory and gives you better performance. Remember, if worksets are closed, you can't do anything with them. If a workset isn't visible, it won't print. To print a current copy of the whole model, you'll need to turn the worksets back on.

Break up your model. For larger projects, or campus-style projects, you can break up your model into smaller submodels that are referenced together. You can also do this on a single building. If you decide to divide your project, make your cuts are along lines that make sense from a holistic-building standpoint. Don't think of the cuts as you would in CAD, but think about how the actual assemblies will interact in the building. So, for example, don't cut between floors 2 and 3 on a multistory building unless you have a significant change in building form or program. Here's a list of some good places to split a model (for example, Figure 21.6 represents one project split into the four models you see):

◆ At a significant change in building form or massing

◆ At a significant change in building program

◆ Between separate buildings on a site

◆ Creating the site as a separate model

FIGURE 21.5
Worksets can be closed to reduce the amount of memory used to open a file.

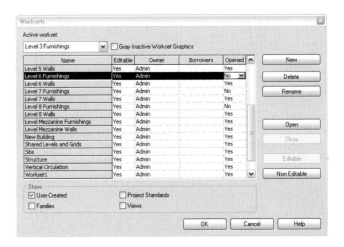

Print DWFs or PDFs before you print paper. Printing big Revit files can sometimes take a long time. Enabling raster printing speeds up printing, although there is a trade-off compared to the quality that vector printing offers. Depending on the printer, you may get better line quality by creating a DWF or PDF first and then printing your physical sheets. It's best to experiment on a few sheets to see what your printer responds to best before sending your entire set. Printing a digital set first will also give you a record copy of what you have just printed as well as a quick way to make additional copies later if needed.

FIGURE 21.6
Splitting up a
model can improve
performance.

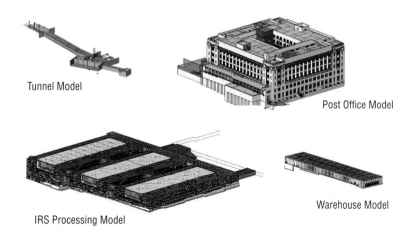

Tunnel Model

Post Office Model

IRS Processing Model

Warehouse Model

Model just what you need. Don't fall into the trap of overmodeling. Just because you *can* doesn't mean you *should*. Be smart about the level of detail you choose to model based on the complexity and size of your project. Some data is just easier and better to show in a 2D detail rather than as 3D model data. The amount of information you model or do not model should be based on your project size and complexity, your timeframe, and your comfort level with the software.

Don't overconstrain. User-defined relationships and constraints are important to embed in the design to help keep important dimensions constant. However, if you don't need to lock a relationship, don't. Even though the option to lock all alignments is available, it's often not necessary to do so. Overconstraining the model can cause problems later in the project process when you want to move or modify an element and you need to figure out (or remember) what you locked or where to allow the particular element to be moved or modified.

Fix overconstrained objects. If you keep encountering a dialog box telling you the model is overconstrained and this is impeding your workflow, you can unlock the constraint. If it is a simple element (such as a wall with no openings or sections), it might be easier to simply delete and re-add the troubled object.

Open your project, not a new empty project file. Each time you launch Revit, it opens with a blank default template. This template is often rich with data, and your computer will need a minute or two to open it. However, once a project is under way, the need to open a default template is removed—you most likely just need to open the file you're working on. Instead of opening Revit and then opening your project file, drag the project file over the Revit icon or double-click the file from Windows Explorer. Doing so launches Revit without first opening a template file. Also, if you do open Revit with the default template, close the file if you're not using it for anything.

Close Revit with an empty view. To avoid long opening times for really large files, establish an office standard that you always close your last view as a drafting view or Legend that is empty or maybe contains only some text with the project name. This way, when Revit first opens the project, it will need much less processing time. By default, Revit always opens with the view from when the project was last saved. We've seen some nice looking "project pages" made with a drafting view using text and some simple instructions (Figure 21.7).

FIGURE 21.7

An example of an "empty" view to STC, open, and close the Project

STC, OPEN AND CLOSE AND HAIKU VIEW

PARAMETRIC THOUGHTS
WHICH MOVES THROUGH THE SPRINGTIME SUN?
MASSING AND LIGHT COMBINED

LAST PURGED AND OPTIMIZED 7-31

File Corruption

On the odd chance your file becomes corrupt and begins to crash frequently, there are a few things you can do to help fix the problem before you call Revit Support in a panic. All of these steps can be taken before you get into trouble. Remember, the best way to keep a file from having issues is to practice good modeling techniques and review warnings regularly (Tools ➤ Review Warnings). Otherwise, here are some suggestions on what to do when you begin get into trouble.

Audit the file. When a file is audited, the data structures are reviewed and problems that are found with the model are corrected. An audited file won't look any different when the audit is completed; however, it should (ideally) not crash. This is not a cure-all, by any means, but it can help you get out of a tight spot when necessary.

You (or the project manager) should first get everyone out of any worksets and local files and have them relinquish their permissions. Then take the following steps:

1. Open the file using File ➤ Open. The resulting Open dialog box lets you browse to a project location.

2. Select your project and, before clicking the Open button to open the file, select the Audit check box in the lower-right corner.

3. Revit will give you a warning before performing an audit on your file. The audit itself can take several minutes to complete.

4. When this process is finished, save the project with a new name or in a new file location; don't save this file over the old Revit file. Saving over an existing Revit file can sometimes lead to instability.

5. When you're finished, have everyone make a new local file, and the team can get back to work.

Review warnings. Each time you make something that Revit considers a problem, a warning is issued. Warnings will accumulate if left unresolved. Think of all these errors as unresolved calculations. The more there are, the more your computer will have to struggle trying to resolve them. Revit provides an interface for reviewing all the warnings in the project and fixing problems.

Try to read and react to the warnings that Revit sends. You don't have to do it when you're under a tight deadline or when doing so will interrupt your work. But once a week, you should spend 30 minutes reviewing the warnings because this can improve your model's overall performance. You can find the list of warnings in your file under Tools ➢ Review Warnings (Figure 21.8).

FIGURE 21.8
The Review
Warnings dialog

Purge Unused.   We referred to this earlier in the chapter, but it can also be used to get rid of poorly built families that might be causing havoc in your file.

Tips for Getting Started in Revit

Although this list isn't complete by any means, it should help steer you in the right direction.

Begin with your end in mind.   When you begin any project, planning is always a good way to start. You can set yourself up for a successful implementation from the beginning by using a bit of forethought about your process, workflow, and desired outcome.

Get your template and office standards in place first.   As design professionals, we have a tendency to develop unique graphic conventions and styles for our documents. This is a specific area in which good planning leads to a good project. If possible, get your standards in place before you begin a project. Revit does an excellent job of getting you started with a good template of graphic standards to work with. However, if you're like most architects, an application right out of the box is never quite nice enough. Revit provides a good starting point for customization, and with some up-front time, you can soon have your project and office standards up and running. See chapters 4 and 5 for more information about standard project templates.

Remember that the first project you do in Revit is a change in methodology.   You're leveraging technology to help you change the way you approach design and documentation. Don't expect the process to have the same workflow as it did in a CAD-based system. Try to stay flexible in your expectations and schedule, and allow yourself time to adapt to the change.

Don't try to conquer the world on the first project.   There are many advantages to using BIM as a design and documentation methodology. As this process becomes more mainstream within the industry, those benefits will only increase. All of these things and more are possible with the use of Revit, but it will take a couple of projects to get there. Tailor the use of BIM to the project, and use the features that will maximize the benefits of using BIM. Choose your goals realistically based on the expertise of your project team, and plan in advance so you can be successful.

Model correctly from the beginning. One of the most important rules to follow as you begin your project is to model the building as it will be built. We can't stress this enough. It's critical to begin modeling correctly from the beginning, so that as the design is refined you don't have to fix things later. What does this mean? If you can begin to think about how your project will be assembled, it will save you a lot of time at the end.

Get information into the project as soon as it becomes known. A key advantage of using Revit is the ability to change your project schedule. In a traditional design process, most of the effort on a project is realized during the construction document phase. At that time, more people are typically working on the project, and it can be fairly difficult to implement major changes to the project design. By this time, the documents are complex, and it would require a great amount of effort for the team to redraw all the changed information. You'll find that with Revit, design change is largely managed by the software itself, which gives you a great deal of flexibility in both your design and documentation. Take advantage of this shift in the process, and add information to your model early. It can be in the form of more detailed content or it can show the material construction of your wall system. Remember that you can change all this information much more quickly and easily than you ever could in CAD, so don't assume you're locked into the information you displayed early in the design process.

Plan for better communication among team members early in the process. Communication within a team is critical for understanding a project and documenting it successfully. One of the limitations of a CAD-based system is that there is no direct connection between the different files that make up the drawing set. This phenomenon carries through to the project team and is inherent in the project workflow and management. In CAD, it's possible for team members to work in some degree of isolation. They aren't forced to immediately reconcile their changes with changes made by their teammates. Revit's single-file environment forces a much higher degree of team communication.

Don't try to model everything. Most of us have drafted in a 2D environment until now. Moving to a 3D world is a significant change. Do you have to model every single screw? That's a good question. Like any BIM system, Revit doesn't require 100 percent 3D information. Typical workstations aren't capable of handling all the data of a building in model form. Additionally, few projects have the time in their schedule to model the screws in a sheet of gypsum board or the sealant around all the windows; some of that information is best presented in 2D or in the specifications. This still leaves you with a wide range of options for modeling. In the beginning, err on the side of simplicity. It's far easier to add complexity to your model later on as you gain experience and confidence than it is to troubleshoot overconstrained parameters early in the process. Start with the big ideas: walls, openings, roofs, and so forth. Work your way down to a comfortable level of detail for both you and your computer.

Organize your team. A BIM project team includes three basic technical roles. These roles are interchangeable, especially on smaller projects with fewer team members. No matter how small the team, it's useful to make sure all these roles are filled.

Content / Family Creator   The Family Creator's primary role is to create the parametric content in the Revit model. This is typically someone with 3D experience who also has a firm understanding of Revit and Revit families. The families, as you saw in Chapters 4 and 5, have parameters that can control visibility, size, color, proportion, and a number of other things.

Designer   This is the person or team whose primary responsibility is to figure out what the project will look like and how it will be made. They create walls, floors, and roofs and locate windows, doors, and other building elements.

Documenter   This role supplies the bulk of the documentation. It consists of drafting some of the 2D linework over portions of the 3D model to show detail, adding annotations and keynotes, and creating details.

Additional Resources

If you get stuck along the way, don't assume you're alone. There are myriad resources to help you find a specific solution to your problem. Chances are, someone has tried the same thing before. In our digital age, a wealth of information is available online, so before you spend hours trying to work through a particular problem, try tapping some of the existing resources.

Revit Help menu   Your first stop, if or when you get stuck, should be the Revit Help menu. It's one of the easier and more robust Help menus out there, and it can give you a lot of useful information very quickly. It's also the most accessible help source. As with most applications, it's at the far right of the menu bar.

Subscription Support   If you have bought Revit on subscription, Revit Subscription Support offers an exemplary web-based support system. Their responses are speedy, and their advice is top-notch. If you need information more quickly, Revit also has an online knowledge base of FAQs that is available without a subscription. Both of these resources can be accessed at `www.autodesk.com/revit`.

AUGI   Autodesk User Group International (AUGI) is also an excellent source for tips and tricks. It's an online community of Autodesk product users and is free after you register on the site. It has a host of information and forums populated by others in the industry. Because it's a forum, you can post and answer questions or engage in discussions surrounding an array of topics. The address is `www.augi.com`.

Revit City   Looking for content and families? Revit City, another free online service, has a growing database of free families posted by other users. Its address is `www.revitcity.com`.

Revit OpEd   This blog is created and edited by Steve Stafford and is a great resource for discussions and Revit-related information. The site also has an extensive list of national and international BIM- and Revit-based blogs: `revitoped.blogspot.com`.

The Bottom Line

Knowing how to model correctly and keep your model running smoothly will save you a lot of time and frustration. Practicing good modeling practices and keeping your model efficient will only help you as you get further along in the project process.

Keep your files lean and keep file performance optimized   Keeping your file optimized will save you a lot of time in the long run. It will shorten the time it takes to open the file and the time it takes to save. Regular maintenance can quickly translate into a better bottom line for the project.

Master It   How do you keep your file performance optimized?

Create best practices for project workflow   Keeping your project file running smoothly not only helps your project process, but also the mental well-being of the people working on the project. If everyone on the project team understands the team's preferred workflow, it makes things just that much easier.

Master It   How do you create a best practice workflow for your project or office?

Repair some of the errors that can happen in Revit files   Working with a file that has become unstable can be a nightmare. You are uncertain of whether it will crash or when and you spend more time than usual saving your work. If a file does begin to behave abnormally, it's important to understand some quick and easy ways to get back on the right path.

Master It   Your file is running slowly or crashing. How do you repair the file before you begin losing time and data?

Appendix A

The Bottom Line

Each of The Bottom Line sections in the chapters suggest exercises to deepen skills and understanding. Sometimes there is only one possible solution, but often you are encouraged to use your skills and creativity to create something that builds on what you know and lets you explore one of many possible solutions.

Chapter 1: Understanding BIM: From the Basics to Advanced Realities

The advantages of Building Information Modeling   The traditional architectural design tools you've mastered are probably serving you well. New software and a new conceptual model of the building process will inevitably involve some adjustments, so they need to provide significant benefits.

> **Master It**   What are some of the advantages of using BIM over traditional CAD tools?

> **Solution**   BIM is a model-based tool that keeps your documents coordinated in a single file. As a modeling tool, representational drawings such as plan and section are by-products of modeling, not separately managed drawing files. BIM is also well suited for making early design decision and iterating in the design, because you can run analysis early and frequently.

What to expect from Building Information Modeling   A BIM project is based on a single, centralized database of information. You need to anticipate how that change can affect work-flows based on more independent functions.

> **Master It**   How can the work process be affected by the adoption of BIM?

> **Solution**   BIM changes the way projects are managed and worked on. You'll find that teams must communicate on a regular basis when working on a shared BIM model. This encourages members of the team to take active responsibility for their parts of the model and understand the impact that design changes have on other parts of the model. Using BIM also means you have to shed some old habits and expectations and be willing to change the way you think about producing construction documents. Moving from a drafting-centric work-flow to a model-based workflow can be jolting at first, but once you take the plunge, you're unlikely to look back.

Chapter 2: Revit Fundamentals

Work with and understand Revit parametric elements   Although you can find references to objects, families, instances, and components, in the end everything is an element.

> **Master It**   What are Revit elements, and how are they managed graphically?

Solution   Anything you can select in the view is a Revit element. By using a fixed category structure, Revit lets you quickly identify elements, control their visibility and graphics, and generate reports based on this information. The data is highly structured, but you have tremendous liberty when it comes to the representation of that data.

Use the Revit user interface   As in any software application, you need to know where all the major components are and what tasks they support.

Master It   How do you change the graphics of a category for all views? What if you need to change the graphics for only one view?

Solution   Use the Object Styles dialog to set up and edit the graphics for all elements in the model. This establishes a default behavior for all views. To change the graphics on a per-view basis, use the Visibility/Graphic Overrides dialog, which you can access from the context menu when elements are selected or by pressing the VG keyboard shortcut. The sooner you embrace this concept and start exploring the opportunities it presents, the better. If you can't get your drawing to look just right, chances are you haven't dug deep enough.

Use the Project Browser   This UI component provides access to all elements in your model. Get used to using it to locate views, families, groups, and links.

Master it   Knowing how to navigate views in Revit is essential to completing work. What are some of the ways to open views in Revit?

Solution   You can open views from the Project Browser by double-clicking any view. In addition, you can double-click view tag symbols directly (level heads, section heads, elevation tags, and callout bubbles) to open the view.

Navigate views and view properties   Views are also elements. Just like the walls, floors, and roofs you add to the model, you'll also add views. They have properties you should become familiar with.

Master it   You need to change the scale of a plan view from $\frac{1}{8}''$ to $\frac{1}{4}''$. How do you do this with Revit?

Solution   Using either the View Properties option on the view's context menu or the view controls at bottom of the view, change the scale. The annotations and hatch patterns will update automatically. You can change the scale of any view at any time.

Chapter 3: Know Your Editing Tools

Selecting, changing, and replacing elements   Learning the basic mechanics of the interface is crucial to just about everything you'll do in Revit.

Master It   Selecting elements in the model happens all the time. What are some of the affordances that the Revit UI provides when you select elements?

Solution   Any time an element is selected, you'll notice that a few things change in the UI. First, the element changes color, indicating that it's selected. Second, if you select a model element, you get temporary dimensions to help you position the element. Third, icons appear for graphic controls such as drag grips, check boxes, and flip arrows. And finally, the Options bar updates with element-specific tools. All these features help keep the UI out of your way until you need it.

Editing elements interactively   The architectural process inevitably involves revision, so be sure you know how to make changes on the fly.

> **Master It**   You need to make some major changes to a floor plan, moving the bathroom 20´ down a corridor. How might you do this with Revit?
>
> **Solution**   Box-select all the walls, fixtures, and doors that are part of the bathroom. Use the Filter tool to make sure you have the right categories selected. Then, select the Move tool in the toolbar. Click anywhere in the model, and move the mouse in the direction you need to move the bathroom. Type **20´**. The whole set of elements then moves 20´.

Using other tools   Revit provides a wide range of tools for making changes in a project.

> **Master It**   In a section view, you notice that the walls and floors aren't cleaning up neatly— you're seeing lines overlap. What tool could you use to try to clean that up?
>
> **Solution**   For quick join cleanups, use the Join Geometry tool. Activate the tool, and then select the elements you want to join. With each click of the mouse, you see the overlapping lines disappear, and your drawings start to clean up immediately.

Chapter 4: Setting up Your Templates and Office Standards

Create your own template with custom annotations and settings   Creating a template that incorporates your firm's styles and preferences is an essential first step in putting Revit to work.

> **Master It**   Your firm has some deeply established graphic conventions that were defined in AutoCAD. How would you go about matching these graphics and setting up a Revit template?
>
> **Solution**   Using object styles to customize how elements appear in both projection and cut, you can get model and annotation categories to match the line weight, color, and pattern of those used in AutoCAD.

Create custom annotation families in the Family Editor   Styles for annotations, dimensions, and text are all governed by office standards, and the Family Editor is your tool for setting up those standards in Revit.

> **Master It**   You need to create dimensions, text, and annotations that match your office standards. How do you do this with Revit?
>
> **Solution**   Make new types of system families for text and dimensions. With these families, you can control font, color, and size. For tags, open an existing tag and customize its graphics to suit your needs. Be sure to add parametric labels to make your tags smart and associative. This will save you huge amounts of time later!

Create custom title blocks in the Family Editor   Title blocks are another important element of office standards that you can configure in the Family Editor.

> **Master It**   Most offices have several title blocks with lots of information embedded in them. How would you add multiple title blocks to your project template file?
>
> **Solution**   Make your own title blocks as parametric families, and then load them into the template using the Load From Library option. With smart labels, you need to define these only once in the Family Editor; they will adapt to whatever project you load the title block into.

Chapter 5: Customizing System Families and Project Settings in Your Template

Creating new types in the Family Editor for common building components such as walls, floors, ceilings, roofs, and stairs Incorporating common building components in your project template is fundamental to using Revit effectively.

Master It How do you add/remove wall, floor, and roof types to your template?

Solution Start with an existing template, and draw all the walls, floors, and roofs you're likely to need in your own projects. Then, purge unused wall, floor, and roof types from the file using the File/Purge tool. That way, all unused types will be removed from the template. If you need to add additional types, duplicate a type, name it, and make changes as needed. When you're done save your file as a new Revit template (RTE file).

Creating a type catalog to organize types for accessibility Revit's type catalogs are an important tool for keeping the types you create accessible in a project.

Master It What are type catalogs used for?

Solution A type catalog is a tool that lets you easily and quickly create many types of a family that have different dimensions and sizes. The type catalog is a text file connected with a Revit family. This text file can store many definitions of family types. It is imperative that the type catalog has the same name and is located in the same folder as the family for which it defines additional types, otherwise there will be no association between them and the type catalog will fail. When you load a family with an associated type catalog, you can selectively load types from the catalog.

Creating view templates for specific requirements View templates allow you to tailor views according to the requirements of a project.

Master It How would you set up a new view template for plan views where the surface pattern of floors is turned off?

Solution You can turn off categories and patterns and override the graphics for any view, and store these settings in a view template so they can be applied to many views. First, choose Settings ➤ View Templates. Duplicate an existing plan-view template type, and give it unique name. Next, click the Visibility/Graphic Overrides button, which takes you the Visibility/Graphic Overrides dialog. Scroll down to the Floors category, and click the Surface Pattern Override button. Deselect the Visible option, and click OK twice to get back to the View Templates dialog. You can now apply this view template to your plan views by right-clicking the view name in the Project Browser and using the Apply View Template feature.

Chapter 6: Modeling Principles in Revit

Using Revit's essential form making tools (Extrusion, Sweep, Revolve, and Blend) These four tools are at the root of practically all form modeling.

Master it Having learned the basics of Revit's form making tools, imagine how you would build this faucet designed by Philippe Starck.

Solution: Start a new Generic Model family. In the family, use Revolves, Sweeps, and Blends to create the faucet. In this example you would model the base as a Revolve, the spout a sweep, and the toggle switch as a blend.

Master it: In some cases, a form is made of multiple sketch lines to generate its form. What form making tools in Revit use more than one set of 2D sketches to generate the form?

Solution: Sweeps have a Profile sketch and a Path sketch.

Revolves have a Profile sketch and an Axis line.

Blends have two sketches: one for the Base and one for the Top.

The Underlying Concept of Sketch Based Design

Master it: Revit uses a 2D sketch based approach to modeling. What modeling elements in Revit use this 2D sketch principle to generate their form?

Solution: Every model element in Revit has at least one 2D sketch in it. Even walls, while not made initially using a sketch mode, have a sketch that can be edited. All 3D content is composed of combinations of forms that all derive from 2D sketches.

How Work Planes, Datums, and Reference Planes are used in modeling

Master it: In order to sketch a form, the form must reside on a Work Plane. How do you define and visualize the Work Plane in Revit?

Solution: To see the active Work Plane in a view, press the Work Plane visibility toggle in the Options bar. Right next to that button is the Work Plane tool, that will allow you to change the Work Plane by choosing an exiting Level, or picking on an existing model face.

Combining Solids and Voids to create complex and intriguing forms

Master it: To make more complex forms, the use of both solids and voids can be used. Think of a case where the using Voids as a subtractive element makes sense.

Solution: If create an extrusion in plan form, and then need to edit it in elevation, a Void is a perfect match. With the Void, you will be able to carve the top of the extrusion to give it a more unique shape.

Chapter 7: Concept Massing Studies

Understanding massing workflows supported by Revit Using generic forms, you can create early conceptual models and then use the mass to create the walls, floors, and roofs.

Master It You need to explore a design idea early on, in 3D, using abstract forms. How would you do this with Revit?

Solution One way to start work on a project is with an early conceptual sketch and massing study. Revit tools allow you to create massing studies and work through iterations to arrive at the design solution you need. You can import a hand sketch or a DWG and model from it or start from zero using the modeling tools. Once you've created some forms, you can make views, do shadow studies, and calculate area and volumes.

Creating massing elements in the project environment and Family Editor In the project environment, you can make massing forms at any time. For generic forms that might appear in multiple projects, consider using the Family Editor and create Mass Families.

Master It You've imported a 2D site plan, and now you need to start building up a massing study model in the project. How would you approach this with Revit?

Solution Start the Massing tool on the Massing Design bar, Create Mass and use the extrusion tool while picking the existing 2D shapes of the imported site plan as a base reference. Create a new massing form to begin experimenting with your design, and see how it impacts the surrounding context.

Understanding how massing can be used downstream as the design progresses Making a mass is one thing, but leveraging that mass for quantity take-offs can further aid and inform the design process.

Master It Once you've settled on a basic massing study, what information can you derive from it? How can this be represented?

Solution Using levels, the mass can be sliced into floors to perform area calculations. These can then be used to track progress of the design against the design requirements. You can also attach walls, floors, and roof to the mass, which can in turn be scheduled very early in the process.

Chapter 8: From Conceptual Mass to a Real Building

Leverage a massing study for program validation and early feasibility studies You can use massing studies to validate a design against the program requirements.

Master It Conceptual modeling is used early in the design process to explore building shape and program. How do you approach schematic design using Revit and perform feasibility studies?

Solution Revit lets you import a site DWG file and begin building a 3D massing study of the surroundings using the linework coming from the CAD import. Then, using the massing tools, you can model your conceptual composition. Using the design options, you can make a few different proposals. With mass and floor schedules, you can measure what you've done and test-proof the fit to the local regulations as well as the program.

Convert a mass into a building using the Building Maker tools   Moving from massing to actual building components is easily done with Revit.

> **Master It**   You've got the basic massing nailed down, and now you need to study more details such as wall and window fenestrations. How do you approach this with Revit?

> **Solution**   Once a final design is selected, you can use the Building Maker concept to quickly turn the mass model into a BIM model that contains walls, floors, roofs, and other architectural elements. In the early stage of this conversion, you can keep the dependency with the mass model so that if you decide to make changes you can use the Remake functionality to update the converted building accordingly. The idea is simple—you move from mass to a final building seamlessly, without data loss.

Import files from other sources when working on massing   You can make your own conceptual massing forms using standard Revit form-making tools or by importing geometry from other applications.

> **Master It**   How can you reuse conceptual models created in other modeling applications and turn them into a measurable and documentable building in Revit?

> **Solution**   The concept of Building Maker allows you to import models from SketchUp, Rhino, 3ds Max, and Inventor. You import early concept studies into a mass element and then apply real components (walls, roofs, floors, and so on) to its faces:

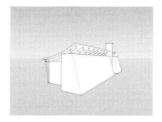

Chapter 9: Working with Design Options

Understanding how design options work in Revit   Design options provide a means to maintain two or more alternative designs for the same project or component.

Master It   What are design options in Revit?

Solution   Design options allow you to explore alternatives to your current design direction. By creating option sets from the Design Options dialog, you can make an unlimited number of variations to your design theme. These can be controlled with the Visibility/Graphic Overrides dialog, which lets you see the options in any number of view types: plans, elevations, sections, perspectives, schedules, and so on.

Creating new design options   Learning to add new options to a set is crucial to getting the most out of this tool.

Master It   Your client has asked you to explore an $8' \times 8'$ seating arrangement option in their office space. It's currently designed for $8' \times 10'$ and $6' \times 8'$ options. Add a new design option to explore the new scheme.

Solution   You've already created a design option for each of the two schemes ($8' \times 10'$ and $6' \times 8'$) using the Design Options toolbar. Both of these options are currently children of the same option set. You need to add a new option. Select one of the two, and copy the option. Now, choose Edit Option, and arrange the existing furniture into the new configuration without fear of losing the other two design schemes. Once this is done, duplicate one of the furniture plans, and you can show the new option by changing the Visibility/Graphics Overrides parameter.

Presenting multiple design options   Presenting multiple options makes it possible for your client and other project stakeholders to explore the alternatives.

Master It   You need to show a client five different design solutions for the new main entrance to the project you're working on.

Solution   Use design options. Add all the host elements, including walls, floors, and roofs, that relate to the area of interest to five separate design options in an option set. Remember to add only elements that will affect the entrance. Edit each design option by adding new elements or editing the elements you copied into the design option. Make 3D and plan views showing the entrance, and duplicate each view five times. Set the visibility of each view to show the desired design option, and put the views on sheets for your presentation.

Showing quantities and cost schedules for multiple options   Making quantitative differences visible is an essential part of presenting multiple alternatives.

Master It   You need to look at some seating layout options for an auditorium space based on different-sized seating and show the seating counts.

Solution   Using design options and a Revit Auditorium Seat family, you can create two design options for the layout: one for seating 20″ wide and one for seating 24″ wide. Once these are laid out in their respective design options, you can create a schedule to count the seating based on size. By creating a seating schedule and then duplicating it, you can change the Visibility/Graphics Overrides parameter of the second schedule to count the second design option. In the following views, the two schemes have 276 and 234 seats, respectively.

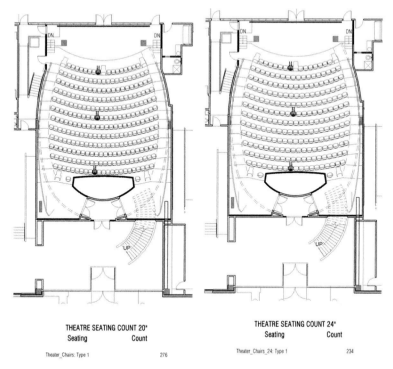

THEATRE SEATING COUNT 20"	
Seating	Count
Theater_Chairs: Type 1	276

THEATRE SEATING COUNT 24"	
Seating	Count
Theater_Chairs_24: Type 1	234

Consolidating your options and settling on a final solution   The end result of exploring multiple options is to choose one alternative and implement that choice.

> **Master It**   You've explored a number of design options for an entry scheme. Your client has selected one, and you need to incorporate it into the rest of the model and remove the unwanted alternates.
>
> **Solution**   In the Design Options dialog, select the desired option, and click Make Primary. Doing so pushes that option into all your views in the project as the default option. Now, select the option set and click the Accept Primary button. Each of your other unwanted options is eliminated, and your primary option is incorporated into the design.

Chapter 10: Creating Custom 3D Content

Understanding the different types of model families you can make   When you're making a new family, consider how it will be used in the model, and choose an appropriate template.

> **Master It**   You found a ceiling-mounted lighting fixture that you want to use in your existing project, but you can't find a Revit family for it in any libraries or online communities. How would you start?

Solution   Knowing that you need to build a lighting fixture from scratch, begin by opening the `Lighting Fixture ceiling based.rft` template file. This will ensure that the family is hosted by ceilings and will thus move and stay connected with the ceiling in which the light is placed.

Look carefully at how the fixture is built, and consider what Revit form-making tools are best suited for building it. Proceed to build the family, and assign it materials and any dimensional parameters using reference planes and labeled dimensions. When you think you're done, save the file with a unique name, load it into your project, and place it. Remember, if you need to make edits, the process is simple: Select the family, and then click the Edit Family button on the Options bar. You'll be taken directly into the Family Editor, where you can tweak the design. Clicking the Load Into Project button reloads the family into your project and updates all instances of the type with your changes.

Leveraging nested families for flexibility and efficiency   The ability to nest families in other families lets you create content that's easier to manage and improves your workflow.

Master It   Building components are often composed of a series of subcomponents that form an overall assembly. Think of some common examples and what strategies you could use to build such content in Revit.

Solution   Consider an office workstation. Typically, a workstation is made of modular components: the desk surface, vertical partitions, file cabinets, bookshelves, and a chair. You could load these elements into a project and manually manage all the parts, maybe even using groups to do so. A more efficient and easier-to-manage method is to nest various parts into one family. Starting with a blank Furniture Systems family template, you could load the desk, partitions, cabinets, and chair into one family. By making each nested family a shared family, you can tag and schedule all the elements.

Building relationships between parameters with formulas   Create smart connections between geometry and dimensions to create efficient and parametric content.

Master It   You can use dimensional relationships to tie the size of one object to the size of another. How do you do this in the context of a family?

Solution   Using the Family Types dialog, you can add new parameters and then create formulas that tie the value of one or more parameters to any other parameter. Using a conventional mathematical formula, you can create families that are extremely flexible and dynamic.

Chapter 11: Extended Modeling Techniques

Take advantage of advanced wall features   Many design situations require more than just the basic wall features; learn to use the more advanced Revit tools.

Master It   A design calls for a horizontal soldier course in a brick wall every 12´ on the façade. Using Revit, how would you build this into a wall element?

Solution   Create a new wall type and add integrated wall sweeps into the wall definition. Each wall sweep can have a material assigned to it, so you just need to define the correct size and materials to the sweep to get it to look correct. Place several instances at 12´ intervals. You can change the preview sample size of the wall to be any height in order to add additional sweeps above the default 20´.

Work with advanced roofs and slab editing   Roofs are another seemingly simple element that present architectural challenges, and Revit has tools for them.

> **Master It**   You are working on a flat roof retail project, but of course the roof is not really flat and will need to drain. Using Revit roof tools, how would you go about modeling this?
>
> **Solution**   Create your roof flat initially, and then select it. Use the shape modification tools to add ridges and low points to the roof. By selecting points, you will get temporary dimension controls to accurately set the height and get correct slopes for drainage.

Work with railings   Railings are another bread-and-butter architectural element whose design can be streamlined with Revit.

> **Master It**   You've found some nice-looking railing panels and balusters while scouring the Web for interesting rail designs. How do you go about building the railing in Revit?
>
> **Solution**   Start by figuring out what is baluster and what is rail. For the rails, you'll need to make custom profile families and use those when you define the rails in the system. For the balusters, use the baluster family templates as a starting point and break the system down into Revit-centric constructs: extrusions, blends, revolves, and sweeps. One you have the baluster made, load it into your project, make a new railing type, set up the baluster spacing, and establish the rail pattern.

Chapter 12: Presenting Your Design

Using shadows for analytical and presentation purposes   Presenting your design to stakeholders is a critical part of your workflow and allows you to sell your ideas. Having tools that make this process easier without compromising your creativity is essential to being successful.

> **Master It**   You've been asked to show the effect of your building's shadow on its surrounding site during the winter solstice. How would you do this with Revit?
>
> **Solution**   Use a site-plan view, and enable shadows from the View Control bar. Set the Sun And Shadows Settings to the correct date, time, and place. Remember to set the correct place, because this affects how shadows are calculated!

Creating elevations that convey depth   2D drawings can be hard for clients to read, which makes shadows a useful mechanism for illustrating recesses and projections.

> **Master It**   You need to give your elevation view more variation in line weight to convey depth beyond the default line styles established in the Object Styles dialog. How do you do this?
>
> **Solution**   Use the Linework tool to apply heavier lines to element edges in the foreground. Use element overrides to apply halftone or thin line weights to elements in the background.

Creating plans and sections for a print publication   Creating clean, easy-to-read plan and section views using Revit is a huge time saver.

> **Master It**   Your latest design is all the rage, and you've been asked to publish the plans and sections in a magazine. How do you make these?
>
> **Solution**   Turn off all the clutter in the view by selecting unwanted categories and elements and hiding them in the view. Then, give the walls, columns, roof, and floors a bold solid fill hatch override when cut. This will make the drawings punch on the printed page.

Creating photo-realistic renderings of your building   You know those signs that are put up at the site before and during construction—the ones with the nice rendering showing the final product? Well, you can generate those directly in Revit!

Master It   You've been asked to produce an exterior rendering of the building. Can you do this in Revit? Can you tweak the results in Photoshop?

Solution   Set up some dramatic exterior camera shots, and assign your materials photo-realistic material image maps that you bought off the Web. Fill the view with entourage such as trees, cars, and people. Raytrace the view, and then export the image so it can be touched up in Photoshop. Send the image to the print shop, and get the rendering up on a billboard.

Chapter 13: Fine-Tuning Your Preliminary Design

Create your own dynamic area plans   Once your plans are established, create your own area plans to dynamically track changes in the project.

Master It   Establish your preliminary design, and then create area plans so you can keep up-to-date with space sizes, allocations, and your project program.

Solution   Use the tools for figuring gross area and rentable area to establish these baseline plans.

Perform an initial cost estimate for the project   Create a schedule that tracks project costs based on an estimated sq. ft. cost.

Master It   Many developers and facilities managers use BOMA calculations for figuring rentable area, gross area, and R/U (rentable/usable)ratios. Establishing area plans and schedules can help you find these numbers much quicker than a legacy CAD system would have allowed.

Solution   Establish the schedules as part of your default templates, and as you create your area plans, the schedules will dynamically fill. Also, become familiar with the typical methods of calculating space. These are some of the formulas you can also incorporate in your default templates:

building rentable area + pro rata building common area = rentable area
gross rentable area / usable area = R/U ratio (load factor)
usable area × (1 + load) = rentable area

Create a schedule of materials from the model   One of the benefits of Revit is the ability to manage not only your drawings, but also other information about the project. Create schedules for your project templates to manage the materials within the project.

Master It   Schedules have a multitude of uses and value at all levels of the project. Explore a variety of schedules to optimize your workflow and maximize what you can get from the model.

Solution   Here is a list of schedules you might try:

◆ Wall schedules showing length and area by wall type

◆ Multicategory schedules showing a full list of all the families in a project

◆ Material schedules—for example, a schedule for reporting the cubic volume of concrete in the project

- ◆ Auditorium seating schedules
- ◆ Door schedules
- ◆ Parking stall schedules for parking counts by type (stalls, accessible stalls, and so on)

Chapter 14: Evaluating Your Preliminary Design: Sustainability

Incorporate a sustainable approach from project inception Sustainability is quickly becoming a core approach to any design. Learn to leverage the Revit model for a more holistic approach to sustainability.

> **Master It** BIM is also a computational database that can report information about the virtual building. The important thing about a sustainable approach is to know which questions to ask and to ask them at the right time.

> **Solution** Come up with your sustainable goals early on in the project process and revisit them regularly to make sure you stay on track.

Use Revit to track sun and shade patterns Understanding the sun's effect on a building is paramount to sustainable design.

> **Master It** Use the tools within Revit to produce still and animated solar studies from interior and exterior views in order to understand shading and the sun's effect on the building and space.

> **Solution** Use the Advanced Model Graphics dialog box to set the global location of the project. Next, establish a time of day to view the effects of the sun. Create key interior and exterior views of the project and apply these sun settings to the new views. To see the effects of the sun at that time throughout the year, animate the solar study for each week throughout the year.

Track recycled materials and other sustainable strategies using schedules Keeping track of project goals is an important part of any project process. By using the schedules and other tools in Revit, you can also track key sustainability goals.

> **Master It** Tracking recycled material usage is key to LEED credits and sustainability. Create a material schedule that tracks recycled content volume for concrete.

> **Solution** Create a schedule for the concrete in the building. Using a custom calculated field, apply your percentage of recycled content by building a formula to multiply the percentage of recycled content by the volume of concrete in the model. As you build and refine the design and the model, this value will dynamically update.

Chapter 15: Annotating Your Model

Create rooms and tag them Room elements are highly useful tools for a number of different applications in a set of documents. Learning how to use them and tag them will help you find areas, create finish schedules, and identify spaces.

> **Master It** Once the model has been largely built out, you need to start adding information about rooms and finishes. What tools would you use?

Solution   Once the areas in the project are roughly defined by walls, you can use the Room tool to add room elements to your project. After these are defined, use the schedule key in combination with a room finish schedule to quickly create finish values for each room that are easy to control and define.

Combine rooms and tags with schedules   Adding information to the room elements is only part of the documentation and design process. Knowing how to schedule that information allows you to communicate effectively with owners and contractors.

Master It   Tags are used to report information about an element. How do tags work in Revit so that they always report accurate and consistent information about the elements they tag?

Solution   Elements defined in Revit such as walls, doors, and rooms all have parameters. These parameters can be used to drive information into tags by adding labels to the tag families. If you change the parameter value, the tag will update automatically. Likewise, by editing the value in the tag, you are affecting the element.

Understand the different ways to note a project   Revit supplies you with three ways to annotate your model and the project. Knowing when to use each and planning for them early in the documentation phase saves time and frustration.

Master It   It is important to understand the relationships between elements and materials in Revit early. How does this help streamline the process of keynoting your project when you reach the documentation phase?

Solution   If this is your first project in Revit, discuss the keynoting strategy used within your office and see how easily that transitions into Revit. Set up your keynotes and schedules for those notes long before you need to document the project. This will ensure that when the time comes to begin laying out your sheets, you can do it with a minimum amount of disruption to your workflow.

If this is not your first project in Revit, begin embedding notes into your project template, building from the experiences of past projects.

Create and modify Keynotes   No set of drawings is complete without keynotes or textnotes. Understand how to create and modify them for a complete set of documents.

Master It   You will need to add notes in every stage of design to communicate your design intent on a project. How do you create and modify the notes to ensure accuracy throughout all the sheets in the set?

Solution   Use the Keynote tool on the Drafting tab to insert element, material, and user notes. As these notes are all tied to a single file and are not modifiable within the project, they will always be identical. To modify the notes, simply modify the linked text file found under Settings ➤ Keynotes.

Chapter 16: Developing the Design with Smart Workflows

Gain understanding of the principles of groups   Groups are a powerful design tool. Anyone working with repetitive elements needs to understand how they work.

Master It   Describe a fundamental benefit of using groups.

Solution   When you make a group of elements and then duplicate it many times, it is important to maintain consistent and predictable results. Using groups, you are guaranteed that a change to one instance will propagate to all other instances in the model. At the same time, Revit recognizes that some group instances might need to be slightly different from the rest and that it needs to be flexible enough to support slight differences without the necessity of creating a separate new group.

Understand workflows where groups can be used   Many projects have repetitive elements and can benefit by using groups efficiently.

Master It   Think of a scenario in your own practice where elements repeat and how you might use Revit groups to solve the problem.

Solution   A hotel room in a multistory tower is a good example of where groups could come in handy. You can draw the walls, add the bathroom and all the fixtures for one unit, and then group them in what will be a typical hotel room. Once they're grouped, you can place instances of the group throughout the model to fill out the design. From there on out, any change to any group will propagate to the other group instances.

Gain understanding of the principles of links   Links are Revit's second major tool for repetitive elements, avoiding the file size and performance issues associated with groups.

Master It   Using a link paradigm means that the BIM model now depends on links to external files. Even so, the links can be scheduled, dimensioned to, and graphically altered. Despite that, there are still some limitations. What are they?

Solution   One of the major limitations is how walls in a linked file interact with walls in the host file. For example, when a Revit link is used, none of the walls in the link will clean up with the host walls and rooms will not be calculated.

Understand workflows in which links are best applied   Knowing when to link a file can improve file performance and provides an easy way to operate on large clusters of building data. You can hide links, remove them, and work on them independently.

Master It   Knowing that links can reduce the overall file size, and thus improve performance when working in Revit, imagine a scenario in which you would most certainly want to employ links over groups.

Solution   A campus layout master plan would be a great candidate for using Links. By building a master site file and building each campus building as a separate file, you could then link them all together in the master file and have good performance in each of the separate files. This also keeps levels and grids from neighboring buildings from interfering with your workflow.

Chapter 17: Moving from Design to Detailed Documentation

Create drafting views   Not every drawing or view in Revit is created with model elements. Some of the views on sheets will be made solely with 2D drafting views. Knowing how to create and use these views is critical to any documentation package.

Master It   Keeping views hyperlinked together is a key benefit to using Revit. How do you draw simple, 2D details in Revit but still keep them parametrically linked to sheets?

Solution   By creating drafting views, you can use detail lines (found on the Drafting tab) to draft 2D details in from within Revit. These drafting views can then be placed on sheets, keeping all the same parametric values maintained by any other view created in Revit. You can also reference these drafting views with the Callout tool.

Import CAD details Even if you've been using Revit for years, you will need to import 2D geometry from an old library of standards or manufacturer drawings. Understanding how to do this effectively will keep you from having performance issues with your model.

Master It Your office has a huge repository of standard details. How do you reuse details drawn in CAD in a Revit project?

Solution Make sure the CAD detail is free of extraneous information and then import it into a drafting view at a 1:1 scale. Reset the scale to the proper scale of the view and place the new drafting view in the appropriate sheet. When forming a new detail callout from a plan or section, check the box Reference Other View on the Options bar and select the CAD detail from the list. This will give the new detail a SIM (similar) annotation.

Create 2D detail components Detail components can be used again and again within a model to graphically show in 2D different typical building components. Mastering their use keeps your use of time efficient and your frustration low.

Master It Detailing is a process of adding more granular layers of information and graphics to the model and view. What tools would you use to add 2D detail?

Solution Create detail components for content that can be reused in other views. Add as much detail to the component that is applicable, including nesting components within one another.

Use masking regions (also referred to as whiteout) to cover unneeded model geometry, taking care to balance proper modeling techniques with efficiency and productivity.

Use filled regions to add additional levels of detail and materiality to the view.

Use repeating details in lieu of copying or arraying simple 2D elements.

Finish the detail by drafting necessary areas with detail lines.

Chapter 18: Advanced Detailing Techniques

Creating 3D details 3D axonometric details are a great way to demonstrate more complex assemblies and conditions in any document set. Know how to create them in Revit to expand the ways in which you can detail.

Master It Use a 3D axonometric detail to demonstrate constructability in a unique assembly condition.

Solution Locate the new detail in a wall section or enlarged plan. Navigate to the default 3D view, and using the Orient To View tool, orient the 3D view to match the desired detail. By orbiting the orientated view, you can begin adding annotations and dimensions to describe the construction of the assembly.

Add detail components to 3D families Adding detail components to 3D families can save time by embedding the linework of a detail within the family itself and making it instantly available throughout all the locations that family is placed.

Master It Create a detail by embedding it into a family so it can be expressed by simply modifying the view detail level.

Solution Open the family in the Family Editor. By adding detail components to the family, we can begin building the corresponding detail (flashing, blocking, sealant, trim, etc.). Next, select these elements and modify their visibility to make them viewable only in specific conditions (in this case, fine level of detail). Reinserting the family into the project allows you to control what is displayed in any view by modifying the view detail in each view.

Export details for use in other Revit projects   There are times when details are common between projects. Knowing how to use details from other Revit projects will cut down on your documentation time.

> **Master It**   Use details you created in your other Revit projects.
>
> **Solution**   After finishing the detail or project, choose File ➤ Save to Library ➤ Save Views to select a variety of views and export them to your project or office standards library.

Chapter 19: Tracking Changes in Your Model

Add revisions to your project that automatically get tracked on sheets   You need the ability to track changes in your design after sheets have been issued. Adding revisions to a drawing is an inevitable part of your workflow.

> **Master It**   Add revisions to your project that automatically get tracked on your sheet.
>
> **Solution**   Use the Settings ➤ Revisions dialog to add, edit, and manage revisions. Be sure to set the numbering scheme to By Sheet.

Create revision clouds   Making an actual revision to a construction document involves adding graphics and coordinating the clouds with revisions.

> **Master It**   You need to cloud a design change. How would you do this using Revit?
>
> **Solution**   Draw clouds with the Revision Cloud tool. Next, tag your revision clouds with parametric tags. In turn, your title block will also be parametrically tied to each revision placed on the sheet.

Export your designs in a lightweight file format for review   You'll often need to allow people who don't have Revit to examine your design.

> **Master It**   How can you export your designs in a lightweight file format?
>
> **Solution**   Publish your sheets to Autodesk Design Review by choosing File ➤ Publish to DWF. You can publish either 2D or 3D data.

Chapter 20: Worksharing

Set up a project with worksets   Knowing how to activate worksharing and set up the project file for more than one person at a time is critical in any office environment.

> **Master It**   How do you work in a single Revit file on a project team with more than one member in the file at a time?
>
> **Solution**   Worksharing allows for multiple users in a Revit environment. Understanding and using worksharing is a vital part of any large-scale project where you will have more than one person doing the drawing. Worksharing will be the most successful when implemented in an organized, well-thought-out division of model assemblies. To set up worksets, first enable worksharing (File ➤ Worksets). Then save the file as a central file and inform team members to make their own local files.

Move elements between worksets   Inevitably, you will put the right element on the wrong workset. It happens. You will need to know how to move elements quickly between worksets to keep your drawings and project organized.

Master It   How do you move elements between worksets?

Solution   By selecting any element or groups of elements, you can access the element properties and change the Workset field at the bottom of the Element Properties dialog box to correspond to the workset you'd like to move the elements to.

Create a central file and local files   Once you've enabled worksharing, you'll need to understand the dynamics of central and local files to fully leverage working in a worksharing environment.

Master It   Once you have enabled worksets to allow for multiple users, what's the best way to implement and use the file?

Solution   Set up a central file on your network. Each of your users makes new, local files from the central file on their local drives and work directly in these copies. These files are smart enough to be able to manage changes between all the members of the project team while updating the central file.

Save to and load from the central file   Saving to and loading from the central file allow you to view other team members' work and allows them to see what changes to the project you have added.

Master It   How can you translate the changes you've made in your local file to the central file on the network? How do you download changes from other team members to your local file?

Solution   Use the Save To Central command on the File menu. This will copy all of your changes up to the networked central file *and* download their changes to your local file. If you are simply looking for changes others have made to update your local copy (without posting your own changes), you can use the File ➢ Reload Latest command.

Request permission to use elements owned by other team members and grant others permission to use your elements   Editing elements in a central file means you have sole ownership over further changes to those elements. Understanding the permissions will be critical to working in a team.

Master It   How do you edit an element in the model if someone has already taken permission of it in a worksharing environment?

Solution   By simply trying to edit the element, you can request permission for the object from another user on the team if permission is not readily available. They can similarly grant or deny you permission for any element they own by using the Editing Requests button on the Worksharing toolbar.

Chapter 21: Troubleshooting and Optimizing Tips

Keep your files lean and keep file performance optimized   Keeping your file optimized will save you a lot of time in the long run. It will shorten the time it takes to open the file and the time it takes to save. Regular maintenance can quickly translate into a better bottom line for the project.

Master It   How do you keep your file performance optimized?

Solution   You keep your file performance optimized by practicing good modeling techniques and performing regular file maintenance. About once a week (depending on use), you should perform the following tasks:

1. Audit your file.

2. Purge unused elements (being careful not to eliminate things you will need in the future).

3. Save to Central and compact the file.

4. Create new local files.

Create best practices for project workflow   Keeping your project file running smoothly not only helps your project process, but also the mental well-being of the people working on the project. If everyone on the project team understands the team's preferred workflow, it makes things just that much easier

Master It   How do you create a best practice workflow for your project or office?

Solution   Using Revit is an organic process, and you will find new and quicker ways of doing things the more experience you gain. Make sure to revisit your office or project library and your project templates to keep them updated with your latest families.

Repair some of the errors that can happen in Revit files   Working with a file that has become unstable can be a nightmare. You are uncertain of whether it will crash or when and you spend more time than usual saving your work. If a file does begin to behave abnormally, it's important to understand some quick and easy ways to get back on the right path.

Master It   Your file is running slowly or crashing. How do you repair the file before you begin losing time and data?

Solution   Begin with getting everyone out of the file (if it is a central file), opening it from a single station, and performing an audit on it. (In the File ➤ Open dialog box, check Audit before opening the file.) After this is complete and the file is open, choose File ➤ Purge Unused and then save to a new central location. Have each team member create new local files.

Index

A

Absolute keynote paths, 506
accelerators, **78–79**, *78*
AccuRender library, 420, *420*
AccuRender option, 90
AccuRender rendering. *See* rendering
Acquire Coordinates option, 233, 536
activating
    Project Browser views, **39**, *39*
    worksets, 619, *619*
active planes, 161
Add Link dialog, 535–536, *536*
Add Parameter option, 489–490
Add to Design Option Set dialog, 262–263, *263*
Add to Group tool, 521
additive selection, 62
Advanced Model Graphics dialog
    sun and shadows, 398–399, *398*
    sun studies, 456–457, *457*, 459
    sunlight, 416
    true-color shading, 410
AEC (Architecture, Engineering, Construction)
    world, 3, 11
Align tool, 148, *149*
aligned dimensions, 96
aligning
    elements, **72–73**, *72–73*, 148, *149*
    fill patterns, 92, *92*
    sketch lines to reference planes, 221–222
Always Vertical parameter, **292**, *292*
analytical drawings, **395–399**, *396–399*
angles
    elevation tags, 113
    extrusions, 337, *337*
    fill patterns, 92–93
    joins, 387, *387*
    railings, 382, *383*
    reference lines, 159, *159*
    revolves, 178–180, *178–179*
    roof slope, 342, 346
    rotation, 67, 69
    segments, 189, *189*
    shadows, 399
    sun, 397–398, 416–417, 458
    sweeps, 185, *186*
    units, 142, 146
    void shapes, 223
angular dimensions, 96
animation
    sun studies, **458–460**, *459–460*, **462**, *462*
    walkthroughs, **423–424**, *424*
annotations, **471**
    3D detail, **585–586**, *586*
    callouts 109, *109*
    crop regions, 571
    keynotes. *See* keynotes
    material definitions, 84
    object categories, **17**
    revision clouds, 604, *605*
    rooms. *See* rooms
    schedule keys, **481–484**, *482–484*
    separation lines, **475–476**, *475–476*
    shared parameters. *See* shared parameters
    tags. *See* tags
    text, **502–503**
    views, **471**, *471*
    visibility, 444
appearance
    materials, **90**
    schedules, 124, 440, 448, *448*
Apply Nosing Profile option, 137
Apply View Template option, 150
architecture
    history, 1–2
    sustainability in, **451–452**

Architecture, Engineering, Construction (AEC) world, 3, 11

archiving with DWFs, 610

Area Boundary tool, 432, 435

area plans

    area calculations, **430–432**, *430–432*

    vs. room areas, 479

area schedules, 438

areas

    adding, **436–437**, *436–437*

    calculating, **429–433**, *429–432*

    rooms, **478–480**, *479–481*

    settings, **145**, *146*

arrays

    creating, **304–305**, *304–305*

    elements, **70–71**, *70–71*

    in Family Editor, **297**, *297*

    formulas for, **300–301**, *301–302*

Arrow Angle setting, 113

arrowheads

    keynotes, 510

    leaders, 100

articulation, wall, **315–318**, *315–318*

artificial lighting, 417, 453

Associate Family Parameter dialog box, 306

associations

    arrays, 71

    bidirectional, 22

    shutter width, 300

asymmetric slopes on gable roofs, 346, *346*

At Library Locations method, 506

Attach Detail tool, 521

attached detail groups, 516, 524–525, *524*

auditing files, **642**, *642*

auditorium railings, 392

auto-hiding sections, **53**

Autodesk Design Review. *See* Design Review

Autodesk User Group International (AUGI), 645

automated dimensioning, 148, *148*

automating area calculations, 433

axes for revolves, 178, *178*, 180, *181*

axonometric 3D views, **56**

B

background

    rendering, **419**, *419*

    text, 100, *100*

balusters

    main patterns, **383–385**, *383–385*

    placement, 381–383, *382*

    railings, 379, *379*

    per tread on stairs, **385–387**, *386–387*

barrel roofs, 336, *336*, 338, 370, *370*

Base blend setting, 190

Base Level property, 334

base molding, **571–572**, *572*

Base Offset From Level property, 334

Basics tab

    design bar, 51, 272

    rooms, 472

    text, 502

Begin with a Riser setting, 137

Beginning setting for baluster patterns, 384, *385*

behavior of keynotes, **504–505**

bidirectional associations, 22

bidirectional relationships, **19–22**, *20–22*

BIM. *See* Building Information Modeling (BIM)

binding links, 533, 538, *539*

black and white high-contrast effects, **400**, *400*

blends, **190–191**, *190–191*

    examples, **197**, *197*

    for lamp, **194–196**, *194–196*

    troubleshooting, **192**, *193–194*

    vertices, **191**, *192*

blocks, 19

Bold setting, 101

BOMA (Building Owners and Managers Association) area calculations, 430

Boolean joins, 251

borrowing elements, **629**

Bottom view range for floor plans, 41, *42*

boundary lines, 432, *432*

bounding boxes, 480, *480*

Break Symbol in Plan setting, 136, *137*

Broken Section Display Style setting, 103, *103*

broken section lines, **52**, *52*

building area schedule updates, 443

Building Information Modeling (BIM), **1**
    advantages, **1–4**
    for creativity, **4**, *5*
    documents, **7**, *8*
    Family Editor, **8**, *8*
    interaction, **6**
    layers and X-References, **9**
    as new technology, **10**
    problem-solving designs, **7**, *7*
    as process change, **9–10**
    properties, **6**, *6*
    working with, **10–11**, *11*
Building Maker tools, 207
    advantages, **238**
    design verification, **239–243**, *240–244*
    Floor Area, **239**, *240*
Building Owners and Managers Association
    (BOMA) area calculations, 430
By Category tag option, 485, 488
By Date, Time, and Place sun angle setting, 398, 458
By Host railings option, 389
By Keynote numbering option, 506
By Project revision numbering option, 602
By shared coordinates option, 233, 536
By Sheet option
    keynote numbering, 506
    revision numbering, 602
By Type railings option, 389, *389*

C

CAD files and formats
    details, **545–547**, *546–547*
    exploding, **636**
    linking, **543–545**, *544*
calculated fields, 447, *447*
calculations
    areas, **429–433**, *429–432*
    room volume, 636, *636*
    stairs, **135**, *136*
Callout tool, 559
callouts and callout tags
    custom, **108–112**, *109–112*
    elevation, 114
    working with, **556–557**, *556–557*

cameras
    3D views, 56, *57*, 413
    sun studies, 454–456, *455–456*
carbon footprints, 451
Cascade option, 31
Cast Shadows option, 457
categories, **13–15**, *14–15*
    annotation, **17**
    imported, **18**, *18*
    Model Object, **15–17**, *15–16*
    for shared parameters, **495–497**, *495–496*
CDs (Construction Documents), 6
ceilings
    floor connections and details, **573–574**, *573–574*
    plans, 42, *42*
    types, **134–135**
Center setting, 384, *385*
Center-to-center option, 232, 536
Centerline Pattern option, 98
Centerline Symbol option, 98
Centerline Tick Mark option, 99
central files, 617
    saving, 621
    workflows, **625–626**, *626*
    working on, 623
    in worksharing, 618, *618*
CFDs (computational fluid dynamics), 467
chain selection, 62
chairs
    arrays, **304–305**, *304–305*
    nesting, **303**, *303*
    visibility, **306–307**, *306–307*
Change Sweep Return option, 322
change tracking, **601**
    Design Review. *See* Design Review
    parametric modeling and supplemental
        drawings, **607**
    revisions, **601–607**, *601–607*
classification system, 14
Close Hidden Windows option, 31, 636
closed loops
    blends, 197, *197*
    profiles, 283, *283*
    revolves, 179–180, *179–180*
    sketches, 156, *156*
    sweeps, 185

closing unused DWGs, 636

coarse settings
    Scale Fill parameter, 407
    wall detail, 132

color
    dimensions, 99
    elevation tags, 113
    elevations, **410**, *410*
    fill schemes, 151, **402–405**, *403–405*
    legends, 403
    level tags, 115
    lines, 85
    text, 100

color-coded plans and sections, **401–402**, *402*
    fill schemes, **402–405**, *403–405*
    presentation plans, **405–408**, *406–407*
    sections, **405**, *405–406*

combining revisions, 603

commas (,) in type-catalog syntax, 141

common edges, 143–145, *144*

communication with teams, 643

complex roofs, 199, *199*

compound walls, 315, *315*

computational fluid dynamics (CFDs), 467

conceptual design and early studies, **229**, *230*
    3D context building, **233**, *234–235*
    Building Maker tools
        advantages, **238**
        design verification, **239–243**, *240–244*
        Floor Area, **239**, *240*
    building mass and underlying mass relationships, **256**, *256–257*
    imported geometry. *See* imported files and geometry
    massing best practices, **244–246**, *245*
        curtain systems by face, **249**
        design options, 237
        Floor by Face tool, **246–247**, *247–248*
        roofs by face, **249**
        scheduling, **249–251**, *250–252*
        Wall by Face tool, **246**
    program check and feasibility, **235–236**, *236*
    site data and context, **230–233**, *231–232*

conditional visibility, **296**, *297*

cone roofs, 368, *368*

constraints
    design stage, **22**, *23*
    move, 66, **75**, *76*
    in performance, 641

Construction Document set, 289

Construction Documents (CDs), 6

context, building, **230–233**, *231–232*

converting groups into links, 533, *533–534*

copies in performance, 637

Copy tool, 67

copying
    area boundaries, 436, *436*
    color, 404, *406*
    with Copy, 67
    groups, 526
    with Move, 66
    options, **63–64**, *63*
    sweeps, 186
    system families, 24, *25*

cores, walls, **309–311**, *310–311*

Corner Radius option, 108

corruption, file, **642–643**, *642–643*

cost estimates, **446–448**, *447–448*

cost schedules, **272**, *272*

Create Floors tool, 246

Create Instance group option, 526

Create Mass tool, 207, 212, 233, 253

Create Roof tool, 255

Create View Template From View option, 35, *35*

creativity, **4**, *5*

crop regions
    annotations, 571
    perspective views, 58, *59*

cupolas, 180, *181*

Current View copying option, 64

Current View Only option, 545

Curtain Grid tool, 327

Curtain Grid Line tool, 330

curtain panel families, **290**, *290*

curtain systems
    by face, **249**
    with Rhino, 255–256

curtain walls, **325–326**, *325–326*
    designing, **326–329**, *327–329*
    doors and windows, **330**, *331*
    panels, **330**, *331*

custom 3D content, **279**
    encoding design rules, **298–302**, *299–302*
    families
        building, **303–307**, *303–307*
        categories and parameters, **291–293**,
            291–292
        curtain panel, **290**, *290*
        detail component, **289**, *289*
        face-based, **287**, *287*
        generic, **289**
        host-based, **282–283**, *282*
        line-based, **285–286**, *286–287*
        linking parameters, **295–296**, *295–297*
        modeling, **279–280**, *279*
        nesting, **292–295**, *293–295*
        profile, **283–285**, *283–285*
        RPC, **288**, *288–289*, 292
        template selection, **280**, *280–281*
        types, **280**
        work plane-based, **288**
    parametric arrays, **297**, *297*
custom keynotes, **120**, *120–121*
custom line types, **551**, *552*
custom patterns, **92–95**, *92, 95*, 389
custom tags, **101–103**, *102*, **116–119**, *116–119*,
    606–607, *607*
custom templates, **81–84**, *82*
custom title blocks, **121–125**, *121–125*
custom walls, **128–129**, *129*
    default wrapping, **131–132**, *132*
    layers, **129–131**, *130–131*
    preview window, **129**
Cut Geometry tool, 209–210, *210*
cut graphics, 16, *16*
Cut Line Styles, 143
Cut Pattern option, 90
Cut Plan Profile tool, 169, *169*, 337, *337*
Cut planes, **41–44**, *43–44*
Cutoff Level property, 334
Cutoff Offset property, 334
cylinder mass elements, 214, *214*

D

datum planes, 160, *160*
defaults
    element settings, **147–151**
    graphics settings, 145
        keynote text files, 505
        view templates, 150
        wall wrapping, **131–132**, *132*
        Work Planes, **166–170**, *166–170*
Defines Slope option, 333–334
Delete Dedicated Options Views dialog, 267, *267*
Delete Inner Segment option, 74
deleting
    dimension types, 99
    markups, 615
    materials, 88
    tags, 473, *473*
    text type, 101
    unused DWGs and views, 636
Deny/Retract option, 631
dependent views, 17
depth
    blends, 190
    elevations for, **408–412**, *408–412*
    extrusions, 175
    view, **44–46**, *44–46*
Design bar, 30, *31*
    for massing creation, 209, *209*
    Rendering tab, **416–419**
    tools, **32–33**, *32*
design cycle, 453
design options, **259–260**, *259*
    design-option sets, **260–261**, *261*
    displaying, **264–266**, *265–266*
    editing, **262**, *263*
    elements for, **261–264**, *262–263*
    enabling, **260**
    in practice, **268–271**, *268–271*
    quantities and cost schedules, **272**, *272*
    rooms, **272–275**, *273–275*
    selecting, **266–267**, *267*
Design Review, **607**, **609**
    importing markups, **614–615**, *614*
    interface, **609–610**, *609–610*
    model markup in, **613**, *613–614*
    publishing to, **610–612**, *611–613*
design rules, encoding, **298–302**, *299–302*
Designer role, 645
designing curtain walls, **326–329**, *327–329*
detail groups, 516, **531–532**, *532*, **547–548**

details and detail components, 15–16, *15*, **541**
   3D, 581
      annotations, **585–586**, *586*
      creating, **581–586**, *582–586*
   callouts, **556–557**, *556–557*, 559
   creating, **548**
   drafting views, **541–542**, *542*
   embedding within families, **586–590**, *587–590*
   exporting, **594–595**, *595–596*
   families, **289**
   groups, **524**, *524*
   importing and linking, **542–547**, *543–544,*
     546–547
   importing views, **595–597**, *596–597*
   information for, **557–559**, *558–559*
   keynotes, 509, *509*
   line tools. *See* line tools
   for line types, **551**, *552*
   nesting, **576**, *576–577*
   properties, **550–551**, *551*
   repeating, **548–551**, *549–552*, **575**, *575*
   rotating, 551
   shaft opening, **598**, *598*
   symbolic lines for, **592–594**, *592–594*
   tips, **578**
   visibility settings, **591–592**, *591–592*
   wall sections
      model details, **566–578**, *567–578*
      SIM condition, **560–566**, *560–566*
.dgn files, 544
Dimension tool, 217, 390
dimensions
   defaults, **148**, *148*
   in family details, 588, *588*
   formulas for, **299–300**, *299–300*
   in moving elements, **65–66**, *65*
   styles, **96–99**, *96–99*
   in views, 471
Direct Editing tool, 373
directions in Reference Planes, **177**, *177*
Directly sun angle setting, 398
Disallow Join option, 313, *313*
Disassociate option, 165
disjoining
   hosted elements, 66
   walls, **313**, *313*

displaying design options, **264–266**, *265–266*
Dist. from Previous setting, 384
documentation. *See* annotations
Documenter role, 645
documents, 7, *8*
dome roofs, 180, *181*, 337, *338*, 369, *369*
Door category, 46
door knobs, 182, *182*
doors
   curtain wall, **330**, *331*
   defaults, 148
   host-based families, 282, *282*
   in modeling principles, 171, *171*
   rotating, **68**, *68*
   symbolic lines for, **594**, *594*
   tags, 472, **486–488**, *488*
      custom, **117–119**, *117–119*
      shared parameters for, **497–501**, *498–501*
   types, **135**
dormers, hipped roofs with, 359, *359–360*, 362,
   362–364, 366, *366–367*
drafting lines
   for elevations, **409**
   reusing, **567**, *567*
drafting patterns, 90–91
Drafting tab
   keynotes, 504, 506
   tags, 485–487, *485*
   text, 502
drafting views, **541–542**, *542*
drainage points, 374
Draw Points tool, 373
Draw Split Lines tool, 373–374, *374*
drawing list schedules, 438
Duplicate option
   groups, 526
   materials, 88
Dutch gables, 355, *355–358*, 357
DWF files, 607
   archiving, 610
   in performance, 641
   sharing, 609
DWG files
   importing and linking, **230–233**, *231–232*, 544
   in performance, 637
   with SketchUp, 252

.dxf files, 544
Dynamic View dialog, 58, *58*, 413, *413*

E

edges
    common, 143–145, *144*
    silhouette, **414**, *414–415*
Edit Assembly dialog
    floors and roofs, 134, *134*
    split sections, 318, *318*
    sweeps and reveals, 319
    wall cores, 309, *310*
    wall tools, 315, *316*
    walls, 128–129, *129*, 132
Edit Baluster Placement dialog, 381–383, *382*
Edit Base blend setting, 190
Edit Color Scheme dialog, 403, *403*
Edit Joins tool, 388, *388*
Edit option
    extrusions, 175
    groups, 526
Edit Rails dialog, 381, *381*
Edit Roof Structure dialog, 375, *375*
Edit Shared Parameters dialog, 492–495, *492–494*, *496*
Edit Top blend setting, 190
Edit Wall Joins tool, 312, *312*
Edit Work Plane option, 165, **175–176**, *176–177*
editable worksets, 620, *620*
editing
    actions for, **61**
        aligning, **72–73**, *72–73*
        arraying, **70–71**, *70–71*
        constraints, **75**, *76*
        copying and pasting, **63–64**, *63*
        joins, **76**, *77*
        keyboard shortcuts, **78–79**, *78*
        moving, **64–67**, *65–67*
        offsetting, **74**, *75*
        painting, **76**, *77–78*
        pinning, **75**
        Place Similar, **64**
        resizing, **71–72**, *72*
        rotating and mirroring, **67–70**, *68–70*
        selecting, **61–63**, *61–62*
        splitting, **74**, *74*, **76**, *77–78*

        trimming and extending lines and walls, **73–74**, *73–74*
    blend vertices, **191**, *192*
    design options, **262**, *263*
    groups, **531**, *531*
    keynotes, **504–505**
    materials, **88–90**, *89*, **420**, *421*
    schedules, **448–449**, *448–449*
    sketches, 157
    wall joins, **312**, *312*
    Work Planes, 165
Editing Requests dialog box, 631–632, *631–632*
electrical lighting, 417, 453
Element Properties dialog, **6**, *6*
    callout tags, 111
    cost schedules, 272
    door tags, 118
    elevation tags, 114
    Height Offset From Level parameter, 243, *243*
    revision clouds, 604, *605*
    scope boxes, 161, *161*
    section tags, 108
    stairs, 135–136, *136*
    system families, 24
    templates, 150, *150*
    text, 100
    visibility, 306
    wall wrapping, 319
    walls, 128
    worksets, 623–624, *623–624*
elements
    aligning, **72–73**, *72–73*
    arraying, **70–71**, *70–71*
    borrowing, **629**
    for design options, **261–264**, *262–263*
    for keynotes, 119, 504, **511–512**, *512*
    moving, **64–67**, *65–67*
    ownership, **628–632**, *628–632*
    pinning, **75**
    resizing, **71–72**, *72*
    rotating and mirroring, **67–70**, *68–70*
    tagging, 472
elevations, **408**, *408*
    default settings, 149, *149*
    images in, **411–412**, *412*
    Linework tool, **408–409**, *408–409*

Project Browser views, **53–56**, *54–55*

tags for, **112–115**, *112–114*

transparent materials, **411**, *411*

true-color, **410**, *410*

embedding details within families, **586–590**, *587–590*

Empty glazing setting, 370

enabling

design options, **260**

design rules, **298–302**, *299–302*

shadows, **397–398**, *398*

End setting for baluster patterns, 384, *385*

End angle resolve setting, 178, *178*

End with a Riser setting, 137

energy analysis, **466–468**, *467–469*

Entire Walls option, 148

Environment dialog, 419, *419*

Exclude feature, 528

Exclude Options option, 263

Explain Error tool, 477, *477*

exploding imported CAD files, **636**

exporting, **424**, *425*

details, **594–595**, *595–596*

to gbXML, **467–468**, *468*

sun studies, **461**, *461*

sun views, 459

expressive drawings, shadows for, 395, *396*, **399–401**, *400–401*

Extend Below Base setting, 136

extending

datum planes, 160

lines and walls, **73–74**, *74*

extending pergola, gable roofs with, 351, *351*

exterior skins, **265**, *265*

external text files, 504

extruded roof dormers, hipped roofs with, 366, *366–367*

Extrusion end setting, 175

Extrusion start setting, 174, *175*

extrusions

roofs by, **166–170**, *166–170*, **336–337**, *336–337*

working with, **174–177**, *174–177*

F

face-based families, **287**, *287*

faces with extrusions, 176

families and Family Editor, **8**, *8*, **13–15**, *14*, **23**

3D. *See* custom 3D content

vs. blocks, 19

callout tags, 108–111, *111*

ceilings, **134–135**

for custom title blocks, **122–125**, *122–125*

door tags, 498

doors and windows, **135**

elevation tags, 114

embedding details within, **586–590**, *587–590*

floors and roofs, **133–134**, *134*

in-place, **27–28**, *28*

loadable, 171, *171*

managing, 101

mass placement, 212

parametric mass family creation, 215, 218, *219*

for primary forms, 174, *174*

profiles, 319

Project Browser views, **38**, *39*

section view tags, **104–107**, *106*

stairs, **135–139**, *135–139*

standard, **25–27**, *25–27*

system, **23–24**, *24–25*

templates, **280**, *280–281*

types. *See* types and type catalogs

visibility settings, 284, *284*, 591–593, *591–593*

wall wrapping, 319, *319*

walls, 131

worksets, 620

Family Category and Parameters dialog, 291, *291*

Family Creator role, 645

Family Types dialog

arrays, 304, *304*

dimensions, 299–300, *300*

parametric mass family creation, 218, *219*

RPC, 288, *288*, 292

visibility, 306

FAR (Floor Area Ratio), 235

feasibility, program, 205, *205*, **235–236**, *236*

feet units, 146

fences. *See* railings

Field of View tab, 58, *58*

Fields tab, 440, *440*, 447, 482

File Locations tab, 82, *82*
File Save Options dialog, 626, *626*
filenaming conventions, keynotes, **505**
files
    corruption, **642–643**, *642–643*
    linking, **535–536**, *536*
    workflow, **626–627**, *626*
Fill Available Space modes, 551
Filled Region tool, 405, **553–554**, *553–554*
fills and fill patterns
    color, 115, **402–405**, *403–405*
    custom title blocks, 123
    for details, 573–574, *573–574*
    elevation tags, 113
    graphics, 407, *407*
    materials, **90–95**, *91–93*, *95*
    regions, **553–554**, *553–554*
filtering
    keynotes, 507, *508*
    schedules, 440, 442, *442*
    selections, **62**, *62*
Fine level of detail, 132
First end blend setting, 190
Fixed Distance modes, 551
Fixed Number modes, 551
Flat railing option, 389
flat roofs, 345, *345*
flexing models, 218
flip controls, 68, *69*
Flip Orientation option, 254
Flipped Dimension Line Extension option, 98
Floor Area tool, **239**, *240*
Floor Area Faces tool, 239, 246
Floor Area Ratio (FAR), 235
Floor by Face tool, 242, **246–247**, *247–248*
Floor Edit tools, 246
floor plans, **40**, *41*
    Cut planes, **41–44**, *43–44*
    primary range, **43–44**, *43–44*
    View Depth, **44–46**, *44–46*
    View Range, **40–42**, *41–42*
floors
    bidirectional relationships, 20–21
    ceiling connections and details, **573–574**, *573–574*
    in modeling principles, 170–171

sketch-based design, **154–157**, *155–156*
    types, **133–134**, *134*
Font setting, 136
footprint roofs, **332–335**, *332–336*
force units, 142
formats
    CAD, **543–547**, *544*, *546–547*
    exporting to, **424**, *425*
formatting schedules, 440–441, *441*, *447*, *449*, *449*
formulas
    arrays, **300–301**, *301–302*
    dimensions, **299–300**, *299–300*
Foundation model, **427–428**
    area calculations, **429–433**, *429–432*
    areas and tags, **436–437**, *436–437*
    change tracking, **608**, *608*
    rentable area plans, **433–435**, *433–435*
    schedules. *See* schedules
    worksets, **621–623**, *622–623*
four-sided gable roofs, 364, *364–365*
freestanding elements
    railings, 378, *378*
    rotating, **68**
Function column for wall layers, **130**
Furniture category, 46
Furniture System category, 46

G

gable roofs, 350, *350*
    with asymmetric slopes, 346, *346*
    Dutch gable with glazed roofs, 355, *355–356*
    Dutch gables, 357, *357–358*
    with extending pergola, 351, *351*
    four-sided, 364, *364–365*
    hip and gable, 352, *352–353*
gambrel roofs, 353, *353–354*
gbXML, **467–468**, *468*
generic 3D families, **289**
Generic Models category, 15
Generic template, 119
glazed panels, 326
Global Project Settings, 145
globally unique identifiers (GUIDs), 501
Go to View dialog, 163, *163*, 561, *561*
granting permissions, **630–632**, *631–632*

graphic appearance
consistency settings
dimension styles, **96–99**, *96–99*
Fill Patterns, **90–95**, *91–93*, *95*
Line Patterns, **87–88**, *87–88*
Line Styles, **85–86**, *86*
Materials Editor, **88–90**, *89*
Object Styles, **84–85**, *85*
text, **100–101**, *100–101*
markups, 613–615
schedules, **448–449**, *448–449*
graphic overrides, **143–145**, *143–144*, 407, *407*
graphical selection, **476–477**, *477–478*
graphics cards, 637, *637*
Green Building Studio service, **468**, *469*
Green Building xml, **467–468**, *468*
grids, **160–161**, *160*
curtain walls, 325, *325–326*, 328, *328*
tags, **116**
Work Planes, 164, *164*
Grids worksets, 619
gross area
calculations, 430
floors, 241–242, *241*
plans, **431–432**, *431–432*
gross building schedules, 438
Group Edit mode, 520–521, *520*, *522*
Group Edit toolbar, 521
Group Editor, 520
Group Properties dialog, 521
groups, **516**
adding rooms to, **521–522**, *522*
arrays, 70–71, *71*
best practices for, **532–533**
creating and managing, **517**
detail, **531–532**, *532*, **547–548**
detail elements for, **524**, *524*
editing, **531**, *531*
vs. links, **538–539**, *539*
moving elements in, **530–531**, *530*
nesting, **523–525**, *523–525*, 529
parameters, **493–494**, *493–494*
as parts of projects, **529**, *530*
Project Browser views, **39**
repeating, **516–521**, *516–521*, **528–529**, *529*
variations, **525–528**, *526–528*
GUIDs (globally unique identifiers), 501

H

half hipped roofs, **360–362**, *360–362*
hatch patterns, **90–95**, *91–93*, *95*
head graphics in section tags, **107–108**, *107–108*
heads, callout, 109, *110*
Height setting for cylinder mass elements, 214, *214*
Height Offset At Head setting, 343
Height Offset From Level setting, 243, *243*
Help menu, 645
hiding
markups, 615
sections, **53–54**, *54*
high-contrast black and white effects, **400**, *400*
hip and gable hybrid roofs, 352, *352–353*
hipped roofs, 348–349, *348–349*
with extruded roof dormers, 366, *366–367*
half, **360–362**, *360–362*
with sloped arrow dormers, 359, *359–360*
with two dormers, 362, *362–364*
historical data, 468
History dialog box, 627
history of design and documentation, **1–2**
Horizontal tag orientation, 487
host-based elements, 263
host-based families, **282–283**, *282*
Host Layer Line Styles dialog box, 143–145, *144*
host objects in graphic overrides, **143–145**, *143–144*
Host Sweep tool, 322

I

identical buildings on shared sites, **535**
Identity Data property, 479
Identity tab, 90, 491
IES <Virtual Environment> application, **467**, *467*
Image Mapping dialog, 421, *421–422*
images in elevation views, **411–412**, *412*
Imperial library, 508
imperial units, 146
Import Instance Query dialog, 547, *547*
imported files and geometry
categories and subcategories for, **18**, *18*
exploding, **636**
Inventor for, **256**
limitations, 18
in performance, 637

positioning, **232–233**

Rhino for, **255–256**, *255–256*

SketchUp for, **252–254**, *253–254*

importing

3D conceptual models, **224–225**, *224*

Design Review markups, **614–615**, *614*

details, **542–547**, *543–544, 546–547*, 588, *589*

DWG/DGN site information, **230–233**, *231–232*

patterns, **94–95**, *95*

with SketchUp, 253, *253*

views, 537, **595–597**, *596–597*

in-place families, **27–28**, *28*, 171, *172*

in-place roofs, **337–338**, *338*

in-place walls, **324**, *324*

inches units, 146

infill wall types, 326

information for details, **557–559**, *558–559*

Insert 2D Elements dialog, 597, *597*

Inside detail option, 551

instance parameters, **19**

Insulation Bulge to Width Ratio setting, 552

Insulation tool, **552**, *553*

intensities, sun, 399, *399*

interaction, **6**

interface. *See* user interface

interior lights, **417–418**, *418*

Interior Tick Mark option, 99

Interiors workset, 621

Inventor software, **256**

invisible lines, 118

Is Reference parameter, 216

issuing revisions, 602–603

Italic setting, 101

J

jogged sections, **52**, *52*

Join Geometry tool, **76**, *77*, 210, 249

joins, **76**, *77*

masses, 210, *211–212*, 249–251, *250–251*

walls, **312**, *312*

K

Keep Readable option, 92, *92*

keyboard shortcuts, **78–79**, *78*

Keyboard.txt file, 79

Keynote command, 504

keynote legend schedules, 439

Keynote Text style, 509

keynotes, **119–120**, *120–121*, **503–504**, *503*

behavior and editing, **504–505**

elements for, **511–512**, *512*

family, **508–512**, *508–511*

filenaming conventions, **505**

legends, 439, **507**, *507–508*

predefining, **512–513**, *512–513*

schedules, **508**

settings, **147**, *147*

in views, 471, **506**, *506*

wall sections, **509–510**, *509–511*

keys, schedule, **481–484**, *482–484*

Koolhaas, Rem, 534, *535*

L

labels

custom title blocks, 123

keynotes, 120

section view tags, **104**

shared parameters, 500

lamp, **194–196**, *194–196*

lampshade, 197, *197*

Landing Carriage Height setting, 139

Landing Overlap setting, 136

landings, **387**, *387*

layer joins cleanup, **311–312**, *312*

layers, **9**

custom walls, **129–131**, *130–131*

importing and linking, 545

merging, 318, *318*

overrides, 143–145, *144*

position, **132**, *132*

splitting, **317–318**, *317–318*

Layout modes, 551

LCR (Lot Coverage Ratio), 235

Le Corbusier, 2

Leader Arrowhead setting, 100

leader lines, 607, *607*

Leadership in Environmental and Energy Design (LEED) system, 452, 465

legends, keynotes, 439, **507**, *507–508*

length
keynotes, 120
lines, 98
nosing, 137
units, 142, 146
Level tool, 239
levels, **159–160**
bidirectional relationships, 20–21, *21*
default settings, 149
floor plans, 40, *40*
rooms, 478
tags, **115**, *115*
levels of detail
families, 586
in performance, **638–639**
walls, **132**, *133*
Libeskind, Daniel, 3, *3*
libraries
keynotes, 508
materials, 420, *420*
organizing, **26–27**, *26–27*
lifecycle costs, 203
lighting, **416–418**, *417–418*
lighting fixtures, 282, *282*
Limit Offset property, 478
line-based families, **285–286**, *286–287*
line patterns
creating, **87–88**, *87–88*
elevation tags, 113
level tags, 115
line tools
custom title blocks, 122
Filled Region, **553–554**, *553–554*
Insulation, **552**, *553*
Linework, **408–409**, *408–409*, **555–556**, *556*
Show Hidden Lines, **554–555**, *554–555*
linear arrays, 70
lines
boundary, 432, *432*
invisible, 118
offsetting, **74**, *75*
repeating details for, **551**, *552*
separation, **475–476**, *475–476*
splitting, **74**, *74*
styles, **85–86**, *86*, 143
symbolic, **592–594**, *592–594*
trimming and extending, **73–74**

lineweights, 85, *86*
dimensions, 98
elevation tags, 113
level tags, 115
text, 100
links and linking, **533**, *533–534*
common uses, **534–535**, *535*
details, **542**, *543*
CAD details, **545–547**, *546–547*
CAD formats, **543–545**, *544*
files, **535–536**, *536*
vs. groups, **538–539**, *539*
markups, 614
parameters, **295–296**, *295–297*
Project Browser views, **38**
special features, **536–537**
unloading and reloading, 537
visibility, **537–538**, *538*
live connections, links for, 543
Load from Library dialog box, 26, *26*
loadable family types, 171, *171*
loaded profiles for sweeps, 185
loading
group files, 525, *525*
mass families, 212, *213*
shared work, **628**
tags, **485**
from type catalogs, **142**, *143*
local files
in performance, 637
in workflows, **626–627**, *626*
Lockable Door parameter, 500
loops
blends, 197, *197*
profiles, 283, *283*
revolves, 179–180, *179–180*
sketches, 156, *156*
sweeps, 185
Lot Coverage Ratio (LCR), 235

M

M_Generic Tag.rtf template, 119
M-Miscellaneous Wide Flange-Column.rfa family, 141
Main Model, 260–264, 266

Make Elements Editable option, 628, *628*
Make Workset Editable option, 619
Manage Links dialog, 543, *544*
Manage Place and Locations dialog, 397, *397*, 458
manual dimensioning, 148
Map tab, 421, *421*
markups
    Design Review for, **613**, *613–614*
    importing, **614–615**, *614*
masking regions, **548**, *549*
Mass.rft template, 213
Mass Element.rft template, 213, 215
massing and massing studies, **201–203**, *201–203*
    3D contexts, 233
    best practices, **244–246**, *245*
        curtain systems by face, **249**
        design options, 237
        Floor by Face tool, **246–247**, *247–248*
        roofs by face, **249**
        scheduling, **249–251**, *250–252*
        Wall by Face tool, **246**
    Design bar, 32
    Floor Area tool, 239
    importing 3D conceptual models, **224–225**, *224*
    mass creation, **208–210**, *209–212*
    mass element creation, **207–208**, *207–208*
    mass family creation, **213–214**, *214*
    mass family placement, **212–213**, *212–213*
    mass joining, 249–251, *250–251*
    mass scheduling, **224**
    mass tags, **223**
    parametric mass family example, **215–223**, *215–223*
    primary forms, 173–174, *174*
    rapid prototyping and 3D printing services, **225–226**, *225–226*
    tools, **206–208**, *206–208*
    uses, **204–205**, *204–206*
    workflows, 172, *173*, **203–204**
Match option for groups, 526
Match Properties option, 63
Material column for wall layers, **130**
Material Editor, 420–421, *421*
Material Library dialog, 420
material takeoff schedules, 438

materials
    editing, **88–90**, *89*, **420**, *421*
    fills, **90–95**, *91–93*, *95*
    keynotes, 119, 504, **509–510**, *509–511*, 512
    non-image based, **422**, *422*
    parameters, 491, *491*
    rendering, **419–422**, *420–422*
    stairs, 137
    tags, 486
    texture maps for, **420–421**, *421–422*
    tracking, **463–464**, *464–465*
    for types, 140
    wall finish, **316–318**, *316–318*
Maximize Extents option, 160
Maximum Riser Height setting, 137
Maximum Segment Angle setting, 189, *189*
Maximum Spacing modes, 551
mechanical, engineering, and plumbing (MEP) consultants, 451
Medium level of detail, 132
Membrane Layer option, 130
merging layers, 318, *318*
metal decks, 575–576, *575–576*
Metric library, 508
Metric Mass.rft template, 215
metric units, 146
Middle Stringers setting, 138
Minimum Tread Depth setting, 137
Mirror tool, **70**, *70*
mirroring elements, **67–70**, *68–70*
mistakes in worksharing, **629**
Miter joins, 312, *312*
model groups, 516
Model Object categories, **15–17**, *15–16*
model patterns, 90–91
Modeling design bar, 171, *171*
modeling principles, **153–154**, *154*
    blends, **190–197**, *190–197*
    extrusions, **174–177**, *174–177*
    overview, **170–174**, *171–174*
    revolves, **178–182**, *178–183*
    sketch-based design, **154**
        floors, **154–157**, *155–156*
        Work Planes, **157–162**. *See also* Work Planes
    solids and voids, **198–199**, *198–199*
    sweeps, **183–189**, *184–189*

Modeling tab, 173, *174*

models

3D physical, **202–203**, *202*

details, **566–578**, *567–578*

importing, **224–225**, *224*

objects, **84**, *85*

rapid prototyping, **225–226**, *225–226*

Modify Sub Elements tool, 373

Modify Vertical Structure options, 319

Monolithic Stair setting, 136

More Tools flyout, 33, *33*

Move To 2nd option, 70, *70*

Move tool, **66**, *66*

moving elements, **64**

in groups, **529–531**, *530*

with nearby elements, **67**, *67*

nudging, **66**, *66*

with temporary dimensions, **65–66**, *65*

between worksets, **623–625**, *624–625*

mullions, 325, 326, 328, *328–329*

Multi-Category tags, 485

Multi-Day sun settings, 457, 459–460, *460*, 462, *462*

multicategory schedules, 438

multipitch roofs, 371, *371–372*

Multiple Alignment option, 72

multiple buildings on shared site plans, **534–535**, *535*

Multiple Copy or Array command, 239

multiple massing design options, **237**, *237–238*

muntins, 299, *299*

N

names

callout tags, 111, *111*

dimension types, 99

door tags, 499–500, *499–500*

elevation tags, 113–114

line patterns, 87

materials, 88

section tags, 107

text type, 101

Work Planes, 162

natural daylight, 453

navigator pane, 610

Nearby Elements feature, **67**, *67*

nesting

chairs, **303**, *303*

detail components, **576**, *576–577*

families, 214, **292–295**, *293–295*

groups, **523–525**, *523–525*, 529

links, 537

New dialog

door tags, 498

parametric mass family creation, 215

New Area Plan dialog, 431, *431*

New Drafting View dialog, 542, *542*, 546, *546*

New Pattern dialog, 91, 93–95, *93*, *95*

New Schedule dialog, 438, 440, 481, *482–483*

No Edge option, 145

non-image based materials, **422**, *422*

non-linear sections, 103

nonstraight segments, 375

Nosing Length setting, 137

Nosing Profile setting, 137

note block schedules, 439

notes

keynotes. *See* keynotes

text, **119–120**, *120–121*

nudging elements, **66**

numbering

keynotes, 506

revisions, **602**

NURBS shape, 224, *224*

NURBS surfaces, 255–256, *255–256*

O

Object Styles dialog, 14, *14*

Annotation Objects tab, 17, 101, *102*

floor plans, 40

for graphic consistency, **84–85**, *85*

graphics rules, 143, *144*

Imported Objects tab, 18, *18*

Model Object tab, 15–16

revision clouds, 604, *605*

standard families, 25

offsets

Floor by Face tool, 247, *248*

lines and walls, **74**, *75*

opaque filled regions, 553, *553*

Open dialog
    auditing files, 642
    libraries, 27, *27*
Open Stringer Offset setting, 139
optimizing. *See* troubleshooting and optimizing
   tips
Options bar, 30, *31*
    parts, **33**
    railings, 388, *388*
orientation
    3D views, **56**, *57*, **584–585**, *584–585*
    fill patterns, 92, *92*
    imported site data, **231–232**, *231–232*
    tags, 487
    walls, 254
Origin-to-origin option, 232, 536
origins
    groups, 518–519, *518*
    linked files, 232, 536
    orienting, 92
    rotation, 68–69, *69*
overconstrained objects, 641
Overhang parameter, 333
overlapping items
    rooms, 474–475, *474–475*
    walls, 518
overrides. *See* Visibility/Graphic Overrides dialog
ownership of elements, **628–632**, *628–632*

P

Paint tool, 76, *77*
Palladio, Andrea, 1
panels
    curtain, **290**, *290*, *325*, *326*, *327*, **330**, *331*
    SIPs, 567–568
parameters and parametric elements, **13–15**, *14–15*
    3D models and families, 3
        building, **303–307**, *303–307*
        modeling, **279–280**, *279*
    Annotation object categories, **17**
    arrays
        creating, **304–305**, *304–305*
        in Family Editor, **297**, *297*
    base molding, 572, *572*
    bidirectional relationships, **19–22**, *20–22*
    change tracking, **607**

    constraints, **22**, *23*
    dimensions, 299–300, *300*
    door tags, 499
    families, **23–28**, *24–28*
    imported categories/subcategories, **18**, *18*
    linking, **295–296**, *295–297*
    mass family creation example, **215–223**,
       215–223
    Model Object categories, **15–17**, *15–16*
    overriding, **29–30**, *29–30*
    shared. *See* shared parameters
    subcategories, **17–18**, *17–18*
    sun shades, **302**, *302*
    type and instance parameters, **19**
    views, **18–19**
    visibility, 306, *306*
parametric change engines, 19
Partial Explode option, 636
pasting, **63–64**, *63*
.pat files, 93
paths
    keynotes, 506
    parametric mass families, 221
    sweeps, **183–184**, *184–185*
patterns
    balusters, **383–385**, *383–385*
    custom, **93–95**, *95*
    fill, **90–95**, *91–93*, *95*
    importing, **94–95**, *95*
    line, **87–88**, *87–88*
PDFs in performance, 641
performance
    best practices, **637–642**, *637–638*, *640–642*
    recommendations, **635–636**, *636*
Perimeter property, 479
periods (.) in type-catalog syntax, 141
permissions
    granting, **630–632**, *631–632*
    requesting, **629–630**, *630*
perspective views
    3D, **56–58**, *57–59*
    overview, **412–414**, *413–415*
Phase property, 479
Physical tab, 90
Pick option, 245

Pick a line and use the Work Plane it was sketched in option, 163, *163*

Pick a plane option, 163, *163*

Pick Level Graphics option, 64

Pick Path option
    parametric mass families, 221
    sweeps, 184

Pick Plane option, 164

Pick Supports tool, 373

Pick Walls method, 332

pinning elements, **75**

Place by Face mode, 213

Place Mass tool, 207, 209, 212

Place on Face mode, 213

Place Request option, 630

Place Similar tool, **64**

Place tab, 397, *397*

placing
    balusters, 381–383, *382*
    mass families, **212–213**, *212–213*
    repetitive units, **517–521**, *517–521*
    revision clouds, **603–604**, *604–605*
    rooms, **472–475**, *472–475*
    tags, **485–486**, *485*

Plan/RCP option, 591

plan regions, 50

plan views, 40–41, *41*
    default settings, 149
    Project Browser views, **46–51**, *47–51*
    visibility in, 591

planes. *See* Work Planes

planning projects, 643

plywood, **286**, *286*

positioning imported files, **232–233**

posts, railings, 379, *379*, **381–383**, *382–383*

predefined color schemes, 404

predefined profiles, 185

predefining keynotes, **512–513**, *512–513*

preliminary cost estimate schedules, **446–448**, *447–448*

preliminary designs, **427**
    Foundation model. *See* Foundation model
    sustainability. *See* sustainability

presentation plans, **405–408**, *406–407*

presenting designs, **395**
    animated walkthroughs, **423–424**, *424*

color-coded plans and sections, **401–408**, *402–408*

drawings with shadows, **395–401**, *396–401*

elevations, **408–412**, *408–412*

exporting, **424**, *425*

perspective views, **412–414**, *413–415*

rendering, **415–423**, *416–423*

previewing
    custom walls, **129**
    sun studies, **461**

primary design set options, 260

primary range for floor plans, **43–44**, *43–44*

principles of modeling. *See* modeling principles

printing
    3D services, **225–226**, *225–226*
    Design Review, 611, *612–613*
    in performance, 641

problem-solving designs, **7**, *7*

Profile Family template, 319

profiles
    3D content, **283–285**, *283–285*
    reveals, 319–320, *321*
    revolves, 178, 180, *181*
    subtractive, 320
    sweeps, 183–186, *184–186*, 319

programs
    feasibility, **235–236**, *236*
    verification, 205, *205*

Project Browser, 30, *31*, **33–34**, *34*
    for callouts, 557, *557*
    details, 595, *595*, 597, *597*
    for family details, 586
    for groups, 519, *519*
    nesting links in, 537
    views, **34–36**, *34–36*
        3D, **56–58**, *57–58*
        activating, **39**, *39*
        custom organization, **36–37**, *36–38*
        elevations, **53–56**, *54–55*
        families, **38**, *39*
        floor plans, **40–46**, *40–46*
        groups, **39**
        links, **38**
        plan views, **46–51**, *47–51*
        section views, **51–53**, *51–53*
        sheets, **38**

project environment types, **140**

project parameters, **224**, **489–491**, *489–491*, **495–496**, *495–496*
project standards worksets, **620**
Project Units dialog, 146, *147*, 342, *342*
projection graphics, 16, *16*
properties
    elements, **6**, *6*
    rooms, **478–479**
prototyping, **225–226**, *225–226*
Publish Coordinates option, 233, 536
publishing to Design Review, **610–612**, *611–613*
Purge unused dialog, **638**, *638*, 643
Purge Unused Elements dialog, 101
Pyramid Mass family, 214, *214*

Q

quantities for design options, **272**, *272*

R

radial arrays, 70–71, *71*
radial dimensions, 96
Radius setting
    arrays, 304, *304*
    cylinder mass elements, 214, *214*
Rafter property, 335
Rafter Cut property, 335
railings, **376–378**, *376–378*
    in auditoriums, 392
    balusters per tread on stairs, **385–387**, *386–387*
    construction, 380, *380*
    main pattern, **383–385**, *383–385*
    miscellaneous controls, **387–389**, *387–389*
    post settings, **381–383**, *382–383*
    rails, 380, *380*
    subelements and principles, **378–380**, *379–380*
    on walls, **390–392**, *390–392*
rapid prototyping, **225–226**, *225–226*
raytracing, **422–423**
RCP (Reflected Ceiling Plan) view, 561
Read Convention setting, 100
recessed walls, hip roofs following, 349, *349*
Rectangular Handrail profile, 381
recycled materials, **463–464**, *464–465*
Reference Label settings, 113–114
Reference Lines, **159**, *159*

Reference Planes, **157**, *158*, **177**, *177*
Reflected Ceiling Plan (RCP) view, 561
regions
    filled, **553–554**, *553–554*, 573
    masking, **548**, *549*
Rehost elements, 165
Related to Mass property, 334
relationships
    bidirectional, **19–22**, *20–22*
    building mass and underlying mass, **256**, *256–257*
Relative keynote path method, 506
relinquishing permissions, 629
reloading
    groups, 526
    links, 537
Remove from Group tool, 521
renaming
    dimension types, 99
    door tags, 499, *499*
    materials, 88
    text type, 101
rendering, **415–416**
    background, **419**, *419*
    best practices, **423**, *423*
    Design bar, **416–419**
    families, 288, *288*, **292–293**
    lighting, **416–418**, *417–418*
    materials, **419–422**, *420–422*
    raytracing, **422–423**
rentable area
    calculations, 430
    plans, **433–435**, *433–435*
    schedules, 438
        making, **439–443**, *440–443*
        on sheets, **443–445**, *444–445*
repetitive details and elements, **515**
    creating and placing, **517–521**, *517–521*, **548–551**, *549–552*
    floors, **575**, *575*
    groups, **516**, *516*, **528–529**, *529*
    for line types, **551**, *552*
Report Shared Coordinates option, 233, 536
requesting permissions, **629–630**, *630*
resizing elements, **71–72**, *72*
Restore All Excluded option, 528

reusing details, **594–597**, *595–597*
Reveal Hidden Elements mode, 53
reveals, **319–322**, *320–324*
Review Warnings option, **643**, *643*
revision clouds
    placement, **603–604**, *604–605*
    tagging, **606–607**, *606–607*
    visibility, **603**, *603*
revision schedules, 124, *124*
Revision Settings dialog, 602, 604
Revisions dialog, 602–603, *602–603*
Revit City service, 645
Revit OpEd blog, 645
revolves, **178–182**, *178–183*
.rfa files, 26
Rhino software, **255–256**, *255–256*
Rich Photorealistic Content (RPC) families, **288**, *288–289*, 292
ridge skylight roofs, **340–343**, *340–343*
Rise/1000 setting, 342
Riser Thickness setting, 137
Riser to Tread Connection setting, 138
Riser Type setting, 137, *138*
Roof by Extrusion tool, 337, *337*
roofs, 332
    barrel, 336, *336*, 338, 370, *370*
    bidirectional relationships, 20–21, *20*
    complex, 199, *199*
    cone, 368, *368*
    dome, 180, *181*, 337, 338, 369, *369*
    by extrusion, **166–170**, *166–170*, **336–337**, *336–337*
    by face, **249**
    flat, 345, *345*
    footprint, **332–335**, *332–336*
    gable, 350, *350*
        with asymmetric slopes, 346, *346*
        Dutch gable with glazed roofs, 355, *355–356*
        Dutch gables, 357, *357–358*
        with extending pergola, 351, *351*
        four-sided, 364, *364–365*
        hip and gable, 352, *352–353*
    gambrel, 353, *353–354*
    half hipped, **360–362**, *360–362*
    hipped, 348–349, *348–349*
        with extruded roof dormers, 366, *366–367*

        with sloped arrow dormers, 359, *359–360*
        with two dormers, 362, *362–364*
    in-place, **337–338**, *338*
    in modeling principles, 170–171
    multipitch, 371, *371–372*
    ridge skylight, **340–343**, *340–343*
    shed, **344**, *344*, 347, *347*
    sloped, 20, **373–375**, *373–375*
    sloped arrows, **343–344**, *343–344*
    sloped glazing, **338–339**, *339*
    types, **133–134**, *134*
    with warped surfaces, **376**, *376*
Room/Area Reports, 465, *466*
Room Bounding property, 334, 472, *472*
rooms, **472**
    area calculations, **429–430**, *429*, **479–480**, *479–481*
    area plans, 430–431, *430–431*
    creating and placing, **517–521**, *517–521*
    design options for, **272–275**, *273–275*
    groups for, **516**, *516*, **521–522**, *522*
    overlapping, 474–475, *474–475*
    placing, **472–475**, *472–475*
    properties, **478–479**
    in section views, **478**
    selecting, **476–477**, *477–478*
    separation lines, **475–476**, *475–476*
    settings, **145**, *146*
    styles, 484, *484*
    tags, **429–430**, *429*, **472–475**, *472–475*
    volume calculations, **479–480**, *479–481*, 636, *636*
    window surface percentage, **465**, *466*
rotating
    detail components, 551
    elements, **67–70**, *68–70*, 213
    orientation, 232
    sweeps, 185, *186*
RPC (Rich Photorealistic Content) families, **288**, *288–289*, 292

S

Same Place option, 64
SAT files
    importing and linking, 544
    with Inventor, 256
    with Rhino, 255

Save As dialog
    animated walkthroughs, 424, *424*
    sun studies, 461, *461*
Save Group option, 526
Save to Central (STC) dialog, 627, *627*
saving
    shared work, **627–628**, *627*
    sun studies, 461, *461*
scale
    coarse scale fill patterns, 407
    imported site data, 231
    in importing and linking, 545
Scene Lighting dialog, 417–418, *418*
schedules
    capabilities, **445–446**, *446*
    cost, 272, *272*
    creating, **437–439**
    custom parameters, 492, *492*
    graphic appearance of, **448–449**, *448–449*
    keynotes, **508**
    keys, **481–484**, *482–484*
    link elements, 536
    massing, **224**
    nested families, **294–295**
    preliminary cost estimates, **446–448**, *447–448*
    rentable area, **439–443**, *440–443*
    on sheets, **443–445**, *444–445*, 450
    technical details, **249–251**, *250–252*
schemes
    color fill, **402–405**, *403–405*
    settings, 151
scope boxes, **161**, *161*
Second end blend setting, 190
section boxes, **583**, *583*
Section Head setting, 103
Section Tail setting, 103
sections and section views
    colored, **405**, *405–406*
    creating, **405–408**, *406–407*
    Project Browser views, **51–53**, *51–53*
    rooms in, **478**
    split, 318, *318*
    tags, **103–108**, *103–108*
    walls
        details, **560–578**, *560–578*
        keynotes for, **509–510**, *509–511*

segmented sweeps, 189, *189*
selections, **61–63**, *61–62*
    for copying, 24, *25*, **63–64**, 404, *404*
    Design Review, **610**, *610*
    element editing by, **264**, *264*
    floor areas, 246
    instances, **62**, 526, 625
    layers, 588, *589*
    levels, 529
    parameters, 123, *123*, 498, *498*
    rooms, **476–477**, *477–478*
    view templates, 150, *151*
separation lines, **475–476**, *475–476*
Set Host option, 392
sets, design-option, **260–261**, *261*
Settings menu, 145, *145*
shades, 186, *186*
shadows and shading, **395–396**, *396*
    for analytical purposes, **395–399**, *396–399*
    enabling, **397–398**, *398*
    for expressive drawings, 395, *396*, **399–401**, *400–401*
    high-contrast black and white effects, **400**, *400*
    materials, 90
    performance, **401**, 639
    with SketchUp, 254, *254*
    soft, 400, *401*
    sun, 453–454, *453–454*
    sun and shadow studies, **397–399**, *397–399*
shaft opening, **598**, *598*
shapes
    elevation tags, 112
    floors, 133
    roofs, 133, **372–373**, *372–373*
Shared Coordinates settings, 233
Shared Levels worksets, 619
Shared Levels and Grids workset, 621
shared parameters, **292**, **489**
    creating, **491–495**, *492–494*
    door tags, **497–501**, *498–501*
    groups, **493–494**, *493–494*
    notes and cautions, **501–502**
    project, **489–491**, *489–491*, **495–496**, *495–496*
shared site plans, buildings on, **534–535**
shared work, saving, **627–628**, *627*
shed roofs, **344**, *344*, 347, *347*

sheets
  Project Browser views, **38**
  publishing, **611–612**, *612–613*
  schedules on, **443–445**, *444–445*, 450
  views on, **125**, *125*
Shell and Core workset, 621
shortcuts, keyboard, **78–79**, *78*
Show Hidden Lines tool, **554–555**, *554–555*
Show option, 631
Show Opening Height option, 99
Show View Name setting, 113
shower fixture, 187, *187*
shutters, 299–300
silhouette edge displays, **414**, *414–415*
SIM (Similar) condition, **560–566**, *560–566*
Simple fill pattern option, **92–93**, *92*
Single-Day sun settings, 457, 459–460, *460*
SIPs (structurally insulated panels), 567–568
site data, **230–233**, *231–232*
site studies, **204**, *204*
Site workset, 622
size
  elements, **71–72**, *72*
  text, 100, 113, 136
  type catalogs for, 140
Sketch 2D Path option, 184
sketch-based design, **154**
  floors, **154–157**, *155–156*
  Work Planes, **157–162**
sketch mode, 23
SketchUp software, **252–254**, *253–254*
skins, exterior, **265**, *265*
SKP format
  importing and linking, 544
  with SketchUp, 252–254
skylight roofs, **340–343**, *340–343*
skylights, *282*
slicing volumes, 239, *240*
Sloped Glazing Curtain Panel type, 370
slopes
  floors, 133
  railings, 389, 391
  sloped roofs, 20, 133, **373–375**, *373–375*
    barrel, 370
    ridge skylight roofs, 342

  slope arrows for, **343–344**, *343–344*
  sloped arrow dormers, hipped roofs with,
    359, *359–360*
  sloped glazing roofs, **338–339**, *339*
smart workflows
  groups. *See* groups
  links. *See* links and linking
  repetitive elements, **515**
snap distance for dimension lines, 99
soft shadows, 400, *401*
Solid Form options, 174, *174*
solid panels, 326
solid shapes
  characteristics, **198–199**, *198–199*
  with extrusions, 176, *177*
Sorting tab, 447
Sorting/Grouping tab, 440–441, *441*
Space parameter for railings, 383
Spacebar for rotation, **68**, *68*
Spacing detail option, 551
Specify Coordinates at a Point option, 233, 536
Split Face tool, 76, *77*
Split Region tool, 317, *317*
Split Segment tool, 103
splitting
  layers, **317–318**, *317–318*
  lines and walls, **74**, *74*
Spread Pattern To Fit setting, 384, *385*
stacked walls, **313–314**, *313–314*
Stafford, Steve, 645
Stair Calculator dialog, 135, *136*
stairs, **135**, *135*
  balusters per tread, **385–387**, *386–387*
  properties, **135–139**, *136–139*
standard families, **25–27**, *25–27*
Start angle revolve setting, 179, *179*
startup tips, **643–645**
static text, **104**
Still settings for sun studies, 457, 459
.stl files, 226
String Reference Planes, 158, *158*
Stringer Carriage Height setting, 139
Stringer Left/Right setting, 138
structurally insulated panels (SIPs), 567–568
Structure option for wall layers, 130

styles
    dimensions, **96–99**, *96–99*
    lines, **85–86**, *86*, 143
    objects. *See* Object Styles dialog
    rooms, 484, *484*
subcategories, **17–18**, *17–18*
submodels, 639, *641*
Subscription Support, 645
Substrate option for wall layers, 130
subtractive profiles, 320
sun and shadow studies, **397–401**, *397–401*,
    452–454, *453–454*
    animated, **458–462**, *459–460*, *462*
    exporting, **461**, *461*
    making, **454–458**, *455–458*
    multi-day, **460**, *460*
    previewing, **461**
    settings, 416–417, *417*
    time of day, 457
    time of year, 459
    true-color shading, 410, *410*
Sun Shade family, 296
sun shades, 186, *186*
sunlight, rendering, **416–417**, *417*
sunny vs. overcast days, 468
supplemental drawings, **607**
surfaces
    materials, 90
    NURBS, 255–256, *255–256*
    units, 142, 146
    warped, **376**, *376*
sustainability, **451**
    in architecture, **451–452**
    energy analysis, **466–468**, *467–469*
    LEED rating system, 452
    recycled materials, **463–464**, *464–465*
    sun studies. *See* sun and shadow studies
    window surface percentage vs. room area, **465**,
      466
sweeps, **183**
    examples, 187–188, *187–188*
    lamp from, **194–196**, *194–196*
    paths, **183–184**, *184–185*
    profiles, 183–186, *184–186*
    trajectory segmentation, 189, *189*
    walls, **319–322**, *320–324*

Symbol setting, 115
Symbol at End 1/2 Default settings, 115
symbolic lines, **592–594**, *592–594*
system families, **23–24**, *24–25*, 127
System Panel Glazed panel, 330
System Panel Solid panel, 330

T

Tab Size setting, 100
tables, revision, 602
tags, **484**, *484*
    adding, **436–437**, *436–437*
    changing values, **486**, *486*
    custom, 101, *102*, **116–119**, *116–119*, **606–607**,
      607
    doors, **486–488**, *488*
    loading, **485**
    mass, **223**
    placing, **485–486**, *485*
    revision clouds, **606–607**, *606–607*
    rooms, **429–430**, *429*, **472–475**, *472–475*
    untagged elements, **486–488**, *487–488*
    in views, **102–103**, 471
    visibility, **603**, *603*
    walls, 488, *488*
tail graphics in section tags, **107–108**, *107–108*
Tangent Joins tool, 387
teams
    communication with, 643
    organizing, **644**
templates
    creating, **81–84**, *82*
    custom 3D content, **280**, *280–281*
    custom title blocks, 122
    family, 28, *28*
    fill patterns, 407
    in performance, 641–642
    strategies, **83–84**
    views, 146, **150**, *150*, 407, *407*
temporary dimensions, **65–66**, *65*
testing design options, 205, *205*
text
    annotating, **502–503**
    dimensions, 99
    elevation tags, 112–113, *113*

for graphic consistency, **100–101**, *100–101*

section view tags, **104**, *104*

stairs, 136

in views, 471

textnotes, **119–120**, *120–121*, **503**. *See also* keynotes

texture maps, **420–421**, *421–422*

Thermal/Air option, 130

Thickness column for wall layers, 130

Thickness/Height of Stringers setting, 138

3D DWF option, **611**, *611*

3D models, **4**, *5*

conceptual, importing, **224–225**, *224*

context, **233**, *234–235*

custom content. *See* custom 3D content

details

annotations, **585–586**, *586*

creating, **581–586**, *582–586*

physical, **202–203**, *202*

printing services, **225–226**, *225–226*

3D views

axonometric, **56**

orienting, **56**, *57*, **584–585**, *584–585*

perspective, **56–58**, *57–59*, 413, *413*

section boxes in, **583**, *583*

/3GB switch, **635**

tick marks, **96–99**, *97–99*

Tile option, 31

title blocks

custom, **121–125**, *121–125*

revision tracking in, **604**, *604*

updates in, 606

TMY2 (Typical Meteorological Year 2) data, 468

toolbars, 30, 521, 609

Top setting

blends, 190

railings, 383

Top view range for floor plans, 41, *42*

tower shapes, **198**, *199*

tracking changes, **601**

Design Review. *See* Design Review

parametric modeling and supplemental drawings, **607**

revisions, **601–607**, *601–607*

tracking recycled materials, **463–464**, *464–465*

Trajectory Segmentation option, 189, *189*

transferring color-fill schemes, **404–405**, *404–405*

transparency

elevation views, **411–412**, *411*

filled regions, 553, *553*

Tread Thickness setting, 137

Trim Stringers at Top setting, 138

trimming

lines and walls, **73–74**, *73*

railings, 387

troubleshooting and optimizing tips, **635**

best practices, **637–642**, *637–638*, *640–642*

blends, **192**, *193–194*

file corruption, **642–643**, *642–643*

performance, **635–636**, *636*

resources for, **645**

startup tips, **643–645**

true-color elevations, **410**, *410*

Truss property, 335

Twisting blend setting, 191

2D DWF option, **611–612**, *612–613*

2D elements, importing, 597

2D line-based families, **285–286**, *286–287*

Type Mark field, 486

Type Properties dialog

callouts, 110–111, *111*

color fill schemes, 403, *403*

detail elements, 548, 551, *551*

dimensions, 96, 97, 99

door tags, 118, 499–500

elevation tags, 112–114, *112*

filled regions, 554, *554*

grid tags, 116

for keynotes, 512, *512*

linking parameters, 295–296, *295*

profile families, 284–285, *284*

railing construction, 380, *380*

text, 101

tick marks, 96, *97*

view tags, 103, 107, *107*

walls, 128, 132

Type Selector

materials, 76, *77*

selection by, 63

text, 502

types and type catalogs, **139–140**, *140*
    3D content. *See* custom 3D content
    creating, **140**, *141*
    loadable, 171, *171*
    loading from, **142**, *143*
    parameters, **19**
    in project environment, **140**
    syntax, **141–142**
    units, **142**
Typical Meteorological Year 2 (TMY2) data, 468

U

Unbounded Height property, 479
Underline setting, 101
Underside of Winder setting, 136, *137*
unenclosed room errors, 473, *474*
units
    settings, **146**, *147*
    type catalogs, **142**
Unjoin Geometry option, 210, 251
unloading
    links, 537
    unused DWGs and views, 636
unused elements
    in performance, **638**, *638*, 643
    unloading, 636
updates
    building area schedules, 443
    in title blocks, 606
Upper Limit property, 478
usable area calculations, 430
Use Baluster Per Tread On Stairs option, 385, *386*
Use Common Edge Style option, 145
Use Function option, 145
Use Landing Height Adjustment option, 387, *387*
Use OpenGL Hardware Acceleration option, 637
Use overlay planes to improve performance option, 637
Use Project Settings option, 448
user interface, **30**, *30*
    Design bar, **32–33**, *32*
    Design Review, **609–610**, *609–610*
    Options bar, **33**
    Project Browser. *See* Project Browser
    View window, **30–31**, *31*
user keynotes, 120, 504, **512**

V

Variable property, 134, *134*
variations to group instances, **525–528**, *526–528*
vaults, **198**, *198*
verifying
    designs, **239–243**, *240–244*
    programs, 205, *205*
Vertical tag orientation, 487
vertices, blend, **191**, *192*
video card options, 637, *637*
View Control bar, 31, *31*
view depth
    floor plans, **44–46**, *44–46*
    in performance, 639
    plan views, 48–50, *48–51*
    section views, **53**, *53*
View/Floor Plan tool, 239
view tags, **102–103**, *102*
    callouts, **108–112**, *109–112*
    elevation, **112–115**, *112–114*
    grid, **116**
    levels, **115**, *115*
    section, **103–108**, *103–108*
View window, **30–31**, *31*, 609
views, **18–19**
    annotating, **471**, *471*
    default settings, **150**, *150–151*
    dependent, 17
    drafting, **541–542**, *542*, 559
    elevation tags, 113
    importing, **595–597**, *596–597*
    keynotes in, **506**, *506*
    lists of, 438
    in performance, 638, 642
    perspective, **412–414**, *413–415*
    plan, 40–41, *41*
        default settings, 149
        Project Browser views, **46–51**, *47–51*
        visibility in, 591
    Project Browser. *See* Project Browser
    on sheets, **125**, *125*
    for sketches, 157
    templates, 146, **150**, *150*, 407, *407*
    worksets, 619–620

visibility
    chairs, **306–307**, *306–307*
    conditional, **296**, *297*
    details, **591–592**, *591–592*
    extrusions, 175, *175*
    link, **537–538**, *538*
    mass elements, **207–208**, *207–208*
    revision clouds and tags, **603**, *603*
    Work Planes, **164**, *164*
    worksharing files, 618
Visibility/Graphic Overrides dialog, 9, *9*, 29, *29*
    CAD details, 546
    cost schedules, 272, *272*
    design options, 266, *266*
    exterior skins, 265
    fill patterns, 407
    graphics, **143–145**, *143–144*
    imported CAD files, 636
    line patterns, 87
    mass elements, 207–208
    Project Browser views, 35
    room elements, 273
    room separation lines, 475, 477
    schedules, 444
    site data, 230
    worksets, 621, 623–625
    worksharing files, 618, *618*
Void Form options, 174, *174*
void shapes, 176, *177*, **198–199**, *198–199*
Void Sweep option, 221
volume
    rooms, **479–480**, *479–481*, 636, *636*
    slicing, 239, *240*
    units, 146

W

walkthroughs, 58, 413, **423–424**, *424*
Wall by Face tool, **246**
Wall Editor, 131
walls, **127–128**, *128*
    articulation, **315–318**, *315–318*
    bidirectional relationships, 20–22, *22*
    compound, 315, *315*
    cores, **309–311**, *310–311*

    curtain, **325–326**, *325–326*
        designing, **326–329**, *327–329*
        doors and windows, **330**, *331*
        panels, **330**, *331*
    custom, **128–129**, *129*
        default wrapping, **131–132**, *132*
        layers, **129–131**, *130–131*
        preview window, **129**
    defaults, **148**
    disjoining, **313**, *313*
    finish materials, **316–318**, *316–318*
    functions, 133
    host-based families, 282, *282*
    in-place, **324**, *324*
    join editing, **312**, *312*
    layer join cleanup, **311–312**, *312*
    levels of detail, **132**, *133*
    in modeling principles, 170–171
    offsetting, **74**, *75*
    overlapping, 518
    railings on, **390–392**, *390–392*
    rotating, 68
    sections
        details, **560–578**, *560–578*
        keynotes for, **509–510**, *509–511*
    splitting, **74**, *74*
    stacked, **313–314**, *313–314*
    sweeps and reveals, **319–322**, *320–324*
    tags, 472, 484, *484*, 488, *488*
    trimming and extending, **73–74**, *73–74*
    wrapping, **319**, *319*
warnings
    reviewing, **643**, *643*
    tags, 473, *474*
warped surfaces, **376**, *376*
Weak Reference Planes, 158, *158*
Weld setting, 387
width
    elevation tags, 113
    Insulation tool, 552
    shutter, 300
    text, 101
Window.rft template, 282
window surface percentage, **465**, *466*

windows
curtain wall, **330**, *331*
defaults, 148
host-based families, 282, *282*
in modeling principles, 171, *171*
with muntins, 299, *299*
rotating, **68**
selection, 62
types, **135**
witness lines, 98
work plane-based families, **288**, **292**
Work Planes, **157**
grids, **160–161**, *160*, 164, *164*
levels, **159–160**
operations, **164–165**, *164–165*
overview, **161–162**, *162*
Reference Lines, **159**, *159*
Reference Planes, **157**, *158*
roofs by extrusion, **166–170**, *166–170*
visibility, **164**, *164*
working with, 162–165, *163*, *165*
workflows, **625**
central files, **626**, *626*
local files, **626–627**, *626*
massing studies, **203–204**

smart
groups. *See* groups
links. *See* links and linking
repetitive elements, **515**
worksets, 623
worksets, **617–618**, *618*, 620–621, *621*
moving elements between, **623–625**, *624–625*
organization, **621–623**, *622–623*
in performance, 639
permissions, 630, *631*
worksharing, **617**
basics, **619–621**, *619–620*
element ownership, **628–632**, *628–632*
mistakes in, **629**
in performance, 637
saving shared work, **627–628**, *627*
workflows, **625–627**, *626*
workset methods. *See* worksets
wrapping walls, **319**, *319*
Wraps column for wall layers, **131**, *131*

X

X-References, **9**